Formatting Legal Documents With Microsoft Word 2016

Tips and Tricks for Working With
Pleadings, Contracts, Mailings,
and Other Complex Documents

Jan Berinstein, Ph.D.

Formatting Legal Documents With Microsoft Word 2016
Tips and Tricks for Working With Pleadings, Contracts, Mailings, and Other Complex Documents

Copyright © 2016 by Jan Berinstein, Ph.D.

All rights reserved. No part of the contents of this book may be reproduced, stored in a retrieval system, or transmitted in any form or by any means—electronic, mechanical, photocopying, photostating, recording, or otherwise—without written permission of the author. No patent liability is assumed with respect to the use of the information contained herein.

Warnings and Disclaimers

The views and opinions expressed in this book are solely those of the author.

Mention herein of a particular product or service does not constitute an endorsement of that product or service.

Although every precaution has been taken in the preparation of this book, the author / publisher assumes no responsibility for errors or omissions. Nor is any liability assumed for damages resulting from the information contained herein, which is provided without any express, statutory, or implied warranties.

All names used in the tutorials herein are fictitious. Any resemblance to real persons, living or dead, is unintended and entirely coincidental.

Trademarks

Microsoft and Windows are registered trademarks of Microsoft Corporation.

WordPerfect is a registered trademark of Corel Corporation.

Screenshots

Microsoft product screenshots reprinted with permission from Microsoft Corporation.

Printed and bound in the United States of America.

First printing: February, 2016.

For Barry
who changed everything

CONTENTS

PAGE

INTRODUCTION

PART I: LAUNCHING WORD

Getting Started With Word 1
   The Start Screen 1
   Using a "Featured" Template 1
   Starting a Blank Document 2
   Opening an Existing Document 2
   Working Offline Versus Signing into OneDrive 3
   Opening Documents From OneDrive 3
   Signing Out of OneDrive 4
   Opening Documents From Your Computer 5
   Opening Recent Documents 6
   "This PC" 6
   Browse 7
   Bypassing the Start Screen / Going Directly to the "Open" Dialog 8
      A Temporary Fix 8
      A Permanent Fix 8
   What's New and Different in Word 2016 10

PART II: THE WORD INTERFACE

The Word Interface (Screen) 13
Overview 13
   Choosing a Screen Color / Office Theme 13
The Ribbon, Tabs, and Groups 15
   The Permanent (Main) Tabs 15
   The Groups 15
   Dialog Launchers 16
The Logic of the Tabs 17
      SIDEBAR: Document Views 21
      SIDEBAR: The Tabs at a Glance 23
   The Contextual Tabs 26
   The Optional Tabs 27
      SIDEBAR: Working With the Contextual Tabs 28
      SIDEBAR: Minimizing (Collapsing) and Restoring the Ribbon 31
The Backstage View / File Tab 35
   Navigating the Backstage View 36
   The "Open" Screen 38
   The "Recent" Screen 38
      "Pinning" Documents 40
      Quick Access to Recent Documents 41
   "This PC" (Revisited) 42
      Recover Unsaved Documents 42

CONTENTS (Cont'd.)

PAGE

Tips About the "Open" Dialog..42
The "Save" Command..45
    The Save Options 47
The "Save As" Screen..47
    "This PC"...48
    OneDrive / SharePoint...48
    Add a Place...48
    Browse 49
"Close" 49
    The "Unsaved Documents" 51
    The AutoRecover Files (Versions) 53
        Configuring Automatic Saves (AutoRecover) 54
SIDEBAR: Closing a Document Without Closing Word........................56
The "Info" Screen 57
    Properties..58
    Advanced Properties..58
    Changing Certain Attributes of a Document 59
SIDEBAR: The Word File Formats...60
    Converting Documents From Compatibility Mode 62
    Should You Convert (Upgrade)?...63
    Protect Document...63
    Mark as Final 64
    Apply a Password...64
    Remove a Password 65
    Restrict Editing 66
    Add a Digital Signature 66
    Inspect Document / Check for Issues 66
    The Document Inspector 67
    The Accessibility Checker 68
    The Compatibility Checker 68
    Manage Document 69
The "New" Screen..70
    Blank Document...71
    Featured Templates 71
    Custom / Personal Templates 72
Print ("Print Place") 73
    The Print Preview 73
    Add a Print Preview Edit Mode Icon to the QAT..............................74
    Print Settings 75
    The "Print All Pages" Menu 76
        Print Selection 77
        Print Current Page 77
        Custom Print 77
        Only Print Odd Pages..78

CONTENTS (Cont'd.)

PAGE

Only Print Even Pages 78
The Printing Specs 78
Page Setup 80
Print What / Document Info 80
Configuring the Print Options 82
The "Share" Screen 84
Share With People 84
WHERE IS IT? Dictionary 86
SIDEBAR: Real-Time Co-Authoring 87
The Email Option 89
Present Online 91
Post to Blog 91
The "Export" Screen 91
Create PDF/XPS Document 92
Change File Type 95
The "Account" Screen 96
The Word Options 97
A Few Important Options Worth Tweaking 98
The Word Options at a Glance 102
Exit (Close Word) 104
Bypassing the Backstage View 105
Closing the Backstage View 105
Other Important Screen Elements 106
The Quick Access Toolbar ("QAT") 106
The Status Bar 106
The Scrollbars 108
The Ruler 108
The Mini Toolbar 109
Live Preview 110
Galleries 111
The Style Gallery (Quick Style Gallery) 113
Show / Hide the Non-Printing Characters (Formatting Marks) 114
Help! Where Did "Help" Go?? 116
SIDEBAR: Protected View 118

PART III: WORD "UNDER THE HOOD": UNDERSTANDING WORD'S LOGIC

The Key to How Word Works: Paragraph Formatting 123
Paragraph Formatting vs. Section Formatting 133
WordPerfect vs. Word—Some Fundamental Differences in "Logic" 135
Not Just for WordPerfect Users: Troubleshooting Without Reveal Codes ... 137
The Paragraph Dialog 137
The Page Setup Dialog 138
Show / Hide (Show the Non-Printing Characters) 139

vii

CONTENTS (Cont'd.)

PAGE

Reveal Formatting 139
Switching to Draft View 141
Select, Then Do 141
When All Else Fails...Try "Undo" 141
More About the Non-Printing Characters 142
The Format Painter 143
    SIDEBAR: Select All Text With Similar Formatting 144
    SIDEBAR: How to Clear Paragraph and Font Formatting 145

PART IV: GETTING WORD TO WORK THE WAY YOU WANT

Disabling or Enabling Certain Features in Word 149
Customizing the Word 2016 Interface to Make It More User-Friendly 151
    Customizing the Ribbon 151
        Adding a Custom Tab and a Custom Group 152
        Adding Commands / Icons to a Custom Group 155
        Adding Another Tab, Group, or Command 157
        Renaming a Custom Group or Tab 159
        Moving a Tab or Group 159
        Hiding a Tab 160
        Removing Groups 161
        Restoring a Removed Group 162
        Removing Commands 163
        Restoring a Removed Command 164
        Renaming Commands or Changing an Icon 164
        Hiding Command Labels in a Custom Group 165
        Resetting Customizations to the Factory Defaults 167
        Importing / Exporting Your Customizations 168
        TIP: Reassigning Ctrl O to "File Open" 174
    Customizing the Quick Access Toolbar 175
        Adding a "Close" ("Close File") Command to the Quick Access Toolbar 180
    Customizing the Status Bar 182
Making Word 2016 Work Like Older Versions of Word 185
    The Role of Style Sets and Themes in Determining Default Settings 186
    Changing the Default Font 187
    Changing the Default Font for Headings (and Other Styles) 188
    Modifying the "Normal" Paragraph Style 189
    Applying a Different Style Set – or Creating Your Own 190
    Themes 192
    Creating Custom Theme Fonts 193
    Modifying the Normal Template 195
    A Last Resort: The Manage Styles Dialog 197
        QUICK TIP: Enable "Use the Insert Key to Control Overtype Mode" 198

CONTENTS (Cont'd.)

PAGE

PART V: EVERYDAY FEATURES DEMYSTIFIED

General Formatting Tips 201

PARAGRAPH FORMATTING

General Rules About Paragraph Formatting 207

Justification (Alignment) 208

Using Left, Center, and Right Alignment on One Line 209

Different Ways to Apply Line Spacing 211

Adjusting Line Spacing – Simplified Steps 214

SIDEBAR: What Are Points, Anyway? 215

QUICK TIP: Setting Line Height 217

TROUBLESHOOTING TIP: Where'd That Line Come From? 218

Indenting Paragraphs 220

SIDEBAR: Why Do Those Thunderbolts Keep Popping Up? 223

Setting (and Deleting / Clearing) Tabs 224

SIDEBAR: Alignment Tabs 228

Creating Bulleted Lists 229

PAGE FORMATTING

Understanding Page (Section) Formatting 235

Changing Page Margins 237

Working With Headers and Footers 239

Using Section Breaks to Create Multiple Headers / Footers 241

SIDEBAR: A Few Tips About Section Breaks 243

Using the "Different First Page" Option 244

Creating and Editing a Letter Template 245

Inserting the File Name and Path into a Footer 248

TROUBLESHOOTING TIP: Restoring the Pleading Paper if It
Disappears 250

Page Numbering 251

Inserting a Page Number Code 251

Don't Use "Bottom of Page" (It's Broken) 251

"Suppressing" a Page Number 252

Changing the Number Format 253

Changing the Number Value (Restarting or Continuing) 254

Footnotes 256

Changing the Footnote Separator 260

Watermarks 261

SIDEBAR: The Curious Case of the Mutating Section Breaks 263

CHARACTER (FONT) FORMATTING

A Few Tips About Fonts 267

Applying Fonts to an Entire Document 267

Applying Fonts to Certain Portions of a Document 268

Font Attributes 268

Changing Case 270

CONTENTS (Cont'd.)

PAGE

Inserting Symbols..270
   SIDEBAR: Keyboard Shortcuts Related to Fonts...............................272
MISCELLANEOUS FEATURES
The Navigation Pane..275
   Searching...276
   Clearing the Search Box...278
   Pausing and Resuming a Search...278
   The Pages Tab (Thumbnail View)...278
   The Headings Tab...280
   Moving the Navigation Pane..283
   Closing the Navigation Pane..283
   A "Sticky" Setting...283
   Additional Search Commands...284
   The Find Options...285
Two Other Organizational Tools..289
   Collapsible Headings..289
   Outline View...291
Using the Traditional "Find" Dialog...292
   Finding Text...292
   Replacing Text..293
   Searching for Formatted Text..294
   Replacing Formatted Text..295
   Replacing Tabs, Section Breaks, Styles, etc..295
   Replacing Other Formatting..296
   Clearing Your Search Criteria...298
   "Reading Highlight" and "Find In"..298
   The "Go To" Dialog...299
   TROUBLESHOOTING TIP: "Find" Disables Page Up and Page Down......301
Copying and Pasting: The Paste Options...304
   Paste Preview...304
   The Paste Drop-Down in the Home Tab..304
   Paste Special..305
   The Right-Click Menu...306
   The Paste Options Button...307
   Pasting an Object..311
   Pasting a Numbered List..312
   Adding a "Paste and Keep Text Only" Icon to the Quick Access Toolbar......313
   Adding a Keyboard Shortcut for "Keep Text Only"................................314
   Configuring the Default Paste Options...315
   Pasting Text From WordPerfect and Other Programs...............................316
   Other "Paste" Settings..317
Opening PDF Files Directly into Word..319
Spell-Checking...322
Creating a Custom Dictionary...325

x

CONTENTS (Cont'd.)

PAGE

QUICK TIP: Frequently Confused Words (Contextual Spelling) 329
The Advanced Grammar Settings 330
The Mini-Translator 331
Built-in Text-to-Speech 334
Sorting Text, Numbers, or Dates 335
    Sorting – Simplified Steps 340

PART VI: WORKING SMARTER AND FASTER (AUTOMATING WORD)

Save Time With Keyboard Shortcuts and Document Automation 343
    Creating Your Own Keyboard Shortcuts 345
       SIDEBAR: Some Cool Built-In Keyboard Shortcuts 348
    Keyboard Shortcuts That Use the Control ("Ctrl") Key 349
      Favorite Ctrl Key Tips 352
    Selected Function Key Shortcuts (Listed by Keystrokes) 353
    Selected Function Key and Ctrl Key Shortcuts (Listed by Feature/Function) 355
    Mnemonics and Keyboard Shortcuts for Tabs and Dialog Boxes 357
Keyboard Shortcuts—Miscellaneous Tips 360
Using Field Codes 361
    What *Are* Field Codes? 361
    Reformatting a Date Code 363
    Creating an Unformatted Page X of Y Code 364
      Creating a Page X of Y Quick Part 366
      Changing the Page Number Format 366
    Locking, Unlocking, and Unlinking Field Codes 367
Fill-in Fields 368
      WHERE IS IT? Macros 371
Creating a Simple Macro to Print the Current Page 372
Creating and Using "Quick Parts" 377
    Saving Quick Parts When Exiting From Word 380
    Managing / Deleting Quick Parts Entries 382
    Sharing Quick Parts 383
Working With Styles 385
    What Are Styles? 385
    Advantages of Using Styles 385
    Potential "Gotchas" 386
    The "Normal" Style 387
    Applying Styles 387
    Creating Custom Styles 389
    Modifying Styles 391
    Copying a Style Between Documents or Templates 392
    Copying Styles With the Organizer 393
    Assigning a Keyboard Shortcut to a Style 395
    Viewing the Styles in a Document 396
    What Are Those Weird-Looking Styles in the Style Pane? 397

CONTENTS (Cont'd.)

PAGE

The Style Gallery 398
    SIDEBAR: The Style Inspector 405
    SIDEBAR: Why the "Automatically Update" Option Is a Bad Idea 407
SIDEBAR: Creating a Style (and Keyboard Shortcut) for Indented Quotes 408
Creating Your Own Templates 409
    Creating a Template From an Existing Document 409
    Saving a Template 410
    Word Template File Formats 411
    Where Personal (Custom) Templates Are Stored 411
    Where Shared Templates Are Stored 413
    Creating a Document Based on Your Custom Template 414
    Creating Another Template Based on Your Custom Template 415
    Editing a Template 416
    Miscellaneous Tips About Templates 416

PART VII: WORKING WITH MAILINGS AND FORMS

Merges (Mail Merges) 419
    Overview 419
        Data Files 419
    Using the Mail Merge Wizard 420
        Using an Existing List (Data File) 421
        Editing a List (Data File) 422
        Creating a New Data File 423
    Form Files 426
        Inserting Individual Address Fields 427
        Typing the Form and Inserting Merge Codes 428
    Previewing the Merge 429
        Including / Excluding Recipients (or Records) 429
    Performing the Merge 430
    Printing the Merged Letters / Forms 431
    Performing a "Manual" Merge (Bypassing the Wizard) 431
        What Is the "SQL Command" Prompt? 437
    Creating a Sheet of Different Labels Using Mail Merge 438
        QUICK TIP: Make the Mail Merge Pane Go Away 446
    Setting Up and Printing Labels 447
    Printing Labels 449
    Adjusting Text on the Labels 449
    Setting Up and Printing Envelopes 451

PART VIII: WORKING WITH PLEADINGS AND CONTRACTS

Aligning Text With Pleading Line Numbers 457
Using Line Breaks (Soft Returns) to Fix Formatting in Pleadings 462
Working With Tables 464
    Inserting a Table 464

xii

CONTENTS (Cont'd.)

PAGE

The Table Tools Tab..466
The Layout Tab..467
Adding Rows and Columns..467
Deleting Rows and Columns..468
Deleting the Entire Table...468
Selecting Parts of the Table...469
Merging or Splitting Cells or Splitting the Table..470
Header Rows...470
Row Height...474
Allowing or Not Allowing Rows to Break Across Pages............................475
Setting the Table Alignment and Size..475
The Design Tab...475
The Table Styles Gallery..475
Table Borders and Gridlines...476
Practical Applications: Signature Blocks and Pleading Captions................478
Some Additional Tips About Tables...479
Sorting Within a Table...481
Using the Numbering Button..487
    QUICK TIP: Using the ListNum Field..495
Multilevel Lists...497
Applying a Multilevel List...497
Creating a New List or List Style..501
Basing a New List Style on an Existing List...501
Checklist for Formatting Each Level of the List Style................................506
Modifying the Heading Styles..507
Double-Checking to Make Sure Everything Works.....................................511
Applying Your List Style..511
Changing List Levels..511
Modifying a Multilevel List: Tips and Caveats...511
Changing the Numeric Formatting...512
    QUICK TIP: Setting Up a "Simple" Multilevel List and Saving It
        as a Style..514
    QUICK TIP: Sharing Your Custom List Style..............................517
Using the "SEQ" Field for Automatic Numbering in Discovery Headings
    and Exhibits...519
Cross-Referencing Exhibit Letters and Automatic Paragraph Numbers...........525
    SIDEBAR: Cross-Reference Tips and Caveats..............................529
    QUICK TIP: Striking Text (Without Redlining or Using Track Changes).....532
Generating and Troubleshooting a Table of Contents (TOC)............................533
Documents That Use Heading Styles..533
How to Tell if Heading Styles Have Been Applied......................................533
Applying Outline Levels to "Manual" Headings..535
Appling TC Codes to "Manual" Headings..536
The "Add Text" Option...537

xiii

CONTENTS (Cont'd.)

PAGE

Style Separators 537
Generating the Table of Contents 538
Tweaking the Formatting of the Generated TOC 540
Troubleshooting the TOC 542
Marking Citations and Generating a Table Authorities (TOA)........543
Modifying the TOA Styles..549
Compare Documents (Redlining) 551
Track Changes..555
Removing Metadata With the Document Inspector 563
More About Metadata 566
    SIDEBAR: What Does "Mark as Final" Do?.............................568
Restrict Editing (Apply a Password for Editing)...........................569

PART IX: TROUBLESHOOTING TIPS

Troubleshooting Tips and Best Practices 573
Consider the Context 573
Test One Potential Cause at a Time 574
Start With the Simple and Obvious Solutions...............................574
The Paragraph Dialog 574
The Word Options 576
The AutoCorrect Options...576
The Display Options 577
Advanced Editing and Display Options..578
    SIDEBAR: Conflicts Between Word and Other Programs (Add-Ins) 580
Preventing, Diagnosing, and Repairing Document Corruption 581
Common Causes of Corruption 581
Symptoms of Corruption..581
Some Possible Remedies and Workarounds................................582
Deleting or Renaming the Normal Template 583
Good Computer "Hygiene"...584
Resources 585
    SIDEBAR: Backing Up Your Normal Template 586

PART X: FILE CONVERSION ISSUES

Opening .docx Files With Older Versions of MS Word 589
WordPerfect to Word Conversions 590
Word to WordPerfect Conversions 592
Avoid Round-Tripping Your Documents 592

APPENDIX A: Quick Start Guides and Other Resources

APPENDIX B: Where Important Word 2016 Files Are Stored

INDEX

Acknowledgments

This book was something of a stealth project, conceived late in 2015 and pursued with little fanfare during a lull in my schedule. Only a few people even knew I was working on it. However, I couldn't have gotten it done without the inspiration, influence, and/or moral support of a close circle of family and friends, as well as a wider circle of acquaintances.

Among the latter, I'm grateful to Donna Payne and her company, Payne Consulting, for laying the groundwork with their superb Word for Law Firms series. Their early books were invaluable when I was first learning to use Word (back when dinosaurs walked the Earth and almost all law firms used WordPerfect). Donna's decision not to write about Word 2007 or Word 2010 left a tremendous gap, which I tried to fill – as best I could – with my own books. In addition to being a role model for me, Donna has been a gracious and supportive colleague.

My trainees have kept me sharp by asking challenging questions that compelled me to learn the material inside-out and to explain complex issues clearly, but without oversimplifying.

My friends and family contributed to this effort primarily through their unstinting emotional support. My mother, Norma J. Baron, also participated in a more tangible way; she served as my proofreader once again, a tedious and thankless task for which I actually do thank her – profusely. She did an outstanding job. (I am solely responsible for any remaining errors.)

My sister, Paula Berinstein, continues to inspire me with her own writing projects – hooray for Amanda Lester! – and with her incredibly creative marketing ideas. I am dazzled by her imagination and tenacity.

My dad, Nathan W. Berinstein, has been gone for nearly ten years, but he's still with me in spirit. He would have been my biggest booster.

Sue Kane, my dear friend and delightful travel buddy, has kept me laughing – and contemplating the meaning of life – over a span of more than 25 years. I feel very lucky to be able to talk with her about anything and everything, however small, silly, or serious.

Linda Hopkins, another treasured friend, has always been there for me, lending support with both words and deeds. Her unwavering belief in me has humbled and touched me. I appreciate her encouragement more than I can say. And she's funny, too!

Marilyn Thomas, who also has been an important part of my life for many years, has taught me much. She has been a companionable and thoughtful friend and a calming influence. We also manage to have an unreasonable amount of fun, even at tech conferences. Go figure.

And Barry – the incomparably funny and charming man with the twinkling eyes – has been my leitmotif, the sweet and sultry background music of my life. He has supplied laughter, succor, adventure, and an abundance of joy. It sounds like hyperbole, but meeting him all those years ago truly did change everything, and only for the better. I have dedicated the book to him as a very small token of my gratitude. And, after all, it's about damn time.

About the Author

Jan Berinstein runs her own software-training company, CompuSavvy Computer Training & Consulting. She provides hands-on classes and on-site training, and also creates customized templates, for law firms and government agencies (among others). She has been involved in dozens of software upgrade projects just in the past five years. Recently, she spent more than 18 months as a consultant to the U.S. Department of Justice in Southern California, assisting with their transition from WordPerfect to Word. In that capacity, she created templates, taught hands-on computer classes, and provided user support.

In 1986, she applied for a part-time job as a legal word processor, and somehow landed the job with no experience – something that would never happen today. She ended up working as a legal word processor for many years, and still takes on word processing projects once in a while for longstanding clients. Those rare exceptions notwithstanding, she made the transition to full-time software trainer a few years ago.

Starting in the mid-1990s, she taught computer classes for legal secretaries and paralegals, as well as "Computers for Seniors" workshops, at UCLA Extension. She also conducted computer classes at the University of West Los Angeles and Learning Tree University, and she led "Internet Legal Research" classes in Los Angeles, San Francisco, and San Jose for the Center for Professional Education / Center for Legal Education.

Ms. Berinstein has given presentations about various computer-related topics at LegalTech Los Angeles, before the Beverly Hills Bar Association, and for several legal secretaries' groups.

A native of Los Angeles, Ms. Berinstein holds a Bachelor's degree in political science from UCLA as well as an M.A. and Ph.D. in government from Cornell University. After working for several years as a freelance writer and editor, she enrolled in UCLA Extension's journalism program and obtained her certification in print journalism in 1993.

She has written two other highly acclaimed books, Formatting Legal Documents With Microsoft Office Word 2007 (published in 2009) and Formatting Legal Documents With Microsoft Word 2010 (published in 2010). She served as a contributing author on Laura Acklen's Absolute Beginner's Guide to WordPerfect 12 (Que Publishing, 2005) and as a technical editor on Ms. Acklen's Absolute Beginner's Guide to WordPerfect X3 (Que Publishing, 2006).

Ms. Berinstein, who uses both Word and WordPerfect to format legal documents on a daily basis, offers article-length tips about both programs in her popular, well-respected blog at http://compusavvy.wordpress.com. She also serves as the webmistress and administrator of the WordPerfect Universe web site, a user-to-user support group (www.wpuniverse.com).

One of these days, she will update her company's web site, which has been accumulating cobwebs for quite some time at www.compusavvy.com.

Introduction

This book is not merely an update of my Word 2010 book. Although it covers some of the same topics, a great deal of the material is brand-new – that is, written completely from scratch. Moreover, I have cut or pared down numerous sections and have added a host of new ones, based partly on my own intuition but also on feedback from a number of people I've trained to use Word in the five-plus years since I published the previous book.

The book aims to help people in the legal profession master the features of Word that are necessary to produce the large volume of paperwork – pleadings, contracts, estate plans, mass mailings, forms, and other documents – that they generate on a daily basis. My goal, as always, is to improve efficiency and ease of use.

I offer practical step-by-step instructions for accomplishing specific tasks, as well as detailed explanations of how Word works "under the hood." Although such explanations might seem extraneous (one reviewer groused that the Word 2010 book reads "like a novel"), they're actually essential for a deeper understanding of Word – why it doesn't always behave as expected and, more importantly, how to fix the problems that arise every now and then (usually when you're on a tight deadline). At the same time, I understand the pressures of the legal profession and the need to get work done quickly, so I have made an effort to include simplified instructions whenever possible.

My target audience spans the entire range of Word users – from novices (including but not limited to long-time WordPerfect users) to word processors and other advanced users who still occasionally run into a problem that leaves them feeling flummoxed.

Topics

As is inevitable in a book such as this one, the choice of which topics to include and which ones to exclude is somewhat subjective. In making those decisions, I was guided by nearly 30 years of experience as a legal word processor and as a software trainer catering primarily to the legal profession. Having trained (and provided support for) hundreds, if not thousands, of people since the early 1990s, I have a very clear sense of which features and functions of Word people find most perplexing. I focus largely on those features and functions, as well as a number of others that I believe people will find useful.

Methodology

I have been using Word 2016 since approximately October of 2015, when I decided to write the book. In fact, I have written the entire book using Word 2016. And rest assured that I tested features extensively while writing about them – even the vast majority of features that existed in prior versions. Sometimes a feature worked as expected; other times, it didn't. In the latter instances, I re-tested and based the "how-to's" on the results of my tests. I also provided workarounds for a few problematic features, as appropriate.

Incidentally, all of the screenshots are from Word 2016, as well. For most of them, I used the White Office Theme (background) because the text is somewhat easier to read on a white background than on blue or dark gray.

Note that any book about a technical subject is a snapshot in time. Because Microsoft routinely updates its software (and also because Microsoft offers a few different "flavors" of the program), your version of Word 2016 might not look or behave exactly like the version I am using in January, 2016.

Organization of the Book

I have revamped the organization substantially in an attempt to improve the logic and flow. It's still a bit quirky in that I arbitrarily put certain features into the section dealing with pleadings and contracts, as opposed to the "everyday features" section. Also, if the placement of some of the tips and sidebars seems a bit odd, it's not your imagination. Although I made an effort to keep all of them with related topics, I had to move a few of the shorter ones around – use them as "fillers" on blank pages – in order to ensure that major sections of the book start on right-facing (recto) pages. (You'll understand if you ever self-publish a technical book.)

The book begins with a "Getting Started" section, describes the screen elements, then explains Word's "logic." This somewhat theoretical discussion about the importance of paragraph formatting, and how it contrasts with section and character formatting, is the key to mastering Word. When I teach classes on this topic, even advanced users often express surprise at how much the information helps to decode Word's occasionally mystifying behaviors.

After presenting those essentials, I discuss several ways to tweak Word to make it more user-friendly – from customizing the Ribbon and the Quick Access Toolbar to changing the default font and the default paragraph settings.

Next, I go over what I refer to as "everyday" features, at the same time emphasizing how those features fit into the program's logical framework.

From there, I provide tips for automating Word with keyboard shortcuts, field codes, simple macros, styles, and templates.

The next two sections focus on features commonly used for formatting specific types of legal documents, including mailings, pleadings, and contracts. Many of the tutorials in this section, including those related to creating and generating a Table of Contents and a Table of Authorities, are completely new (i.e., written specifically for this book).

To wrap things up, I offer some generalized troubleshooting tips; advice about preventing, diagnosing, and repairing document corruption; recommendations about file conversions; information about where key Word files – documents and templates that contain user customizations and critical settings – are stored; and other resources.

Conventions Used in the Book

When describing keyboard shortcuts, I simply list the sequence of keys to be used in combination, such as Ctrl Alt 1, without any "linking" character such as a plus sign between the keys. The context should make it clear that the keys are intended to be used together.

I have attempted to make it easier to follow step-by-step instructions by using boldface to emphasize items that should be clicked or pressed, such as a particular tab of the Ribbon, a group within a tab, a dialog box or task pane, a button or icon, or a keyboard shortcut.

In places, I use boldface and capital letters to make the following advisories stand out:

TIP or **QUICK TIP**: A helpful hint for using a feature more efficiently or, sometimes, for working around a problem. Also, rarely, a **TIPLET**.

TROUBLESHOOTING TIP: A recommendation based on my experience resolving a particular problem I've encountered while using the software.

WORKAROUND: Just that. A method of bypassing something that you find problematic, whether an actual bug in the program or whether an issue that is "Working As Designed."

NOTE: Something to keep in mind – typically, advice that is worth taking into account when you are working with a feature.

CAUTION: A warning about a potential glitch or unexpected/unintended result.

SIDEBAR: A brief section that is peripherally related to the previous section or chapter.

My Style

The book, like my training, is highly task-oriented. My foremost goal is to help people get their work done – as accurately, efficiently, smoothly, and quickly as possible. Toward that end, I always try to use real-world, or at least realistic, examples.

Mixed in with the realism, I sometimes employ offbeat humor to keep my trainees alert during lengthy sessions. I've tried to use this device sparingly in the book so that it doesn't get in the way of the substantive points I'm trying to make.

Also, as I said earlier, I often include "background" or contextual information about features in order to clarify *when* to use the feature as well as *how* to use it. Often the in-depth explanation also helps users recognize the limits of a feature or work around its quirky behavior.

Like the previous books, this one can be somewhat redundant at times. However, I truly believe that most of the redundancy serves a legitimate purpose: It underscores important information that can be easy to miss on first reading.

Lastly, I recognize that there are many different ways to accomplish a particular task in Word. If you have a favorite method that I haven't described in the book, keep using it! There's no compelling reason to change the way you do things, as long as your preferred method works – that is, it accomplishes what you intend (and doesn't cause other problems).

Also, I'm aware that I tend to emphasize certain methods at the expense of others – for example, I'm not much of a right-clicker, so sometimes it slips my mind to mention that method – but if you prefer to accomplish tasks by right-clicking, go for it! I would never be so presumptuous as to claim that my way is the best way, although from time to time I *will* offer the benefit of my experience and point out which methods I have found to be more or less effective. And I will also alert you to glitches and dead ends, and provide workarounds whenever possible.

*　*　*　*　*

Many thanks for purchasing the book! I hope it proves to be a useful resource that helps to make your everyday work significantly easier, more efficient, and more trouble-free.

Jan Berinstein, Ph.D.
CompuSavvy
Computer Training & Consulting
Northridge, California
compusavvy2@earthlink.net
Winter, 2016

PART I: Launching Word

Getting Started With Word

This section of the book is intended to get you up and running quickly. We'll take a much closer look at the Word interface (screen) in the next section.

The Start Screen

When you first open Word, you will not go directly to a new blank document. Rather, you will see a start screen that looks something like this:

The Word 2016 Start Screen

You'll notice immediately that there is a large "**Recent**" link below the program name. After you've saved some documents in Word, links to your recent documents will appear in that area. However, the first time you launch Word, there won't be any recent documents displayed. Instead, you have three choices: You can begin working on a new blank document, create a document based on one of Microsoft's templates, or browse for an existing document that is located on your computer or that you have stored in the "cloud."

Using a "Featured" Template

Most of us in the legal profession seldom use Microsoft's built-in or online templates. But if you decide, after scrolling through the "Featured" templates on the Start screen, that you want to use one of them as the basis for a new document, simply click that template's icon. Then click "Create," which opens a new doc based on the template and downloads the template to your computer. Also, if you are not familiar with Word, you might find the "Take a tour / Welcome to Word" template useful. It offers a few tips about the new features of Word 2016.

Starting a Blank Document

To begin working on a new blank document, simply click the large "**Blank document**" icon to the right of the solid-colored vertical pane (which I sometimes refer to as a Navigation Pane). Doing so will take you directly to a new document editing screen.

Opening an Existing Document

To locate and open an existing document, click the "**Open Other Documents**" link at the left side of the screen (below "Recent").

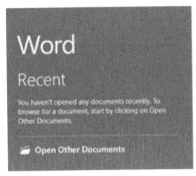

Open Other Documents

NOTE: Whereas in most recent versions, File > Open goes directly to the Open dialog in Windows, the "Open Other Documents" link in Word 2016 (and Word 2013) takes you to the "**Open**" screen (shown below) so that you can browse on your computer or, if you have a (Microsoft) OneDrive account and you have been saving documents to the cloud, you can work on a document that you have stored there. This changed functionality is one of the most significant differences between Word 2013/2016 and previous versions.

The Open Screen

Working Offline Versus Signing into OneDrive

Despite Microsoft's friendly reminder at the right side of the Start Screen to "Sign in to get the most out of Office," you don't necessarily need a OneDrive / Microsoft account in order to work in Word – assuming that you have offline access to the program. (If you use Office 365, it's possible that you will have to sign in.) The main advantage of creating and signing into a OneDrive account is that you can save documents online (to the "cloud"). Doing so gives you access to those docs from any computer, tablet, or phone that has Internet access.[1]

When you are signed in, you also have access to a few additional features, such as online video and online pictures (formerly known as Clip Art).

However, if you have Word installed on your computer, you can work offline as a matter of course and periodically sign into your OneDrive account to save certain documents to the cloud. (That is my preferred way to work. I typically save documents to the computer, but occasionally – as with drafts of my books – store copies of important documents online. I can sign into OneDrive at any time, and then sign out after I've uploaded my documents.)

You can always set up a OneDrive / Microsoft account later on, if you wish.

Opening Documents From OneDrive

If you already have documents stored in OneDrive, you can sign into your account, then open a document by clicking "OneDrive" in the Open screen.

Open - OneDrive

---

[1] For those of you who use Word 2016 at work, be aware that your organization might not allow you to use OneDrive to save documents to the cloud.

You'll be prompted to sign in. If you already have an account, just sign in with either an e-mail address or a phone number, plus your password.

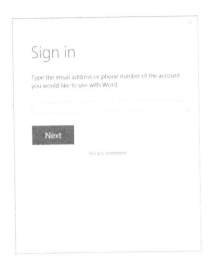 

If you don't have an account, type the e-mail address or phone number you want to use, then follow the prompts to set up an account.

Once you have signed in, you will see your user name in the upper right corner of the Word screen.

My User Name (Upper Right-Hand Corner)

Close-Up of My User Name

Signing Out of OneDrive

If you see your user name in the upper right-hand corner, you can sign out by clicking it, then clicking "**Account settings**" in the drop-down menu. That will take you to the Account screen so that you can sign out.

4

Sign Out

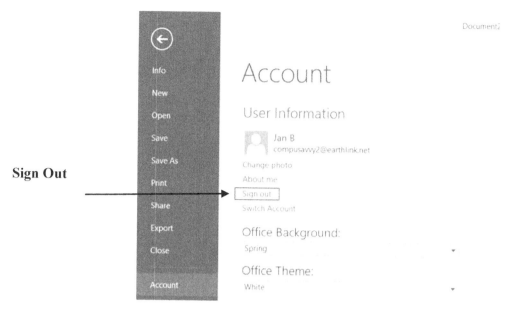

Account Screen (Partially Shown)

If you ***don't*** see your user name in the upper right-hand corner of the Word screen, you can sign out by clicking the **File tab**, **Account**. That will take you directly to the Account screen pictured above. When you click "Sign out," you'll see the following message:

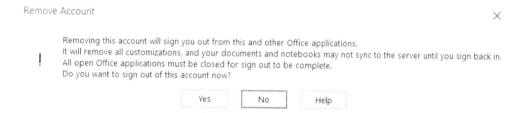

Don't be concerned about the part that says "All open Office applications must be closed for sign out to be complete." Obviously, you can sign out while you're still working in Word. This message is simply a reminder that signing out of Word – i.e., so that the program isn't linked directly to the cloud – also will sign you out of any other Office programs you have open, such as Excel. All of your programs will continue to work; you just won't be able to save to the cloud (the Web).

CAUTION: If you have been saving a document (or several documents) to the cloud and you sign out before you have saved your most recent edits, you will see a prompt warning you that you need to sign in to your OneDrive / Microsoft account again in order to upload the latest changes.

Opening Documents From Your Computer

The Open screen provides a few different ways to open documents on your computer. As shown in the screenshot below, there are submenus labeled Recent, This PC and Browse. ("Add a Place" is for adding a link to your OneDrive / Microsoft account, if any, or to SharePoint.

However, if you work for an organization that uses SharePoint, your IT department probably will set this link up for you.)

Opening Recent Documents

The "**Recent**" link typically shows up to 25 of your recently used documents. As discussed in the next section (in the long portion about the File tab), you can configure Word to show no recent documents at all or any number from 1 to 50. Also, you can "pin" documents to the Recent list. Unpinned documents will rotate off the list as you open more than the maximum number set in the Word Options.

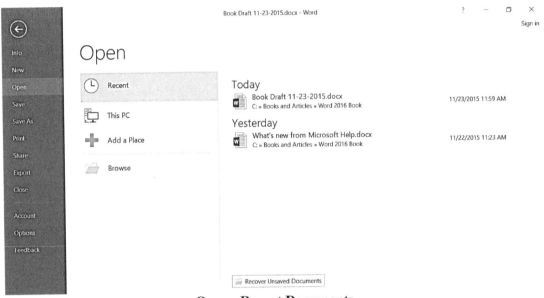

Open - Recent Documents

"This PC"

When you click "**This PC**," Word displays recently opened folders and subfolders, plus any documents contained in the top-level folder (the one above the horizontal line – see the screenshot below).

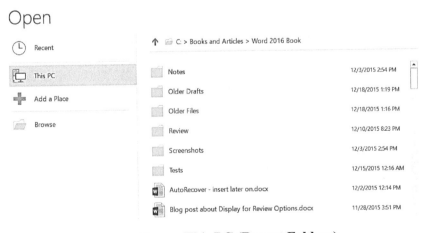

Open - This PC (Recent Folders)

Because I recently opened a draft of this book, "This PC" shows my "Word 2016 Book" folder above the horizontal line. Below the line, you can see subfolders of that folder, as well as a few files stored in the main "Word 2016 Book" folder. (They appear to display in alphabetical / name order regardless of the order you've set from within a dialog box.) [2]

Clicking a file opens the file; clicking a folder opens the folder. You also have the option of opening a file or folder by right-clicking it.

For example, when I click the "Notes" subfolder of my "Word 2016 Book" folder, Word shows the contents of that subfolder (see the screenshot). Clicking the "**Up**" **arrow** opens the higher-level folder. In this case, it returns to the "Word 2016 Book" folder (not shown).

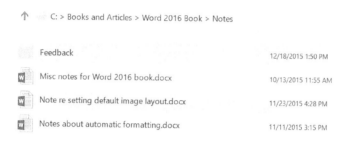

My "Notes" Subfolder

Clicking "Up" again goes up one more level – to my "Books and Articles" folder.

My "Books and Articles" Folder

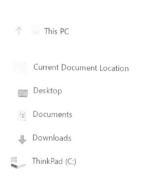

If you keep clicking the "Up" arrow, eventually you will reach the very top level (in my case, and the arrow will be grayed out; you'll see something similar to the screenshot at right. Clicking "**Current Document Location**" opens the most recently opened folder.

Browse

Finally, if you can't find the document you need under recent folders, you can "**Browse**" to go to the familiar **Open dialog**.[3]

---

[2] Your screen might look somewhat different, especially on a computer at your job site.

[3] The Open dialog looks somewhat different depending on which version of Windows you use.

7

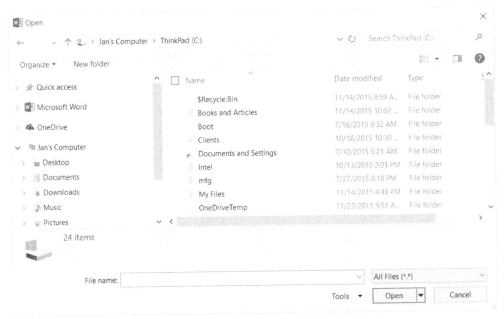

Open Dialog Box (Windows 10)

At this point, you might be wondering, "Do I have to go through all of these steps every time I want to open a document? After all, in earlier versions of Word, I just clicked File > Open or used a keyboard shortcut to go directly to the Open dialog in Windows." The answer is a resounding "No!"

Bypassing the Start Screen / Going Directly to the "Open" Dialog

A Temporary Fix

You'll be pleased to learn that you can bypass the start screen and go directly to the Open dialog in Windows Explorer / File Explorer by pressing **Ctrl F12**, one of the keyboard shortcuts for "**Open**" in Word and other Microsoft Office programs.

Note that pressing Ctrl O, another keyboard shortcut for "Open," does not bypass the start screen. Rather, it takes you to the File > Open screen, where you have to click Recent, This PC, or Browse.[4] And, at least on my computer, clicking the "Open" icon on the Quick Access Toolbar also produces the File > Open screen, rather than the Open dialog in Windows.

A Permanent Fix

If you want to bypass the Start Screen altogether, you can configure the Word Options to do so. Just follow the steps below.

---

[4] You can, however, reassign the keyboard shortcut Ctrl O to the standard "File Open" command, rather than the "File Open From Backstage" command that Microsoft has assigned to that keyboard shortcut in both Word 2016 and Word 2013. For instructions, see the tip on page 174.

8

1.   Click **File**, **Options**.

     The Word Options dialog opens, with the General category at the forefront.

2.   Navigate to the section labeled "**Start up options**."

3.   *Uncheck* "**Show the Start screen when this application starts**." (It is checked by default.)

Start up options

Choose the extensions you want Word to open by default: Default Programs...

☐ Tell me if Microsoft Word isn't the default program for viewing and editing documents.

☑ Open e-mail attachments and other uneditable files in reading view

☑ Show the Start screen when this application starts

4.   Click **OK** to save your changes and close the Word Options dialog.

CAUTION: Don't click the red "X" at the top right side of the Word Options dialog. If you do so, Word won't save your configuration changes.

Now that you've gotten started, let's explore the rest of the Word interface in detail.

What's New and Different in Word 2016

This chart lists – in no particular order – a few of the major and minor changes in Word 2016 (some of which were introduced in Word 2013).

Feature	What It Does	See page(s)
Tell me what you want to do...	Interactive Help / Search – provides an easy and readily available way to look up a feature	116
Open PDF directly into Word	Allows you to open a PDF directly into Word for editing.	319
Real-Time Co-Authoring	Allows simultaneous editing of a document by different people.	87
Header & Footer Tools - Insert Document Info	Makes it easy to insert codes for document information such as the file name and path	248
Smart Lookup	Replaces "Research" function; provides definitions of words and phrases as well as info from Wikipedia and other web sites	116, 322
Auto-Numbering - changes to right-click menu	Microsoft removed some of the options previously available on the right-click menu. Now, you must click the Numbering Button drop-down in the Paragraph group on the Home tab to locate those options.	490
Track Changes – Display for Review options have changed	"All Markup" – shows all revisions "Simple Markup" – hides revisions but shows "change lines" in the margins "No Markup" – displays the document as if changes had been accepted "Original" – displays the document as it looked before revisions	559
Collapsible Headings	You can collapse headings in order to see an "outline" view of your document by clicking a triangle to the left of the heading	289

PART II: The Word Interface

The Word 2016 Interface (Screen)

For those of you who have been working with a "Ribbonized" version of Word – that is, Word 2007, 2010, or 2013 – Word 2016's interface (screen) won't seem terribly different. Microsoft has not radically changed the overall design, or the placement of most of the commands. The most obvious change has to do with the File tab, which I'll discuss in detail shortly.

There are a few other minor differences from earlier versions: a new Design tab (actually added in Word 2013), an Add-Ins group in the Insert tab (also added in Word 2013), an Insights group in the Review tab (new to Word 2016), slight changes to the methods for minimizing / collapsing and then restoring the Ribbon (introduced in Word 2013), and a brand-new interactive help / search function labeled "Tell me what you want to do…"

Also, in both Word 2013 and Word 2016, Microsoft revamped the Status Bar in at least one important way – by removing Draft View from the View Shortcuts section.

For folks who have been using a version of Word older than Word 2007 – i.e., before the introduction of the Ribbon-based interface – Word 2016 will seem like a completely different animal. The same holds true for WordPerfect users (and yes, some law firms and government agencies still use WordPerfect!).

This part of the book provides both an overview of and an in-depth look at the Word 2016 interface.

Overview

Choosing a Screen Color / Office Theme

When you first start using Word (or any of the MS Office programs), you might want to change the screen color, also known as the Office Theme. Microsoft has provided only three choices: White, Colorful, and Dark Gray. Whichever one you choose will be applied to **all** of your MS Office programs (Word, Outlook, Excel, PowerPoint, etc.).

To change your screen color / Office Theme, do the following:

1. Click the File tab (at the top left side of your screen);

2. Navigate to the bottom left and click "Options";

3. Locate the section of the Word Options screen labeled "Personalize your copy of Microsoft Office"

4. Click the Office Theme drop-down and choose White, Colorful, or Dark Gray (see the screenshot).

If you have signed into OneDrive, you will also have the option of choosing among various "Office Backgrounds" that decorate the upper right-side of the screen.

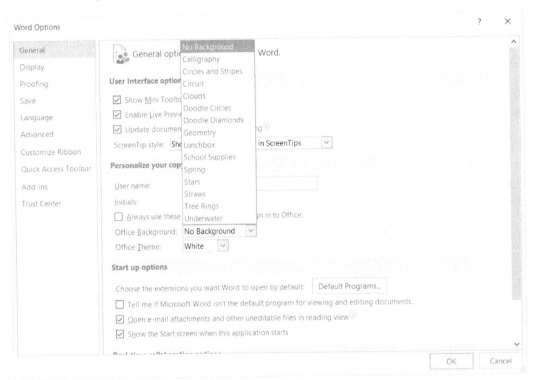

The screenshots below show the "Spring" background with the White Office Theme.

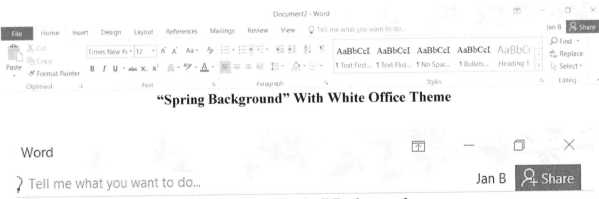

"Spring Background" With White Office Theme

Close-up of "Spring" Background

Backgrounds are not available unless you sign in to your OneDrive / Microsoft account.

The Ribbon, Tabs, and Groups

With the introduction of Office 2007, Microsoft abandoned the menus and toolbars that had been standard in nearly every program running on Windows. In place of those familiar screen elements, the newer versions of MS Office programs (Word, Excel, PowerPoint, and Outlook) prominently feature a single thick toolbar called "the **Ribbon**." The Ribbon consists of several "**tabs**"; within each tab, there are bite-sized "**groups**" of commands.[1]

The Permanent (Main) Tabs

In Word 2016, there are nine permanent "tabs" on the Ribbon (also sometimes referred to as the Main tabs): File, Home, Design, Insert, Layout,[2] References, Mailings, Review, and View. By default, the Home tab is at the forefront. See the screenshot below. (Note that your screen might look somewhat different, both because you might be using a different screen color / Office Theme and because you or your employer might have added some custom tabs and/or moved some items.)

The Ribbon - The Permanent Tabs
(White Office Theme)

The Groups

Each "tab" consists of "groups" of related commands (with commands shown as icons, most of which have text labels as well as images[3]). The groups, separated by thin vertical divider lines, have labels across the bottom. Each group contains several related commands. For instance, at the left end of the Home tab, there is a Clipboard group that contains commands for cutting, copying, and pasting text, as well as using the Format Painter to copy paragraph formatting. (More on the Format Painter elsewhere.)

---

[1] Although some people refer to the tabs as "Ribbons," there's actually only one Ribbon, which is divided into separate tabs. In using these terms, I am adhering to Microsoft's own terminology (dating back to the company's blog posts when it introduced Office 2007, and internally consistent within the program itself – for instance, when you customize the Ribbon, you'll choose icons from the "Main Tabs," "Tool Tabs," and so forth). Just be aware that when people speak of, say, "the View Ribbon," they mean the same thing as when I speak of "the View tab."

[2] In versions prior to Word 2016, "Layout" was called "Page Layout."

[3] The main exceptions are the commands in the Font and Paragraph groups on the Home tab.

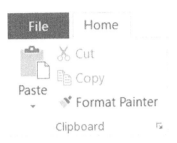

To the right of the Clipboard group, there is a Font group. It contains commands for working with fonts – changing the font face and/or size and/or color, changing case, applying attributes such as bold or underlining, using strikeout, inserting a subscript or superscript, adding highlighting, etc. You get the idea.

Dialog Launchers

Some groups, such as the Font group and the Paragraph group on the Home tab, contain a dialog launcher (an arrow pointing down and rightward diagonally) in the lower right-hand corner. Because the dialog launchers – also called dialog box launchers – are small and unobtrusive, people sometimes overlook them. That's unfortunate, because they come in handy at times. When you click the arrow, the dialog box opens, offering more advanced options than what is available in the Ribbon.

Dialog Launcher (Magnified)

When you point to a dialog launcher, you'll see a description of what the dialog box does. (Some descriptions are lengthy; some are very abbreviated.) In a couple of cases, you'll also see the keyboard shortcut that opens the dialog box. See the screenshot below for an example.

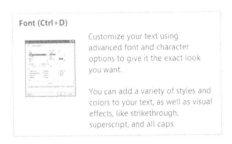

Clicking the Font dialog launcher or pressing the keyboard shortcut **Ctrl D** opens the Font dialog:

The Logic of the Tabs

To my mind, there is a certain logic to the tabs. This logic might be helpful to you as you are trying to locate specific commands.

The File Tab – Commands for File Management, Including Printing and Sharing Files

The File tab is where you'll find the familiar commands for opening, saving, and closing files, as well as for starting a new document based on a template. In addition, this tab is the location of commands for printing files, sharing files (via e-mail or the cloud), changing the file type of an existing document, reviewing a document's properties, and stripping metadata from a document.

Because the File tab is so important, and because it has changed dramatically in recent versions of Word, I have dedicated a separate section of the book to it. My in-depth discussion of the File tab follows the discussion of the other tabs.

The Home Tab – Common Commands for Everyday Formatting

In all of the Office programs – not just Word – Microsoft has placed the commands that people use most commonly for basic formatting. For example, the commands for cutting, copying, and pasting text are on Home, as are all of the commands related to fonts as well as paragraph formatting (justification, line spacing, borders, etc.) and automatic numbered and bulleted lists.

Options for finding and replacing text are also located on the Home tab. So is the Style Gallery (previously called the Quick Styles Gallery), along with a dialog launcher that opens the Styles Pane. From the Styles Pane, you can create, modify, and apply styles and determine which ones appear in the Style Gallery – and in which order.[4]

The Insert Tab – For Inserting Tables, Images, Charts, Shapes, Text Boxes, Symbols

This tab is almost self-explanatory, or at least fairly logical. It is the Insert tab that stores commands for adding tables, images (pictures), shapes, text boxes, and symbols to your documents. The Insert tab also features an icon for inserting a date, either as a code that automatically updates or as plain text. Plus, the QuickParts drop-down is very useful for creating and inserting boilerplate text, as I'll explain later.

There are a few commands on the Insert tab that either aren't heavily used in the legal profession or that I consider to be the long and clunky way of doing things – such as inserting headers, footers, and page numbers. For adding a page number to the bottom of a simple document (as opposed to a pleading or contract), those commands might work perfectly well, however.

The one command that you might expect to be on the Insert tab that isn't there is Footnotes. Rather, you insert footnotes from the References tab, which will make more sense after I explain what I consider to be the logic of *that* tab.

NOTE: Some icons, including all of those in the Add-ins group, are grayed out – i.e., unavailable – when you are working in a document that has been saved in the older .doc format, as opposed to the newer .docx format.

The Design Tab – "Themes" (Colors / Fonts / Effects), Watermarks

Much of what is on the Design tab isn't particularly useful for the legal profession, in my opinion. The left-hand portion of the tab features Themes and Style Sets, "canned" formatting options that typically don't meet strict Court requirements such as those imposed by the California Rules of Court and the Federal Rules of Civil / Criminal Procedure. Although I explain Themes and Style Sets later in the book, neither is widely used by law firms or government agencies.

Watermarks, which are more common in legal documents, have been moved to the Design tab.

Layout (Page Layout) – Page Formatting, Paragraph Spacing, and Arrange Objects

The Layout tab, formerly called "Page Layout," harbors most of the commands that affect the formatting of an entire page: page margins, orientation (landscape versus portrait), page size, and section breaks. Section breaks, as noted in the section starting on page 241 and in

---

[4] Styles will be defined, and discussed in depth, in the section starting on page 385.

the Sidebar starting on page 243, are necessary when you want to change page formatting (such as page numbering) within a document.

In Word 2007 and 2010, this tab also featured a Page Background group that included icons for inserting watermarks, for changing the page color, and for adding page borders. To me, that made perfect sense, since the features in the Page Background group, like most of the other items on the tab, affect an entire page, rather than a paragraph. However, starting with Word 2013, Microsoft moved the entire Page Background group (Watermark, Page Color, and Page Borders) to the Design tab, while retaining the Paragraph group on Layout. Even though I understand the rationale behind placing the features in the Page Background group on the Design tab, it seems to me that the change undermined the logic and integrity of the Page Layout tab.

Having a Paragraph group on the Layout tab makes it easy to set left and right indents as well as before and after spacing, but it's really not necessary since you can do the same thing easily enough by opening the Paragraph dialog from the Home tab (or by right-clicking). Plus, it confuses functions that, to me, are better kept separate – i.e., page formatting and paragraph formatting. See the portion of the book about Word's logic, beginning on page 121, for a discussion of the very essential differences between page and paragraph formatting.

Just my two cents.[5]

The other portion of the Layout tab that doesn't neatly fit into my logical scheme is the Arrange group. This group includes commands used for formatting images and other objects (text boxes, shapes, charts, and the like). The one advantage of the Arrange group, as far as I can tell, is that it is always available (unlike the contextual tabs for each type of object, which appears only when you click on an object). However, since you have to click on the object to apply the commands from the Arrange group anyway, I'm not entirely sure what the purpose of this group is. Like the duplicate Paragraph group, it strikes me as somewhat redundant. I can appreciate the logic of placing commands for arranging objects on the Layout tab, however.

The References Tab – Features That Refer to Another Part of the Document

I used to get confused between the two tabs that start with the letter "R" – References and Review. What finally clarified the essential difference(s) was the realization that References primarily is for features that refer from one part of the document to another, such as footnotes, a Table of Contents, and/or a Table of Authorities. Not surprisingly, the References tab also contains commands for adding a bibliography and/or an index (such as the index for this book).

This tab also is the place to look if you want to insert a cross-reference in your document. (That command doesn't really fit in the Captions group, since you can use cross-references to refer to a numbered paragraph or other items that are not captions or part of a table of figures.)

---

[5] As I sometimes say during training sessions, Microsoft has never asked my opinion about such matters – even though I'm waiting patiently by the phone.

WATCH OUT: Insert Citation does not allude to a legal citation. Note that the command is in the "Citations and Bibliography" group, which is significant. It relates to a bibliographic citation, not a legal one.

Review – Features You Use Before Sharing a Document

By contrast with References, the Review tab is home to the functions you use before sharing a document – whether with colleagues at work, with co-counsel, with opposing counsel, or with a client. These functions include Spelling, Word Count, Comments, Track Changes, and Compare Documents.

Mailings

The Mailings tab has icons for setting up envelopes and labels, as well as tools for performing a mail merge (where data is pulled from a data file such as a mailing list or service list into a form such as a letter, an envelope, a Proof of Service, etc.).

View – Change the Display of Various Items

The View tab, unsurprisingly, features commands that affect what you display on screen and how it looks. The commands on this tab include Document Views, Zooming, Display Ruler, Display Navigation Pane (not the same as the pane in the File tab!), View Side by Side, and Switch Windows.

For reasons unknown, there is also a drop-down at the right side of the View tab for working with Macros.

TIPLET: When you have enabled or turned on an item such as automatic numbering or Track Changes, the icon for that item is highlighted in the Ribbon. Depending on which Office Theme (color) you've chosen, the highlighting might be light blue or light gray – in earlier versions of Word, it was orange.

SIDEBAR: Document Views

To change your document view, go to the **View tab**, **View group** and choose among the following:

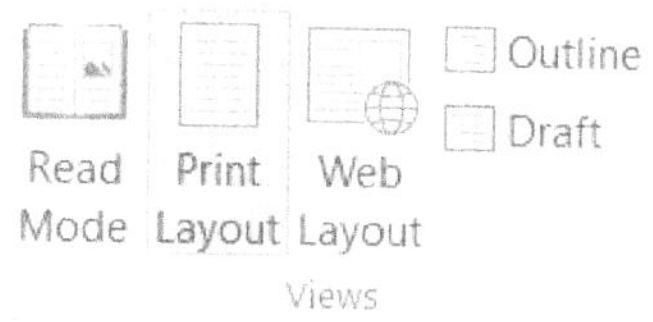

Read Mode | Print Layout | Web Layout | Outline | Draft

Views

Read Mode – By default, all Word documents you receive by e-mail will open in Read Mode, a very basic, stripped-down view of the document and the Word screen. (Also, such documents will be set as **read-only**, which means you will have to save them with a new name). It can be difficult to figure out how to return to the normal Word editing screen.

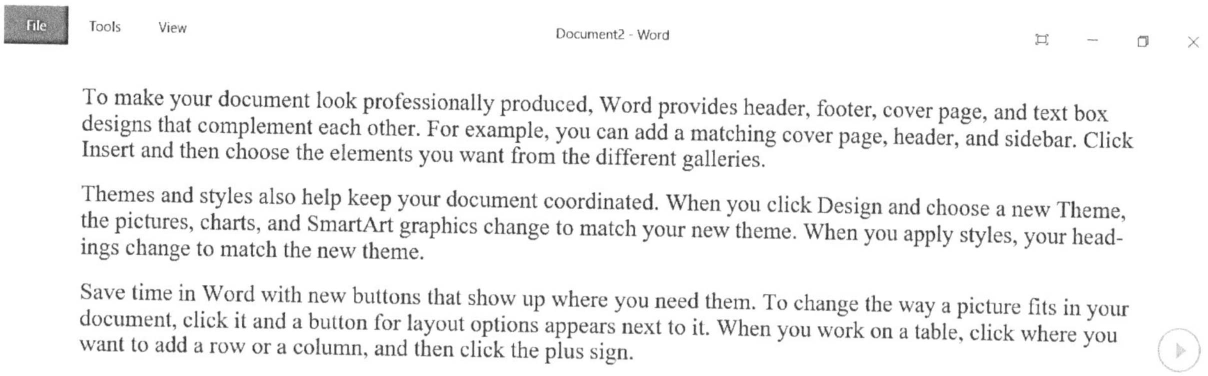

File   Tools   View   Document2 - Word   ☐ — ☐ ✕

To make your document look professionally produced, Word provides header, footer, cover page, and text box designs that complement each other. For example, you can add a matching cover page, header, and sidebar. Click Insert and then choose the elements you want from the different galleries.

Themes and styles also help keep your document coordinated. When you click Design and choose a new Theme, the pictures, charts, and SmartArt graphics change to match your new theme. When you apply styles, your headings change to match the new theme.

Save time in Word with new buttons that show up where you need them. To change the way a picture fits in your document, click it and a button for layout options appears next to it. When you work on a table, click where you want to add a row or a column, and then click the plus sign.

View

Edit Document

Navigation Pane

Show Comments

Column Width   ›

Page Color   ›

Layout   ›

Note the View menu at the top left side of the screen. Click **View**, then click the first command, **Edit Document**, to close Read Mode and return to the Print Layout view that you're accustomed to.

You can configure Word so that it does not automatically open attachments in Read Mode. Click **File**, **Options**, and while in the General category, navigate to "**Start up options.**" *Uncheck* "**Open e-mail attachments and other uneditable files in reading view**" and **OK** out.

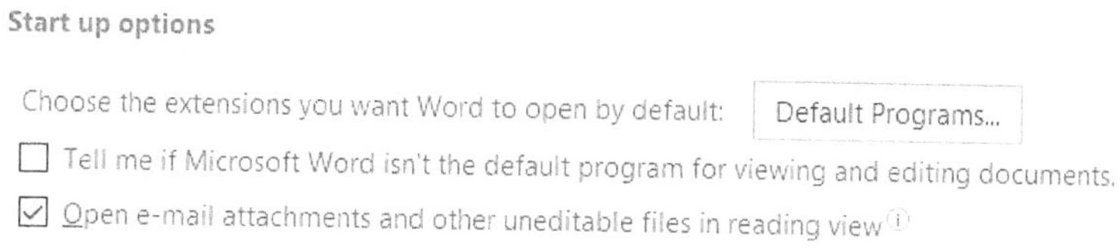

Start up options

Choose the extensions you want Word to open by default: Default Programs...

☐ Tell me if Microsoft Word isn't the default program for viewing and editing documents.

☑ Open e-mail attachments and other uneditable files in reading view ⓘ

Print Layout – This is the view most people prefer. It displays the document as it will look when printed, which means it is a "WYSIWYG" (What You See Is What You Get) view.

Draft View – Formerly called Normal (although it wasn't the view that most people normally used, which is probably why Microsoft renamed it), Draft view hides headers, footers, and other graphical elements. Somewhat less cluttered than Print Layout view, it's useful when working on legal documents because it can be configured to show the styles (if any) that have been applied in the document.[1] It also makes section breaks and page breaks easier to see.

Web Layout – Seldom used in the legal field, this view shows what your doc would look like as a web page.

Outline View – Outline view shows your document as if the headings and text were in outline form. You can apply up to nine heading styles quickly, collapse and expand the outline to show only certain heading levels, and move headings (and associated text) easily. For more about the Outline View, see the sidebar on page 291.

In addition to changing document views from the View tab, you can click one of the **View Shortcuts** on the Status Bar (but you're limited to Read Mode, Print Layout, and Web Layout; there is no way to add the others to the Status Bar).

Or you can use keyboard shortcuts:

- Read Mode — Alt W, F
- Print Layout — Ctrl Alt P
- Web Layout — Alt W, L
- Outline – Ctrl Alt O
- Draft – Ctrl Alt N (for Normal)

If you like, you can add icons for the various document views to the Quick Access Toolbar (also known as the "QAT").[2]

---

[1] Instructions on pages 396 and following.

[2] For general instructions on adding items to the Quick Access Toolbar / QAT (the narrow toolbar where you can put icons for the commands you use most often), see the section starting on page 175.

SIDEBAR: The Tabs at a Glance

The Permanent (Main) Tabs

There are nine permanent (Main) tabs, as follows:

The Home Tab

Groups on the Home tab: Clipboard, Font, Paragraph, Styles, Editing

The Insert Tab

Groups on the Insert tab: Tables, Illustrations, Media, Comments, Header & Footer, Text

The Design Tab

Groups on the Design tab: Document Formatting, Page Background

The Layout Tab

Groups on the Layout tab: Page Setup, Paragraph, Arrange

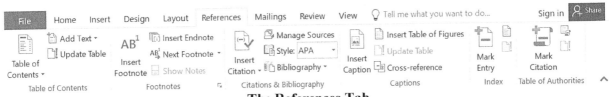
The References Tab

Groups on the References tab: Table of Contents, Footnotes, Citations & Bibliography, Captions, Index, Table of Authorities

The Mailings Tab

Groups on the Mailings tab: Create, Start Mail Merge, Write & Insert Fields, Preview Results, Finish

The Review Tab

Groups on the Review tab: Proofing, Insights, Comments, Tracking, Changes, Compare

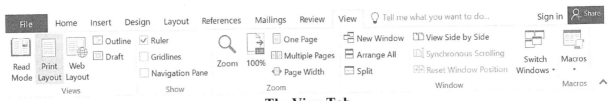
The View Tab

Groups on the View tab: Views, Show, Zoom, Window, Macros

When you click the File tab, it opens full screen. There is a vertical menu or navigation pane[1] at left; clicking any menu item opens a "screen" that extends across the entire screen.

The File Tab

Commands on the File tab include Info, New, Open, Save, Save As, Print, Share, Export, Close, Account, Options, and Feedback. Also, you can configure Word to show a few Recent documents at the bottom of the vertical menu.

---

[1] As I mention elsewhere, I'm not sure what Microsoft calls this part of the File tab, but the "Navigation Pane" terminology is consistent with how the company refers to many of the vertical menus in the Microsoft Office suite.

The Contextual Tabs

Some additional tabs, called "Contextual tabs" or "Context-Sensitive tabs," appear when you perform specific tasks (e.g., when you're working with tables, with headers and footers, or with images). Perhaps the most important, and among the most frequently used, are the Header & Footer Tools tab (which appears only when your cursor is within a header or footer), the Table Tools tab (which appears only when your cursor is within a table), and the Picture Tools tab (which appears only when you click on an image). The Table Tools tab is divided into two parts: Design (with commands that affect the *appearance* of the table) and Layout (with commands that affect the table *structure*).

A few of the contextual tabs, with summaries of the command groups they contain, are shown below.

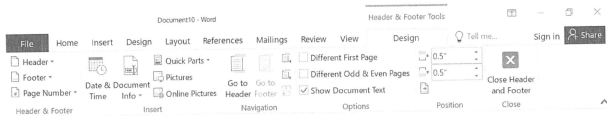
Header & Footer Tools

Groups on the Header & Footer Tools tab: Header & Footer, Insert, Navigation, Options, Position, Close

Table Tools - Design

Groups on the Table Tools – Design tab: Table Style Options, Table Styles, Borders

Table Tools – Layout

Groups on the Table Tools – Layout tab: Table, Draw, Rows & Columns, Merge, Cell Size, Alignment

Picture Tools

Groups on the Picture Tools tab: Adjust, Picture Styles, Arrange, Size

The Optional Tabs

Word comes with a couple of optional tabs (the Developer tab and the Add-Ins tab) that can be added permanently to the Ribbon, as well. The Developer tab is particularly useful because it provides easy access to commands for working with macros. The Add-Ins tab appears to be enabled – checked – by default in Word 2016, but I have no Add-Ins for Word yet (I'm working on a new computer) so that tab is not displayed on my system.

The Developer Tab

Groups on the Developer tab: Code, Add-ins, Controls, Mapping, Protect, Templates.

SIDEBAR: Working With the Contextual Tabs

As mentioned in the previous section, recent versions of Word come with a variety of **contextual tabs**, also known as **context-sensitive tabs**. The context-sensitive tabs appear only when you are performing a specific task or using a certain feature, such as when your cursor is in a header or footer editing screen or within a table or when you have clicked an image.

Sometimes with contextual tabs, the tab label seems to disappear. For example, if you are working in a header or footer and you click the Home tab in order to change a font setting or adjust paragraph formatting, the Header & Footer Tools tab label vanishes, taking with it some icons you might wish to use—including the all-important Close Header and Footer button.

Never fear! The tab is still there, though it has faded into the background. You should see the tab toward the top of the screen. Just click it to bring it to the forefront again. The same is true with the Picture Tools tab and many of the other context-sensitive tabs. (In the case of the Table Tools tabs, simply click somewhere within the table to make the tabs visible.)

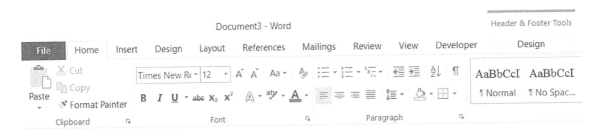

Note that if you use the .doc format (compatible with Word 97-2003) rather than the .docx format, some of the context-sensitive tabs either will not be available or they will work differently from the way they work .docx files. For example, when you insert Smart Art into a .doc in Word 2016, you have access to only the diagrams and organizational charts (as opposed to the Smart Art graphics), and after you insert one of those, you will see just the Diagram Tools tab or the Organizational Chart tab, as appropriate. Even in Word 2007, by contrast, you can insert Smart Art into a .doc – as well as into a .docx – and you have access to the full range of Smart Art options (and the Smart Art contextual tab is visible).

Here is a complete list of the context-sensitive tabs and commands in Word 2016. (You can display the full list by **right-clicking the Ribbon** (or the QAT) and clicking "**Customize the Ribbon…**," then navigating to the right-hand side of the Word Options screen and changing the "**Customize the Ribbon" drop-down** from "Main Tabs" to "**All Tabs**." You'll probably have to scroll to see everything.)

Most of the items are self-explanatory.

- Blog Post
- Insert (Blog Post)
- Outlining
- Background Removal

(The Background Removal command, part of the Picture Tools tab, appears when you click a photo. It provides a method for removing the background from your images. Note that it becomes active only in a .docx or one of the other Open Office XML file formats.)

- Smart Art Tools
  - Design
  - Format
- Chart Tools
  - Design
  - Format
- Drawing Tools
  - Format
- Picture Tools
  - Format
- Table Tools
  - Design
  - Layout
- Header & Footer Tools
  - Design 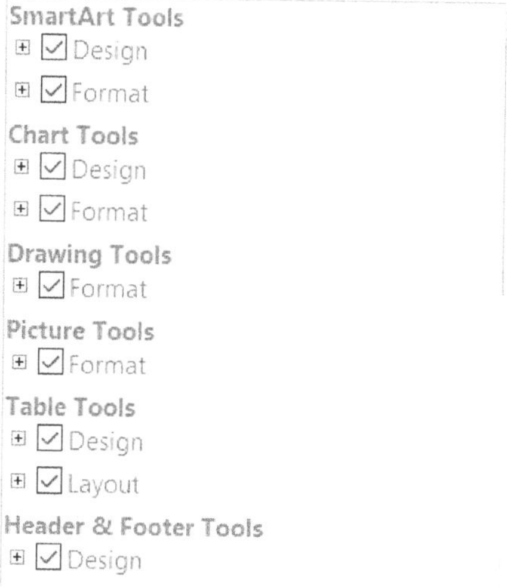
- Equation Tools
  - Design
- Ink Tools
  - Pens
- Text Box Tools (Compatibility Mode)
  - Format
- Drawing Tools (Compatibility Mode)
  - Format
- WordArt Tools (Compatibility Mode)
- Diagram Tools (Compatibility Mode)
- Organization Chart Tools (Compatibility Mode)
- Picture Tools (Compatibility Mode)

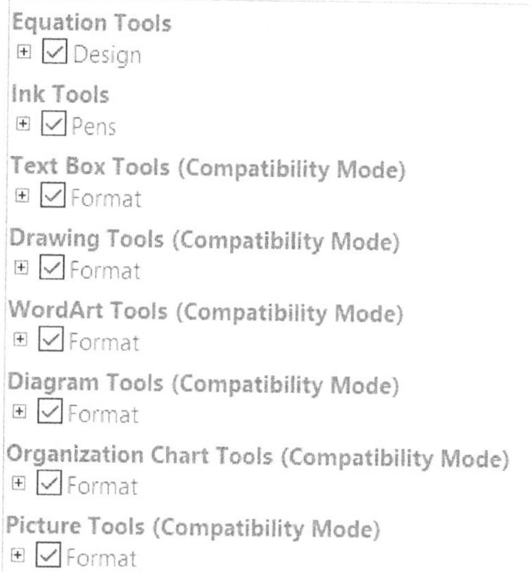

Where Is It?

This chart gives you a quick way to locate some of the hard-to-find features in Word. I've included features that my trainees commonly ask about, as well as a few that are located in places I don't find particularly obvious or logical – and some that were in a different spot in Word 2010.

Feature	Location
Footnotes	References tab (Footnotes group)
Spell-Checker	Review tab (Proofing group)
Find / Find & Replace	Home tab (Editing group)
Symbols	Insert tab (Symbols group)
Change Case	Home tab (Font group)
Superscript / Subscript	Home tab (Font group)
Strikeout	Home (Font group)
Section Breaks	Layout tab (Page Setup group)
Track Changes	Review tab (Tracking group)
Comment	Review tab (Comments group); also Insert tab (Comments group)
Compare Documents	Review tab (Compare group)
Tables (Columnar Tables)	Insert tab (Tables group)
AutoCorrect	File tab > Options > Proofing
Dictionary ("Smart Lookup")	Review tab (Insights group)
Sort (Sorting)	Home tab (Paragraph group); also Table Tools, Layout tab (Data group)
Watermark	Design tab (Page Background group)
Bookmarks	Insert tab (Links group)
Cross-References	Insert tab (Links group); also References tab (Captions group)
Macros	View tab (Macros group); also Developer tab (Code group)

SIDEBAR: Minimizing (Collapsing) and Restoring the Ribbon

The Ribbon can be "minimized" (collapsed) to gain more room on the screen. Essentially, you have two choices: You can **minimize** the Ribbon so that it (along with the Quick Access Toolbar [QAT], if it's positioned below the Ribbon) disappears completely – leaving only the tab labels (names) visible.[1] Alternatively, you can **hide** the entire Ribbon, the tab labels, and the QAT (assuming you've positioned it below the Ribbon), showing only the document editing screen (and the Ruler, if it was already displayed).

When you have minimized the Ribbon, single-clicking a tab label will temporarily expand the Ribbon so that you have access to all of the commands you need to get your work done. As soon as you click within the document editing screen, the Ribbon reverts to its collapsed state.

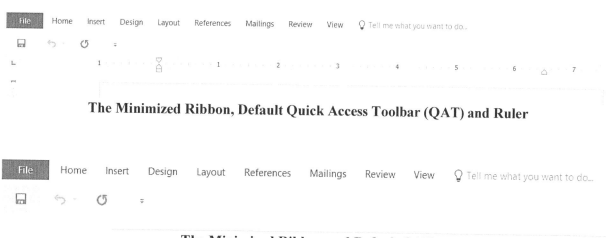

The Minimized Ribbon, Default Quick Access Toolbar (QAT) and Ruler

The Minimized Ribbon and Default QAT

Various Ways to Minimize – and Restore – the Ribbon

There are a few different ways to accomplish this task. For one, there's a "**Collapse the Ribbon**" icon. It takes the form of a carat (arrow) that appears at the right end of the Ribbon, approximately in line with the "Close" icon in the Word Title Bar. (See the screenshot at right.)

When you point to the carat, you'll see the pop-up pictured immediately below:

---

[1] If you have previously displayed the Ruler, it remains visible when you minimize the Ribbon.

To minimize the Ribbon, simply click the carat (arrow).

In Word 2010, the carat remains visible after you've clicked it, but merely changes its orientation (pointing down rather than up). You can click it again to maximize (restore) the Ribbon to its full size. In both Word 2013 and Word 2016, however, the carat disappears after you click it. That can be very confusing if you are accustomed to the way this feature works in 2010.

So how do you maximize the Ribbon again? One solution is to locate the "**Ribbon Display Options**" icon in the Title Bar, click it, and choose from among the three available options. See the screenshots below, which show the Ribbon Display Options icon by itself and as it appears in context (to the left of the Minimize, Restore, and Close Word buttons in the Title Bar).

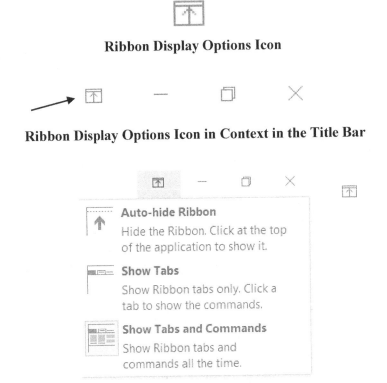

This button also gives you the option of hiding the Ribbon completely. Just click the first choice, "**Auto-hide Ribbon.**" When you do so, everything vanishes – with the exception of the Ruler, if you previously had it displayed. (Note that the Quick Access Toolbar disappears in Auto-hide mode, even if it was positioned above the Ribbon.)

The middle option, "**Show Tabs**," collapses the Ribbon itself but leaves the tab labels and the Quick Access Toolbar visible.

Show Tabs

Show Tabs – Close-Up View

Note that the "Show Tabs" option produces the same results as double-clicking a tab label (see below).

Finally, the bottom option, "**Show Tabs and Commands**," maximizes the Ribbon and the related screen elements, so that you can see the entire Ribbon, the tab labels, and the QAT.

Incidentally, these three options can be applied separately to individual documents that you have open on different screens at the same time. (The same is not true for the location of the QAT – i.e., if you place it below the Ribbon in one document, it appears below the Ribbon in all of the others.)

A second way to minimize the Ribbon is by pressing **Ctrl F1**, the keyboard shortcut to collapse the Ribbon. (It's a toggle; simply press Ctrl F1 again to restore the Ribbon.)

Another way is by **double-clicking any tab label** – something that many people do by accident. You can double-click a tab label again to maximize the Ribbon (doing so will bring the tab you double-click to the forefront). **NOTE**: As mentioned earlier, if you minimize the Ribbon and then *single*-click a tab heading, the Ribbon expands, but the Quick Access Toolbar disappears (if you normally display your QAT below the ribbon).

And finally, you can *right-click* somewhere within the tab headings, the Ribbon, or the QAT, and select "**Collapse the Ribbon**" from the context-sensitive menu. When you have Collapsed the Ribbon, a checkmark appears next to the "Collapse the Ribbon" command to show that the Ribbon has been hidden.

There is no "Maximize the Ribbon" command on that menu. Instead, right-click within any tab label or in a white space on the QAT – if the tab labels and the QAT are visible – and click the "Collapse the Ribbon" command again to uncheck it, and the Ribbon will reopen at full size.

Auto-Hiding (and Restoring) the Ribbon

Whereas clicking the carat and double-clicking a tab label merely collapse the Ribbon, the first option in the Ribbon Display Options drop-down - Auto-hide option – hides the whole shebang (Ribbon, tab labels, QAT). It leaves only the document editing screen (along with the Ruler, if you previously displayed it, and the vertical scrollbar). The Ruler is visible in the screenshot below only because I enabled it before I applied the Auto-hide option.

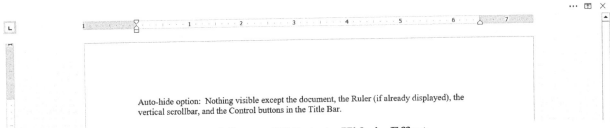

Word Screen With Auto-Hide in Effect

After you hide the Ribbon, you will see only three icons in the Title Bar: a sort of menu consisting of three dots, the Ribbon Display Options icon, and the Close icon.

Clicking the three-dot menu icon will restore the Ribbon (plus the tabs and the QAT), but only *temporarily*. As soon as you start typing, it will disappear again. (Double-clicking the Title Bar has the same effect.)

Incidentally, clicking Ctrl F1 does not restore the Ribbon – or do much of anything, as far as I can tell – when you are using the "Auto-hide" view.

To expand the Ribbon, tabs, and commands, click the **Ribbon Display Options** icon and choose the bottom option, **Show Tabs and Commands**.

The Backstage View / File Tab

Because of its importance, and because it is one of the most complex and significantly altered features in Word 2016, I have saved the File tab for last. You can think of this tab, which Microsoft has dubbed the "**Backstage view**,"[1] as a replacement for the traditional File menu found in pre-Ribbon versions of the program. It also replaces the Office button found in the first "Ribbonized" version, Word 2007 (the multicolored orb in the upper left-hand corner of the Word 2007 screen).

Like the Office button and the File menu in previous versions, the Backstage view gives you access to your recently used files; provides commands for opening, saving, and closing documents and for starting a new document based on an existing template; displays print and page setup options; makes it easy to share documents via e-mail and other means; and displays information about the current document. The Backstage view also serves as the portal to most configuration options for Word (called "Options" or "Word Options" in Word 2016).

Here is an overview of the commands on the File tab's vertical menu (which I sometimes call a "Navigation Pane,"[2] since it helps users navigate the various File tab options).

Back arrow – returns to the document editing screen

Info – shows the properties of the current document

New – provides access to built-in and personal templates

Open – offers various ways to open existing documents

Save – lets you save an unsaved document or unsaved edits

Save As - lets you save an unsaved doc or save as a new doc / doc type

Print – opens a combined Print / Print Preview screen

Share – makes it easy to share documents via e-mail, the cloud, etc.

Export – gives you another way to save docs in a different format

Close – provides one method for closing an open document

Account – provides a button for signing in to your OneDrive account

Options – opens the Word Options dialog so you can configure features

Feedback – lets you send comments / feature requests to Microsoft

---

[1] Throughout this book, I use the terms "**File tab**" and "**Backstage view** "(or, simply, "**Backstage**") interchangeably, although I prefer "**File tab**."

[2] Not to be confused with the Navigation Pane feature invoked by pressing Ctrl F.

Navigating the Backstage View

To open the Backstage view, either (1) click the **File tab** at the upper left-hand side of the Word 2016 screen or (2) press **Alt F**—the same keyboard shortcut that opens the File tab or menu in all earlier versions of Word.[3] To return to your document, either click the (un-labeled) **Back** arrow at the top left side of the Backstage view or press the **Esc** key.

Back Arrow

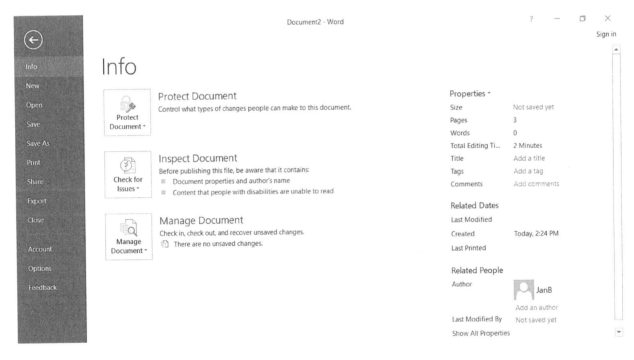

Click the File Tab (at Left) to Open the Backstage View

The first thing you'll notice when you click File is that the resulting menu (a sort of "**fly-out menu**"[4]) fills the entire screen.

---

[3] Tapping **the Alt key alone** triggers **KeyTips**, also known as "**mnemonics**" or "**badges**," that appear on the screen, making it easy to use keyboard shortcuts to carry out commands. See page 357.

[4] In my Word 2010 book, I refer to the various Backstage view screens as "fly-out menus." I'm not crazy about that term, but haven't found a better one, except perhaps simply "screen." I will alternate between the two terms.

Which screen you see depends on whether or not you have a document open. Specifically:

- When you first launch Word, before you open a file, the Backstage view displays the "**Recent**" screen (so that you can easily open a recent document).

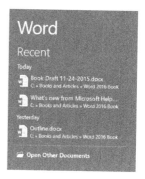

- When you already have a file open on your screen, the Backstage view opens to "**Info**" (so that you can see the document properties at a glance, apply a password, or check for and remove metadata).

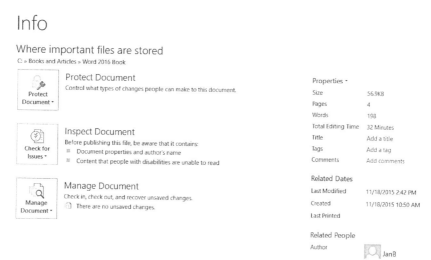

In addition to Info, the Backstage view provides four other full-screen menus: **New**, **Print**, **Share**, and **Export**. Each screen groups related commands that were somewhat scattered in old versions of the program. For example, the **Print** screen (sometimes called "**Print Place**") includes not only all of the configuration options available in the standard Print dialog – which is no longer available, by the way – but also a large print preview window.

Toward the bottom, there's a link to an **Account** screen where you can sign into your OneDrive / Microsoft account so that you can save documents to the "cloud" (i.e., the Web).

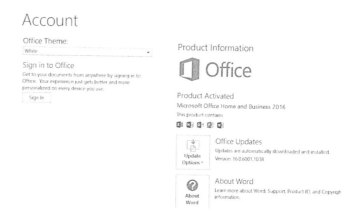

This screen contains some additional information about the program and lets you choose when to download updates.

You'll also see the familiar commands for working with documents: **Open**, **Save**, **Save As**, and about 2/3 of the way down, **Close**. Significantly, there is no "**Exit**" command. (For more about that issue, see the sidebar on page 56 about closing a document without closing Word.) And there's a link to the **Word Options**, which opens a large window where you can configure the program to work according to your personal preferences.

Let's take a closer look at the various "fly-out menus" on the File tab. We've already gone over the basics of opening new and existing documents, but it's worth exploring the "Open" screen, and exploring additional ways to open documents, in more detail.

The "Open" Screen

As discussed in the section about opening an existing document (starting on page 2), File > Open does not work the same way it worked in Word 2010 and earlier versions. Rather than taking you directly to the Open dialog in Windows, it takes you to the Open screen in the Backstage view. To bypass Backstage and go directly to the Open dialog, press Ctrl F12 or, for a more permanent solution, configure the Word Options as outlined in the "Bypassing the Start Screen" section on page 8.

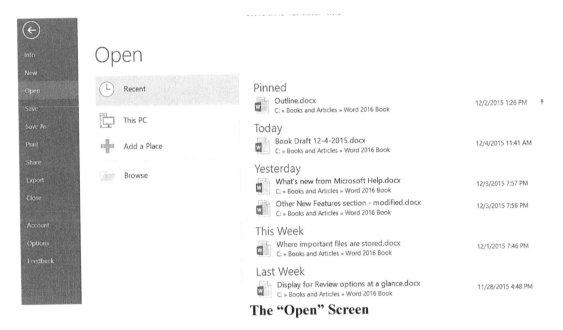

The "Open" Screen

The "Recent" Screen

Also as mentioned earlier, the "Recent" screen appears when you first launch Word, before you have opened any documents. Unlike in Word 2010, there is no separate Recent command in the File tab's navigation pane, but clicking **Open** reveals a "Recent" submenu. Clicking the link to open that submenu produces a screen similar to the one shown below:

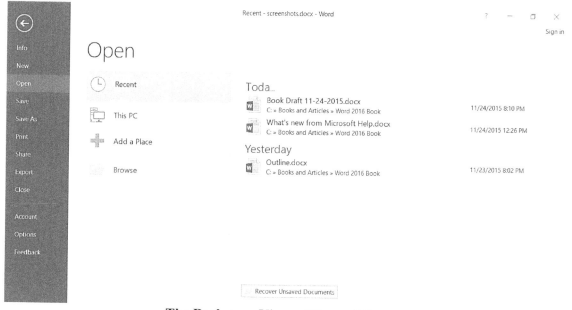

The Backstage View – "Recent" Screen

The number of recent documents displayed on the Recent screen is determined by a setting in the **Word Options**. The default is 25, but you can change that to any integer between 1 and 50. Or, if you prefer not to show any recent documents, you can change the setting to 0 (zero). To change the setting, click the **File tab** (or press **Alt F, T**), then click **Options**, **Advanced**, scroll to the **Display** category, "**Show this number of Recent Documents**."

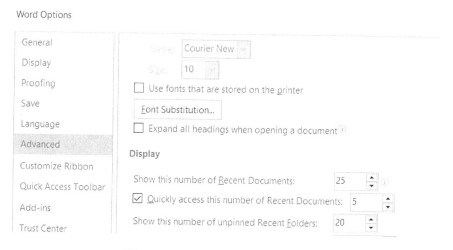

Word Options, Advanced, Display

NOTE: Depending on the size of your screen and your screen resolution, you might have to scroll to see all of the documents in the Recent Documents list.

"Pinning" Documents

You can "pin" one or more of your recent documents to the top of the Recent Documents list to prevent it / them from scrolling off the list as you open additional files. To pin a document, click the pin to the right of the document name in the list (see the screenshots below).

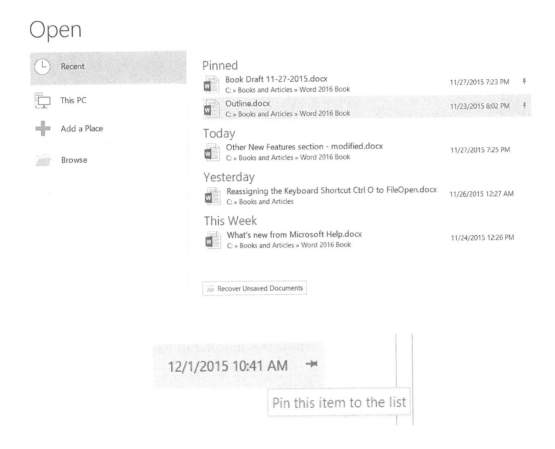

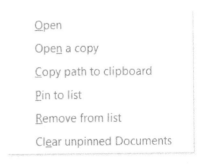

Alternatively, you can right-click a document in the "Recent" list and choose the "Pin to list" option. To unpin a pinned file, click the pin again or right-click and choose "Unpin from list."

In addition to pinning, you can right-click an item in the list to open a particular document (or open a copy), copy the file's path (i.e., the drive letter and folder / subfolder where it's stored), pin it to the list, remove it from the list, or clear all of the unpinned documents from the list.

NOTE: This right-click menu does *not* appear if you right-click a recent document in the "Quick Access" list toward the bottom of the File tab's Navigation Pane. See the next section.

Quick Access to Recent Documents

In old versions of Word, you could view a list of your recently used files just by clicking "File." But in the versions that use the Ribbon interface, clicking "File" doesn't produce the "Recent Documents" list." Rather, you must click" Open" to display the list (in Word 2010, you click "Recent"), and the list disappears if you click a different fly-out menu, such as Print.

However, there is a way to configure Word 2016 to show your recent files whenever you open the File tab, and regardless of which menu is at the forefront. See the screenshot below. (There's a Quick Access file list at the bottom of the File tab's Navigation Pane.)

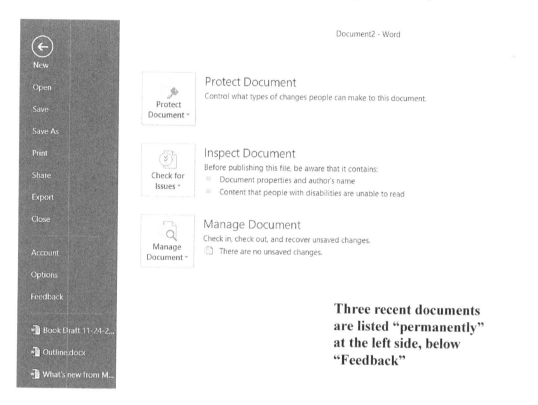

Three recent documents are listed "permanently" at the left side, below "Feedback"

To activate the option, you must **check the box labeled "Quickly access this number of Recent Documents"** in the Word Options, as in the screenshot immediately below this paragraph. You can set the number of documents to display at left by typing an integer or by using the up / down arrows ("spinners").

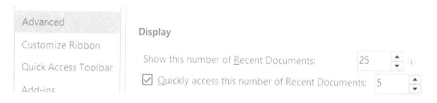

The number of files you choose to display in the Quick Access area does not have to match the number of files in the Recent Documents list. (However, it's probably best to keep the

41

number fairly small. In any case, the maximum number of docs you can display in the Quick Access area is 25, whereas the maximum number you can display in the Recent list is 50.)

The documents in the Quick Access area will remain visible regardless of which screen (Info, New, Open, Print, etc.) is at the forefront. Again, you'll probably have to scroll to see all of them.

NOTE: The "Quick Access" list puts documents you've pinned to the Recent list (if any) first and then lists the next items in date and time sequence.

"This PC" (Revisited)

Another option on the Open screen is "This PC." As discussed earlier, this option shows your recently opened folders. For more details, see the section starting on page 6.

Recover Unsaved Documents

The "**Recover Unsaved Documents**" option, located at the bottom right side of the screen, will be discussed in detail starting on page 51.

Tips About the "Open" Dialog

Most people open files from the Windows Open dialog by either double-clicking the file or single-clicking it, then clicking the "Open" button at the bottom right side of the dialog. But there are a few additional options available from the "Open" button that you might find useful – especially if you've never noticed them before. (Did you realize that there is an arrow at the right side of the button and that clicking the arrow produces a drop-down menu with more commands?)

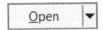

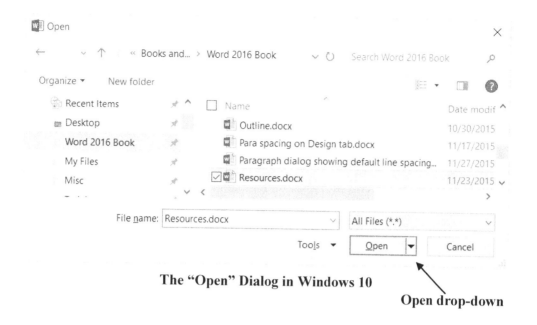

The "Open" Dialog in Windows 10

Open drop-down

Let's take a quick look at these options, even though you might already be aware of at least some of them. Knowing a few alternate methods for opening files can help you avoid accidentally overwriting an existing document – and can help to minimize problems when you are working with a corrupted document or with a document that originated in another program (WordPerfect, Open Office, etc.).[5]

Always try to follow "best practices" when you are creating a new document based on an existing one or creating a new draft (version) of a document. There are at least three methods that will preserve the original file:

(1) Instead of using Open, use "**Open as Copy**" (see the screenshot at right), and then *immediately* press **F12** (or use **File**, "**Save As**") to save the copy with a different name; or

(2) Use the "**Open Read-Only**" option and *immediately* press **F12** (or use **File**, "**Save As**") to save the file with a different name; or

(3) Open the existing document and then *immediately* press **F12** (or use **File**, "**Save As**") and save the document with a different name from that of the original.[6]

---

[5] Of course, if your organization uses a document management system (DMS), you probably won't work with these options.

[6] This practice reduces the likelihood that you will accidentally overwrite the existing file.

"**Open as Copy**" and "**Open Read-Only**" function in essentially the same way. Either of those options is a good choice if you want to ensure that the original file remains intact.

Yet another option for opening files into Word is to click the **Insert tab**, navigate to the **Text group**, click the **Object drop-down**, and click "**Text from File**." If you start from a blank document screen, Word will insert the text of the document you select into the blank screen, ready to save as a separate file. If you have an existing document on the screen, Word will insert the text of the selected document *at the cursor position* in that document. This function comes in handy if, for example, you want to insert an existing, separate Proof of Service or Certificate of Service, or an Exhibit, at the end of a pleading. It also can be useful for bringing the text from a WordPerfect document into a Word document, although the complex formatting in the WordPerfect file often won't convert well when you pull up the file in Word. (The less complex the formatting in the WordPerfect doc, the better it will convert. For example, simple columnar tables usually convert fairly well. Pleadings with vertical lines and line numbers usually convert poorly.)

Note that this option will knock out some of the formatting and/or convert styles and automatic numbering schemes from the original document into your default ("destination") styles.

"Open and Repair"

The "Open and Repair" command can be helpful if a document you're working on appears to be corrupted.[7] It is a method of last resort, to be used when nothing else you've tried works. And, to be on the safe side, *make a copy of the document* **before** using "Open and Repair."

To use the "Open and Repair" function, select the document, then click the "Open" button and choose "Open and Repair." Word will fix the document, open it, and display a dialog box showing the items that were repaired (if any).

It's unnecessary (and usually an exercise in futility) to attempt to view the errors by clicking the "Go To" button. However, it's a good idea to close the "Show Repairs" dialog and then save the repaired file.

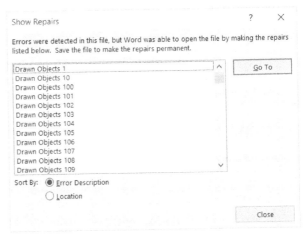

---

[7] Symptoms of document corruption include, but are not limited to: sudden, unintended changes in formatting; inability to save a file; inability to open a file (or the program crashes when you do); unusual delays in opening or saving a file; uncontrollable movement of the cursor (and/or the cursor skips certain pages); constant repagination; and error messages about "insufficient memory."

If you close the file without saving, the repairs will be lost.

For more information about the "Open and Repair" feature, see this Microsoft Knowledge Base article entitled "How to troubleshoot damaged documents in Word":

http://support.microsoft.com/kb/918429

For a fuller discussion about identifying and repairing document corruption (as well as steps you can take to prevent corruption), see the section starting on page 581.

"Open with Transform"

The "Open with Transform" option, which ordinarily is grayed out, is pretty much for techies only (folks who work with XML files and, specifically, with .xsl or .xslt files); most people who work in the legal field won't ever need or use that option.

"Open in Protected View"

"Open in Protected View," however, is useful for opening a file you've downloaded from e-mail or or from the Internet or, for that matter, any other document you want to view but not edit. Protected View allows you to see the contents of the file while limiting your computer's exposure to any malicious code that might be embedded in the file. For more information, see the section about the Protected View on page 118.

The "Save" Command

"Save" works the same way as in previous versions of Word. You can save brand-new docs or revisions to your previously saved docs by doing any of the following:

- Clicking File > Save,

- Pressing Ctrl S, or

- Clicking the "Save" (floppy disk) icon on your Quick Access Toolbar.

The Save Options

To view or change the Save options, click the File tab, Options, and click the Save category at left.

45

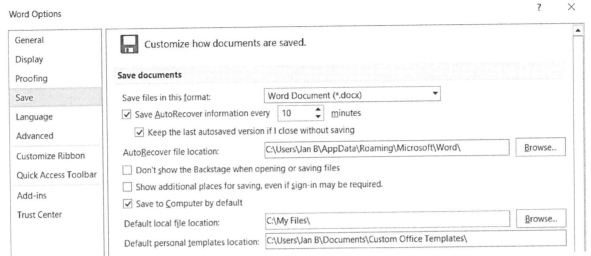

The Save Options in Word (File > Options, Advanced)

The first option determines the default "Save" file format, which is set to "Word Document (*.docx)." In general, there's no reason to change that setting.

I'll discuss the AutoRecover options ("Save AutoRecover information every __ minutes"; "Keep the last autosaved version if I close without saving: and "AutoRecover file location") in detail later in this section.

One important setting to be aware of is the one labeled "Don't show the Backstage when opening or saving files." If you enable this setting by checking the box, then clicking "OK," you will be able to open and save files without going through the intermediary of the Backstage view – and Word will reassign the keyboard shortcut Ctrl O so that it goes directly to the Open dialog in Windows, rather than to the "Open" screen in the Backstage view.

Also, be aware that if you are constantly prompted to save files to OneDrive or some other location besides your computer, you can click the checkbox labeled "Save to Computer by default."

Note that this screen is where you set your default file location, as well as the location of your personal (custom) templates, if any. You can also change these settings by clicking File, Options, Advanced, and then scrolling almost all the way down to "File Locations."[8] Your ability to change these settings might be restricted by your employer, though.

---

[8] Make sure that the "**Default personal templates location**" set in the Word Options under **Save**, "**Save documents**" matches the location of the "**User templates**" set in the Word Options under **Advanced**, "**File Locations**." When the settings in both places in the Word Options match, all of your custom templates will be displayed in the Backstage view (when you click File, New, Custom), as well as in the "New" dialog. When the settings don't match, any templates stored in the location set for "User templates" will *not* appear in the Backstage view (File, New, Custom) – but *will* appear in the "New" dialog. For more about this confusing change, first implemented in Word 2013, see the discussions on pages 411 and 597.

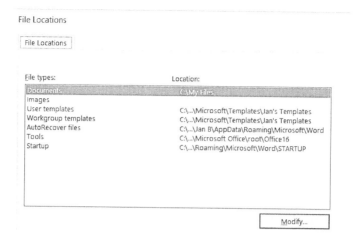

The "Save As" Screen

Like the "Open" screen, "Save As" is very different in Word 2016 (and Word 2013) from the "Save As" screen in Word 2010 and earlier. Depending on whether you are signed into OneDrive, the screen shows Save As options that include This PC, OneDrive, "Add a Place,"and Browse. (If you have Office 365 and/or SharePoint, you might see those options, as well.)

"Save As" Screen – Not Signed into OneDrive

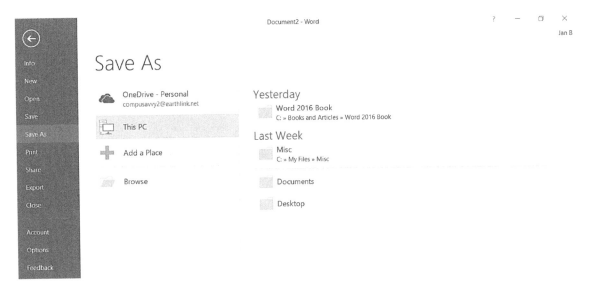

"Save As" Screen – Signed into OneDrive

"This PC"

The folders shown under "This PC" are the recently used folders – that is, the folders where you recently saved documents – *on your computer* (as opposed to folders in OneDrive). Sharp-eyed readers might notice an interesting discrepancy in the two previous screenshots. Although both of the screenshots show the "This PC" category within the "Save As" screen, different folders appeared when I clicked "This PC," depending on whether I was or was not signed into my OneDrive account.

I can think of at least a couple of possible reasons for this discrepancy: First, I seldom use OneDrive, so perhaps the "This PC" list in the second screenshot reflect the folders on my computer where I saved documents as of the last date I was signed into OneDrive. Secondly, it's possible that I manually removed some of the folders from one of the lists by right-clicking the folders and then choosing "Remove from list."

In any case, "This PC" can be a useful option if you wish to save a document to one of your recently used folders on your computer.

OneDrive / SharePoint

If you have a OneDrive account and/or if your firm uses SharePoint, you will have the option of saving files to one or both of those locations.

Add a Place

The "Add a Place" option is available so that you can add OneDrive or SharePoint to the list of "Save As" locations, if those options aren't already shown.

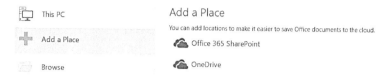

Browse

The "Browse" option, which is self-explanatory, works the way it did in previous versions.

Use F12 to ByPass Backstage

We've already discussed bypassing the Backstage view when *opening* files. To do the same when *saving* files, use the keyboard shortcut for "Save As," which is **F12**.

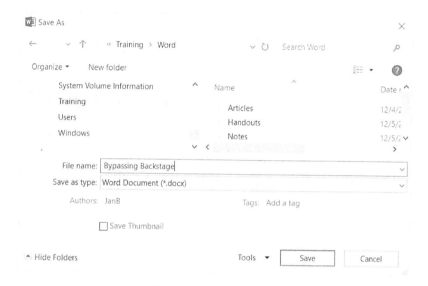

The "Save As" Dialog

"Close"

You probably know that there are several ways to close an open document in Word:

- File, Close;

- Ctrl W;

- Ctrl F4;

- The red "X" ("Close" button) in the upper right corner of the Word program window; and

- A "Close" icon on the Quick Access Toolbar (which you have to add to the QAT if your employer hasn't already done so).

Regardless of the method you use, if you have saved your revisions, the active / current file simply closes. If you have not saved your revisions (or have never saved the document), you'll see the familiar "Save / Don't Save" prompt:

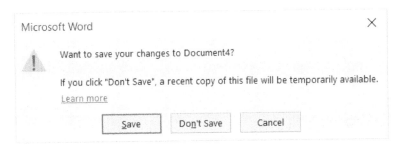

"Save" and "Cancel" are self-explanatory; they work the same way they've worked in previous versions. "Don't Save" closes the file without saving, but creates a temporary backup of the file (an "Unsaved Document," described below) – which can come in handy if you need to recover the file.

Different Types of Temporary Backup Files

All recent versions of Word automatically create a temporary backup copy of any previously saved document that has been open on your screen for at least ten minutes (the default autosave interval).[9] [10] These traditional "**AutoRecover**" **files**, intended as emergency backups that you can use to recover at least some of your work in the event of a computer crash, power outage, or similar situation, are deleted when you exit from Word.

In addition, Word creates temporary backups of documents that you close without saving, and it keeps them for four days.[11] These backup files, called "**Unsaved Documents**," fall into two categories:

(a) documents that you have worked on but then closed, either accidentally or deliberately, *without ever saving*; and

---

[9] As discussed later in this section, you can – but probably shouldn't – change this interval in the Word Options.

[10] You might notice that the autosave intervals appear somewhat irregular. The reason is that the autosave function doesn't kick in at the normally scheduled time if you save a document manually before the ten-minute interval for automatic backups has elapsed. Apparently the clock starts ticking again after you manually save the document.

[11] That is, unless you open one of them and save it normally before four days have elapsed. In that event, Word deletes the backup file sooner.

(b) documents that you *have saved at least once* but have modified since your last save and closed without saving your changes.

The two types of Unsaved Documents are stored in different locations, and are opened in different ways.

The "Unsaved Documents"

When you attempt to close a document that you haven't saved manually for several minutes, the "**Close**" **prompt** appears, offering three choices: "**Save**," "**Don't save**," and "**Cancel**."

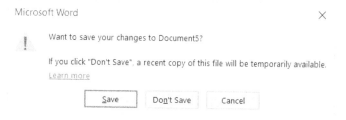

The "Close" Prompt in Word 2016

The first and third choices are self-explanatory. However, the middle choice, "**Don't Save**," doesn't merely discard any unsaved edits and then close the doc. In Word 2016 and other recent versions, when you click "Don't Save," the program creates a temporary backup copy of the file, including any unsaved edits, that you can restore later on if you wish. These temporary backups are the **Unsaved Documents**.

When Does the "Unsaved Documents" Backup Kick In?

The "Unsaved Documents" backup works as long as the "**Keep the last autosaved version if I close without saving**" option is enabled (checked) in the **Word Options** – which it is by default.

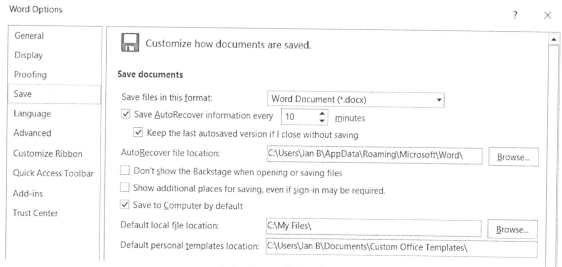

The "Save" Options

51

With this option enabled, the autosave appears to kick in immediately. I tested by opening a new blank document, typing two characters, then clicking "Close," and clicking "Don't Save." When I attempted to recover the Unsaved Document using the first method described in the next section, I was able to do so.

Recovering an Unsaved Document

You can recover an Unsaved Document from two different places in the Backstage View:

- from the **Manage Document drop-down** on the **Info screen** (click the "**Recover Unsaved Documents**" button); and/or

- from the "**Recover Unsaved Documents**" **link** at the bottom of the **Open > Recent screen**.

When you click the "Recover Unsaved Documents" link, Word opens an "UnsavedFiles" folder so that you can open one or more of the temporary files into Word if you so choose. Once you've done so, you can save it (and, of course, rename it) in the same way you would save any other document.[12]

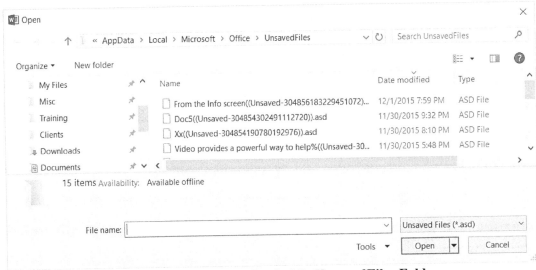

Temporary (Unsaved) Files in My UnsavedFiles Folder

---

[12] It can be difficult to tell from the names that Word assigns the Unsaved Files which is which. You can guess by looking at the date/time stamp or, if necessary, open each one and view the contents.

Unsaved Files open in Read Mode (a stripped-down view of the document that hides the Ribbon and the Quick Access Toolbar), as read-only files. A message bar across the screen indicates that the document is a recovered unsaved file that is temporarily stored on your computer. (As previously mentioned, it will be deleted within four days unless you click the "Save As" button at the right side of the message bar.)

If you don't want to save the file, just click the Close button (the red "X") at the upper right side of the screen to close the file.

If you want to keep the file permanently, click the "**Save As**" button. When the "Save As" dialog opens, you'll be prompted to save the file as a Word Document (*.docx).

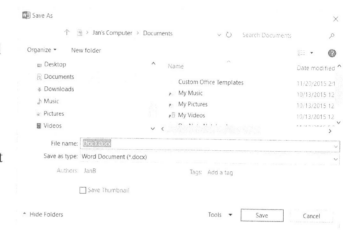

Interestingly, in my tests, Word opened the "Save As" dialog to the Documents folder, even though I have set my default file location elsewhere. Obviously, you can rename the file and save it to any folder you choose.

The AutoRecover Files (Versions)

Keep in mind that the Unsaved Documents are different from the "**AutoRecover**" **files** that Word creates every few minutes while you are working on a document. If it helps to distinguish the two, think of the AutoRecover files as different versions or drafts of the document that is open on your screen. If necessary, you can restore a previous autosaved version of the document and either overwrite the existing version or save it as a completely different doc.

To restore an earlier version of a document that is open on your screen, click the **File tab**, **Info**, and check to see if there are any autosaved versions of the document listed to the right of the **Manage Document button**. See the screenshot below for an example.

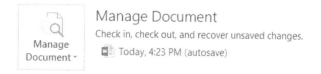

Click the version you want to recover. Like the Unsaved Documents, the AutoRecover file will open in Read Mode. A message bar that spans the top of the screen indicates that it is an autosaved version and that a newer version is available.

There are two buttons in the message bar: "**Compare**" and "**Restore**." To determine which version you want to keep, click the "**Compare**" button.

Word will perform a document comparison – i.e., a redline – and will open the results in a new window. (To get a better understanding of what you're seeing on the document-comparison screen, see the tutorial about the document comparison feature, starting on page 551.)

If you decide to keep the backup version instead of the one you last saved manually, click the "**Restore**" button. A pop-up will appear, warning that you are about to overwrite the last-saved version with the temporary backup file.

If you're sure you wish to do so, click "**OK**"; otherwise, click "**Cancel**" and click File, Save As (or press F12) to save the AutoRecover version as a separate document.

Although Word automatically saves temporary backup files, try to remember to save your documents often, especially those that are "mission critical." Keep in mind that the Unsaved Documents are stored for only four days, and the AutoRecover files – intended as a last resort in an emergency – are deleted when you close out of Word. Neither type of automatic backup is an adequate substitute for mindful, and frequent, saves.

Configuring Automatic Backups

As mentioned in passing previously, the backup interval for both the AutoRecover files and the Unsaved Documents is determined by a setting in the **Word Options (File tab, Options, Save category, Save documents)**, as shown in the next screenshot. The setting is labeled "**Save AutoRecover information every __ minutes**," and, as we've discussed, the default setting is ten minutes.[13]

---

[13] **CAUTION**: Although you can change the time interval at which "AutoRecover" drafts are saved, it's not a good idea to save more frequently than every 5 minutes. Doing so can tie up the computer's processor and prevent you from getting your work done normally.

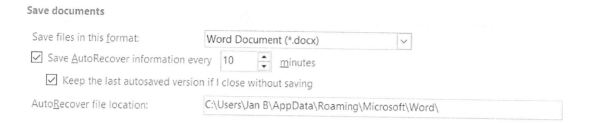

Word Options, Save Documents

The option labeled "**Keep the last autosaved version if I close without saving**" is the key to preserving the Unsaved Documents. By default, it is enabled (checked). Unless you are working on a public computer (or a shared one), it is a good idea to leave the option checked.

Additionally, you can modify the AutoRecover file location and/or your default file location from this screen, although there's no obvious or compelling reason to do so.

File Type and Storage Locations

The AutoRecover Files and the Unsaved Documents both use the .asd extension (presumably "asd" stands for AutoSaved Document).

The AutoRecover Files are stored in this location in Windows 7, 8, and 10:
C:\Users\<User Name>\AppData\Roaming\Microsoft\Word

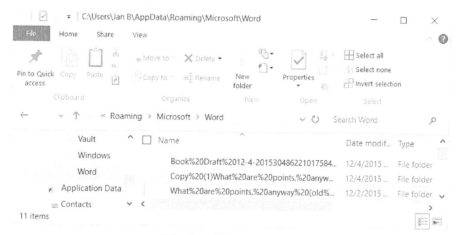

My AutoRecover Files

If you navigate to this folder, you'll see that the AutoRecover files are actually saved within folders.

The Unsaved Documents are saved in this location in Windows 7, 8, and 10:
C:\Users\<UserName>\AppData\Local\Microsoft\Office\ UnsavedFiles

SIDEBAR: Closing a Document Without Closing Word

Many people are accustomed to closing individual documents by clicking the "X" (the "Close" button) at the upper right-hand corner of a document window. That option has been available in Word (and in numerous other programs, including WordPerfect) through many, many versions.

Starting with Word 2007, the program no longer displays a "Close" button for individual documents (or, for that matter, the separate "Minimize" and "Maximize/Restore" buttons that used to be available for documents). The only "Control buttons" visible in recent versions of Word are the ones at the right side of the Title bar – i.e., the ones that affect *the program*. Thus, when people click on the "X" in the upper right-hand corner of the screen, the program itself closes (if only one document is open), to some people's surprise – and, occasionally, consternation.

There are other ways to close a document, of course. If you are a "mouse person," you can simply click the **File tab**, then click **Close**. If you are a "keyboard person," you can use any of the following key combinations:

- **Ctrl F4**

- **Ctrl W**

- **Alt F, C**

Or you can add a "**Close**" ("**Close File**") **icon** to the **Quick Access Toolbar** (QAT). For instructions, see page 180.

The "Info" Screen

When you have at least one document open (even a blank one), clicking the File tab produces the "Info" screen, which gives you easy access to in-depth information about the active document (the one at the forefront of the document-editing screen).

The Backstage View – "Info" Screen

Word 2016's Info screen keeps track of a tremendous amount of information about the current document. The left side of the screen is a sort of "action" area, where you can do any of the following:

(1) convert a .doc file to the newer .docx file format;[14]

(2) apply a password;

(3) check for metadata and other potential issues that might arise when you share the document with others;

(4) open an earlier "autosaved" version of the active document; or

(5) open a draft of one of the documents that Word automatically backed up when you closed without saving.[15]

---

[14] You won't see the "Convert" button if the document you're working on is a .docx – that is, if it has been saved in the newer Word file format.

[15] The way that options (4) and (5) work can be somewhat confusing. For a more complete discussion, see the section starting on page 51.

57

The right side is a collection of statistics, divided into a few subcategories (Properties, Related Dates, Related People, and Related Documents).

Properties

The **Properties** section of the screen provides information about various characteristics of your document: Size, Pages, Words, Total Editing Time, Title, Tags (if any), Comments (if any). Most of those characteristics automatically populate. As for the ones that don't, you can add a title, tags, or comments if you like by clicking in a fill-in field, then typing some text.

Under **Related Dates**, it shows the Last Modified date/time, the Created date/time, and the Last Printed date/time.

Under **Related People**, it shows the author and the person who last modified the document (who is often the author). Note that you can add other authors by clicking "Add an author."

Under **Related Documents**, there is a folder icon labeled "Open File Location." When you click that icon, Word opens Windows Explorer / File Explorer to the folder where the current file is stored so that you can view or work with other files in that folder.

Advanced Properties

To view more characteristics of the document, click the **Properties drop-down** at the top, and then click **Advanced Properties**. Doing so opens the traditional Properties dialog, with the familiar tabs: General, Summary, Statistics, Contents, and Custom.[16]

---

[16] In case you were wondering, the Document Panel has been removed from Word 2016.

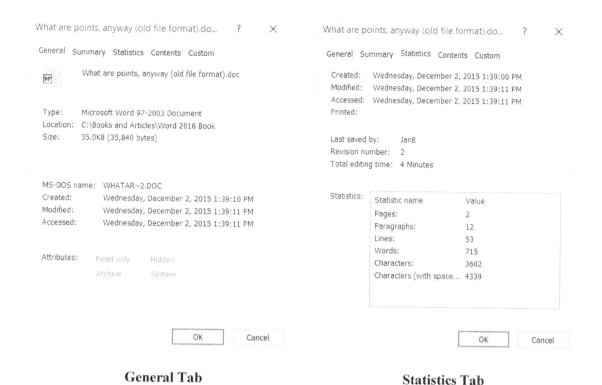

General Tab   **Statistics Tab**

At the bottom of the Properties list, there is a link labeled "**Show All Properties**." When you click the link, Word displays additional document properties; the link label then changes to read "**Show Fewer Properties**."

"**Show All Properties**" displays the name of the underlying template and adds fill-in fields for Status, Categories (which enables you to mark the document with one or more searchable tags), Subject, Hyperlink Base, Company, and Manager.

Click the "**Show Fewer Properties**" link to collapse the properties list.

Changing Certain Attributes of a Document

At the left side of the Information screen, there are a few tools for changing a few important attributes of the active document.

SIDEBAR: The Word File Formats

There are several different Word file formats: .docx, .doc, .docm, .dotx, .dotm, and .dot. The first three are **document** formats; the last three are **template** formats.

By default, when you save a brand-new Word 2016 document, it is saved in an XML-based Word file format called **.docx**. ("XML" stands for "eXtensible Markup Language," a kind of coding commonly used for web pages but also used in other applications, such as Word.) The .docx file format was first used in Word 2007. Initially, its use caused many problems because the format is not backwards-compatible with some older versions of Word. In fact, in order to open / read .docx files, users of older versions had to download a special "compatibility pack" from Microsoft's web site.[1]

Microsoft modified the .docx file format somewhat in Word 2010 and again in Word 2013 / 2016. For the most part, the three different .docx versions are interchangeable, although newer iterations include enhancements that don't function at all, or in the same way, if you save a newer .docx to an older file format.[2]

The original Word file format, standard in versions prior to Word 2007, is called **.doc**. You can save Word documents in this older format by choosing "Word 97-2003" as the file type. Note that when you have a .doc file open on your screen, you will see "[Compatibility Mode]" following the document name in the program's Title Bar. (Somewhat confusingly, the "[Compatibility Mode]" designation also appears when you have an older "build" of a .docx file – that is, a Word 2007 .docx or a Word 2010 .docx – open.)

Files saved in the .docx format are not capable of containing macros created in the programming language Visual Basic for Applications (VBA). As a workaround, Microsoft created another XML file format that can contain VBA macros, called **.docm** ("m" for "macro-enabled").

The standard XML file format for Word templates is the **.dotx**. Like .docx files, .dotx files aren't macro-enabled, so there is also a macro-capable file format for Word templates, the **.dotm**. Older Word templates are based on the **.dot** (**D**ocument **T**emplate) file format.

---

[1] If you have an older version of Word and are unable to open .docx files, go to Microsoft's site, https://products.office.com/en-us/microsoft-office-compatibility-pack-for-word-excel-and-powerpoint for more information about the Compatibility Pack, as well as a download link.

[2] For a handy chart comparing the features available in each version of the .docx format, see the Microsoft Help article entitled "Use Word 2016 to open documents created in earlier versions of Word" (available on the Internet and also by typing "compatibility" – without quotation marks – in the "Tell me what you want to do box" and then clicking "Get help on Compatibility").

File Type	Description	Comments
.docx	Word 2007 – 2016 files	.docx files cannot contain macros Word 2013 and Word 2016 use a newer version of the .docx; Word 2010 and Word 2007 use older versions
.docm	Macro-enabled Word files	
.doc	Word 97-2003 files	
.dotm	Macro-enabled Word template	
.dotx	Word template	.dotx files cannot contain macros
.dot	Word 97-2003 template	

If you wish, you also have the option of saving Word documents in other formats. In Word 2016, you can save files directly in PDF format (**.pdf**),[3] as well as Rich Text Format (**.rtf**), Open Document Text (**.odt**), Plain Text (**.txt**), a regular or filtered web page (**.htm** or **.html**); a single-file web page (**.mht** or **.mhtml**), XML (**.xml**), and XPS (**.xps**). (XPS is one of Microsoft's proprietary file formats; it isn't widely used except by IT people and other techies).

```
Word Document (*.docx)
Word Macro-Enabled Document (*.docm)
Word 97-2003 Document (*.doc)
Word Template (*.dotx)
Word Macro-Enabled Template (*.dotm)
Word 97-2003 Template (*.dot)
PDF (*.pdf)
XPS Document (*.xps)
Single File Web Page (*.mht;*.mhtml)
Web Page (*.htm;*.html)
Web Page, Filtered (*.htm;*.html)
Rich Text Format (*.rtf)
Plain Text (*.txt)
Word XML Document (*.xml)
Word 2003 XML Document (*.xml)
Strict Open XML Document (*.docx)
OpenDocument Text (*.odt)
```

The "Save As" File Formats Available in Word 2016

Incidentally, the option to save as a WordPerfect file (.wpd) has not been available in Word for the last few versions.

---

[3] Also, Word 2016 (and Word 2013) now have the capability to **open** PDF files directly for editing. The conversion might result in certain layout changes (especially to page breaks), but it's still a handy new feature. For details and instructions, see the section starting on page 319.

Converting Documents From Compatibility Mode

When you are working on a document that has been saved as a .doc file – or even a .docx file created and saved in Word 2010 or earlier[1] – you will see an additional button on the Info screen. It is labeled "Convert / Compatibility Mode."[2]

The button provides a way for you to "upgrade" documents that were saved in an older Word file format to the Word 2013/2016 format, an enhanced version of the .docx. If you upgrade, you will be able to take advantage of all of the bells and whistles available in the latest format. However, most of those bells and whistles aren't essential, particularly for the type of document formatting common in the legal profession. So upgrading is by no means necessary.

If you do decide to upgrade, click the "**Convert**" button. Doing so produces a message box with a warning that converting the document might result in some layout changes (see the screenshot below). Note that there is a button labeled "**Tell Me More...**"

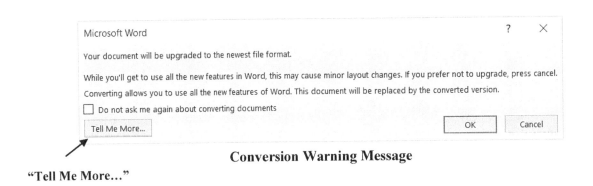

"**Tell Me More...**"   **Conversion Warning Message**

---

[1] As mentioned in the accompanying Sidebar, there are actually a few different .docx file formats: the original .docx, which is the default format for Word 2007, a modified Word 2010 version; and a modified Word 2013/2016 version. Note that .doc files, as well as the older .docx file formats (the Word 2007 and 2010 versions), will open in Compatibility Mode in Word 2016 (and in Word 2013). As a visual cue that your document is based on an older file format, you will see "[Compatibility Mode]" following the document name in the Title Bar.

[2] The Convert icon also appears (as does the [Compatibility Mode] designation after the file name in the Title Bar) if you open a document that is in a different file format, such as a .wpd (WordPerfect document), a Rich Text Format file (.rtf), or an XML file (.xml).

If you click "**Tell Me More…**," Word opens a very informative Help article entitled "Use Word 2016 to open documents created in earlier versions of Word." The article explains that there actually are four different Word file types: .doc, the standard file format for Word 97-2003, as well as separate Word 2007, Word 2010, and Word 2013-2016 versions of the newer .docx file format.

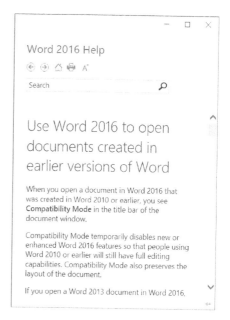

According to the article, the original Word 2007 .docx format doesn't support certain newer features of the program, including new shapes and text boxes, text effects, alternative text in tables, OpenType features, the ability to block authors (part of the innovative Co-Authoring function), new WordArt effects, and new content controls. The Word 2010 .docx format doesn't support certain newer features, either.

If you decide to proceed, click **OK**, and the program will convert your document into the latest .docx file format. However, the .docx extension might not appear in Word's Title Bar until after you save the file.

CAUTION: This method overwrites your existing document, rather than creating a new version of the file. That might or might not be your intention. Also, if you send the converted .docx file to someone who uses an older version of Word and doesn't also have Office 2013 or 2016 installed, the recipient won't have access to any newer features the document contains. In addition, the document layout might be somewhat different for that person. You can always use F12 or File > Save As to create a *copy* of the document in the newer file format.

Should You Convert (Upgrade)?

In most circumstances, you don't need to change (upgrade) the file format. You will seldom have a pressing reason to convert from an older file format (whether a .doc or a .docx) to the newest one (the Word 2013/2016 version of a .docx). In fact, most training and IT professionals consider it a best practice to leave your document format as is. If at some point you need to use some of the features of Word that are disabled (or that have reduced functionality) in the older file format, you could make an exception to this general rule. But whatever you do, don't "round-trip" – go back and forth between different file formats! That is a sure-fire route to document corruption, as explained in the section starting on page 581.

Protect Document

Protect Document encompasses several different methods for limiting access to the current document:

- Mark as Final
- Encrypt with Password
- Restrict Editing
- Add a Digital Signature

NOTE: Your ability to apply these types of protection might be limited by your organization's policies and procedures.

Mark as Final

As discussed in detail on page 568, the **Mark as Final** choice is not particularly restrictive (and it's much less restrictive than Encrypt with Password). When you mark a document as final, Word applies the "Read-Only" attribute to it and disables formatting commands. However, it's a trivial matter to turn off the "Read-Only" attribute and re-enable editing. By contrast, when you password-protect a document, no one can open it unless they know the password. Of course, that's a rather extreme measure and is useful only in limited circumstances. If your goal is to share the document with other people but limit their ability to make changes, Restrict Editing might be a better choice. More on that option momentarily.

Apply a Password

To apply a password to the current document, click the **Encrypt with Password** button.[3] An "**Encrypt Document**" **dialog** will open. **Type a password** into the box—make note of the password (mentally and/or in writing), keeping in mind that passwords are case-sensitive—and click "**OK**." Doing so will open a "**Confirm Password**" **dialog**; **type the password again** (with care to type it exactly as you did the first time), and then click "**OK**."

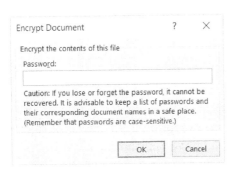

---

[3] Also, you can add a password the first time you save a document. After naming the document, click the **Tools button** at the lower left side of the **Save As dialog**, then click "**General Options**." When the **General Options dialog** opens, **type a new password** – be sure to make note of it – then click "**OK**." When prompted, type it again and click "**OK**," then click "**Save**."

After you apply a password to your document, the Info screen will add this notification:

CAUTION: *You must save the document* in order for the password to take effect. If you close without saving, the password will not be applied, and anyone with access to your computer will be able to open the document.

Assuming that you have saved the document (and have succeeded in applying the password), the next time someone attempts to open the document, a **Password dialog** will appear and prompt the user to **type a password**. The password must match—exactly—the password you applied when you saved the document. If it does, clicking "**OK**" will open the file.

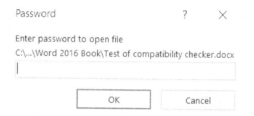

Remove a Password

To remove a password, open the password-protected document, then click File, Protect Document, Encrypt with Password again. Delete the (hidden) password. The warning that the file is password protected should disappear. Immediately save the document.

If you are working in Compatibility Mode, you'll see a message similar to the following when you first save the document after adding a password:

Essentially, the message is asking if you want to convert the file to the latest .docx format. If you don't want to do so, just click "No."

Restrict Editing

The **Restrict Editing** command effectively prevents certain types of editing and/or keeps certain individuals from working on the document.

When you click "**Restrict Editing**," the **Restrict Formatting and Editing Pane** opens at the right side of the screen (see the screenshot at right). You can change the settings in this pane to prevent people from altering the current document at all (by making it read-only). You can also limit other people's ability to create their own styles within the document or to turn off track changes, and you can allow them to insert comments only in certain "regions" of the document. In addition, you can control their ability to fill in form fields in the document.

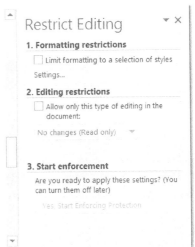

To apply any restrictions that you have selected from the various drop-downs in the pane, be sure to click the "**Yes, Start Enforcing Protection**" button.

For more information about the Restrict Editing option, see page 569.

Add a Digital Signature

Finally, if your organization has purchased a digital signature (or if you have done so), you can add one to a document by clicking the **Add a Digital Signature** button. (A digital signature can be a useful way of assuring the recipient of a document that it did, indeed, come from its purported—legitimate—source.) Note that you need to save the file (as a .docx) before adding a digital signature.

If neither you nor your organization has obtained / installed a digital signature, clicking the button will produce a message box similar to the one shown below:

As with some of the other document protection options, your ability to use this feature could be limited by your organization's IT department or the company's management.

Inspect Document / Check for Issues

The Inspect Document / Check for Issues option reminds you to review your document before sending it to someone else to make sure it doesn't contain sensitive, confidential, or otherwise problematic content. In particular, it is designed to prevent you from forwarding a document that includes "metadata" – certain identifying information about the document (dates created or modified, location in the computer, length, size, revision number, etc.), the computer(s) on which it was created and/or modified, the author(s), and so forth – as well as hidden text, comments, and revision marks (redlining and strikeout).

As soon as you open the Info. screen, Word starts searching the current document for any possible "issues."

It looks for document properties that you might not want others to see (author's name, printer path, related dates, etc.); headers and footers; hidden text; custom XML data; and so forth. See, for example, the warning in the screenshot immediately below:

Inspect Document
Before publishing this file, be aware that it contains:
- Document properties and author's name
- Characters formatted as hidden text
- Content that people with disabilities are unable to read

For more information and/or to address the issues, click the "Check for Issues" drop-down. It offers three different ways of reviewing your document for potential problems: Inspect Document, Check Accessibility, and Check Compatibility.[4]

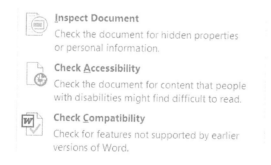

The Document Inspector

The Document Inspector, a built-in metadata removal utility, was introduced in Word 2007. I discuss this feature in detail later in the book. See the section starting on page 563.

---

[4] In Word 2007, Inspect Document and Run Compatibility Checker were part of the Prepare screen from the Office button / File drop-down. There was no equivalent to the Accessibility Checker.

The Accessibility Checker

The Accessibility Checker works only in .docx files (i.e., not in .doc files). When you click the "**Check Accessibility**" button, the utility examines your document, looking for various items that, according to Microsoft, can make a document harder to read, especially for a person with disabilities. These items typically have to do with the way that tables, headings, hyperlinks, images, and so forth are laid out and formatted in your document.

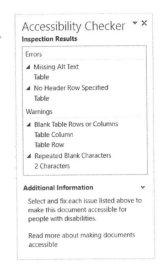

For instance, the Accessibility Checker will point out potential problems such as a table that lacks a header row, headings that are formatted as body text, and/or excessive white space. When the utility finds problems, it identifies the problems in an pane that opens at the right side of the screen. Clicking one of the items in the top portion of the pane produces an "Additional Information" box that explains why the item merits attention and provides information about how to fix it.

Obviously, you can choose to make the suggested changes or leave the document as is. Either way, it can be helpful to know how accessible the document is to people with disabilities.

The Compatibility Checker

You can run the compatibility checker to find out which of the newer features of Word won't translate well if someone opens your Word 2016 .docx file with an old version of the program that isn't optimized for the .docx file format – or if you save the file as a .doc. The Compatibility Checker dialog box summarizes the feature(s) that are affected, what will happen on backwards conversion, and how many occurrences of the feature exist in the document.

For instance, if you have inserted SmartArt into a .docx, when you click the button to run the compatibility checker, a dialog box will open and advise you that the SmartArt "features may be lost or degraded when opening this document in an earlier version of Word or if you save this document in an earlier file format." (See the screenshot below.)

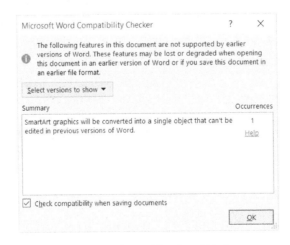

The Compatibility Checker Dialog

Some of the other features (besides Smart Art) that don't work in prior versions of Word, or that don't work the same way, include:

- Charts and diagrams (will be converted to images that can't be edited)
- Equations (will be converted to images that can't be edited; however, converting to a .docx format will change the equations back to editable text)
- Themes (will be converted permanently to *styles*)
- Content Controls (will be converted permanently to *static text*)
- Citations and bibliographies (will be converted permanently to *static text*)
- Tracked Moves (will be converted permanently to **Insertions** and **Deletions**)
- Embedded objects will not be editable unless you right-click the object, click Convert, choose "Convert to…" and click "Microsoft Word 97-2003 Document."
- Text Boxes with Vertical Alignment (will be converted permanently to use *Top vertical alignment*)
- Relative Positioned Text Boxes (will be converted permanently to *absolute positioned* text boxes)

For a comprehensive list of features that might work differently (or not at all) in older versions of Word, see the Help article entitled "Compatibility changes between versions." (To locate the article, type "compatibility" – without quotation marks – in the "**Tell me what you want to do**" box above the Ribbon, then click "Get Help on compatibility." The Help window will open and display a list of relevant articles. The titles are hyperlinks; click a title to open the article.)

If you attempt to save a .docx as a .doc, you'll see a slightly different version of the Compatibility Checker dialog, notifying you of the features that will be lost or degraded and prompting you to continue or cancel. Clicking "Continue" will convert the file. Note that if you ever convert the .doc back to a .docx, some of the newer features that aren't functional in Compatibility Mode will work again. These features include SmartArt, Charts, Images, and Equations.

Manage Document

The Manage Document section of the Info screen is a little confusing because it encompasses two related but different features: (1) the AutoRecover files, or autosaved backup versions of documents that you're working on, as discussed in the section starting on page 53, and (2) the Unsaved Documents (documents that you closed without saving), as discussed in the section starting on page 51.

To the right of the Manage Document icon, you'll see the autosaved backup drafts of the current (active) document – i.e., the AutoRecover files.

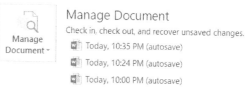

As discussed earlier, you can click one of the autosaved versions and run a comparison/redline with the most recent version; save the earlier version (preferably as a separate file); or discard it.

The "Manage Document" Button

As discussed earlier, you can restore an Unsaved Document from the "Open" screen; there's a link at the bottom right side (under "Recent"). You can do the same thing from the "Info" screen – by clicking the Manage Document button.

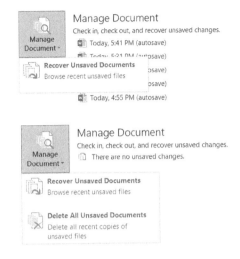

When you do, a drop-down opens. It will offer either the single choice, "**Recover Unsaved Documents**," or that choice plus the option labeled "**Delete All Unsaved Documents**," depending on whether you have or haven't already saved the current (active) document. If yes, then you'll see only the single choice. If not, then both choices will be available.[5]

The "New" Screen

The "New" screen is for creating a blank document or creating a document based on a built-in or customized (personal) template. The "Featured" templates shown there are provided by Microsoft; clicking "Custom" displays your own personal templates (if any)[6], along with shared ("Workgroup") templates.

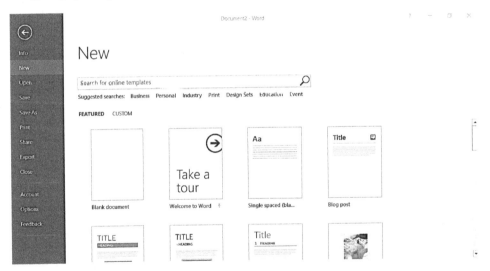

The Backstage View—"New" Screen

---

[5] There might be occasions when you don't want to retain Unsaved Documents – for instance, when you are using someone else's computer (or a computer in a public place).

[6] **CAUTION**: This screen displays only those templates that are stored in the Default personal templates location" in the "Save" category of the Word Options, as explained below.

Blank Document

This aspect of the New screen is self-explanatory. You can create a new blank document by clicking the Blank Document icon.[7]

Featured Templates

In the "Featured" group – which, by default, is at the forefront – Microsoft has provided about two dozen templates, including a fax cover sheet, a couple of different letters, a resume, a brochure, an APA report, and so forth. There are also a few templates for special occasions such as birthdays and weddings.

If the templates shown don't meet your needs, you can type a search term in the box toward the top of the screen or, if you prefer, click a category label below the search box (such as Business) to look for relevant online templates.

As a test, I typed "legal," which turned up a few samples of pleading paper. When I held the mouse pointer over each sample, a pop-up appeared with information about the line numbers. I downloaded one that indicated it had 28 line numbers.

When I clicked it, a preview opened (see the screenshot below).

Because Microsoft created the template, I figured it was safe to proceed. When I clicked "Create," the template opened in Word. (It needed some tweaking to comply with California court rules and be reasonably functional, but would have done the job if someone put in the time and effort to fix it.) The downloaded template is now listed in the "Featured Templates" area.

---

[7] Another way to create a new blank document is by pressing the key combination **Ctrl N** (for "New"). Or you can add a blank document icon to the Quick Access Toolbar (QAT) by clicking the "**More**" drop-down at the right end of the QAT, then clicking "**New**."

Custom / Personal Templates

The Custom Templates section gives you easy access to any custom (personal) templates that you have created – as long as they are stored in certain folders where Word looks for them.

In particular, clicking the "**Custom**" heading[8] displays the folder designated as your "**Personal templates default location**" in the "**Save**" category of the **Word Options**. It also displays the folder you have set, if any, for the "**Workgroup**" (shared) **templates** in the "**Advanced**" category of the **Word Options** under "**File Locations**."[9]

However, this screen does *not* display any custom templates stored in the "**User templates**" folder designated in the Advanced category of the Word Options under "File Locations." For a fuller explanation of this very important but also very confusing issue, see pages 597 and following.

The screenshot below left shows my Workgroup templates folder (CompuSavvy Templates) and my personal templates folder (Custom Office Templates). (By default, personal templates are saved to a Custom Office Templates subfolder of your Documents folder, although you can change this setting in the "Save" category of the Word Options.) The screenshot below right shows a "Legal" subfolder I created within the Custom Office Templates folder, along with a template that I put in the main Custom Office Templates folder.

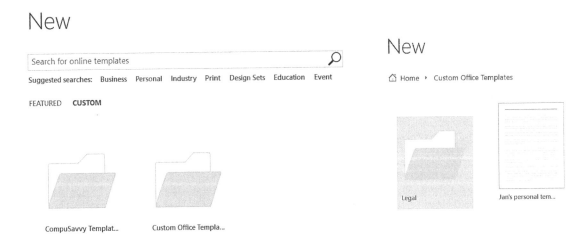

Clicking a folder (such as the Custom Office Templates folder) displays any existing subfolders, as well as thumbnails of any templates contained within the folder. To create a document based on one of the templates, just single-click that template's thumbnail.

For more about using (and creating) templates, see the section starting on page 409.

---

[8] If you don't see any "Custom" (or "Personal") heading, it's because you haven't set a "Personal templates default location" in the "Save" category of the Word Options.

[9] Any subfolders you have created within those folders will be available from this screen, too.

Print ("Print Place")

In all Office 2016 applications, including Word, the traditional Print dialog has been replaced by what Microsoft sometimes calls "**Print Place**," a full page of print configuration options combined with a large print preview area. (And yes, in anticipation of your question, **Ctrl P** now opens Print Place rather than the old-fashioned print dialog.) I'll discuss the print preview feature, which takes up the right side of the screen, before describing the print options.

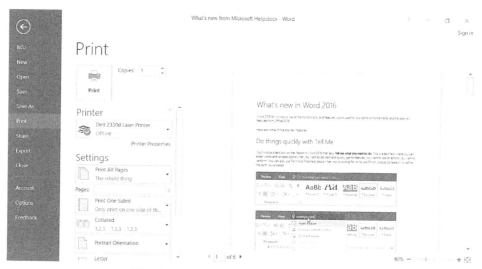

The Backstage View—"Print Place"

The Print Preview

There are a few important points to note about the way the print preview works in Print Place. First, the underlying document can't be edited from within the preview, which is a change from prior versions of Word. (You can retain the functionality of the older versions if you add a "Print Preview Edit Mode" icon to the Quick Access Toolbar, however. See the discussion on page 74.)

Normally, the print preview displays a single page at a reduced size. You can use the slider at the bottom right to zoom in (increase the magnification) or out (decrease the magnification). In a multi-page document, zooming out displays two or more pages at once. A "zoom to page" button to the right of the slider restores the normal full-page magnification.

To move to a different page from within the preview screen, you can either use the arrows at the bottom center (see the screenshot on the next page) or press Page Up / Pg Up or Page Down / Pg Dn. (You might find that you have to click on the image of the document in the preview in order to get the Page Up and Page Dn keys to work properly—presumably because until you do so, another portion of Print Place has the focus.)

Add a Print Preview Edit Mode Icon to the QAT

In Word 2016, there is no editable Print Preview feature. The keyboard shortcut that, in some older versions, opened a separate Print Preview screen that included a way to edit the doc while previewing it – **Ctrl F2** – now merely opens Print Place. However, you can emulate the Print Preview functionality found in earlier versions of Word by adding a "**Print Preview Edit Mode**" icon to the Quick Access Toolbar. That icon produces a fully editable preview, separate from Print Place, that works the same way as in previous versions of Word.

To add the icon to the QAT:

1. Position the cursor anywhere within the QAT and *right-click*. You'll see a mini-menu like the one below. (If you haven't moved your QAT, yours will read, "Show Quick Access Toolbar Below the Ribbon.")[10]

2. Click "**Customize Quick Access Toolbar…**"

3. When the Word Options screen appears, change the "**Choose commands from:**" drop-down from "Popular" to "**All Commands**."

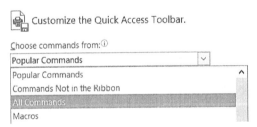

4. Click in the command list underneath the "Choose commands from:" drop-down and press the letter "**P**" (which will move the cursor to the first command that starts with "P") and scroll down to the "Print Preview" commands. There are a few of them. The one you want is labeled "**Print Preview Edit Mode**."

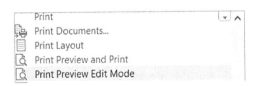

---

[10] Another way quick way to open the Quick Access Toolbar in the Word Options is by clicking the "**More**" **drop-down arrow** at the right side of the QAT, then choosing "**More Commands…**" For a more complete discussion of customizing the QAT, see pp. 175 and following.

5. Click that command, then click the "**Add**" **button** in the middle of the screen. (Or you can double-click after clicking the command.)

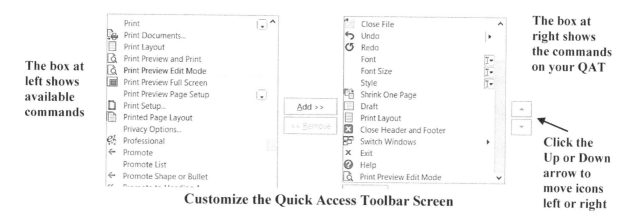

Customize the Quick Access Toolbar Screen

(**NOTE**: The screenshot shows my customizations; your screen will look somewhat different.)

6. If you wish, you can change the location of the "Print Preview Edit Mode" icon on the QAT. First, click the command in the box at the right side of the screen (which displays the icons on your customized QAT), then click either the **Up arrow** (to move the icon to the left) or the **Down arrow** (to move it to the right). Note that one or both of the arrows will be grayed out until you click a command.

7. Click "**OK**" to save your setting, close out of the Word Options, and return to the document editing screen.

When you click the "Print Preview Edit Mode" button, you will see the current document in the traditional print preview mode, not within the framework of Print Place. A context-sensitive "Print Preview" tab will appear, offering pertinent commands (including a "Close Print Preview" button that returns you to the normal editing screen).

NOTE: If you can't click in or edit the document in the preview screen (because the mouse pointer turns into a magnifying glass and clicking merely zooms in and out), click to *uncheck* "**Magnifier**" in the Ribbon.

Contextual Print Preview Tab

Print Settings

The entire left-hand side of the "Print Place" screen is devoted to various print settings. For the most part, the choices available are the same as those offered in the traditional Print dialog, but the graphical interface is different.

75

At the top, there is a large **Print button** with a printer icon, plus a box to set the number of copies. Your active printer appears below that; click the drop-down to one of your other printers (if any), add a new printer, or print to a file. The "**Printer Properties**" link below the drop-down is useful if you need to change your printer's configuration options – for example, I use it for automatic duplex (double-sided) printing from the Printer Properties dialog because the "Print One Sided" drop-down offers only a manual duplexing option. Also, you can change the active printer tray from within the Printer Properties dialog.

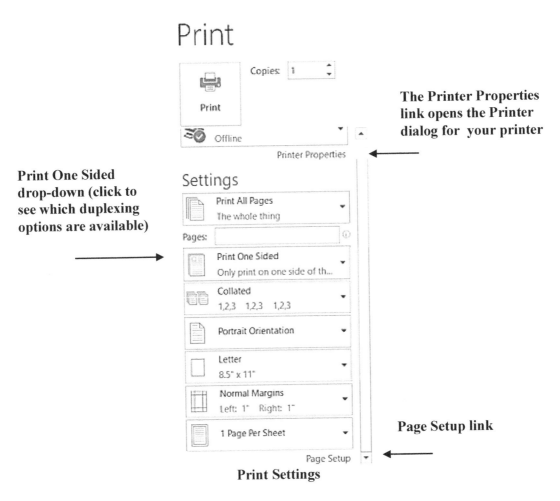

Print Settings

The "Print All Pages" Menu

Below "**Settings**," you'll find the all-important "**Print All Pages**" menu. By default, the menu is collapsed. When you click it, the menu expands and displays several choices about which pages to print: "Print All Pages" (the default setting), "Print Selection" (grayed out unless / until you select some text), "Print Current Page," and "Custom Print."

76

Note that there's a "Pages" box underneath the menu, where you can type a custom page range (see the screenshot in the "Custom Print" section for examples of the syntax to use).

Print Selection

This option works as you might expect: After you have selected some text, the "Print Selection" option becomes available from the drop-down "Settings" menu. Click it, then click the Print button to print the selected text.

TIP: As you might know, in recent versions of Word, it is possible to select non-contiguous portions of text. To do so, select the first portion, then press the Ctrl key, move the mouse pointer, select another portion, and so on.

Print Current Page

It's easy to miss the "Print Current Page" command because it's not visible when the "Print All Pages" menu is in its normal collapsed state.

I haven't found a way to add "Print Current Page" to the Quick Access Toolbar. However, some IT departments create a command button for printing the current page and add the button to a customized tab (or to a custom QAT that they distribute to everyone who works at the organization).

Custom Print Range

Using "Custom Print," you can specify not merely a series of contiguous (1-3) or non-contiguous (2,5,11) pages, but also—if your document consists of multiple *sections*—a series of pages within a single section of the document. For example, you can print pages 1 through 7 of section 3 of a document by typing "p1s3-p7s3" (without quotation marks) in the "Print Range" portion of the Print dialog. In fact, it is possible to print a few different portions of one section, and/or a few different portions of multiple sections, and/or one or more entire sections.

Indeed, if you position the mouse pointer over the "Information" button to the right of the "Pages:" field under "Settings," you'll see a pop-up that explains the syntax to use in order to print a custom page range. (Keep in mind that the examples are not exhaustive.)

The Pages Box   **Syntax for Printing a Custom Range**

Only Print Odd Pages

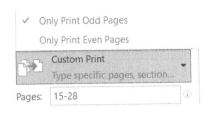

At the bottom of the menu, there is a command labeled "Only Print Odd Pages." You can use the command to print all of the odd-numbered pages in your document or to print the odd pages within a certain page range by clicking "Custom Print," then entering the range in the "Pages" box. See the screenshot for an example of the latter.

Commonly used for manual duplex (double-sided) printing, "Only Print Odd Pages" can be used with the Print option labeled "Print on front of the sheet for duplex printing" described below, under "The Printing Specs."

Only Print Even Pages

The "Only Print Even Pages" option works exactly the same way as "Only Print Odd Pages." Again, you can use the option by itself—and print all of the even-numbered pages in your document—or in conjunction with the "Print Custom Range" choice.

The Printing Specs

In addition to determining which pages to print, you can choose among various printing specifications available from drop-downs in the "Settings" section. These options include:

One sided or duplex	Print One Sided — Only print on one side of the page Manually Print on Both Sides — Reload paper when prompted to print the second side Note that the duplex option says "Manually Print on Both Sides," suggesting that you must remove the paper from the printer manually, turn it over, and replace it in order to print on the other side. If your printer allows *automatic* duplexing, you can set this option *via the Printer Properties link*.
Collated or uncollated	Collated 1,2,3 1,2,3 1,2,3 Uncollated 1,1,1 2,2,2 3,3,3 This option is fairly straightforward.
Portrait or landscape orientation	Portrait Orientation Landscape Orientation Also straightforward.

Paper size	The paper size choices include standard Letter and Legal sizes (which are common in the U.S.), A4 and A5 (common in Europe), a variety of envelopes, and more (you have to scroll down to see the entire list). Note that there is a "More Paper Sizes…" option at the bottom of the menu. Clicking that option opens the Page Setup dialog with the Paper tab at the forefront so that you can scroll to find additional choices.
Margins	This menu offers assorted print margins, ranging from whatever your normal margin settings are to Microsoft's idea of "Narrow" and "Wide" margins. At the bottom of the menu there is a "Custom Margins" option. Clicking that option opens the Page Setup dialog with the Margins tab at the forefront so that you can configure custom margins.
Pages per sheet	This option lets you print booklets, deposition summaries, and the like by subdividing a page into two or more virtual pages.

Page Setup

At the bottom right side of the Settings menu, there is a link labeled "Page Setup." Clicking the link opens the Page Setup dialog so that you can change the document's margins, the orientation, the paper type, the paper size, the paper source (i.e., which tray the printer pulls from), and so on directly from within that dialog.

Of course, the Page Setup dialog is also available from the dialog launcher in the Page Setup group on the Layout tab. (Keyboard users can open it by pressing **Alt P, S, P**.)

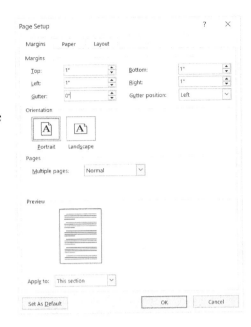

Print What / Document Info

In earlier versions of Word, the Print dialog included a "Print what" option. This little known but handy feature made it simple to print objects other than the current document. The other "Print what" choices in the traditional Print dialog included the following:

- Document

- Document properties

- Document showing markup

- List of markup

- Styles

- Building Blocks entries

- Key assignments

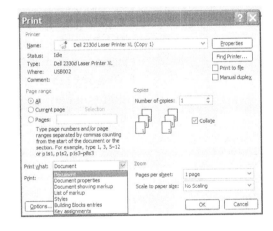

If you chose "Document properties," a list of several properties of the current document printed. If you chose "Document showing markup," the document printed, with any revision marks therein (redlining, strikeout, comments, etc.) displayed. If you chose "List of markup," only a *summary* of the revision marks in the current document printed, not the document itself.

If you chose "Styles" or "Key assignments," a list and description of any customized (user-created) styles or keyboard shortcuts used – or available for use – in the current document printed.

If you chose "Building Blocks entries," Word printed the customized (user-created) Building Blocks entries[11] embedded in the template underlying the current document (usually the Normal template), as well as in any other templates attached to the document.

In Word 2016, the "Print what" drop-down has been replaced by a menu labeled "**Document Info**" that is somewhat difficult to find. Like many of the other advanced options, it is buried in the "**Print All Pages**" menu.

The list of printable document attributes and objects appears below the catch-all label "**Document Info**." As you can see from the previous screenshot, you must scroll to see all of those attributes. If you scroll through the items in the menu, you'll see almost the same list of printable items as in the "Print what" drop-down in the old Print dialog:

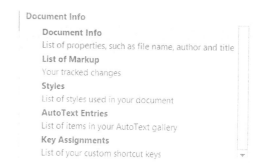

- Document Info
- List of Markup
- Styles
- AutoText Entries (more or less comparable to Building Blocks Entries in the traditional Print dialog) [12]
- Key Assignments

When you select an object to print by clicking that object in the list, your choice will appear in the Settings area and the object (such as AutoText entries, shown in the screenshot below) will print when you click the Print button.

Document Properties

As in earlier versions of Word, choosing the "Document Properties" option will print an extensive list of the properties of the current document, including the filename, folder, template, title (if you've typed anything in the title field within the Info screen), subject (if you've typed anything in the subject field), author, keywords (if you've typed any), comments (if any), creation date, change number, last date saved, person who last saved the document, total editing time, last date printed, number of pages, number of words, and number of characters.

---

[11] "Building Blocks," also known as "Quick Parts," are discussed in detail starting on page 377.

[12] The term "AutoText Entries" appears to mean only AutoText entries that have been imported from an earlier version or Word or new Quick Parts that you save to the AutoText gallery.

Styles, Key Assignments, and AutoText Entries

Choosing "Styles" will print a list and description of any built-in and customized (user-created) styles used—or available for use—in the current document.

Choosing "Key assignments" will print a list and description of customized (user-created) keyboard shortcuts used—or available for use—in the current document. As the next screenshot clearly implies, the list does *not* include built-in shortcuts.

Key Assignments
List of your custom shortcut keys

Choosing "AutoText entries" will print the AutoText entries used – or available for use – in the current document, including both built-in entries and customized (user-created) entries. In my tests, the results included custom AutoText entries stored in my Normal template (Normal.dotm), as well as custom Quick Parts entries stored in my personal Building Blocks template.[13] Note that the output consists of both the names of the AutoText and Quick Parts entries and the expanded AutoText and Quick Parts entries themselves.

Print Markup

At the very bottom of the "Print All Pages" menu, there is an item labeled "Print Markup." This last item is comparable to the old "Print what" option called "Document showing markup."

NOTE: Because this option *is enabled by default*, any revision marks in the current document will appear in the printed document unless you take the deliberate step of *unchecking* the "Print Markup" checkbox (by clicking it) before printing.

✓ Print Markup

Configuring the Print Options

To view or change one or more of the default Print Options, click the **File tab**, **Options**, **Advanced**, and scroll a little more than halfway down to the **Print** category. It's unlikely that you'll have occasion to tweak most of these settings. However, a few of them might be useful on occasion. For example, if you are working on a very long document and you want to speed up the print process, you can try selecting the "Use draft quality" option. Just keep in mind that the quality of the printout might not be as sharp as normal.

---

[13] As mentioned elsewhere in the book, there is one Building Blocks template for built-in entries (entries that come with the program) and a separate one for custom (user-created) entries.

```
Word Options

  General            ☑ Show vertical ruler in Print Layout view
  Display            ☐ Optimize character positioning for layout rather than readability
  Proofing           ☐ Disable hardware graphics acceleration
  Save               ☑ Update document content while dragging ⓘ
  Language           ☑ Use subpixel positioning to smooth fonts on screen

  Advanced           Print
  Customize Ribbon   ☐ Use draft quality
  Quick Access Toolbar ☑ Print in background ⓘ
                     ☐ Print pages in reverse order
  Add-ins            ☐ Print XML tags
  Trust Center       ☐ Print field codes instead of their values
                     ☑ Allow fields containing tracked changes to update before printing
                     ☐ Print on front of the sheet for duplex printing
                     ☐ Print on back of the sheet for duplex printing
                     ☑ Scale content for A4 or 8.5 x 11" paper sizes
                     Default tray:  [ Use printer settings            ▾ ]

                     When printing this document:  ☑  [ Book Draft 12-3-2015.docx    ▾ ]
                     ☐ Print PostScript over text
                     ☐ Print only the data from a form
```

The Print Options

The "Print in background" option is enabled by default because it allows you to continue to work while a document is printing. If a particular print job seems to be exceptionally slow, you can try unchecking this option (which will allocate more memory to the printer), but you'll have to wait until the document finishes printing before you can edit another document.

"Print Postscript over text" is seldom used except with documents converted from Word for the Mac.

"Print pages in reverse order" is self-explanatory. Microsoft's support site points out that you shouldn't use this option when printing envelopes.

Most people probably will never use the "Print XML tags" option. This option is designed for people who work with XML coding.

"Print field codes instead of their values" is used to show the codes that are normally hidden, such as PAGE or SEQ codes. See the section about field codes, starting on page 361, for more information.

If your printer doesn't automatically print duplex (double-sided), you can use the "Print on front of the sheet for duplex printing" option to print the odd pages of a lengthy document, then flip the document over and print the even pages. Microsoft indicates that the pages *will print in reverse order* "so that when you flip the stack to print on the back, the pages will print in the proper order."

83

"Print on back of the sheet for duplex printing" – the same as above, except that this option prints the even pages of the document.

"Print only the data from a form" will print just the data you have input into a form, not the underlying form itself.

The "Print pages in reverse order" option might come in handy at some point.

"Allow fields containing tracked changes to update before printing," which is enabled by default, ensures that field codes that you inserted while tracking changes are updated to reflect the current information.

The "Share" Screen

The "Share" screen in Word 2016 lets you share the current / active document with others in several different ways.

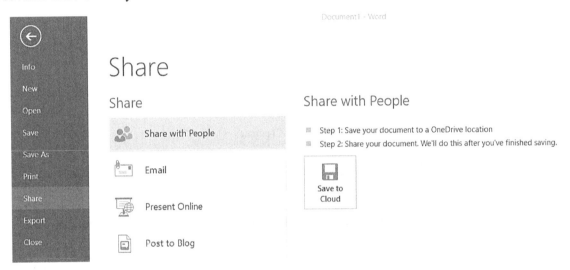

The "Share" Screen

In particular, you can share it with others via OneDrive, upload it to SharePoint, e-mail it, present it on the Internet using a Microsoft presentation service, or publish it as a blog post. Click a category heading to see an expanded menu with options for that category.

Share With People

The first option, Share with People, walks you through the process of saving a document to the OneDrive or to SharePoint (if available) and then sharing the document with others. After you save a document to a OneDrive or SharePoint account, a Share with People button appears.

Clicking the button opens a Share pane at the right side of the document. The pane includes a link to your address book so that you can invite people to edit, or simply to view, your document. If you want colleagues to be able to work on the document, be sure to choose "Can edit" when you send invitations.

Another option, which is useful if you want to use the new "Real-Time Co-Authoring" feature (see the Sidebar on the next page), is to click the "Get a sharing link" command at the bottom of the "Share" pane.

When the "Get a sharing link" dialog opens, click either the "Create an edit link" button or the "Create a view-only link" button.

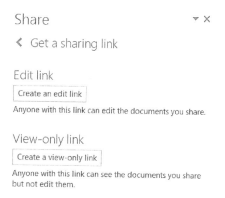

The resulting link (URL) appears with a "Copy" button so that you can copy the link and forward it to other people. When they click the link, the document will open in their version of Word or in Word Online, where they can edit or view the doc, depending on the type of link you created.

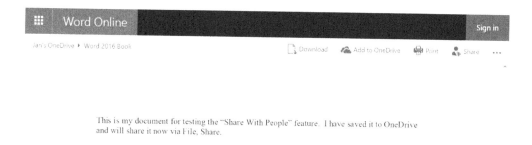

(Note that Word online isn't as full-featured as the regular versions of Word.)

WHERE IS IT? Dictionary

This one is tricky. In earlier versions of Word, the dictionary feature was located at the left side of the **Review tab**, in the Proofing group, under "**Research**." Although the dictionary is still on the Review tab in Word 2016, it is in its own separate group ("**Insights**") under the somewhat obscure name "**Smart Lookup**."

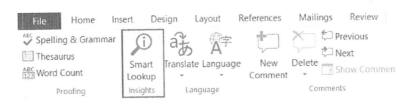

To define a word or phrase, right-click a word or phrase (select / highlight the phrase first), then click "**Smart Lookup**." Alternatively, click within a word or select / highlight a phrase, then click the "Smart Lookup" icon in the Ribbon. When you do so, the **Insights Pane** opens at the right side of the screen.

It has two tabs: "**Explore**" and "**Define**." **Define** is self-explanatory (the definitions appear to be based on the Oxford Dictionaries / Oxford University Press and/or on Bing, Microsoft's search engine). **Explore** takes you to web pages (via Wikipedia) for further information about the word or phrase.

When you click the Explore tab, be sure to scroll down to see all of the information from Wikipedia.

At the bottom right side, there is a "**More**" link you can click to get additional information / definitions from the Web (Bing).   See the screenshot at right.

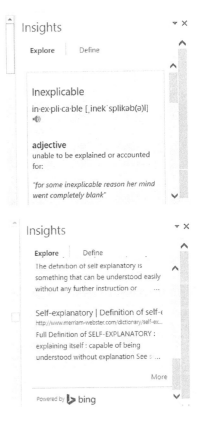

If you click the icon without selecting text first, you'll get an error message:

Just select the text, then give it another go.

SIDEBAR: Real-Time Co-Authoring

A new feature in Word 2016 called **Real-Time Co-Authoring** lets you and your colleagues work on a document simultaneously – and see one another's changes "live."

To use the feature, you must save your document to a shared online location. Start by clicking the **File tab**, **Share**, clicking the **Save to Cloud button**, and selecting **OneDrive** or **SharePoint Online**, as appropriate.

Word will open the "**Save As**" screen.

If necessary, click "**Add a Place**," then sign in to your OneDrive or SharePoint Online account and save the document to your preferred folder.

After you save the document, if a Share pane doesn't open at the right side of the doc, click the **File tab**, **Share** again and click the "**Share with people**" button.

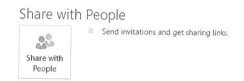

When the **Share pane** opens, you have two options. You can use the "**Invite people**" option at the top (either type an e-mail address yourself or click the address book icon at right and browse through your contacts), choosing either "Can edit" or "Can view"; or you can click "**Get a sharing link**" at the bottom, then click either "Get an edit link" or "Get a view link."

To make sure everyone is able to view your changes, be sure to choose either "**Ask me**" or "**Always**" from the drop-down toward the middle of the pane. If you forget, Word will prompt you later to share your changes.

87

After you send sharing invitations or links, other people will be able to open your document either in Word 2016 or in Word Online. They, too, will have the choice of automatically sharing their changes. If they do, you will be able to see their edits as they work on the document. (Be careful not to leave the "**Don't ask me again**" checkbox checked if you want Word to prompt you to share changes automatically the next time you engage in Real-Time Co-Authoring.)

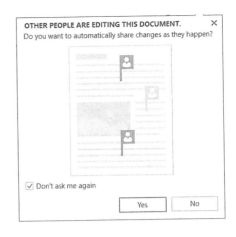

Colored flags will show you exactly where the other co-authors are working. When you hold the mouse over a flag, a pop-up displays the co-author's name (see the screenshot below).

Next, you invite people to edit it with you. When they open and work on the document in Word 2016 or Word Online, you'll see each other's changes as soon as they're made. Like this!

The appearance of the "Save" icon changes (you'll see green "Refresh" arrows superimposed on the icon) and, when you hold the mouse pointer over the icon, you'll see the pop-up shown in the next screenshot:

Note that if other people are working on the document at the same time you are but have not agreed to share their changes, you will see indicators that they are in the document, but won't be able to see their edits until after they have saved the doc.

Word will alert you when a co-author closes the document or stops sharing.

The Email Option

The second option, Email, offers a few different ways to forward a document: Send as attachment, Send a link, Send as PDF, Send as XPS, and Send as Internet fax (which requires you to have an Internet faxing service).

Send as Attachment

If you have Outlook installed on your computer, clicking the "Send as attachment" button opens a new mail message (i.e., a message composition screen) in Outlook, with the document already attached. See, for example, the next screenshot.

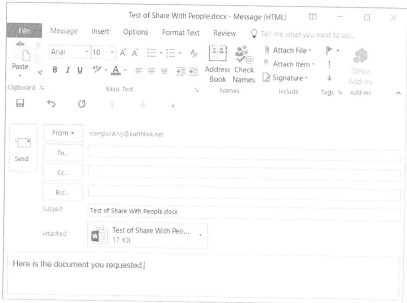

Send as Attachment – Opens a New Mail Message in Outlook

Send a Link

If your document is saved in a shared location (such as OneDrive, a SharePoint library, or a network drive), you can use this option to send other users (typically other members of your organization) a link to the document via e-mail. This option is particularly useful because everyone who opens the link will see the latest version of the document. Note that the "Send a Link" button is grayed out if the current document is not saved in a shared location (e.g., it's stored in a folder on your C: drive).

89

Send as PDF

If you click the "Send as PDF" icon, two things occur: Word makes a copy of the active file and converts it into a PDF, and Outlook opens a new mail message with the PDF attached. As far as I can tell, Word doesn't actually save the new PDF to your hard drive; if you wish to create and store a permanent copy, you'll need to right-click it from within Outlook and click "Save As."

- Everyone gets a PDF attachment
- Preserves layout, formatting, fonts, and images
- Content can't be easily changed

Send as XPS

The "Send as XPS" option lets you save a copy of the document in Microsoft's proprietary XPS format and send it to others. Note that XPS files require a special reader.[14] Because XPS is a generic format, the document appears the same on most computers, and fonts, formatting, and images are preserved. However, it can be difficult to edit an XPS file.

- Everyone gets an XPS attachment
- Preserves layout, formatting, fonts, and images
- Content can't be easily changed

Most people who work in the legal field probably won't have much occasion to use this option. (I have never met anyone who used, or admitted to using, the XPS file format.)

Send as Internet Fax

You need a fax Internet service provider in order to use this option.

- No fax machine needed
- You'll need a fax service provider

---

[14] There is an XPS viewer built into recent versions of Windows.

Present Online

The Present Online option lets you use a Microsoft presentation service to show your document to others on the Internet. (The service is free, but you have to sign up for it.)

Present Online
Present the document to people who can watch in a web browser
- No setup required
- A link is created to share with people
- Anyone using the link can see the document while you are presenting online
- The document will be made available for download

You will need a Microsoft account to start the online presentation.

By clicking Present Online, you agree to the following terms:
Service Agreement

☐ Enable remote viewers to download the document

Post to Blog

The "Publish as Blog Post" option, albeit not something you're likely to use at work, nevertheless might come in handy if you have Word 2016 on a personal computer and want to use it to create posts for a new or existing blog.

When you click the Post to Blog button, you'll be asked to register your blog with Microsoft. After you do so, a contextual Blog Post tab appears. You can just start typing, then use icons on the Blog Post tab for to publish, either as a draft or in final.

Post to Blog
Create a new blog post using the current document.

Some supported blogging sites include:
- SharePoint Blog
- WordPress
- Blogger
- Telligent Community
- TypePad

If this is your first blog post from Word, you'll be prompted to register your blog account. You can add additional accounts anytime.

The "Export" Screen

The items on the "Export" screen, "Create PDF/XPS Document" and "Change File Type," were part of the Save & Send screen in Word 2010.

Export

Create PDF/XPS Document

Change File Type

Create a PDF/XPS Document
- Preserves layout, formatting, fonts, and images
- Content can't be easily changed
- Free viewers are available on the web

Create PDF/XPS

The "Export" Screen

91

Create PDF/XPS Document

This option is one of several ways you can convert a Word document into a PDF (Portable Document File) in Word 2016. (You can also use this option to convert a Word doc to an XPS file, although most people in the legal profession don't work with XPS files.)

Recent versions of Word do a much better job of converting Word docs to PDF files than older versions. Even Word 2007 initially didn't include a built-in converter that allowed users to save .docx or .doc files in PDF format. Until 2009, when Microsoft released a patched version of Word 2007 that incorporated the PDF converter, anyone wishing to publish to PDF had to download a separate add-in. Happily, Word 2016 comes with a PDF conversion filter, so users no longer have to download an additional utility in order to turn a Word document into a PDF. And the quality of the converted file is, for the most part, very good.

To save a document as a PDF file, click the **"Create a PDF/XPS" button**. When you do, you might see a prompt asking which program (or app) you want to use to open the PDF after creating it. I chose Adobe Reader; the other options listed (available on my Windows 10 computer) were Microsoft Edge (Microsoft's new browser), Word 2016 – this version of Word can open PDFs directly for editing! (See the section starting on page 319) – and "Look for an app in the Store."

The first time you use this feature, there should be a box you can check to have Word always open PDF files you create in this manner with the program you select.

After you click OK, a **Publish as PDF or XPS dialog** will open.

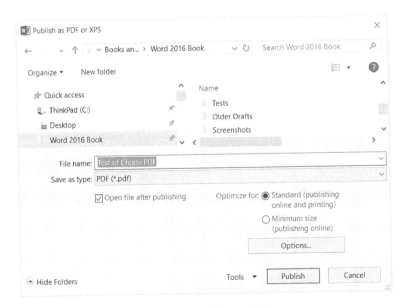

Publish as PDF or XPS

If the dialog box opens with the "Save as type" set to "XPS Document (*.xps)," click the "Save as type" drop-down and change it manually to PDF.[15]

Before clicking "Publish," change the file name (and/or the "Save in" location) if you like, and then make note of the various configuration options at the bottom of the dialog. By default, Word uses "**Optimize for: Standard (publishing online and printing)**"; you can change this setting so that Word creates a smaller PDF file for publishing online (i.e., one that takes up less space in the computer, not one with smaller fonts).

If you check the "**Open file after publishing**" **box**, Word will open the PDF file in the program you chose earlier. (An XPS file will open in the XPS reader included in your version of Windows.)

To see what other configuration options are available to you, click the "**Options**" button in the lower right-hand corner of the dialog. Incidentally, as you will see from the screenshot at right (toward the bottom), you can convert the Word document into a PDF/A file, the format that many courts in California now require.

NOTE: The Document Properties *will be included* in the resulting PDF (or XPS) file unless you specifically *uncheck* the "**Document properties**" **box** (in the section of the dialog labeled "**Include non-printing information**"). In other words, by default the PDF will contain some metadata.

CAUTION: The "Document properties" checkbox is grayed out – meaning you won't be able to uncheck it – if you select the PDF/A file format. See the screenshot at left.

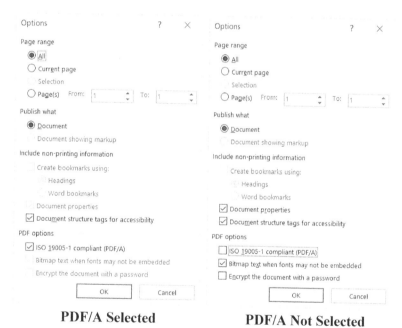

ANOTHER CAUTION: Don't assume that unchecking the "Document properties" box is sufficient to remove all metadata from the converted document. In fact, it might be a good idea to take additional steps to scrub the Word document prior to conversion. For more information, see the discussion of metadata starting on page 566.

---

[15] The process of creating an XPS file works essentially the same way.

AND: If the document contains markup, the "**Document showing markup**" radio button, which normally is grayed out (as it is in the screenshot above), will be active. Unless you click the "**Document**" radio button instead, the PDF or XPS file will display the markup in the document.

You can convert the entire document, the page the cursor is on (Current page), or a range of pages. Note that the conversion utility automatically creates bookmarks in the PDF or XPS file using headings. If your document contains bookmarks and/or headings configured with styles, the bookmark option will be available. Otherwise, it will be grayed out.

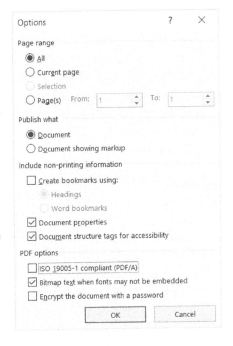

You also have the option of adding a password so that only people who know the password can open the doc.

Once you have set the configuration options the way you like, click "**OK**" to confirm your choices and close the Options dialog, and then click "**Publish**."

Assuming that you left "Open file after publishing" checked, a converted PDF file will open in the program you chose earlier; a converted XPS file will open in the XPS reader that comes with your version of Windows.

It's important to keep in mind that a converted PDF file might not look exactly the way it would if you used a PDF-creation program such as Adobe Acrobat to perform the conversion.

Printing to a PDF Printer

As an alternative to saving a file as a PDF as outlined above, you should be able to print the document to a PDF printer. Just click the **File tab**, **Print** (or press **Ctrl P**), choose an available PDF printer, and click **OK**. If you have access to Adobe Acrobat or a similar PDF-creation program, you should see at least one PDF Printer in the list of available printers. And if you are running Word 2016 on Windows 10, you can use the **Microsoft Print to PDF** option that comes with Windows 10.[16]

Your list of available printers probably looks somewhat different from the screenshot below; what appears in the list depends on which specific printers and print drivers are available to you.

---

[16] I have a copy of Acrobat on one of my laptops, but not on the one I'm using to write this book – which I chose for the task because it has Office 2016 installed. However, because this is a Windows 10 machine, I've got access to the Microsoft Print to PDF option.

Microsoft Print to PDF →

CAUTION: If you use the print-to-PDF option instead of the Save As option, *be sure to change back to your normal printer before attempting to print another document*. (Click the **File tab**, **Print** [or press **Ctrl P**], choose your regular printer from the printer list, and click **OK**.)

<u>Change File Type</u>

The "Change File Type" option allows you save the current document in several different formats. These include: the XML-based Word file format (.docx), the older Word 97-2003 file format (.doc), Open Document text – i.e., the file format used by the word processing program Open Office (.odt), Word template (.dotx), Plain Text (.txt), Rich Text Format (.rtf), a Single-File Web Page (.mht or .mhtml), or "Another File Type."

If you click "**Save As Another File Type**," then click the large "**Save As**" **button**, the "Save As" dialog opens, offering all of the above file types, plus macro-enabled Word files (.docm), macro-enabled Word templates (.dotm), Word 97-2003 templates (.dot), PDF files, two different types of XML (.xml) files, other types of web pages (.htm and .html), and XPS files (one of Microsoft's proprietary file formats; it isn't widely used except by IT people and other techies).

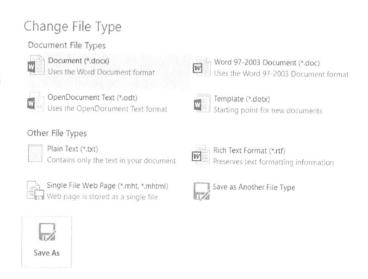

Note that you will not find WordPerfect files (.wpd) in the list; you can't save Word 2016 documents in WordPerfect format.

As an aside, you don't have to use this option to save a document as a different file type. You can simply use "Save As" and change the File type from the drop-down in the "Save As" dialog.

The "Account" Screen

There's not much to the "Account" screen. As mentioned elsewhere, it provides a convenient way to sign into and out of your OneDrive / Microsoft account.

Also, clicking the "**Update Options**" button opens a menu with a few options for configuring your Office 2016 updates. You can disable them (probably not a good idea because the updates include security patches); go online to see the latest updates; check for and apply updates (if your version of Word supports that feature); or learn more about updates. When you click "About Updates," you'll see a message similar to the one below – depending on which version of Word 2016 you're using – i.e., one that is part of Office 365 or one that isn't.

Updates to this Office product are enabled by default and are downloaded through your Internet connection and installed automatically. To check your update status and turn on or off updates, select the File tab, and then click Account. Under Office Updates, you can view your current update status and turn automatic updates on or off.

Because I have a "perpetual-license" version of Word 2016 (a stand-alone version, not Office 365, which is a subscription version), I receive automatic updates on a monthly basis. In fact, I recently noticed a (beneficial!) change in Word's behavior and, when I checked the "Account" screen, I saw that the version of Word had changed since I took the screenshot above.

The Word Options

Clicking **Options**, the next-to-last item on the File tab's Navigation Pane, opens the **Word Options dialog** – the primary tool for configuring many, if not most, everyday features of the program. For example, you can choose which elements of the Word screen to display or hide; change settings for automatic formatting, the spell-checker, and the grammar-checker; select the default "paste" behavior; and set your default file and template locations. You can also use the Word Options to customize the Ribbon and the Quick Access Toolbar.

One important thing to keep in mind is that the categories at the left side of the dialog are of limited value as a guide to where particular settings are located. For example, although it's true that many display settings are in the "**Display**" category – as you would expect – several other display settings have been tucked away under "**Advanced**." In fact, the "Advanced" category appears to be something of a catch-all for all of the configuration options that Microsoft couldn't fit elsewhere.

"Display" Category   "Advanced" Category, "Display" Section

The takeaway from that fact is that if you can't locate a particular setting in the category that seems the most logical to you, take a look at the options in the Advanced category.

97

There are a few rather obscure options that it's worth pointing out in case you ever encounter problems with the way that text is aligning with the line numbers in a pleading. In particular, toward the end of the **Advanced** category, under **Layout options**, you'll see "Don't center 'exact line height' lines," "Suppress extra line spacing at bottom of page," and "Suppress extra line spacing at top of page." If text at the top of the page – particularly on the first page – rises above the first line number, and changing the line spacing to match that of the line numbers doesn't help, try "Don't center 'exact line height' lines." In my experience, that option frequently fixes that specific issue. If it doesn't, try one or both of the "Suppress" options.

☐ Don't center "exact line height" lines
☐ Don't expand character spaces on a line that ends with SHIFT+RETURN
☐ Draw underline on trailing spaces
☐ Suppress extra line spacing at bottom of page
☐ Suppress extra line spacing at top of page

A Few Important Options Worth Tweaking

Here are a few other configuration options that you might want to adjust:

- **Bypass Backstage When Opening and Saving Files (Disabled)**. The option to bypass the Backstage view when opening and saving files in Word is located in the **Save** category, under "**Save documents**." It's labeled "**Don't show the Backstage when opening or saving files**."

- **Show the Start Screen When This Application Starts (Enabled)**. You can disable this option, located in the **General** category under "**Start up options**," to go directly to a blank document screen, rather than to the Word Start screen, when you launch the program.

Start up options

Choose the extensions you want Word to open by default: [Default Programs...]

☐ Tell me if Microsoft Word isn't the default program for viewing and editing documents.
☑ Open e-mail attachments and other uneditable files in reading view ⓘ
☑ Show the Start screen when this application starts

- **Attachments Open in Read Mode (Enabled)**. You can disable the option to open attachments in Read Mode (which is enabled by default). This option, in the **General** category under "**Start up options**," is labeled "**Open e-mail attachments and other uneditable files in reading view**." Note that even if you disable this option, e-mail attachments will open as read-only files.

- **Speller Ignores UPPER CASE Words (Enabled)**. By default, the spell-checker skips – i.e., it doesn't check the spelling of – words typed in UPPER CASE. (I'm guessing this option is designed to prevent the spell-checker from stopping frequently in documents that use a lot of acronyms or abbreviations – such as for government agency names.) You might want to disable this option. It's toward the top of the **Proofing** category, under "**When correcting spelling in Microsoft Office Programs**."

- **Insert Key Toggle for Insert/Overtype Modes (Disabled)**. In recent versions of Word, Microsoft has disabled the option to toggle between Insert and Overtype mode by pressing the Insert key. (No, your keyboard isn't broken!) You can enable it in the **Advanced** category of the Word Options under **Editing** (click to check "**Use the Insert key to control overtype mode**"). CAUTION: If you prefer Insert mode – and it does seem to be the more common choice – don't also enable "Use overtype mode." Note that you can add "Overtype" to the Status Bar (just right click and check that option) and then click the link on the Status Bar to toggle between the two modes.

- **Show White Space Between Pages (Enabled)**. If all of a sudden you can't see your headers and footers, and there doesn't appear to be any blank space between the pages of your document, it's possible that you need to enable "**Show white space between pages in print layout view**." This option is located in the **Display** category, under "**Page display options**." The other way to toggle between showing and hiding the white space between pages (i.e., when viewing pages vertically – stacked on top of one another) is to position your mouse pointer between two pages and double-click. In fact, that's probably how it got disabled in the first place.

- **Default Paste Is Set to "Keep Source Formatting."** The default paste format for pasting within the same document, pasting between Word documents, and pasting into a Word document from another program is "Keep Source Formatting." The only circumstance in which the default paste format is set to "Use Destination Styles" is for pasting between Word documents when style definitions in the two docs conflict – that is, there are styles in the documents that have the same name but different formatting.

In reality, you'll seldom want to retain the source formatting when you are pasting from another program – or even when you are pasting between documents. Depending on the situation (and on how you typically work), you might want to change one or more of these options from "Keep Source Formatting" to "Keep Text Only." To do so, go to the **Advanced** category and scroll to "**Cut, copy, and paste**."

Note that whichever option you choose becomes the default behavior when you click the top of the Paste icon in the Home tab (the clipboard), and also when you use the keyboard shortcut Ctrl V.

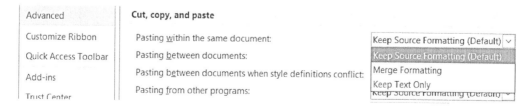

99

- **Default Personal Templates Location**. It is *essential* that you set the "**Default personal templates location**" in the **Save** category, under "**Save documents**," to point to the folder where you store your custom templates. In a departure from how previous versions of Word worked, both Word 2016 and Word 2013 populate the "**Custom Templates**" (or "Personal Templates") area of the **File tab**'s "**New**" screen based on this setting, *not* on the setting in the Advanced category of the Word Options under "File Locations."

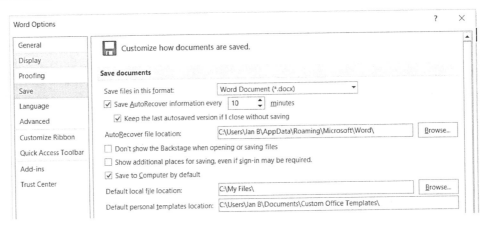

- **File Locations**. It's a good idea to review, and if necessary modify, the **File Locations** settings (found by scrolling almost all the way to the bottom of the **Advanced** category, by clicking the "**File Locations**" button). Note that any custom templates stored in the location set in the "**User templates**" area will *not* appear on the File tab's "New" screen under "Custom Templates" unless the location matches the setting in the Save category under "Default personal templates location." Therefore, I strongly recommend that you put all of your custom templates in one place and make sure the settings in both locations (Save, "Default personal templates location" and Advanced, File Locations, "User templates") are identical. Also, make sure that the "Workgroup templates" setting points to the location of any shared templates at your organization.

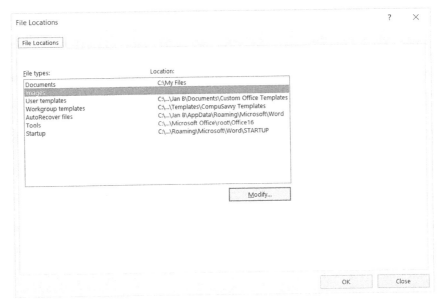

- **Show Bookmarks (Disabled)**. If your documents contain bookmarks (typically used for purposes of adding cross-references – "see paragraph ##," "see page ##," and the like[17] – it can be helpful to display the gray brackets that serve as bookmark indicators so that you don't accidentally delete them. If you do delete a bookmark, any cross-reference based on the bookmark will no longer work. (Because the bookmark indicators are somewhat hard to see, someone might delete a bookmark anyway, but enabling "Show bookmarks" – located within the **Advanced** category under "**Show document content**" – should reduce the likelihood of such an accident.)

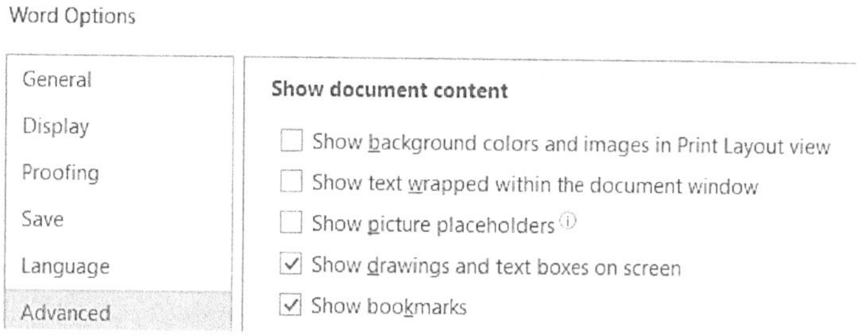

Word Options

General	**Show document content**
Display	☐ Show background colors and images in Print Layout view
Proofing	☐ Show text wrapped within the document window
Save	☐ Show picture placeholders ⓘ
Language	☑ Show drawings and text boxes on screen
Advanced	☑ Show bookmarks

---

[17] Bookmarks are essential for the proper functioning of hyperlinks within your documents, as well. For example, if clicking a Jury Instruction number in the Table of Contents takes you to that Jury Instruction, there are bookmarks, hyperlinks, and cross-references at work. Breaking the bookmark would impair the functionality of the hyperlink.

The Word Options at a Glance

Options Menu	Features You Can Enable/Disable, Show/Hide, or Otherwise Adjust (Partial List)
General	• The Mini Toolbar • Office Themes (colors) • Open e-mail attachments in Read Mode • Display the Start screen when Word opens • Real-time collaboration options
Display	• Show white space between pages • Display formatting marks (non-printing characters) • Display / print highlighting • Print drawings and other graphics • Update fields before printing
Proofing	• AutoCorrect • AutoFormat As You Type (tabbing sets indents, straight vs. curly quotes, automatic border lines, ordinals, etc.) • Spell-checking o Ignore UPPER CASE WORDS • Grammar (including grammar rules)
Save	• The default file format • The autosave (AutoRecover) backup interval • Show the Backstage view when opening or saving files • Save files to the computer (rather than the cloud) by default • The default location for files • The default location for personal (custom) templates
Language	• Your default editing and help screen languages
Advanced	• Insert / Overtype • Autocomplete • Default paste options within and between documents and from other programs • Paste Options button

Options Menu	Features You Can Enable/Disable, Show/Hide, or Otherwise Adjust (Partial List)

Advanced (cont'd.)	• Keep track of formatting
	
	• Field shading
	
	• Print in the background
	
	• Show bookmarks
	
	• Number of Recent Documents
	
	   o Number of Recent Docs in the Quick Access Area
	
	• Width of Style Area Pane in Draft and Outline Views
	
	• Show scrollbars
	
	• Show vertical ruler
	
	• Allow fields containing tracked changes to update when printed
	
	• Layout options
	
	   o Don't center "exact line height lines"
	
	• Default file locations, including User templates and Workgroup templates

Customize Ribbon	• Add custom tabs, groups, commands • Remove groups or commands • Show / hide tabs • Rename tabs or groups
Quick Access Toolbar	• Add frequently used commands to the QAT • Change the order of commands on the QAT • Export (back up) or import (restore) your customized QAT
Add-ins	• View / manage add-ins such as PDF programs, third-party programs for generating a Table of Authorities, etc.
Trust Center	• Trusted publishers and/or trusted locations • Protected View • Warn before printing, saving or sending a file that contains tracked changes or comments

Feedback

You can use the Feedback link at the bottom of the File tab's Navigation Pane to let Microsoft know what you think of various features. Note that you will need to sign in with your OneNote or Microsoft account to use this feature.

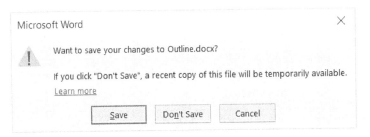

Exit (Close Word)

In Word 2016, there is no Exit button on the File tab. Not only that, but the "X" at the top right side of the Word window (i.e., in the Title bar) is actually a "Close" button and doesn't act quite the same way as an "Exit" button. If you have multiple documents open, clicking the "X" closes one document at a time – prompting you to save the document if you haven't done so since making some revisions.

For the most part, this method is straightforward. But people who are accustomed to the way that older versions of Word worked might not realize that when only *one* document is open, clicking the "Close" button will close the document *and* exit from Word. That can be a problem if you intended merely to close the doc and then either work on a new blank document or open another existing file.

There are a few workarounds for this issue. One is to use a keyboard shortcut to close your documents without closing Word. You can use either **Ctrl W** or **Ctrl F4**. (Both will prompt you to save your changes, if you haven't recently done so.)

Alternatively, you can add a "Close" button to the Quick Access Toolbar (QAT). And, if you want, you can also add an "Exit" button that behaves like the old-fashioned "Exit" command. For instructions, see page 180.

Bypassing the Backstage View

Experienced users might find the Backstage view somewhat cumbersome. After all, it obscures the current document, and most of the screens (fly-out menus) are somewhat cluttered. Fortunately, it's possible to use keyboard shortcuts when opening and saving documents – typically the same shortcuts as in previous versions of Word – to bypass the Backstage view and go directly to many of the familiar dialog boxes.[18]

As mentioned earlier (see p. 49), you can use **F12** to open the **Save As** dialog. This keyboard shortcut is the same one used in prior versions of Word to invoke **Save As**. Here are a few other "bypass" key combinations:

Ctrl F12 for **Open**: This keyboard shortcut goes directly to the Open dialog. Note that Ctrl O, another keyboard shortcut for Open, no longer works as it did in previous versions. Instead, it takes you to the Open screen in the Backstage view.

Ctrl S for **Save**: This keystroke still saves the revisions you have made to the current document without the necessity of opening the Backstage view (clicking File, Save). As always, you can click the "Save" icon on the Quick Access Toolbar, too.

Ctrl F4 or **Ctrl W** ("W" as in "Window") for **Close**: Both of these shortcuts close the current document without going into the Backstage view. Note that **Alt F, C** also works, although you might see the Backstage View flash momentarily as the command is working.

Ctrl N for **New**: This shortcut creates a new blank document. No need to use File, New. You also have the option of adding a "New" icon to the QAT.

Alas, I don't know of any built-in keyboard shortcut you can use to bypass "Print Place."

Closing the Backstage View

CAUTION: Because the Backstage view takes up the entire screen, you might be tempted to click "Close" in order to return to the document editing screen. That would be a mistake. "Close," like the "Close" command in previous versions, closes *the active document*. To dismiss the Backstage view and resume work on your documents, do either of the following:

- Click the **Back button** (left-pointing **arrow**) at the top left side; or

- Press the **ESC key**.

---

[18] Or, as mentioned on page 98, you can configure the Word Options to bypass Backstage when opening and saving documents – a more permanent solution than using keyboard shortcuts.

Other Important Screen Elements

The Quick Access Toolbar ("QAT")

An essential component of the modern "Ribbonized" interface, the **Quick Access Toolbar** (also known as the "**QAT**") is a fully customizable toolbar. Like the dialog launchers, it is sometimes overlooked because when you first start using Word, it is small—consisting of a few icons—and scrunched into a tiny portion of the upper left-hand corner of the screen.

The Default QAT

However, the QAT is exceptionally useful. You can move it below the Ribbon so that it expands into a full-sized toolbar, then add icons for the features you use most often. That way, you can find commands easily, even if you can't remember where they're located in the Ribbon.

Because the QAT is stationary, it's a good place to add items that you want visible at all times, regardless of which tab is active. For example, if you want to keep track of the font face, the font size, and the styles at various places in your document, you can add a font face box, a font size box, and a style box to the QAT, as I've done.

My Customized QAT (Partial)

For instructions on customizing the QAT (including how to move it), see the section that starts on page 175.

The Status Bar

Another screen element that most people never notice is the Status Bar. In Word 2016, it appears as a dark blue, blue-gray, or dark gray horizontal bar across the bottom of the Word window. It contains information about the number of pages in your document (and which page your cursor is on), how many words your doc contains, and the current magnification (zoom).

Status Bar – Left Side (Page X of Y, Word Count, Proofing Errors, Macros)

In addition, you can click icons on the Status Bar to check for "proofing errors" (e.g., misspelled words); to create or run a macro; to change document views; and to zoom in and out.

Status Bar – Right Side (View Shortcuts, Zoom Slider, Zoom Level)

To check for proofing errors, click the icon to the right of the word count (it looks like a small book with a pen across one page). If Word finds what it considers to be proofing errors, clicking the icon open the Spell-Checker at the right side of the screen so that you can review and correct any problems.

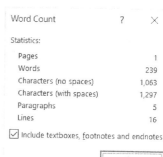

Clicking the word count opens the Word Count dialog, which also contains information about the number of pages, characters, paragraphs, and lines in your document. (By default, the count includes text boxes, footnotes, and end notes, but you can exclude those items by unchecking the checkbox at the bottom of the Word Count dialog.)

Note that there is also a Word Count icon on the Review tab.

View Shortcuts

At the right side, there are three icons you can click to change your document view. From left to right, the icons represent Read Mode, Print Layout, and Web Layout. (For some reason, starting with Word 2013, Microsoft removed the icon for Draft view, even though those of us in the legal profession use that view much more often than Web Layout.) The icons work exactly the same way as the **Document Views** icons in the **Views group** on the **View tab**.

Zoom Slider

The Zoom controls on the Status Bar give you a quick way of changing the document magnification. If you're good with the mouse, you can use the Zoom Slider to change the zoom in and out. I find it difficult to use, so I simply click the plus or minus sign. Each click zooms in (plus) or out (minus) by an additional ten percent.

To fine-tune the magnification, you can click the Zoom Level (the percentage) at the right side of the Status Bar, which will open the Zoom dialog. This dialog is the same one that opens when you click the Zoom icon in Zoom group on the View tab.

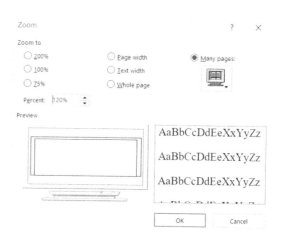

Click the Zoom Level (Percentage)...

...to Open the Zoom Dialog

107

The Scrollbars

You probably don't give the vertical and horizontal scrollbars much thought. Yet they can be very handy ways to move through your documents. The scrollbars are enabled by default, although the vertical scrollbar appears to "hide" while you are typing and appear, as if by magic, when you move the mouse or other pointing device. The horizontal scrollbar seldom makes its presence known. Typically, it shows up if you zoom in so far that your document fills the entire screen *or* if you resize the Word program window (for instance, by positioning it side by side with another window).

To show or hide one or both scrollbars, click the File tab, Options, click the Advanced category, and scroll down to "Display." There are checkboxes labeled "Show horizontal scroll bar" and "Show vertical scroll bar."

The Ruler

Word actually comes with two Rulers: a **horizontal Ruler** and a **vertical Ruler**. The horizontal Ruler is particularly useful because you can use it to set tabs and indents. Also, you can double-click the very bottom of the horizontal Ruler to open the Tabs dialog for a more precise way to set tabs; if you double-click elsewhere within the horizontal Ruler, or anywhere within the vertical Ruler, the Page Setup dialog will open.

Horizontal Ruler

To display or hide the horizontal Ruler, click the **View tab**, then check (display) or uncheck (hide) the **Ruler checkbox** in the **Show** group. **NOTE**: When the option to show the horizontal Ruler is checked, it will appear in Print Layout View *and* in Draft View, but *not* in Outline View or Read Mode.

Ruler Checkbox in the View Tab (Show Group)

The vertical Ruler displays by default at the left side of your screen when you are working in the Print Layout view. To disable / hide the vertical Ruler, click **File**, **Options**, then click the **Advanced category** at the left side of the **Word Options** dialog. Scroll down to **Display** and *uncheck* "Show vertical ruler in Print Layout view." (That option is checked in the screenshot below.)

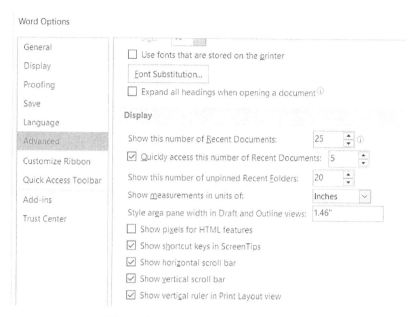

Word Options, Advanced, Display

CAUTION: As always, be sure to click "**OK**" (bottom right side of the Word Options dialog) to save your new settings. If you click the red "X" at the upper right side, Word will not save your changes.

NOTE: The vertical Ruler does not appear in any document view except Print Layout, even if you have checked the option to display it.

The Mini Toolbar

Word 2007 was the first version to make use of a floating Mini Toolbar that materializes when you select text. The Mini Toolbar also appears—above a context-sensitive menu—when you right-click selected text. It includes commands for working with fonts (font face, font size, size up, size down, bold, italics, underlining, highlighting, font color), for applying bullets or automatic numbering, for copying paragraph formatting via the Format Painter, and for applying styles.

The Mini Toolbar

Certain additional commands become available depending on the context (for example, if you select text within a table, commands for borders and shading appear along with most of the other commands).

Mini-Toolbar for Selected Text in a Table

When you select text, the Mini Toolbar first appears as a sort of hazy apparition. It solidifies when you move the mouse closer to it.

You can disable the Mini Toolbar. Click **File**, **Options**, and, when the **Word Options** dialog opens with the General screen at the forefront, *uncheck* "**Show Mini Toolbar on selection**." **CAUTION**: Be sure to click "**OK**" afterwards to save your new setting. Closing the Word Options dialog by clicking the red "X" at the top right side won't save your change.

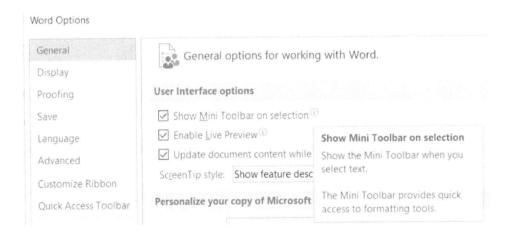

Word Options - Show or Hide Mini Toolbar

TIPLET: Selected (Highlighted) Text Turns Gray, Launches Mini Toolbar

In this version of Word, selected text turns light gray. (In some earlier versions of Word, it turns blue-gray.) Also, when you select text, you will see the Mini-Toolbar.

Live Preview

Because of a feature called **Live Preview** (introduced in Word 2007), you can see what your document would look like before you actually apply a particular style or font attribute. To preview a paragraph style, simply click within some text and then position your mouse pointer over a style icon in the **Style gallery**; to preview a character style, select the text and then hold the mouse pointer over a style icon.

110

To preview a font attribute, select some text and then click one of the drop-downs in the **Font group** on the **Home tab**. In addition to font faces, you can preview font sizes, underlining styles, highlighter colors, font colors, and text effects. (You can also preview paragraph background colors with the shading drop-down in the **Paragraph group** on the **Home tab**, and you can preview page colors by using the page color drop-down in the **Page Background group** on the **Design tab**.)

<u>Galleries</u>

Word 2016 provides several "Galleries" that consist of built-in formats (or styles) for headings, headers and footers, page numbering, watermarks, tables, a Table of Contents, numbered lists, and other commonly used document elements. You can select one of the built-in styles or, if you prefer, simply create your own.

For example, the Watermark gallery (Design tab, Page Background group) incorporates several different built-in watermarks; you have to scroll down to see all of them. The screenshots below show about 2/3 of the items in the gallery.

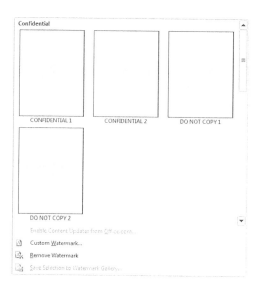 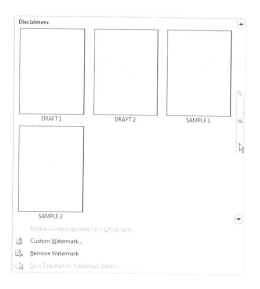

Similarly, there is a **Footer drop-down** on the **Insert tab** (in the **Header & Footer group**) that offers various pre-configured footers, including one with three columns (so that you can type some text at the left, in the center, and at the right side of the footer.)

The gallery contains several other sample footers; you need to scroll down in order to see them.

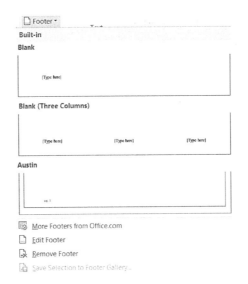

The Footer Gallery

And if you want to change the page margins in your document, you can use the old-fashioned method of launching the Page Setup dialog (by clicking the **dialog launcher** in the lower right-hand corner of the **Layout tab, Page Setup group**)…

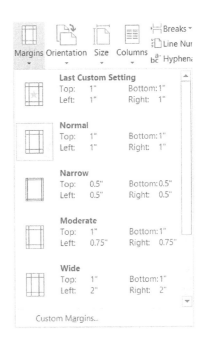

…*or* you can click the **Margins drop-down** in the **Page Setup group** and choose one of the options in the gallery. (Clicking the "Custom Margins" command opens the Page Setup dialog.)

Of course, you don't have to use any of the built-in styles in any of the galleries – and many of them aren't particularly suitable for legal documents – but they give you some additional choices. You might want to experiment and see how you like them.

The Style Gallery (Quick Style Gallery)

The Style Gallery (called the Quick Style Gallery in previous versions of Word), was introduced in Word 2007. Situated at the right side of the Home tab, it puts some of the most commonly used built-in styles, as well as the other styles in your document (if any), within easy reach. Moreover, the icons in the gallery feature mini-samples of the styles, so you can see at a glance what each style will look like.

The Style Gallery

To apply a style to a paragraph, place the cursor within the paragraph and then click the icon for the style in the gallery. (To apply a character style rather than a paragraph style, select the text you want to reformat before clicking the icon.)

Note that when you position the mouse pointer over a style (either deliberately or accidentally), Word displays the text in your document at the cursor position *as if you had applied the style*. That's because of the **Live Preview** feature mentioned on page 110. It's a useful feature, but can be disconcerting if it happens unexpectedly. Watch out for it, and don't panic! The style won't be applied unless and until you actually click it. Just move the mouse so that it is not pointing to the style, and your text will appear normal again.

For more details about styles and the Style Gallery, see the section starting on page 398.

Show / Hide the Non-Printing Characters (Formatting Marks)

Clicking the **Paragraph icon** in the **Paragraph group** on the **Home tab** toggles between displaying and hiding the **non-printing characters**, also referred to as "**formatting marks.**" These characters include the paragraph mark found at the end of every paragraph (including "empty" paragraphs), created when you press the Enter key; dots representing spaces between words, created when you press the Spacebar; arrows representing tab characters, created when you press the Tab key; bent/broken arrows representing Line Breaks (Soft Returns), created when you press Shift Enter; end-of-cell markers in tables; and the like.

In addition, this feature, commonly known as "**Show / Hide,**" displays or hides "Hidden Text" – which includes, among other things, Table of Authorities codes – as well as graphical representations of section breaks and page breaks.[1]

When you turn on "Show / Hide" (enable "Show" mode), the Paragraph icon in the Ribbon becomes shaded; when the characters are hidden, the icon loses its shading.

Most people work with Show / Hide turned off (i.e., in "Hide" mode) because displaying the non-printing characters can make the screen look cluttered. However, enabling Show / Hide can be helpful when you are performing certain tasks, such as copying and pasting. It's also useful as a troubleshooting tool.[2] For example, in "Show" mode it's easy to tell if you've accidentally pressed the Spacebar or the Tab key too many times.

"Show" mode can be helpful in other ways. It enables you to view the paragraph marks in your document, which in turn enables you to clean up certain formatting problems.

For example, because each paragraph mark contains the formatting instructions for the paragraph that precedes it (see pages 123 and following), you can fix the formatting of a "misbehaving" paragraph simply by copying and pasting the paragraph mark from a well-formatted paragraph to the troublesome one. This cleanup method is very similar to using the Format Painter (see pages 143 and following). But of course, you have to see the paragraph

---

[1] Ordinarily, you can't see Section Breaks or Page Breaks in Print Layout View. You have to switch to Draft View *or* turn on "Show / Hide" in order to see graphical representations of both types of breaks.

[2] However, it doesn't provide the same functionality as WordPerfect's Reveal Codes, even though people sometimes compare the two features.

114

mark in order to select and copy it, and that's where turning on "Show / Hide" (switching to "Show" mode) comes in handy.

Here's another real-world example: Sometimes, after you have applied highlighting or a font attribute such as bolding, italics, or underlining to a paragraph – typically in a bulleted or numbered list – you try to strip out the highlighting or font formatting, but it remains in part of the paragraph (such as the bullet or number at the beginning of the paragraph). What usually fixes that issue is turning on "Show / Hide" (switching to "Show" mode), selecting the paragraph mark at the end of the problematic paragraph, and then turning off highlighting or the font attribute.

As mentioned in the section about marking citations and generating a Table of Authorities (TOA) starting on page 543, "Show / Hide" *__must be turned off__* (i.e., you must switch to "Hide" mode) before generating a TOA.

If you have toggled Show / Hide off but you can still see some or all of the non-printing characters and/or hidden text, it's probably because of a setting in the Word Options. To check, click the **File tab**, **Options**, click the **Display category**, and look to see if anything under "**Always show these formatting marks on the screen**" is checked. If so, *__uncheck__* those items and click "**OK**." That should fix the problem.

Always show these formatting marks on the screen

☐	Tab characters	→
☐	Spaces	...
☐	Paragraph marks	¶
☐	Hidden text	abc
☐	Optional hyphens	¬
☑	Object anchors	⚓
☐	Show all formatting marks	

Incidentally, the keyboard shortcut to toggle between show and hide is **Ctrl Shift *** [asterisk].[3]

---

[3] Some people refer to this shortcut as Ctrl Shift 8, but I prefer to make reference to the asterisk to avoid confusing with the number 8 on the Numeric Keypad.

Help! Where Did "Help" Go??

As you might have noticed, there's no "Help" command on the File tab (i.e., in the Backstage view), as there is in Word 2010. Nor is there a Help icon (question mark) above the Ribbon, as in Word 2010. (There *is* a question mark at the top right side of each Word Options screen, but clicking it provides help only with the Options.)

Instead, there is a new feature called "**Tell me what you want to do…**" This feature, which usually appears to the right of the View tab, is a combined "Help" and interactive search function. In this sense, it is similar to Microsoft's search utility, Cortana (which comes with Windows 10).

When you click in the box to the right of the lightbulb and type a search term (word or phrase), Word suggests topics related to your search term. If you search for a specific feature, such as Table of Authorities, you'll see a few items related to that feature. Clicking one of the items (such as "Insert Table of Authorities") opens a dialog box – such as, in this case, the Insert Table of Authorities dialog or the Mark Citation dialog – or otherwise provides more information.

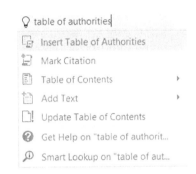

If the topics that Word suggests don't meet your needs, you have two additional options: "Get Help on [your search term]" or "Smart Lookup on [your search term]." Clicking "Get Help" takes you to Word's online Help, which can be very useful – although sometimes it provides a large number of search results, and it's not always obvious which ones are relevant. There's a printer icon in the Help window, so you can print a Help article if you like.

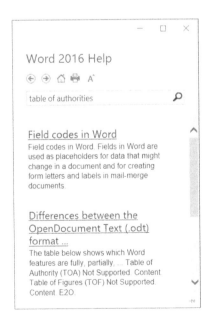

116

"Smart Lookup" uses Microsoft's search engine, Bing, to research your term on the Internet. It typically provides a definition of your term as well as additional information from Wikipedia and other sites.

If you like, you can add the old familiar Help icon to the Quick Access Toolbar (QAT). To do so, follow these steps:

1. Right-click within the QAT and choose "**Customize Quick Access Toolbar**."

2. When the **Word Options dialog** opens, change the "**Choose commands from**" **drop-down** at the top left from "**Popular Commands to All Commands**."

3. Click in the **Commands box** and press the letter "**H**" to move to the first command that starts with that letter.

4. Scroll to the "**Help**" **command** and click to select it.

5. Click the "**Add**" **button** in the middle of the screen to add it to the box at right (which represents your QAT).

6. If you like, you can move the command to the left or right on your QAT by clicking the command in the box at right, then clicking either the "**Up**" **arrow** (to move it to the left) or the "**Down**" **arrow** (to move it to the right).

7. Click "**OK**" to save your settings and close the Word Options dialog.

SIDEBAR: Protected View

Protected View, introduced in Word 2010, is intended to help users avoid accidentally triggering a virus, worm, or other malicious content in documents they receive in e-mail messages or download from the Internet. Protected View is enabled by default for all documents originating from those locations. Thus, when you open a Word document directly from an Outlook e-mail message, it will open in Protected View. You will see a message bar at the top of the screen (Microsoft calls it the "Trust Bar") that warns that the document might be unsafe.

> PROTECTED VIEW Be careful—email attachments can contain viruses. Unless you need to edit, it's safer to stay in Protected View.   [Enable Editing] ×

When a document opens in Protected View, both the Ribbon and the QAT are hidden. As with Read Mode, you'll see three menus at the top of the screen (the File tab, a Tools menu, and a View menu), but many of the commands are grayed out / unavailable. You won't be able to edit, save, or print the document, even though the Save and Print commands appear to be available from the File tab.[1]

If you try to re-save a file that opens in Protected View, an error message appears, indicating that saving is disabled – and providing a handy "Enable Saving" button so that you can save the file if you dare. Similarly, if you try to print, you'll see a warning that printing is disabled, along with a handy "Enable Printing" button.

To view – or change – the Protected View settings, click **File**, **Options**, click the "**Trust Center**" category, click the "**Trust Center Settings**" button, then click "**Protected View**." Make any changes you like, then be sure to click "**OK**" to save your settings.

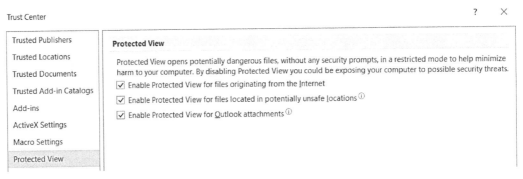

It's usually fairly easy to turn off Protected View. If you are certain the document comes from a trusted source and is free of malware, you can click the button marked "**Enable Editing**." That will allow you to edit, save, and/or print the doc. (The Trust Bar will close, the Ribbon and QAT will be maximized, and commands that were grayed out will become available again.)

---

[1] Also, so-called active file content is disabled – including add-ins, ActiveX controls, database connections, hyperlinks, and macros written with Visual Basic for Applications (VBA).

PART III: Word "Under The Hood": Understanding Word's Logic

This section of the book explains what I often refer to as Word's logic, or, more colloquially, how the program "thinks." Understanding this logic is the key to mastering Word – as opposed to being at its mercy. It will make both formatting and troubleshooting significantly easier, and that is true regardless of whether you have been using Word for many years or you're a relatively new user with long experience with WordPerfect.

If you are more familiar with WordPerfect and you are having trouble getting Word to work the way you want – and trying to function without WordPerfect's ever-helpful Reveal Codes – be sure to read the sections about paragraph formatting, paragraph formatting versus section formatting, and the main differences between Word's logic and that of WordPerfect. If the information therein doesn't sink in fully the first time you read it, don't worry. The more you work with Word, the more "aha!" moments you will have.

But even if you have no experience with WordPerfect, or your experience with that program is distant in time and memory, the discussions in this entire section will give you a much clearer sense of what's going on "under the hood" in Word – why it does what it does, how to make it stop doing the things you don't like, and how to fix it when things go wrong.

The Key to How Word Works: Paragraph Formatting

The first thing to understand about Word's "logic" is that Word is ***paragraph-centric***. (In this regard, it is very different from WordPerfect.) By paragraph-centric, I mean that:

- The paragraph is the primary formatting unit in Word;

- Word interprets all text as belonging to a paragraph;

- Most formatting attributes are applied to an entire paragraph[1], rather than to discrete bits of text; and

- Formatting such as line spacing, tab settings, indents, and justification (some of the attributes that I refer to as "paragraph formatting") is applied paragraph by paragraph (it doesn't simply flow forward from the cursor position).

With regard to the last point, when you type a document from scratch, formatting ordinarily carries over from one paragraph to the next. That's because the formatting instructions (codes) ***are contained within the paragraph mark*** (¶) at the end of the paragraph, which is copied to the next paragraph when you press the Enter key.[2] However, if you have already typed a substantial amount of text and you want to change the formatting – such as the line spacing – of some or all of the text, you need to select / highlight the text before applying the formatting attributes.

These concepts have other significant implications. They explain why it's difficult to have left-aligned, centered, and right-aligned text on the same line in Word (in WordPerfect, that task is easy to accomplish because you can format bits of text individually, whereas in Word, those pieces of text all belong to a single paragraph – and, quite logically, you can't apply different types of alignment / justification to one paragraph[3]). They also explain why pressing the Enter key doesn't simply reset the formatting, as it usually does in WordPerfect.

And, although many people don't realize it, because you typically apply formatting to an entire paragraph, you don't have to select / highlight a paragraph before applying formatting. Instead, you can simply position your cursor somewhere in the paragraph first.

---

[1] In WordPerfect, by contrast, formatting such as alignment and indents can be applied separately to smaller units (text strings or streams). This approach is called "text-stream formatting."

[2] The paragraph mark is also known as a ***pilcrow***. Although you can't literally crack open the pilcrow and see the codes it contains (and Word has no single feature comparable to WordPerfect's vaunted Reveal Codes), there's an easy way to figure out a paragraph's formatting. Simply open the Paragraph dialog and have a look at the configuration options therein. More on that momentarily.

[3] There are workarounds that let you accomplish this task, however. See pages 209 and following.

123

So what, exactly, constitutes paragraph formatting? Basically, the term refers to any attribute of paragraphs that you can change through the **Paragraph dialog box**, depicted below:

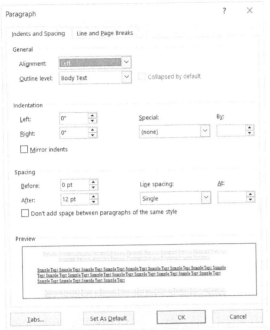

Indents and Spacing tab   **Line and Page Breaks tab**

In other words, it encompasses the following:

- **alignment** (justification);

- **indentation** (i.e., the left and right margins of the paragraph, as well as the first line thereof);

- **line spacing**;

- **spacing before and after the paragraph**; and

- **tabs**.

It also includes the items in the Paragraph group on the Home tab:

- **bulleted lists**;

- **numbered lists**;

- **multilevel lists**;

- **paragraph background color** (if any); and

- **paragraph borders** (if any).

124

In addition, paragraph formatting encompasses **line breaks** and **page breaks** (whether you allow lines or paragraphs to break across pages).

The Paragraph dialog serves two extremely important purposes. For one thing, you can use it to apply formatting.[4] It's also an essential tool for troubleshooting formatting issues. In fact, I consider the Paragraph dialog similar to WordPerfect's "Reveal Codes" feature – in the sense that you can use it to diagnose (and often resolve) many, if not most, formatting problems. After you become familiar with the configuration options within the dialog, you'll be able to spot quirky settings or discrepancies in no time at all.

Opening the Paragraph Dialog

There are several different ways to open the Paragraph dialog to apply formatting (or for troubleshooting purposes):

- Navigate to the **Home tab, Paragraph group**, and click the dialog-launcher arrow at the bottom right; *or*

- Navigate to the **Layout tab, Paragraph** group, and click the dialog launcher; *or*

- Right-click within any paragraph and then choose **Paragraph**; *or*

- Press **Alt O, P**. (Think "**O**pen **P**aragraph.")

Formatting Tips

To apply formatting changes to a single paragraph, position your cursor somewhere in the paragraph before opening the Paragraph dialog. (As mentioned previously, you do not have to select the paragraph, because options within the dialog will be applied to the whole paragraph.) To apply formatting changes to multiple paragraphs, select / highlight the paragraphs first.[5]

As you change various settings from within the Paragraph dialog, periodically take a look at the Preview at the bottom of the dialog, which shows what the new settings will look like. When you have finished, be sure to click "OK" to save your settings. Clicking the "X" at the top of the dialog box, or clicking "Cancel," will discard your changes.

Let's take a closer look at the types of formatting that you can apply from the Paragraph dialog.

---

[4] Formatting that is applied through the Paragraph dialog is often called "***direct formatting***" or, occasionally, "manual formatting." People often contrast direct formatting with formatting that is applied via ***styles***. If your organization uses properly designed templates that incorporate styles, you probably won't use the Paragraph dialog very often to apply formatting. Still, it's useful to know which formatting attributes can be applied in this way.

[5] Also, you can apply certain types of paragraph formatting from the Paragraph group on the Home tab and from the Paragraph group on the Layout tab. Be sure to explore both.

Alignment / Justification

Although I typically don't apply paragraph alignment / justification from within the Paragraph dialog – I use keyboard shortcuts or the alignment buttons in the Paragraph group on the Home tab – it's possible to do so. The options available from the Alignment drop-down are Left, Centered, Right, and Justified (i.e., full justification).

Outline Level

The Outline Level option lets you designate a paragraph as an outline level. This option is used mainly as a way of marking headings for inclusion in a Table of Contents (TOC) when the headings in the document have been formatted manually (i.e., without the benefit of heading styles). For more on this technique, see the section starting on page 535.

Indentation

The **Indentation** section of the dialog is where you set the left and/or right indentation – i.e., the margins – of the paragraph your cursor is in (or of paragraphs that you've selected). Just navigate to and type a figure (such as 1", .5", etc.) in the **Left** box and in the **Right** box. (Note that you don't have to type the inches symbol.) Or click the "**spinner**" **arrows** ("up" for a higher number or "down" for a lower number).

Incidentally, this method is commonly used in the legal profession to set the left and right indentation for block quotations in pleadings.

The "**Special**" box in the same section of the dialog determines the indentation of *the first line of the paragraph*. There are three options under "**Special**": **(none)**, **First line**, and **Hanging**. The "**(none)**" option means that the first line of the paragraph will be the same as the left indent you've set for the paragraph as a whole. So if you've set a left indent at 1", the first line also will begin at 1".

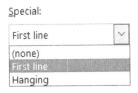

The "**First line**" option means that the first paragraph will be indented more than the other lines – as if you had pressed the Tab key. By default, the first-line indent will be half an inch (.5"), but you can change this setting to suit your needs.

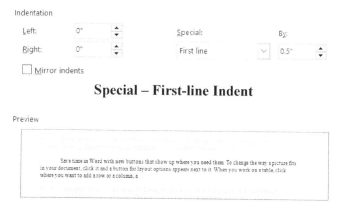

Special – First-line Indent

Preview of the First-line Indent

     Save time in Word with new buttons that show up where you need them. To change the way a picture fits in your document, click it and a button for layout options appears next to it. When you work on a table, click where you want to add a row or a column, and then click the plus sign.

The Formatted Paragraph

The "**Hanging**" option means that the first line of the paragraph will be farther to the left than the other lines – i.e., "outdented" (ugh!). By default, the first line will be the same as your Left indent setting, and every line except the first will be half an inch (.5") to the right of that. As always, you can change the default setting to suit your needs.

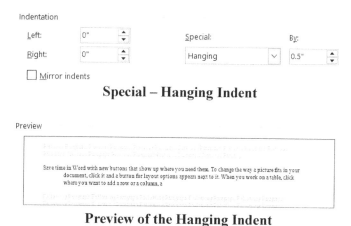

Special – Hanging Indent

Preview of the Hanging Indent

Save time in Word with new buttons that show up where you need them. To change the way a picture fits in your document, click it and a button for layout options appears next to it. When you work on a table, click where you want to add a row or a column, and then click the plus sign.

The Formatted Paragraph

127

Incidentally, although a paragraph with an automatic First-line indent looks the same as a paragraph with a first line that has been indented with the Tab key, the two paragraphs usually behave differently. That is because of the fact that the paragraph formatting typically carries over from one paragraph to the next when you press the Enter key (thereby copying the paragraph mark, along with the instructions it contains), as mentioned on page 123.

You can test this phenomenon for yourself. Type two paragraphs that consist of at least two or three lines of text. Apply a First-line indent to paragraph from within the Paragraph dialog. Press the Tab key to indent the first line of the other paragraph manually. If a button with a thunderbolt icon appears, hover over it with the mouse pointer, click the drop-down, and choose "Change Back to Tab." Next, click at the end of the first paragraph and press the Enter key. Make a mental note of where your cursor goes. (It should retain the same indent as the previous paragraph.) Then click at the end of the second paragraph and press the Enter key. This time, the cursor should appear at the left margin – because you applied the indentation manually, not by setting a First-line indent from within the Paragraph dialog. In other words, pressing the Tab key does not apply true "paragraph formatting." (If you open the Paragraph dialog while your cursor is within the second paragraph of text, you'll see that the "Special" box, which determines the indentation of the first line of a paragraph, is set to "(none).")

This example should help clarify how paragraph formatting works.[6]

Understanding How Word Handles Line Spacing

Think about it for a moment: In Word, line spacing is an aspect of paragraph formatting. Therefore, it is typically applied from the Paragraph dialog, affects the entire paragraph, and in most cases is copied from one paragraph to the next when you press the Enter key.

In Word, the **Line Spacing drop-down** offers the standard choices (single, double, 1.5 lines), but it also provides some unusual configuration options, including "**Exactly**," "**At Least**," and "**Multiple**." What do those choices do?

"**Exactly**" allows you to set very precise custom line spacing in *points*. As explained in greater detail in the Sidebar starting on page 215, points refer to the height of the characters. There are 72 points in an inch; 12 points approximates one line of text, although it is not true single spacing.

"Exactly" spacing is typically used for pleadings. Prior to Word 2007, the program included a "Pleading Wizard" that generated pleading paper based on criteria entered by the user. To accommodate the line numbers – 28 of them for most California pleadings – as well as top and bottom margins of approximately one inch, Microsoft spaced the line numbers *Exactly 22.75 points* apart. True double spacing, which is less compressed vertically ("taller"), didn't work because the added height prevented some of the line numbers from fitting on the page.

---

[6] It also underscores the importance of using "Show / Hide." With "Show / Hide" enabled, you can see the Tab character (an arrow) at the beginning of the second paragraph – a helpful graphical representation of the difference between the first and second paragraphs.

The Exactly 22.75 pt spacing accomplished the goal, but it created widespread confusion among users. Most people set their line spacing for the body text to double (2), unaware that the line spacing configured by the Pleading Wizard (which I call "pleading double spacing"[7]) was more condensed than true double spacing. Not surprisingly, the text quickly got out of alignment with the line numbers.

It's important to understand this very common issue for purposes of troubleshooting. Note that not all pleading paper uses 22.75 points for "pleading double spacing"; some people have tweaked the "pleading double spacing" setting, resulting in a wide variety of figures (I've seen 22.65 pt, 23.15 pt, 23.75 pt, and 24 pt). Regardless, you're likely to experience alignment problems unless the line spacing of the "pleading double spaced" text in your document matches that of the line numbers – and the "pleading single spaced" text is set at exactly half that figure.

Because the line spacing can vary from pleading to pleading, you'll need to do some detective work. To determine the spacing of the line numbers in the document you're working on, open the document's header, click somewhere within the line numbering, and then right-click to open the Paragraph dialog. Make note of the line spacing (write it down if necessary). Then, after you exit from the header, apply the same line spacing to all of the "pleading double spaced" text. Then make sure to apply exactly half that line spacing to all of the "pleading single spaced" text. That should do the trick. For more information and tips, see the sections starting on page 215 and 457.

"**At Least**," an option that also is based on points, sets a *minimum* line spacing. Word can - and will - adjust the spacing if necessary to accommodate graphics (or other characters) that wouldn't fit otherwise. (This option is more suitable for desktop publishing than for pleadings or any other type of document that is subject to strict formatting rules.) Because the line spacing can change without warning, I strongly advise against using the At Least option.

The "**Multiple**" option is for setting line spacing – measured in lines, not points – at an interval other than single, double, or 1.5. For example, if you wanted triple spacing, you would select the "Multiple" option and type "3" in the "At" box. (Sometimes Word automatically changes the "By" figure to 3 when you choose "Multiple." Or, if you are working on a document where the text spills over onto the last page by just one or two lines, you can select the text of the document and change the line spacing from single to a percentage of one line, such as .95 or .97 lines. That usually shrinks the text just enough, while maintaining readability.

Paragraph Spacing ("Spacing Before" and "Spacing After")

You can insert additional white space between paragraphs by using "**Spacing Before**" and/or "**Spacing After**." This extra white space—usually measured in points—is built into the paragraph to which you add it. In other words, it becomes a property of the paragraph, just like indents and line spacing.

---

[7] I coined the terms "pleading double spacing" and "pleading single spacing" to differentiate the line spacing required for pleadings from standard double and single spacing, both of which are significantly less compressed vertically (taller) than their "Exactly" line spacing counterparts.

Spacing Before and Spacing After are commonly incorporated into styles to achieve uniform spacing between paragraphs in a document. Template designers often use it to provide extra white space after components of a pleading that use "pleading single spacing," such as headings and block quotes.

If you add "Spacing After" to a paragraph, you'll notice that when you press the Enter key, the cursor skips a blank line – as if you had pressed the Enter key twice.

Spacing		Line spacing:	At:
Before:	0 pt		
After:	12 pt	Single	

☐ Don't add space between paragraphs of the same style

CAUTION: People who use this feature have to get into the habit of not pressing the Enter key twice after typing a paragraph.

ANOTHER CAUTION: There is an additional item in the Paragraph dialog labeled **"Don't add space between paragraphs of the same style."** This option is disabled by default for most text, which means that in most instances you can increase the "Before" and/or "After" paragraph spacing and your changes will go into effect as expected. However, the option is *enabled* by default for bulleted and numbered lists. As a result, even if you have configured Word to add space between bulleted or numbered paragraphs, Word *will ignore* those settings – which can be very confusing. If it happens, select the entire bulleted or numbered list, open the Paragraph dialog, *uncheck* that option, then click "**OK**."

Line and Page Breaks

Always keep in mind that this feature is found in the **Paragraph** dialog box. That means that each option under "**Line and Page Breaks**" applies to *an entire paragraph*.

Thus, "**Keep lines together**" means keep the entire paragraph – all of its lines – on one page. In other words, it's intended to prevent splitting a paragraph across pages. When this option is checked (enabled), if the entire paragraph won't fit at the bottom of one page, Word bumps the paragraph to the next page.

Note that this feature is different from Widow/Orphan Control. With "**Widow/Orphan Control**" checked (enabled), Word does allow paragraphs to split across pages, but won't allow *a single line of a paragraph* to dangle by itself at the top or bottom of a page.

"**Keep with next**" also differs from "Keep lines together." Whereas "Keep lines together" refers to the lines of a single paragraph, "Keep with next" refers to the relationship between a paragraph and the one that immediately follows. When "Keep with next" is checked (enabled), Word will attempt to keep the paragraph that contains this setting with the following paragraph, and if the following paragraph is on the next page, Word will bump the current paragraph to the next page, as well.

130

One common use of this feature is to keep a heading on the same page as the body text that follows the heading. Note, however, that you might have to apply the "Keep with next" setting to *both the heading and the blank line below the heading*, because Word considers the blank line a separate (if empty) paragraph that requires its own formatting. If you apply the setting only to the heading, it will keep the heading together with the blank line / paragraph below it, but it won't keep the blank line / paragraph together with the text that follows.

CAUTION: This feature sometimes causes text to move around within your document for no apparent reason! If text won't stay where you type it, put the cursor into one of the meandering paragraphs, open the **Paragraph dialog**, and look to see whether "Keep with next" is checked. If it is, uncheck it. You might have to select the entire document, or several paragraphs, and then uncheck that option. (In general, "Keep with next" shouldn't be applied to body text – precisely because of this potential issue. The option is intended mainly for use with headings.)

"**Page break before**" means exactly what it sounds like. When this option is checked, Word will insert a page break before the paragraph that contains that setting. This result also can be achieved by pressing **Ctrl Enter** (the keyboard shortcut for page break). The Ctrl Enter method is probably preferable, if only because – as discussed earlier – any options you apply from the Paragraph dialog will be copied to the next paragraph when you press the Enter key. With "Page break before," that can lead to unintended, and very confusing, consequences.

Other Paragraph Formatting Options

There are three additional paragraph formatting options -- **Outline level**, **Suppress line numbers**, and **Don't hyphenate**. Of the three, you probably will find the "Outline level" option the most useful.

In truth, I never use Suppress line numbers or Don't hyphenate. As for the former, it's difficult to imagine a situation where you would want to suppress line numbering in a legal document. As for the latter, hyphenation options in Word are set from the **Layout tab**, **Hyphenation drop-down**, **Hyphenation Options**. By default, hyphenation is turned off. If you enable automatic hyphenation, you can use the **Paragraph dialog** to exclude certain paragraphs from automatic hyphenation.

The Set As Default Button

There is a **"Set As Default" button** at the bottom of the Indents and Spacing tab of the Paragraph dialog. This feature, first introduced in Word 2007, allows you to change the default paragraph settings for the existing document *and all future documents* with a couple of clicks.[8]

---

[8] **CAUTION**: In versions of Word prior to Word 2007, you could set defaults for the Normal paragraph style and they would remain in place unless and until you deliberately changed them. In Word 2016 (and Word 2007), the Normal paragraph style *can be overwritten by Style Sets*, template-like objects that use XML coding to determine most of the basic formatting of your documents. See the discussion of Style Sets starting on page 186.

Simply go through the dialog and modify any settings you wish. Then, before closing the dialog, click the "**Set As Default**" **button**. A message box will open, prompting you to confirm that you wish to change the underlying template so that the default paragraph style in future documents will reflect the changes you are making now. If you want to do so, click "**Yes**." Otherwise, click "No" or "Cancel." ("No" closes both the message box and the Paragraph dialog; "Cancel" closes only the message box, leaving the Paragraph dialog open.)

Another enhancement first introduced in Word 2007 is the **"Mirror Indents"** command on the **Indents and Spacing tab**. Essentially, that command allows you to set either a left or right indent for a paragraph that goes into effect on even pages only and is indented (usually by the same amount) from the other margin on odd pages only. For example, you might set a 2" **left indent** that goes into effect on even pages and then becomes a 2" **right indent** on odd pages. Note that when you use this feature (by checking the "Mirror Indents" box), the labels in the Indentation section of the dialog change from "Left" and "Right" to "Inside" and "Outside."

Stripping Out Paragraph Formatting

You can remove direct formatting – that is, formatting that you applied by using the Paragraph dialog, the commands in the Paragraph group on the Home tab, the commands in the Paragraph group on the Layout tab, and/or keyboard shortcuts – in a few different ways.

One very quick way to remove direct formatting is to click within a paragraph (or select multiple paragraphs) and press the key combination **Ctrl Q**. Essentially, Ctrl Q resets the formatting to your default settings. (This method does not remove any formatting that has been applied by way of a *style*.)

You can also click within a paragraph or select multiple paragraphs and click the icon for the **Normal style** in the **Style Gallery** (assuming it is displayed there, which it might or might not be).

The "Normal" Icon in the Style Gallery

See the Sidebar starting on page 145 for additional methods of clearing both paragraph and font formatting.

Paragraph Formatting vs. Section Formatting

As you know by now, formatting in Word is applied mainly to *paragraphs* or to *sections* of a document. The types of formatting you can apply to paragraphs (usually via the **Paragraph dialog box**) are listed in the left-hand column of the chart below. For more detailed information, see the discussion of paragraph formatting in the preceding section and in the section starting on page 137.

Page layout actually is applied section by section in a document in Word. When you need to *change* page layout, you must insert a **section break (next page)** in order to apply different formatting. The break goes *on the page before* any formatting change.[1] (If you don't want to change the page layout anywhere in your document, you don't need a section break. You simply apply the formatting to the entire document or to one or more paragraphs.) The types of page formatting that are applied section by section – and for which a section break is needed if you wish to make a change – are listed in the right-hand column of the chart.

Paragraph Formatting	Section Formatting (Page Layout)
Alignment (Justification)	Margins (page margins)
Indentation—Left and Right	Headers and footers (especially multiple headers and footers)
Indentation—First Line, subsequent lines (hanging indent)	Page orientation—portrait vs. landscape
Spacing before / Spacing after	Columns (i.e., mixed with regular text on the same page)
Line spacing	Page numbering
Tabs	Footnotes
Widow and orphan	Page borders
Keep with next (paragraph)	
Keep together (i.e., keep entire paragraph together on one page)	
Page break before	

---

[1] In Word 2016, you add a section break by clicking the **Layout tab, Breaks (Alt P, B)**.

Practical Implications

What does the chart on page 133 mean in practical terms?

It means that if you want to change the page margins somewhere in your document (as opposed to the margins of one or two isolated paragraphs), you need to insert a section break on the page before the page where the change is to go into effect.

It means that if you need to format one page of a document so that it has a "landscape" (sideways) orientation, you have to insert a section break on the last "portrait"-oriented page before the landscape-formatted material (and, if you're changing back to portrait orientation afterwards, you need a second section break on the page before the formatting reverts to portrait).

It means that if you are writing a book or other material where footnotes in the various chapters or sections are supposed to start over with the number 1, you need to insert a section break on the page before the renumbering is to start.

It means that if you are working on a pleading that includes a Table of Contents and a Table of Authorities and you need the page numbering to restart – and/or you need to switch from Arabic numerals to Roman numerals and back again – you must insert section breaks ahead of the page(s) where the value and/or style of the page numbering will be different.

And it means that if you want to use more than one header or footer in your document, you need to insert a section break on the page before any page where a new/different header or footer is to begin (or, if appropriate, use the Different First Page option, which automatically sets up a first-page header or footer that is distinct from any header or footer that follows).

Keep these general rules in mind when you are working with page formatting, and eventually they will become second nature.

WordPerfect vs. Word—Some Fundamental Differences in "Logic"

The following chart makes it easy to compare the essential differences between WordPerfect's "logic" and that of Word. Understanding how the two programs work "under the hood" gives you more control over document formatting in at least two significant ways: (1) it makes the behavior of the software less mysterious / easier to predict; and (2) it provides clues about how to troubleshoot problematic formatting.

The information in this chart, together with the explanations that follow about paragraph and section formatting, is the key to mastering Word.

WordPerfect's Logic	Word's Logic
Based on *text-stream formatting*:	Based on *paragraph formatting*:
You insert a code at the cursor position, and everything that follows—i.e., in the stream of text—is governed by that code (until you insert a new code that supersedes the first one).	The paragraph is the basic formatting unit in Word. (*Section formatting* is used for features like page orientation, margins, and headers/footers; *character formatting* is used for attributes like bold and italics that can be applied to individual characters).
Examples: Font face / size Text alignment (left, center, right) Line spacing	Examples: Justification (left, center, right) Indentation
Implications:	Implications:
Easy to format small bits of text – for instance, you can indent or center part of a line	Harder to format individual pieces of text, because Word sees everything as a paragraph
Formatting codes are visible with Reveal Codes (and many codes can be expanded)	Formatting codes are contained in the paragraph mark (¶); they're not directly visible[1]
Formatting you apply to a specific paragraph usually *does not* carry over to the next paragraph	Formatting you apply to an entire paragraph *carries over to the next paragraph* when you press the Enter key

---

[1] This aspect of paragraph formatting in Word is critical to understand because it means, among other things, that you can modify the formatting of one paragraph by copying and pasting the pilcrow from the end of another paragraph—an extremely handy "fix-it" tool.

WordPerfect's Logic

Uses "*select, then do*" to some extent, but generally more stream-based than Word

Extensive use of function keys, both alone and in combination with Alt, Ctrl, and/or Shift key

Reveal Codes simplifies troubleshooting because 90% of problems with the document can be diagnosed and fixed by using Reveal Codes. (It's very easy to delete offending codes, move codes around, and/or double-click codes, thereby opening dialog boxes so you can change configuration settings.)

"*Plain vanilla*" unless you apply formatting (but is becoming more like Word—using more automatic formatting features)

Word's Logic

Much formatting requires "*select, then do*" (example: changing fonts in the document)

Extensive use of Ctrl key + letter

Word has no single feature comparable to Reveal Codes, but there are at least four different ways you can get information about document formatting:

1. **Paragraph dialog** (available from the Home tab and also from the Layout tab)—very useful!

2. **Page Setup dialog** (available from the Layout tab)—also quite useful

3. **Reveal Formatting** (Select text, then press **Shift F1** *or* launch the **Style pane** and press **Style Inspector / Reveal Formatting**)—somewhat useful

4. **Show / Hide Non-Printing Characters**—helpful in a variety of circumstances

Automatic formatting (which can be great if it's what you want, but can be annoying if it isn't)

Not Just for WordPerfect Users: Troubleshooting Without Reveal Codes

Those of you who are moving from WordPerfect to Word, or who use both programs, might feel somewhat stymied by the fact that Word doesn't have any single feature comparable to WordPerfect's Reveal Codes - the highly esteemed troubleshooting aid. But Word has several other powerful troubleshooting tools, and you don't need to be a WordPerfect user (or ex-user) to find them helpful!

The Paragraph Dialog

My favorite troubleshooting tool in Word, and the one that strikes me as closest to Reveal Codes in its utility, is the **Paragraph dialog box**.

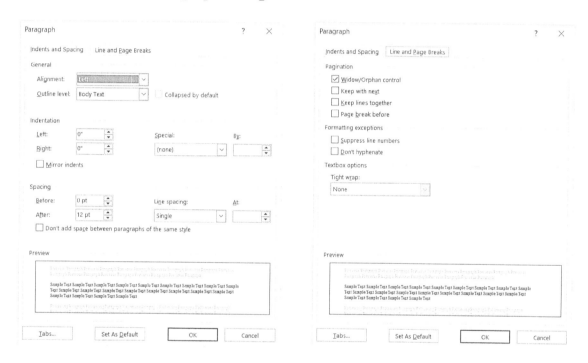

To troubleshoot a paragraph, place your cursor anywhere within the paragraph and open the Paragraph dialog by clicking the **dialog launcher** in the **Paragraph group** on the **Home tab** or by **right-clicking** within the paragraph, then choosing "**Paragraph**."

When the dialog opens, look for any quirky settings that might be throwing things off. For example, there might be some Before or After spacing that is creating too much white space between paragraphs, or line spacing in a pleading that is set to Single or Double rather than some "Exactly" figure. (For more about that issue, see the section starting on page 457, as well as the Sidebar about Points starting on page 215.) Or there could be a "First-line indent" or "Hanging indent" that is wreaking havoc with the text wrapping.

I've even seen a situation in which someone accidentally set a Left indent of 5", rather than .5", resulting in a lopsided paragraph that left her completely flummoxed. A quick review of the Paragraph dialog revealed the problematic setting.

Be sure to examine both the **Indents and Spacing tab** and the **Line and Page Breaks tab** of the dialog box to see if any of the settings need to be changed.

Incidentally, note that you can use the Paragraph dialog to change the formatting of a paragraph even if a style has been applied. "Direct" (manual) formatting overrides the formatting of the style.

As you continue to use this tool, you'll get better at it – so that any peculiar settings practically jump off the page when you look at the dialog box.

The Page Setup Dialog

The **Page Setup dialog** is another useful troubleshooting tool. You can use it to check margin settings and other page formatting information. To open the dialog, click the **dialog launcher** in the **Page Setup group** on the **Layout tab** or press the **Alt key**, then **P**, **S**, **P**. In particular, look at the **Margins** and **Layout tabs**. (The Paper tab is less important unless you are experiencing printing problems that could be affected by the paper format or paper source.) The Layout tab contains information about headers and footers.

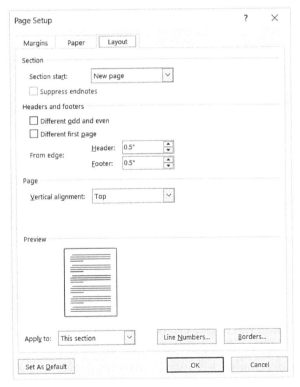

TIP: Be sure to look at the "**Apply to:**" box on both tabs, since occasionally formatting that should have been applied to the whole document has been applied to just one section.

Apply to:	Whole document ⌄		Apply to:	This section ⌄		Apply to:	This point forward ⌄

Show / Hide (Show the Non-Printing Characters)

As discussed earlier (see page 114), when you are having formatting problems, it can be helpful to turn on **Show / Hide** – that is, to display the **non-printing characters**, such as paragraph marks, tab marks, and spaces, as well as hidden text and codes such as those used to mark citations for a Table of Authorities (TA codes). Show / Hide can help you to discern extra spaces between words or between paragraphs, tabs, end-of-cell markers (in a columnar table), and so forth, and can help you locate section breaks and page breaks.

Also, remember that the paragraph marks contain the formatting codes – which affect the justification, indentation, line spacing, before and after spacing, line and page breaks, and automatic numbering – for the immediately preceding paragraph. Sometimes you can fix a problem by deleting a paragraph mark that represents an empty paragraph, or by copying a paragraph mark from a correctly formatted paragraph to the end of a paragraph that isn't cooperating (similar to using the Format Painter).

To display the paragraph mark in order to delete or copy it, turn on Show/ Hide – in other words, switch to "Show" mode – by doing either of the following:

- clicking the **Paragraph icon** in the **Paragraph group** on the **Home tab**; or

- pressing the key combination **Ctrl Shift * (asterisk)**.

To turn off Show / Hide – in other words, switch to "Hide" mode – just click the Paragraph icon or press the keyboard shortcut a second time. (Both methods act as "toggles" that turn the feature on and off.)

Reveal Formatting

One troubleshooting tool that many legal secretaries swear by is **Reveal Formatting**. Reveal Formatting provides some information about paragraph formatting in your document, such as indentation and alignment, and about character formatting, such as the font and whether the text is bolded or italicized.

To use Reveal Formatting, either start by pressing **Shift F1** and then select some text (or click within a paragraph) *or* start by selecting some text (or clicking within a paragraph) and then press **Shift F1**. The Reveal Formatting Task Pane opens at the right-hand side of the screen. In the box labeled "**Formatting of selected text**," you'll see detailed information about the font, paragraph, and section formatting of your text.

139

The font information includes the font face, size, color, and any attributes such as bolding or underlining. The paragraph information includes the alignment, indentation, and spacing, as well as which style has been applied (if any). The section information – which typically is hidden; just click the white triangle labeled "Section" to display the info – includes the page margins, layout, paper size, and header and footer margins.

The blue underlined links (FONT, LANGUAGE, ALIGNMENT, etc.) are hyperlinks. Clicking any of them opens a dialog box – usually either the Font dialog or the Paragraph dialog – where you can select more advanced options.

By the way, be sure to use the vertical scrollbar in order to view additional formatting information, typically about section (page) formatting.

The Reveal Formatting Task Pane also can be used to compare the formatting of selected text with other text in the document, or to determine whether a style has been applied.

Start by selecting some text or simply clicking within a paragraph. Some or all of the text appears in the "Selected Text" box.

Next, click the checkbox labeled "**Compare to another selection**." A second box appears below the "Selected Text" box (you might see the words, "Sample Text").

At this point, select some additional text or click within a different paragraph.

Major differences between the two paragraphs or bits of text appear in the larger box, which is now labeled "**Formatting differences**."

Position the mouse pointer over the second box in the "**Selected text**" area to display an arrow for a drop-down menu that includes options to select all text in the document with similar formatting, apply the formatting of the original selection, or clear the formatting altogether. For more about these options, see the sidebar on page 144.

140

Switching to Draft View

Most of the time, you probably work in Print Layout View – in which what is displayed on the screen is the same as what displays in the printed document. However, switching to Draft View (by clicking the "Draft" icon at the left side of the View tab or by pressing Ctrl Alt N) actually can be useful for troubleshooting.

For one thing, if you have applied bullets or automatic numbers, but suddenly they seem to disappear, switching to Draft View and then back to Print Layout View (by clicking the Print Layout icon on the View tab or pressing Ctrl Alt P) usually restores the bullets or numbers. Also, you can update certain codes by switching to Draft View and back again.

For another thing, you can configure the Word Options so that styles that have been applied within your document display at the left side of the screen when you change to Draft View. That can be very helpful because you can see at a glance whether the wrong style has been applied. For instructions, see page 396 and following.

Select, Then Do

There are a couple of other things to keep in mind that can help you with troubleshooting. Remember that Word is based on the concept, "Select, Then Do." Occasionally you will try to apply paragraph formatting, such as a first-line indent, and it won't "take." If that happens, *select* the paragraph you want to apply the formatting to, and *then* perform the steps to apply the formatting.

When All Else Fails…Try "Undo"

Also, don't forget that you can undo actions (up to the last 300 actions, in fact!) with the **Undo icon** on the **Quick Access Toolbar** (or **Ctrl Z**). Occasionally something as simple as using the Undo command will fix your problem.

More About the Non-Printing Characters

There are several non-printing characters that ordinarily are not displayed on the screen. These include the paragraph mark (pilcrow), tabs, spaces between words or letters (created by pressing the spacebar), end-of-cell markers in tables, hidden text, and more.

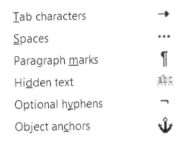

**The Non-Printing Characters
(End-of-Cell Markers Not Shown)**

End-of-cell markers (they look somewhat like little suns) ¤	¤	¤
¤	¤	¤

Displaying those characters can be useful for troubleshooting purposes (e.g., to determine if you really did press the spacebar twice between two words, when you meant to press it once). Also, it's useful when you want to copy one paragraph's formatting to another paragraph—remember that the formatting codes for any given paragraph are contained within the paragraph mark at the end of that paragraph.

You might want to hide the non-printing characters in certain circumstances, too. When you mark headings for inclusion in a Table of Contents or citations for inclusion in a Table of Authorities, Word displays the non-printing characters and TOC/TOA field codes. Those characters and codes actually take up space in the document, such that they can bump headings or citations down to the next page. As a result, when you generate the TOC and TOA, the generated page numbers will be incorrect. In order to avoid that problem, you need to hide the non-printing characters before generating a TOC or TOA.

To display the non-printing characters, either

- click the **Paragraph icon** in the **Paragraph group** on the **Home tab** *or*

- press **Ctrl Shift * (asterisk**, which is above the number 8 at the top of the keyboard).

Repeat either of those steps to hide the non-printing characters again (it's a toggle).

The Format Painter

Strictly speaking, the Format Painter isn't a troubleshooting tool. At least, it's not a diagnostic tool that will help you pin down what's wrong with your document. However, it's an extremely helpful tool for cleaning up problems – whipping those misbehaving paragraphs into line.

To copy paragraph formatting (line spacing, before and after spacing, justification, indents, tabs, automatic numbering, etc.) from a "model" paragraph to one or more other paragraphs, position your cursor within a paragraph[1] that is formatted to your liking, and then:

- Locate the **Format Painter** at the left side of the **Home** tab (in the **Clipboard** group);

- **Single-click** the paintbrush icon if you plan to apply the formatting to *one* other paragraph; or

- **Double-click** the paintbrush icon if you plan to apply the formatting to *multiple* paragraphs;

- After your mouse pointer turns into a small paintbrush, **click within** – or **drag the mouse pointer across** – the target paragraph(s).

The target paragraphs should take on the same formatting as the original (source) paragraph.[2]

Incidentally, if you prefer, you can use keyboard shortcuts to copy and paste paragraph formatting. First, position your cursor in the source paragraph, then press **Ctrl Shift C** to copy the formatting. Next, click within a target paragraph (or select several paragraphs) and press **Ctrl Shift V** to paste the formatting. Nice, eh?

Also nice: You can paste formatting between open documents. This option works best when you have positioned the source and target docs side by side.

---

[1] **CAUTION**: Because the Format Painter also copies the *character / font formatting* that is in effect at the cursor position, *be careful where you place the cursor in the "model" paragraph*. If, for instance, you click within a part of the paragraph that has bold or italics applied, you'll end up copying the boldface or italics to the other paragraph(s). Those attributes will be pasted into the target paragraph at the cursor position or, if you drag the mouse pointer across target paragraphs, the font attributes will affect entire paragraphs. With respect to copying *paragraph* formatting, the placement of the cursor doesn't matter because, as you know by now, paragraph formatting is applied to the entire paragraph.

[2] Be aware that the Format Painter doesn't let you pick and choose which types of paragraph formatting to copy from one paragraph to another. It's all or nothing.

SIDEBAR: Select All Text With Similar Formatting[1]

As mentioned in passing in the section about Reveal Formatting (see page 139 and following), there is a very useful option in the Reveal Formatting pane labeled "Select All Text With Similar Formatting." This command, also available from the Editing group in the Home tab, is a great way to reformat several paragraphs at once without using styles.[2]

To start, click within a paragraph or select some text that you want to reformat.

Next, click the "**Select**" drop-down at the right side of the **Home** tab and choose "**Select All Text With Similar Formatting**." (If you don't click within a paragraph or select some text first, you will see "(No Data")" after the command name.

Any other text in the document that has the same formatting as the paragraph your cursor is in or the text you selected at the outset becomes selected / highlighted. While it is highlighted, apply any paragraph and/or font formatting you desire. And that's all there is to it!

Note that you can do the same thing from within the Reveal Formatting Pane.

Click **Shift F1** to open the pane. Next, click within a paragraph or select some text, and then hold the mouse over the "**Selected Text**" box. When the arrow appears, click it to open the drop-down menu and choose "**Select All Text With Similar Formatting**." Any other text in the document that has the same formatting as the paragraph your cursor is in or the text you selected at the outset becomes selected / highlighted. Apply any paragraph and/or font formatting you desire.

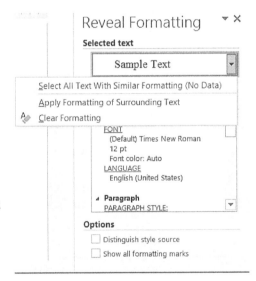

So quick and easy – now that you know about this feature.

---

[1] Thanks to Simona Millham, whose short tip about this feature inspired me to write this one.

[2] Although well-designed styles make such reformatting a breeze, not everyone has access to documents that use styles. This technique is a real time-saver for people who fall into that category. For more about working with styles, see the section that starts on page 385.

SIDEBAR: How to Clear Paragraph and Font Formatting

Even if you have been using Word for a long time, you might not realize how easy it is to remove paragraph and/or font formatting from text. This Sidebar highlights a few different methods for stripping formatting, all of which work in recent versions up through and including Word 2016.

You can clear paragraph and/or font formatting with the mouse or with keyboard shortcuts.

Using the Mouse

The following techniques require just a mouse click or two.

The "Clear Formatting" Icon in the Font Group (Home Tab)

Did you ever notice the icon in the top row of the Font group on the Home tab that looks like a little eraser? Most people probably don't even see it, especially in versions prior to Word 2013, where the icon is so pale that it blends in with the background of the Ribbon. (In the two most recent versions, the eraser has a reddish tint, so it stands out slightly.) In any case, despite its location in the Font group, that icon – labeled "Clear Formatting" in some versions and "Clear All Formatting" in others – actually can be used to remove both font formatting and paragraph formatting from text.

If you have applied a paragraph style, such as a heading style or block quote, you can strip the style by placing your cursor anywhere in the paragraph and then clicking the "Clear Formatting" icon. This method won't clear any font formatting that you have applied directly to text after you've applied a paragraph style. However, if the paragraph style itself incorporates font attributes (e.g., bolding, italics, a size or font face other than the default, etc.), clicking the icon clears those font attributes as well – even if you don't select / highlight the entire paragraph first.

If you have manually applied a font attribute to some text, you can strip the font formatting by selecting / highlighting the affected text, then clicking the "Clear Formatting" icon. (If you want to remove font formatting from a single word, just place your cursor somewhere within the word and click the icon.)

What's particularly useful about this tool is that you can use it to remove both the paragraph style ***and*** any "direct" font formatting within a paragraph by selecting / highlighting the entire paragraph, then clicking the icon. And yes, you can clear formatting from multiple paragraphs by selecting all of them and then clicking "Clear Formatting."

By the way, it's super-easy to add "Clear Formatting" to your Quick Access Toolbar (QAT). Just right-click the icon and choose "Add to Quick Access Toolbar." The icon will appear at the right side of your QAT.

145

The "Clear All" Style in Styles Pane

Another item you might never have noticed is the "Clear All" style at the very top of the Styles Pane. (To open the Styles Pane, either click the dialog launcher at the right side of the Styles group on the Home tab – or press Ctrl Alt Shift S.) This style works exactly the same way as the "Clear Formatting" icon in the Font group on the Home tab.

Incidentally, there's also a "Clear Formatting" icon toward the bottom of the Style Gallery drop-down menu.

Using Keyboard Shortcuts

Ctrl Shift N – Apply the Normal Paragraph Style

Clicking within a paragraph to which a style has been applied and pressing Ctrl Shift N strips out the style and reverts to your Normal (default) paragraph style. Like the "Clear Formatting" icon, Ctrl Shift N will not strip font formatting unless the font attributes are part of the paragraph style.[1]

Ctrl Q – Clear Manually Applied Paragraph Formatting

The keyboard shortcut Ctrl Q clears "direct" (manual) paragraph formatting. Typically, that means any attributes applied via the Paragraph dialog. It also means formatting applied from commands in the Paragraph groups on the Ribbon, formatting applied with keyboard shortcuts, and formatting applied by moving the indent markers on, or clicking, the Ruler.

Ctrl Q does *not* remove paragraph styles or font formatting.

Ctrl Spacebar – Clear Font Formatting

Ctrl Spacebar is a handy keyboard shortcut to clear direct (manually applied) font formatting. You can remove font formatting from a single word by placing your cursor somewhere within the word and then pressing Ctrl Spacebar, but more often you'll select / highlight a larger block of text to which you've applied font formatting, and then press the key combination to remove that formatting.

Keep in mind that Ctrl Spacebar does *not* remove font formatting that is incorporated into a paragraph style. For example, if you use heading styles that apply boldface and underlining as part of the style, Ctrl Spacebar won't remove the bolding and underlining.[2]

---

[1] In my tests, Ctrl Shift N sometimes did remove manually applied font formatting if I selected the entire paragraph first – but sometimes it didn't do so.

[2] You can, however, press Ctrl U or Ctrl B (or click the underlining and/or bold icons), then right-click the style in the Styles Gallery and choose "Update style to match selection," which will clear those attributes from the style within the current document. For more about updating styles on the fly, see the section starting on page 391.

PART IV: Getting Word to Work
the Way <u>You</u> Want

Disabling or Enabling Certain Features in Word

Microsoft has chosen to enable (or disable) certain features by default that you might prefer to turn off (or on). These features include the paragraph option, "Don't add space between paragraphs of the same style," which is turned *off* by default in the Normal paragraph style but turned *on* by default in numbered and bulleted lists. This option can thwart your efforts to increase the visual separation between items in a list, and the problem can be perplexing unless you know about the setting.

The following chart provides some tips about changing the default settings of a few features operating in the background that might make it more difficult for you to format your document to your (or your firm's) specifications.[1]

Feature	Comments	How to Disable (or Enable)
Don't add space between paragraphs of the same style (Paragraph dialog)	This Paragraph formatting option is *unchecked* (*disabled*) by default in the Normal paragraph style but *checked* (*enabled*) by default in bulleted and numbered list styles. Thus, even if you add "Spacing Before" or "Spacing After" to increase the visual separation between items in list paragraphs, Word suppresses the extra space between paragraphs.	Select the affected paragraphs, then launch the **Paragraph dialog** and click to uncheck the "Don't add space between paragraphs of the same style" option. Click "**OK**" to save your changes. Note that these steps will disable the option only within the selected list. For a more permanent solution, you can change the default settings for this option by modifying the List Paragraph style, which is the style typically applied to bulleted and numbered lists, and then saving the modified style to your Normal.dotm template. From within a blank document, open the Styles Pane, then locate the List Paragraph style. Right-click it and choose "Modify…" When the Modify Styles dialog opens, click the "Format" button at the bottom left side and choose Paragraph. Set the line spacing you want, plus any spacing after, and then uncheck the "Don't add space…" option. Be sure to click the "New documents based on this template" radio button, then click "OK."

---

[1] Thankfully, the ubiquitous Clippy was removed in Word 2007, so it is no longer necessary to include instructions for disabling him.

Feature	Comments	How to Disable (or Enable)
Paste Options Button	On by default in Word 2016 Some people find this pop-up distracting, but it can be helpful in that it gives you a second chance to choose a different Paste Option after you have pasted text.	Click the **File tab**, **Options**, **Advanced**, navigate to the **Cut, copy and paste** section, and *un*check "**Show Paste Options button when content is pasted.**"
Set Left- and First-Indent With Tabs and Backspaces	This option is on by default in Word 2016. With this setting enabled, pressing the Tab key applies an automatic first-line indent (and, in some circumstances, changes the indentation of an entire paragraph) rather than applying a manual tab. This setting also enables you to promote or demote outline levels by pressing the Tab key or Shift Tab.	**File tab, Options, Proofing, AutoCorrect, Options…, AutoFormat As You Type tab**, *un*check Set left- and first-indent with tabs and backspaces.
Expand all headings when opening a document	This option, which automatically expands collapsed headings when a document is opened, is disabled by default in Word 2016. As a result, you might inadvertently miss seeing some of the text in a document.	**File tab, Options, Advanced, Display.** *Check* to enable.
White space between pages	This feature is turned on by default in Word 2016, which is desirable in most circumstances. It can be turned off accidentally if you double-click in the area between the bottom of one page and the top of another. When white space is hidden, *headers and footers also are hidden* (though footnotes and endnotes are not).	**File tab, Options, Display, Show white space between pages in Print Layout view**, *check* to enable. You also can this setting turn on and off (temporarily) by double-clicking the gray area or hairline division between pages.

Customizing the Word 2016 Interface to Make It More User-Friendly

For both long-time Word users and WordPerfect users, the Ribbon-based interface can be disorienting. But, in addition to the tips I've provided about the logic of the tabs, there are lots of other ways to increase your efficiency in Word. For one thing, you can use keyboard shortcuts for many everyday tasks. If you have been using keyboard shortcuts in an earlier version of Word, you'll find that nearly all of the same shortcuts work in this version.

Also, you can customize the interface in several ways that make the program much easier to use – without having to master XML coding or Visual Basic for Applications (VBA), a macro programming language that is often used to customize Microsoft Office programs.[1]

In this section of the book, I explain how to make Word more user-friendly by tweaking several different elements of the interface.

Customizing the Ribbon

It is possible to customize the Word 2016 Ribbon in a number of ways. This capability, which was not available in the first version of Word with a Ribbon interface (Word 2007), makes the program significantly easier to use. It compensates to a great extent for the absence of customizable toolbars such as those available in earlier versions.

In particular, you can make any of the following changes to the Ribbon in Word 2016:

- You can create entire new tabs.

- You can create new groups within custom tabs and/or within built-in tabs.

- You can add commands to custom groups (but *not* to built-in groups).

- You can rename *any* tab, group, or command.

- You can change the icons for commands.

- You can move tabs around in the Ribbon.

- You can hide custom tabs and/or built-in tabs.

- You can remove groups from custom tabs and/or from built-in tabs.

- Once you have customized the Ribbon, you can export your customizations to a file and install them on another computer.

This section provides detailed instructions for performing each of these tasks, as well as more information about the various options for—and limitations on—customizing the Ribbon.

---

[1]**NOTE:** There are several third-party tools available that allow you to customize the Ribbon; some of these utilities emulate the traditional interface, with old-style menus and toolbars.

Creating a Custom Tab Plus a Custom Group

To create a new tab plus a new group, do one of the following:

- **Right-click** the **Ribbon** (or the **Quick Access Toolbar**) and click the "**Customize the Ribbon…**" option (see the screenshot immediately below); *or*

- Click the **File tab**, **Options**, then click the "**Customize Ribbon**" category at the left side of the Options window (as in the next screenshot).

Either of those methods will take you to the Customize Ribbon screen within Word Options.[2]

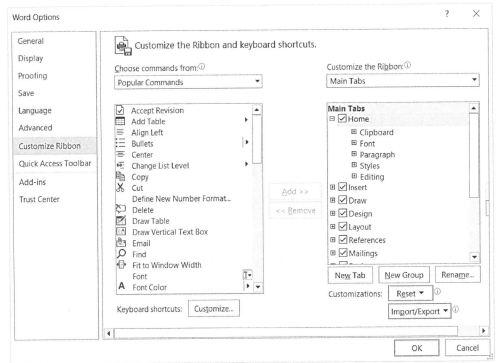

Customize Ribbon Screen Within the Word Options

---

[2] As an aside: It is from this section of the Word Options, not from the Customize the Quick Access Toolbar section, that you create **customized keyboard shortcuts**. Note the item at the bottom left side of the screen, labeled "**Keyboard shortcuts:**," followed by a "**Customize**" button. I will reiterate and expand on this point later on.

To add your own tab, do as follows:

1. First, **decide where** you want the new tab to appear in the Ribbon.[3]

2. Next, click to **select (highlight) the built-in tab** that you want displayed in the Ribbon *to the left of* your new custom tab. (Alternatively, you can click that tab before opening the Word Options to the Customize Ribbon screen. If you do so, that tab will be highlighted when you open the Word Options.)

3. Navigate to the **right-hand side** of the screen. You should see the "New Tab" button at the bottom, below the diagram of the Main Tabs.

4. Click the "**New Tab" button**.

   Word creates both a new tab and, within the tab, a new group.

   The new tab appears below the tab you selected (highlighted) in step 1 (or the tab that was at the forefront before you opened the Word Options). In the screenshot, my new tab appears below the Home tab, which means it will appear to its right in the Ribbon.

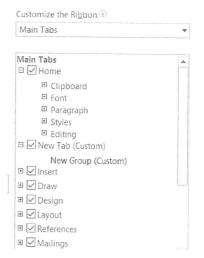

New Tab (Custom) and New Group (Custom)

5. Word assigns generic names to the new tab and new group, but it's easy to rename them.[4] To rename the new tab, first make sure *New Tab* rather than *New Group* is selected / highlighted within the box showing the tab names. If it isn't (note the Step 4 screenshot), click it. (Otherwise, clicking the "Rename" button as in step 6 will rename the *group*, not the *tab*.)

6. Next, locate the "**Rename...**" **button** (toward the bottom right) and **click it**.

---

[3] Don't worry about the placement of the new tab at this point. You can always move it later.

[4] You can rename the new group first if you prefer.

153

7. When the **Rename dialog box** opens, **type a name** for the new tab, then click **OK**. (I typed "Jan's Stuff," as you can see in the screenshot below.)

Rename Your Custom Tab

8. To rename your custom group, **select / highlight) it** and **repeat steps 6 and 7**. (If you don't see the group, click the **plus sign (+)** to the left of the label for your custom tab. That will expand the tab and show the custom group underneath it.) **NOTE**: this time, when the Rename dialog opens, it displays dozens of icons.[5]

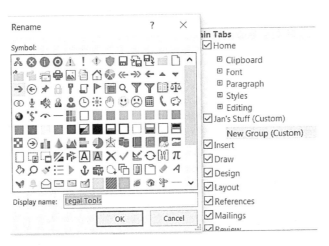

Rename Dialog for a Custom Group (at Left)

9. **Type a name** for the new group—I chose "Legal Tools," but you could use a name like "Numbering," "Everyday Features," "My Goodies," or anything that makes sense to you—and then **click OK**.

You should see your new tab in the Ribbon. Note that in Word 2010, you'd also see your new group within the custom tab, but in Word 2016, I'm not seeing the tab label. The label should appear when I add commands to my custom group, which I'll do next.

---

[5] There is one dialog for renaming tabs and a different one for renaming groups. The inclusion of icons in the latter is misleading because it isn't possible to apply an icon to a group. Rather, they are used to designate *individual commands within a group*.

Adding Commands to a Custom Group

To add commands to your new group, return to the Customize Ribbon screen in the Word Options and do the following:

1. First, **select (highlight) the group**. (Again, if you don't see the group, click the plus sign to the left of the custom tab to expand the tab and display the group.)

2. Next, scroll through the items under "**Popular Commands**." If the command you're looking for isn't there, change the **"Choose Commands From:" drop-down** from "Popular Commands" to "**All Commands**."

   NOTE: There are other choices besides "All commands": "Commands Not in the Ribbon," "Macros," "File Tab," "All Tabs," "Main Tabs," "Tool Tabs," and "Custom Tabs and Groups." I prefer "All Commands" because that option makes it easy for me to find every available command (it's not always obvious which commands are located on a particular tab). However, the other lists let you narrow the available choices, which can make the process somewhat less overwhelming.

3. Once you have selected a "Choose commands from:" option, **scroll down** to locate the commands you wish to add to your new group. The commands are listed in numeric order and then in alphabetical order.

TIP: To find a command quickly, click within the command list and press the letter the command starts with. For example, to find the "Overtype" command, press the letter "O." That moves to the first command that begins with that letter. Next, scroll to the command you want.

4. **Click to select (highlight) a command**, then click the "**Add**" **button** at the center of the screen or **drag the command** to your new group.[6]

Select a Command (at Left), Then Click "Add"

As you can see from the screenshot above, I selected "Shrink One Page."

---

[6] You can drag commands or command groups to custom groups (but *not* to built-in groups).

The new command should appear below your custom group in the Main Tabs section of the Word Options screen.

My New Tab, New Group, and New Command

5. You can add more commands at this point, but let's stop here so we can to save your new stuff and see what it looks like in the ribbon. To do so, click "**OK**" at the bottom right side of the Options screen. (**CAUTION**: Always be sure to click "OK" after you add, rename, or otherwise modify a custom tab, or your changes won't be preserved when you close out of the Word Options.)

6. After you click OK, you should see your new tab in the Ribbon.

Success!
(My New Tab, Group, and Command in the Ribbon)

You can see from the (truncated) screenshot above that I have successfully added a new tab called "Jan's Stuff," which appears between the Home Tab and the Insert Tab, as well as a new group labeled "Legal Tools" and a Shrink One Page command. As I add commands to the "Legal Tools" group, it will expand accordingly (see the screenshot below.)

My Custom Tab and Group With a Few More Commands

Now that you've added a new tab and a new group, let's return to the Customization Screen in the Word options and experiment some more. We can do any or all of the following:

- Add another custom tab;

- Add another group to your custom tab (or add a group to a built-in tab);

- Add more commands to your new group;

156

- Change the icons for commands you've placed in a custom group;

- Rename a custom or built-in tab or group;

- Move a tab or group to a different location in the Ribbon;

- Hide a tab;

- Remove commands from a custom group;

- Remove built-in or custom groups or custom tabs;

- Reset all customizations to the factory default settings; or

- Export your customizations to a file in order to use them on another computer.

Remember that there are two different ways to get to the Customize Ribbon screen in the Word Options. Either:

1. **Right-click the Ribbon** (or the **Quick Access Toolbar**) and click **Customize the Ribbon...** *or*

2. Click the **File tab**, **Options**, **Customize Ribbon**.

The following sections provide instructions for all of the additional customization options outlined above.

Adding Another Tab, Group, or Command

Adding a new tab should be fairly self-explanatory at this point. It's pretty simple to add more groups, too. Just keep in mind that you need to click to select the tab you want to contain your group, either before or after you open the Word Options screen. Also, note that you can add groups to both *custom* tabs and *built-in* tabs.

Commands, however, can be added only to custom groups.

To add another tab to the Ribbon:

1. Select (highlight) an existing tab (the one you want to appear in the Ribbon to the left of your new tab), if it isn't already selected.

2. Click the "New Tab" button.

3. If necessary, click to select (highlight) the new tab within the diagram of tabs and groups, then click the "Rename" button.

4. Type a name for your new tab and click OK.

157

5. Select (highlight) the new group that Word created within your new tab.

6. Click the "Rename" button.

7. Type a name for your new group and click OK.

8. Click the OK button at the bottom right side of the Word Options screen to save your changes.

<u>To add a group (to either a custom tab or a built-in tab)</u>:

1. Click the tab you want to contain your new group.

2. Click the "New Group" button.

3. Click the "Rename" button.

4. Type a name for your new group.

5. Click the OK button at the bottom right side of the Word Options screen to save your changes.

<u>To add another command (to a custom group only)</u>:

1. First, **click the group** where you want to insert the command. Before moving on to step 2, note the following:

    (a) If you plan to use the "drag-and-drop" method to add a command, either expand the group by clicking the plus sign (+) to the left of the group's name or hold the mouse over the group name until it expands. Otherwise, Word won't let you drop the command.

    (b) If you plan to use the "click 'Add' button" method, you don't need to expand the group.

2. If necessary, change the "Choose commands from:" drop-down at the top left side of the screen to "All Commands" (or any other list you prefer).

3. Next, locate the command you wish to add by using the scrollbar or by clicking within the command list and pressing the letter of the alphabet that matches the first letter of the command name, then scrolling down.

4. Do one of the following:

    (a) Click to select (highlight) the command, then click the "Add" button; ***or***

    (b) Click the command, keep the left mouse button depressed and drag the command to your group, then position the mouse pointer where you want the command to go and release the mouse button to drop the command.

5. If necessary, click the "Up" arrow or the "Down" arrow to reposition the command.

6. Continue adding commands in this fashion if you like. (Remember that you can add more commands later on.)

7. When you're finished, be sure to click the OK button at the bottom right side of the Word Options screen to save your changes.

CAUTION: Remember that you can't add commands to built-in groups. If you try to do so, you will get a warning prompt, as follows:

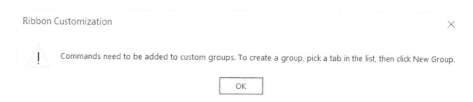

Renaming a Custom Group or Tab

From within the Customize Ribbon screen in the Word Options:

1. Click the group or tab you want to rename.

2. Click the "Rename" button.

3. Type a new name and click OK.

4. Click OK to save your changes when you exit from the Word Options.

Moving a Tab or Group

It's easy to move a tab or group within the Ribbon. Navigate to the right-hand side of the Customize Ribbon screen in the Word Options and do the following:

1. First, **locate the tab or group** you wish to move.

2. Click to **select (highlight) the tab or group**.

3. Next, click the "**Up**" arrow or the "**Down**" arrow at the right side of the screen. The "**Up**" arrow repositions the tab or group to the left in the Ribbon; the "**Down**" arrow moves it to the right.

4. Click the "**OK**" button at the bottom right side of the Word Options screen to save your changes.

In the next screenshot, you can see that I moved my custom tab ahead of (to the left of) the Home tab. To do so, I simply clicked my custom tab and then clicked the "Up" arrow at the right side of the screen.

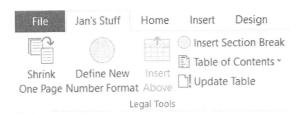

CAUTION: If you choose to place your custom tab first, ahead of the Home tab, the custom tab will appear at the forefront when you launch Word. That might or might not be desirable; you'll have to experiment and decide what you prefer.

Hiding a Tab

You can't hide a group, but you *can* hide an entire tab (even one that is built in). To do so, return to the Customize Ribbon screen in the Word Options and do as follows:

1. **Click** to **uncheck the checkbox** to the left of the tab name.

The screenshot at right shows that I have unchecked the box next to my "Jan's Stuff (Custom)" Tab.

2. **Click OK** at the bottom right side of the Word Options screen to save your changes.

Ribbon (Partial) With "Jan's Stuff" Tab Hidden

3. To un-hide a tab, **click the checkbox again** in order to put a check back in the checkbox, then **OK** out.

160

Removing Groups

You can remove custom groups and/or built-in groups. To do so from within the Customization Screen of the Word Options:

1. First, if you can't see the group you want to remove, expand the tab the group is in by **clicking the plus sign (+)** to the left of the tab name.

2. **Click to select (highlight) the group** you want to delete.

   I've clicked the Add-Ins group, a built-in group within the Insert tab (screenshot at right). Since I'm unlikely to use the commands in that group (for the Microsoft Store, Wikipedia, and "My Add-ins"), I'll remove the group and make the tab less cluttered.

   **Click the Group,
   Then Click "Remove"**

3. **Click** the **"Remove" button** in the middle of the screen.[7]

4. Remember to **click "OK"** to save your changes when you exit from the Word Options.

After you close the Word Options, the group you removed will not appear in the Ribbon.

The Insert Tab Before Removing the Add-ins Group

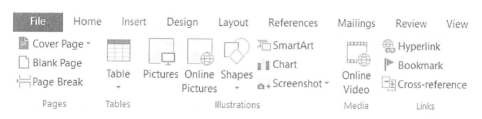

The Insert Tab After Removing the Add-ins Group

---

[7] You can restore the removed group later on if you so choose, as explained on the next page.

161

Restoring a Removed Group

If you change your mind after removing a group or deleting a command, not to worry—you can restore it. To do so, return to the Customization Screen in the Word Options and do the following:

1. Change the "**Choose commands from:**" drop-down to "**All Tabs.**"[8]

2. **Locate the tab** where the group you deleted normally resides (in the example below, the Insert tab) and **click the plus sign (+)** to the left of the tab name in order to expand it and display the groups contained in that tab.

3. Click to **select (highlight) the group** you want to restore.

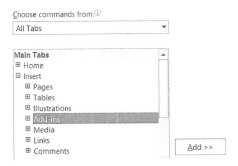

Click the Group You Want to Restore

4. Click the "**Add**" button.

5. Look at the right side of the screen and, if necessary, click the "**Up**" or **Down**" arrow to move the group to the location in the Ribbon where you want it. In the screenshot at right, you can see that when I added the "Add-ins" group back to the tab, it appeared in a different location from where it was before. I'd like it between the "Illustrations" and "Media" groups, so I'll click the "Up" arrow to move it.

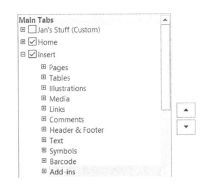

6. Remember to **click "OK"** to save your changes when you exit from the Word Options.

---

[8] If you are restoring a group that belongs to a Main Tab, you can choose "Main Tabs" instead.

The Insert tab With the "Add-ins" Group Restored

Removing Commands

You can remove a command from a custom group, but not from a built-in group. When you try to select a command in a built-in group in order to remove it, you'll see that the commands are grayed out, as are the "Add" and "Remove" buttons in the Customize Ribbon screen of the Word Options.

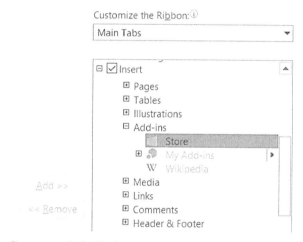

**Commands in Built-In Groups Are Grayed Out,
As Are the Add and Remove Buttons**

To remove a command from a *custom* group:

1. First, expand the group if necessary (in order to show the commands) by **clicking the plus sign (+)** to the left of the group name.

2. **Click the command** you want to remove.

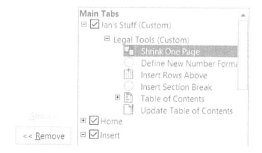

Click to Select (Highlight) the Command You Want to Remove

163

3. **Click** the "**Remove**" **button**.[9]

4. Remember to **click** "**OK**" to **save** your changes when you close the Word Options.

My Custom Tab With "Shrink One Page" Removed

Restoring a Removed Command

Perhaps the most difficult aspect of restoring a deleted command is locating it in the command list at the left side of the Customize Ribbon screen. Again, I find it easiest to change the "Choose commands from:" drop-down to "All Commands," but if you know where the command is located, you can choose a different drop-down, such as "Main Tabs."

Remember that you can move quickly through the command list by positioning your cursor in the list and then pressing the letter of the alphabet that is the first letter of the name of the command you're seeking.

Once you have chosen a drop-down command list and have located the command you want to restore, just do the following:

1. **Click the command**,

2. **Click** the "**Add**" button,

3. Remember to **click** "**OK**" to save your changes when you exit from the Word Options.

Renaming Commands or Changing an Icon

It's easy to rename a command. From within the Customize Ribbon screen in the Word Options, do the following:

1. Expand the tab and/or the group that the command is in if necessary. Then **click the command or icon** you want to change or rename.

2. To rename a command, click the "**Rename**" **button**, then **type a new name** for the command and click **OK**. (Or **right-click** the command, then click "**Rename**.")

---

[9] You can add the command back later on if you so choose.

164

3. To change a command's icon, click the "**Rename**" **button**, then locate an icon you prefer in the "**Rename**" **dialog box, click it**, and click **OK**.[10]

4. Remember to **click "OK"** to save your changes.

**Custom Icons for "Define New Number Format"
and "Insert Section Break" Commands in My Custom Tab**

Hiding Command Labels in a Custom Group

You can hide the icon labels for the commands in a custom group—in effect, leaving only the icons, and no text, by doing the following:

1. From within the Customize Ribbon screen in the Word Options, first make sure you can **see the group** with the commands whose labels you want to hide (if necessary, **click the plus sign [+]** to the left of the name of the tab containing the group in order to expand the tab).

2. Next, *right-click* the group and, when the pop-up menu appears, click "**Hide Command Labels**."[11]

3. Remember to **click "OK"** to save your changes when you exit from the Word Options.

The screenshot on the next page shows the results of hiding the command labels in my "Legal Tools" custom group. All you can see is the icons (buttons) for the commands. It's not a pretty sight…

---

[10] As you'll see, the options in the Rename dialog box are limited. It's possible to create custom icons, although the process sounds more complicated than in older versions. See Word MVP Greg Maxey's tips for creating custom icons in Word 2007, which likely work the same way in Word 2016: gregmaxey.mvps.org/Ribbon_Custom_Icons.htm

[11] This option applies to all commands within a custom group. In other words, you can't hide the label for one or more individual commands; it's an all-or-nothing proposition.

My Custom Group With the Command Labels Hidden

…so I think I'd better restore the command labels (even though I can see a pop-up label for every icon, and a description for some of them, when I hover over one of the icons with the mouse).

To restore the command labels, just repeat the steps you took to hide the labels. (Clicking "Hide Command Labels" a second time toggles the labels back on.)

Here are the steps again:

1. From within the Customize Ribbon screen in the Word Options, first make sure you can **see the group** with the commands whose labels you want to restore (if necessary, **click the plus sign [+]** to the left of the name of the tab containing the group in order to expand the tab).

2. Next, *right-click* the group and, when the pop-up menu opens, click "**Hide Command Labels**" again, which will remove the checkmark enabling that option.

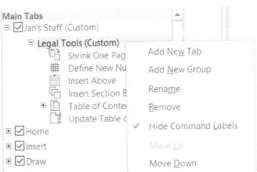

3. Remember to **click "OK"** to save your changes when you exit from the Word Options.

That looks much better. At least now I can figure out what the icons actually do.

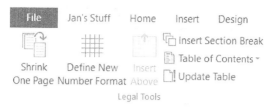

My Custom Group With the Command Labels Restored

Resetting Customizations to the Factory Defaults

You can restore the default "factory" settings for an individual tab or for the entire Ribbon. For example, I have added a custom "Watermarks" group, with commands related to inserting and removing watermarks, to the Layout tab to emulate Word 2010. But perhaps I'm going to do a training session, and I want to reset the tab to its default settings so as to avoid confusing my trainees.

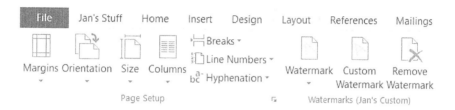

Open the Customize Ribbon screen in the Word Options and then proceed as follows:

1. To restore the default settings for one tab, **locate the tab** and **click it**.

2. Click the "**Reset**" **button**, which opens a drop-down.

3. From the drop-down, click the "**Reset only selected Ribbon tab**" button.

Word immediately resets the tab, removing any new group / commands you added to that tab.

4. When you have finished resetting tabs, **OK out** of the Word Options.

Let's say you decide to restore everything – both the Ribbon and the Quick Access Toolbar – to the factory defaults.[12] Reopen the Word Options and do as follows:

1. Click the "**Reset**" **button**, then click "**Reset all customizations**."

2. A warning message will appear, asking if you're sure you want to delete all of the customizations for the ribbon and the QAT.

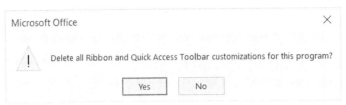

3. If you aren't sure you want to delete all of the customizations, click "**No**."[13]

4. If you do wish to proceed, click "**Yes**."

    Word immediately reverts to the factory default settings, removing all custom tabs, groups, and commands from the Ribbon and all custom commands from the QAT. (It doesn't move the QAT back above the Ribbon if you have placed it below the Ribbon, however.)

5. At this point, you can click "**OK**" to close out of Word Options. (Note that clicking the "Cancel" button *does not* restore the customizations.)

Importing / Exporting Your Customizations

You can back up the customizations that you have made to the Ribbon, as well as to the Quick Access Toolbar. Doing so is a smart preventive measure in case a power outage or other unexpected problem causes you to lose your customizations. (It's also possible that your IT department might swap out your computer at some point, in which case you would have to start customizing everything from scratch – unless you had backed up your personalized settings onto external media, such as an external hard drive or USB drive.) Another reason to back up your customizations is so that you can copy them to another computer.

---

[12] **CAUTION:** You can't reset the Ribbon without also resetting the QAT. If you don't want to lose the customizations you've made to your QAT, ***don't use this option***! Instead, try making incremental changes to individual tabs and groups to restore the defaults. Note that it *is* possible to reset the QAT without resetting the Ribbon. From the Word Options dialog, Quick Access Toolbar category, click the "Reset" button. You'll see two choices: "Reset only Quick Access Toolbar" and "Reset all customizations." (If you see only one choice, close and then reopen the Word Options.) Choose the former.

[13] To be on the safe side, use the "Export" option to save a backup copy of your customizations prior to experimenting with the "Reset" button. That way, you can use "Import" later on to restore the customizations that are discarded when you revert to the factory defaults.

To do so, *either* **right-click the Ribbon** (or the **Quick Access Toolbar**) and click **Customize the Ribbon...** *or* click the **File tab, Options, Customize Ribbon**.

1. When the Customize Ribbon screen appears, navigate to the lower right-hand side and locate the **Import/Export button**.

Note that if you place the mouse pointer over the "information" icon to the right of "Import/Export," a pop-up appears:

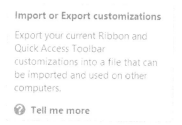

You can click "Tell me more" to open a Help screen with additional information.

2. Click the button to open the drop-down list. You'll see two choices: **Import customization file** and **Export all customizations**.

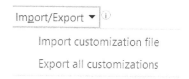

3. To save your Ribbon (and/or QAT) configurations to a file, click **Export all customizations**.

4. A "**File Save**" dialog, similar to the one in the screenshot on the next page, will open.[14]

As you can see, the program automatically assigns the name "Word Customization" to the configuration file, but you can rename it. (Just be sure to use a name that clearly describes the file's contents). I usually add the current date to the file name, like so: "Word Customizations 12-19-2015.exportedUI."

---

[14] By default, Word will save the configuration file in your "Documents" folder, but you can use the drop-down at the top of the dialog to save it to a different folder. Note that your "File Save" dialog might look somewhat different, depending in part on which version of Windows you use.

That can be helpful if you make additional customizations later on but decide you also want to keep previous customizations of your Ribbon and QAT.

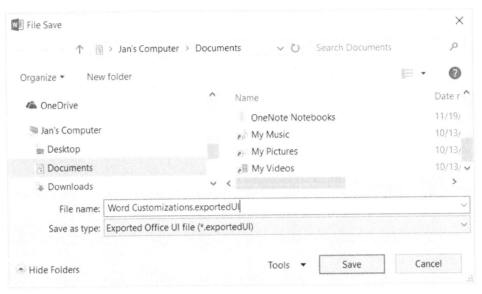

The File Save Dialog (Windows 10)

5. Optional step: **Change the file location** if you wish.

6. Optional step: **Rename the file** if you wish.

7. **Click "Save."**[15]

After you have saved this file to your hard drive, you can copy it to a USB drive, an external drive, a CD or DVD, or some similar medium, paste the copy into another computer, and then import the configuration file on that machine. Or, as I've suggested, you can import it to the same computer if you lose your customizations for some reason.

1. To import the file, go into the Customize Ribbon screen of the Word Options and click the **"Import / Export" button**, then click **"Import Customization File."**

---

[15] Word saves the file as an "Exported Office UI file" ("UI" stands for "User Interface").

2. **Browse** to the location of the file.

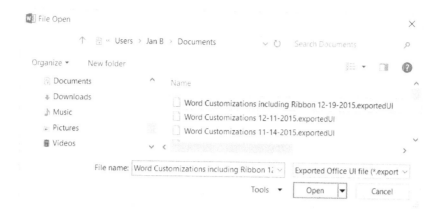

3. Click to select (highlight) the file, then click the "**Open**" button.

4. A warning message appears, giving you a chance to change your mind.

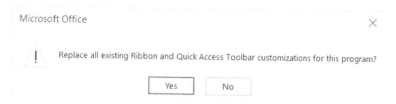

5. If you are unsure whether you want to replace all customizations to the Ribbon and the Quick Access Toolbar, click "**No**."

6. If you are sure you want to proceed, click "**Yes**."

The changes will go into effect regardless of whether you click "OK" or "Cancel" when you close out of the Word Options.

CAUTION: When you import the configuration file on another computer, you will overwrite all customizations the user has made to the Ribbon and the Quick Access Toolbar on that machine (the "target" or "destination" computer). It's a good idea to export the original configuration file on the "destination" computer – not just the one on the "source" computer (the one you're copying from) – *before* you import the new configuration file to the destination machine. That way, you have a backup copy you can use to restore the original settings if need be.

Right-Click Options for Working With Tabs, Groups, and Commands

Word 2016 provides helpful context-sensitive menus when you right-click a group or tab from within the Customize Ribbon screen within the Word Options. The right-click options make it easy for you to add a new tab, add a new group, rename an existing tab or group, show or hide a tab, show or hide command labels, remove a tab or group, and/or move a tab or group up or down (left or right in the Ribbon).

The options available in the pop-up menus vary depending on *what type of object* you right-click (for instance, a built-in tab versus a custom tab) and *whether you have modified it* in any way. As an example, right-clicking **a custom tab** produces the pop-up menu you see on the left, and right-clicking **a custom group** produces the pop-up menu you see on the right:

A Custom Tab   **A Custom Group**

The difference between the two is that—logically enough—the menu for the custom tab includes the "Show Tab" option but not the "Hide Command Labels" option, whereas the menu for the custom group has the "Hide Command Labels" option but not the "Show Tab" option. (If you have hidden a custom tab, the "Show Tab" command appears in the menu without a check mark next to it. Click that command to un-hide the tab.)

NOTE: The "Hide Command Labels" option appears *only* when you right-click on the name of a custom group (*not* a custom tab, a built-in group, or a built-in tab—or on an individual command).

Right-clicking a command that you have added to a custom group produces a pop-up menu similar to the one that follows:

Right-Clicking a Command in a Custom Group

Whether both the "Move Up" and "Move Down" options are available depends on where the command is located in your group – i.e., whether there are other commands above it (to the left of it in the Ribbon) or below it (to the right of it in the Ribbon). No pop-up menu appears when you right-click a built-in command because you can't modify built-in commands.

Right-clicking a **built-in tab** produces one of the following pop-up menus. The difference between the two has to do with whether or not you have modified the tab (i.e., by adding a custom group to it). If you've modified the tab, the "Reset Tab" option that is normally grayed out becomes available.

Right-Clicking an Unmodified Built-in Tab   **Right-Clicking a Modified Built-In Tab**

These commands can be useful for changing the default settings to suit your needs. For example, I considered using the "Rename" command to change the name of the "Layout" tab to "Page Layout," which is what Microsoft called the tab in Word 2010. (In Word 2013, I used the command to change the tab labels from ALL CAPS, which was the default setting in that version of Word, to Initial Caps.)

Right-clicking a **built-in group** produces the following pop-up menu:

Right-Clicking a Built-In Group

Note that it lacks a "Show Tab" option and a "Reset Tab" option, but it includes a "Remove" option. (You can remove, rename, or relocate a built-in group, but you can't add any commands to it.)

Limitations on Customizing the Ribbon

The main limitations on customizing the Ribbon at this point are that you can't add commands to built-in groups, and you can't hide groups. Also, it is difficult to create custom icons, though it can be done (if you are adventurous, very computer-literate, and patient, and if you have the appropriate permissions).

TIP: Reassigning Ctrl O to "File Open"

1. Click the **File tab**, **Options,** and when the Word dialog opens, click the **Customize Ribbon** category at left.

2. Click the "**Customize…**" **button** toward the bottom left side of the Word dialog. The **Customize Keyboard dialog** will open.

3. At the left side of the Customize Keyboard dialog, under "**Categories**," **File Tab** should be highlighted. Navigate to the right side of the dialog, under "**Commands**." Scroll down to **FileOpen** and click it.[1]

   You might notice that some keyboard shortcuts already have been assigned to the command. (If so, they appear in the "**Current keys:**" box at left.)

4. Click in the "**Press new shortcut key**" box and press and hold the **Ctrl** key, then tap the letter **O**. (Be careful to press the letter O, not a zero.)

5. Note the message below the "**Current keys**" box: "**Currently assigned to: FileOpenUsingBackstage**." (This is essentially a warning in case you didn't realize that the key combination you chose is already assigned to another feature or function. If you want to retain the original assignment to that other feature or function, you can select a different key combination.)

6. **OPTIONAL STEP**: Note the "**Save changes in**" **drop-down** at the lower left side of the dialog box. By default, Word saves your keyboard reassignment to the Normal template (which is the basis for new blank documents). If you have created customized templates and wish to reassign keyboard shortcuts within one of your own templates, you can click the "Save changes in" drop-down and choose a different template.

7. The "**Assign**" button is now active (no longer grayed out). To proceed with the key reassignment, click the button.

8. Click **Close**, then be sure to click **OK** to save your new shortcut.

   CAUTION: If you click the red "X" in the upper right corner to close the Word Options dialog, Word will not save your configuration changes!

   Now Ctrl O should bypass the Backstage view and go directly to the Open dialog in Windows. And now you know how to create your own custom keyboard shortcuts!

---

[1] The item immediately below FileOpen, labeled FileOpenUsingBackstage, is the command to which the keyboard shortcut Ctrl O is assigned by default. If you click that command, you will see Ctrl O listed in the "Current keys" box at left.

<u>Customizing the Quick Access Toolbar</u>

The **Quick Access Toolbar** (sometimes referred to as the "**QAT**") is highly customizable, which makes it invaluable. In its original state perched above the Ribbon, the QAT is teeny-tiny and it contains only a few icons. However, if you move it below the Ribbon, it expands to fill the entire width of the screen. That makes it easier to see, and it gives you plenty of room to add the features and commands you use most often. (Also, in that location, it won't overlap the document name in the Title Bar.)

To move the QAT below the Ribbon, **right-click** anywhere within it and choose **Show Quick Access Toolbar Below the Ribbon**. (To put it back above the Ribbon, **right-click** it and choose **Show Quick Access Toolbar Above the Ribbon**.)

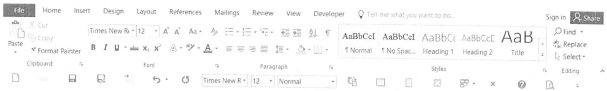
My Customized QAT Below the Ribbon

Moreover, the QAT remains stationary—which means your frequently used icons are always available, regardless of which tab of the Ribbon happens to be at the forefront.

You can add command icons, drop-down menus (e.g., the Font Size drop-down), dialog launchers (e.g., the Paragraph dialog launcher), and even entire groups (e.g., the Font group) or galleries (e.g., the Style Gallery).

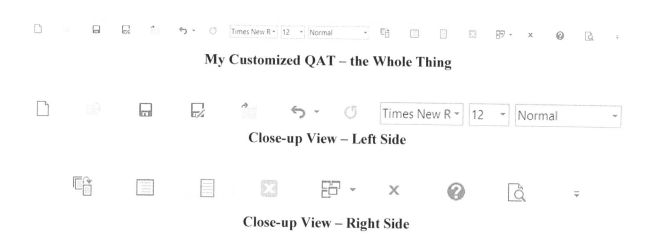
My Customized QAT – the Whole Thing

Close-up View – Left Side

Close-up View – Right Side

The screenshots show the icons on my customized QAT, from left to right: Blank document, Open, Save, Save As, Close, Undo, Redo, Font, Font Size, Style, Shrink to Fit, Draft View, Print Layout View, Close Header & Footer, Switch Windows, Exit, Help, and Print Preview Edit Mode.

175

Other commands that you might want to add include Quick Print (which immediately sends the entire document to your default printer), the Paragraph dialog, Paste and Keep Text Only, Keep With Next, Insert Footnote, Insert Table Row, Delete Table Row, Insert Symbol, and Section Break – just a few ideas to get you started. There are lots of other possibilities.

You can add icons for commands, entire groups or galleries, and/or dialog boxes to the QAT by using one of the following methods:

1. Right-click any command, group, or dialog launcher in the Ribbon, then choose "**Add to Quick Access Toolbar**"); or

2. Click the "**More**" drop-down (i.e., the **Customize Quick Access Toolbar menu**) at the right side of the QAT and choose any of the commands on the menu; and/or

3. Go into the **Word Options** and add icons from there. To get there, do one of the following:

    (a) *Right-click* anywhere within the QAT and choose "**Customize Quick Access Toolbar…**"; or

    (b) Click the "**More**" drop-down (the arrow) at the right side of the QAT, then choose "**More Commands…**"; or

    (c) Click the **File tab**, **Options**, **Quick Access Toolbar**.

For detailed instructions, keep reading.

<u>Right-Click a Command in the Ribbon</u>

My favorite method, and one of the easiest, is to right-click a command or drop-down menu – or even a dialog launcher – in the Ribbon. For instance, let's say you want to add a "Footnote" icon to the QAT. Just locate the "Footnote" command in the Ribbon (it's on the "References" tab), right-click the icon, and choose "Add to Quick Access Toolbar."

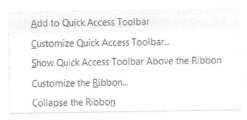

The icon will be added at the right side of the QAT. If that's not where you want it, not to worry; you can move it later on. For instructions, see page 179.

To add an icon, a group of commands, or a dialog launcher to the QAT, simply **right-click it** and choose **Add to Quick Access Toolbar**.

The "Customize Quick Access Toolbar" Drop-Down

You might have noticed a drop-down arrow at the right side of the QAT. (If you use the "Colorful" Office Theme, in which the area above the Ribbon is bright blue, you might not have noticed the arrow, because it doesn't appear unless / until you position the mouse over it... which you probably wouldn't think to do if you didn't know of its existence!)

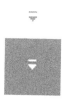

The arrow (sometimes called a "**More**" button) opens a **Customize Quick Access Toolbar** drop-down that gives you an easy way to add several commonly used commands to the QAT: New, Open, Save, Email, Quick Print (which sends the current document directly to the printer), Print Preview and Print, Spelling & Grammar, Undo, Redo, Draw Table, and Touch/Mouse Mode (for tablets and other touch-capable devices).

Simply click to put a checkmark next to the one(s) you want to add to the QAT. (Save, Undo, and Redo are checked—i.e., placed on the QAT—by default.) To remove one or more of the commands in this list from the QAT, click to *uncheck* it.

The "**More Commands…**" option at the bottom of the drop-down menu opens the "Quick Access Toolbar" screen in the Word Options (similar to right-clicking the QAT, then choosing "Customize Quick Access Toolbar.") This option is useful because the menu provides so few choices. (For instance, although it offers an "Open" command, there is no "Close" command.)

Also at the bottom of the menu, there's an option to change the position of the QAT (to show it above the Ribbon if you've moved it down, or show it below the Ribbon if you haven't).

The Word Options

When the Word Options screen opens, by default the "**Choose commands from:**" drop-down shows what Microsoft calls "**Popular Commands**."

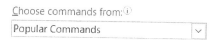

However, "Popular Commands" offers a very limited – and some might say quirky – assortment of commands, and you might not find what you are looking for.[1] If you don't, click the drop-down list at the top left side and choose "**All Commands**." Although the resulting list of commands can be somewhat overwhelming – there are literally hundreds of commands available

---

[1] An example I frequently give in class is the "Close" command, which most of us probably consider fairly popular. Apparently Microsoft doesn't agree, however, because that command is conspicuously missing from both the "Customize" drop-down and the "Popular Commands" list.

– at least you'll be able to locate the command you want, assuming that Microsoft created one for the feature you have in mind.[2] (Surprisingly, there isn't a command for every feature.)

In the command list immediately below the drop-down, the commands are listed in numeric and then alphabetical order. To move quickly through the list, first click somewhere within it – this is a critical step – and then press a key that corresponds with the first letter of the command you're looking for. It usually won't take you directly to that command, but it will get you close. For example, to find the "Close" command, press "C" to move to the first command in the list that starts with the letter "C," and then scroll down. Or you can simply scroll through the entire command list by using the scrollbar or your mouse wheel.

After locating one that you wish to add, **click it** and click the **Add button**.

For example, to add a font-face drop-down (which shows the font in effect at the cursor position and also lets you choose a different font), , use the scrollbar in the command list to locate the icon labeled "Font" that displays both an arrow pointing down and what looks like an I-beam pointer (see the screenshot).

Font

Click the icon in the command list, then click the **Add button** (or double-click). You can add a Font Size and Style box in the same manner (you can't select more than one icon at a time, however; you must add each icon separately).

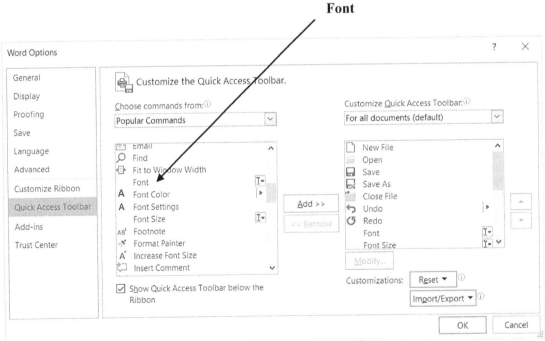

Click to select an icon from the "Command List" on the left, then click "Add"

---

[2] You can narrow down the options by choosing to display only the commands available from a specific tab, such as the File tab, the Home tab, or the Review tab, or by choosing from commands that aren't on the Ribbon.

Changing the Order of Icons on the QAT

After you've added an icon to the QAT from the Word Options dialog, you can change its location if you like. (**NOTE**: You can't move icons around on the QAT – or remove them altogether – by dragging them. This is the only method you can use to change the order of icons on the QAT.) First, click the command for the icon in the box on the right side of the dialog, then click either the **up arrow** (to move the icon to the **left**) or the **down arrow** (to move it to the **right**). Note that one or both of the arrows will be grayed out until you click a command.

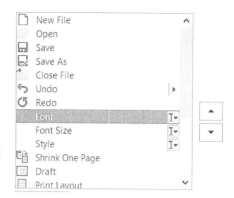

Removing Icons from the QAT

The easiest way to remove an icon from the QAT is to **right-click** it, then click **Remove from Quick Access Toolbar**. Alternatively, you can use any of the methods described on page 176 to open the Word Options to the Quick Access Toolbar category, then click to select an item in the box *at right* (which represents your customized QAT) and click **Remove**.

When you have finished customizing the QAT, be sure to click "**OK**." (**CAUTION**: Clicking the "X" at the upper right side of the Word Options dialog will close the dialog *without saving your changes*.)

Limitations of the QAT

The QAT has a couple of built-in limitations:

(1) There is no way to display more than one row. You *can* add more icons after filling the entire row, but those "extra" icons will be visible only by clicking the chevron (double arrow) at the right side of the QAT (see the screenshot); and

(2) You can't change the size of the buttons without tinkering with your screen resolution, which usually isn't advisable for the uninitiated because, done incorrectly, it can cause display problems.

Exporting (Backing Up) and Restoring Your Customizations

It's a good idea to back up your customized QAT in case a power outage or some other unexpected event causes the QAT to revert to its default settings. That doesn't happen often, but it does happen occasionally (I've seen it at a few law firms where I've provided training and/or floor support). For instructions on exporting (backing up) and restoring your customized QAT, see the section starting on page 168.

Adding a "Close" ("Close File") Command to the Quick Access Toolbar

I like to use this example in class because it demonstrates not merely how to add a specific command – "Close" to the Quick Access Toolbar (QAT), but also how the three different options for adding items to the QAT work.

First, you might recall that you can add a command to the QAT by right-clicking the icon for that command in the Ribbon. Ordinarily, the only place you'll find the "Close" command in the Ribbon is on the File tab.[3] But when you click the File tab, then right-click "Close," nothing happens. Hm.

So then it might occur to you that you can add some commands by clicking the "Customize Quick Access Toolbar" drop-down menu at the right side of the QAT, then clicking to put a checkmark next to the command label. Great! …except that there's no "Close" command on the menu. Double-hm.

Now what? Oh, yes – the third way to add a command to the QAT is by opening the Word Options, usually by right-clicking the QAT (or the Ribbon) and choosing "Customize Quick Access Toolbar) or by clicking the "Customize…" drop-down and choosing "More Commands…" That sounds like a good plan.

When the Word Options dialog opens to the Quick Access Toolbar category, by default "Choose commands from" displays only the "Popular Commands." "Close" must be there – after all, isn't that a popular command?

You and I might think so, but for some reason Microsoft didn't include that one, even though it *did* include "Open."

So what's the solution?

You have to change the "**Choose commands from:**" drop-down from Popular Commands to either "**All Commands**" or "**File tab**," then press the letter "**C**" (to go to the first command that starts with "C") or scroll down… and voilà! There's that hard-to-find command, called "**Close File**" in this version of Word.

See the screenshots on the next page.

---

[3] Of course, it's possible that the IT department at the organization where you work has added a custom tab that includes the "Close" icon. If so, they've probably added a "Close" icon to the QAT, too.

180

**Choose commands from:
File Tab**

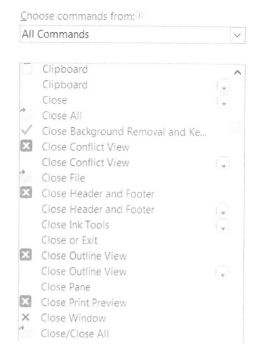

**Choose commands from:
All Commands**

In previous versions the command was called "Close," which made it difficult to differentiate from another command with the same name. Because Microsoft now calls this command "Close File," that's no longer a problem.

But if you encounter two other commands with the same name when you are trying to add an icon to the QAT, how do you determine which is the correct one? Just position the mouse over the command name for a few seconds, and a pop-up appears with more information about the command.

When I hover over "Close," I see the pop-up depicted in the accompanying screenshot. I might not know what "Background Removal Tab | Close (GroupBackgroundRemovalClose)" refers to, but I can be pretty certain it's not the same as "Close File."

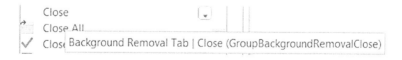

By contrast, hovering over "Close File" produces the following pop-up. *That* sounds more like what we were looking for.

181

Customizing the Status Bar

You can customize the Status Bar by adding such useful information as Section number (which, in a departure from all previous versions of Word, is ***not*** displayed by default), Overtype mode, Track Changes, and—perhaps a nod to WordPerfect users—Vertical Page Position. The full range of options, and the status of each item (On or Off, etc.) is shown in the screenshot below.

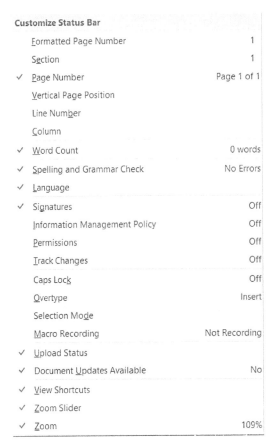

Status Bar Menu

To add or remove Status Bar icons/text, ***right***-click within the Status Bar, then **click** to check or uncheck individual items.

Just press the **Esc key** or click somewhere outside the menu in order to close it.

Default Settings

By default, the following items are ***not enabled or displayed*** in the Status Bar in Word 2016:

- Formatted Page Number
- Section
- Vertical Page Position
- Line Number
- Column
- Information Management Policy
- Permissions
- Track Changes
- Caps Lock
- Overtype
- Selection Mode
- Macro Recording

The items that ***are enabled*** by default (and are displayed if the feature they relate to is activated / in use) are:

- Page Number
- Word Count
- Number of Authors Editing
- Spelling and Grammar Check
- Language
- Signatures
- Information Management Policy
- Permissions
- Upload Status
- Document Updates Available
- View Shortcuts
- Zoom Slider
- Zoom

The Information Management Policy and Permissions options are set to "Off" if you are not using Word in a networked office environment that makes use of SharePoint.

The "Number of Authors Editing" and "Document Updates Available" items are related to the co-authoring feature (see the Sidebar about Real Time Co-Authoring that starts on page 87). The "Number of Authors Editing" does not display unless the co-authoring feature is active.

Making Word 2016 Work Like Older Versions of Word

Once upon a time, Word's default font was Times New Roman and the default line spacing was single, with no "After" spacing – just like in WordPerfect and most other word processing programs. Starting with Word 2007, Microsoft changed these default settings. In Word 2016, the defaults are as follows:

- The default font for regular (body) text is **Calibri 11 pt**;

- The default font for heading styles is **Calibri Light**[1];

- The default line spacing is **1.08 lines**; and

- The default "spacing after" paragraphs is **8 points**.

Microsoft has stated, in blog posts and elsewhere, that it increased the line spacing and the "spacing after" (white space between) paragraphs in order to improve readability. (I'm not sure why the company changed the default font). However, those modifications pose problems for those of us who work in the legal field because of the strict formatting rules in effect for litigation-related documents that have to be submitted to a court or other judicial body. Hence, one of the first things you'll probably want to do after installing Word 2016 is to restore the default formatting you used in prior versions.

In this section, I will explain how to change the default font and the default settings for the Normal paragraph style (the style that determines the paragraph formatting – indents, line spacing, spacing after, etc. – of most body text in your documents) – and I'll provide a tip about a last resort you can try in case your modified settings don't stick. I'll also walk you through the process of editing the Normal template (Normal.dotm).[2]

We'll also take a look at a couple of features first introduced in Word 2007: **Style Sets** and **Themes**. These two obscure but important features, which work together, determine some of the document default settings[3] – and can undermine your efforts to change those defaults.

---

[1] Also, the default font color for at least some of the heading styles is blue rather than black.

[2] I strongly advise you to make a backup copy of your Normal template (Normal.dotm), since many of your customizations are stored there. If Word crashes, you could lose those customizations, because Word will create a new – and generic –Normal.dotm that will take effect when you reopen the program. Having a backup Normal.dotm makes it easy to restore your customizations after a crash. For instructions, see page 586.

[3] For more about how the newer versions of Word determine so-called "Document Defaults," see http://blogs.msdn.com/microsoft_office_word/archive/2008/10/28/behind-the-curtain-styles-doc-defaults-style-sets-and-themes.aspx. I have borrowed the term "Document Defaults" from this blog article because it strikes me as particularly clear and succinct.

The Role of Style Sets and Themes in Determining Default Settings

You probably don't realize it, but right out of the box, Word 2016 applies a Style Set and a Theme to your documents.[4] That initial Style Set, working together with its companion Theme, is what sets most of the default paragraph and font formatting in your documents. You can take back control of that formatting, but first you have to understand what is going on under the hood.

In all recent versions of Word, the so-called Document Defaults are based on an XML-coded **Style Set** that determines the font size, line spacing, "After" spacing, and certain other formatting in every document. In particular, it is the "**Word**" **Style Set**, operating unobtrusively in the background, that imposes the 11-point font size, the 1.08 line spacing, and the 8 points of "After" spacing in effect in every new document in this version of Word.[5]

A **Theme** called "**Office**," also operating in the background when you first start using Word 2016, is what produces the Calibri font face for regular (body) text and Calibri Light for built-in heading styles and tints the heading fonts blue.

In general, Style Sets establish a document's *paragraph formatting*: the indents (including first-line indent), the line spacing, the before and/or after spacing, and tab settings. Style Sets also can dictate *font attributes* such as font size, boldface, italics, and the like. Typically, however, it is a companion Theme that determines the *font face and color* of regular (body) text and headings, as well as of certain "accents" such as hyperlinks and shapes.

The program comes with a number of different Style Sets and Themes. You can switch Style Sets and/or Themes (they can be mixed and matched) whenever you want to change the appearance of a document without actually using another template. The good news is that there's a "**Word 2003**" Style Set that applies single spacing with zero (0) spacing after (and also applies a 12-point font to body text); you can choose that Style Set from the drop-down on the Design tab and then make it the default, so that new blank documents use that line spacing. Or you can save the formatting of one of your own documents as a custom Style Set and make *that* the new default. (Instructions follow later in this section.)

However, that's only a partial solution because the default Theme still determines the default font face and color for body text, headings, and many other styles. Fortunately, it's easy to create custom Theme Fonts, and you can change the Theme Colors, too (and make them the defaults), if you're so inclined. But before we start fiddling with Style Sets and Themes, let's go over how to change the default font and the default paragraph formatting.

---

[4] If you work for an organization with an IT Department, it's likely that they have already changed the default settings for you.

[5] This Style Set resides in a file (a template) called **Default.dotx**.

Changing the Default Font

The default font works with the **Normal paragraph style** in a particular template. Changes you make to the default font will affect *only* that one paragraph style (as well as any other styles that are *based on* the Normal paragraph style) in *only* that one template. This limitation is important to understand from the outset because it explains why changing the default font isn't a complete solution – and why those ornery headings still use Calibri Light (and are blue!) or some other font that's not appropriate for legal documents. Still, it's a good place to start.

Incidentally, changing the default font is a much better option than selecting an entire document with Ctrl A and then applying your preferred font (as people often do). There are two main reasons: First, it's a temporary solution that affects only a single document, but secondly – and even more importantly – applying a font to the document affects only the text of the document, *not* the other "substructures" within the document such as headers, footers, and footnotes. For example, the font for the pleading line numbers, which are within the header, won't change if you use this method to change the font in the document.

If you change the default font from within a new blank document, the underlying template that will be affected is your Normal template (Normal.dotm). To change the default font for a different template, open either the template itself or a document based on the template.

Then open the **Font dialog**, using either of the following methods:

- Click the **dialog launcher** in the **Font group** on the **Home tab**; *or*
- Press **Ctrl D**.

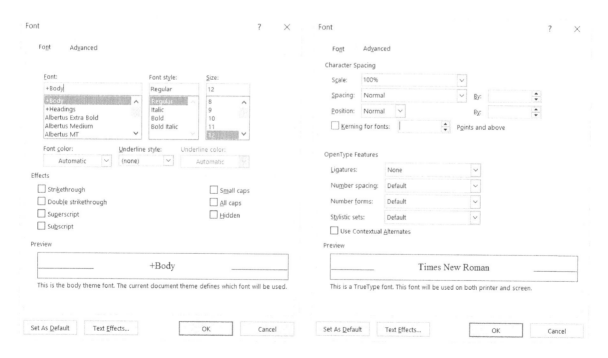

Font Dialog – Font Tab   **Font Dialog – Advanced Tab**

187

You might see a +Body designation at the top of the Font list. The +Body font, like the +Headings font, is a *placeholder* or *variable* that changes depending on which Theme has been applied. (Remember that Themes determine the default font face.) Because the font can change unexpectedly, ***avoid using the +Body placeholder*** for your default font.

Instead, select a specific ("fixed") font, such as Times New Roman, Courier New, or Helvetica. Be sure to choose the Regular style (as opposed to Italic, Bold, or Bold Italic) and a font size that is appropriate for body text (usually, that means 12 points).

CAUTION: Again, you might not think to do so, but you also need to check the font color settings. Locate the **Font color drop-down** underneath the font list and, if it says "**Automatic**," click the drop-down and then click one of the black squares ("Black, Text 1") to ensure that the default color will be black. Otherwise, the font color also could change depending on which Theme is applied to a particular document.

When everything looks correct, click the "**Set As Default**" **button** at the bottom of the dialog box. Word will prompt you to confirm that change, asking whether you want to change the default font to a certain typeface, size, and color, and if so, for "**This document only?**" or for "**All documents based on the Normal.dotm template?**" (If you are changing the font for some other template, you will see the name of that template instead of "Normal.dotm.")

If in fact you want all new documents based on the underlying template to use the font face, size, and color you've just selected, ***make sure to click the radio button to the left of "All documents..."*** – ordinarily, the other button ("This document only") is selected – and then click "**OK**." Otherwise, Word will change the default font ***only in the current document***, which probably is not your intention.

Click "All documents...," Then Click "OK"

It is important to recognize that modifying the default font in a particular template will not change the default font in any of your other templates. So you might need to repeat the above steps for other templates you use.

Changing the Default Font for Headings (and Other Styles)

Even after you have made the changes described in this section – changing the default font for body text as well as tweaking Style Sets and Theme Fonts – you might find that certain styles, including heading styles, still use a font you don't want. If that is the case, you'll have to modify those styles (to change the font from a +Headings or +Body placeholder to whichever specific font you wish to use). For instructions on how to modify a style, see the tutorial starting on page 391.

Modifying the "Normal" Paragraph Style

In addition to changing the default font for the underlying template, you might want to modify the **Normal paragraph style**. As mentioned previously, this style controls the default line spacing, justification, indentation, before and/or after spacing, and tab settings for most text, as well as for any styles that are *based on* the Normal style. Keep in mind that you can have different Normal paragraph styles for different templates.

The easiest way to modify the Normal paragraph style in the underlying template is by doing the following:

- Open the **Paragraph dialog** by clicking the **dialog launcher** in the **Paragraph group** on the **Home tab** (or using any other method you like).

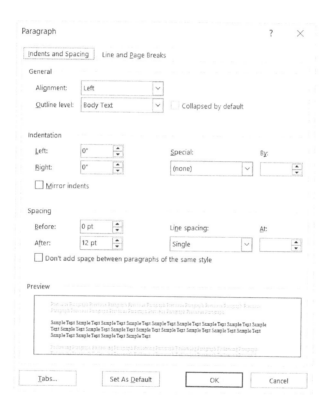

- Change the settings (on both tabs) to reflect your preferences.

    At a minimum, you'll want to set the default line spacing, as well as any spacing after that you desire. You can add a first-line indent if you want that to be the default. Also, you can turn Widow / Orphan control (on the Line and Spacing tab) on or off.

    Give each of these options some thought, since they will become the new default settings.

- Click the "**Save As Default**" button at the bottom of the dialog.

A prompt will appear, asking if you want to set the default alignment, indentation, and spacing of the paragraph for "**This document only?**" or "**All documents based on the Normal template?**" (if you are modifying the Normal style in a different template, you will see the name of that template instead).

- To apply the new settings to all future documents based on the underlying template, be sure to click the "**All documents...**" option.

- Finally, click "**OK**" to save your changes.

Easy, no? (You can repeat these steps in other templates if necessary.)

Next, I will walk you through changing the default Style Set – or creating a custom Style Set based on settings in one of your own documents. Both options are surprisingly easy.

Applying a Different Style Set – or Creating Your Own

Word 2016 comes with a number of different Style Sets, any of which you can make the default. They reside in a gallery that takes up the entire left side of the **Design tab**. (Like the Style Gallery on the Home tab, the Style Set Gallery consists of multiple rows, so be sure to expand the Gallery to see all of the available Style Sets.)

The Style Set Gallery

When you hold the mouse pointer over one of the icons, you'll see the name of that Style Set and, if there is text in your document, a Live Preview of how the text would look if you applied the Style Set by clicking it. You might not discern major differences, but if you apply one of the Style Sets and then right-click within the text and open the Paragraph dialog, you'll notice distinct variations in the line spacing and spacing after.

Another good way to see the differences among the Style Sets is to type a couple of paragraphs, then apply one of the Style Sets, such as Basic (Elegant), Minimalist, or Shaded. Then switch back to the Home tab and hold the mouse pointer over two or three of the heading styles to see how the various Style Sets would change the appearance of headings in your document.

As you can tell, most of the built-in Style Sets aren't appropriate for legal documents. However, toward the bottom of the gallery you'll find a "**Word 2003**" Style Set that looks pretty serviceable. It applies single spacing with no spacing after, and also applies a 12-point font, to regular (body) text. (In other words, it modifies the Normal paragraph style to use those settings.) Since most people seem to prefer those settings, why not simply apply that Style Set and choose it as the default?

You can. Just keep in mind that the Word 2003 Style Set isn't a total solution because it doesn't change the default fonts for body text and headings. *Those* settings derive from the default ***Theme*** ("Office"). So, unless you also create and apply your own Theme Fonts, you'll still end up with Calibri as your default font for body text and Cambria as your default font for headings.

In the next section, I will walk you through the process of creating your own custom Theme Fonts. But before doing so, I want to point out that if you aren't 100% sold on the Word 2003 Style Set, you can create your own custom Style Set simply by saving the settings in one of your own documents. Just open a document that is already formatted to your liking (i.e., with your preferred indents, line spacing, and before / after spacing).

When you position the mouse pointer over the first Style Set shown in the Gallery on the Design tab, you'll see the pop-up depicted at right. You can either follow the instructions and right-click the icon in the Gallery and then choose "**Save**" *or* click the **drop-down** at the right side of the Gallery and then click "**Save as a New Style Set...**"

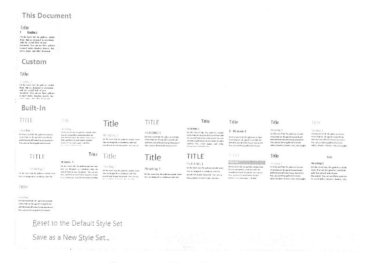

Save as a New Style Set...

Either way, a "**Save as a New Style Set**" dialog will open to the folder where Word stores and looks for Style Sets. Give the new Style Set a descriptive name (I've called mine "Single Spacing With 12 Pt After") – this is the name you'll see when you hover over the icon for the Style Set in the Gallery – and then click "**Save**." Word automatically assigns the file extension .dotx because Style Sets are templates.

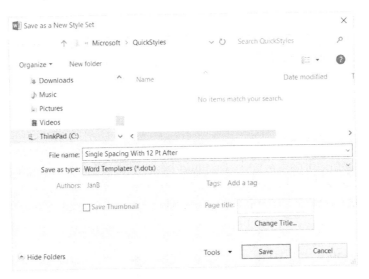

After you save your custom Style Set, it will be available in the Gallery and you can apply it to various documents. If you want to use that Style Set for all future documents, you can make it the default. First, however, let's review how Themes work and set up a custom set of Theme fonts.

Themes

Themes, which can be thought of as a layer placed on top of an underlying Style Set, consist of three main elements:

1. A set of **font faces** for regular (body) text and headings;

2. A **color scheme** similar to those found in PowerPoint presentations (matching various colors with various design elements, namely text, background, and "accents"); and

3. Styles for "**effects**" like graphic lines and fill.

For our purposes, the only aspect of Themes you really need to understand is how Themes affect font faces and font colors.

As mentioned earlier, each Theme has its own distinct fonts for body text and headings. When a particular Theme is in effect, its font attributes (font face and color) are applied by default to regular (body) text and heading styles.[6] Thus, if the Office Theme is active (as it is by default), body text will use Calibri font and headings will use Calibri Light, colored blue. It doesn't matter which Style Set you're using. If you superimpose the Office Theme on any of the various built-in Style Sets, the font faces and colors for body text and headings will change accordingly.

Just as a refresher, here is what is going on behind the scenes:

Many built-in paragraph styles in Word – including all of the Heading styles – use *variables* (*placeholders*) in lieu of specific fonts. These variables use the designation **+Body** (for regular body text) or **+Headings** (for heading styles). Whenever there is a +Body or +Headings designation associated with a style, the font for that style *will change depending on which Theme is applied*.

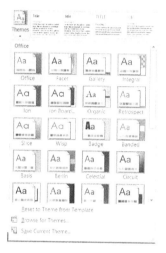

You can see this phenomenon in action by applying one or more of the built-in heading styles to some text (assuming that no one has modified the styles so that they use a specific font rather than the +Headings placeholder), then clicking the **Themes drop-down** at the left side of the **Design tab** and slowly moving the mouse pointer over a few of the icons that represent different themes. The formatting of the text appears to change – an example of the Live Preview feature.

Again, the font face and color change depending on the Theme that is in effect, even if you have changed the default font. The reason is that, as you'll recall, the default font *is applied only to the Normal paragraph style* (and any other styles that are based on Normal), not necessarily to any other built-in styles.

You'll also observe the same effects if you insert a shape such as an arrow or rectangle (Insert tab, Shapes) into your document. By default, the shape outline is blue, not black. That's because the shape takes on the "Accent 1" color assigned by the Office Theme, which is blue.

Creating Custom Theme Fonts

Although we found a built-in Style Set ("Word 2003") that works reasonably well for legal documents, none of the built-in Themes or sets of Theme Fonts is particularly apt. However, it's easy to create your own customized Theme Fonts for body text and headings and then make them the default. Doing so will ensure that your preferred font settings take effect in styles that use a placeholder (+Body or +Headings) instead of a specific font.[7]

---

[6] Keep in mind that themes work only in .docx files. They are disabled / grayed out when you are working on a .doc file (i.e., a file saved in Compatibility Mode).

[7] As an alternative, of course, you can modify styles that normally use a placeholder font – such as heading styles – and assign a specific font, then save the modified styles to the underlying template.

To create your own Theme Fonts, start from within a .docx file, rather than a .doc. (Remember that Themes are disabled in .doc files.) If necessary, just save a new blank document and make sure that the "Save as type" is "Word Document (*.docx)."

Navigate to the **Fonts drop-down**, which is about 2/3 of the way across the **Design tab**.

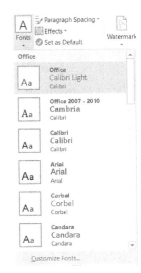

Click to open the drop-down, then click the "**Customize Fonts**" command at the bottom.

A **Create New Theme Fonts dialog** will open (see the screenshot below).

First, type a succinct and descriptive **name** for the new Theme (I've chosen "TNR" for mine, as shown in the screenshot below). Then use the drop-downs at the left side of the dialog to select a specific **Heading font** and a specific **Body font**. (Note that there is no option to choose a font *size* or a font *color*.) Finally, click **Save**.

After you save your Theme, you should see it in the "**Custom**" section at the top of the **Themes drop-down** on the **Layout tab** (screenshot at right).

To make your custom Theme the default, click to apply the theme in the current document, then click the green "**Set as Default**" **button** to the right of the "Fonts" drop-down.

A prompt will appear, asking if you want to set the current Style Set and Theme including Fonts, Colors, Effects and Paragraph Spacing as your default. The prompt indicates that the settings will be applied to all new blank documents.

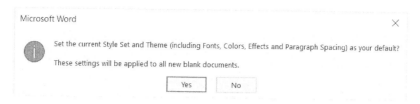

If you are certain you want to make both your new Theme and the current Style Set the default, click "**Yes**." Afterwards, your new Theme (as well as your new Style Set, if you created one), will be applied automatically to all new .docx files.

Modifying the Normal Template

One final item you might wish to change is the Normal template (Normal.dotm).[8]

Each user has a unique Normal template. It is located on the user's hard drive, not on a shared drive.[9] Under most circumstances, this template is the basis for all new documents. It contains default page formatting settings – page margins, margins for headers and footers, paper orientation (portrait versus landscape), and so forth – as well as default paragraph and font settings.

In addition, the Normal.dotm stores a number of user customizations, including formatted AutoCorrect entries (unformatted AutoCorrect entries are located in the user's application data folder in Windows); styles; keyboard shortcuts; and macros. In Word 2016, the Normal.dotm also stores AutoText entries.

Also, the "Zoom" (magnification") setting for documents based on this template – i.e., new blank documents – is stored in the template.

Should you wish to make "permanent" changes to any of these settings, you can do so by editing the Normal template directly.

To open your Normal template, press **Ctrl F12** or click **File**, **Open** and browse to this location: **C:\Users\<UserName>\AppData\Roaming\Microsoft\Templates**. (This is the location where the Normal.dotm template typically resides in Windows 7, 8, and 10.) If you see a file named Normal.dotm that appears to be relatively current, click to select it, then click "**Open**."[10]

---

[8] **NOTE**: The Normal template and the default Style Set are not the same thing, although they appear to work in concert. Among other differences, the latter does not store customized styles, macros, or keyboard shortcuts.

[9] Many organizations also make use of shared templates located on a network drive. You might or might not be able to modify any such shared templates.

[10] Be sure to *close all other documents* prior to opening the default template for editing.

CAUTION: Do *not* double-click the Normal.dotm template to open it, or you will open a new blank document based on the template, not the template itself. (You can tell if you have opened the template because you will see the file name – Normal.dotm – in the Word Title Bar.)

If you don't see the Normal.dotm template in that location, look in this location instead: **C:\ Users\<UserName>\Documents\Custom Office Templates**.

When the Normal.dotm template opens, make any modifications you want to the font face, size, and color; the line spacing (and spacing after); and the page margins.

ANOTHER CAUTION: Because the Normal.dotm is the basis for new blank documents, don't actually incorporate any text into the template. If you have inserted text while creating styles, Quick Parts, and the like, be sure to delete it before you save your modifications.

To change the zoom, click the **View tab**, click the Zoom button, and set your preferred magnification. Then click "**OK**" to save your changes.

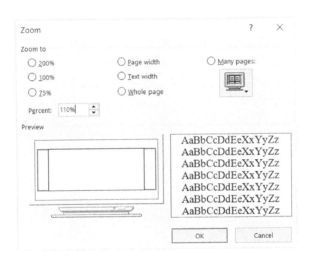

Before you click "Save" and close the template, you'll probably need to take one more step. The newer versions of Word won't save modifications that they don't recognize as substantive changes, so you might have to make a small change such as typing a character (or pressing the Spacebar) and then pressing the Backspace key. To determine whether this "change" is sufficient for Word to permit you to save the modified template, glance at the **Undo** button. If the button is grayed out (dimmed), you won't be able to save the template; if it isn't grayed out, you'll be able to save the template.[11]

Assuming that you have backspaced over the character or space and that the Undo button is active, click "Save" or press Ctrl S, then close the Normal.dotm template.

---

[11] Thanks to Word MVP Suzanne Barnhill for this tip. See in particular her very extensive FAQ, "How to change the default settings for new Word documents," which you can find here: http://wordfaqs.mvps.org/CustomizeNormalTemplate.htm.

A Last Resort: The Manage Styles Dialog

Every now and then, even after you have changed your default settings, you might notice that the font and/or paragraph settings in your new documents have changed. That is, for some reason your defaults didn't "stick."

What usually works in that even is to change the defaults from within the **Manage Styles** dialog.

1. To do so, open the **Styles Pane** by clicking the **dialog launcher** in the **Styles group** at the right side of the **Home tab** or press **Ctrl Alt Shift S**.

2. Navigate to the bottom of the **Styles Pane** and click the third button from the left.

3. When the **Manage Styles dialog** opens, click the "**Set Defaults**" tab.

4. Make any necessary changes.

5. Before closing the dialog, be sure to click the "**New documents based on this template**" radio button at the bottom so that the defaults will apply to all new blank documents.

6. Finally, click "**OK**."

QUICK TIP: Enable "Use the Insert Key to Control Overtype Mode"

Hiding demurely in the middle of the "Editing options" subcategory of the Advanced Word Options is an option labeled "**Use the Insert key to control overtype mode**."

You might be surprised to find that this setting is turned off by default. That is a change from pre-Word 2007 versions of Word—and from nearly all other Windows programs—in which the Insert key toggles between Insert mode (where new typing bumps existing text over to the right, rather than replacing it) and Typeover or Overtype mode (where new typing actually erases existing text).

Advanced	☐ Use the Insert key to control overtype mode
Customize Ribbon	☐ Use overtype mode

Upon reflection, it makes sense that Microsoft chose to disable this feature by default, considering how commonly people press the Insert key and end up overwriting existing text by accident. Still, considering what a radical departure this change represents, many people are caught off guard by it.

If you want to enable the option, making Word 2016 behave more like traditional Windows programs, click the **File tab**, **Options**, **Advanced**, locate the settings in the "**Editing options**" section, and just click the first checkbox ("**Use the Insert key to control overtype mode**"). Watch out, though: The *second* checkbox (labeled "Use overtype mode") makes Typeover / Overtype the default, which is neither the norm nor the mode that most people prefer.

PART V: Everyday Features Demystified

General Formatting Tips

Before we jump in and explore specific features, let's review some helpful general tips about the types of formatting that are available in Word and how to apply them.

We've already discussed paragraph formatting (but we'll go over that again momentarily). Besides paragraph formatting, there is page (section) formatting and character formatting. Let's take a closer look at each.

Paragraph Formatting

Paragraph formatting mostly encompasses features that you can apply from the Paragraph groups on the Home and Layout tabs, as well as from the Paragraph dialog. In other words, it includes the following:

- Justification
- Indentation
- Line Spacing
- Before and After Spacing
- Bulleted Lists
- Numbered Lists (and Multilevel Lists)
- Tabs
- Widow / Orphan Control
- Keep with next
- Keep lines together
- Paragraph Borders
- Paragraph Shading

To apply paragraph formatting, do one of the following:

- Click anywhere within a single paragraph (you don't need to select / highlight the paragraph), and then apply the formatting; or
- Select / highlight multiple paragraphs, and then apply the formatting.

To select / highlight several paragraphs that are contiguous (next to one another), select the first one, then drag the mouse pointer across the other paragraphs.

To select / highlight several paragraphs that are *not* contiguous (next to one another), select the first one, press and hold the Ctrl key, and then drag the mouse pointer across the other paragraphs.

Again, you can apply formatting directly from the icons and/or drop-downs in either of the Paragraph groups in the Ribbon (Home tab, Layout tab); from the Paragraph dialog; or by using a keyboard shortcut.

Keyboard Shortcuts for Working With Paragraphs

Alt, O, P: Opens the Paragraph dialog

Ctrl 1:   Applies Single Spacing

Ctrl 2:   Applies Double Spacing

Ctrl 5:   Applies 1.5 Spacing

Ctrl 0 (zero):   Press once to add 12 pt Before spacing; press again to remove the added spacing.

Ctrl Shift C: Copy paragraph formatting from the current paragraph

Ctrl Shift V: Paste paragraph formatting

Ctrl Q: Remove direct (manually applied) paragraph formatting (revert to default paragraph settings)

Ctrl M: Increase the Left indent by one tab stop each time you press the key combination

Ctrl T: Increase the Hanging indent by one tab stop each time you press the key combination

Page (Section) Formatting

Page formatting, also known as section formatting, is applied to one or more entire pages. It includes features that you can apply from the Page Setup group on the Layout tab or from the Page Background group in the Design tab, as well as a couple of other important ones:

- Page Margins
- Orientation (Portrait or Landscape)
- Page (Paper) Size
- Columns
- Line Numbers
- Watermarks
- Page Color
- Page Borders
- Headers and Footers
- Page Numbering

Character Formatting

In general, character formatting means anything having to do with fonts, including the features that can be applied from the Font group in the Home tab or from the Font dialog:

- Font face
- Font size
- Color
- Bold, underlining, italics
- Case of letters (CAPS, lower case, Sentence case., Capitalize Each Word, tOGGLE cASE)
- Strikeout
- Subscript / Superscript
- Font effects (also known as Text Effects), such as reflection, glow, outline, engraving, etc.
- Small caps / All caps
- Highlighting

Keyboard Shortcuts for Applying Font Formatting

Ctrl D: Opens the Font dialog

Ctrl]:   Increases the font size of selected text by one point each time you press the key combination

Ctrl [:   Decreases the font size of selected text by one point each time you press the key combination

Ctrl Shift >:   Increases the font size of selected text by two points each time you press the key combination

Ctrl Shift <:   Decreases the font size of selected text by two points each time you press the key combination

Ctrl Alt H – Applies highlighting to selected text

Applying Formatting to an Entire Document

To apply paragraph formatting or font formatting to an entire document, you can select the document by pressing Ctrl A, then applying the desired formatting. Note, however, that this method typically will not change the formatting of document "substructures" such as headers, footers, and footnotes.

To change the paragraph or font formatting of the entire document *including* headers, footers, and footnotes, open the paragraph or font dialog, make your desired changes, and click the "Set As Default" button at the bottom of the dialog. A prompt will appear, asking if you want to apply the default settings to the current document or to the template underlying the document. If you want to change the paragraph or font formatting only in the current document, choose that option.

* * * * *

The remainder of this section of the book covers a range of features that are commonly used to format legal documents. To the best of my ability, I've tried to follow the same organization as in the general introduction – that is, starting with paragraph formatting, then moving to page (section) formatting, then character (font) formatting. Toward the end of this section, I review a few features that don't fall neatly into any of those three main categories.

PARAGRAPH FORMATTING

General Rules About Paragraph Formatting

As I have mentioned elsewhere, the paragraph is the basic formatting unit in Word. Even in a blank document, before you start typing, a paragraph mark appears when you turn on Show / Hide. That's because Word is already "thinking" in terms of paragraphs.

I've also mentioned that paragraph formatting is stored in the (ordinarily hidden) paragraph mark at the end of a paragraph and – usually – gets copied to the next paragraph when you press the Enter key. (There is a significant exception to this rule, which involves Styles. For more details, see the section about Styles starting on page 385, and especially page 391.)

It's worth repeating that the features in this section are applied paragraph by paragraph, and they affect the entire paragraph. These features are available from the Paragraph dialog and/or from the Paragraph group in the Home tab and/or the Paragraph group in the Layout tab. They include:

- Justification / Alignment
- Indents (paragraph margins, as well as the indentation of the first line of a paragraph)
- Line Spacing
- Before and After Spacing
- Tabs
- Widow / Orphan Control
- Keep with next
- Keep lines together
- Bulleted lists
- Automatic numbered lists
- Multilevel lists
- Paragraph Background (if any)
- Paragraph Borders (if any)

To apply paragraph formatting to a single paragraph, click anywhere within the paragraph and then apply the attribute(s) (you don't have to select / highlight the paragraph first).

To apply paragraph formatting to multiple paragraphs, select / highlight the paragraphs and then apply the attribute(s). **NOTE:** This step is necessary only when you are applying formatting to text that has already been typed.

By the way, you can select paragraphs that are not contiguous – next to each other – by selecting / highlighting one paragraph, pressing and holding the Ctrl key, and then dragging the mouse pointer across other paragraphs. When you release the Ctrl key, the paragraphs should remain selected so that you can apply formatting to all of the paragraphs at once.

207

Justification (Alignment)

Justification (alignment), which like the other features described in this section is applied paragraph by paragraph and affects the entire paragraph, is one of the easiest features to use.

To change the justification of a single paragraph, click within the paragraph and then do one of the following:

- Click the appropriate justification button in the Paragraph group on the Home tab; *or*

- Apply justification from the Alignment drop-down on the Indents and Spacing tab of the Paragraph dialog; *or*

- Press the keyboard shortcut for the type of justification you wish to use (Ctrl L for Left; Ctrl R for Right; Ctrl J for Justify / Full Justification; or Ctrl E for Center).

NOTE: Because justification is applied to an entire paragraph, it is more difficult in Word than in WordPerfect to have left-aligned, centered, and right-aligned text on a single line. (In WordPerfect, you can apply formatting to individual bits of text within one line, but Word thinks of those bits of text as belonging to the same paragraph and gets confused. After all, how can a paragraph be left justified, centered, and right justified at the same time?)

For the solution(s), keep reading.

Using Left, Center, and Right Alignment on One Line

WordPerfect's text-stream formatting makes it easy to put left-aligned, centered, and right-aligned text on the same line. In Word, this task is complicated by the fact that Word considers text typed on the same line to be part of paragraph—and, not surprisingly, the program can't figure out how to format one paragraph so that it uses three different types of justification.

Fortunately, there are a few reasonably good workarounds available. To left justify, center justify, and right justify text on the same line in Word, do one of the following:

1.   Use Word's "**Click and Type**" feature (similar to the Shadow Cursor in WordPerfect): Type some text at the left margin, then slide the mouse pointer to the right until you see an I-beam with a "shadow" that looks like several centered lines. **Double-click** to position the cursor, and then type the text you want centered.

     Then slide the mouse pointer farther to the right until you see an I-beam with a "shadow" that consists of lines at the left side of the I-beam. **Double-click**, then type the text you want right-justified.[1]

2.   Alternatively, use the Tab dialog or the horizontal Ruler to set a center tab and a right tab at appropriate intervals. If you are using 1" left and right margins, the center tab should be at approximately 3.25" and the right tab at approximately 6.5". If you are using the Ruler, you might have to position the right tab shy of the 6.5" mark and then drag it over. (**NOTE**: It's best to set the tabs *before* you begin typing; that way, your settings will apply to the entire document.)

     A corollary to this tip: Headers and footers in Word are automatically configured with a center tab and a right tab, so all you need to do to center and/or right-align text in a header or footer is press the Tab key the appropriate number of times.

     CAUTION: Depending on the document margins, you might have to adjust the center tab and the right tab within your header and footer screen. You can do so by dragging each tab stop to the correct position, or you can "alignment tabs," which are positioned relative to the page margins (and which automatically adjust if you change the margins). For an extended discussion of this feature, see the section starting on page 228. Keep in mind that alignment tabs work only in .docx files (and other Open Office XML file types), *not* in .doc files (Word's older file format).

---

[1] This feature must be enabled in the Word Options. It is enabled by default, but if it doesn't appear to be working, click the **File tab**, **Options**, **Advanced**, and click to check "**Enable click and type**." Note that when you double-click to position the cursor at the center, Word inserts a center tab at that position; when you do the same at the right margin, Word inserts a right tab.

It's easy to change the tab settings within headers and footers within a particular document by turning on the Ruler and dragging the tab markers. (You'll need to do so within both the header editing screen and the footer editing screen if you want the header and footer settings to be the same. Also, if you have multiple headers and/or footers, you'll have to change the settings in each section.) However, if you want to use the new tab settings in all future documents, you must either (1) modify the Footer style and save the modified style to the template or (2) modify the underlying template.

3.   Create a three-column table and apply different justification in each of the three cells. (**NOTE**: If you use this method, you probably will have to turn off the table border to prevent it from printing along with the text. To do so, insert your cursor into a table, then click the **Borders drop-down arrow** at the right side of the **Table Styles group** and click **No Borders**.)

Different Ways to Apply Line Spacing

Many people – including lots of long-time Word users – don't realize that line spacing is considered an attribute of a paragraph. Because it falls into this category, line spacing can be applied from the Paragraph dialog box (though there are other ways, which I'll discuss below and in the "Simplified Steps" section).

Like all of the other features described in this "Paragraph Formatting" section, line spacing can be applied to one paragraph at a time by clicking anywhere within a single paragraph and then choosing the spacing (you don't have to select / highlight the paragraph).

As you know by now, if you set line spacing before you start typing, the spacing will carry over from paragraph to paragraph until you change it. However, as you also know, to change the line spacing of more than one paragraph of *existing* text, you must select the text first.[1]

Line Spacing Options and How to Apply Them

Keyboard Shortcuts

For simple single or double spacing (which is fine for most documents, with the notable exception of legal pleadings where the text has to align with line numbers in the left margin), you can use the keyboard shortcuts **Ctrl 1** (single spacing) and **Ctrl 2** (double spacing). For 1.5 spacing, you can press **Ctrl 5**.

Line and Paragraph Spacing Drop-Down

There's also a **drop-down** toward the middle of the **Paragraph group** in the **Home tab** that provides several different choices.

The Line Spacing Button in the Paragraph Group

As shown in the screenshots, you can apply single spacing, 1.15 line spacing (the default line spacing for Word 2007 and Word 2010, but *not* for Word 2016[2]), 1.5 spacing, 2.0, 2.5, or 3.0. Or you can click "Line Spacing Options…" to open the **Paragraph dialog** and choose among more advanced options.

---

[1] Unlike in WordPerfect, changing the line spacing of a single paragraph will not affect subsequent existing text. That is, the line spacing you set in Word doesn't flow forward.

[2] The default line spacing for Word 2016, and for Word 2013 as well, is 1.08 lines.

The bottom two options will alternate depending on whether Before and/or After spacing has been applied to the paragraph your cursor is in. You will see some combination of "Add Space Before Paragraph," "Remove Space Before Paragraph," "Add Space After Paragraph," and "Remove Space After Paragraph," as appropriate.

When you add Before or After spacing with this method, Word typically adds 12 points.

The Paragraph Dialog

For anything more complex, use the **Paragraph dialog** and choose one of the other options. As discussed in more detail in the section starting on page 128, those options include At Least, Exactly, and Multiple spacing.

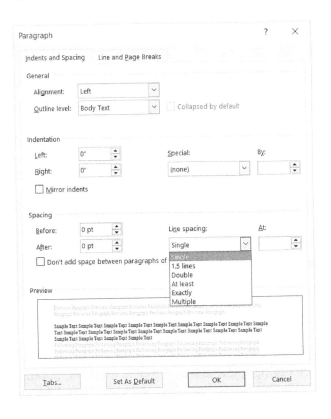

Paragraph Spacing Drop-Down on the Design Tab

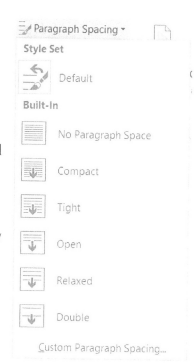

Another method of applying line spacing is by using the **"Paragraph Spacing" drop-down** toward the right side of the **Design tab**.

I don't recommend this method because (1) I think it's confusing; and (2) most of the choices aren't appropriate for legal document formatting. But let me walk you through what this drop-down does.

Essentially, it offers built-in "Style Sets" (mini-styles created by Microsoft) that apply specific line spacing and before / after spacing. Note that these "Style Sets" become the default line spacing for *the entire document*. You still can apply your preferred spacing (including any before/after spacing) to one or more paragraphs, and your manual formatting of those paragraphs will override the Style Set, but *the underlying line spacing for that document* will change to whichever Style Set you choose. That can lead to unexpected, and undesirable, results.

The Style Sets available are as follows:

- Default = 1.08 line spacing with 8 points after;

- No Paragraph Space = single spacing with 0 before / 0 after;

- Compact = single spacing with 4 pts after;

- Tight = 1.15 line spacing with 6 points after;

- Open = 1.15 line spacing with 10 points after; and

- Relaxed = 1.5 with 6 points after

Note that if you click "**Custom Paragraph Spacing**," Word does *not* open the Paragraph dialog. Instead, it opens the **Manage Styles dialog**. If you like, you can change the default font as well as the default line spacing (and before / after spacing) for the underlying template from within this dialog. However, *this feature can be quirky*. I prefer to set those defaults from the Font dialog and the Paragraph dialog. To me, the Manage Styles dialog is a last resort to use if your settings don't stick. More on this feature / issue on page 197.

Adjusting Line Spacing – Simplified Steps

For each of the methods described below, start by placing your cursor anywhere within a single paragraph *or* select multiple paragraphs. Then follow the steps.

Keyboard Shortcuts

- For single spacing, press **Ctrl 1**
- For double spacing, press **Ctrl 2**
- For 1.5 spacing, press **Ctrl 5**

Line and Paragraph Spacing Drop-Down in Paragraph Group on Home Tab

- Locate the Line and Paragraph Spacing drop-down in the Paragraph group on the home tab and click the arrow;

- Choose one of the pre-sets (1.0, 1.15, 1.5, 2.0, 2.5, or 3.0); or

- Choose "Line Spacing Options," which opens the Paragraph dialog so that you can choose one of the options under Spacing, Line spacing.

    o Those options include Single, Double, 1.5, Exactly, At Least, and Multiple.

      ▪ For a discussion of Exactly, At Least, and Multiple, see the section starting on page 128.

Paragraph Dialog

- Open the Paragraph dialog in one of the following ways:

    o Right-click and choose Paragraph; *or*
    o Click the dialog launcher in the Paragraph group on the Home tab; *or*
    o Click the dialog launcher in the Paragraph group on the Layout tab, and then:

- Choose one of the options under Spacing, Line spacing

    o Those options include Single, Double, 1.5, Exactly, At Least, and Multiple.

      ▪ For a discussion of Exactly, At Least, and Multiple, see the section starting on page 128.

For a discussion of Spacing Before and Spacing After, which you can use to add white space *between* paragraphs ("paragraph spacing"), see the section starting on page 129.

SIDEBAR: What Are Points, Anyway?

One of the line spacing options in Word is "Exactly" line spacing, which usually is configured in *points*. In my experience, although many people have heard the term "points," few have a clear understanding of what it means.

In typography, a point (abbreviated "pt") is a fixed unit of measurement representing the *height* of the characters. (The term "*pitch*" represents the *width* of the characters.)

There are 72 points in an inch. Twelve (12) points – 1/6 of an inch – is approximately one line. However, Exactly 12 pt line spacing *isn't* the same as single spacing. Text to which Exactly 12 pt line spacing has been applied is more compressed vertically (i.e., more "squished") than single-spaced text created with the same font. Likewise, text to which Exactly 24 points line spacing has been applied is more compressed vertically than double-spaced text.

You can test for yourself. Type two short paragraphs that are at least two lines long. Apply single spacing to one of the paragraphs and Exactly 12 pt spacing to the other. Can you see a difference in terms of the height of the characters and how much white space exists between the lines of the paragraphs? It is even more noticeable if you apply double spacing to one of the paragraphs and Exactly 24 pt to the other.

When should you use points ("Exactly" line spacing)? Typically, you'll use points only in pleadings (litigation documents) where the text is supposed to align with line numbers embedded in the left margin. (This is a standard requirement for pleadings filed in California courts, including Federal District Court in California, and for certain other jurisdictions.) Because the line numbers use "Exactly" line spacing, *you must use that same spacing for all of the "pleading double spaced" text* (my term), or the text will get out of alignment with the line numbers. And your "pleading single spaced" text must be half that size.

For letters, contracts, estate documents, and the like, simple single and double spacing usually work fine. Pleadings with line numbers are different because of the importance of getting the text to align with the line numbers.

The ideal setting for a California pleading template, in my opinion, spaces the line numbers Exactly 24 points apart. (Again, the line spacing of the pleading line numbers is what determines the line spacing for your "pleading double spaced" text.) What makes that figure ideal is that it is easy to halve for the "pleading single spaced" text (Exactly 12 points).

Don't assume that every pleading uses Exactly 24 points / Exactly 12 points. The spacing of the pleading line numbers can vary from document to document, especially if you are working with pleadings obtained from other organizations. To determine the correct setting for line spacing in a specific document, you must go into the document's header, right-click within the line numbers, choose "Paragraph," and make note of the line spacing – that is, the number of points displayed under Spacing, Line spacing, Exactly. Your "pleading double spacing" must match that figure; your "pleading single spacing" must be half that figure. (Word usually rounds up to the first decimal place, so if your pleading line numbers are set at Exactly 22.75 points and you configure your "pleading single spacing" to be 11.375 points, Word probably will change that figure to 11.4.)

If you are still confused by the concept of "pleading double spacing" based on points, this summary might help:

- Points (often abbreviated as "pt") indicate the *height* of typed characters;

- There are 72 points in an inch;

- Exactly 12 pt spacing approximates one line of text, although it isn't the same as single spacing;

- Pleadings that embed line numbers in the left margin use line spacing based on points;

- The "pleading double spacing" you should use in your document is determined by *the line spacing of the line numbers in the left margin*, typically a figure such as Exactly 22.75 pt, Exactly 22.65 pt, Exactly 23.15 pt, Exactly 24 pt, or something similar;

- The "pleading single spacing" in your document must be *exactly half* the "pleading double spacing" (again, based on the line spacing of the pleading line numbers);

- "Exactly" spacing is more compressed vertically (more "squished," if you prefer) than true double (or single) spacing; and

- If you use true double and single spacing, rather than the "Exactly" figure that has been applied to the pleading line numbers, the document text will get out of alignment with the line numbers. The same is true if you use an incorrect "Exactly" figure, such as Exactly 24 points when the pleading line spacing is actually set to Exactly 22.75 pt or Exactly 23.15 pt.

- To determine the spacing of the line numbers, go into the header of any page of the pleading (by double-clicking in the white space at the top of the page or by right-clicking in the same location, then choosing "Edit Header"), right-click somewhere in the line numbers, click "**Paragraph**," and when the **Paragraph dialog** opens, make note of the line spacing.

This issue is discussed in detail in other sections of the book, including "Aligning Text With Pleading Line Numbers" (see pages 457 and following).

QUICK TIP: Setting Line Height

In Word, you can approximate the "Line Height" feature found in WordPerfect in a couple of ways.

One way is to use "**Exactly**" line spacing. As noted in the previous section, as well as in the discussion about line spacing starting on page 128, this option – found in the **Paragraph dialog** on the **Line spacing** drop-down menu – lets you fine-tune character height down to fractions of a point. (For what it's worth, there are 72 points per inch; one point is one-twelfth of a pica.)   You might have to experiment somewhat to get the precise measurement you want; if you normally use 12-point spacing, try 11 or 11.5 (unless, of course, you are formatting a pleading or other type of document that requires you to use a 12-point or larger font).

Another way is to use "**Multiple**" line spacing and set the spacing to a number less than 1 – for example, .97 or .94. Again, you might have to experiment to get the setting just right.

TROUBLESHOOTING TIP: Where'd That Line Come From?

If the automatic borders feature is turned on – which it is by default in Word 2016 – pressing the hyphen key three times, then pressing Enter, produces a horizontal line. That's great if you intended to create a line, but disquieting if you didn't! How do you get rid of it?

If you're quick enough, you can undo the line by clicking the **Undo button**, by pressing **Ctrl Z**, or by clicking the **AutoCorrect Options icon** that pops up when you insert an automatic border. Clicking the AutoCorrect Options icon opens a drop-down that offers three choices: **Undo Border Line**, **Stop Automatically Creating Border Lines** (which turns off the automatic borders), and **Control AutoFormat Options** (which takes you into Word Options so that you can configure the AutoCorrect options to your liking).

If you don't notice the line immediately, or you notice it but don't take action right away to remove the line, you can delete it later. To do so, display the non-printing characters by clicking the **Paragraph icon (¶)** in the **Paragraph group** on the **Home tab** (*or by pressing* **Ctrl Shift * [asterisk]**). Locate and delete the paragraph mark just *above* the line. (That almost always works, but if it doesn't, try deleting the paragraph mark *below* the line.)

Another way to delete the line – it's actually a paragraph border – is to click on the line, then locate the **Borders drop-down** in the **Paragraph group** on the **Home tab** (it's just below the Paragraph icon / pilcrow), click the Borders drop-down, then click **No Border**. See the screenshot at right.

To turn off automatic borders altogether, click the **File tab**, **Options**, **Proofing**, **AutoCorrect Options**, **AutoFormat As You Type tab**, and *uncheck* **Border lines**.

218

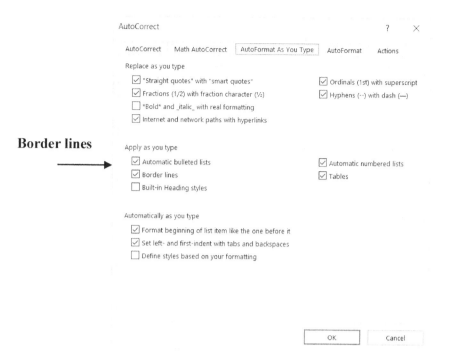

Border lines →

AutoFormat As You Type Tab

NOTE: Be sure to explore the AutoCorrect Options on the AutoFormat As You Type tab and uncheck any that you don't want (note that some options appear on both that tab and the AutoFormat tab; however, the options on the AutoFormat tab don't go into effect automatically, so you don't need to uncheck any of them).

You can learn more about automatic formatting options by clicking the question mark in the upper right-hand corner of the **AutoCorrect dialog**. That opens the Word 2016 Help screen pictured at right.

If you scroll down, you'll see descriptions of each automatic formatting option.

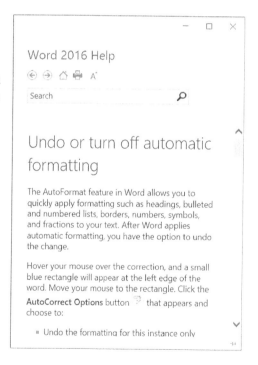

219

Indenting Paragraphs

Like line spacing, indentation is an attribute of paragraphs that you set from the **Indents and Spacing tab** of the **Paragraph dialog box**. Again, you can open the Paragraph dialog by clicking the **dialog launcher** in the **Paragraph group** on the **Home tab**; by **right-clicking** within a paragraph and choosing "**Paragraph**"; or by pressing **Alt O, P**). By default, the Paragraph dialog opens to the Indents and Spacing tab. See the screenshot below; both tabs of the Paragraph dialog are shown on page 124.

Using the Paragraph Dialog to Set Indentation

People frequently ask me how to set the left and right indentation of a paragraph (the paragraph margins) in order to format block quotes in a pleading. Typically you set the indents manually from the Paragraph dialog.

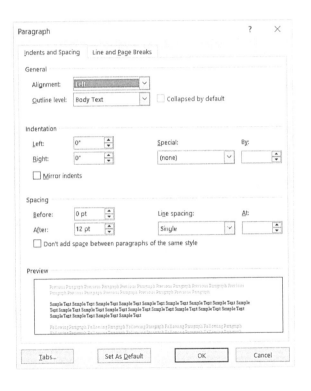

"**Left**" and "**Right**" set the indents for the whole paragraph

"**Before**" and "**After**" spacing – to add white space between paragraphs

"**Special**" – options for indenting the first line of a paragraph (**none, First Line Indent,** or **Hanging**)

There is no single key combination built into Word for setting a left and right indent for the paragraph, as there is in WordPerfect. However, you can create *a style* to set a left and right indent and then assign a keyboard shortcut to that style. For instructions, see the Sidebar starting on page 408.

To indent the whole paragraph *from the left only*, you can set the Left indent within the Paragraph dialog *or* use the keyboard shortcut **Ctrl M**. Each time you press Ctrl M, the left indent increases by one tab stop. (This function is similar to using the F7 key in WordPerfect – or F4 if you use WordPerfect's DOS-compatible keyboard.) To reverse the indent by one tab stop, press **Ctrl Shift M** (hold down Ctrl and Shift and tap "M.")

The "**Special**" drop-down in the Paragraph dialog is used for formatting the indentation of ***the first line of the paragraph***. If "Special" is set to "**(none)**," the first line indentation is the same as the left indent of the entire paragraph.

If you choose the "**First line indent**" option, Word automatically indents the first line – i.e., positions it farther to the right than the rest of the paragraph – by whatever measurement you choose. The default is .5" (half an inch) (so that the first line starts half an inch to the right of the Left indent set for the whole paragraph), but you can change this setting by typing a different figure or using the "spinner" arrows to increase or decrease the number.

Another choice under "Special" is **Hanging Indent**. With a hanging indent, Word "outdents"[1] the first line—i.e., positions it farther to the left than the rest of the paragraph. The default setting is .5" (half an inch) (so that the first line starts half an inch to the left of the Left indent set for the whole paragraph), but again, you can change this setting.

Hanging indents are commonly used in bibliographies. They are seldom used in legal document formatting, but be on the alert because this type of indent ***is the default setting for numbered lists*** and certain other items in Word. When you encounter it, you might have to change the setting, which you can do either from within the Paragraph dialog or from the Ruler.

Hanging indents actually are very useful for certain types of formatting. For instance, they are used with numbered and lettered headings so that the number or letter is out to the left, but if the heading goes beyond a single line, the text of the heading wraps back to the first word in the first line of the heading, not all the way back to the position of the number or letter. Sometimes when people don't use a hanging indent with a numbered or lettered heading, they end up tabbing subsequent lines of the heading to try to line them up with the first word in the first line, which – as you know if you've been in this situation – causes all kinds of problems.

Using the Ruler to Set Indentation

You might find that you prefer using the Paragraph dialog to adjust indents because this method can be more precise than using the Ruler. However, you can use the Ruler to accomplish the same task.[2]

To set indents with the Ruler, position your cursor in the paragraph you want to adjust and drag one or more of the **Indent Markers**.

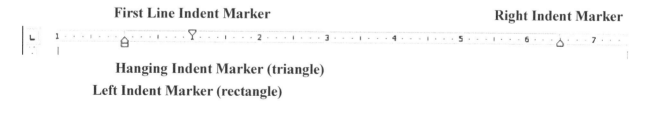

---

[1] I don't like that term – it strikes me as "technobabble" – but it gets the point across.

[2] If the Ruler is not displayed, click the **View tab** and click to check the "**Ruler**" check box (toward the left side, in the **Show group**).

The down-pointing triangle (shown at the 1" mark in the screenshot above) controls the first line of the paragraph your cursor is in. You can drag that triangle—appropriately called the **First Line Indent Marker** – to indent the first line of the paragraph by as much as you like. (This function is the equivalent of using "Special, First Line Indent" in the Paragraph dialog.) At the 1" position as in the screenshot, it sets a first-line indent of one inch. If it were in its default position at the left side of the Ruler, there would be no first-line indent – i.e., the first line would begin flush with the left margin.

The up-pointing triangle at the bottom of the Ruler controls the indentation of the remainder of the paragraph – i.e., *every line except the first*. It is the **Hanging Indent Marker**. If you click within the triangle and then drag it, dragging the marker does not affect the first line of the paragraph. In fact, you'll note that the First Line Indent Marker doesn't move. This function is the equivalent of using "Special, Hanging Indent" in the Paragraph dialog.

By contrast, the rectangle at the bottom left of the Ruler (the **Left Indent Marker**) controls *the left indentation of the entire paragraph*. When you click within the rectangle and then drag it, *both the First Line Indent and the Left Indent markers move*. They retain the same relationship with each other as before you dragged the Left Indent marker to one side. So, for example, if you originally had a first-line indent of .5" and a left indent of 0 (zero) – meaning that the left margin of the paragraph was flush left, not indented at all – and you drag the rectangle (Left Indent Marker) over to the 1" mark on the Ruler, the First Line Indent Marker will move over .5" to the right of the Left Indent Marker and will end up at 1.5".

CAUTION: The fact that the Hanging Indent Marker (triangle) and the Left Indent Marker (rectangle), which are attached, work independently of each other – and produce different results – can be very confusing. And it is easy to click and drag the Left Indent Marker by accident when you are trying to drag the Hanging Indent marker. It takes a certain amount of practice to get it right.

To see how these indent markers work in practice, experiment with them. You'll quickly see their utility.

SIDEBAR: Why Do Those Thunderbolts Keep Popping Up?

Sometimes when you press a key (or key combination), a small icon with a thunderbolt on it pops up. Many people barely notice – I can't tell you how many times my trainees have said, "Oh, I did see that, but I didn't know what it was, so I ignored it."

The thunderbolts – technically, they're called AutoCorrect Options icons – actually can be important. They are Word's way of signaling you that the program is about to apply some automatic formatting, and it's asking if it has guessed correctly about what you are trying to do.

For example, you might see a thunderbolt icon when you press the Tab key to indent the first line of a paragraph. Word guesses that you might prefer to indent the first line automatically, so that you don't have to press Tab every time you start a new paragraph. That might be your intention, but it might not be – so Word applies an automatic indent instead of a Tab, but then checks with you.

When you position the mouse pointer over the thunderbolt, an arrow appears. Clicking the arrow reveals a menu with three different choices. In this case, those choices are: Change Back to Tab (i.e., change the automatic indent back to a Tab just this once), Stop Setting Indent on Tabs and Backspace (i.e., change it back and *never do it again*!), and Control AutoFormat Options… (i.e., take me to the AutoFormat As You Type tab in the Word Options so that I can play with the configuration options directly).

Whenever you see a thunderbolt, there will always be three choices with respect to the automatic formatting Word has applied: (1) change it back to the way it was ***this time only***; (2) change it back and ***never do it again***; and (3) take me to the Word Options so that I can fiddle with the settings myself.

Incidentally, the thunderbolt icon disappears as soon as you resume typing. Be aware that when you do, Word retains the automatic formatting that it applied. The assumption seems to be that if you didn't intend to use it, you would have opened the drop-down and chosen the second or third option. At least now you know!

Setting (and Deleting / Clearing) Tabs

There are a couple of ways to set tabs in Word 2016. You can set them directly on the **horizontal Ruler**, or you can use the **Tabs dialog box**.

Using the Ruler

To display the horizontal Ruler, click the **View tab**, navigate to the **Show group** (toward the left), and click to check the **Ruler** checkbox.

By default, tab stops are set every half inch.

To insert custom tab stops directly on the Ruler, choose the appropriate tab type (if necessary) by clicking the **Tab type button** at the far left of the Ruler. The "L" symbol sets Left tabs; the upside-down "T" symbol sets Center tabs; the backwards "L" symbol sets Right tabs; and the inverted "T" with a period to the right of the bar of the "T" sets Decimal Tabs.

Centered　　　　　　　**Right**　　　　　　　**Decimal**

Once you have the Tab type button set the way you want, just left-click at the point on the Ruler where you want to insert a tab stop. If you need to reposition the tab indicator, you can drag it to the left or right. (To clear tab settings, just drag the tab indicator off the Ruler.)

Tab type button　　　　　　　　　　　　　　　　　　　**Click to add tab stop**

CAUTION: Be aware that when you set individual tabs, *any existing tabs to the left of your custom settings will be cleared*. In other words, if you add a tab at 1.5", Word will delete the tabs set at .5" and 1"! "! In other words, you are not merely *adding* a tab stop; you're actually *replacing* any and all of the existing tabs set to the left of your first tab stop.

Again, keep in mind that in Word, tab formatting is associated with *paragraphs*. Thus, if you change tab settings before you start typing or while you are typing, the new settings (which are stored in the paragraph mark at the end of the paragraph) will be copied to successive paragraphs when you press the Enter key. However, if you need to adjust tab settings in a portion of the document you have already typed, *you must select the paragraph(s) you want the new settings to affect* before changing the tab settings.

Using the Tabs Dialog

You can open the **Tabs dialog** in at least three different ways.

For one, there is a **Tabs…** button at the bottom left side of the **Paragraph dialog**.[1] Click that button to open the **Tabs dialog**.

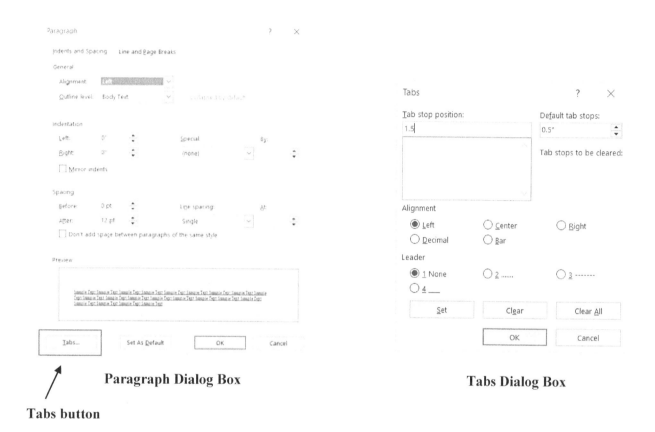

Paragraph Dialog Box   **Tabs Dialog Box**

Tabs button

Note as well that you can open the Tabs dialog directly by double-clicking a tab stop on the Ruler, although this method requires a certain amount of manual dexterity. (**CAUTION**: If you double-click the top border of the Ruler or a portion of the Ruler that is outside the page margins, the Page Setup dialog opens instead).

Or you can use the keyboard shortcut **Alt O, T**.

---

[1] To open the Paragraph dialog, click the dialog launcher in the Paragraph group on the Home tab *or* click the dialog launcher in the Paragraph group on the Layout tab *or* right-click within a paragraph *or* hold down the Alt key and tap the letters O, P in sequence (think "**O**pen **P**aragraph")

As mentioned earlier, the default setting for tab stops is every half inch. To change this setting (perhaps you'd prefer default tab stops every .25" or every inch), just type a new setting in the Default tab stops field or use the arrows ("spinners") to adjust the setting.

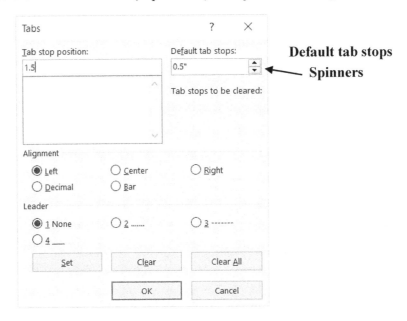

To set custom tabs by using the Tabs Dialog Box, do the following:

1. Type a setting (a number corresponding to the tab position) in the **Tab stop position box**.

2. Set the **alignment** if necessary (Left, Center, Right, Decimal, or Bar[2]).

3. Set any desired **Leader** (dots, hyphens, underscores, etc.).

4. Next – *and this is a critical step!* – click **Set**.[3]

5. When you're finished, be sure to click **OK**.

CAUTION: As mentioned earlier, when you set individual tabs, *any default tabs to the left of your custom tabs will be cleared*. For example, if you type 1.75" in the Tab stop position box, Word will clear / delete the default tabs set at .5", 1", and 1.5"! (You will have to add those tab stops back yourself.) In other words, you are not merely *adding* a tab stop; you're actually *replacing* the default tabs to the left of your first custom tab stop. (However, this procedure does *not* clear any of your other custom tabs!)

If you intend to clear existing tab stops, you can **click the tab** below the **Tab stop position box** and then click the **Clear** button. To delete all tabs, click **Clear All**.

---

[2] Definitions of Left, Center, Right, Decimal, and Bar tabs follow below.

[3] Many people forget this step, but your settings *will not stick* unless you click **Set**.

Types of Tabs

(**NOTE:** In the following examples, **X** marks the location of the tab stop.)

Left tabs (the most commonly used type): Text moves *to the right* from the tab stop.

                    X
                    This is an example of a Left tab (set at 1.5") .

Right tabs: Text moves *to the left* from the tab stop.

                                                                            X
                                    This is an example of a Right tab (set at 6").

Center tabs: Text *centers around* the tab stop.

                                    X
                    This is an example of a Center tab (set at 3.5").

Decimal tabs: Text (consisting of numbers) *aligns at a decimal point.*

                                                                    .**X**
        This is an example of a Decimal tab (set at 5")[4]   1,279,567.85
                                                                        734.27
                                                                      3,561.04

Bar tabs[5]: Word inserts *a vertical line* at the tab stop.

This is an example of a Bar tab (set at 3.2").

| You can type text on either side of the "bar." However, it's tricky because you have to tab to move to the right side. |

Note: Word extends the bar when you press Enter (which, as you know, copies the paragraph mark that contains the tab settings from one paragraph to the next) or if you press the Tab key repeatedly.

TYPES OF LEADERS

   NOTE: Leaders work with **Right tabs**. They move *to the left* from the leader tab stop to the previous tab stop.

Dot...**X**
Dash --**X**
Underline_____ **X**

---

[4] I've also added a Left tab at .5" so that I could tab the introductory text over slightly.

[5] Not to be confused with your running account for drinks you've bought at the local tavern.

SIDEBAR: Alignment Tabs

In Word 2007, Microsoft introduced a new form of tabs called "Alignment Tabs." Similar to WordPerfect's longstanding Relative Tabs feature, alignment tabs readjust automatically if you change the page margins in a way that alters the location of the left, right, and/or center point of the document – or you insert a page with a different orientation (such as landscape). This feature works particularly well if you need centered page numbers in a document that has both portrait and landscape pages. (A regular center tab in the footer of a portrait-oriented page will not be in the correct position in the landscape page.)

NOTE: Alignment tabs work only in .docx files (and other Open Office XML file types). They are not available in .doc files.

These new tabs are something of a "stealth" feature because there's no reference to them anywhere on the Ribbon (or in any dialog boxes) unless you happen to be working with headers or footers. When your cursor is in a header or footer editing screen, you will see an "**Insert Alignment Tab**" command in the **Position group** on the **Header & Footer Tools tab**.

Clicking the command opens a dialog that lets you set a left, center, and/or right tab—with or without a leader—in the header or footer and align it relative to either the margin or an indent. (You can set more than one alignment tab.) Because tabs are an element of paragraph formatting, when you insert an alignment tab on one line of a header or footer, the setting will apply *only to the paragraph your cursor is in*. However, if you press the Enter key after inserting an alignment tab, the tab setting will carry over to the next paragraph.

Unlike the left, center, and right tabs built into headers and footers, alignment tabs do not appear on the Ruler. (Microsoft recommends that you remove any pre-existing tabs from the Ruler before adding alignment tabs—which you can do by dragging the tabs off the Ruler—to avoid confusion about where the tabs exist in your headers and footers.)

Although the "Alignment Tab" command appears only on the Header & Footer Tools tab, you can add it to the Quick Access Toolbar so that you can use alignment tabs in the body of your document. To do so, either (1) go into a header or footer editing screen, **right-click** the "**Insert Alignment Tab**" **icon**, and then click "**Add to Quick Access Toolbar**" *or* (2) **right-click** the **QAT**, click "**Customize the Quick Access Toolbar…**," change the "Choose commands from" drop-down at the top left side of the Word Options screen to "**All Commands**," scroll to the "**Insert Alignment Tab**" command, click the "**Add**" **button**, and then click "**OK**" to save your settings.

Creating Bulleted Lists

You can created a bulleted list in Word 2016 by inserting a bullet first and then typing text or by typing some text first and then applying bullets to the text.

Perhaps the easiest way is simply to click the **Bullets button** in the **Paragraph group** on the **Home tab** and then type some text. When you press the **Enter key**, Word inserts another bullet of the same type and with the same indentation so that you can type another bulleted paragraph. To end the bulleted list, click the **Bullets button** again.

Alternatively, you can type some text first and then click the **Bullets button**. To apply bullets to several consecutive paragraphs, **select the paragraphs** and then click the **Bullets button**.

If you wish, you can insert bullets in a couple of other ways:

- By pressing **Ctrl Shift L**; or
- If Automatic Bulleted Lists has been enabled in the Word Options, by **typing an asterisk** and pressing either the **Spacebar** *or* the **Tab key**

To enable or disable Automatic Bulleted Lists, click the **File tab**, **Options**, **Proofing**, **AutoCorrect Options**, and click the **AutoFormat As You Type tab**.

Changing the Indentation of the Bulleted List

By default, the first level of Word's built-in bulleted lists indents the bullet by .25" and begins the text at .5". You can change the indentation of any list level by **right-clicking** somewhere within a paragraph, choosing **Adjust List Indents**, changing the indentation of the bullet and/or the text, then clicking **OK**. Note that doing so will change the indentation of all paragraphs in the current list that are at that level, but will not affect other bulleted lists in your document.

One way to change the indentation of those lists is to use the **Format Painter** (the **paintbrush icon** in the **Clipboard group** on the **Home tab**). With your cursor somewhere within one of the paragraphs whose indentation you wish to copy, **double-click the Format Painter**, then click on **every bulleted paragraph** that you want to adopt the indentation of the "model" paragraph. Be sure to click the Format Painter again to turn it off.

Changing the Spacing Between Bulleted Paragraphs

In recent versions of Word, Microsoft made a change that suppresses before and after spacing in bulleted and numbered lists. In other words, even if you add before and/or after spacing to a list, that spacing will not go into effect unless you change a somewhat obscure setting within the Paragraph dialog. This setting, "Don't add space between paragraphs of the same style," *is enabled (checked) by default for bulleted and numbered lists*. Many people, unaware of this setting, have been nonplussed by the fact that despite adding spacing after paragraphs in a bulleted or numbered list, the paragraphs remain scrunched together.

The "Don't add space…" Option in the Paragraph Dialog

If you have already typed an entire list, select / highlight the list, then open the Paragraph dialog, uncheck this option, and click "OK." If you have just started typing the first item in the list and your cursor is within the list, open the Paragraph dialog, uncheck the option, and click "OK." When you press the Enter key to insert another bulleted paragraph, the modified setting will be copied to the next paragraph.

Changing the Bullet Size

It can be somewhat tricky to change the bullet size without also changing the size of the text in a bulleted paragraph.

The trick is to turn on **Show Nonprinting Characters** (by clicking the **paragraph icon**/pilcrow [¶] in the **Paragraph group** or by pressing **Ctrl Shift *** (asterisk—the asterisk is above the number 8 at the top of the keyboard), then **select the paragraph mark** at the end of the paragraph and use any method you like to decrease or increase the font size. (You might find it helpful to insert a space between the last character in the paragraph and the paragraph mark at the end.) **NOTE**: *Changing the size of the paragraph mark changes the size of the bullet but not the size of the text*.

After you change the size of the bullet in one paragraph, you should be able to copy the formatting by using the Format Painter. If that doesn't work, try **copying the paragraph mark** from a "successful" paragraph and **pasting it** at the end of the paragraph you are trying to modify.

Another method that appears to work is to click within a bullet and, if / when all of the bullets in the list turn gray, use the Font drop-down or the Font dialog to change the size of the bullets.

Changing the Bullet Character

To change the appearance of a bullet, insert the cursor into a paragraph whose bullet you wish to modify, then open the **Bullets drop-down** and select a bullet from the gallery.

If none of the existing choices appeals to you, click **Define New Bullet**. The **Define New Bullet dialog** will enable you to browse through various font sets to locate another symbol or to browse through a picture gallery and find an image that you can use for your bullet.

Creating a Multilevel Bulleted List

After you have inserted a bullet and typed some text (or applied a bullet to existing text), you can change the level of a bulleted paragraph by doing any of the following:

- pressing **Alt Shift →** to "demote" the paragraph to a lower list level or pressing **Alt Shift ←** to "promote" the paragraph [1]; or

- pressing the **Tab key** to "demote" the paragraph level or **Shift Tab** to "promote" the paragraph level[2]; or

- clicking the **Increase Indent icon** in the **Paragraph group** on the **Home tab** to "demote" the paragraph level or clicking the **Decrease Indent icon** to "promote" the paragraph level; or

---

[1] You can "demote" any paragraph in the list, but you can't "promote" the first paragraph, for reasons that should be obvious. (You can "promote" any other paragraph in the list.)

[2] If Tab and Shift Tab don't work as expected, you might need to change a setting in the Word Options. Click the **File tab, Options, Proofing, AutoCorrect Options, AutoFormat As You Type tab**, and if necessary, click to check (enable) "**Set left- and first-indent with tabs and backspaces.**" (When this setting is unchecked, the Tab key inserts a tab but does not change the paragraph level.

- opening the **Bullets drop-down**, choosing **Change List Level**, and clicking on one of the **list level icons**.

Multiple Bulleted Lists and Nested Lists

Word allows you to insert different bulleted lists in different parts of your document ***and/or*** to nest various types of lists (up to nine separate lists) inside one another.

In this context, "nesting" merely means changing the level / indent of some of the bulleted paragraphs. You can change the level by positioning your cursor at the beginning of a bulleted item and pressing the Tab key (to "demote" the level) or Shift Tab (to "promote") the level ***or*** you can click the Increase Indent button in the Paragraph group on the Home tab (to "demote" the level) or the Decrease Indent button (to "promote" the level).

You also have the option of clicking the arrow to the right of the Bullets button and choosing "Change List Level," then clicking one of the options on the fly-out menu.

After you have changed the level of a bulleted paragraph, right-clicking within the bullet produces a menu that includes a "Separate List" command. If you choose that command, the "Join To Previous List" command (which is grayed out before you separate the list) will become active - in case you change your mind.

Note that you can apply automatic numbering or lettering to some of the paragraphs within your list. Simply select the paragraphs, then click the drop-down to the right of the Numbering button in the Paragraph group on the Home tab and choose from among the existing icons or click "Define New Number Format" and create your own. You can adjust the indents of the numbers / letters separately from the indents of the bullets. See the screenshot below for an example.

- Video provides a powerful way to help you prove your point.
- When you click Online Video, you can paste in the embed code for the video you want to add.
  - (a) You can also type a keyword to search online for the video that best fits your document.
  - (b) To make your document look professionally produced, Word provides header, footer, cover page, and text box designs that complement each other.
- For example, you can add a matching cover page, header, and sidebar.

QUICK TIP: If you have applied bullets (or numbers) to a list, but suddenly you can't see some or all of the bullets, switch from Print Layout View to Draft View and back again. That usually fixes the problem.

PAGE FORMATTING

Understanding Page (Section) Formatting

We've focused on paragraph formatting thus far, largely because the paragraph is the primary unit of formatting in Word. But page formatting is important, too, and like paragraph formatting, it's not entirely intuitive – either in theory or in the way it actually functions in your documents.

The critical thing to understand about page formatting in Word is that whenever you want to change the page formatting (page layout) *in a portion of your document*, you must insert a "**section break**." Otherwise, Word applies your formatting changes to the entire document. I typically demonstrate this phenomenon in my classes by trying to change the orientation of a single page of a multi-page document from portrait to landscape. Without a section break, the whole document changes to landscape – not what we intended.

That example is so graphic that people understand the concept immediately. First, you insert a section break at the bottom of the page *before* the part of the document where you want the different page format (e.g., landscape orientation) to go into effect. Then you can change the format of the new section. If you want to change the format again –in this example, back to portrait orientation – you need to insert another section break.

What makes things tricky is (1) understanding what Microsoft considers "page formatting"; and (2) figuring out how section breaks work. They are somewhat complicated (and are *not* the same as page breaks).

So what constitutes "page formatting," according to Microsoft? With respect to legal documents, "page formatting" mainly means headers, footers, and page numbering. It also includes page margins, footnotes, watermarks, page color, page borders, and, of course, page orientation. (See the section on page 133 for a summary – and a comparison with paragraph formatting.)

After you insert one or more section breaks, the document is divided into different sections for purposes of page formatting. But there's more to it than that. In most situations, all of the sections you create are "**linked together**" – which means that *they are identical*. (My classroom example with portrait/landscape formatting is a significant exception to this rule.) When sections are linked / identical, what you type in a footer in one section – and, importantly, which page numbering format you use – is reflected in the footers in all of the other sections. So you need to take the additional step of *unlinking* sections from each other if you want them to be different in some substantial way – for instance, the text in the footers will be different in each section, or some footers will have page numbering and others won't.

Furthermore, you can't unlink all of the sections at once. You must unlink the sections one at a time (well, two at a time – you unlink the later section from the earlier section.). But once you have unlinked the sections, you can change the formatting in one section without affecting the other(s).

I'll review these points and go into more detail in the parts of the book that cover headers, footers, and page numbering. Hang in there. It will start to make sense as you read more – and practice more.

Changing Page Margins

In Word, document margins are considered an attribute of *page layout*. That means that you set margins for the entire document (as opposed to only a few paragraphs) via **Page Setup** on the **Layout tab**.[1]

From the **Layout tab**, you can choose one of the margin settings available on the "**Margins**" **drop-down menu** (see the screenshot at right) or, if you prefer, open the **Page Setup dialog** to review and adjust the margin settings from there.

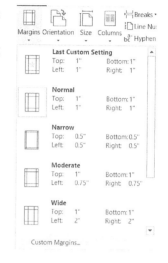

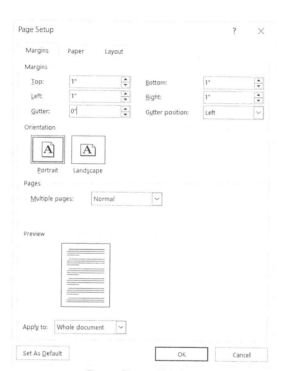

Page Setup Dialog

To open the dialog box, do one of the following:

- Click the **Custom Margins** command at the bottom of the drop-down menu, which will open the **Page Setup dialog**; or

- Click the **dialog launcher** in the **Page Setup group**; or

- Press the key combination **Alt P, S, P**

---

[1] When WordPerfect was still in relatively wide use, many people referred to "paragraph margins" as well as "page margins." However, in recent years, the term "paragraph margins" has lost favor and has been replaced by the term "left and right indents."

When the Page Setup dialog opens, you can simply type numbers for the Top, Bottom, Left, and/or Right margins directly in the respective boxes (or, if you prefer, use the "spinner" arrows). You don't need to type the inch symbol after typing a number.

Before closing the Page Setup dialog, make sure that the "**Apply to:**" **drop-down** is set to "**Whole Document**," or your custom margins might be applied to only a portion of the document.[2]

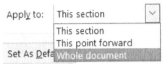

If you want your custom margin settings to apply to all future documents based on the underlying template, click the "**Set As Default**" button at the bottom of the dialog before clicking "OK." When the prompt appears, asking if you want to change the default settings for page setup, click "**Yes**."

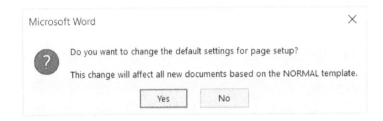

To save your settings, click "OK."

<u>Changing Page Margins for Part of Your Document</u>

Suppose you want different page margins for a particular section of a document. You can apply page margins to a portion of your document as by choosing "This Point Forward" or "This Section" from the "Apply to" drop-down, as mentioned in footnote 2. Or, if the paragraphs are adjacent to one another, you can do the following: **Select the text**, launch the **Page setup dialog**, and **change the margin settings**. *Before clicking OK*, navigate to the **"Apply to:" drop-down** at the lower left-hand side of the dialog box and make sure it is set to "**Selected Text**." Then click "**OK**" to save your settings and close the dialog box.

Word will insert section breaks before and after the text you selected in order to set that portion of the document off from other portions that use different margin settings.

---

[2] If you choose one of the other "Apply to:" options ("This point forward" or "This section"), word automatically applies your margin setting to the portion of the document that your cursor is in. If you have not already divided your document into sections, Word inserts a next-page section break on the page above the cursor location.

Working With Headers and Footers

If you have used WordPerfect recently, you probably know that headers and footers work very differently in Word from the way they work in WordPerfect. In WordPerfect, it is easy to insert two separate headers and two separate footers (or more than two) and to format each one independently of the other(s).

In Word, although you can create multiple headers and footers, there is a bit of a trick to doing so. First, as I mentioned in the introduction to the Page Formatting section, you have to break the document into *sections* – separate units that can be formatted differently.

After you do so, all headers and footers in the various sections are *linked together*. Because they are linked, if you change the formatting and/or the contents (the text) of one header or footer, the others change as well. In order to use different formatting or content within a particular header or footer, you must navigate to the document section where you want to make the change and *break the link* between that header or footer and the one in the previous section.[1] After you break the link, you can make changes without affecting the previous header or footer. I'll provide step-by-step instructions below.

Headers and footers in Word are considered a separate, "hidden" layer of the document. (They appear grayed out when you are working in the document editing screen.)[2]

To work on a header or footer, you can click the **Insert tab**, then click **Header** or **Footer** (as appropriate) and click "**Edit Header**" (or "**Edit Footer**") at the bottom of the drop-down. (If you like, you can select one of the pre-formatted header or footer styles from the gallery, although most of them aren't well suited for legal documents.)

Actually, I never use that method nowadays. It's faster to **double-click** within the white space at the very top or bottom of any page (depending on whether I'm creating a header or a footer).[3] Or, since I'm not particularly skilled at double-clicking, I **right-click** in the white space, then click "**Edit Header**" or "**Edit Footer**."

Edit Footer

Whichever method you prefer, Word opens the header or footer editing screen, and the Ribbon morphs into a context-sensitive **Header & Footer Tools Design tab** (see the screenshot on the next page).

---

[1] The main exception to this rule is if the footers are identical in every respect other than the page number format. If there are no substantive differences besides the page number format, you actually don't have to unlink the sections. However, it's good to get into the habit of doing so.

[2] That "hidden" attribute might explain why the Headers and Footers command was found on the View menu in pre-Word 2007 versions of Word.

[3] Your mouse pointer should be within the area spanning half an inch from the top or bottom.

The Header & Footer Tools Tab

This contextual tab[4] provides commands for most of the features and formatting options you need in a header or footer: a Page Number drop-down, where you can insert a page number code, select a number format, and restart or continue page numbering; a Date & Time dialog, where you can insert date and/or time codes (or fixed text); a Document Info drop-down, where you can insert a code for the file name and path (a terrific new feature first introduced in Word 2013); boxes where you can change the distance of the header and/or footer from the very top or bottom of the page[5]; and more.

In the screenshot above, in the **Navigation group**, "**Go to Header**" is active and "**Go to Footer**" is grayed out because my cursor was in the footer editing screen when I took the screenshot. If I had moved my cursor to the header editing screen, the reverse would be true.

You can move between the header and footer editing screens by either (1) clicking "**Go to Header**" (or "Go to Footer") in the **Navigation group**, *or* (2) pressing the **up arrow** or the down arrow on the keyboard as appropriate (up arrow to move from the Footer screen to the Header screen, down arrow to move from the Header screen to the Footer screen).

Headers and footers in Word are pre-configured with a center tab at 3.25" (dead center in an 8 ½" by 11" document with 1-inch left and right margins) and a right tab at 6.5". That makes it easy to insert a centered page number and a right-aligned file name and path code. However, be aware that if you use L/R margins that differ from the default margins, tabs at 3.25" and 6.5" might not work well for you. In order to compensate, you'll have to drag the tab markers on the ruler bar in both the header and the footer editing screens – or, better yet, use alignment tabs.[6] For more about alignment tabs, see the section starting on page 228.

If all you want to do is insert one header and/or one footer, just type the text you want (and/or insert the codes you want) and click the **Close** button, and you're done.

---

[4] "Contextual tabs" appear only when you are performing a specific task, such as creating a header or footer, working in a columnar table, resizing a photo, editing a text box, etc.

[5] Note that header and footer margins are *not* the same as page margins. Header and footer margins control how far the text in the footer (as opposed to the text in the document itself) is from the very top or bottom of a page.

[6] To change the tab settings in the underlying default template, see the instructions for modifying the default template at page 195.

Using Section Breaks to Create Multiple Headers / Footers

If you want to create additional headers or footers, things become a little more complicated. As mentioned previously, in order to have different headers and footers, you must divide the document into *sections*.

Let's assume you want to create two different footers. First, you need to insert a **section break**, which will split the document into two sections. Make sure that you start from within the document, not from within the footer editing screen. Then proceed as follows:

1. Position the cursor at the bottom of *the page immediately before* the page where you want the new footer to go into effect.

2. Click the **Layout tab, Breaks, Section Breaks, Next Page**.[7]

    Make sure to choose the Next Page section type. Continuous section breaks are used only when you want to change formatting *within* a page – e.g., for a newsletter with a title that spans the entire page and three columns below the title.

    If you have displayed the non-printing characters (either by clicking the Paragraph icon in the Paragraph group on the Home tab or by pressing Ctrl Shift *), the section break will appear as a dotted double line at the cursor position. See the screenshot below.

    ....Section Break (Next Page)............................

3. Next, open the Footer editing screen, either by double-clicking or by right-clicking and then choosing "Edit Footer."

4. Note which section you're in (a label at left should say **Footer -Section 2-** or **Footer -Section 1-**). If you are in the Section 1 footer, click the "**Next**" button in the Navigation group in the Header & Footer Tools tab to move to the Section 2 footer.

5. Note as well whether the words "**Same as Previous**" appear at the right-hand side of the footer editing screen. If so, the two footers / sections are linked, which means that whatever changes you make to one of the footers will be reflected in the other one.

---

[7] If you have displayed the Section indicator per the instructions on page 248, the Status Bar should indicate that your cursor is in Section 2.

6. Click the "**Link to Previous**" button to ***unlink*** the Section 2 footer from the Section 1 footer—allowing you to have different formatting and/or text in the footers. (You always unlink the later footer from the earlier one.) After breaking the link, you can type the text for the Section 2 footer without affecting the Section 1 footer.

Link to Previous button

NOTE: ***This is a critical step***. If you don't turn off "Link to Previous," whatever you type in the Section 1 footer will replace what you have typed in the Section 2 footer—and vice versa.

7. When you have finished typing the text in the Section 2 footer (and the Section 1 footer), click the **Close Header and Footer** button (or double-click somewhere in the grayed-out document text) to return to the document.

8. If you want to create another (different) footer, you need to insert another "Next Page" section break on the page before the page where you want the new footer to start. After you've done so, go into the footer editing screen for the new footer (make sure your cursor is in the correct section) and, before you start typing any text, ***turn off "Link to Previous"*** by clicking the Link to Previous button. If necessary, also turn off "Different First Page."[8]

The same general steps, and precautions, apply to the creation of multiple headers.

---

[8] When your document contains a header or footer that uses the "Different First Page" option, any new sections you insert will ***inherit*** that setting – i.e., the new sections also will have a "Different First Page" header / footer as well as a main header / footer. Typically, it's best to have a different first page header / footer ***only in the first section*** of your doc.

SIDEBAR: A Few Tips About Section Breaks

- Legal documents almost always use "Next Page" section breaks rather than "Continuous" section breaks. The latter are used to change formatting *within* a page – for example, a newsletter with a title spanning the entire page and three columns below the title.

- Sometimes "Next Page" section breaks insert an extra page. To delete it, display the non-printing characters, click on the page break, and press the "Delete" key.

- As mentioned earlier, you must unlink sections when you want them to be *substantively* different. That usually means one of the following:

  o One footer has a page number and another footer does not;
  o The footers contain different text; or
  o One footer contains a field code (e.g., the file name and path) and another footer does not.

- By contrast, you actually don't need to unlink sections that are identical except for the page number format. It won't hurt to do so, however.

- You always unlink a *later* section from an *earlier* one. For example, you unlink section 3 from section 2, rather than the other way around, and you unlink section 2 from section 1. (For obvious reasons, section 1 can't be unlinked from an earlier section.)

- There are two visual cues that tell you whether sections are or aren't linked: If they are linked, "**Same as Previous**" is displayed at the right side of the later footer / section, and the "**Link to Previous**" button in the Header & Footer Tools tab is shaded.

Section 2 is Linked to Section 1

Not Linked

- You might find it helpful to switch to **Draft view** when you work with section breaks. In Draft view, section breaks are graphically represented as double lines across the page, so it's easy to see them. Of course, **displaying the non-printing characters** (changing "Show / Hide" to "Show" mode) does the same thing, as mentioned on page 114.

Section Break Shown in Draft View

243

Using the "Different First Page" Option

The "Different First Page" option, available from the Header & Footer Tools tab, is a very useful feature when you want a different header or footer only on the first page of a document. It works extremely well for letter templates, for example, because you can reserve the first-page header for letterhead and create a main header for the remainder of the letter that contains placeholders for the recipient's name, the date, and the page number (as well as the matter number or other similar information).

"Different First Page" is also a good option for pleadings. It lets you "suppress" the page number on the first page of the pleading (you actually delete the page number code) without affecting the other pages.

But, you might be wondering, why not insert a section break at the bottom of the first page, go into the footer editing screen, navigate to the Section 2 footer, and unlink Section 2 from Section 1? Wouldn't that accomplish the same thing?

Indeed, it would (I'm glad you asked!). However, using that method creates a potential problem: ***Section breaks move around*** as text above them is inserted and deleted. So if your pleading text starts on page 1, and the author of the pleading adds or deletes text, the section break could end up on the next page, so that the first section of the pleading consists of page 1 and page 2. In that situation, if you delete the page number from the Section 1 footer, the page number won't appear on either page 1 or page 2.[1]

By contrast, with the "Different First Page" option enabled, the author(s) can add or delete text on the first page of the pleading without adversely affecting the footers. Make sense?

Incidentally, note that the "Different First Page" option doesn't actually create a new section. Rather, it splits one section into two parts that you can format differently.

The main disadvantage of using this option in a pleading is that it sometimes deletes the pleading paper in one or more sections of the document. However, there's an easy way to restore the pleading paper. See the sidebar on page 250 for instructions.

To apply the "Different First Page" option, do the following:

1. Go into the **footer editing screen** on the first page of your pleading (or other document) by either double-clicking in the white area at the bottom of the page or right-clicking in the white area, then choosing "Edit Footer."

2. Locate the "**Different First Page**" checkbox in the **Options group** on the **Header & Footer Tools** tab.

3. **Click** to put a check in the box.

---

[1] If the pleading text doesn't start on page 1, this method should work well.

That's all there is to it.[2]

CAUTION: If you use the "Different First Page" option in the first section of your document, be sure to ***turn that option off*** (i.e., ***uncheck*** it) in the other sections. Otherwise, ***each section*** will have both a First Page Header/Footer ***and*** a regular Header/Footer – which can be very confusing as well as problematic.

Creating and Editing a Letter Template

Your organization might have set up a letter template already, but in case you want to create your own, just follow these instructions.

1. First, within a blank document, create a page break (probably the easiest method is to press **Ctrl Enter**). For now, don't be concerned about the fact that most of your letters probably will be only a single page.

2. Next, go into the Header editing screen and navigate to the **Options group** in the **Header & Footer Tools tab**.

3. Click to put a check in the "**Different First Page**" box.

4. Note whether your cursor is in the **First Page Header** or the main **Header**. (Word sometimes opens to a different header editing screen from what you expected.)

5. If necessary, move the cursor from the First Page Header to the Header by clicking the **Next button** in the **Navigation group** of the Header & Footer Tools tab. To move back to the First Page Header, click the **Previous button**.

6. If you're going to use pre-printed letterhead, remember to leave the First Page Header blank. You can press the Enter key as many times as necessary to accommodate the text on the printed letterhead.[3] Doing so will not affect the main Header in the document.

7. Next, navigate to the main header. Add a placeholder for the recipient's name (remember, templates should be generic; you shouldn't insert any specific information that you don't want to appear in every new letter based on the template). Then press the Enter key to move the cursor to the next line.

8. To insert either a date code or a date text placeholder, click the Insert tab, Insert Date & Time (in the Text group), choose the date format, and, to use a code that will update

---

[2] That is, unless you lose your pleading paper after enabling the option. If so, use the workaround described on page 250.

[3] You might have to experiment to get the right amount of space. Or just measure the text on the pre-printed letterhead with a ruler and adjust the size of the header accordingly.

when you open / print the letter, click to check the "Update automatically" box at the lower right side of the dialog box. Click "OK" to save your changes.

9. Press the Enter key to move the cursor to the next line.

10. Type "Page" and press the spacebar.

11. To insert a page number code, do one of the following:

   a. Click the Page Number drop-down in the Header & Footer group, then choose "Current Position," "Plain Number"; or

   b. If you prefer a "Page X of Y" format – where "X" is the current page and "Y" is the total number of pages, click the Page Number drop-down, choose "Current Position," "Plain Number," but before clicking, scroll down below "Plain Number" and choose the "Page X of Y" option. The number codes will appear in bold, but you can select / highlight them and turn bold off by pressing Ctrl B or pressing the Bold icon in the Font group on the Home tab.

12. Make any other desired changes, then close out of the Header editing screen.

13. Delete the page break that you inserted in Step 1.

Finally, save the document as a template by clicking "Save As" or pressing F12, then making sure to choose "Word Template (*.dotx)" as the "Save as type."[4]

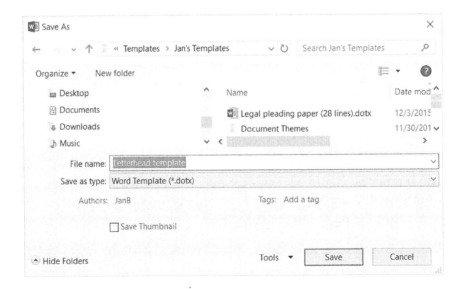

---

[4] When I changed the "Save as type" to "Word Template (*.dotx)," Word immediately opened the folder I had designated as my template location. If that doesn't happen, you can browse to your preferred template folder.

14. When you've finished, close the template.[5]

15. Test to see if it works as expected by clicking File, New, Custom, browsing to the template, and double-clicking it. A new letter based on the template should open. (Note that as you add pages, you will see the Main header at the top of page 2 and following.)

To edit the template, you must open the actual .dotx file, not a document based on the template.

1. Navigate to the location where your custom / person templates are stored. (Do *not* click File, New and click "Custom"; that will open a new document based on the template, rather than the template itself). If you can't remember the location, click File, Options, Save, and take note of (or copy) the path listed under "Default personal templates location." See the screenshot below.

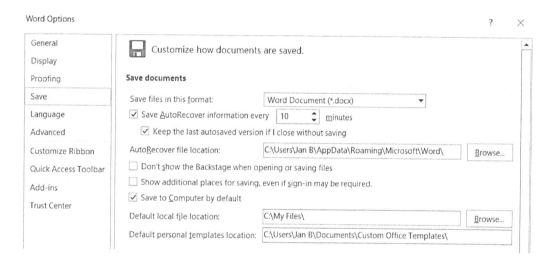

2. Open the template as you would open any file.

3. If you need to edit the Main (second-page) header, be sure to insert a page break before going into the header. If you forget to do so, click to **uncheck** "Different First Page," then click "Next" to go to the Main header. **CAUTION**: Be sure to check "Different First Page" again before closing the header.

4. Make any desired changes and close out of the header.

5. Delete the page break and save the template.

---

[5] **CAUTION:** When "Different First Page" is checked, sometimes the main header or footer editing screen becomes hidden. This behavior can be confusing. If you are having trouble finding the main header or footer editing screen, try **unchecking** "Different First Page"—if only temporarily. The hidden header or footer editing screen should reappear.

Inserting the File Name and Path into a Footer

A new icon on the Header & Footer Tools tab, introduced in Word 2013, makes it extremely easy to insert a code for the file name and/or the file path (drive letter and folders / subfolders where the doc is stored in the computer). This handy drop-down, labeled "**Document Info**," is in the **Insert group**, toward the left side of the tab.

Position your cursor where you want the code to go, click the Document Info drop-down, and choose either File Name or File Path. (The File Path includes both the name and the path.) If you haven't yet saved / named your document, the code for the name will reflect the temporary name / document number assigned by Microsoft. The code might not update immediately after you save the document, but should do so when you print the doc or click the File tab, Print.[6]

Document2   C:\Books and Articles\Word 2016 Book\Test of File Path code.docx

After you insert a code, you can select it and then apply font formatting such as bolding, choose a different font face, or increase the font size.

Adding a Section Indicator to the Status Bar

You can add a Section indicator to the Status Bar so that you can tell at a glance which section of the document your cursor is located in.[7] Just right-click within the Status Bar, then click "**Section**" to put a checkmark next to it. Finally, click anywhere outside the pop-up menu to close it.

Section Indicator in the Status Bar

---

[6] Some field codes in Word, including the FILENAME code, don't update until you print the document (or click File, Print and then return to the document editing screen).

[7] Even a blank Word document already consists of one section for purposes of page formatting, so you'll see Section 1 when you are working in a new blank document.

Deleting a Section Break

To delete a section break, you need to display the section breaks in your document, which normally are hidden. To do so, either enable **Show mode** (click the Paragraph icon in the Paragraph group on the Home tab, or press Ctrl Shift *) or switch to **Draft View** (View tab, Draft or Ctrl Alt N). Then click the section break you want to delete and press the Delete key. Sometimes it's necessary to press Delete more than once.

CAUTION: The page formatting in your document is contained in the section breaks. In the same way that each paragraph mark stores the paragraph formatting codes for the preceding paragraph, each section break stores the page formatting codes *for the preceding section*. If you accidentally delete a section break, the text will take on the page formatting of the *following* section (i.e., it will be affected by the codes within the next section break). That can lead to unexpected, and often undesirable, changes. So be sure to click the **Undo button** on the **Quick Access Toolbar** (or press **Ctrl Z**) as soon as you realize what happened.

Troubleshooting Section Breaks

Sometimes Word will change a "Next Page" section break into a "Continuous" section break with no warning and for no apparent reason. If that happens, it can cause problems with your document. (To see which type of section breaks exist in your document, display the non-printing characters or switch from Print Layout view to Draft view by clicking the **View tab, Draft**.) For a solution, see the sidebar on page 263.

TROUBLESHOOTING TIP: Restoring the Pleading Paper if It Disappears

As mentioned earlier, using the "Different First Page" option in a pleading can cause the pleading lines and numbers to disappear. The coding for the pleading paper is contained in the first-page header, and headers and footers are linked, so choosing "Different First Page" in order to create a different first-page footer sometimes wipes out the first-page header (i.e., the pleading paper), as well.

If that happens, immediately click "**Undo**" (or press Ctrl Z, the keyboard shortcut for Undo) and then do as follows:

1. Go into the header editing screen on the first page of your document if you're not already there.

2. Display the **non-printing characters (Show / Hide)** by clicking the Paragraph icon in the Paragraph group on the Home tab or pressing Ctrl Shift * [asterisk].

3. **Copy** the first **paragraph mark** (pilcrow) in the header.

    That paragraph mark contains the formatting codes for the header, including the graphics (pleading lines and numbering).

4. Next, **click** to check (enable) the "**Different First Page**" option.

5. Don't panic if the pleading paper disappears. Instead, simply **paste the paragraph mark** back into the header.

    Be sure to use a standard paste – using Ctrl V or "Keep Source Formatting" – rather than a "Paste and Keep Text Only." Although I generally advise people to use "Paste and Keep Text Only" in order to avoid pasting unwanted formatting into your document, in this situation you want to retain the formatting of the pleading paper (the vertical lines and line numbers).

    Pasting the paragraph mark should restore the pleading paper, at least on that page. If there is another paragraph mark in the header, delete it.

6. Scroll through the rest of the pleading to see if the pleading paper disappeared anywhere else when you applied the "Different First Page" option. If so, go into the header at the top of the page that doesn't have pleading paper and paste the paragraph mark.

When you've finished, you can proceed to "suppress" the page number on the first page of your pleading and use a different footer, with a page number displayed, in the remainder of the document.

250

Page Numbering

Now you know how to create sections, go into the footer editing screen, and unlink one footer / section from the previous one. So how do you actually insert a page number code and format the number? And how do you restart or continue numbering in one footer / section?

Inserting a Page Number Code

You can insert a page number code by clicking the **Insert tab**, navigating to the **Header & Footer group**, clicking the **Page Number drop-down**, and choosing one of the options – such as "**Bottom of Page**," "**Plain Number**." In a very simple document where there is nothing in the footer but a page number, that method works just fine. However, for documents with text or complex formatting in the footer, I don't recommend that method because:

(1)   It doesn't give you as much control over the formatting of the footer as if you go directly into the footer editing screen and apply formatting; and, more importantly,

(2)   Although the "Bottom of Page" option sounds like a logical choice, it's actually problematic because *it will delete any existing text in the footer*. Yes, really.

Don't Use "Bottom of Page" (It's Broken)

The "Bottom of Page" option is broken (as is the "Top of Page" option). That has been the case since at least Word 2010. You can test it yourself by typing some text in a footer, then clicking the Page Number drop-down at the left side of the Header & Footer Tools tab and hovering over "Bottom of Page," then choosing "Plain Number 2" (or either of the other "Plain Number" options). Whoops! Your text disappears. This behavior is considered a bug.

So what should you do instead?

A better option, in my opinion, is to insert a page number code from within the footer editing screen. After going into the footer editing screen, type any text you want at the left margin. Then press the **Tab key**, which should move the cursor to the center of the footer (there's a center tab built into the footers, as well as the headers, in Word).[1] In other words, position the cursor where you want the page number code to go before inserting the code.

---

[1] In a pleading, the center tab might not be set at true center. There are two possible solutions: (1) you can drag the center tab to true center; or (2) delete the existing center tab and then click "Alignment Tab" and insert a Center tab relative to the margin. Alignment tabs adjust based on your document margins, so the new Center tab should be in the correct place. (Alignment tabs don't appear on the Ruler, but you will know if it worked the cursor appears to move to the true center of the document when you press the Tab key.) See the Sidebar about Alignment tabs starting on page 228.

Next, click the **Page Number drop-down** in the **Insert group** toward the left side of the tab and choose "**Current Position**," "**Plain Number**."

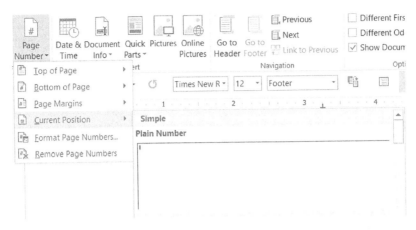

Current Position, Plain Number

Unlike the "Bottom of Page" option, "Current Position" offers only one "Plain Number" choice, which appears to be at the left side of the screen. However, the image displayed under "Plain Number" is not a live preview and doesn't represent the actual location where the page number code will appear. Rather, the code will appear at the current cursor position, which is why you should move the cursor first.

You should see a page number code in the center of the footer.

Typically, the code turns gray when you click within it. If the number does not turn gray when you click in it, you can determine that it is a code by pressing the key combination **Alt F9** – the keyboard shortcut to toggle between "field codes" in your document and the code results. You'll see a Page Number field code that looks something like this:

{ PAGE * MERGEFORMAT }

Be sure to press **Alt F9** again to show the code result (the page number) again.

To change the setting that determines whether codes turn gray when you click within them, click the **File tab**, **Options**, **Advanced**, scroll to the **Show document content** section, and change the "**Field shading**" drop-down to "**When selected**" (as opposed to "Never" or "Always").

Then click "OK" at the bottom right side of the Word Options dialog to save your new setting.

"Suppressing" a Page Number

After you have inserted a page number code in your footer, it's easy to "suppress" the page number in the first-page footer. With your cursor in that footer, click to enable the "Different First Page" option, and then select / highlight the page number code and press the Delete key. (Note that California Rules of Court, Rule 3.1113(h)(1) requires that the caption page(s) in a motion that exceeds ten (10) pages have no page numbering.)

Changing the Number Format

California Rules of Court, Rule 3.1113 requires that a memorandum in support of a motion that is longer than ten (10) pages have a Table of Contents and Table of Authorities[2]; that the pagination of the Tables be in lower-case Roman numerals[3]; and that the pagination of the text be in Arabic numerals, starting on page 1[4].

In order to change the number format within a pleading to conform to the Court rules, you need to insert a next-page section break on the page before the first page of the Table of Contents (TOC) and another one on page before the Memorandum of Points and Authorities. Without section breaks, you won't be able to change from Arabic numerals (used in the Notice of Motion that typically precedes the TOC) to lower-case Roman numerals or vice versa.

Remember that you must insert a section break from the document editing screen, not from within a footer editing screen. Start by positioning your cursor at the bottom of the page before the TOC and click the **Layout tab**, **Breaks**, **Section Breaks** > **Next Page**. Then do the following:

1. Go into the footer editing screen.

2. Make sure you are in the correct section (sometimes Word puts you in a different section from what you expect).

3. With your cursor anywhere within the footer – you don't have to select / highlight the page number – click the **Page Number drop-down** in the **Header & Footer group** at the left side of the tab.

4. Choose "**Format Page Numbers…**"

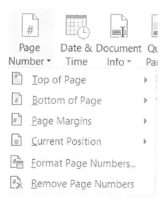

---

[2] CRC Rule 3.1113(f).

[3] CRC Rule 3.1113(h)(2). The Roman numerals begin on the first page of the Table of Contents (TOC) (i.e., that is page i) and continue consecutively through the last page of the Table of Authorities (TOA).

[4] CRC Rule 3.1113(h)(3).

5. When the **Page Number Format dialog** opens, click the "**Number format**" **drop-down** and select the number type you want to use (for the TOC, choose lower-case Roman numerals).

6. Make sure that "**Start at**" (at the bottom of the dialog) has been enabled and is set to i.

7. Click "**OK**" to save your changes.

8. Repeat these steps for the Memorandum of Points and Authorities, but in Step 5, choose Arabic numerals.

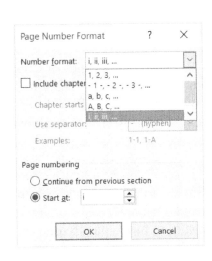

9. Note that you don't need to unlink the sections if the only substantive different between the sections is the page number type. However, unlinking the section might be a good idea if you think you might want to change the text in one or more sections. (You won't be able to do so unless you break the link.)

Changing the Number Value (Restarting or Continuing)

To restart (or continue) numbering in a particular section, do the following:

1. Go into the footer editing screen.

2. Make sure you are in the correct section (sometimes Word puts you in a different section from what you expect based on the location of your cursor before you opened the footer editing screen).

3. With your cursor anywhere within the footer – you don't have to select / highlight the page number – click the **Page Number drop-down** in the **Header & Footer group** at the left side of the tab.

4. Choose "**Format Page Numbers…**"

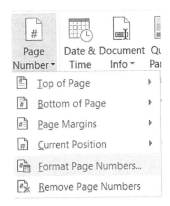

254

5. When the **Page Number Format dialog** opens, click "**Start at**" and, if the number doesn't change to 1, type the number 1.

   Or, if Word restarted numbering when you meant to continue numbering in the new section, click "**Continue from previous section**."

6. Click "**OK**" to save your changes.

7. Repeat these steps in other sections as necessary.

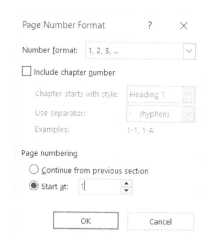

Footnotes

Contrary to what many people think – and to what your intuition might tell you – the Footnote feature is not located on the Insert tab; it's on **References**. Remember my tip about the References tab: It's where you'll find features that refer from one part of the document to another (footnotes, Table of Contents, Table of Authorities, cross-reference, etc.).

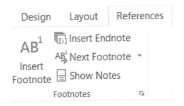

To create a footnote, position the cursor within the text where you want the footnote to go and do any of the following:

- Click the **References tab**, **Footnotes group**, **Insert Footnote** (toward the left side of the Ribbon); *or*

- Use the keyboard shortcut **Ctrl Alt F**; or

- Use the keyboard shortcut **Alt I, N, N** – think "N" for "Note"; or

- If you or someone else at your organization has added an **Insert Footnote icon** to your **Quick Access Toolbar**, click the icon.

Word inserts a footnote number code in both the body of the document (the footnote reference number) and the footnote area (the footnote text), and places the cursor in a special footnote editing screen so you can begin typing the note.

To move the cursor back to the document at the point where you left off, either double-click the footnote number or click the "**Show Notes**" button in the Footnotes group. (This button acts as a toggle that moves the cursor between the footnote reference in the document text and the footnote text itself.)

CAUTION: Whichever method you use, Word puts the cursor *to the left of* the footnote number, not to the right of it. Be sure to move the cursor past the footnote number before you continue typing.

Note that you can see the text of the footnote without scrolling down to the footnote screen. Just position the mouse pointer over the footnote reference number in the document and Word will display a pop-up box containing the text of the footnote.

Changing the Footnote Options

Should you wish to change any of the footnote options, click dialog launcher in the Footnotes group to launch the **Footnote and Endnote dialog**.

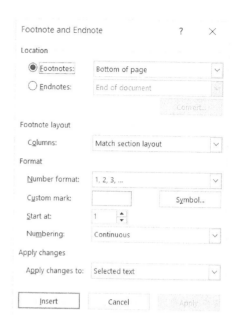

When the Footnote and Endnote dialog box appears, you can change the placement of the footnotes (bottom of page or below text), the number format, the starting number, and whether numbering is continuous (which is the norm in legal documents) or restarts on every page (or every section of the document).

And in this version of Word, there is an additional option labeled "Footnote layout" that you can use to put footnotes side by side in columns (as opposed to the traditional layout, where each footnote spans the entire width of the page).

You are limited to the number formats available from the drop-down. You *can* use symbols instead of numbers. However, if you choose symbols from the Number format drop-down, they will rotate through the symbol set Microsoft created (i.e., each note will be different). If you insert a custom mark, you'll have to open the dialog box and insert the mark for every footnote. (I tried selecting the entire document and applying the changes to "Whole document," and then to "Selected text," but still had to use the dialog box to apply my custom mark to each footnote.)

Deleting, Moving, or Editing a Footnote

To **delete** a footnote, simply select the footnote number *in the text* and press the **Delete key** (or cut it using **Ctrl X** or by **right-clicking** the number, then choosing "**Cut**").

To **move** a footnote, simply select the footnote reference number in the text and cut it (with **Ctrl X** or any method you prefer), then position the cursor where you want the number to be and paste it (with **Ctrl V** or any method you prefer). Alternatively, if you are good at using the mouse, you can drag the reference number to a different position.

To **edit** a footnote, simply go into the footnote (by clicking in the footnote editing screen *or* by double-clicking the footnote reference number in the document) and make your changes. (Watch out! As mentioned previously, if you double-click the number, your cursor will end up to the left of the number in the footnote text.)

Modifying the Footnote Text Style

If you like, you can change the appearance of the footnote (such as the line spacing or the font face or size) by modifying the Footnote Text style.

1. Navigate to the **Home** tab, **Styles** group and click the dialog launcher to open the **Styles Pane**.

2. When the Styles Pane appears, scroll down to **Footnote Text** and **right-click** it.

    If you don't see the Footnote Text style in the pane, click the **Options…** link at the bottom right corner, then change the "**Select styles to show**" drop-down to "All styles" and change "**Select how list is sorted**" to Alphabetical. Click "**OK**."

3. Click **Modify.**

4. When the **Modify Style dialog** opens (see the screenshot on the next page), make any changes you desire. (To change line spacing and/or indents, click the "**Format**" button at the bottom left, then click "**Paragraph**" to open the **Paragraph dialog**. After changing the settings in that dialog, click "**OK**" to save your changes and return to the Modify Style dialog.)

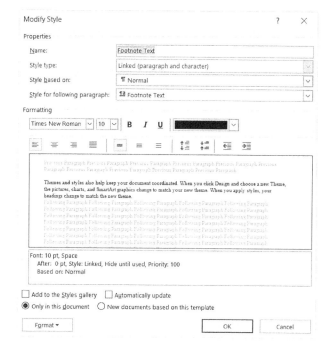

Click the Format button and choose "Paragraph"

The Modify Style Dialog

5. If you want your changes to take effect in all new documents that are based on the underlying template, click the "**New Documents based on this template**" radio button at the bottom of the dialog. (If you don't click that radio button, the changes will apply only in the current document.)

6. Once you have finished, **OK** out of the dialog and then click the **X** at the upper right-hand side of the Styles Pane to close it.

NOTE: If for some reason you need footnotes to start re-numbering with the value of 1 at some point in your document, you *must insert a section break (next page)* on the page before the page where you want the numbering to restart. Otherwise, the note numbers will be continuous throughout your document.

<u>The Note Pane</u>

If you switch to **Draft View** (by clicking the **View tab**, **Draft** or pressing the key combination **Ctrl Alt N**[1]), then click the **Show Notes button** in the **References tab**, a footnote bar appears, splitting the screen so that you can see both the footnote editing area (sometimes called the **note pane**) and the document at the same time. Switching back to Print Layout view closes the note pane. (There's also an **X** at the far-right side of the note pane that you can click to close it.)

---

[1] "N" presumably because Draft View used to be called "Normal View."

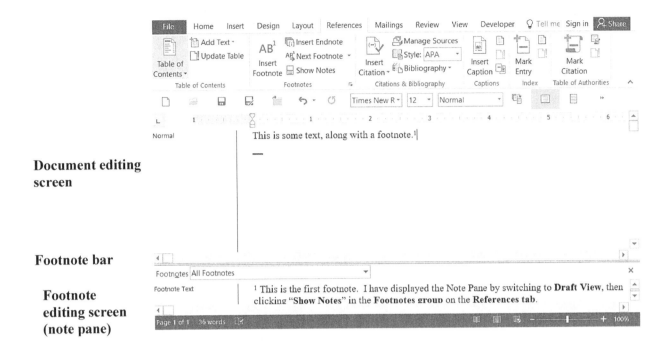

Document editing screen

Footnote bar

Footnote editing screen (note pane)

Note that you can drag the footnote bar up or down in order to view more or less of the footnote text / document text.

Changing the Footnote Separator

If you have attempted to change the footnote separator line in Word, you might have noticed that you can't select the line with the mouse. Left-clicking, right-clicking, and double-clicking are exercises in frustration; they move you between the note text and the note reference or they offer a command for opening the Footnote Options dialog, but they don't let you anywhere near the line itself.

To delete or change the separator line, do the following:

1. Switch to **Draft view**. (**View tab**, **Document Views**, **Draft** or press **Ctrl Alt N**.)

2. Click the **References tab**, **Footnotes group**, **Show Notes**.

3. In the **Note Pane**, locate the **drop-down** and change it to display "**Footnote Separator**."

Now you can delete the separator if you like and replace it with a different line. (If you just want to make the line longer – that is, wider – the easiest way is to select / highlight the existing line, copy it, place the cursor at the right side of the line, and paste.)

Watermarks

The Watermark feature is now found on the **Design tab** in the **Page Background group**. When you click the drop-down, you have the option of using one of the built-in watermarks available in the gallery (be sure to scroll down to see all of them) or creating your own customized watermark.

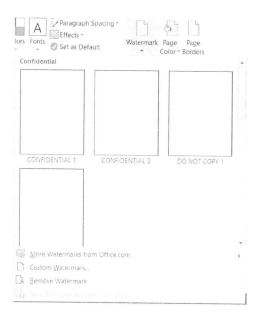

Clicking "**Custom Watermark**" opens a dialog box with options to create a watermark consisting of text or a picture. By default, "No watermark" is selected, so be sure to click either "**Picture watermark**" or "**Text watermark**" to activate the feature.

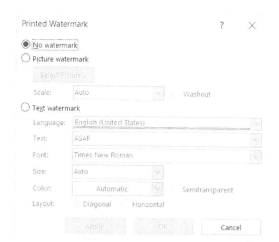

The Watermark Dialog Box ("No Watermark")

The "Text watermark" drop-down is pre-populated with some slogans you can use, but you can type your own words (as I've done in the example on the next page).

You can set the font, size, color, and layout (diagonal or horizontal) from the dialog. You might have to change the color—by default, it's set to a very light shade of gray—in order to see the watermark.

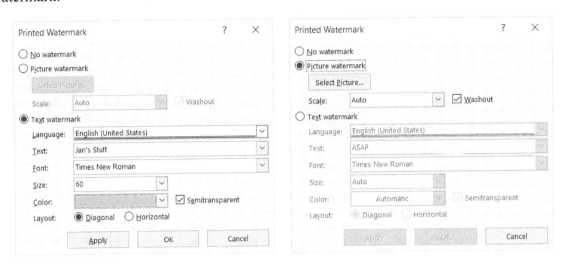

If you choose "Picture watermark," the "Select Picture…" button becomes active so that you can browse to the image file you want to use. As with text watermarks, you can adjust the size (scale) as well as the intensity of the image ("Washout").

After you have inserted the watermark, you must go into the Header editing screen – watermarks are embedded in the header – to edit it. Clicking on the picture opens the Picture Tools contextual tab, which provides tools for resizing the image, changing the brightness or contrast, and so forth.

If you like, you can save your custom watermark to the gallery. (That option is grayed out until you go into the Header editing screen and click the watermark. If you created a picture watermark, the Picture Tools tab will come to the forefront when you click the image, so you'll need to click the Design Tools tab to get access to the Watermark drop-down.)

To remove a watermark, you can click the "**Remove Watermark**" option in the Watermark drop-down. Alternatively, you can go into the header editing screen, click the watermark, right-click, and choose "Cut." (It can be tricky to select the watermark.)

By default, the watermark will appear on all pages of your document. To have the watermark appear only on certain pages, you'll need to insert one or more section breaks and then unlink the sections, as described on pages 235 and following. After you unlink the sections, you can delete a watermark altogether or insert a different one.

SIDEBAR: The Curious Case of the Mutating Section Breaks

Perhaps the most confounding aspect of working with section breaks is their tendency to mutate spontaneously from one type of break to another (for instance, from a "next page" break to a "continuous" break), which can create all sorts of headaches. Trying to delete the offending section break often makes things worse; you might find that section breaks that had been formatted correctly suddenly go bad, too.

::::::::::::::::::::Section Break (Next Page)::::::::::::::::::

::::::::::::::::::::Section Break (Next Page)::::::::::::::::::

::::::::::::::::::::Section Break (Continuous)::::::::::::::::::

::::::::::::::::::::Section Break (Next Page)::::::::::::::::::

What makes things particularly confusing is that each section break stores the formatting for the document section that *precedes* it. So when you delete a section break, the text ahead of it takes on the formatting of the section that comes immediately *after*.[1]

But, complicating the situation further, the information that determines each section break's *type*—that is, whether an individual section break is a "Next Page" or "Continuous" break—actually is stored in the section *after* that specific break. (***Huh?***)

What that means is that when you delete a section break, the prior section break takes on the characteristics of the one you deleted. (In other words, although it is completely counter-intuitive, deleting a rogue "Continuous" section break doesn't help matters because it ***turns the previous break into a "Continuous" section break***.) Are you tearing your hair out yet?

Not to worry. Here's a workaround:

- First, switch to **Draft view** so that the section breaks in the document are easier to see / identify.

- Suppress your impulse to delete the misbehaving section break. Instead, put your cursor on—or, better yet, select—the ***next*** section break.[2]

---

[1] In this regard, section breaks are similar to paragraph marks, which store the formatting information for the preceding text.

[2] Alternatively, you can double-click the section break, which will open the Page Setup dialog.

- Open the **Page** Setup **dialog**, click the **Layout tab**, and click to open the **Section start drop-down**.

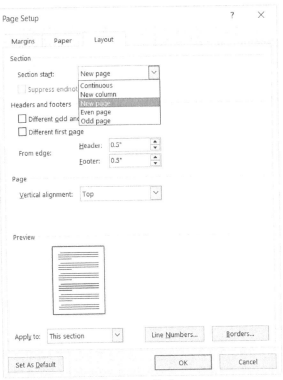

Page Setup dialog

- Select the type of section break you want, which probably is "**New page**."

- Make sure that choice is displayed, then click **OK**.

The "bad" section break should change to reflect your "Section start" choice. Problem solved!

CHARACTER (FONT) FORMATTING

A Few Tips About Fonts

This section offers selected tips for working with fonts and font-related features. It is not meant to be an exhaustive discussion of fonts.

Applying Fonts to an Entire Document

By default, new blank documents in Word 2016 use the Calibri font face, with a size of 11 points.[1] Although you *could* change the current font by selecting the entire document (with the keyboard shortcut Ctrl A) and then applying a different font (either from the Font drop-down in the Font group on the Home tab or from the Font dialog box), doing so won't change the font in "substructures" like headers, footers, and footnotes. The formatting of those items is determined by header, footer, and footnote *styles*.

A better method is to set a default font for the document – or for all new documents. One easy way is to click the **dialog launcher** at the bottom right side of the **Font group** *or* press **Ctrl D**. When the **Font dialog** opens, select the font face, style, and size (plus the color and any other attributes you want to use), and then click the "**Set as Default**" button at the bottom left side of the dialog.[2]

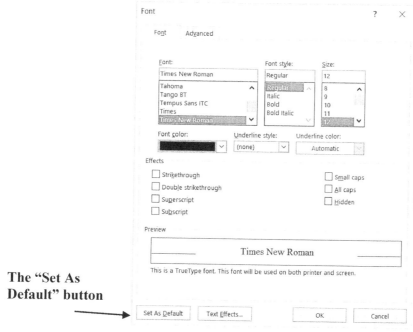

The "Set As Default" button

The Font Dialog

---

[1] The default font is part of the "Normal" style embedded in the Normal.dotm template, which is the template that determines the font and paragraph settings for your blank documents. (Each user – that is, each login ID – has his or her own Normal.dotm template.)

[2] **CAUTION**: Don't choose a font that is followed by "(+Body)," and don't choose bold face, underlining, etc. for the default font, or everything you type will appear with those attributes.

A message box will appear, asking if you want to set the default font for:

- **This document only?** or

- **All documents based on the Normal.dotm template?** (or, if you are changing the font from within an existing document, rather than a new blank document, whichever template that document is based on)

The first option, "This document only?" is automatically selected.

To apply the font throughout the entire document, click "**OK.**" (**CAUTION**: Do ***not*** click the "All documents based on the XX template?" choice unless you are absolutely certain you want to apply the font to all new documents!)

After you change the default font for the document, the font you have chosen will be used in the body of the document as well as in headers, footers, footnotes, and similar document "substructures."

Applying Fonts to Certain Portions of a Document

To apply a font only to certain portions of a document that you have typed already, select those portions before applying the font.

TIP: To select non-continuous areas of text, press and hold the **Ctrl key** while selecting the text.

Font Attributes

Font Color

It's a good idea to choose a specific font color, rather than using the "Automatic" setting, which actually is the default in this version of Word. When the "Automatic" setting is in effect, Word determines the font color based on the Style Set and Theme, if any, that currently are in effect. If your fonts appear in a color you don't like, check the font dialog to make sure that the "Font color" drop-down shows your preferred color, rather than "Automatic."

Underline Style

As you would expect, the default underline style in Word is "(none)" (i.e., the program doesn't apply underlining unless you choose to underline certain text). To toggle underlining on or off, just press **Ctrl U** or click the underlined "U" in the **Font group** on the **Home tab**.

When you select contiguous words and apply underlining, Word automatically underlines both the text and the spaces between words. However, you can change this setting by clicking the **Underline style drop-down** in the **Font dialog** and choosing the "**Words only**" option.

QUICK TIP: You can use the keyboard shortcut **Ctrl Shift W** (for **W**ords?) to underline just the words. As with all font attributes that you are applying to only a portion of the text, be sure to select the text first.

The drop-down also offers options for double underlining, plus a variety of line styles that you can apply to selected text. (Be sure to scroll down to see all of the choices.) If you prefer, you can use the keyboard shortcut **Ctrl Shift D** (for **D**ouble?) to apply double underlining.

Note that if you have typed and underlined some text already, you must select that text to change the underline style applied to that text.

All Caps and Small Caps

You can apply the "All Caps" attribute to text by checking that option in the Font dialog; you can do the same with respect to the "Small Caps" attribute (remember to click "OK" to save your settings when you close the dialog). Or you can use keyboard shortcuts. For All Caps, press the key combination **Ctrl Shift A**; for Small Caps, press the key combination **Ctrl Shift K**.

As with most other font attributes, these formatting options can be applied to selected text or turned on and applied from the cursor position forward.

The Advanced Tab

The **Advanced tab** of the Font dialog provides options for changing the **scale** of selected characters (i.e., you can make them a certain percentage larger or smaller than "normal," where normal is defined as 100%); the **spacing between characters** (which can be expanded or condensed); the **vertical position** relative to a line of text (in other words, you can raise or lower characters relative to the normal line position, somewhat like superscripting or subscripting); and **kerning** (which has to do with the distance between pairs of fonts). Use these options with care.

269

There are also several advanced typographic features related to OpenType and the use of ligatures. Most people who work on legal documents won't use these options, but at least now you know where to find them in case they are of interest.

Changing Case

To change case, **select** the text and press **Shift F3**. If you press Shift F3 repeatedly, the text will alternate among **UPPER CASE**, **lower case**, and either **Capitalize Each Word** (also known as **Initial Caps**) or **Sentence case**, depending on the context—i.e., whether the selected text includes a period, which will trigger Sentence case. (With Sentence case, all words except the first use lower case.)

Note, as well, that there is **a Change Case drop-down** in the top row (toward the right) of the **Font group** on the **Home tab**. The button shows an upper-case "A" next to a lower-case "a."

The drop-down includes **Sentence case** and **tOGGLE cASE**. The latter is not available via the Shift F3 keystroke.

Inserting Symbols

The **Symbol dialog** is available from the **Insert tab**, **Symbols group**.

Ω Symbol ▾

Clicking the **Symbol drop-down** opens the **Most Recently Used (MRU) list**, giving you easy access to the last 20 symbols you used. (When you first install the program, you'll see an MRU list that contains 20 symbols chosen by Microsoft, but the list changes to reflect your personal choices as you insert different symbols. Your default MRU list might look different from the screenshot at right, which shows some symbols that I've used recently.)

To open the **Symbol dialog**, click the **More Symbols** label at the bottom of the **MRU list**. When the dialog opens, you can choose symbol sets by selecting a **Font** (from the drop-down at the top left) and/or a **subset** of symbols for that font (from the drop-down at the top right). To insert a symbol, either double-click it or click once, then click the **Insert button**. Afterwards, the label on the **Cancel** button changes to **Close**.

 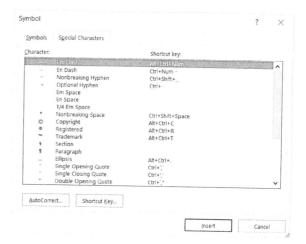

    To assign a keyboard shortcut to a symbol, click the symbol and then click the "**Shortcut key…**" button at the bottom of the dialog. Word indicates whether the key combination you choose is already assigned to another feature so that you can proceed or choose a different key combo. (**TIP**: The Alt key plus any number at the top of the keyboard is a good choice, typically not assigned to any other feature.)

    A second tab labeled "**Special Characters**" displays commonly used symbols, such as the paragraph mark (pilcrow) (¶), the section sign (§), the copyright symbol (©), non-breaking hyphens (if you don't want a hyphenated item such as a phone number to split between lines), and em-dashes (wide dashes), among others. Most of those symbols already have keyboard shortcuts assigned to them, but you can change or add shortcuts if you like.

    An **AutoCorrect** button lets you create AutoCorrect entries. For example, when I clicked the inch symbol ("), then clicked the AutoCorrect button, Word opened the AutoCorrect dialog with the inch symbol in the "With" box and the cursor positioned in the "Replace" box so that I could type an abbreviation to use when I want to insert the inch symbol as I type. I chose "\inch." (I used the backslash because otherwise, the symbol would appear whenever I type the word "inch" and press the spacebar.) Now, when I type "\inch" and press the Spacebar, Word automatically converts my abbreviation into the symbol. This feature can come in very handy and is worth exploring.

SIDEBAR: Keyboard Shortcuts Related to Fonts

Ctrl B	Applies **Bold**
Ctrl I	Applies *Italics*
Ctrl U	Applies <u>Underlining</u>
Ctrl D	Opens the Font Dialog
Shift F3	Changes case of selected text (toggles among cases)
Ctrl Shift A	Applies ALL CAPS
Ctrl Shift K	Applies THE SMALL CAPS ATTRIBUTE
Ctrl Shift W	Underlines words only (<u>not</u> <u>spaces</u> <u>or</u> <u>tabs</u>)
Ctrl Shift D	Applies <u>Double Underline</u>
Ctrl Spacebar	Removes character formatting
Ctrl]	Increases font size of selected text by 1 point
Ctrl [	Decreases font size of selected text by 1 point
Ctrl Shift >	Increases font size of selected text by 2 points
Ctrl Shift <	Decreases font size of selected text by 2 points

MISCELLANEOUS FEATURES

The Navigation Pane

The Navigation Pane is a feature first introduced in Word 2010 that combines aspects of four different functions: Find, the legacy feature known as the Document Map, another legacy feature called Browse Objects, and Thumbnails. Like the traditional "Find" dialog, it allows you search for text strings in your document. In addition, it provides an easy way for you to move quickly through a long document by jumping from one heading—or page—to another. And, like the Document Map, it serves as an organizational tool, displaying your document's headings and subheadings in outline format, and making it easy to move sections of the document around by dragging and dropping headings within the Navigation Pane.

You can open the Navigation Pane by doing any of the following:

- Clicking the **Find** icon (the magnifying glass, not the drop-down) in the **Editing group** at the right side of the **Home tab;** *or*

- Pressing **Ctrl F**[1]; *or*

- Clicking the **Navigation Pane checkbox** in the **Show group** on the **View tab, Show group** (if it isn't checked already, which by default, it isn't).

Whichever method you use, the Navigation Pane opens at the left side of the screen (though you can move it). There are three "tabs": **Headings**, **Pages**, and **Results** (as in "Search Results"). Clicking a tab label makes it the active one.

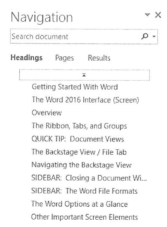

The Navigation Pane (Headings Tab)

---

[1] This keyboard shortcut no longer opens the "Find" dialog box, as it did in older versions.

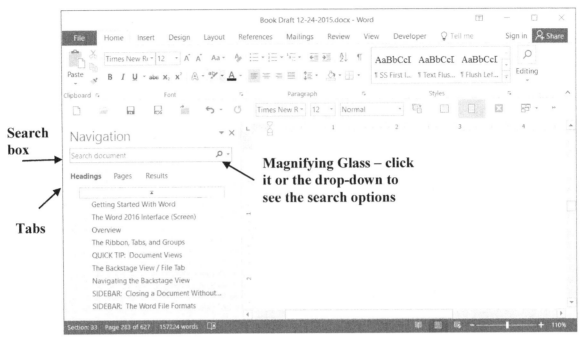

Navigation Pane at Left Side of Screen (With Headings Tab at the Forefront)

The screenshots below depict the three "tabs": **Headings** (the left-most tab), **Pages** (the center tab), and **Results** (the right-most tab). When your document contains Heading styles, you'll see them depicted in the Navigation Pane under Headings. The Pages tab shows thumbnails of each page. The Results tab shows the results of any search you perform from the search box.

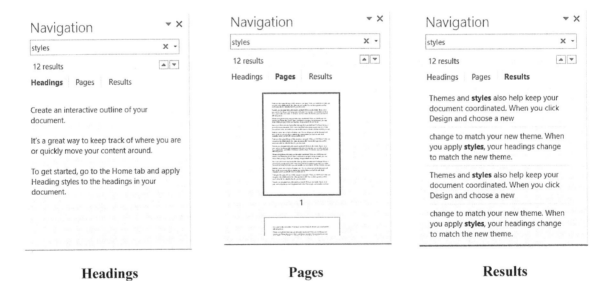

          Headings   **Pages**   **Results**

Searching

    Always visible and available for use at the top of the Navigation Pane, regardless of which tab is at the forefront, there is a search box where you can type a word or phrase to find in your document. Searching is not case-sensitive, so it doesn't matter what case you use when you type your search term.

When you type a term in the search box and press the Enter key, Word provides a tally of how many times the term appears in the document; scrolls to a page containing your search term; shows all of the search results in context in the Results tab; and highlights all instances of the term in the document in yellow so that you can see them more easily. The highlighting disappears when you stop the search—and clear the search box—by clicking the "X" to the right of the search box. (Be careful not to click the "X" at the very top of the Navigation Pane unless you want to close the pane itself.)

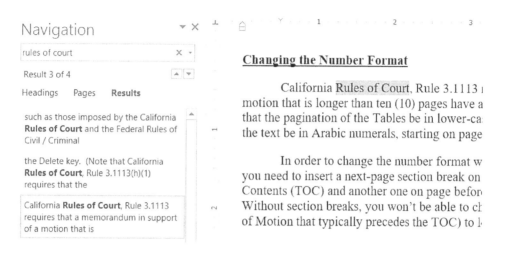

CAUTION: If you click the "X" to the right of the search box without first clicking to position the cursor in the page where the search took you, *Word will return you to the page your cursor was on when you started the search*. This action is by design.[2] Indeed, if you position the mouse pointer over the "X" in the search box, you'll see a pop-up that says: "Click or tap to end your search *and scroll back to your original place in the document*" (emphasis mine).

To avoid scrolling back to your last edit point, be sure to click somewhere within the search result page you intended as your destination *before* clicking the "X" to stop the search.

You can move to any other page that appears in the Results tab – that is, a page that contains your search term – by clicking on the boxed text in the Results tab, or by using the up or down arrow above the tabs.

Incidentally, Word uses an "incremental find" function, which means that it looks for text *as you type* and displays matches within the Search tab. For example, if your document contains the words "plaintiff," "plan," and "plant," Word shows instances of each of those words after

---

[2] Clicking the "X" that closes the Navigation Pane can have the same effect—that is, it sometimes scrolls back to the page your cursor was on when you began the search. This behavior doesn't appear to occur consistently, however.

277

you type the letters "pla." But as you type additional letters, some of the words get filtered out of the search results. The final results depend on which character you type next.

Clearing the Search Box

To reiterate, you can clear the search box (either to start a new search or simply to stop Word's incremental search feature from operating in the background) by clicking the "X" at the right side of the box.

Pausing and Resuming a Search

In this version of Word, the search process automatically pauses when you start editing the document. This feature represents an improvement over Word 2010, in which the search box sometimes clears itself when you click a contextual result to go to that page.

The Pages Tab (Thumbnail View)

The **Pages** tab, like the Thumbnail option in some older versions, provides a "thumbnail" view of your document, with each page displayed individually within the Navigation Pane. The current page (the one your cursor is in) appears within a box with a dark border. The display changes in real time – albeit sometimes with a slight lag – as you move around in your document while you are working.

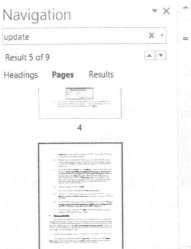

The Pages Tab

278

You can also use the Pages tab to scroll through your document. Dragging the scrollbar moves you through the document and displays a page indicator. Clicking the "Up" and "Down" arrows takes you from page to page if you haven't typed a search term, or to *the previous or next instance of your search term* if you have done so. If your search term isn't within a specific page, that page won't be displayed.

Scroll Here

Top

Bottom

Page Up

Page Down

Scroll Up

Scroll Down

Right-clicking the Navigation Pane scrollbar while the Pages tab is at the forefront opens a context-sensitive menu that offers a few scrolling options. These options change what is displayed in the Pages tab, but they don't actually move the cursor within the document or change what you see in the document editing screen.

Which pages appear in the thumbnail view when you click the "Scroll Here" option depends on the position of your mouse pointer in the scrollbar. For instance, if the mouse pointer is about halfway down the scrollbar, clicking "Scroll Here" will present a thumbnail view of two or three pages located approximately in the middle of your document. If the mouse pointer is toward the top of the scrollbar, the command will result in the display of pages near the beginning of the document. And so forth.

The "Top" command displays the very first page of the document; the "Bottom" command displays the very last one. "Page Up" and "Page Down" show the page before or the page after whatever is currently displayed in the Pages tab.

"Scroll Up" and "Scroll Down" move the thumbnails up or down incrementally.

Note that you can't actually move pages around in your document via the Pages tab (i.e., you can't drag and drop entire pages the way that you can drag and drop headings and subheadings via the Headings tab).

TIP: If you like, you can widen the Navigation Pane by positioning the mouse pointer over the right border and, when the double-headed arrow appears, dragging the border farther to the right. That will allow you to see more pages, displayed in two or more columns, in thumbnail view. When you change the display to show thumbnails in multiple columns (as in the screenshot at right), the "Page Up" and "Page Down" commands on the context menu actually jump more than a single page at a time.

It's worth repeating that the "Search" function of the Navigation Pane acts as a filter on the Pages tab. That is, if you have entered a word or phrase in the search box, the Pages tab will display *only those pages that contain your search term*. In order to see all pages, be sure to clear the search box by clicking the "X" at the right side of the box.[3]

---

[3] The "Find" function doesn't work quite the same way with respect to the Headings tab. See page 282 for more information.

The Headings Tab

The Headings tab is very useful if you have applied heading styles in your document. Any headings formatted with styles are automatically pulled into the Navigation Pane, where they are displayed in a condensed outline view.

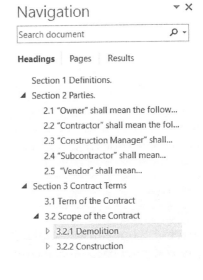

The Navigation Pane doesn't merely *reflect* the structure of your document; it also provides an easy way to reorder topics. Dragging and dropping headings from within the Headings tab actually moves those sections in the document. Assuming the headings use automatic numbering, they should renumber accordingly.

Be sure to double-check. If they ***don't*** renumber properly, look at the document and locate the first heading that should have incremented but did not. **Right-click** within the paragraph number and, when the context-sensitive menu appears, choose the "**Continue Numbering**" command.

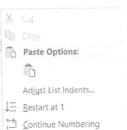

Numbers Right-Click Menu (Partial)

CAUTION: Consider making a backup copy of your document before experimenting with this feature, just in case you change your mind afterwards and have difficulty restoring the document's original organization.[4]

It's easy to change how the headings are displayed in the Headings tab. When you right-click on one of the headings, a context-sensitive pop-up menu appears, offering several highly useful commands for organizing your document.

For example, the "**Expand All**" command shows all of the heading levels in the document, whereas "**Collapse All**" shows only the level 1 headings.

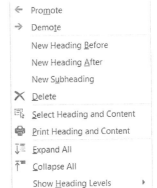

Headings Right-Click Menu

---

[4] You should be able to undo any moves by pressing Ctrl Z or clicking the Undo button on the Quick Access Toolbar, assuming you act quickly.

In the screenshots below, you can see a sample Trust document with the headings collapsed (at left) and expanded (at right).

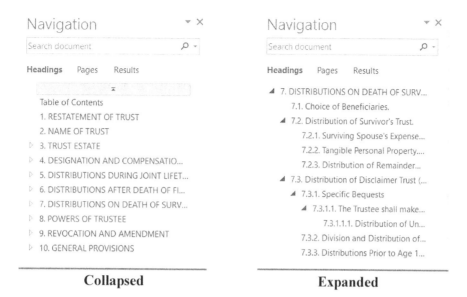

Collapsed   **Expanded**

The right-click menu also provides a "**Show Heading Levels**" command that you can click to specify exactly how many levels to display in the Headings tab. (You can display any number of heading levels in your document from one to nine.) Note that choosing a particular level means displaying headings *up to and including* that level. For instance, clicking "Show Heading 2" will show two levels of headings (i.e., all headings to which a Heading 1 or a Heading 2 style has been applied). See the screenshots below.

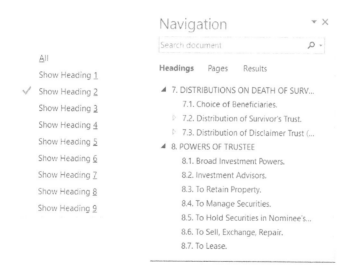

Individual headings that contain at least one section with a subheading can be expanded or collapsed. In the screenshots, you'll notice a small white triangle to the left of those headings that contain sections with subheadings. The black triangles show headings that have been expanded; the white ones show headings that have been collapsed. Clicking a white triangle expands a heading "family"; clicking a black one collapses it.

Also, you can use the right-click menu to insert a new heading before or after an existing heading. From within the Navigation Pane, right-click the heading you want the new heading positioned before or after and, when the context menu appears, choose "New Heading Before" or "New Heading After," as appropriate.

When I right-clicked paragraph 7.2.3 and then clicked "New Heading After," Word added a new (blank) paragraph 7.2.4. in both the Navigation Pane and the document. See the screenshots below.

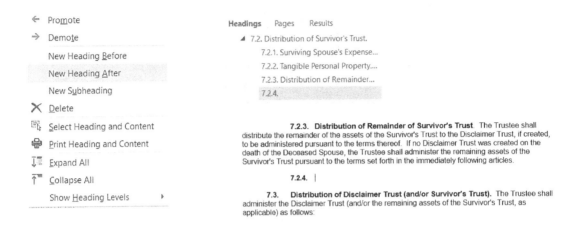

The right-click menu also contains a "New Subheading" command. Be aware that when you right-click a specific heading or subheading, then click the "New Subheading" command, Word does indeed create a new subheading, but places it *after the last existing subheading* at that level. (In other words, if you right-click a Level 2 subheading and click "New Subheading," Word will create a new Level 3 subheading and place it after any pre-existing Level 3 subheadings, not after the Level 2 subheading itself.)

That placement is logical, but it might not be what you intended. If the new subheading doesn't appear where you want it, just drag and drop it within the Headings tab to position it in the correct order. The numbering of the other subheadings should update automatically.

You can also use the right-click menu to promote or demote headings or subheadings (i.e., change their outline level); to delete them altogether; to print them (along with any text that follows); or to select them and then apply formatting. To do the latter, right-click a heading or subheading, choose "Select Heading and Content" (the content includes the heading family and associated text), and then apply character or paragraph formatting or a style.

A final word about the Headings tab: If you recently used the "Find" feature to search for a word or phrase, your search term acts as a filter on what is displayed in the Headings tab. That is, all of the headings and subheadings in your document to which styles have been applied will appear there, but you might notice that some of them – the ones that contain your search term – are highlighted.

The screenshot at right shows headings and subheadings in my family trust document after I searched for the word "bequest." The headings that contain my search term are highlighted in yellow.

To remove the highlighting (and clear the filter), just click the "X" at the right side of the search box.

Moving the Navigation Pane

There are a couple of ways to move the Navigation Pane. You can drag it by its title bar and drop it in a new location. Or you can click the down-pointing triangle at the top right side of the Navigation Pane to open the drop-down (the "**Control Menu**"), then click **Move**, and then do a drag-and-drop operation. Note that after you drop the Nav Pane, you should *click to anchor it in position*. Otherwise, it might continue to move when you reposition the mouse pointer.

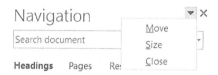

The Navigation Pane's "Control Menu"

You also have the option of resizing the Navigation Pane, as mentioned previously, by dragging its right border *or* by clicking the Control Menu and clicking Size, then moving the mouse pointer. Be sure to click again when you're finished to stop the resizing operation.

Closing the Navigation Pane

You can close the Navigation Pane by doing one of the following:

- Clicking the "X" at the top right side of the Pane; or
- Pressing the Esc key[5]; or
- Clicking the drop-down at the top of the Navigation Pane, then clicking "Close."

A "Sticky" Setting

The state of the Navigation Pane (i.e., whether it is displayed or hidden) is "sticky." In other words, if it's displayed when you close out of Word, it will be displayed when you re-launch the program and vice versa.

---

[5] In my tests, this method worked only some of the time. I had the most success shortly after opening / displaying the Navigation Pane.

Additional Search Commands

When you click either the magnifying glass or the arrow to the right of the Search box, a menu with additional search commands appears.

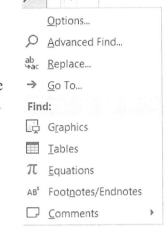

This menu is similar to the "Browse by Object" screen that appears in versions of Word prior to Word 2013 when you click the circle at the bottom of the vertical scrollbar. However, the menu in the Navigation Pane uses words, as well as icons, to label the commands. (Also, the drop-down menu contains fewer objects.) Both let you search for objects other than text in your document.

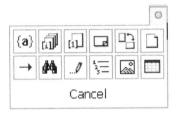

The Browse by Object Screen From Word 2010

The drop-down (much like the Browse by Object screen) includes the following commands / selections:

- Options…
- Advanced Find…
- Replace…
- Go To…
- Graphics
- Tables
- Equations
- Footnotes/Endnotes
- Comments

I will backtrack and discuss "**Options…**" in the next section.

"**Advanced Find**" invokes the traditional Find dialog box, complete with tabs for Replace and Go To; "**Replace**" produces the same dialog, but with the Replace tab at the forefront, and **Go To** opens the dialog with the Go To tab at the forefront.

When you click the "**Graphics**" command, Word immediately searches the document for images. It stops at the first one it comes to – that is, the first one that appears in or after the page your cursor is in when you start the search.

To see the next graphic in the document, click the down arrow to the right of the tabs. (If you prefer, you can use the scrollbar to move more quickly through the Pages display.)

Searching for graphics (or other objects), like searching for text, serves as a filter on the Pages tab. In other words, if you click the Pages tab after searching for graphics in the document, you'll see that the tab displays *only thumbnails of pages that contain graphics*.

Searching for the other types of objects (tables, equations, footnotes / endnotes, or comments) works essentially the same way. When you search for **comments**, however, you need to select a particular "reviewer" (commenter) or "**All Reviewers**."

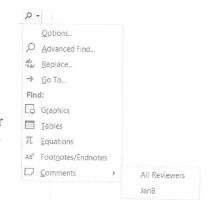

After you search for a certain type of object, remember to click the "X" at the right side of the search box to clear it—and make the magnifying glass visible again—so that you can start a new search. You must do so regardless of whether the new search involves a different type of object or text.

The Find Options

The first command on the menu that appears when you click the magnifying glass (or the "Down" arrow to its right) is **Options…** Clicking **Options…** produces a dialog that displays several different "**Find Options**" you can use to delimit complex searches involving text.

"Highlight all" and "Incremental find" already are checked because they are default settings. You can change them if you like. If you uncheck "Incremental find," Word will stop searching for text strings as you type them in the search box. You will need to type the entire word or phrase and then press the Enter key or click the magnifying glass to carry out the search.

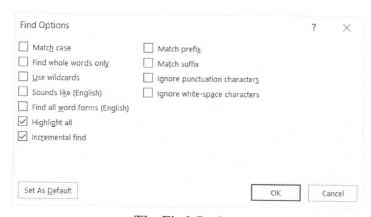

The Find Options

285

Once you have selected the options you wish to use, you can click the drop-down again, then click the binoculars to start a "Find" operation using the filters you've selected.

Here is a brief explanation of each option.

- **Match case**

    When this option is checked, Word will search for a word or phrase in the case that you use to type the word in the search box (or in the Find dialog): UPPER, lower, Initial Caps, etc. If the word or phrase occurs in the document in a different case from what you type in the search box (or Find dialog), those instances of the word or phrase will not appear in the search results.

- **Find whole words only**

    This option can be helpful if you are looking for a word that might be subsumed within a longer word. For instance, let's say you want to find all occurrences of the word "he" in estate documents so that you can replace the male gender with the female gender (a common practice when creating estate docs for a husband and wife). Obviously, searching for the letters "he" without limiting the search to whole words will turn up all sorts of irrelevant results, such as "she," "whether," and "the." Applying the "whole words" filter will make the search results more meaningful.

- **Use wildcards**

    You might be familiar with wildcards from searches you've performed with Lexis or Westlaw or on the Internet. Wildcard characters such as the question mark (?), the asterisk (*), or the exclamation point (!) typically stand in for other characters, so that you can find all forms of certain words in your document or find a particular word even if you're not sure how it's spelled.

    In Word, some wildcards are fairly simple to use. For example, the question mark character (?) stands in for a single character. Thus, the search term "f?rm" (without quotation marks) will find the words "farm," "firm," and "form" (if those words appear in your document). Some of the other wildcards work in a less straightforward manner. The asterisk (*), for example, stands in for multiple contiguous characters.[6] In theory, it lets you search for words when you're not certain of the spelling or when a word is spelled differently with American English ("color") and British English ("colour"). You would use the search term "col*r" (without quotation marks), where the asterisk stands for multiple characters between the letter "l" and the letter "r." That would find both "color" and "colour."

---

[6] This usage is somewhat different from searches in Lexis and/or Westlaw.

In Word, however, the asterisk can produce results that include *multiple consecutive words*. So, a search that turns up both "color" and "colour" might also highlight text in your document such as "column or"—because the asterisk wildcard apparently encompasses spaces (and punctuation marks), as well as alphabetical and numeric characters. Thus, it does not limit a search to individual words.

You *can* perform wildcard searches and limit the results to individual words, but to do so requires the use of a more complex "expression." Advanced searches involving so-called regular expressions are beyond the scope of this book.[7]

- **Sounds like**

  You can use the "Sounds like" filter to search for words you're not sure how to spell. (For instance, suddenly you can't remember if it's "supercede" or "supersede," "admissible" or "admissable." "Sounds like" will find either.)

- **Find all word forms**

  This nifty option looks for all forms of a particular word. For example, a search for "navigate" also turns up "navigation," "navigated," and "navigating."

  CAUTION: If you choose to *replace* word forms, it's advisable to review each instance of the word rather than using "Replace All." Word, while smart enough to *find* all of the forms of a particular word, isn't necessarily smart enough to *replace* with the correct word form.

- **Match prefix**

  This option looks for letters at the beginning of a word (or that form an entire word). As an example, if you click the "Match prefix" option and then search for the word "fix" (not within quotation marks), Word will find "fix" by itself, and also at the beginning of words (such as "fixed," "fixing," and "fixated") but not at the end of words ("prefix," "suffix," "affixed").

- **Match suffix**

  This option works like "Match prefix," but looks for words that appear at the end of a word rather than at the beginning. (It also finds whole words.) Hence, if this option is checked and you search for the word "fix," Word will find "prefix" and "suffix," but not the words "fixed," "fixing," "fixated," "fixer," "fixed," and so on.

---

[7] For detailed instructions on using wildcards and complex expressions, see the Microsoft article, "Replace text using wildcards," located here: https://support.office.com/en-US/article/Replace-text-using-wildcards-5CDA8B1B-2FEB-45A6-AF0E-824173D3D6E4 and Microsoft MVP Graham Mayor's article: http://www.gmayor.com/replace_using_wildcards.htm

- **Ignore punctuation characters**

  This option finds words whether they appear before a comma, a period, an exclamation point, a question mark, etc. But if you check this option and then specify a punctuation character as part of your search term, Word includes that character—and excludes other punctuation—in the search results (if it finds any matches).

  For instance, if I enable the "Ignore punctuation characters" option and then search for "WordPerfect." (i.e., my search term is WordPerfect followed by a period, but without quotation marks), Word finds only those instances of "WordPerfect" that are followed by a period. It does not return instances of "WordPerfect" followed by a comma. If I use the "Ignore punctuation characters" filter and then remove the comma from the search term, Word finds all instances of "WordPerfect," whether in the middle of a sentence or followed by a comma or a period.

- **Ignore white-space characters**

  This option will find a search term whether it appears with or without white space incorporated into the term. For example, if you check this option and then search for "WordPerfect," Word will find both "WordPerfect" and "Word Perfect"; likewise, a search for "screenshot" will turn up both "screenshot" and "screen shot" (assuming your document contains both terms).

- **Highlight all**

  As mentioned previously, this option is enabled by default. It acts to highlight all instances of your search term in the document (in yellow) to help you locate them. The temporary highlighting disappears when you clear the search box by clicking the "X" to the right of your term.

- **Incremental find**

  Also mentioned previously, this default setting lets Word look for text strings, and filter the search results, in real time as you type characters in the search box. You don't have to press the "Enter" key to carry out the search.

CAUTION: After you have finished using one or more of these filters, remember to open the Find Options dialog and ***uncheck*** (clear) them. Otherwise, ***they will remain enabled*** and, in future searches, will exclude certain results you probably did not intend to screen out. The same advice holds if you have used any other advanced search options available from the "Format" or "Special" buttons in the Find dialog. For more tips about using the Find feature, see the section starting on page 292.

Two Other Organizational Tools

The Headings tab within the Navigation Pane can be useful when you want to view your document in outline form – that is, that is, to see a "collapsed" version of your document that displays only headings, or only the first couple of levels of headings, rather than all of the headings plus the text of the document. There are a couple of other tools you might want to consider to help you organize your document.

Collapsible Headings

With Word 2013, Microsoft introduced another way of producing an outline view of documents that use heading styles: **Collapsible Headings**. When a heading style has been applied to text, a triangle appears to the left of the heading when you hold your mouse there. As in Windows Explorer / File Explorer, a dark triangle that points down means that the heading is "expanded" – in other words, you can see the text and any subheadings that follow. A white triangle that points to the side means that the heading is "collapsed" – in other words, you can see only the heading, but the text and any subheadings are not visible. In the example below, the first and second headings are collapsed, and the third is expanded.

▷ 1.   RESTATEMENT OF TRUST

▷ 2.   NAME OF TRUST

◢ 3.   TRUST ESTATE

        The property listed in the attached Schedule(s) and its proceeds, as well as any other property held in the name of the trust, shall be referred to as the trust estate.

Right-clicking in or near a triangle produces a pop-up menu that includes an Expand/Collapse command with options to expand or collapse an individual heading (depending on whether it is already collapsed or expanded) or to expand or collapse all headings in your document.

By default, if you close a document with some or all of the headings collapsed, the document will open with the headings expanded. If you prefer to have the headings stay collapsed when you open the doc, open the Paragraph dialog, click within a heading and then click / enable the new "**Collapsed by default**" checkbox (see the screenshot on the next page).

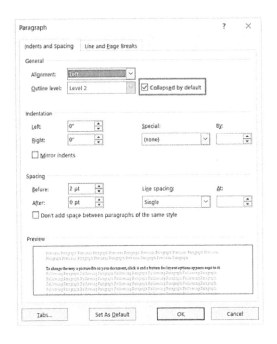

If you are concerned that you might inadvertently miss seeing important text when headings are collapsed, you can configure the Word Options so that collapsed headings automatically expand when you open a document. This option, which is disabled by default, is located in the Advanced category (**File**, **Options**, **Advanced**) under "**Show document content**."

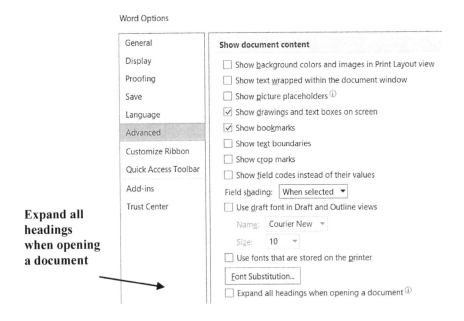

Incidentally, note that Word's Document Inspector, which you can use to search for metadata in a document, looks for and alerts you to any collapsed headings (among other content you might want to check or remove before sending the document outside your organization). See the partial screenshot on the next page.

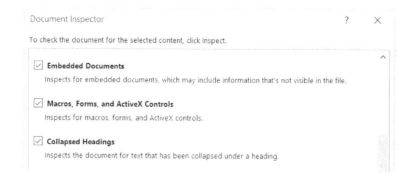

If the Document Inspector finds collapsed headings, it notifies you with a red exclamation point. If you then click "Remove All," Word expands all of the collapsed headings (it doesn't actually remove them!) so that you can see the text below them.

Outline View

Another feature you can use to help you organize your document is Outline View. This is not a new feature, but you might not be aware of it. To enable the Outline view, navigate to the left side of the View tab and click the "Outline" icon. The Outlining tab will appear.

You can use the commands on this tab to collapse text and view only the headings, move "families" of headings, sub-headings, and text, and show only certain heading levels.

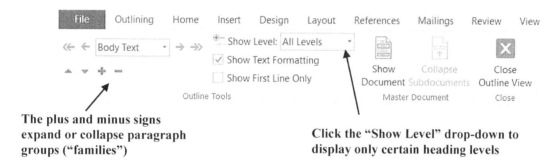

One significant difference between this feature and the Collapsible Headings feature is that in Outline View, headings and text don't necessarily appear the way they look in Print Layout view. For example, headings that are formatted to be center-justified won't appear to be centered in Outline View.

Note that Outline View is intended mainly as an organizational tool. To apply or create different types of outlines, use the Multilevel List feature (see the section starting on page 497).

Using the Traditional "Find" Dialog

You can still use the traditional Find dialog if you like. There several ways to invoke it:

- From within the Navigation Pane, click the **magnifying glass** at the top of the Search tab or **the arrow** to the right of it to display a drop-down with various options. Click "**Advanced Find**" to open the traditional Find dialog; or

- Navigate to the right side of the **Home tab**, click the **Find** drop-down, and choose "**Advanced Find**"; or

- Press **Ctrl H** to open the Find and Replace dialog with the "Replace" tab at the forefront, then click the "**Find**" tab; or

- Press **Ctrl G** to open the Find and Replace dialog with the "Go To" tab at the forefront.

Finding Text

Performing a simple, straightforward "find" works the same way as in previous versions, although there are a couple of relatively new bells and whistles (see the section about advanced Find features that starts on page 298). Just enter your search term in the "**Find what**" box, and then either click the "**Find Next**" **button** *or* use the keyboard shortcut **Alt F** to move to the next instance of your term.

Word typically searches from the cursor position forward ("Down"), although you can change the direction if you like. (Instructions follow.) When Word has finished searching the document, a pop-up appears, asking if you want to start over. This feature is useful in case your cursor was not at the very beginning of the document when you started your search.

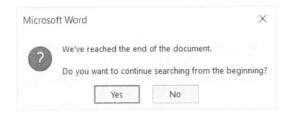

292

To see the advanced options, click the "**More**" button at the bottom left side of the Find dialog.

The expanded dialog provides access to the advanced options discussed in the previous section, as well as additional options available from the "**Format**" and "**Special**" buttons at the lower left side. I will explore those options in the next section.

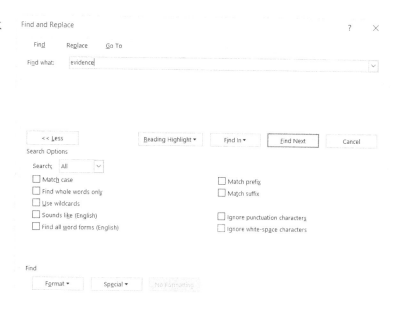

Toward the middle of the dialog, just above the advanced options, there is a "**Search**" drop-down that you can click to change the direction of the search.

By default Word searches forward, but if your cursor is at or near the end of your document, you can change the dropdown to "Up" and search backwards.

CAUTION: Settings in the Find dialog are "sticky" (persistent), so be sure to change this setting back to "All" before performing another search.

Replacing Text

Replacing unformatted text (i.e., text without font attributes such as underlining, bolding, and/or italics) is straightforward. Type your search term in the "**Find what**" box and the term you want to use instead in the "**Replace with**" box. Then click "**Find Next**" (or press **Alt F**) and click "**Replace**" as appropriate or, if you're sure you want to replace all instances of a word or phrase with another one, click "**Replace All**."

Use "Replace All" with caution. It's easy to replace text by accident that you didn't mean to replace.

Options such as "**Match case**" and "**Whole words only**" can help. For instance, if you want to replace "plaintiff" with "Plaintiff," you'll get better results if you check "**Match case**" before proceeding.

Similarly, to replace "he" with "she" you'll get better results by clicking "**Find whole words only**" first.

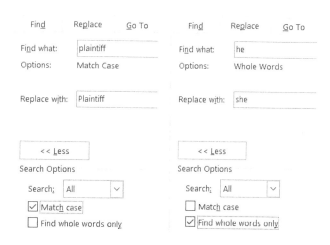

293

Searching for Formatted Text

It can be surprisingly difficult to search for formatted text. Here's how:

1. Open the **Find dialog**.

2. Click the "**More**" button to expand the dialog.

3. Click to position the cursor in the "**Find what**" box.

4. Type your search word or phrase. (**NOTE**: You can perform this step before or after choosing the font formatting.)

5. Click the "**Format**" button at the bottom left side of the dialog and choose "**Font**."

6. When the **Font dialog** opens, do one of the following:

    (a) For underlining, click the "**Underline style**" drop-down and choose the **single underline style** shown in the screenshot below;

    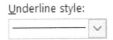

    (b) For bolding, click "**Bold**" in the "**Font style**" box (and, if necessary, make sure that the "Underline style" drop-down is set to ("none") so that you don't end up with both bolding and underlining);

    (c) For italics, click "**Italic**" in the "**Font style**" box (and, if necessary, make sure that the "Underline style" drop-down is set to ("none") so that you don't end up with both italics and underlining).

7. Click "**Next**" or press **Alt F** to search for the formatted word or phrase.

Be sure to *clear the formatting* from the "Find what" box before performing another search. If you don't, Word will look for your new search term *with formatting applied to it* (leaving you mystified as to why the program couldn't find the term). To start a new search without formatting, click within the "**Find what**" box, then click the "**No Formatting**" button at the bottom of the expanded Find dialog.[1]

---

[1] Clearing the formatting before closing the dialog won't accomplish anything, because settings in the "Find what" and "Replace with" boxes persist until you perform another find or replace operation – or exit from Word.

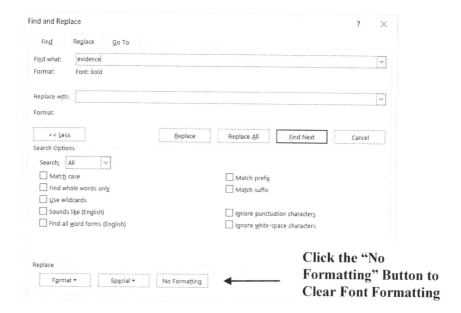

Click the "No Formatting" Button to Clear Font Formatting

Replacing Formatted Text

To find and replace formatted text, open the Find dialog to the Replace tab (an easy way to do so is by pressing the keyboard shortcut **Ctrl H**). Then follow the steps outlined above for both the "**Find what**" box and the "**Replace with**" box – choosing the appropriate font attribute for each.

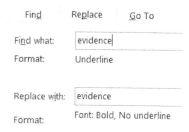

If necessary, turn off the Bold attribute within the Font dialog by either clicking "Regular" instead of bold or simply deleting any text within the "Font style" box, as shown in the screenshot at right.

Replacing Tabs, Section Breaks, Styles, etc.

Another handy option is to use Find and Replace to delete extraneous tabs (especially the leading tabs that are imported when you paste from WordPerfect – even with the Keep Text Only option, which strips out nearly all of the formatting from the source document). Or you can delete section breaks. As an example, here are the instructions for replacing tabs:

1. First, **select the paragraphs with leading tabs** (or other text that has tabs you want to delete).[2]

---

[2] **CAUTION**: As a general rule, it's probably not a good idea to select the entire document and replace all of the tabs. Most documents contain what I think of as "beneficial tabs," such as tabs between a heading number and the heading text – and ordinarily, you wouldn't want to delete those tabs.

2. Press **Ctrl H** or click the "**Replace**" **icon** at the right side of the **Home tab** to open the Find dialog with the Replace tab at the forefront.

3. If necessary, click "**More**" to expand the dialog.

4. Position your cursor in the "**Find what**" box.

5. Click the "**Special**" button at the bottom of the expanded dialog.

6. When the "**Special**" **menu** opens (screenshot at right), click the item you want to find and/or replace.[3] In this example, we're replacing tabs, so, click "**Tab Character**."

7. Leave the "**Replace with**" box **blank**. The process of deleting the tabs essential boils down to replacing them with nothing.

8. If you have selected only certain paragraphs that have tabs you know you want to delete, click "**Replace All**." Otherwise, click "Find Next" and click "Replace" when appropriate.

NOTE: Some of the options in the "Special" menu might not work if "Wildcards" is checked. (However, when I tested finding and replacing Tab Characters, I did not experience any problem, even with "Wildcards" checked.)

Replacing Other Formatting

In addition to using the "Special" menu to replace various characters, you can use the "**Format**" **menu** at the bottom left side of the Find dialog to replace fonts, paragraph formatting such as line spacing, tab settings (i.e., tab stops, not tab characters themselves), language choices, frames, styles, and highlighting.

For example, if you need to change the Double line spacing throughout the document from to Exactly 24, you could do a find and replace. With your cursor at the beginning of the document, do the following:

---

[3] "Paragraph mark" means the non-printing character mark that appears at the end of each paragraph and contains the formatting codes for that paragraph. "Paragraph symbol" means the character that you insert from the Symbol dialog, as when you refer to a paragraph within another document.

296

1. Press **Ctrl H** (or click "Replace" at the right side of the Home tab) to open the Find dialog with the Replace tab at the forefront.

2. Click the "**More**" **button** to expand the dialog.

3. Place your cursor in the "**Find what**" box.

4. Click the "**Format**" **button** at the bottom left side, and choose **Paragraph**.

5. When the Paragraph dialog opens, navigate to **Line spacing**, choose "**Double**," and click **OK**.

6. Place your cursor in the "**Replace with**" box.

7. Click the "**Format**" **button** and choose **Paragraph**.

8. When the Paragraph dialog opens, navigate to **Line spacing**, choose "**Exactly**" and type the number 24 (or use the "spinner" arrows to increase the points to 24), then click **OK**.

9. Click "**Replace All**."

10. Check to make sure the double-spaced text in the document changed to Exactly 24 points (it should have; in my tests it worked perfectly).

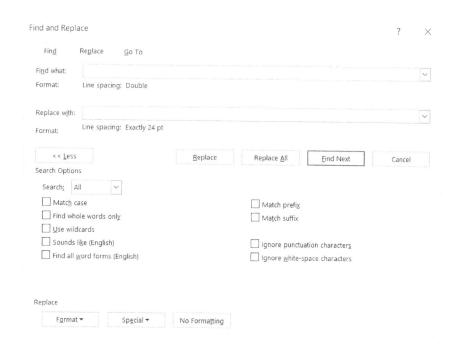

Nice, eh? Keep in mind that you can use this feature to replace highlighting, styles and many other types of formatting.

Clearing Your Search Criteria

Remember to *clear the text as well as any formatting* from both the "Find what" box and the "Replace with" box before performing another find or replace operation. To do so, click within the "**Find what**" box, then click the "**No Formatting**" button at the bottom of the expanded Find dialog; do the same for the "**Replace with**" box. As mentioned previously, settings in these boxes persist until you perform another find or replace – or exit from Word.[4]

As far as I know, the only sure-fire way clear your search criteria completely and start with empty "Find what" and "Replace with" boxes is to exit from Word and reopen the program (be sure to save all of your work before exiting!).

"Reading Highlight" and "Find In"

You might not have noticed a couple of useful, but somewhat obscure, advanced Find options that were introduced in Word 2007. One is the "**Reading Highlight**" option in the "Find" dialog box. When you type a search term in the box and click the **Reading Highlight drop-down**, then click "**Highlight All**," Word goes through your document and highlights all instances of the term in yellow so that you can locate them easily. When you want to turn the highlighting off again, just click "**Clear Highlighting**." ("Clear Highlighting" is grayed out before you apply highlighting; it becomes active afterwards.)

There is also a "**Find in**" button that lets you specify which part of the document to search: the **Main Document**, **Headers and Footers**, **Footnotes**, **Text Boxes in Main Document** or, if you have text selected, **Current Selection**. Note that the options available from this drop-down vary depending on the types of formatting that exist in the current document.

---

[4] Clearing the text and formatting and closing the Find dialog doesn't do the trick, as you'll discover if you perform another Find or Replace.

CAUTION: This feature occasionally goes awry, in that you might assume that the program is searching the entire document, but Word "gets stuck" searching only the footnotes. If you get an error message indicating that the program can't find any more instances of a particular word *in the footnotes*, be sure to click "**Find in**" and reset the search location to "**Main Document**," and then click "**Find Next**" to resume searching the document text.

The "Go To" Dialog

A somewhat under-used option, the Go To portion of the Find dialog can be extremely helpful. This feature, which you can initiate directly by pressing **F5** or **Ctrl G**, gives you a quick way to move to a specific page, section, bookmark, footnote, and so forth.[5]

The complete list of "go to" items includes:

- Page
- Section
- Line
- Bookmark
- Comment
- Footnote
- Endnote
- Field
- Table
- Graphic
- Equation
- Object
- Heading

"Page" is the default object, but you can change that by clicking any other object in the list. You can use the "**Next**" and "**Previous**" buttons to move to next or previous object, or you can type a plus sign (+) or a minus sign (-), then press the "**Enter**" key (or click the "Go To" button). If you type a number, such as 3, after the plus or minus sign, pressing "Enter" or clicking "Go To" will take you that many objects forward or back – say, three footnotes before or after the current one.

---

[5] You can also open the Go To dialog by clicking the **Section indicator** in the **Status Bar**, if you've added it. Or, at the right side of the **Home tab**, click the **Find drop-down, Go To**.

299

For a few object types, a drop-down appears to the right of the "Go to what" box, offering specific choices. If you click "Bookmark," for example, you'll see a drop-down list with the names of all of the bookmarks in your document. Similarly, if you choose "Field" (Field Code) as the object, you'll see a list of available field codes. If you choose "Comment," you can select "Any reviewer" or a specific comment author.

Like the Find dialog, the Go To dialog is "sticky"; it retains the last setting you used. So, for instance, if you invoked Go To and entered a specific page number, that page number will be in the "Enter page number" box the next time you use the feature. The only way to clear the box completely is to exit from Word and then reopen the program.

TROUBLESHOOTING TIP: "Find" Disables Page Up and Page Down

After you use "Find," "Find and Replace," or the Navigation Pane to look for a word, phrase, or object, the keyboard shortcuts for Page Up (**Ctrl Page Up**) and Page Down (**Ctrl Page Dn**) stop working as navigation keys. This seemingly arbitrary change in functionality actually is working as designed – as they used to say, "It's not a bug; it's a feature" – but it's not particularly logical and can be disconcerting if you're not expecting it. It has to do with the "**Browse by Object**" feature used in earlier versions of Word.

This now-discontinued feature made it easy to move through your document page by page – or *object by object*: edits / revisions, headings, graphics, tables, fields, endnotes, footnotes, comments, or sections. In other words, when you chose a particular "browse by" object (such as graphics or comments), you could move quickly from one instance of that object in the document to another.[1] Browse by Object also included a "Find" option; choosing that option opened the Find dialog.

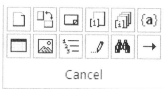

Top: Page, Section, Comment, Footnote, Endnote, Field

Bottom: Table, Graphic, Heading, Edits, Find, Go To

Browse by Object

For some reason, Microsoft assigned the key combination normally used for Page Up (**Ctrl Pg Up**) and Page Down (**Ctrl Pg Dn**) to the Browse by Object feature itself, ***not*** to Page Up and Page Down. That wasn't a problem most of the time, because by default "Browse by Object" was set to browse *by page*. So pressing Ctrl Pg Up or Ctrl Pg Dn worked as expected.

The problem was – and is – that using Find, Replace, or the Navigation Pane's search function resets the "browse by" object from *page* to *Find* (meaning that it browses by the last-used search term). Therefore, after you have performed a search, pressing Ctrl Pg Up or Ctrl Pg Down actually initiates a "Find" rather than moving to the previous or next page.[2] That's why you'll sometimes see a message more often associated with searching:

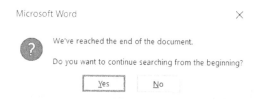

---

[1] You can still do that, either from the Navigation Pane's drop-down or from the Go To dialog.

[2] The keyboard shortcuts are associated with the commands "**BrowseNext**" and "**BrowsePrev**." That means that they move to the next (or previous) object, depending on what type of object, if any, you selected from the Navigation Pane drop-down or from the Go To dialog – or the next (or previous) instance of a search term you entered into the Find dialog..

In versions of Word prior to 2013, most people worked around this problem by clicking the "Browse by Object" icon on the vertical scrollbar and choosing "page," which reset the "browse by" object from Find to Page. However, the icon (shown at right) has been removed, so that solution is no longer available. And the problem still exists, because when Microsoft removed the "**Browse by Object**" feature from Word (starting with Word 2013), the company didn't reassign the keyboard shortcuts to the Page Up and Page Down functions. They are still assigned to BrowseNext and BrowsePrev.

Happily, there are three other workarounds that you can use to fix this issue.

Workaround #1: "Go To" Dialog

The fastest workaround, albeit a temporary one, is to open the "**Go To**" **dialog**, make sure it is set to **Page**, and click "**Next**." In effect, that resets the "browse by" object to page – much like clicking the "Page" object in the Browse by Object icon on the vertical scrollbar.[3] After you do so, close the Go To dialog. Ctrl PgUp and Ctrl PgDown should now move to the previous and next page.

Workaround #2: Add Page Up and Page Down Icons to the QAT

Another workaround is to add Page Up and Page Down icons to the Quick Access Toolbar (QAT). To do so:

1. **Right-click** within the Ribbon or the QAT and choose "**Customize the Quick Access Toolbar**" (*or* click the "Customize Quick Access Toolbar" drop-down at the right side of the QAT, then click "More commands");

2. When the Word Options dialog opens, change the "**Choose commands from**" drop-down at the top left to "**All commands**."

3. Click in the **Commands list** below "All commands" and press the letter "**P**" to move to the first command that starts with that letter, and then scroll to "**Page Down**."

4. Click to **select / highlight** that command, then click the "**Add**" button in the center.

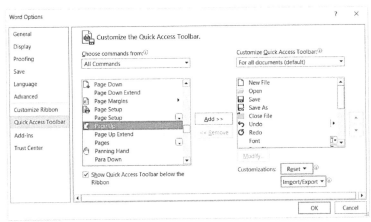

---

[3] Alternatively, you can open the **Go To dialog** by pressing **Ctrl G**, click **Page**, click **Next** (or **Previous**), then click **Close**. CAUTION: Simply clicking Page in the Go To dialog and then clicking Close without clicking Next or Previous *does not* re-set the default search object.

5.   Repeat Steps 3 and 4 for "**Page Up**."

6.   To move one of the commands farther left or right on the QAT, click the "**Up**" or "**Down**" arrow at the right side of the dialog.

7.   Click "**OK**" to save your changes and close the Word Options dialog.

Note that this workaround doesn't affect what the Ctrl PgUp and Ctrl PgDn keyboard shortcuts do. It is a *substitute* for those keyboard shortcuts. If you would prefer to use the keyboard to move from one page to the next (or previous), the third workaround might be the best one for you.

Workaround #3: Reassign Ctrl PgUp and Ctrl PgDn

A permanent, and elegant, solution, although it's also the most time-consuming, is to reassign the Ctrl PgUp and Ctrl PgDn keyboard shortcuts to Page Up and Page Down. [4] To do so, follow these steps:

1.   Click the **File tab, Options, Customize Ribbon**, then click the "**Keyboard shortcuts: Customize" button**.

2.   In the **Categories box**, scroll down to and click **All Commands**.

3.   In the **Commands** box, scroll down to and click **GoToNextPage**.

4.   Next, click in the **Press new shortcut key:** box and press **Ctrl PgDn**.

5.   Word will indicate that the shortcut already is assigned to BrowseNext. To reassign the shortcut, click the **Assign** button.

6.   Then, in the **Commands** box, scroll down to and click **GoToPreviousPage**.

7.   In the **Press new shortcut key:** box and press **Ctrl PgUp**.

8.   Word will indicate that the shortcut already is assigned to BrowsePrev. To reassign the shortcut, click the **Assign** button.

9.   When you've finished, click **Close**, and then be sure to click **OK** (not Cancel) to close out of Word Options.

Now, when you wish to move up or down one full page, you can use the traditional keyboard shortcuts. They'll work regardless of whether you have recently used "Find," "Find and Replace," the Navigation Pane, or "Browse by Object."

---

[4] One advantage of this method is that you can continue to use familiar keyboard shortcuts for those functions. (Note that Page Up and Page Down move only one screen up or down, not a full page.)

Copying and Pasting: The Paste Options

The Paste function has been revamped in a couple of significant respects in recent versions of Word. For one thing, the program offers various options for pasting text that you have copied or cut from another document (or from another location in the current document). For another thing, you can preview the way each option will affect the formatting of the text, which makes it easier for you to determine which one to use.

After you have cut or copied text, you can paste it by doing any of the following:

- press the keyboard shortcut **Ctrl V** (doing so pastes *with formatting*); *or*

- click the clipboard icon at the left side of the Home tab (doing so pastes *with formatting*); *or*

- click the **Paste drop-down** below the clipboard at the left side of the **Home tab**, then choose one of the paste options; *or*

- **right-click** the location where you want the pasted text to go and then choose one of the options from the pop-up menu.

With all of those methods, **Paste Options button** pops up after you paste the text so that you can choose a different formatting option if the pasted text doesn't look the way you want.

Paste Preview

The "live" Paste Preview, introduced in Office 2010, lets you see *before* you paste what the text would look like with different formatting applied to it.[1] This feature is available when you cut or copy some text and then use either the Paste drop-down on the Home tab or the right-click menu for pasting. Both methods display various **Paste Options icons**; when you hold the mouse pointer over an icon, you can see how the text would appear if you applied the formatting option that icon represents. For more about this feature, see the section about the Paste Options.

When you use the keyboard shortcut Ctrl V to paste, you don't get a *preview* of the different paste options. However, a **Paste Options button** that appears after you paste gives you access to the Paste Options icons. Clicking an icon is a quick, easy, and fairly intuitive way to change the formatting *after* pasting the text.

The Paste Drop-Down in the Home Tab

As a legal word processor, I am accustomed to using keyboard shortcuts (such as Ctrl V to paste) most of the time. However, there are many other methods for copying and pasting text.

---

[1] Microsoft implemented this enhancement because of research that showed that the function for which people most frequently used the "Undo" command was Paste.

An easy "mouse" way to paste text is to click the **Paste drop-down** in the **Clipboard group** at the left side of the **Home tab**. (Actually, you can paste just by clicking the Paste icon itself—the big clipboard—*but doing so imports the formatting*, just like pressing Ctrl V. The Paste Options drop-down gives you more choices and also allows you to preview the various formatting options before you actually paste the text.[2])

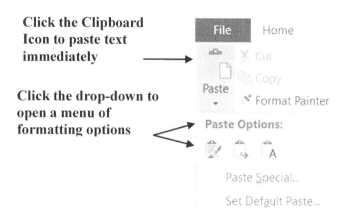

The Paste Drop-Down in the Home Tab

The available choices – presented as icons (each with a text label that pops up when you hold the mouse pointer over the icon) – vary depending on what you have copied, but typically include **Keep Source Formatting (K)**, **Merge Formatting (M)**, and **Keep Text Only (T)**. Those are the options shown in the screenshot immediately above. I will discuss the specific paste options in detail in the section about the Paste Options button.

When you position the mouse pointer over one of the Paste Options icons before you paste, you'll see a preview of what the text you copied would look like if you applied the formatting represented by that icon. To paste and apply a specific type of formatting (Paste Option), either (1) click the icon *or* (2) simply press the letter (i.e., the mnemonic) that appears in the pop-up label for the icon, as described in the previous paragraph.

The Paste drop-down also includes a "Paste Special…" command, as well as a command to "Set Default Paste…"

Paste Special

Clicking the "**Paste Special…**" command produces the **Paste Special dialog**, which is an older method for pasting unformatted text. Most people no longer use "Paste Special" for this

---

[2] Clicking the Clipboard icon will paste the text immediately. However, the Paste Options button will appear after you paste the text (unless you have disabled it), giving you a chance to apply a different formatting option after the fact. See the discussion, *infra*, about the Paste Options button. Note that when you click the Clipboard icon, Word pastes the text according to settings specified in the Word Options, as explained in detail later in this section.

purpose, because recent versions of Word include a paste option called "**Keep Text Only**" that works like "Paste Special," "Unformatted Text," but is even quicker and easier to use.

The Paste Special dialog can be useful if you need to apply non-standard formatting to pasted text or objects. The available formatting options depend on the type of item you are copying and pasting (text, images, lists, etc.). For text, those options (shown below at left) are: Microsoft Word Document Object, Formatted Text (RTF) (Rich Text Format), Unformatted Text, Picture (Enhanced Metafile), HTML Format (the default), and Unformatted Unicode Text. For images, those options (shown below at right) are: Bitmap, Picture (Enhanced Metafile), Picture (GIF), Picture (PNG), Picture (JPEG), and Microsoft Office Graphic Object (the default format).

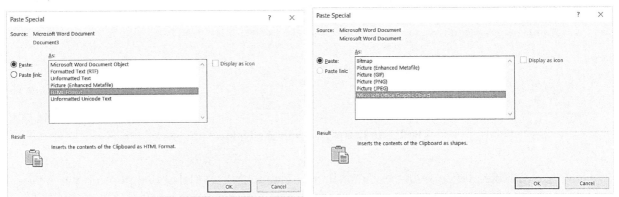

        The "Normal" Paste Special Dialog   The Dialog That Appears
                                                                 When You Are Pasting an Image

Incidentally, you can use the keyboard shortcut **Ctrl Alt V** to open the Paste Special dialog.

As for the "Set Default Paste…" option, see the discussion later in this section about configuring the Word Options for cut, copy, and paste.

The Right-Click Menu

After you have cut or copied some text, you can right-click where you want to paste the text to open a context-sensitive menu that displays the new Paste Options icons. The screenshot at right shows the right-click menu with the Paste Options displayed toward the top.

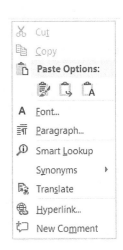

There's not much to say about the right-click menu, other than to point out its existence and the fact that the available options are the same as those offered by the Paste Drop-Down in the Home tab and by the Paste Options button.

The Paste Options Button

The Paste Options button – the pop-up that appears when you paste – typically proffers either three or four choices for formatting pasted text and objects,[3] as well as a "Set Default Paste" option. Clicking the words "Set Default Paste" (or the mnemonic—i.e., the underlined letter "a") takes you directly into the Word Options, where you can configure the settings that control how text is pasted under various circumstances. See page 315 for more information about the Default Paste options.

The Paste Options Button (Collapsed)   **The Paste Options Button (Expanded)**

If you are copying text to which no formatting has been applied – or to which only *direct* (font or paragraph) formatting, as opposed to a style, has been applied – the Paste Options button presents three different icons representing three different formatting choices. When you position the mouse pointer over an icon, a pop-up label appears, indicating what the icon does. From left to right, the options are: Keep Source Formatting (**K**) (depicted as a clipboard with a paintbrush in front of it), Merge Formatting (**M**) (a clipboard with an arrow pointing to the right), and Keep Text Only (**T**) (a large letter "A" appears on the clipboard icon).

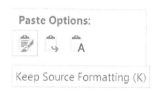 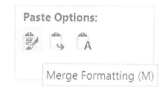 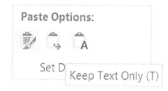

In some situations – such as pasting text into a document that makes heavy use of styles, pasting text to which a style has been applied, or (sometimes) pasting text from the Internet – other options become available: Use Destination Styles (**S**) (a clipboard filled with horizontal lines) and/or Use Destination Themes (**H**) (a clipboard with horizontal lines plus a formatted letter "a"[4]).

---

[3] How many choices – and which ones – are available depends on *both* the formatting of the text you have cut or copied *and* the formatting of the text that already exists at the paste location. The available options also change depending on *what* you are pasting: text, an image, a list, and so forth. **NOTE**: the Paste Options button sometimes offers the Use Destination Styles (S) even when that choice is *not available* via the Paste Options drop-down and the right-click menu. I'm not sure why it doesn't appear consistently on all of the paste menus.

[4] The Use Destination Themes option is not available in .doc files. Themes are enabled only in the newer XML file formats (.docx and similar).

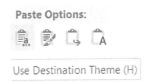 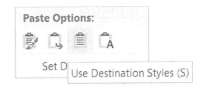

To apply one of the options, either (1) click the icon for that option or (2) press the letter (mnemonic) associated with it (**K** for Keep Source Formatting, **M** for Merge Formatting, **T** for Keep Text Only, **S** for Use Destination Styles, or **H** for Use Destination Themes).

In the sections that follow, I'll explain how each option is intended to work – and how they actually worked in a few tests that I performed.

Keep Source Formatting (K)

Keep Source Formatting retains the ***appearance*** of the text in the source document, but not the ***styles***.

In my tests, I used as a source document a contract containing heading styles formatted with legal-style numbering and regular text formatted with a body text style. All text was formatted with Arial 12 (with bold for the headings).

Heading 1	**Section 3 Contract Terms**
Body Text First Indent	The following material terms shall apply:
Heading 2	**3.1 Term of the Contract**
Body Text First Indent	The Contract shall be in effect for one (1) year from the date that the last party executes the Contract ("Effective Date").
Heading 2	**3.2 Scope of the Contract**
Heading 3	**3.2.1 Demolition**
Body Text First Indent	Contractor shall perform demolition on the Premises according to the following terms and conditions:

My Source Document for Testing

As destination documents, I used two different docs with heading styles formatted with automatic numbering – not the same numbering scheme as in the source document – and regular text formatted with a body text style. All text was formatted with Times New Roman 12.

In my tests, the pasted headings kept the same **font formatting** (font face, font size, and font attributes – in this case, bolding), and the pasted text retained the same **font formatting** and **indents**, as in the source document. Interestingly, the pasted headings also retained **automatic numbering**, but *not* the same numbering scheme as in the original (source) document. (They adopted the numbering scheme in the destination document.)

Both the headings and the body text adopted the **Normal style** – even when pasted into blank paragraphs formatted with a body text style. (Note, however, that if I pasted a heading from the source document *into existing text* – as opposed to a blank paragraph formatted as body text – the heading style from the source document did go into effect at the cursor position.)

In sum, Keep Source Formatting *discards styles* but imports most of the styles' attributes as *direct formatting*.

Merge Formatting (M)

The Merge Formatting option applies the formatting of the surrounding text in the destination document to the text that you paste – assuming that your cursor is within existing text when you paste (as opposed to within a blank paragraph).

But this general rule has some exceptions. Even if you paste into existing text, the results can vary depending on how the existing text itself is formatted. For example, the existing text might be formatted in ALL CAPS, so you might reasonably expect that the pasted text, when merged, would adopt the ALL CAPS formatting. It might or might not do so, and here's the reason: If ALL CAPS has been applied to the existing text from the "Effects" portion of the Font dialog, the pasted text *will* adopt the ALL CAPS formatting. But if the ALL CAPS formatting has been applied to the existing text as "*direct formatting*" – i.e., from the Change Case icon, with the keyboard shortcut F3, or by using the Caps Lock button, the pasted text *will not* change to ALL CAPS.

In my tests, this option stripped out the heading styles and the font face from the source document, but preserved the bolding in the headings as well as font formatting (italics and underlining) applied directly to text. It also retained automatic numbering for the headings (but not the same numbering scheme as in the source document). The automatic numbering incremented according to any existing numbering in the destination document, which is why the heading in the screenshot below is numbered II.

Body Text		
Body Text	**II.**	**Contract Terms**
Body Text		The following material terms shall apply:
Body Text	**A.**	**Term of the Contract**
		The Contract shall be in effect for one (1) year from the date that the last party executes the Contract ("Effective Date").

Pasted Text Using Merge Formatting

The line spacing of the pasted text changed to that of the destination document. When I pasted into blank paragraphs to which a body text style had been applied, all of the pasted text adopted the body text style. When I pasted into text to which a heading style had been applied (just as a test), all of the pasted text adopted that heading style.

In short, Merge Formatting appears to keep *certain font attributes* such as bolding, italics, underlining, and the like, as well as automatic numbering codes, but doesn't retain *styles*.

Keep Text Only (T)

Keep Text Only is essentially the same as "Paste Unformatted Text." It pastes the copied text from the source document, but doesn't import any styles or direct formatting (with one notable exception, described below). This option comes in particularly handy when pasting from a WordPerfect document or from the Internet into a Word doc.

Body Text	Section 3 Contract Terms
Body Text	The following material terms shall apply:
Body Text	3.1 Term of the Contract
Body Text	The Contract shall be in effect for one (1) year from the date that the last party executes the Contract ("Effective Date").

Pasted Text Using the "Keep Text Only" Option

As you can see from the screenshot, the pasted text appears without any formatting. The numbering was converted into plain text. (The paragraphs are indented because I pasted into an empty paragraph formatted with a body text style that uses a first-line indent.)

IMPORTANT: *The pasted text adopts the style and/or direct formatting at the cursor position*. Therefore, it's essential to place the cursor in an empty paragraph before pasting.

CAUTION: When you paste from WordPerfect, any leading tabs used to indent the paragraphs in the source document ***will be imported***. You will need to delete these tabs, either manually or by using Find and Replace (as described in the section starting on page 295).

Use Destination Styles (S)

The Use Destination Styles option replaces any styles and direct formatting that exist in the original document with the styles and direct formatting in the destination document.

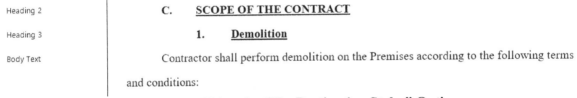

Pasted Text Using the "Use Destination Styles" Option

When I tested this option while working on my Word 2010 book, it appeared somewhat quirky. However, in my current tests, it worked as expected: The pasted text adopted the heading and text styles (including the font formatting, indents, and line spacing) of the destination document. That is, Heading 1, Heading 2, and Heading 3 styles from the source doc remained Heading 1, Heading 2, and Heading 3 styles, but took on the formatting of the heading styles in the destination doc. The automatic numbering in the headings incremented according to the existing numbering in the destination document. The text adopted the formatting of the body text style in effect at the cursor position.

Use Destination Theme (H)

This option appears to work the same way as Use Destination Styles. (As mentioned previously, themes are disabled in .doc files, so this Paste Option appears only in files that use one of the XML formats – usually .docx files.)

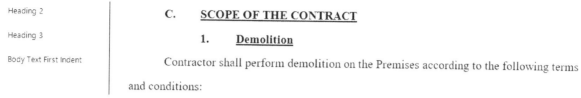

Pasted Text Using the "Use Destination Theme" Option

The main difference – which I can't account for – is that the "Use Destination Theme" option applied a Body Text First Indent style to the text, even though I pasted into blank paragraphs that were formatted with a Body Text style. The regular *source* document does, in fact, use a text style called "Body Text First Indent." (The text in the source doc used single line spacing with 12 points after; when pasted, it adopted the 24 pt line spacing in the destination doc.)

The Upshot: Take Advantage of the Paste Preview Function

The lesson to take away from these experiments is that you should test each option for yourself to see how it works under various circumstances. And be sure to use Paste Preview before pasting; that should help to minimize unpleasant surprises.

Pasting an Object

As mentioned earlier, the available paste options also change depending on *what* you are pasting. For example, when you paste a graphic, you might see only one or two icons, as in the screenshot below. The options shown in the screenshot are **Keep Source Formatting (K)** and **Picture (U)**.

Although I'm not entirely sure of the difference, when I pasted a graphic as a picture, it seemed to lose some resolution (i.e., it pasted as a "second-generation" image), whereas when I pasted it using the "Keep Source Formatting" option, it remained relatively sharp.

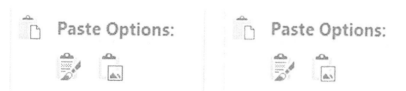

You can see the difference in clarity when you look at the squiggly lines on the clipboard at left in both images ("Keep Source Formatting" at left, "Picture" at right).

Pasting a Numbered List

Other paste options appear in the menus when you are merging into an existing outline or list. If you copy a portion of an existing list and then paste somewhere within another list (either in the same document or in a different document), you will see paste options similar to the following:

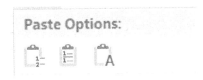

The option on the left is Continue List (**C**); the one in the middle is New List (**N**); the right-most option is Keep Text Only (**T**). Continue List renumbers the pasted portion of the list so that it continues the numbering of the existing list (based on the number of the preceding paragraph). New List, by contrast, restarts the numbering so that the pasted list (or partial list) begins at 1.

Interestingly, when I tested by pressing Enter to start a new numbered paragraph at the third level of a list using legal numbering, then pasting two first-level numbered paragraphs using Keep Text Only, the two pasted paragraphs adopted the third-level numbering – and both used automatic numbering.

> 4.1.5. Reading is easier, too, in the new Reading view. You can collapse parts of the document and focus on the text you want. If you need to stop reading before you reach the end, Word remembers where you left off - even on another device.
> 4.1.6. xx
> 5. Save time in Word with new buttons that show up where you need them. To change the way a picture fits in your document, click it and a button for layout options appears next to it.

Before Pasting

> 4.1.6. xx Video provides a powerful way to help you prove your point. When you click Online Video, you can paste in the embed code for the video you want to add. You can also type a keyword to search online for the video that best fits your document.
> 4.1.7. To make your document look professionally produced, Word provides header, footer, cover page, and text box designs that complement each other. For example, you can add a matching cover page, header, and sidebar. Click Insert and then choose the elements you want from the different galleries.
> 4.1.8.
> 5. Save time in Word with new buttons that show up where you need them. To change the way a picture fits in your document, click it and a button for layout options appears next to it.

After Pasting With "Keep Text Only" Option

A Brief Review

So to review: You can apply different formatting options for text (as well as for lists and objects) by using (1) the Paste drop-down in the Home tab, (2) the right-click menu, or (3) the Paste Options button. The first two methods allow you to preview the formatting *before* pasting; the third method allows you to change the formatting *after the fact* by selecting a different choice from the drop-down. (As long as the Paste Options button remains visible on the screen, you can continue to choose from among the different formatting options.)

To apply an option, you can either (a) click the icon for that option or (b) press the letter of the alphabet (the mnemonic) associated with the option.

Adding a "Paste and Keep Text Only" Icon to the Quick Access Toolbar

If you like, you can add a command to the Quick Access Toolbar (QAT) that will paste text without formatting. Here are the steps:

1. **Right-click** the QAT and then click "**Customize Quick Access Toolbar…**" (or click the **File tab**, **Options**, **Quick Access Toolbar**).

2. When the Word Options dialog appears, change the "**Choose commands from:**" **drop-down** at the top left to "**All Commands.**"

3. Click within the commands box and press the letter "P" to go to the first command that starts with that letter.

4. Then scroll down to "**Paste and Keep Text Only**."

5. Click to **select** (highlight) **that command**, then click the "**Add**" **button** at the center of the screen (or simply double-click the command).

6. The command will appear in the large display area at right under "Customize Quick Access Toolbar." You can change its position in the QAT by clicking the **Up Arrow** (to move it to the left in the QAT) or the **Down Arrow** (to move it to the right).

7. Click the "**OK**" button at the bottom right side of the dialog to save your changes.

The new icon will appear in your QAT. It will be grayed out until you have cut or copied some text or an object in your document, at which point it will become active.

Adding a Keyboard Shortcut for "Keep Text Only"

You also have the option of creating a keyboard shortcut for the **Keep Text Only** option (i.e., **Paste Special, Unformatted Text**). Here's how:

1. Either (1) **right-click** the **Ribbon** (or the Quick Access Toolbar), then click "**Customize the Ribbon…**," or (2) click the **File tab**, **Options**, **Customize Ribbon**. Then:

2. Navigate to the bottom left side of the Word Options screen and click the "**Keyboard shortcuts: Customize…**" button.

3. When the **Customize Keyboard dialog** appears, look at the left side, under "**Categories:**", and scroll all the way down. Click to select (highlight) "**All Commands.**"

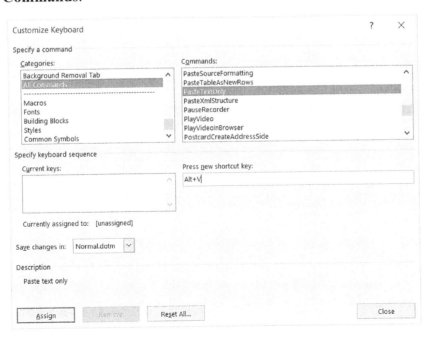

314

4. On the right side of the dialog, under "**Commands**," scroll down about 2/3 of the way until you see "**PasteTextOnly**." Click to select (highlight) that command.

5. Next, click in the "**Press new shortcut key**:" box. With the cursor in that box, press a **key combination** you would like to assign to the command, such as Alt V. If the key combination already has been assigned to another feature, you'll see a message to that effect in the "Currently assigned to:" area below the "Current keys" box. (At that point, you can assign the key combination to the PasteTextOnly command anyway, or you can type another keyboard shortcut in the "Press new shortcut key:" box.)

6. When you are ready, click the "**Assign**" button at the bottom left of the dialog, then close out.

7. Click the "**OK**" button at the bottom right side of the dialog to save your changes.

Configuring the Default Paste Options

You might want to change the default paste options settings at some point. To do so, open the Word Options by clicking the **File tab**, **Options**, click the **Advanced** category, then scroll down about ¼ of the way to **Cut, copy, and paste**. (Alternatively, you can change the default settings from the Paste Options button or from the Paste drop-down in the Home tab.)

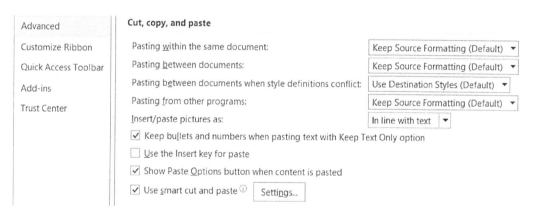

The Cut, Copy and Paste Options (in Word Options)

The options that control the way that pasted text appears in your document include various possible paste scenarios:

- Pasting within the same document
- Pasting between documents
- Pasting between documents when style definitions conflict
- Pasting from other programs

For pasting within the same document, it makes sense to use "Keep Source Formatting" as the default setting. However, it strikes me as somewhat odd – and counterproductive – that

315

the default setting for pasting between documents and for pasting from other programs is also "Keep Source Formatting." (See the screenshot.) Because the source document is almost always formatted differently from the destination document, it's usually better to discard the formatting from the source document. That's especially true if the source document was created with WordPerfect, but also applies to Word documents that originate at other organizations, as is common in law firms and government agencies.

Most software trainers consider it a best practice to use the "Keep Text Only" paste option or "Paste Special, Unformatted Text" in these situations. In fact, if you do paste and keep the formatting from the source document, you'll probably have to click the Paste Options button after pasting and choose the "Keep Text Only" option anyway. So why not simply change the default paste setting to "Keep Text Only?"

If you do so, you'll be able to use Ctrl V (or the Clipboard icon on the Home tab) to paste *without* importing the formatting from the source document.

The third scenario, "Pasting between documents when style definitions conflict," refers to situations where two documents contain styles that have the same name, but are formatted differently. This scenario occurs fairly frequently, particularly with respect to heading styles.

For example, your co-counsel at another law firm might use a Heading 1 style formatted with Arial for the font, bolded but without underlining, with line spacing set at Exactly 12 points with 12 points after, whereas your firm uses a Heading 1 style formatted with Times New Roman, bolded and underlined, with line spacing set at Exactly 24 points. When you paste text from your co-counsel's document into one of your firm's documents, would you prefer that the pasted Heading 1 paragraphs retain the style used in the source document (i.e., the one created by co-counsel) or adopt the style used in the destination document (i.e., yours)? The default setting in the Word Options will determine whose Heading 1 style prevails when you paste with Ctrl V or the Clipboard icon.

Of course, you can simply choose one of the paste options from the Paste drop-down in the Home tab or the right-click menu – or you can choose "Keep Text Only" from the Paste Options button after you paste. However, if you find yourself having to perform this procedure often, you might want to change the setting in Word Options. That way, you can simply click the Paste icon in the Home tab or press Ctrl V – i.e., without selecting a specific paste option each time – and Word will paste the Heading 1 paragraph *based on your default settings*.

Pasting Text From WordPerfect and Other Programs

"Pasting from other programs" might involve pasting from WordPerfect or from Open Office, pasting from Excel, pasting from a legal-specific program, etcetera. Again, you'll probably want to change the default setting to "Keep Text Only," but give it some thought and choose the option that best suits your needs and preferences.

Other "Paste" Settings

Other options that you can configure from this screen include:

- Insert/paste pictures as:
- Keep bullets and numbers when pasting text with Keep Text Only option
- Use the Insert key for paste
- Show Paste Options button when content is pasted
- Use smart cut and paste

The "Insert/paste pictures as" option lets you determine the default wrapping for pasted images (in line, square, behind text, etc.). As with other features, you can change the setting for an individual item that you paste, regardless of the default setting.

The "Keep bullets and numbers…" setting ensures that when you paste a list, the bullets or numbers used in the list are retained even when you strip out other formatting by using the "Keep Text Only" option. In my tests, the pasted text kept numbers, but converted them into plain text, not automatic numbers. Both the "Merge" option and the "Keep Source Formatting" options retained the automatic numbers – but they also retained the other formatting.

If you enable (check) "Use the Insert key for paste," pressing the Insert key pastes any text (or objects) that you have cut or copied. (By default, this option is disabled.)

The "Show Paste Options button…" option, enabled by default, is responsible for the button popping up whenever you paste text or objects. Over the years, many of my training clients have complained about the persistence of this button, but as this section demonstrates, it can be very useful. If it annoys you, simply disable it by unchecking the box.

The **Smart Cut and Paste** options control the appearance and formatting of sentences, words, paragraphs, bulleted and/or numbered list items, tables, as well as content from a PowerPoint presentation or from an Excel spreadsheet, that you cut (or copy) and paste into a Word doc.

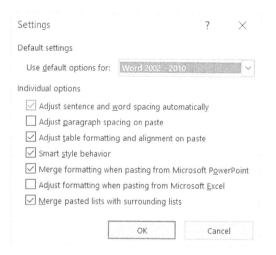

The setting for sentence and word spacing ensures that there is adequate white space between pasted text and any surrounding text into which it is inserted. (This setting also controls the amount of space left between words and sentences when you **delete** text.)

The setting for paragraph spacing is intended to avoid inconsistently formatted paragraphs and/or empty paragraphs when you cut (or copy) paragraphs.

According to Microsoft, when the table adjustment option is enabled, "single cells are pasted as text, table portions are pasted as rows into an existing table (rather than as a nested table), and tables added to an existing table are adjusted to match the existing table."

Microsoft says that the Smart Styles option "has no effect." Rather, it is the "**Pasting between documents when style definitions conflict**" option (also under the **File tab**, **Options**, **Advanced**, **Cut, copy, and paste**) that determines which style takes precedence—the one in the source document or the one in the destination document—when the styles have the same name but are formatted differently.

As always, be sure to click "**OK**" to save your settings when you close the Word Options.

Opening PDF Files Directly into Word

The ability to open PDF files directly for editing is a new feature, introduced in Word 2013. Just browse to a PDF you've stored on your computer, on your network (or in your DMS), or in the cloud and open it as you would open any other file. Word makes a copy of the PDF and opens the copy.

Note that, as with WordPerfect files, the less complex the formatting of the original document, the better the conversion will be. Complex documents that include graphics such as pleading lines, charts, or similar objects are trickier to convert; sometimes Word converts them to images that can't be edited. In addition, paragraphs and/or pages might break differently from the way they break in the original.

Microsoft cautions that the following elements, among others, tend not to convert well:

- Tracked Changes

- Footnotes that span more than one page

- Frames

- Tables that use cell spacing

- Page colors and page borders

- PDF bookmarks

- PDF comments

Nevertheless, the ability to edit a PDF file directly in Word can be useful. And, after you have converted the PDF, you can save the file as a Word document *or* as a PDF – or, for that matter, as any of the other file formats listed in the "File type" drop-down in the "Save As" dialog. Of course, it's a best practice *not* to convert documents to different formats multiple times because doing so greatly increases the risk of corruption.

I decided to test by opening the Word 2016 Quick Start Guide that I had previously downloaded from Microsoft's "Support" web site (http://support.microsoft.com). When I selected the PDF file and clicked "Open," a warning message popped up:

319

I clicked OK, and, after a short delay, the converted document opened on my screen – as a PDF. (See the screenshot of the file name as it appeared in the Title Bar, below.)

WORD 2016 QUICK START GUIDE.PDF - Word

At first glance, it looked as though the conversion was fairly successful. Even the complex graphics came across reasonably well.

However, a closer examination revealed some issues. I took a screenshot of the first page as it appeared when opened in Adobe Reader and then took a screenshot of the converted Word doc – which split the first page into two separate pages, perhaps because the content wouldn't fit on a single page in the converted doc.

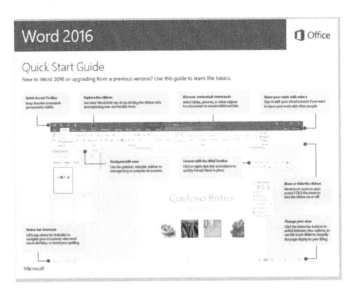

Original PDF – Single Page

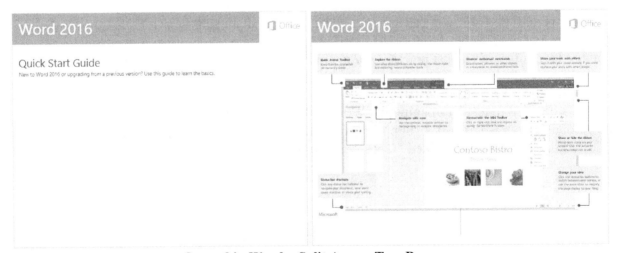

Opened in Word – Split Across Two Pages

There were a few other issues, such as the loss of color saturation. And although I was, in fact, able to edit certain portions of the converted file, some text – especially the text superimposed on a large graphic – was converted to an image and I was unable to edit it. Other text could be edited, but I had to right-click, then click "Edit Text." So it wasn't entirely successful. But on the whole, Word did a respectable job of converting a fairly complex file.

When I went to save the document, Word prompted me to save it as a Word file / .docx, which I did.

See "Why does my PDF look different in Word?" This Microsoft Office support article is located here: https://support.office.com/en-us/article/Why-does-my-PDF-look-different-in-Word-1d1d2acc-afa0-46ef-891d-b76bcd83d9c8

Spell-Checking

Running the Spell-Checker

To run the Spell-Checker, do one of the following:

- Click the "**Spelling & Grammar**" **button** at the left side of the **Review tab** (in the **Proofing group**); or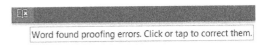

- Press **F7**; or

- Click the book icon on the Status Bar.

In recent versions of Word, the Spell-Checker opens as a separate pane on the right side of the screen.

To replace a flagged word with one of the suggestions from the Speller, click the suggestion (if not already highlighted), then click "**Change**." To change every instance of the flagged word, click "**Change All**."

To ignore a single instance of the flagged word, click "**Ignore**"; to ignore every instance of the word, click "**Ignore All**."

To add the flagged word to the default dictionary, click the "**Add**" button.

In this version of Word, the Speller also allows users to hear the pronunciation of the flagged word. Toward the bottom of the Speller, the word appears with a small icon of a speaker to the right. Clicking the speaker plays an audio file with the pronunciation of the word.

Also, the Speller provides **synonyms** for the flagged word, and a drop-down that you can click to see **definitions** of the word. Note, however, that if you want to see the definition of the word, Microsoft asks you to sign in to your Microsoft online account.

WORKAROUND: As mentioned in the section about the Dictionary / Smart Lookup, you can display definitions without signing into a Microsoft account by simply right-clicking a word or selected / highlighted phrase, then choosing "Smart Lookup."

322

Other Spelling Options

To configure other spelling options, click the **File tab**, **Options**, and click the **Proofing** category at the left side of the Word Options dialog. The spelling and grammar options are located in a section labeled "**When correcting spelling in Microsoft Office programs**."

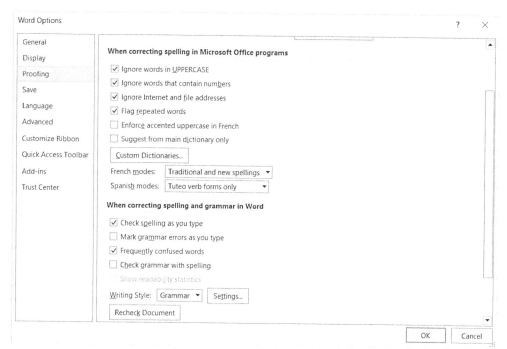

Word Options – Spelling and Grammar
(Scroll Down to See "Exceptions for...")

Ignore Words in UPPERCASE

As mentioned on page 98, an option that has tripped up many a Word user is the very first one, "Ignore words in UPPERCASE." This inconspicuous setting – which is *enabled by default* – means that Word will not flag misspelled words that appear in upper case. My best guess is that someone at Microsoft thought that the spell-checker might choke in documents containing lots of acronyms and initials, but I strongly recommend that you uncheck (disable) this option. If necessary, you can add those pesky acronyms and initials to the dictionary so that the spell-checker won't flag them in the future.

The options to ignore words that contain numbers and/or Internet and file addresses are enabled by default, as is the option to flag repeated words.

Check Spelling as You Type

This option is enabled by default. If you type a word that isn't in the dictionary, Microsoft flags with word with a red wavy underline. Right-clicking produces a shortcut menu with suggested alternatives, as well as the standard options to Ignore All, Add to Dictionary, or use Smart Lookup.

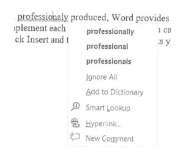

323

Incidentally, you have the option of hiding spelling errors in one particular document, rather than disabling the spell-checker altogether. If you scroll down in the Word Options dialog, you'll see "**Exceptions for**" (not shown in the screenshot on the previous page), where you can select one of your open documents and then check "**Hide spelling errors in this document only**."

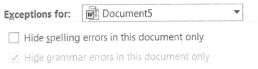

CAUTION: If someone with whom you are collaborating on a document has checked this box, spelling errors might not appear when you perform a spell-check. Be sure to review this option and, if necessary, uncheck it so that the speller works as expected. And, as always, click "OK" to save your settings when you close the Word Options dialog.

Mark Grammar Errors as You Type

This option is enabled by default, but it's easy to disable by unchecking the box at its left. When it is enabled, Word uses a blue wavy underline to flag phrases and sentences that conflict with the default grammatical rules operating in the background. For more about those rules, see the section starting on page 330. Incidentally, you must check "Mark grammar errors as you type" in order to *enable* "Hide grammar errors in this document only."

Check Grammar With Spelling

To have Word flag potential grammar issues when you run the spell-checker, click to enable "Check grammar with spelling."

Re-Check Spelling

The Re-Check Spelling option is very useful, particularly if you are collaborating on a document with someone else who might have clicked "Ignore" with respect to one or more misspelled words that should have been changed. It's also useful because – let's face it – it's easy to click the wrong button while running a spell-check (or at other times), which can result in a final draft that includes misspelled words. Re-checking the spelling before saving the final draft of a document could save you some grief.

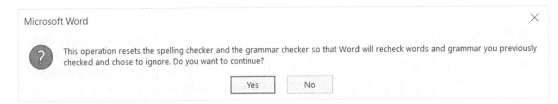

For more about spelling and grammar, keep reading.

Creating a Custom Dictionary

When Word's spell-checker stumbles on a word that it doesn't recognize—such as parol, interpleader, or Trustor—you can click the "**Add to Dictionary**" **button**, and the word will be incorporated into the program's built-in dictionary, a file called "Custom.dic."

While it can be useful to add words to the dictionary "on the fly," you also have the option of creating one or more custom dictionaries—a legal dictionary, a medical dictionary, an architectural dictionary, or even a client-specific dictionary—and adding words without running a spell-check.

To create a custom dictionary, click the **File tab**, **Options**, and click the **Proofing** category in the Word Options dialog Once there, navigate to the section labeled "**When correcting spelling in Microsoft Office programs**."

Before proceeding, make sure the "Suggest from main dictionary only" option is *not* checked. Otherwise, the Speller will suggest alternative words based only on the contents of the main dictionary, not on any custom dictionaries you set up.

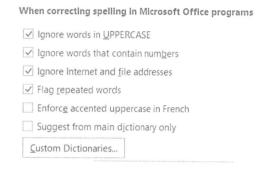

Next, click the "**Custom Dictionaries…**" **button**. A **Custom Dictionaries dialog** will open.

From this very handy dialog, you can edit the existing word list (to add words, delete and retype misspelled words that have been added accidentally, and/or delete words that don't belong in the dictionary). Alternatively, you can create a new dictionary by clicking the "**New…**" **button**.

When you click "New," a **"Create Custom Dictionary" dialog** opens. Type a name for your dictionary, such as "Legal" or "Engineering" (or some other concise description), then click "**Save**." Word automatically adds the ".dic" extension to the file name.

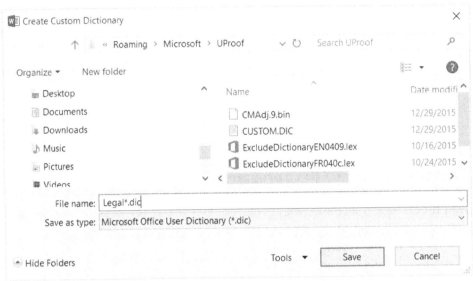

Create Custom Dictionary Dialog

The new dictionary will be added to the dictionary list.

Custom Dictionaries (Including a New "Legal" Dictionary)

As you can see, some dictionaries in the list are checked, and one is marked as the default. What is the significance of those designations?

The "*checked*" dictionaries are *active*. That means that the Spell-Checker compares the words in your document against the content of all of the dictionaries that are checked. (You can uncheck one or more dictionaries if you don't want the Speller to look there).

The *default* dictionary is the one to which the Speller adds words when you click the "**Add**" button during a spell-check. If you wish, you can change the default dictionary from within the "Custom Dictionaries" dialog. Just click the dictionary you want to use as the default, then click the "**Change Default**" button. The dictionary will move to the top of the list, with

326

"**(Default)**" after its name. (The "Change Default button" then becomes inactive until you click a dictionary name again.)

Adding or Deleting Words

It's easy to edit a custom dictionary from this dialog. First, click to select the dictionary, then click "**Edit Word List**." (Don't click "Add.") When the dictionary dialog opens, click in the "Word(s):" box and type a word, then click "**Add**" (the "Add" button is grayed out until you type a word).

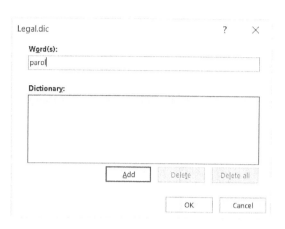

You also can delete a word, or even all of the words in the dictionary (but be careful not to click the "Delete all" button unless that's your intention). Be sure to click "**OK**" to save your changes.

This Warning Appears if You Click "Delete All"

It can be advantageous to add one word at a time, rather than an entire phrase, such as "lis pendens." If you add a phrase, the Spell-Checker will recognize the phrase but not the individual words that comprise the phrase – unless you add them separately. (If the words are always used as part of the phrase, that shouldn't be problematic, but if any of the words ever appear alone, the speller will flag them.)

You can add up to 5,000 words to each custom dictionary. Individual words can consist of one to 64 characters.

Editing the Word List Directly

You can edit the word list for a particular dictionary directly (by opening the dictionary file itself), since word lists are plain-text files. Exit from Word and launch **Windows Explorer / File Explorer**, navigate to the folder where the custom dictionaries are stored,[1] and **right-click the dictionary** you want to edit.

---

[1] In Windows 7, 8, and 10, the location is:
C:\Users\<User Name>\AppData\Roaming\Microsoft\UProof

327

When the pop-up menu appears, choose "**Open with…**" and select **Notepad**. When the dictionary opens, type one word per line, then click the **File menu**, **Save** (not "Save As").

When you have finished, close the edited dictionary file either by clicking the red "**X**" in the upper right-hand corner or by clicking the **File menu**, **Exit**.

QUICK TIP: Frequently Confused Words (Contextual Spelling)

Frequently Confused Words, formerly known as Contextual Spelling, is a nifty feature, albeit one with definite limitations.

When the "**Frequently confused words**" option is enabled, Word flags words that are spelled correctly but aren't appropriate in the context in which you use them. For instance, if you type "Their are many reasons…," Word will either change "Their" to "There" automatically or mark the word with a blue squiggly underline – even if you do not have the grammar checker itself enabled.

Their are many reasons

Right-clicking an item that the contextual spell-checker flags will produce a pop-up menu with one or more suggested alternatives, plus the "Smart Lookup" option.

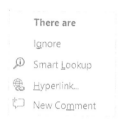

To enable or disable the option, click **File**, **Options**, **Proofing**, and navigate to the section labeled "**When correcting spelling and grammar in Word**." Click to check (enable) or uncheck (disable) the "**Frequently Confused Words**" option. Be sure to click "**OK**" to save your settings when you exit from the Word Options.

A few caveats about this feature:

- It doesn't always catch contextual spelling errors, so you still need to proofread your documents;

- It occasionally produces "false positives";

- If you have less than 1 GB of RAM on your computer, the option will be automatically disabled to save memory; and

- If your computer seems unusually slow or your system resources appear to be low, try disabling the option. According to Microsoft, the option consumes a fair amount of memory.

The Advanced Grammar Settings

As of this writing (in late December of 2015), Word 2016 lacks the advanced grammar settings that were available in Word 2013 and earlier versions. In prior versions, users could select from among different writing styles and also could choose whether to require a comma before the last item in a list, whether to place punctuation inside (American standard) or outside (British standard) quotation marks, and whether to use two spaces between sentences (old-school journalistic standard) or one space (modern typographical standard). For reasons unknown, Microsoft removed those options from this version of Word. (There is only one writing style available, labeled simply "Grammar.")

You still can choose which grammatical and stylistic features the grammar checker adjusts, but it's hard to know how some of them (such as Punctuation and Spacing) work, since there is no explanation within the Grammar Settings dialog where you choose the options. (**File**, **Options**, **Proofing**, "**When correcting spelling and grammar in Word**," **Writing Style**, **Settings**.)

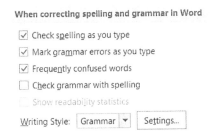

The options for Word 2016 and for Word 2010, respectively, are depicted below.

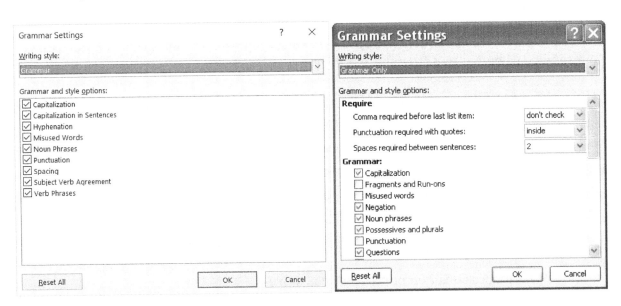

Word 2016   **Word 2010**

On a positive note, it is my understanding that Microsoft is working on an automatic update (a patch) for Office 2016 that might restore these useful options. Keep checking the Word Options just in case.

The Mini-Translator

Word includes a Mini-Translator that you can use to translate words or phrases in your documents into any of several different languages. To use this feature, click the **Review tab**, **Language group**, click the **Translate drop-down**, then click the "**Mini Translator**" command.

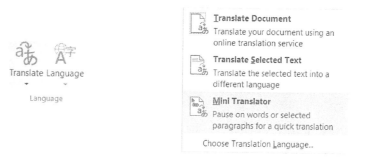

The first time you click the command, a **Translation Language Options** dialog appears, so that you can choose the "Translate from" and "Translate to" languages for the current document. There's also a drop-down for selecting the default language for the Mini Translator. As you can see in the next screenshot, I have chosen to translate text from English to French, but there are several languages available, from Arabic, Chinese, Croatian, Dutch, Hindi, Persian, Russian, and Swedish to Thai.[1]

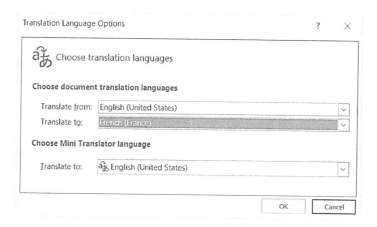

Translation Language Options

After you click "OK," you'll see a pop-up message, warning you that Word needs to send text over the Internet to a third-party translation service provider. Click "**Yes**" to continue. **NOTE**: This pop-up will appear each time you translate text unless you click the "**Don't show again**" box.

---

[1] You can choose a different language for a subsequent translation by clicking the "Choose Translation Language…" option from the "Translate" drop-down.

To translate text, either click within a word or select a block of text, then click the "**Mini Translator**" command). (Alternatively, for selected text, you can click "**Translate Selected Text**.") A **Research Pane** opens at the right side of the screen, showing your original text, the languages to translate from and to, and the translated text. Additional information, including the source used for the translation, appears at the bottom of the Research Pane.

The screenshot below left shows the results when I clicked within the word "matching." The screenshot below right shows the results when I selected the text "Click insert and then choose the elements you want…"

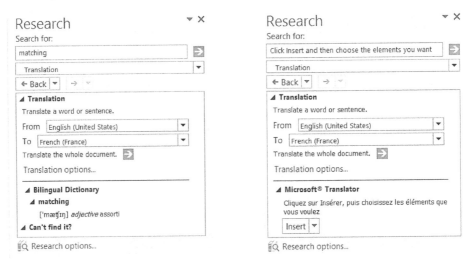

Clicking the "**Back**" button opens a list with the history of terms you've searched for previously (at least, during this work session). After you click the "Back" button, the arrow to the right becomes active and you can click that drop-down to show – and return to – other words or phrases that you previously translated.

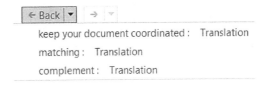

You can use the "**Insert**" button toward the bottom of the Research Pane (if one appears) to insert the translated text into the document or copy the text and paste it into another document.

If you can't find a serviceable translation, you can scroll down to "**Can't find it?**" and click one of the suggested search options.

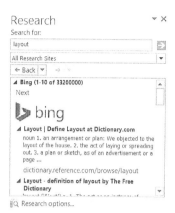

When I did so and then I clicked "**All Research Sites**," the Research Pane displayed definitions and other information about my search term, although not in my chosen "translate to" language. See the screenshot at right.

To see which sources Microsoft uses for its translations and/or to activate other choices, click "**Research Options**." Be sure to scroll through the entire dialog box to see all of the available sources.

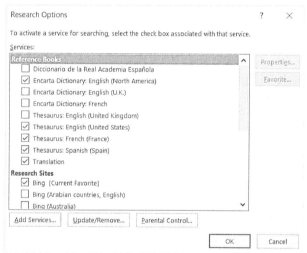

One final note about translations: When I attempted to translate a Latin phrase into English, I discovered that Latin was conspicuously missing from the "translate from" languages.

333

Built-in Text-to-Speech

Word also offers a built-in text-to-speech option that can be used by people who have some visual impairment, as well as by people with a speech impediment (such as a dysphonia). Because it serves these purposes, it can be thought of as an "accessibility" feature.

Text-to-speech makes use of the speech engine built into your version of Windows. The voice software has improved significantly over the past few years and is easy to understand, although it still sounds somewhat mechanical compared to natural human speech.

The Speak command isn't built into the Ribbon, but you can add it to the Quick Access Toolbar. Just do the following:

- Right-click the QAT, then choose "**Customize the Quick Access Toolbar…**"

- When the Word Options screen appears, change the "Choose commands from:" drop-down to "**Commands Not in the Ribbon**" or "**All Commands**."

- Press the letter "S," then scroll to "**Speak**."

- Click to select "Speak," then click the "**Add**" button.

- Click the "**OK**" button to save your changes when you close out of the Word Options.

After you have added a "Speak" icon to the QAT, simply click within a word or select some text, then click the "Speak" icon (shown at right).

If you like, you can add a keyboard shortcut for this function. Just follow the steps for creating a custom keyboard shortcut in the section starting on page 345. The tricky part is figuring out the name for and locating this specific command. After clicking "All Commands" in the Categories list, navigate to the Commands list at right and scroll to (and select) **SpeakStopSpeaking**.

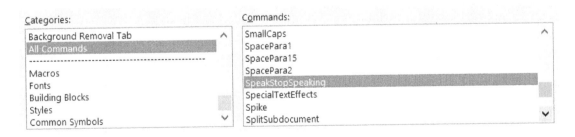

Sorting Text, Numbers, or Dates

To sort text, numbers, or dates, start by selecting the items to be sorted.[1] Next, click the **Sort icon** in the **Paragraph group** on the **Home tab**. (See the screenshot at right.) The **Sort Text dialog** will open.

By default, sorting is performed on *paragraphs*. You can choose to sort text, numbers, or dates. For all sort types, you can sort in either *ascending* or *descending* order (with dates, ascending means older to newer; descending means newer to older).

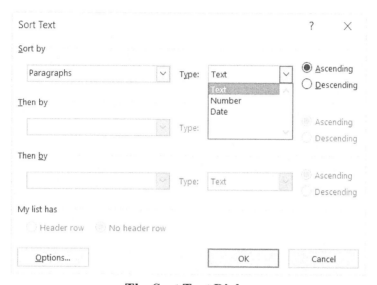

The Sort Text Dialog

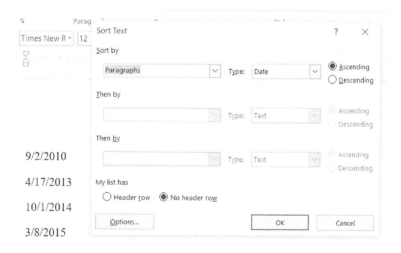

Sort Results - Dates Sorted in Ascending Order (Oldest to Newest)

---

[1] In the rare event that you are sorting all of the text in a document, you don't have to select the text first.

335

Most of the time, you will sort by paragraph. But there might be occasions when the items you want to sort aren't separated into paragraphs but, instead, are separated by tabs or commas (Word calls such items "**fields**"). For example, you might have a list of people in which each individual's last name appears first, followed by his or her first name.

To sort by something other than paragraph – in this case, by a "field" (last name and/or first name) separated by commas – click the "**Options…**" button and choose the appropriate field separator type.

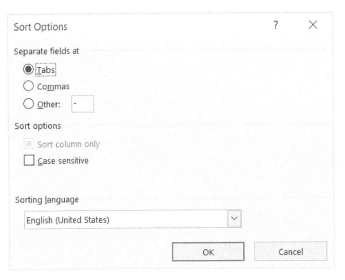

If you select Tabs or Commas, the "Sort by" options will change so that you can sort by field. Using the same example, where Field 1 is the first name and Field 2 is the last name, you can sort first by Field 1, then by Field 2 (that is, you are alphabetizing first by last name and then by first name, in case two or more people share the same last name).[2] See the screenshot below.

---

[2] Field 1 simply refers to the item to the left of the first comma or tab, and Field 2 refers to the item to the right of the comma or tab, etc.

If you prefer, you can change the sort type not by clicking the "Options" button but by clicking the "Sort by" drop-down and choosing something other than "Paragraph." When I performed the search above, I actually clicked "Sort by" and chose "Field 1." Because the items in my list were selected by commas, Word automatically changed the separator type to commas.

The sort results are depicted below. Note that because I chose to sort by last name (Field 1) and then by first name (Field 2), the two Smiths ended up in the correct order.

>Andersen, Mark
>
>Martinez, Efraim
>
>Smith, Anna
>
>Smith, Bart
>
>Stein, Julie
>
>Wong, Shayla

You also have the option of sorting by word, which can be convenient if, for example, you are sorting a list of people's names in which the first name and last name are separated by a space rather than by a tab or a comma. To do so:

1. Click "Options" at the bottom of the Sort Text dialog;

2. Click to select the "Other:" option under "Separate fields at";

3. Delete the character in the box to the right of the label "Other:";

4. Press the Spacebar; and

5. Click "OK."

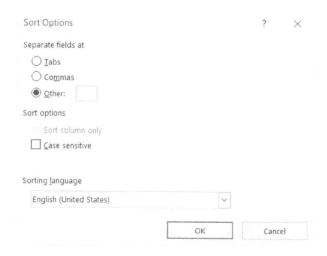

Afterwards, the "Sort by" drop-down provides the option to sort by word, rather than by field.

In this example, I'm sorting by Word 2 and then by Word 1 because I've typed the names in first name / last name order, with a space between the first and last names. I want the primary sort to be on the last names (Word 2) and the secondary sort to be on the first names (Word 1).

Bart Smith
Shayla Wong
Mark Andersen
Efraim Martinez
Julie Stein
Anna Smith

Mark Andersen
Efraim Martinez
Anna Smith
Bart Smith
Julie Stein
Shayla Wong

It worked!

TIP: If you are sorting a list of names and some of the people use their middle initials or middle names or have compound first names, insert a hard space (Ctrl Shift Spacebar) between the first name and the middle initial (or middle name) before sorting.

In the screenshot at right, I've turned on "Show / Hide" so that you can see the hard spaces. They look like degree symbols (or like a tiny letter "o" that has been superscripted). There is one after "Mark" and one between "Anna" and "Louise."

Bart·Smith¶
Shayla·Wong¶
Mark°P.·Andersen¶
Efraim·Martinez¶
Julie·Stein¶
Anna°Louise·Smith¶

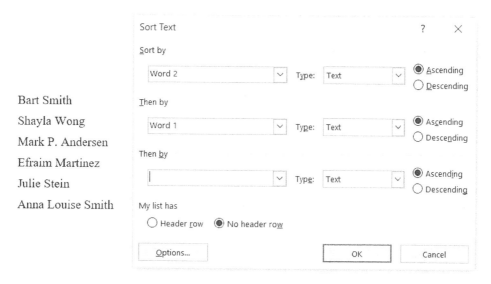

Bart Smith
Shayla Wong
Mark P. Andersen
Efraim Martinez
Julie Stein
Anna Louise Smith

Second Step: Configure and Run the Sort

Mark P. Andersen
Efraim Martinez
Anna Louise Smith
Bart Smith
Julie Stein
Shayla Wong

Search Results – Perfect!

For instructions about sorting text, numbers, or dates within a table, see the section starting on page 481.

Sorting - Simplified Steps

1.   **Select the text** you want to sort.

2.   Click the "**Sort**" button in the **Paragraph group** on the **Home tab**.

3.   If necessary, change the "**Sort by**" and/or the "**Type**."

4.   Choose "**Ascending**" or "**Descending**."

5.   If appropriate, choose a "**Then by**" option.

6.   If appropriate, select from "**Other Options**."

7.   Click "**OK**."

PART VI: Working Smarter and Faster
(Automating Word)

Save Time With Keyboard Shortcuts and Document Automation

This section of the book deals with features that can help you get your work done more efficiently and smoothly. I start with extensive lists of keyboard shortcuts, which save time because you don't have to stop typing to reach for the mouse and which also make it easy to perform tasks when you're not sure where commands are located on the Ribbon. Next, I provide instructions for automating your documents with field codes, Quick Parts, and styles.

Keyboard Shortcuts

As a legal word processor (and a fast typist – I've been known to bang out documents at 85-95 wpm when I'm really cranking), I rely heavily on keyboard shortcuts. They allow me to work much more quickly and efficiently than if I were using the mouse to click my way around the Ribbon, tabs, groups, icons, and dialog boxes. Every time I take my hands off the keyboard, my productivity drops. I couldn't tell you precisely how much, though I remember reading efficiency studies years ago that suggested that people who use keyboard shortcuts shave 20% to 40% off their time. That sounds about right to me.

In any case, the fast typists among you will be pleased to know that Word offers lots of built-in keyboard shortcuts. And it's easy to set up additional shortcuts of your own.

For Users of Prior Versions of Word

Keyboard shortcuts also come in handy because the Ribbon interface isn't entirely intuitive, especially if you are accustomed to working in an older version of Word or with WordPerfect. Luckily, most of the shortcuts you used in prior versions of Word still work in Word 2016 (and if you never learned them, you'll be glad to learn them now).

As in older versions, you can use mnemonics (the Alt key plus a letter or two) to invoke many commands, including the most common "File" commands. So, for example, **Alt F** opens the File tab; **Alt F, S** is Save; **Alt F, A** is Save As; **Alt F, C** is Close; **Alt F, O** is Open (as is **Ctrl O**); **Alt F, P** is Print, as is **Ctrl P** (both key combinations open Print Place); **Alt F, X** is Exit (i.e., from Word).

And the Paragraph dialog, an essential formatting and troubleshooting tool, can be opened from just about anywhere in the program by pressing **Alt O, P**.

For WordPerfect Users

For the most part, Word's standard keyboard shortcuts differ from those you might be accustomed to in WordPerfect. The good news is that many of them are simple to remember because they use the Ctrl key plus a letter of the alphabet that is the first letter of the command, such as Ctrl P for Print. Others will become second nature because you will use them every day.

Should you wish to assign familiar WordPerfect keyboard shortcuts to Word functions, be sure to read the next section, "Creating Your Own Keyboard Shortcuts."

All Manner of Shortcuts

I have provided lists of keyboard shortcuts that are organized in a few different ways. The first list represents many commands that make use of the Ctrl key plus a letter or number; the second offers keyboard commands that use various function keys; the third is organized by feature or function; and the fourth contains keyboard shortcuts for access to tabs of the Ribbon and to dialog boxes. The lists aren't exhaustive, and you'll notice that some of them overlap. My intention and hope in including these lists is that they will familiarize you with the keyboard shortcuts you will use most often.

Document Automation

Word makes it easy to automate many aspects of your document, such as paragraph numbering, page numbering, dates, and document information including the file name and path. It's also easy to insert boilerplate text with just a few keystrokes – once you know how.

Among the many advantages of using automation are that it saves you time, you don't have to remember to keep updating various parts of the document, and – if everyone where you work (or with whom you collaborate on documents) has some basic training in these features – you're less likely to experience problems such as duplicate paragraph numbers (something I used to see at various law firms where some of the secretaries were using automatic numbering and some were not).

Don't be intimidated by the concept of automation. If you follow the instructions in this section for using Quick Parts, you'll soon be using just a few keystrokes to insert boilerplate paragraphs, signature blocks, discovery headings that include automatic numbering, and the like. (In most cases, it's as simple as copying some text, assigning it a short name / abbreviation, saving it, and then invoking it by typing the abbreviation and pressing F3.)

Likewise, field codes and styles are not as daunting as you might think. You can start with the basics and then explore more advanced functionality as your time and temperament permit.

And as for macros, you don't have to create, or figure out how to use, complicated scripts and subroutines. While many brave souls do venture into sophisticated macro coding that involves Visual Basic for Applications (VBA), it's not necessary to do so.[1] In fact, you can create simple macros just by recording keystrokes. I've provided an example to get you started.

Once you start using these time-saving features, you'll probably wonder how you managed without them.

---

[1] I admire, but am not among, those VBA wizards.

Creating Your Own Keyboard Shortcuts

Setting up your own keyboard shortcuts for nearly any function is a relatively simple matter. First, do one of the following:

1. Right-click the **Ribbon** or the **Quick Access Toolbar**, then click **Customize the Ribbon** (or click the **File tab**, **Options**, **Customize Ribbon**);

2. Scroll to the bottom of the **Word Options dialog** and click the **Keyboard Shortcuts: Customize button**.

    You'll see the **Customize Keyboard dialog** (screenshot below).

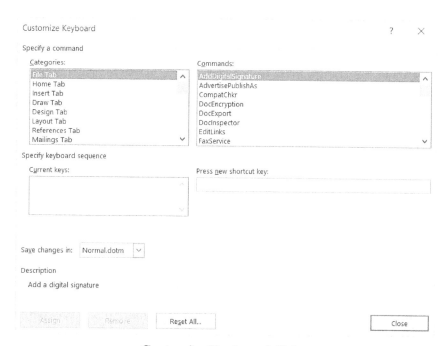

Customize Keyboard dialog

3. Note the **Categories list** on the left and the **Commands list** on the right.

    The item you select in the **Categories list** determines which commands are displayed in the **Commands list**. In the screenshot, the File tab is highlighted on the left, so the commands displayed on the right are items accessible from the File tab.

    The Categories are organized roughly by the tabs in the Ribbon. As you scroll down, you'll see as well the context-sensitive tabs, and then, toward the bottom, **All Commands**. Below **All Commands** there are a few other miscellaneous categories, including **Fonts**, **Macros**, **Styles**, and **Common Symbols**.

4. Click within the **Categories list** and scroll down to the category that is likely to contain the command (feature) for which you want to create a keyboard shortcut.

   TIP: If you're not sure which category to choose, scroll down to the **All Commands** category.

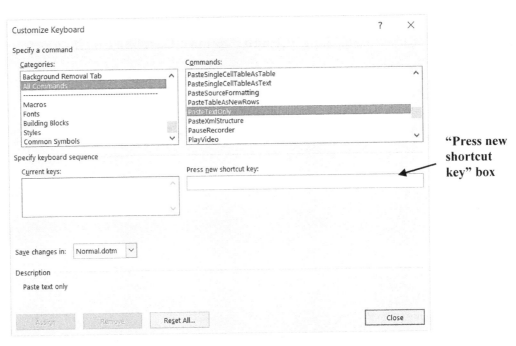

"Press new shortcut key" box

All Commands – PasteTextOnly Command

5. Navigate to the **Commands list** on the right and scroll to the command that activates the feature you want. (You can move quickly through the command list by clicking in the list, then pressing a key that represents the first letter of the command. That will take you to the first command that starts with that letter, so you don't have to scroll very far.)

   The commands are in alphabetical order. However, it can be challenging to figure out what name Microsoft has assigned to a command. The company often uses a verb – and not necessarily the verb that first comes to mind –to name command. So, for example, GrowFont and ShrinkFont are the commands to increase and decrease font size, respectively.

6. After you locate the command you want, click to **select / highlight it**. Then position your cursor in the **Press new shortcut key** box (see the screenshots on this page and on the next page) and press the keys you wish to use.

   For example, if you want to create a shortcut key to insert a table row above the cursor position (command name: **TableInsertRowAbove**) using the Alt key plus the Insert key, press Alt Ins. If you want to use the key combination Alt Ctrl F1, press those keys in sequence.

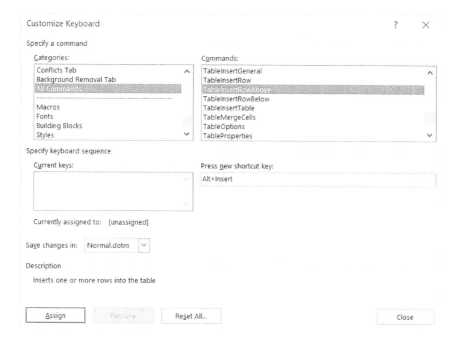

7. If the keyboard shortcut you type in the **Press new shortcut key** box is already assigned to a Word feature or function, you'll see "**Currently assigned to:**" underneath the **Current keys:** box on the left side of the dialog. (See screenshot below for an example.)

8. To use that keyboard shortcut anyway, click "**Assign**."[1] Otherwise, type a different key combination in the **Press a new shortcut key** box. If that combination isn't already assigned to a feature, click **Assign**.[2]

9. After you finish setting up your keyboard shortcut(s), click **Close**.

10. Finally, click **OK** to save your changes and close out of the Word Options.

It's always a good idea to test your keyboard shortcuts to make sure they work as you intended. Also, keep in mind that by default, you are saving your customized keystrokes in your **Normal template (Normal.dotm)**.

---

[1] That removes the keyboard assignment from the feature it was associated with previously and associates it with your chosen feature. **CAUTION**: Word will make this change without warning you, so don't click the Assign button unless you're certain you want to reassign the key combination.

[2] To remove an existing key assignment, click to select the keys displayed in the "**Current keys**" box, then click the "**Remove**" button.

SIDEBAR: Some Cool Built-In Keyboard Shortcuts

Here are a few keyboard shortcuts you might not know about—but you'll definitely appreciate. I've chosen them somewhat randomly. To me they're cool because they make it easy to perform tasks I actually use in my work.

You can apply highlighting to selected text by pressing **Ctrl Alt H**. (After applying highlighting, you can turn it off by selecting the text and pressing Ctrl Alt H again.)

Ctrl Alt C inserts the copyright symbol (©); **Ctrl Alt R** inserts the registered symbol (®); and **Ctrl Alt T** inserts the Trademark symbol (™).

Ctrl Alt F inserts a footnote reference in the text and positions the cursor in the footnote pane. **Alt I, N, N** (maybe for **I**nsert, **N**ote, **N**umber?) does the same thing.

Ctrl Shift A applies the ALL CAPS attribute to selected text. (If subsequent text takes on ALL CAPS formatting, change back to lower case by selecting the text and using **Shift F3** – the keyboard shortcut for "Change Case" – *or* by pressing **Ctrl D** to open the Font dialog and deselecting All Caps, then clicking OK). To remove the attribute, select the text and press **Ctrl Shift A** again (the following three keyboard shortcuts also work as toggles).

Ctrl Shift K applies the SMALL CAPS font attribute.

Ctrl Shift W underlines words only (<u>not</u> <u>spaces</u> <u>or</u> <u>tabs</u>).

Ctrl Shift D applies <u>double underline</u>.

Ctrl Spacebar removes ***character formatting*** (such as the font attributes applied by the four previous keyboard shortcuts).

Ctrl Alt P switches to Print Layout view; **Ctrl Alt N** switches to Draft view (formerly called "Normal" view, which explains the mnemonic); and **Ctrl Alt O** switches to Outline view.

F7 starts the Spell-Checker and **Shift F7** opens the Thesaurus, while **Alt Shift F7** opens the Mini Translator. (For the Thesaurus and the Mini Translator, click within a word or select some text first.)

Press **Shift F5** to move the cursor to the previous editing position. You can repeat this keystroke to go to at least three previous editing positions – even if one of them is within a document that is open on another screen. Very useful!

There is no built-in keyboard shortcut for the section sign (§), but it's easy to create one. Open the Symbols dialog (Insert tab, Symbols group, Symbol drop-down, More Symbols), then click the Special Characters tab. Click the symbol and then click the Shortcut Key button and proceed as described in the section above. See also the discussion about symbols on page 270.

Keyboard Shortcuts That Use the Control ("Ctrl") Key

Keystrokes	Function	Comments
Ctrl A	Select All (i.e., the entire document *or* an entire header or footer *or* an entire table)	
Ctrl B	Bold	
Ctrl C	Copy	
Ctrl D	Opens the Font dialog	
Ctrl E	Center (Center Justification)	Toggles Center Justification on and off
Ctrl F	Opens the Navigation Pane	
Ctrl G	Go To	A quick way to move to a page, bookmark, comment, or other item
Ctrl H	Replace	
Ctrl I	Italics	
Ctrl J	Justify (Full Justification)	Toggles between Full Justification and Left Justification
Ctrl K	Insert Hyperlink	
Ctrl L	Left Align (Left Justification)	Toggles between Left Justification and Full Justification
Ctrl M	Indent Paragraph (i.e., indent entire paragraph from the left) Each time you press Ctrl M, it indents by one additional tab stop	Ctrl Shift M = Decrease Indent
Ctrl N	New Document (blank screen)	
Ctrl O	Open (but goes through the Backstage view)	See also Ctrl F12
Ctrl P	Print and Print Preview	(aka "Print Place")
Ctrl Q	Remove Paragraph Formatting (i.e., formatting applied through the Paragraph dialog)	
Ctrl R	Right Align (Right Justification)	Toggles between Right Justification and Left Justification

349

Keystrokes	Function	Comments
Ctrl S	Save	
Ctrl T	Hanging Indent Each time you press Ctrl T, it increases the hanging indent by one additional tab stop	Ctrl Shift T = Decrease Hanging Indent
Ctrl U	Underline	
Ctrl V	Paste	
Ctrl W	Close (Document Window)	
Ctrl X	Cut	
Ctrl Y	Repeat Action	
Ctrl Z	Undo	
Ctrl 0 (Zero)	Add/Close Space Before Paragraph	Adds or removes extra points before a paragraph.
Ctrl 1	Single Spacing	
Ctrl 2	Double Spacing	
Ctrl 5	One-and-One-Half Spacing	
Ctrl Alt V	Opens the Paste Special Dialog	
Ctrl Alt Enter	Style Separator	Used to prevent the text of a paragraph from being inserted into a generated TOC along with the paragraph heading.
Ctrl Shift * (asterisk)	Show / Hide Non-Printing Characters (Hidden Text)	Toggles the feature on and off
Ctrl Shift D	Double Underline Words	
Ctrl Shift W	Underline Words Only	
Ctrl Shift A	All Caps	
Ctrl Shift K	Small Caps	
Ctrl Shift N	Applies the Normal paragraph style for the template you're using	

Keystrokes	Function	Comments
Ctrl Shift C	Copy paragraph formatting (not text)	The Ctrl Shift C and Ctrl Shift V keystrokes work like the Format Painter in that you can use them to copy formatting from one paragraph to another
Ctrl Shift V	Paste paragraph formatting (not text)	Note that these keystrokes are used for copying and pasting *formatting only*, not text
Ctrl Shift T	Decrease Hanging Indent Each time you press Ctrl T, it decreases the hanging indent by one additional tab stop	Ctrl T = Increase Hanging Indent
Ctrl Shift = (equal sign)	Superscript	
Ctrl = (equal sign)	Subscript	
Ctrl - (hyphen)	Soft Hyphen	
Ctrl Shift - (hyphen)	Hard (Non-Breaking) Hyphen	
Ctrl Shift Spacebar	Hard (Non-Breaking) Space	
Ctrl Delete	Deletes the word to the right of the cursor	Cursor must be on the first letter of the word
Ctrl Backspace	Deletes the word to the left of the cursor	Cursor must be to the right of the last letter of the word
Ctrl] (close bracket)	Increase font size by 1 point	Select text first
Ctrl [(open bracket)	Decrease font size by 1 point	Select text first
Ctrl Shift > (greater than / close chevron)	Increase font size by 2 points	Select text first
Ctrl Shift < (less than / open chevron)	Decrease font size by 2 points	Select text first

Favorite Ctrl Key Tips

Everyone – or nearly everyone – knows that Ctrl B applies boldface, Ctrl I applies italics, Ctrl U applies underlining, and Ctrl A selects the entire document. But not everyone knows about the following Ctrl key shortcuts, which come in very handy. I use them almost every day!

Applying the Normal Paragraph Style

The key combination **Ctrl Shift N** applies the Normal paragraph style (for whichever template your document is based on; different templates can have different Normal styles). It wipes out any formatting that has been applied via a style or manually via the Paragraph dialog: justification, line spacing, indentation, first-line indent, before and/or after spacing, line and page breaks, tab settings. It also restores the default font face, size, and color of the Normal style.

Just insert your cursor within a paragraph that you want to strip of formatting, press **Ctrl Shift N**, and the paragraph should go from fancy to plain vanilla.

NOTE: Ctrl Q also removes paragraph formatting, *with the exception of formatting that has been applied via a style*. If you attempt to use Ctrl Q to strip a paragraph's formatting and it doesn't work, try Ctrl Shift N instead.

Using Keystrokes for Indent and Hanging Indent

In Word, **Ctrl M** (M for Margin?) is like Indent in WordPerfect (F7 or, for those of you who still use the DOS-compatible keyboard, F4). **Ctrl T**, on the other hand, creates a hanging indent (T for indenT?). Each time you press Ctrl M or Ctrl T, you increase the indentation by one tab stop. To reverse the amount of indentation, press **Ctrl Shift M** or **Ctrl Shift T**.

Increasing or Decreasing Font Size on the Fly

A quick way to increase or decrease font size by **1 point** is to select the text and press **Ctrl]** (close bracket—increase) or **Ctrl [** (open bracket—decrease). While the text is selected, you can continue pressing Ctrl] or Ctrl [until the text attains the desired size.

To increase or decrease font size by **2 points**, select the text and press **Ctrl Shift >** (increase) or **Ctrl Shift <** (decrease). **NOTE:** This shortcut increments / decrements font sizes that are under 12 points by 1 point, and increments / decrements fonts that are 12 points and above by 2 points.

Other Faves

I also regularly use **Ctrl D** to open the **Font dialog** and **Ctrl H** for **Replace**.

And I often insert non-breaking spaces with **Ctrl Shift Spacebar**, as well as non-breaking hyphens with **Ctrl Shift -** (hyphen).

Selected Function Key Shortcuts
(Listed by Keystrokes)

Keystrokes	Function	Comments
F1	Help	
Shift F1	Reveal Formatting	
Ctrl F2	Print / Preview	(aka "Print Place"
Shift F3	Change Case (of selected text)	Toggles among ALL CAPS, lower case, and Initial Caps or Sentence case. (Depends on the context of selected text.)
Alt F3	Opens Quick Parts / Building Blocks dialog	Must select text first
F4	Repeat Previous Command	Also Ctrl Y
Ctrl F4	Close Document Window	Also Ctrl W
Alt F4	Exit Word	
F5	Go To (page, section, line, footnote, comment, etc.)	Also Ctrl G
Shift F5	Go To Previous Cursor Position(s)	
Ctrl F6	Next Document Window	Like F3 (Switch Screen) in WordPerfect
F7	Spell-Check	
Shift F7	Thesaurus	
F9	Update Field Codes	(To update an individual field, put the cursor into the field and press F9; to update all fields in document, select the entire document with Ctrl A and press F9)
Alt F9	Toggle Between Field Codes and Code Results in Document	
Ctrl Shift F9	Unlink a Field Code (convert to text)	
Ctrl F11	Lock a Field Code (prevent it from updating)	

Keystrokes	Function	Comments
Ctrl Shift F11	Unlock a Code	
Shift F10	Display Shortcut Menu	
F12	Save As	Bypasses the Backstage View
Shift F12	Save	
Ctrl F12	Open (bypasses the Backstage View)	See also Ctrl O
Ctrl Shift * (asterisk)	Show / Hide Non-Printing Characters, including Hidden Text	This is a toggle; press once to display and a second time to hide
Ctrl Shift D	Double Underline Words	
Ctrl Shift W	Underline Words Only	
Ctrl Shift A	All Caps	
Ctrl Shift K	Small Caps	
Ctrl Shift N	Applies the Normal paragraph style for the template you're using	
Ctrl Shift = (equal sign)	Superscript	Apply to selected text
Ctrl = (equal sign)	Subscript	Apply to selected text
Ctrl - (hyphen)	Soft Hyphen	
Ctrl Shift - (hyphen)	Hard (Non-Breaking) Hyphen	
Ctrl Shift Spacebar	Hard (Non-Breaking) Space	

Selected Function Key and Ctrl Key Shortcuts
(Listed by Feature / Function)

Feature	Keystrokes	Comments
Help	F1	
Reveal Formatting	Shift F1	Click within the paragraph first.
Change Case	Shift F3	Apply to selected text.
Close Document Window	Ctrl F4 *or* Ctrl W	
Go To	F5 *or* Ctrl G	
Go To Previous Cursor Position	Shift F5	
Next Document (Switch Screen)	Ctrl F6	
Previous Document	Shift Ctrl F6	
Spell-Check	F7	
Thesaurus	Shift F7	Click within a word first.
Update Field Codes	F9	
Toggle Between Codes and Results	Alt F9	
Unlink a Field Code (Convert to Text	Ctrl Shift F9	
Lock a Field Code (Prevent Updating)	Ctrl F11	
Unlock a Code	Ctrl Shift F11	
Open (bypasses the Backstage View)	Ctrl F12	
Save As (bypasses the Backstage View)	F12	
All Caps	Ctrl Shift A	Apply to selected text.
Small Caps	Ctrl Shift K	Apply to selected text.
Double Underline	Ctrl Shift D	Apply to selected text.
Underline Words Only	Ctrl Shift W	Apply to selected text.
Normal Paragraph Style	Ctrl Shift N	Apply to selected text.

Feature	Keystrokes	Comments
Display Non-Printing Characters	Ctrl Shift * (asterisk)	
Soft Hyphen	Ctrl - (hyphen)	
Hard (Non-Breaking) Hyphen	Ctrl Shift - (hyphen)	
Hard (Non-Breaking) Space	Ctrl Shift Spacebar	
Superscript	Ctrl Shift = (equal sign)	Apply to selected text.
Subscript	Ctrl = (equal sign)	Apply to selected text.
Increase Font Size by 1 Point	Ctrl] (close bracket)	See * below.
Decrease Font Size by 1 Point*	Ctrl [(open bracket)	See * below.
Increase Font Size by 2 Points*	Ctrl Shift > (greater than / close chevron)	See * below.
Decrease Font Size by 2 Points*	Ctrl Shift < (less than / open chevron)	See * below.
Style Separator	Ctrl Alt Enter	Prevents the text of a paragraph from being inserted into a generated TOC along with the paragraph heading.

*Be sure to select the text first. Note that Ctrl Shift > (greater than / close chevron) and Ctrl Shift < (less than / open chevron) change the text size by 2 points only for font sizes from 12 points and up; below 12 points, they change the text size by 1 point.

Mnemonics and Keyboard Shortcuts for Tabs and Dialog Boxes

In all versions of Word that use the Ribbon interface, tapping the **Alt key** displays **mnemonics** (shortcut keys) that you can use to open the tabs, as well as the icons/drop-downs and commands on your Quick Access Toolbar (QAT).[1] Some people refer to these mnemonics as "**badges**." You might see them referred to elsewhere as **KeyTips**. They can be very useful. If you haven't tried working with them, give them a whirl and see what you think.

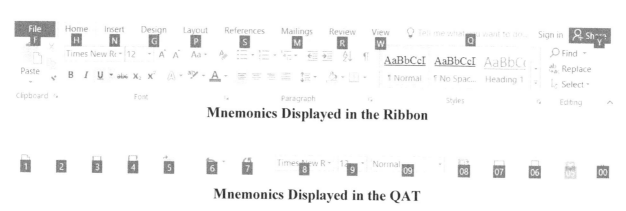

Mnemonics Displayed in the Ribbon

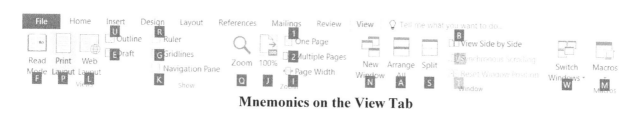

Mnemonics Displayed in the QAT

After tapping the Alt key, you can open a tab by pressing the mnemonic for that tab (such as **F** to open the File drop-down, **N** to open the Insert tab, or **W** to open the View tab). After you press one of the mnemonics to open a tab—as shown in the screenshot below, I pressed "W" to open the View tab—you'll see mnemonics for the commands on that tab.

Mnemonics on the View Tab

To use a command on a tab or on the QAT, press the mnemonic for that command. If more than one letter or number is displayed, press all of the letters or numbers in sequence, such as **Alt P, S, P** or **Alt 09**.

Alternatively, after you have pressed the Alt key, you can press the **Tab key** to move the cursor in sequence from icon to icon on the Ribbon and then from icon to icon on the QAT. To use a highlighted icon, simply press the **Enter key**.

---

[1] To stop the mnemonics from displaying, either press the Alt key again or press the Esc key.

357

The following keyboard shortcuts provide quick access to tabs on the Word 2016 Ribbon and to certain dialog boxes. (This list is not intended to be comprehensive.)

Displaying the Mnemonics (Badges) on the Various Tabs

Alt F—Opens the Backstage View and displays mnemonics (badges) for commands therein.

Alt F, Esc	= Back to document
Alt F, I	= Info
Alt F, N	= New
Alt F, O	= Open
Alt F, R	= Recent (from the Open screen)
Alt F, S	= Save
Alt F, A	= Save As
Alt F, P	= Print
Alt F, D	= Share
Alt F, E	= Export
Alt F, C	= Close
Alt F, D	= Account
Alt F, T	= Options (Word Options)
Alt F, K	= Feedback (to Microsoft)
Alt F, X	= Exit from Word (not displayed, but it works)

If you have recent documents displayed in the Quick Access area below "Feedback," each will have a number, starting with 1. The first one in the list will be Alt F, 1; the second listed will be Alt F, 2, and so forth.

Alt H—Displays mnemonics (badges) for commands on the Home tab

Alt N—Displays mnemonics (badges) for commands on the Insert tab

Alt P—Displays mnemonics (badges) for commands on the Layout tab

Alt S—Displays mnemonics (badges) for commands on the References tab

Alt M—Displays mnemonics (badges) for commands on the Mailings tab

Alt R—Displays mnemonics (badges) for commands on the Review tab

Alt W—Displays mnemonics (badges) for commands on the View tab

Alt L—Displays mnemonics (badges) for commands on the Developer tab (if displayed)

Alt X—Displays mnemonics (badges) for commands on the Add-Ins tab (if displayed)

Using Keyboard Shortcuts to Open Various Dialog Boxes and Panes

Alt O, P—opens the Paragraph dialog (works regardless of which tab is active)

Alt P, M, A *or* Alt P, S, P—opens the Page Setup dialog

Alt Ctrl Shift S—opens the Styles Pane (you can press the first three keys in any sequence; just keep them depressed and then tap "S")

Ctrl D—opens the Font dialog

Alt I, T *or* Alt N, D—opens the Date and Time dialog

Alt I, S—opens the Symbols dialog

Alt I, N, N *or* Alt S, Q—opens the Footnote dialog

Alt O, T—opens the Tabs dialog

Alt V, Z—opens the Zoom dialog (for changing magnification of the document on the screen)

Alt V, Z, E—opens the Zoom dialog and positions the cursor in the Percent box so you can change the magnification easily

Alt H, F, O—opens the Clipboard

Shift F1—opens the Reveal Formatting pane

Miscellaneous

Alt N, H, E—puts the cursor in the Header editing screen

Alt N, O, E—puts the cursor in the Footer editing screen

Keyboard Shortcuts—Miscellaneous Tips

Moving Up or Down One Page

The keyboard shortcut for moving up or down one page at a time depends on which version of Word you use. In Word 2016, **Ctrl Pg Up** (or Ctrl Page Up) moves the cursor up one full page; **Ctrl Pg Down** (or Ctrl Page Down) moves the cursor down one full page. (**Pg Up** and **Pg Down** move the cursor up or down one *screen* at a time.) But sometimes these keyboard shortcuts don't work as expected. For more information about this issue, and a few workarounds, see the section starting on page 301 about how performing a "Find" hijacks the keyboard shortcuts for the Page Up and Page Down functions.

Copying and Pasting Paragraph Formatting

As mentioned in the section about the Format Painter starting on page 143, there are a couple of highly useful keyboard shortcuts that allow you to copy and paste paragraph formatting. **Ctrl Shift C** copies the formatting of the paragraph your cursor is in; to apply that formatting to another paragraph, position the cursor within the "target" paragraph and press **Ctrl Shift V**.

Exactly what are you pasting when you use Ctrl Shift V?

If your cursor is at the beginning or end of the target paragraph (the paragraph you're pasting into), or within white space, Ctrl Shift V will paste only *paragraph formatting* (the types of formatting that can be applied from the Paragraph dialog): justification, indentation, line spacing, before and after spacing, widow and orphan control settings, etc. If your cursor is within text, Ctrl Shift V will apply paragraph formatting and also will apply *direct character formatting*—such as bolding, italics, and/or font face/size—to *the word the cursor is in*. To apply character formatting to the entire paragraph, along with paragraph formatting, select the text of the target paragraph before pressing Ctrl Shift V.

In any case, keep in mind that Ctrl Shift C / Ctrl Shift V copy and paste only formatting, not text.

Using Field Codes

This section explains how to automate your documents with field codes, a powerful, if somewhat under-used, feature.

What *Are* Field Codes?

Fields codes, sometimes referred to as just "fields," are *variables* – that is, placeholders for information that can change, such as a page number, a paragraph number, a date, a complete Table of Contents, a single citation for a Table of Authorities, a file name and path, and so forth. There are also field codes that reflect document information (Author, Title, Subject, Comments, etc.) that is pulled from the File tab's Info screen.

Often, field codes are inserted into your document automatically (behind the scenes, so to speak) when you execute a command. However, you can insert codes directly from the Field dialog box, and you can choose a formatting option (such as upper or lower case for text or a specific starting value for a number) when you do so.[1] Or, if you know how, you can edit the codes yourself after inserting them.

The codes are usually hidden; we see the code results, such as a formatted page number, rather than the coding itself. To toggle between the codes in your document and the code results, press **Alt F9**. (**Alt F9** toggles all of the codes in your document; **Shift F9** toggles only the code your cursor is in.) In the screenshots below, you can see what a page number code and a date code look like when you press Alt F9 to show the codes themselves:

{ PAGE }   { DATE \@ "M/d/yyyy" }

The codes appear inside curly brackets. They have a gray background because of a (default) setting in the Word Options[2] that applies shading when a field is selected – which means when you click somewhere within a field. I recommend retaining this setting, because it provides the best of both worlds: The codes are inconspicuous (and not distracting) most of the time, but it's easy to tell whether a date or paragraph number is a code or plain text by clicking within that item and noticing whether it turns gray. (If you choose "Always," the codes remain gray at all times; if you choose "Never," the codes won't turn gray when you click within them.)

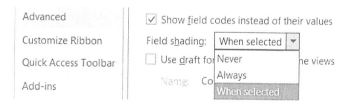

---

[1] These formatting options or parameters are sometimes referred to as "switches."

[2] **File**, **Options**, **Advanced**, scroll to "**Show document content**," "**Field shading**."

361

Updating a Field Code

Field codes are somewhat different from other codes in Word in that, although they are automated to some extent, certain codes occasionally require ***manual updating***.

You can update a single code at any time by either clicking within a code, then pressing **F9** *or* right-clicking within a code, then choosing "**Update Field**." You can update the codes in the ***body*** of the document by pressing Ctrl A to select the entire doc, then pressing F9 or right-clicking. But **CAUTION**: This method ***will not*** update any fields in headers, footers, or footnotes. You will need to go into the header or footer editing screens, and/or into the footnote text area(s), and update from there.

Note that codes can be locked, and that locked codes will not update. For more information, see page 367.

Some codes update automatically when you insert the next code in sequence. Others update when you open a document or when you print (or open the Print / Print Preview screen).

- Page number codes update automatically when pages are added or deleted.

- Date (and time) codes update automatically when you open or print a document containing the codes (or open the Print / Print Preview screen).

- SEQ codes (discussed at length in the section starting on page 519) usually update if inserted in sequence, and they update when you print (or simply open the Print / Print Preview screen, including Print Preview Edit Mode). However, they need to be updated manually if you cut and paste or delete items containing the codes.

- Filename and Filename and Path codes update when you print (or open the Print / Print Preview screen).

Note that the option to update fields before printing (**File tab**, **Options**, **Display** category, scroll all the way down to **Printing options**, "**Update fields before printing**") is ***disabled*** by default. That is intentional. Of course, you can change the setting if you like.

Let's take a look at a couple of useful field codes, starting with a very simple example of a code that you typically wouldn't edit – or even think to edit. (Also, see the discussion starting on page 495 about the ListNum field, a way of inserting an automatic paragraph number such as "(a)" or "(i)" – that is, sub-numbering – within a numbered paragraph.)

Reformatting a Date Code

Ordinarily, you don't need to mess around with field codes in order to change the formatting of an automatic date that you insert by clicking **Insert Date & Time** on the **Insert tab**. When the **Date and Time dialog** opens, you just **click the example date** that is in the format you want – typically, the one with the month spelled out followed by the day in single or double digits as appropriate, a comma, and then a four-digit year. To make that the default format, click the "**Set As Default**" button in the lower left-hand corner before clicking "**OK**." (To insert the date as a code, click "**Update automatically**." Otherwise, the date will be inserted as plain text that does not update when the document is opened or printed.)

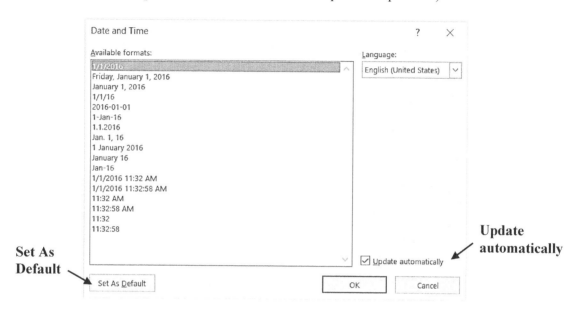

But just for the sake of reviewing how field codes work, let's say that you do an Internet search to find out how to insert a date code in Word, and you learn that you can use the keyboard shortcut **Alt Shift D**. You press Alt Shift D, and the date appears like so:

1/1/2016

You can tell that the inserted date is a code because it turns gray when you click within it. However, if the format you wanted was "January 1, 2016," the fact that it's a code doesn't help much. Or does it?

If you press the key combination **Alt F9** while your cursor is in the code, you'll see the code itself, rather than the code results (the date).[3] It should look similar to the following:[4]

{ DATE \@ "M/d/yyyy" }

---

[3] Or right-click, then choose "**Toggle Field Codes**."

[4] If the current month has two digits, you'll see "MM"; if the current day has two digits, you'll see "dd."

To change the format for this code – although not the default date format for all future documents – just type within the quotation marks, so that the end result looks something like the screenshot below:

{ DATE \@ "MMMM d, yyyy" }

You will need to delete the slashes, add a comma after the code for the day, and insert spaces before the codes for the date and the year. To spell out the name of the month, you need four capital "M's." **CAUTION**: Be careful not to delete the quotation marks!

After changing the format within the code, press **Alt F9** to toggle back to the code results. But wait! You are still seeing something like this:

1/1/2016

That's because you need to *update* the newly formatted code to reflect your changes. So either **click** within the code and press **F9** (the keyboard shortcut that updates a field code) or *right-click* in the code, then choose "**Update Field**." (See the screenshot at right.)

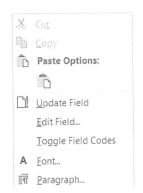

After you do so, you should see something like this:

January 1, 2016

If your cursor is still within the date code, it will have a gray background like the screenshot. Otherwise, it will look just like a regular typed date. Because it's a code, it will update to the current date *whenever you open or print the document*.

NOTE: Codes can be locked; locked codes will not update. See page 367 for more information.

Creating an Unformatted Page X of Y Code

My Word 2010 book included instructions for inserting a code for the file name and path. That seemed like a useful tip because Microsoft had recently removed an AutoText entry, available in older versions of Word, for the file name and path. However, I am happy to report that in Word 2016, you can insert either a FileName code or a FileName and Path code directly from the Header & Footer Tools tab. For instructions, see pages 248 and following.

But it's still difficult to insert a code for "Page X of Y" (where "X" represents the number of the current page and "Y" represents the total number of pages) – at least, without font formatting. The only relevant option available from the gallery under Page Number, Current Page Number uses **boldface** for the page numbers, as shown in the screenshot on the next page. Although it's true that you could insert that code, select / highlight the code, and turn the bold attribute off, you might want to create your own unformatted "Page X of Y" code (and then turn it into a Quick Part / Building Block so that it's readily available in all future documents).

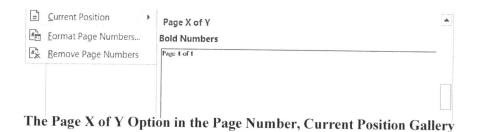

The Page X of Y Option in the Page Number, Current Position Gallery

To create an unformatted "Page X of Y" code, position the cursor where you want the code to appear (typically within the header or the footer) and do the following:

1. Type the word "**Page**" and press the **Spacebar**.

2. Press **Alt Shift P** to insert a page number code. (The format will be Arabic numerals, but you can change the format later if you like.)

3. Press the **Spacebar**, type "of," and press the **Spacebar** again.

4. Open the **Field dialog** by clicking the **Quick Parts drop-down** and choosing "**Field…**" (or press **Alt I, F**).

5. Change the "**Categories**" drop-down from "(All)" to "**Document Information**."[5]

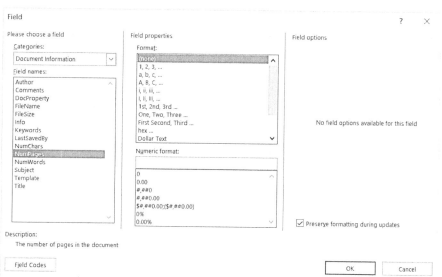

6. From the **Field names** box, click to select "**NumPages**," and click "**OK**."

---

[5] Or, if you leave the "Categories" drop-down set to "(All)," click in the "**Field names**" box and press the letter "**N**" about five times to move to the "**NumPages**" code.

7. You should see something like the screenshot below (i.e., the code result).

Page 1 of 5

8. If you see something more like the next screenshot you are viewing the code itself. Press **Alt F9** to toggle the display from the code to the code result.

Page { PAGE * MERGEFORMAT } of { NUMPAGES * MERGEFORMAT }

That's all there is to it.

Creating a Page X of Y Quick Part

If you like, you can turn your unformatted "Page X of Y" code into a Quick Part (Building Block) so that it is available in future documents. Just follow these instructions:[6]

1. Select the entire code (make sure you are displaying the code *result*) and press **Alt F3**.[7]

2. When the **Create New Building Block dialog** appears, type an abbreviation that is easy to remember, such as PXOY.

3. **IMPORTANT**: Change the "**Save in**" location from Normal.dotm to **BuildingBlocks.dotx**. That will make the Quick Part available in all new documents.

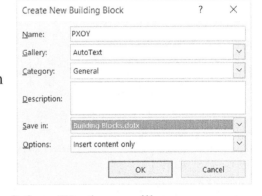

4. Click **OK** to save the Quick Part.

5. **CAUTION**: You're not done yet! When you exit from Word, you will see a prompt warning you that you have made changes to building blocks and asking if you want to save your changes. *Be sure to click "Yes,"* or your new Quick Part will be deleted!

To insert the Page X of Y entry, position the cursor where you want the text and codes to appear, then **type your abbreviation** and **press F3**.

Changing the Page Number Format

As I mentioned earlier, you can change the page number format for both the "X" and "Y" codes after inserting the Quick Part. To do so, press Alt F9 to toggle to the code itself. You should see something like the following:

Page { PAGE} of { NUMPAGES * MERGEFORMAT }

---

[6] For more about Quick Parts, see the section starting on page 377.

[7] Alternatively, click the **Insert tab, Quick Parts, Save Selection to Quick Part Gallery**.

1. To change the number format of the first code (the "Page X" code) to lower-case Roman numerals (i, ii, etc.), click after the word "PAGE," making sure your cursor is within the curly brackets.

2. Press the Spacebar, then type a backslash (\), followed immediately by an asterisk (*).

3. Press the Spacebar again, and then type "roman" in all lower-case letters, without quotation marks.[8]

4. To change the number format of the second code (the "Page Y" code) to lower-case Roman numerals (i, ii, etc.), click after the word "MERGEFORMAT," making sure your cursor is within the curly brackets.

5. Press the Spacebar, then type a backslash (\), followed immediately by an asterisk (*).

6. Press the Spacebar again, and then type "roman" in all lower-case letters, without quotation marks.

    The entire code should now look like the following:

    Page { PAGE * roman} of { NUMPAGES   * MERGEFORMAT * roman}

    If necessary, turn on Show / Hide to make sure you inserted spaces in the appropriate locations. Then press Alt F9 again to toggle back to the code results. And finally, update the code by selecting the entire code and then pressing F9 or right-clicking and choosing "Update Field Code." Voila!

    Page i of i

Locking, Unlocking, and Unlinking Field Codes

It is possible to lock codes (for example, a date code) so that they don't update unless they're unlocked. To lock a field code, click the code and press the key combination **Ctrl F11**. To unlock a field code (assuming it's actually locked), click the code and press **Ctrl Shift F11**.

Also, you can convert certain codes into plain text by ***unlinking*** them. To unlink a code, select it (or insert the cursor into the code), then press **Ctrl Shift F9**.

CAUTION: After codes have been unlinked, you can't link them again – unless you click "Undo" or press Ctrl Z immediately after unlinking.

---

[8] If you want to use upper-case Roman numerals, type "Roman" with a capital "R" instead. I've tested, and that works!

Fill-in Fields

Field codes have many uses. For example, as shown in the section that starts on page 519, you can insert **SEQ codes** from the Field dialog box to produce automatic numbers such as those used in headings for discovery and discovery responses (e.g., Interrogatories and Responses to Interrogatories, or Requests for Production of Documents and Responses to Requests for Production of Documents).

Another example is **Fill-In fields**, which you embed in templates to prompt the person working on the document to enter variable information at certain points in the document. (Fill-In fields are somewhat akin to variables in keyboard merges in WordPerfect.)

How Fill-In Fields Work

In order for Fill-In fields to work properly, you need to do all of the following:

(1)   embed the fields in a template;

(2)   put the template in the default template location in Word (note that you might have to put the templates in a shared network location or copy them to each staff member's computer); and

(3)   open a new document based on the template by clicking the **File tab**, **New**.

Note that after clicking the File tab, New, users might have to click "**Custom**" or "**Personal**" in order to locate the template that contains the Fill-In fields (depending on where you've stored the template).

Creating a Template With Embedded Fill-In Fields

You can start with a blank document or with a form you're already using. In either case, do the following:

1.   Position the cursor at the first point where you want variable information to be inserted.

2.   Open the **Field dialog** by pressing the key combination **Alt I**, **F** or by clicking the Quick Parts drop-down on the Insert tab and clicking "Field..."

3.   Locate the **Fill-In fields** command. You can move to that command quickly by pressing the letter "F" a few times.

   At this point, you have the option of **adding a specific prompt** to help guide the users (see the top center of the dialog box). You also can create a **default response** (see the upper right-hand corner of the dialog box), which will be inserted automatically into the document if the person filling in the fields in response to the prompts leaves that field blank.

368

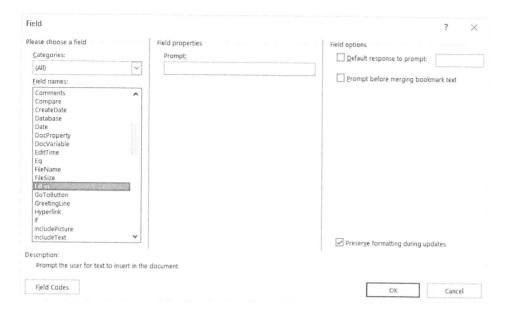

4. When you are ready to insert the field code into the document, click **OK** *or* press the **Enter key**.

5. A **prompt box** will appear. Since you are still in the process of creating the template, don't type anything in the box. (If you like, you can type a placeholder such as an "X," which users will be able to type over when they are prompted to enter text in the box.) Simply click "**OK**," and the code will be inserted at the cursor position.

6. Note that unless you specifically choose to display the codes while creating the template, you won't be able to see them, which can make things somewhat challenging. In order to display the codes, press **Alt F9**. To hide the codes, simply press Alt F9 again (it's a toggle).

7. Continue inserting fill-in field codes at appropriate places in the document. Then, when everything is to your liking, save it as a template.

8. To save the template, click the **File tab** (*or* press Alt F), then click **Save As** (*or* press the letter A). Navigate to the folder where templates are stored. In Windows 7, 8, and 10, the personal templates folder usually is located here:

   C:\Users\<UserName>\AppData\Roaming\Microsoft\Templates

   or it might be located here:

   C: \Users\<UserName>\Documents\Custom Office Templates

   If you prefer (and have the necessary permissions), you can save the template in a shared location. Just make sure that the users' computers point to the correct "Workgroup" templates location by clicking File, Options, Advanced, scroll to

"File Locations"; if necessary, click "Workgroup templates," click "Modify," then browse to the shared folder. Click "OK" to save your changes.

9. Be sure to save the document as a template. Note that you have a choice of saving the template as a Word 2016 template (*.dotx) or as a Word 97-2003 template (*.dot).

Using a Document Based on the Template

After you've saved the template, users should be able to create a new document based on the template by clicking the **File tab, New, Custom** and single-clicking the appropriate personal or workgroup folder. To create a document based on the template, simply click the icon for the template.

When the doc opens, the first prompt will pop up. **Type the information** and click **OK**. (**NOTE**: pressing Enter won't dismiss the prompt. Rather, it will merely move the insertion point down to the next line within the prompt.)

The next prompt (if any) will pop up. Continue as in the previous paragraph.

When you have filled in the last prompt, you'll be returned to the document, where you can make any necessary changes.

Note that if you close the document and reopen it, you won't be prompted to fill in the fields. *Prompting occurs only when you open a new document based on a template that was created with Fill-In fields embedded in it.* However, you can press **F11** to move your cursor to the first field in the document, then press **F9** to open the pop-up for that field, type any text you want, and click **OK** to dismiss the pop-up. To continue, repeat the F11, F9 sequence.

ALSO NOTE: If "Update fields before printing" is enabled in the Word Options, fill-in fields will pop up every time you print a document containing the fields. That can become burdensome. To prevent this behavior, you can turn off the "Update fields before printing" option (**File tab, Options, Display, Printing options,** and *uncheck* "**Update fields before printing**"), *or* you can **select the fill-in fields** and convert the codes to text before you print by pressing **Ctrl Shift F9**.

CAUTION: If there are fields in the document that you want to update, such as a date code, don't select the entire document before pressing Ctrl Shift F9. Select only the fill-in fields.

WHERE IS IT? Macros

If you've scoured the Ribbon for a Macros command, you're probably completely at a loss. Where the heck did it go?

For reasons that aren't entirely clear to me, Microsoft located the macros function on the **View tab**. There's a **Macros group**, with a **Macros drop-down** that you can use to record macros (or to view the built-in macros), at the right end of the tab.

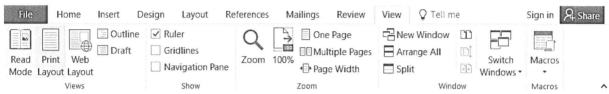

The View Tab – Macros at Right

In addition, the **Developer tab** – which by default is hidden (not on the Ribbon) – contains icons for **Macros** (opens the Macros dialog) and **Record Macro**.

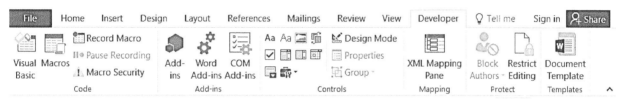

The Developer Tab – Macros at Left

To add the Developer tab to the Ribbon, **right-click** the Ribbon, and click "**Customize the Ribbon….**"

When the **Word Options dialog** opens, navigate to the right side of the screen (underneath "Customize the Ribbon"), and click to put a check in the **checkbox** to the left of "**Developer tab**." Then click "**OK**" to save your changes and close out of the Word Options.

Finally, you can add a **Macros icon** to the **Status Bar**. To do so, **right-click** within the Status Bar, and when the pop-up menu appears, click "**Macro Recording**." Then click anywhere outside the menu to close it.

To record a macro, just **click the button** on the Status Bar, which will launch the **Record Macro** dialog box.

371

Creating a Simple Macro to Print the Current Page[1]

There are three different ways to start recording macros:

1. Navigate to the **View tab**, **Macros group**, click the **Macros drop-down** and then click **Record Macro...**; *or*

2. Display the **Developer tab**, an optional tab that ordinarily is hidden,[2] then click the **Record Macro** button on that tab.; *or*

3. Click the **Macro icon** on the **Status Bar** (if you have added one).

Any of those methods will open the **Record Macro dialog box**.

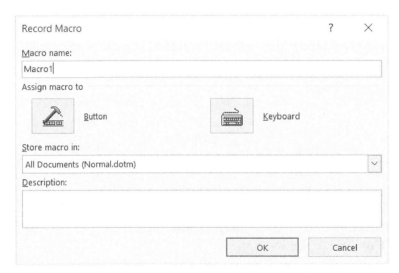

Record Macro Dialog Box

In the **Macro name** box, type a short, memorable name for the macro that identifies what it does, such as PrintCurrentPage. **NOTE**: Spaces are not allowed in macro names.

You can type a description of the macro in the **Description** box. This is an optional step, but it has two advantages: (1) It permits other users who open the Macros dialog box to figure out what the macro does; and (2) if you assign the macro to a button, the description you type

---

[1] This tutorial is intended to introduce you to the process of writing (recording) macros in Word. I've deliberately chosen a very simple macro to get you started.

[2] To display the Developer tab (also detailed on the previous page), **right-click** the **Ribbon** or the Quick Access Toolbar and click "**Customize the Ribbon...**" When the Word Options screen appears, navigate to the right-hand side (the box that shows the names of the tabs). Locate and **click** to put a checkmark in the box to the left of "**Developer**," then click "**OK**."

will appear as a pop-up description when you position the mouse pointer over the button that runs the macro. A good description for our sample macro might be "Prints the current page."

NOTE: By default, the macro will be stored in your Normal template (Normal.dotm). If you prefer, you can click the **Store macro in:** drop-down and choose the current document.

At this point, you can create a **button** so that you can run the macro from the Quick Access Toolbar or designate a **keyboard shortcut** for the macro. Let's start by assigning a keyboard shortcut; later on, we'll also put a button to run the macro on the QAT. (Note that you can perform either step later on.)

First, click the **Keyboard** button in the section of the dialog box labeled "**Assign macro to:**." The **Customize Keyboard** dialog opens. Note that the "**Macros**" category is already selected in the "**Categories**" **box** at top left.

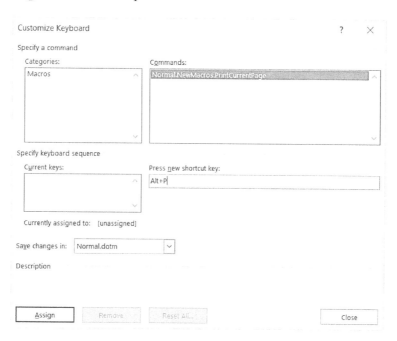

Type a key combination in the "**Press new shortcut key:**" box. In the example, I used Alt P. Be sure to choose a key combination that hasn't already been assigned to another function. If the key combo you type is taken, the area below the "Current keys" box will display "Currently assigned to:" followed by the name of the function using that shortcut. Otherwise, it will display "**Currently assigned to: [unassigned]**." If the key combination is available, click the **Assign** button to assign that shortcut to your macro. Then click **Close**.

Next, create your macro by using the keyboard and/or the mouse as if you were going to print the current page. In other words, press **Ctrl P** (or click the **File tab**, **Print**), then click the **Print All Pages drop-down** and choose **Current Page**. Finally, click the **Print** button. (The page your cursor is in should print, unless you don't have a printer attached or running.)

Lastly, stop recording the macro by clicking the "**Stop Recording**" button on the **Macros drop-down** on the **View tab**; by clicking the "**Stop Recording**" button on the Developer tab; *or* by clicking the **Macro Recorder** icon in the Status Bar.

To run (play) the macro, you can simply press the key combination you assigned to the macro. Or you can open the **Macros dialog** by pressing **Alt F8**,[3] scrolling to the PrintCurrentPage macro, and clicking **Run** (or **double-clicking** the macro name).

You can assign the macro to the Quick Access Toolbar after you have recorded the macro. First, click the **File tab**, **Options**, **Customize Quick Access Toolbar...** (or right-click the **QAT** or the **Ribbon** and choose **Customize Quick Access Toolbar...**). When the Word Options dialog opens, click the **Choose commands from: drop-down** at the top left side and select **Macros**.

The macro will appear in the box at left, using the name you chose for it, preceded by "Normal.NewMacros." **Click to select** the macro, and then click the "**Add**" **button** in the middle column to add the macro to the Quick Access Toolbar.

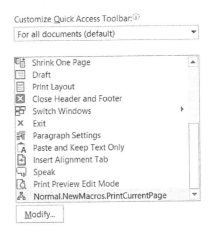

After you've done so, the "**Modify**" button underneath the **Customize Quick Access Toolbar box** (grayed out in the screenshot above) will become active (as in the screenshot at right). **Click** the "**Modify**" button.

---

[3] There are many ways to accomplish the same task. If you like, you can open the Macros dialog by clicking the Macro icon on the View tab or the one on the Developer tab.

374

The "**Modify Button**" dialog will open.

Before Changing the Name   **After Changing the Name and Choosing a Button**

In the "**Display name**" box at the bottom, you can type a user-friendly name for the macro – as opposed to the VBA-coded name Microsoft assigns to it. For example, I've chosen the display name "**Print Current Page**" (without quotation marks). (Unlike macro names, display names can have blank spaces between letters.)

Before clicking "OK," you can select a button to display on the Quick Access Toolbar. (I've chosen one that looks like a printer.) Just single-click, then click "OK" to save the display name and button you've chosen. (You can change them later if you like.)

Here is a screenshot of the icon on my Quick Access Toolbar. I've tested with both my regular printer and a PDF printer, and it works as expected – i.e., it prints only the page my cursor is in.

If you didn't set up a keyboard shortcut when you first created the macro, you can do so at some later date. Just right-click the **Ribbon**, click "**Customize the Ribbon…**," then click the **Keyboard shortcuts: Customize button** (or click the **File tab**, **Options**, **Customize Ribbon**, and then click the **Keyboard shortcuts: Customize button**).

When the dialog opens, navigate to the "**Categories**" box at the top left side, then scroll down to and click **Macros**.

Next, navigate to **Macros** on the right side and **click the macro name**. (If you have created other macros in the interim, you might have to scroll down.)

375

Position your cursor in the **Press new keyboard key:** box and press a key combination. If the keyboard shortcut you wish to use isn't assigned to another function – or if you're willing to reassign that shortcut to your macro – click the "**Assign**" button. If necessary, try a different key combination and, if it's available, click "**Assign**."

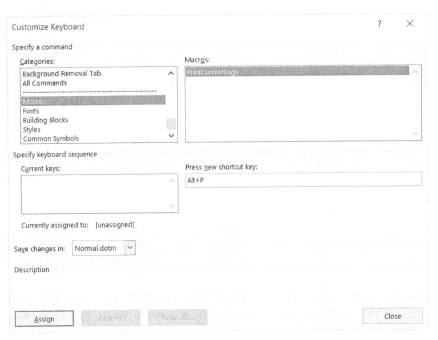

Finally, click **Close** and then click "**OK**" to save your changes and exit from the Word Options dialog.

Creating and Using "Quick Parts"

Word's Quick Parts feature allows you to insert commonly used phrases, boilerplate paragraphs, signature blocks, and other frequently used text and graphics into your documents with just a few keystrokes. Microsoft sometimes refers to Quick Parts as Building Blocks. The terms are interchangeable. (AutoText still exists, but as a sort of sub-set of Quick Parts.)

To create a Quick Parts entry, start by typing and formatting some text, along with any graphics you wish to use. Then select / highlight everything – including any tabs or other formatting you want to incorporate.[1] (If you want a blank line / empty paragraph inserted below the entry, select the next line, too.)

Next, do one of the following:

- click the **Insert tab**, click the **Quick Parts drop-down** in the **Text Group**, and click **Save Selection to Quick Part Gallery...**; *or*

- click the **Insert tab**, click the **Quick Parts drop-down**, scroll to **AutoText**, slide the mouse pointer to the left, and click **Save Selection to AutoText Gallery**; *or*

- press **Alt F3**.

All three methods launch the **Create New Building Block dialog**. However, the first method by default saves Quick Parts entries in the BuildingBlocks.dotx template, whereas the other two methods by default save Quick Parts entries in the Normal.dotm template. That difference has important consequences, as I will explain momentarily.

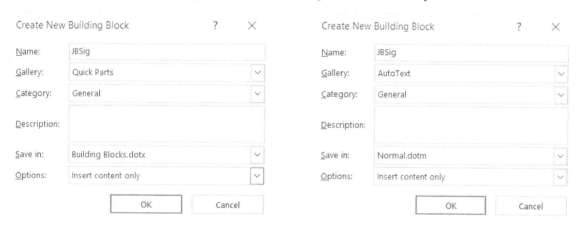

Create New Building Block Dialog
Using "Save Selection to Quick Part Gallery"

Create New Building Block Dialog
Using Alt F3 or "Save Selection to *AutoText* Gallery"

---

[1] Also, if you wish to preserve any paragraph formatting, be sure to select the paragraph mark at the end of the paragraph along with any text and graphics. To ensure that you select the paragraph mark (plus any tabs), turn on Show / Hide by clicking the **Paragraph icon** on the **Home tab, Paragraph group** (or pressing **Ctrl Shift ***) before selecting the text (and graphics).

Type a short, easy-to-remember, and unique name (an abbreviation) in the "**Name**" **field**. This abbreviation, plus the F3 key, is what you will use to insert the Quick Parts entry into your document. (If you want Word to prompt you to insert the entry by pressing the Enter key after typing the abbreviation – using a feature known as **AutoComplete** – the abbreviation must be at least four characters long.)

The Quick Parts feature *is not case-sensitive*. In other words, the abbreviation VTY works the same way as vty, and Vty (and all other permutations).

You can add a brief description in the "**Description**" **field** if it will help you remember what your abbreviation does, but that step is optional.

Remember that the method you use to create the Quick Part determines the template where the Quick Part will be stored by default. If you use the first method described on the previous page (**Insert**, **Quick Parts drop-down**, "**Save selection to Quick Part gallery**"), the default "Save in" location is the **BuildingBlocks.dotx template**. Each user has one.[2]

There are pros and cons to storing Quick Parts in that template. Doing so makes the Quick Parts available globally, i.e., regardless of which template you are using at any given time (such as a pleading template or letterhead).

However, there are two possible reasons why you might want to change the "Save in" location. For one thing, you might wish to create certain entries for use only with one specific template (such as a discovery template). If so, be sure to change the "Save in" location to that template.

For another thing, the AutoComplete feature, described below, doesn't work with Quick Parts entries that are stored in the BuildingBlocks.dotx template. If you change the "Save in" location to Normal.dotm, or in fact to any other template, AutoComplete should work (as long as the abbreviations you assign to your entries are at least four characters long). And fortunately, Quick Parts stored in the Normal.dotm template also are available globally.

To change the "Save in" location, just click the drop-down and select a different template.

---

[2]Actually, there are two different Building Blocks templates for each user. One, located in **C:\Program Files (x86)\Microsoft Office\root\Office16\Document Parts\1033\16** and called **Built-In Building Blocks.dotx**, includes dozens of pre-formatted cover pages, footers, headers, page numbers, tables, text boxes, watermarks, and similar items. This template should not be deleted or edited.

The other, located in **C:\Users\<UserName>\AppData\Roaming\Microsoft\Document Building Blocks\1033\16**, is the "working" copy and is where the user's customized entries are stored. (A copy of the Built-In Building Blocks.dotx template is stored in this location, as well.) **NOTE**: It is a good idea to back up the customized template from time to time (and save it to another location such as an external drive) because it occasionally gets corrupted.

The screenshot at right shows only two templates: Normal.dotm and BuildingBlocks.dotx. If I had started creating the Quick Part from within a different template, that template would be available from the "Save in" drop-down, as well.

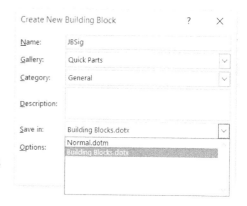

There's no compelling reason to change the gallery where your Quick Part will appear. As you might recall from the part of the book that described the Word screen elements, a "Gallery" usually refers to a collection of pre-formatted items, such as footers, cover pages, or watermarks.

See the screenshot at right for a partial list of available galleries where you can store Quick Parts.

The default gallery for Quick Parts, logically enough, is the Quick Parts Gallery, which is visible only when you open the **Building Blocks Organizer (Insert tab, Quick Parts drop-down, Building Blocks Organizer)**. Another good choice is the AutoText gallery (also located toward the bottom of the Quick Parts drop-down, but less overwhelming because it isn't pre-populated with entries created by Microsoft).

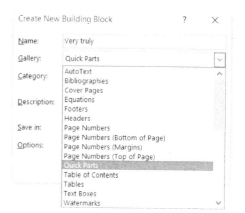

The next screenshot provides a truncated view of the AutoText gallery, where I stored a Quick Part that expands into my signature block.

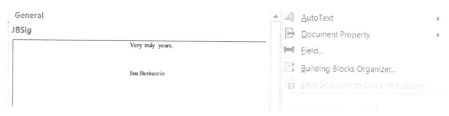

My New Quick Parts Entry in the AutoText Gallery (Truncated)

After creating your Quick Parts entry, click **OK**. Doing so saves the entry for use during the current editing session (i.e., until you exit from Word). To ensure that your Quick Parts entry is available in future editing sessions, see the discussion on page 380.

To insert your Quick Part at the cursor position, do one of the following:

(1) **Type the abbreviation** (assuming you remember it!)[3] and press **F3**; *or*

---

[3] If you have given your Quick Parts unique names / abbreviations, you can use the F3 key to expand a Quick Part without typing the full abbreviation.

379

(2) If the abbreviation is four characters or longer (and if you've stored the entry in a template other than BuildingBlocks.dotx), **type those characters** and, when the **AutoComplete prompt** appears, press the **Enter key**; *or*

(3) Click the **Insert tab**, navigate to the **Text group**, click the **Quick Parts drop-down**, and, if an image of your Quick Part appears there, click it; *or*

(4) Click the **Insert tab**, navigate to the **Text group**, click the **Quick Parts drop-down,** click "**Building Blocks Organizer**," **locate your entry** in the list, click to **select it**, and click **Insert**.[4]

Saving Quick Parts When Exiting From Word

After creating and saving Quick Parts, you must take one additional step to ensure that your new Quick Parts are available the next time you open Word, not merely during the current editing session. This step requires vigilance because it involves a prompt that appears when you exit from Word and, if you aren't paying close attention, it's easy to dismiss the prompt and inadvertently discard your new Quick Parts.

As you know, when you exit from Word, whether at the end of the day or before taking a break, the program prompts you to save any edits you've made, but not saved, in open documents. If you are rushing to leave – as we all do from time to time – you probably click the "Don't Save" option routinely. But *watch out*, because the very last prompt that appears after you have created a new Quick Parts entry is asking whether you want to save those Quick Parts (recall that they are also known as Building Blocks) for future use. See the screenshot below.

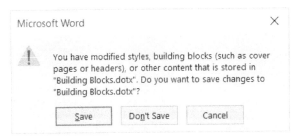

CAUTION / CRITICAL: You *must* click "**Save**," or Word will discard your new Quick Parts!

AutoComplete

As mentioned throughout this section, the AutoComplete feature is a quick method of inserting a Quick Parts entry (or built-in entries such as the names of days and months) into your document. There are a couple of limitations. The feature works only if:

---

[4] The Building Blocks Organizer can be somewhat overwhelming. See the section entitled "Managing / Deleting Quick Parts Entries," starting on the next page, for tips about making the Organizer more user-friendly.

- the name for your Quick Parts entry is at least four characters long; and

- the entry is stored in a template *other than* the default Quick Words / Building Blocks template, BuildingBlocks.dotx.

If the Quick Parts entry satisfies those criteria, you'll see an AutoComplete prompt (sometimes referred to as a "tip") after you type the fourth character of the name / abbreviation. When the prompt appears, you can either press the Enter key to insert the Quick Parts entry into the document or keep typing (if the name / abbreviation you've assigned is a real word and you want to use the word, rather than the full Quick Parts entry, in this specific situation). Of course, you also have the option of expanding your Quick Parts entry by pressing the F3 key.

So, for example, let's say that I create an interrogatory heading – as described in the section about SEQ codes that starts on page 519 – and give it the name / abbreviation "ROGG." (Ordinarily, I'd call it "ROG," but the name has to be four characters long to trigger the AutoComplete prompt. Remember, too, that Quick Parts aren't case sensitive, so I could call the entry "rogg" or "Rogg" and it would work the same way.) When I set up the entry, I make sure to store it in the Normal.dotm template rather than in BuildingBlocks.dotx.

Now, when I type "ROGG" (or "rogg" or "Rogg," etcetera), I see an AutoComplete prompt, as follows:

ROGG (Press ENTER to Insert)

rogg

The prompt merely shows me the name of the entry, followed by the parenthetical instruction, "(Press ENTER to Insert)." If I press the Enter key, my Quick Part is inserted at the cursor position. (See the next screenshot.)

INTERROGATORY NO. 1:

Sometimes, the AutoComplete prompt shows what the entry will look like when expanded, as with a simple Quick Part I set up (using the abbreviation "janb") to insert my name:

Jan Berinstein (Press ENTER to Insert)

janb

If you type a date, or even a day of the week, you will probably see an AutoComplete prompt. For example, I typed "January" (without quotation marks, and when I pressed the Enter key, AutoComplete guessed what I was trying to type:

January 2, 2016 (Press ENTER to Insert)

January |

You get the idea.

381

Managing / Deleting Quick Parts Entries

When you click **Insert**, **Quick Parts**, then click **Building Block Organizer**, you will see that there are already numerous Quick Parts entries that come with the program. As previously mentioned, those items appear in various galleries scattered among the tabs, such as the Page Numbers gallery, the Headers gallery, the Footers gallery, the Table Styles gallery, and the Watermarks gallery. Within each gallery, Quick Parts are assigned to – and divided into – certain categories (Built-In, General, Simple, Plain Numbers, With Shapes, etc.). The categories are used mainly as a way of organizing the galleries.

By default, your new entries go in the Quick Parts gallery, but you can choose a different gallery if you like.

The Organizer can be somewhat overwhelming because of the sheer number of entries and also because of several limitations – e.g., the fact that you can't delete more than one entry at a time and the fact that you can't resize (widen) the Organizer. (You can widen the columns within the Organizer by dragging, however.)

To make things more manageable, you can sort the entries. Clicking the Gallery heading sorts the entries alphabetically by gallery name; clicking the Category heading sorts the entries alphabetically by category name; and clicking the Name heading sorts the entries alphabetically by name (abbreviation).

Consider using an underscore character as the first character when you name a new Quick Part, since items starting with an underscore will rise to the top – following the blank document templates and the simple text box template – when you sort by name. (If you do so, be sure to type the underscore character at the beginning of the abbreviation before pressing F3 to expand it into the full Quick Part. I've tested, and that works fine, but there are pros and cons.)

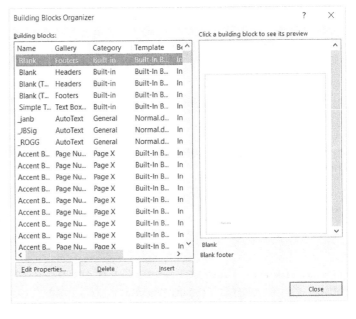

Of course, if you remember the abbreviations, you can insert Quick Parts entries simply by typing the abbreviation and pressing the F3 key.

Also, you can delete entries that you are unlikely to use. Doing so has the added benefit of making it easier to find your own entries in the list. Just go into the **Building Blocks Organizer**, click to select an entry, and click the "**Delete**" **button**. Word will prompt you to make sure you wish to delete the entry. If you're sure, click "**Yes**." Unfortunately, you can't select multiple entries; you have to select and delete one at a time.

Sharing Quick Parts

To share Quick Parts with other users, create a new blank template, preferably in a shared folder on a network drive. Then create Quick Parts from within that template, making sure the "Save in" field displays the name of the new template rather than the Building Blocks template or any other default. Continue creating your entries in and saving them to the new template.

Before distributing the template to others in the firm, delete any content (i.e., the "expanded" Quick Parts) and save the blank template. Even though you have deleted the content, the Quick Parts remain stored in the template.

When you give others access to the template, instruct them to *make a copy* and *store the copy in their custom Building Blocks folder*.

In Windows 7, 8, and 10, the path is:
C:\Users\<UserName>\AppData\Roaming\Microsoft\Document Building Blocks\1033\16.

Note that users might have to close and reopen Word before the entries will appear in the Building Blocks Organizer.

To share *existing* Quick Parts, create a new template and then edit the properties of the Quick Parts entries, one by one, to change the "Save in" location to the new template. (From the Building Blocks Organizer, click to select an entry, click the "**Edit Properties**" button, and when the "**Modify Building Block**" dialog opens, click the "**Save in**" drop-down and select the new template. If prompted to redefine the entry, click "**Yes**." Repeat those steps for each Quick Parts entry you wish to distribute to other users.)

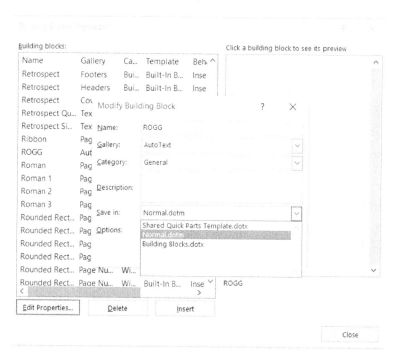

Click "Edit Properties...," Then click "Save in" and Choose the New Template

Note that when you edit the Quick Part properties you are ***moving***, ***not copying***, the entries to the new template, which means they might not be globally available to you (if you are working on a document created with a different template). However, you can make any template a "Global" template by saving it to the STARTUP folder on each user's computer. That folder is located here:

C:\Program Files (x86)\Microsoft Office\root\Office16\STARTUP

The AutoText Gallery

In Word 2016, there is an AutoText gallery that opens as a fly-out from the Quick Parts drop-down. You can insert AutoText entries into your document from the gallery, and you also have the option of saving selected text and/or graphics directly to the AutoText gallery (note the "**Save Selection to AutoText Gallery**" command at the bottom of the fly-out menu, labeled "General," shown at the left side of the screenshot below).

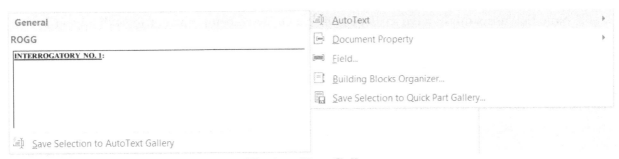

The AutoText Gallery

To move an entry manually to the AutoText gallery (or any other gallery), **select the entry** in the Organizer, then click the "**Edit Properties**" **button**. When the "**Modify Building Block**" **dialog** appears, simply click the "**Gallery**" **drop-down** and click "**AutoText**" (or any other gallery in the list).

Click "**OK**" to save your change. A prompt will appear, asking "Do you want to redefine the building block entry?" Unless you have changed your mind for some reason, click "**Yes**."

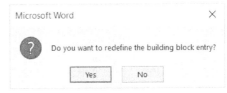

Finally, click "**Close**" to close the Building Blocks Organizer.

Working With Styles

What Are Styles?

A style is merely a "package" of formatting commands that you apply to text all at once, rather than applying one attribute at a time. For example, you could create a style called "Block Quote" that has a left indent of 1", a right indent of 1", and a first-line indent of .5", as well as line spacing of Exactly 12 points plus 12 points after. Then, you could apply the style either before or after typing the text of the quotation, rather than manually tweaking the indents and line spacing each time you want to insert a block quote.

Most styles are *paragraph styles*, which means they are applied to an entire paragraph (or selected paragraphs).[1] They typically affect formatting such as alignment (justification), indents, line spacing, before and after spacing, tabs, automatic numbering, and other attributes of paragraph formatting. Paragraph styles can incorporate font formatting, too (bold, underlining, all caps, etc.).

Word makes heavy use of styles (unlike WordPerfect). The program comes with numerous built-in styles, including interrelated nine heading styles (organized by hierarchic "levels," as in an outline). In fact, built-in styles are responsible for the appearance of various features of your documents, including footnotes and footers. You can use any of the existing styles as is, or you can modify them to suit your needs.

Styles are often contrasted with "direct formatting" (or "manual formatting") – indents, line spacing, and other formatting that is applied *directly* to text rather than using a style.

When you create a style, you can configure it so that it is always followed by another particular style. To use a common example, you can create heading styles and specify that each of those styles will be followed by a text style that uses a half-inch first-line indent. As a result, pressing the Enter key after you type a heading and apply a heading style "turns on" a text style, not another heading style – and places your cursor half an inch from the left margin, ready for input.

Advantages of Using Styles

One advantage of using styles is that they provide a certain uniformity of appearance throughout your documents. If you don't use styles, you might inadvertently use different indents or line spacing for outline-numbered paragraphs or block quotes; if you use styles, the indents and spacing will be the same every time.

---

[1] Actually, Word uses both *paragraph* styles and *character* styles, but paragraph styles are much more common. Generally speaking, character styles primarily involve font formatting attributes such as font face, font size, bolding, italics, small caps, etc., and are applied to small units of text.

Styles save time because they provide a way to apply multiple formatting codes all at once, rather than individually.

Also, styles make it easy to change the formatting of your text because ***modifying the style reformats every paragraph to which you have applied that style***. Perhaps you have set up a heading style with boldface type, but you decide to use underlining instead. When you modify the style, all of the paragraphs to which you have applied that style will update automatically to reflect the change. You don't need to go through the document and reformat individual paragraphs.[2] Very convenient!

And if you use Word's built-in heading or outline numbered styles (after modifying them to suit your needs), Word will pull your headings into a Table of Contents automatically – without your having to mark the headings for inclusion in the TOC.

Potential "Gotchas"

There are a few potential "gotchas" involved in using styles. For one thing, keep in mind that when you create a style, ordinarily the style will be available *only* in the document in which you create the style.[3] That's the default setting for new styles in both Word and WordPerfect. However, you can make the style more widely available by taking the additional step of checking the **"New documents based on this template" radio button** at the bottom of the **Create New Style From Formatting** dialog box before you close the dialog. (When you modify a style, you must check a similar button in the **Modify Styles** dialog in order to make the style available in new documents based on the underlying template.) See the discussions in the sections that follow about creating and modifying custom styles.

Styles can change unexpectedly. There are a few possible reasons why:

1. **"Automatically update"** is enabled, and you have **manually reformatted** a paragraph to which that style has been applied in a document you are working on;

2. You (or someone else) modified **an underlying style** that the style is based on;

3. You (or someone else) modified **the template** in which your style is stored.

4. You are working on a different computer, and there is a style in the Normal template (Normal.dotm) on that machine that has *the same name* as your style but *is formatted differently*. (A document you create from scratch will reflect the formatting of the style in the Normal.dotm of the machine you are working on.)

---

[2] That phenomenon is *not* the same as the "Automatically Update" option. Rather, "Automatically Update" actually *redefines a style* when you make *a manual formatting change* to any paragraph to which that style has been applied. As you might imagine, that can be highly problematic, so use the option sparingly, if at all. See the Sidebar on page 407.

[3] The exception to this rule is styles that you create within a *template*. Often, however, someone else in your organization creates the templates that your documents are based on.

The "Normal" Style

The "Normal" style is the ***default paragraph style*** – i.e., it applies the default paragraph and font settings specified in the template on which your document is based.[4] **CAUTION**: Applying the Normal style strips out any and all indentation, alignment, space before and after, etc. that you have applied manually via the Paragraph dialog.[5] (Many organizations use a custom body text style rather than Normal for plain text.)

Paragraph formatting and font formatting in recent versions of Word are determined partly by built-in "Style Sets" and "Themes" operating in the background. For more information, see the section about Style Sets and Themes starting on page 186.

Applying Styles

To apply a paragraph style,[6] click somewhere within the paragraph to which you want to apply the style (or select contiguous paragraphs), then use one of the following methods:

1. Navigate to the **Style Gallery** at the right side of the **Home tab**, locate the style you want (if it's in the gallery), and click the icon for that style. You might have to scroll row-by-row or open the gallery to see all of the styles therein. Note that when you hold the mouse over an icon, you'll see a live preview of the style in the document text.

   What you see in the Style Gallery depends on which styles are embedded in the document you're using, as well as which styles the template designer chose to display. The screenshot below shows the Style Gallery with a few custom styles in this book.

2. If you don't see the style you want to use, press **Ctrl Shift S** or click the "**More**" button – the arrow with a horizontal line above it – at the right side of the Style Gallery and, when the drop-down opens, click "**Apply Styles**." Click within the **Apply Styles** dialog box, type the name of the style (or choose it from the drop-down), and if Word doesn't automatically apply the style, either press **Enter** or click "**Apply**."

   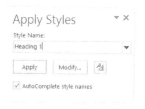

---

[4] **NOTE**: Different templates can have different Normal paragraph styles.

[5] That can be a good thing, if you are deliberately trying to clear manually applied formatting, but it can be problematic if you're not.

[6] To apply a font style, select the text to which you want to apply the style before proceeding.

3. Navigate to the **Styles group** on the **Home tab** and click the **dialog launcher** (or press **Ctrl Alt Shift S**). When the **Styles Pane** opens, locate the style you want to use and click to apply it.

NOTE: Which styles appear in the Styles Pane, and how they look, depends on settings configured in the pane's display options. To change those settings, click the **Options button** at the lower right-hand side of the Styles pane.

By default, the "**Select styles to show**" drop-down is set to "**Recommended**," which displays the built-in styles. If you prefer, choose one of the other options: **All Styles** (to see every built-in and custom style available to you), **In Use** (to see only those styles actually applied in the doc you are using), or **In Current Document** (to see the styles embedded in the current document, whether they have been applied or not).

By default, the "**Select how list is sorted**" drop-down also is set to "**Recommended**," which means that the styles display in an order determined by Microsoft. I typically choose "**Alphabetical**" because that is the sort order that makes the most sense to me (and makes it easiest to find the styles). The other options group the styles by **Font**, **Type**, or **Based On** style (the underlying style).

I typically do not check any of the boxes under "Select formatting to show as styles" because that can lead to a very cluttered Styles Pane (see page 397 for more details).

If you want these settings to apply to new documents based on the template underlying your current document, click the "New documents based on this template" radio button. Then click **OK** to save your changes and close the Style Pane Options dialog.

The appearance of the styles in the Styles Pane is also affected by the state of the "**Show Preview**" checkbox (whether it is or isn't checked). When the box is unchecked, you see the names of the styles in the same font and without formatting. When the box is checked, you see the names of the styles in the font they actually use and with formatting such as boldface, underlining, italics, and indents. (Note that this option does not provide a "live preview" – that is, you won't see a preview of any style in the document itself when you hover over that style in the Styles Pane.)

4. You can use a keyboard shortcut to apply a style. Microsoft has assigned the shortcuts Ctrl Alt 1, Ctrl Alt 2, and Ctrl Alt 3 to the Heading 1, Heading 2, and Heading 3 styles, respectively (for some reason, the company didn't assign shortcuts to any heading style after the third level). If you create your own styles, you can assign custom keyboard shortcuts to those styles.

You also have the option of applying a "**Style Set**" to your document as a whole (as opposed to applying styles paragraph by paragraph).[7] I don't recommend this option because it can produce unexpected, and undesirable results. For more about Style Sets, see the section starting on page 186.

Creating Custom Styles

There are two main ways to create a custom style:

By Example

1. You can create a style by placing your cursor within a paragraph that is formatted to your liking, then opening the **Styles Pane** – either by clicking the dialog launcher in the Styles group on the Home tab or by pressing **Ctrl Alt Shift S** – and clicking the "**New Style**" button at the bottom left side of the pane (enclosed in a border in the screenshot at right).

    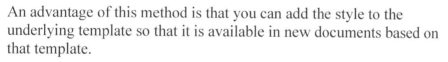

    An advantage of this method is that you can add the style to the underlying template so that it is available in new documents based on that template.

2. Alternatively, place your cursor within a paragraph that is formatted to your liking, press **Ctrl Shift S** to open the **Apply Styles dialog**, type a name in the **Style Name** box, then click "**New**." The "New" button is replaced by a button labeled "**Modify**." Click the "**Modify**" button to modify the style and/or save it to the underlying template so that it is available in new documents based on the template.

    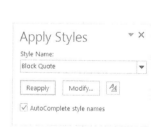

    When the **Modify Styles dialog** opens, be sure to check "**New documents based on this template**," then click "**OK**" to save your changes.

3. You can **right-click** within a paragraph and, when the **Mini Toolbar** appears, click to open the "**Styles**" **menu** and choose "**Create a Style**."

---

[7] The Style Sets include one that Microsoft has labeled "Word 2003." As mentioned on page 191, this label is somewhat misleading because when you apply the Word 2003 Style Set, you still get the Calibri font, which was not the default font in Word 2003.

When the **Create New Style from Formatting** dialog opens, type a **unique name** for the style. To add the new style to the underlying template, click the "**Modify**" **button**, click the "**New documents based on this template**" **radio button**, and **OK** out.

From Scratch:

1. On the **Home tab**, locate the **Styles group** and click the **dialog launcher**. When the Styles Pane opens, click the "**New Style**" button in the lower left-hand corner. That will open an expanded version of the **Create New Style from Formatting dialog box** (see the screenshot).

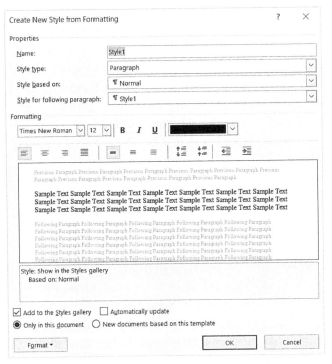

Create New Style From Formatting Dialog

2. When the dialog appears, **type a name** for the style (it must be unique, and it should describe what the style does). Ignore the style type; Word assumes that you're creating a paragraph style, which you are. Therefore, you don't need to change the style type.

3. You can base the style on an existing style. If you wish to do so, type the name of the base style in the "**Style based on**" field or choose the style from the drop-down. **CAUTION**: When you use this option, it's important to remember that ***any modification to the base style will affect your new style as well***. (As mentioned on page 386, a style can change unexpectedly if someone changes the formatting of the underlying style.) In general, it's a good idea not to base the style on another style – and definitely ***do not*** base any of your heading styles on another heading style because any change to the "based on" heading style also changes the other style(s).

390

4. Also, you can specify a style for the following paragraph by typing a style name in the **"Style for Following Paragraph"** field (or choosing the style from the drop-down). Choosing a style for the following paragraph is a good option for heading styles and block quotes, which ordinarily are followed by regular body text.

   If you don't specify a style, the following paragraph will be formatted with the same style, which is a good choice for body text styles, including paragraphs with automatic numbering, such as those in a Complaint or an Answer.

5. To specify formatting details, such as font, tabs, numbering, and so forth, click the **"Format" button** at the lower left side of the dialog and choose the appropriate options.

6. When you have finished, click the **"New documents based on this template"** radio button, then **OK** out of the dialog. (If you don't click the "New documents based on this template" radio button, the style will be available *only in the current document*.)

7. **CAUTION**: *Do not* check "**Automatically update**." If you do, any *direct / manual formatting changes* you make to one paragraph to which that style has been applied actually will redefine the style. As a result, those formatting changes will be reflected in *all* paragraphs to which that style has been applied. For a longer discussion of this issue, see the section starting on page 407.

<u>Modifying Styles</u>

There are a few ways to modify a style, including the following two methods:

1. You can modify a style "on the fly." First, click within a paragraph to which that style has been applied and make any formatting changes you like. Next, locate the icon for the style in the **Style Gallery** at the right side of the Home tab (assuming the style has been added to the Style Gallery), **right-click** it, and choose **Update <style name> to match selection**.

The modifications will be incorporated into the style. Note, however, that this method ***does not add your modifications to the underlying template*** (i.e., it modifies the style only in the current document).

2. Alternatively, from the **Home tab**, click the **Styles dialog launcher**. When the Styles Pane appears, **right-click** the style name, then click "**Modify….**" When the **Modify Style** dialog appears, make any changes you like (by clicking the icons, choosing commands from the drop-downs, and/or clicking the "Format" button at the bottom left side of the dialog, then choosing other options.)

To ensure that your changes take effect in all new documents based on the underlying template, be sure to click the "**New documents based on this template**" radio button before clicking "**OK**" to save your changes and close the dialog.

Copying a Style Between Documents or Templates

It's easy to copy a style between documents and/or templates. Perhaps the easiest method is to use the Format Painter or to use keyboard shortcuts to copy and paste formatting (**Ctrl Shift C** and **Ctrl Shift V**, respectively). Just make sure you start by positioning your cursor within a paragraph to which the style you want to copy has been applied.

Another method is to copy the paragraph mark at the end of a "styled" paragraph within your "source" document or template and paste it into your "destination" document or template. You can copy some text, too, if you like, but *the key is to copy the paragraph mark* because – as you know by now – it contains the formatting codes for that paragraph, *including the style*.

In order to see the paragraph mark so that you can select and copy it, be sure to turn on **Show / Hide** (press **Ctrl Shift ***, or click the **paragraph icon** (¶) in the **Paragraph group** on the **Home tab**).

Copying Styles With the Organizer

In addition to the method described above, you can copy styles between documents and/or templates by using the **Organizer**. To open the Organizer, do one of the following:

1. If you have displayed the **Developer tab**, click the **Document Template icon** in the **Templates group** (at the right side of the tab), and when the **Templates and Add-Ins dialog** opens, click the "**Organizer**" **button** at the bottom left side; *or*

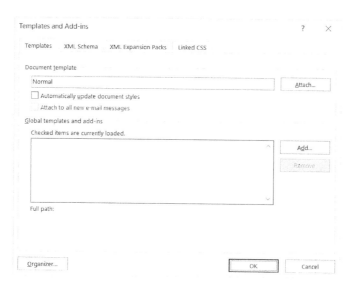

2. Launch the **Styles Pane**, then click the **Manage Styles button** (the right-most button) at the bottom of the pane, and click the "**Import/Export**" **button** at the bottom left side of the **Manage Styles dialog**.

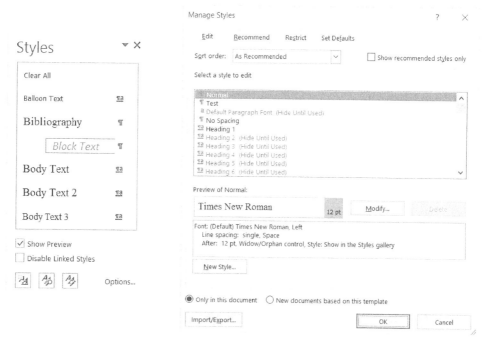

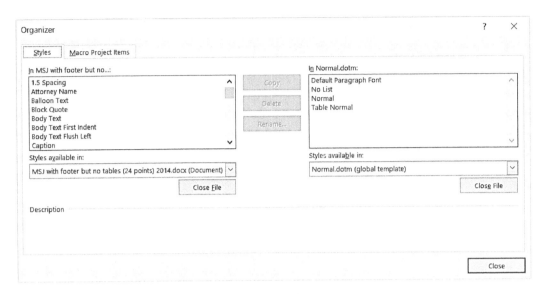

The Organizer

When the Organizer opens, you'll see a box on the left and a box on the right. The left-hand box typically shows the styles available in the document on your screen; the right-hand box typically shows the styles available in your Normal template (Normal.dotm).

To copy a style from one to the other, click the style in the "**source**" document (the one you want to copy *from*). The "**Copy**" **button** will become active, and will display an arrow pointing left or right, depending on which box you're copying into (the arrow points to the "**destination**" document or template—the one you're copying *to*). Click the button to copy a style from one document or template to the other. Note that you can select and copy multiple styles all at once (by pressing the **Ctrl key** before clicking the styles you wish to copy).

CAUTION: If a style in the source document or template has the same name as a style in the destination document or template, Word will warn you and ask if you want to overwrite the style in the destination document. Pay attention to this warning; it is designed to prevent you from accidentally overwriting *a custom style* that might have the same name as a style that actually is formatted differently. Styles with the same name *are not necessarily the same style*!

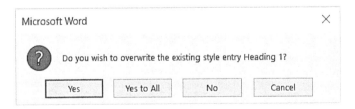

You can delete or rename styles in documents and templates via the Organizer, as well. Again, use caution before deleting or renaming a style, especially from within a template. (On the other hand, people sometimes clutter their documents and templates with lots of styles they never use; if you're sure you don't need particular styles, it's not a bad idea to delete them, since a profusion of styles can lead to document corruption.)

Although the Organizer opens with items in the current document displayed on the left and items in the Normal template displayed on the right, you can display a different document or template on either side simply by clicking the "**Close File**" button underneath one of the boxes, which then becomes an "**Open File**" button. Click the "Open File" button and navigate to the document or template you wish to use instead, then click the "**Open**" button. (If you like, you can repeat the process for the other document or template.)

When you have finished copying, renaming, and/or deleting styles, just click "**Close**" to close the Organizer. (At that point, Word might prompt you to save any changes you've made.) If you're through with the Styles Pane, click the **X** at the upper right-hand side of the Styles Pane to close it.

Assigning a Keyboard Shortcut to a Style

As you can see from the screenshot on page 390, the **Create New Style from Formatting** dialog box has a "**Format**" **button** at the bottom left. Clicking the button opens a menu that has a "**Shortcut key**" command . If you click the Shortcut key command, the "Customize Keyboard" dialog appears.

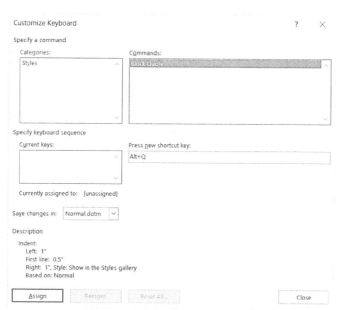

Customize Keyboard Dialog

To assign a keyboard shortcut, type the shortcut you wish to use in the "**Press new shortcut key**" box. (For keyboard combinations that use function keys or the Alt key, the Ctrl key, and/or the Shift key, simply press the keys in the sequence you desire.) If that shortcut already has been assigned to another function, you'll see the words "**Currently assigned to**," followed by the function. If you wish to use the keyboard shortcut (even if it is currently assigned to another function), just click the "**Assign**" button (it is grayed out until you insert a key combination in the "Press new shortcut key" box). Otherwise, choose a different key combination. When you have finished, click the **Close** button.

As also mentioned in the section on keyboard shortcuts, there are a few predefined keystrokes in Word that will apply (or remove) styles. These shortcuts include the following:

- Ctrl Q – removes direct paragraph formatting (*not* applied via a style)
- Ctrl Shift N – applies the Normal paragraph style (strips out paragraph formatting applied manually or via a style)
- Ctrl Shift L – applies the bulleted list style
- Ctrl Alt 1 – applies the Heading 1 style
- Ctrl Alt 2 – applies the Heading 2 style
- Ctrl Alt 3 – applies the Heading 3 style

Viewing the Styles in a Document

There are a few different ways to see which style is in effect at the cursor position. For one, if the style has been added to the Style Gallery, the icon for that style will display there with a prominent border (colored blue, light gray, or dark gray depending on which Office Theme you have applied).

Also, if you have added a Style icon to your Quick Access Toolbar, it will show the style that has been applied to the paragraph your cursor is in.

My QAT (Truncated View) with a Style Icon at Right

A third method involves changing a setting in the Word Options so that when you choose Draft View, all of the styles in your document – except for those within columnar tables – display at the left side of your screen.

To do so, click the **File tab**, **Options**, choose the **Advanced** category, and then scroll down to **Display**. In the box labeled **Style area pane width in Draft and Outline views**, set a width larger than 0" (1" to 2" is usually sufficient), and click "**OK**" to save your changes and close the Word Options.

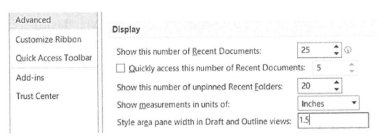

396

Then switch to **Draft view** (by clicking the **View tab**, **Draft** or pressing **Ctrl Alt N**). You should see a **Style Area** at the left-hand side of your document that shows the names of the styles that have been applied to the various paragraphs in the document.

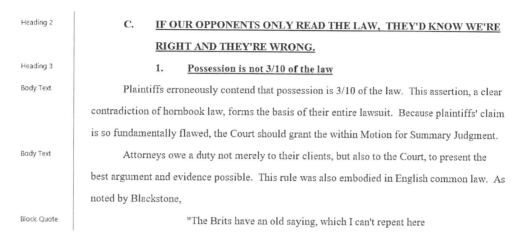

The styles will appear in the left margin whenever you apply Draft View in a document until / unless you change the setting in the Word Options.

What Are Those Weird-Looking Styles in the Style Pane?

Every now and then, you might notice that the Style Pane displays the name of a style in use in the document *plus* any formatting you've applied directly, such as bold, underlining, a first-line indent, or a custom font size. This phenomenon can be both confusing and distracting.

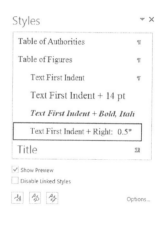

To restrict the display to true styles (rather than both styles and styles-plus-direct-formatting), click the **Options...** link at the bottom right side of the Styles Pane to open the **Style Pane Options dialog**.

When any of the options under "**Select formatting to show as styles**" are checked, the Style Pane displays the name of the original style and also lists "variations" of the style – that is, instances of the style to which direct (manual) paragraph formatting, font formatting, or list formatting has been applied. To remove those bogus styles from the Styles Pane, uncheck the boxes and click "**OK**." (Be sure to click the "**New documents based on this template**" radio button at the bottom right side if you want to turn off this setting for future documents based on the underlying template.)

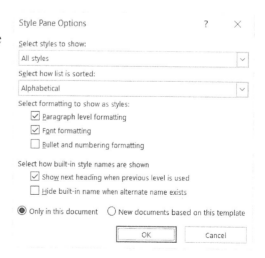

397

The Style Gallery

The **Style Gallery**, a prominent part of the **Home tab** (at the right side, in the **Styles group**), made its debut in Word 2007.[1] Although there are other ways of finding and applying styles (as discussed in the section starting on page 387), the Style Gallery is particularly convenient because it provides easy access to – and a visual representation of – many of the available styles.

The screenshots below show the default Style Gallery in Word 2016. Microsoft provided a number of built-in styles and chose to display them in a particular order, but you can remove any styles that you don't use and add your own custom styles instead. Also, you can customize the built-in styles – such as the heading styles – to suit your needs (and you can display as many levels of headings as you want).

Which styles appear in the gallery, and the order in which they appear, will vary from document to document. If you use custom templates, whoever designed the templates might have chosen to add certain styles to the gallery and to arrange them in a specific order (although sometimes Word assigns the order of the styles and the template designer doesn't make any changes).

**The Style Gallery – Collapsed / Closed
(Default Settings – No Customizations)**

**The Style Gallery – Expanded / Opened
(Default Settings – No Customizations)**

---

[1] Microsoft now calls this feature the "Style Gallery," although I occasionally slip and call it by its previous name, the "QuickStyle Gallery."

The Style Gallery – Expanded / Opened
(Showing Mostly Custom Styles)

Applying a Style

To apply one of the styles in the gallery, simply click the icon for that style.[2] In order to see all the available styles, you might have to scroll up or down or open the entire gallery. Click the up or down arrow to scroll one row at a time (one arrow might be grayed out, depending on which row is active); the bottom arrow (labeled "More" when you hold the mouse pointer over it) expands the gallery so that you can see all of the styles therein.

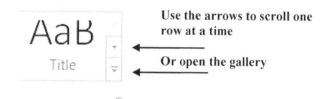

Live Preview

The Style Gallery makes use of another feature introduced in Word 2007, **Live Preview**. Live Preview means that when you position the mouse pointer over a paragraph style in the gallery (either deliberately or accidentally), Word *changes the appearance of the text* at the cursor position in your document, showing what it would look like with that style applied.

The Styles Gallery makes use of another feature introduced in Word 2007, Live Preview. Live Preview means that when you position the mouse pointer over a style in the gallery (either deliberately or accidentally), Word changes the appearance of the text at the cursor position in your document, showing what it would look like with that style applied.

A Preview of the "Intense Quote" Style Applied to the Previous Paragraph

---

[2] Remember that you don't have to select the paragraph to apply a style (or other paragraph formatting) to a single paragraph. You *do* have to select the paragraphs to apply a style to multiple paragraphs. You also have to select text before applying a *character (font)* style.

(The screenshot immediately above shows what happened when I moved my mouse pointer over the "Intense Quote" style in the gallery while my cursor was inserted in the previous paragraph.)

The sudden change can be disconcerting if you don't realize what's going on. Don't panic! It's just a preview, and it's temporary. If you don't click the icon representing that style, the style will *not* be applied to the text. As soon as you move your mouse, the appearance of the text will return to normal.

The Display of Styles in the Gallery

Which styles are displayed in the gallery? And what determines the order in which they're shown?

As mentioned at the beginning of this section, when you first start using Word, the gallery is already populated with certain styles, including heading styles, the Normal style, and a few other paragraph and character styles chosen by Microsoft.[3] However, the display typically varies from document to document. If the current document contains customized heading styles, the Style Gallery likely will show those heading styles in lieu of Microsoft's defaults, and you might see other custom styles, as well.

To some extent, you can control which styles appear in the gallery when you have a particular document on your screen, although you might not be able to change those settings for the template that your document is based on. The next sections explain how to add and remove styles from the gallery and how to change the order in which they appear.

Adding and Removing Styles

It is very easy to add styles to, and remove styles from, the gallery. To remove a style, simply **right-click** it and, when the context-sensitive menu opens, click "**Remove from Style Gallery**."

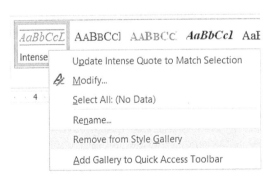

Right-Click a Style to Remove It From the Gallery

---

[3] Presumably Microsoft has chosen those styles based on user feedback, although the default formatting of the styles isn't suitable for most legal documents.

To add an existing style to the gallery, open the **Styles Pane** by either (1) clicking the **dialog launcher** at the bottom right side of the **Styles group** in the **Home tab** or (2) pressing the key combination **Alt Ctrl Shift S**. If necessary, click the "**Options…**" link at the bottom right side of the pane and change the display options so that you can see all available styles. Locate the style you want to add to the gallery, **right-click** it, and choose "**Add to Style Gallery**."

There are a couple of other ways that you can add styles to the gallery. For one thing, when you create a new (custom) style, you can click the checkbox at the bottom of the "**Create New Style from Formatting**" dialog that is labeled "**Add to the Styles gallery**."

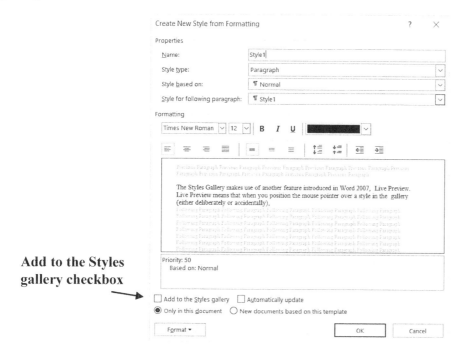

Add to the Styles gallery checkbox

For another thing, any style you create a style "on the fly" from formatted text will be added automatically to the Style Gallery. As outlined in the section starting on page 389, place your cursor within a paragraph that is formatted to your liking, right-click, and when the **Mini Toolbar** appears, click the **Styles menu**, then click "**Create a Style**."

When the condensed version of the "**Create New Style from Formatting**" dialog appears and you click the "**Modify**" **button** (see the screenshot on the next page), the expanded "**Create New Style from Formatting**" **dialog** opens so that you can tweak the style.

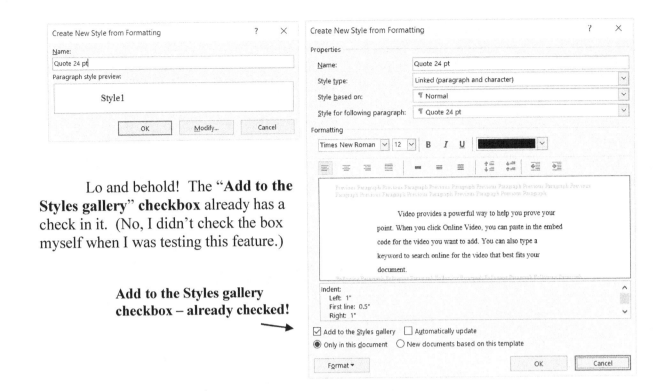

Lo and behold! The "**Add to the Styles gallery**" **checkbox** already has a check in it. (No, I didn't check the box myself when I was testing this feature.)

Add to the Styles gallery checkbox – already checked!

CAUTION: Remember that your new style will be available *only in the current document* unless you take steps to add it to the underlying template. To do so, click the "**New documents based on this template**" radio button at the bottom of the dialog box before clicking "**OK**" to save your changes and close the dialog. If you forget this step when you first set up the style, you can right-click the style in either the Style Gallery or the Styles Pane and click "**Modify**" to open the **Create New Style from Formatting** dialog.

Changing the Order of Styles in the Gallery

The order of the styles in the Style Gallery is based on each style's "value" setting (priority), which in turn is set by Microsoft. You can find, and change, a style's value by opening the Styles Pane and then clicking the right-most button at the bottom of the pane to open the **Manage Styles dialog**.

**The Right-Most Button at the Bottom of the Styles Pane
Opens the Manage Styles Dialog**

When the Manage Styles dialog appears, click the "**Recommend**" tab. (Screenshot on next page.) In that tab, styles appear with their pre-assigned value displayed at left. The values range from 1 to 100; the smaller the number (1), the higher and farther to the left the style will appear in the Style Gallery. If multiple styles have the same value – say, three styles are assigned the value 1 – those styles will appear next to each other in the gallery, in alphabetical order by style name (styles with names that start with the letter "A" will appear to the left of styles with names that start with the letter "B," and so forth).

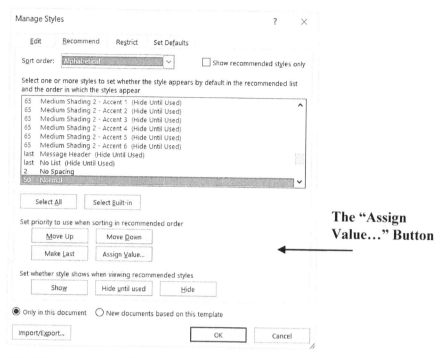

The Manage Styles Dialog – "Recommended" Tab

To change a style's value, locate the style (you might find it helpful to change the **"Sort order"** from "Recommended" – the default – to **"Alphabetical"**) and click to select it, then click the **"Assign Value" button**. Choose a number between 1 and 100, then click **"OK"** and click **"OK"** a second time to close the **"Manage Styles"** dialog box and save your changes.

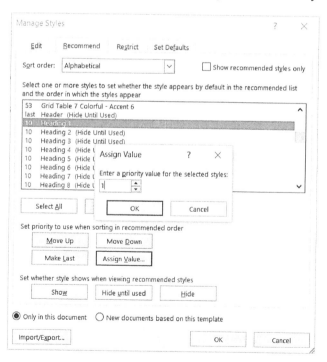

The style should appear in a different position in the Style Gallery, based on the value that you assigned.

403

Other Options

When you right-click a style in the gallery, you'll see a pop-up menu like the one in the screenshot at right. The menu offers several options, including:

- **"Update [Style Name] to Match Selection."**

This option provides an easy way to modify a style on the fly so that the style will match the formatting of selected text.

- **"Modify…"**

This option opens the "Modify Style" dialog so that you can tweak the style.

- **"Select All"**

You can use this option to select all instances of the style (and/or see how many instances there are) in the current document.

- **"Rename…"**

An easy way to rename the style without opening the Modify Style dialog – but this method renames the style only in the current document.

- **"Remove from Style Gallery"**

This option removes the style from the gallery, but again, only in the current document.

- **"Add Gallery to Quick Access Toolbar"**

This command puts an icon for the entire Style Gallery on the QAT so that it is readily available even if the Home tab isn't at the forefront.

Also note that the expanded Style Gallery gives you easy access to three commands (discussed throughout the book) that come in handy when you are working with styles. And the three dots in the lower right-hand corner of the drop-down lets you widen, lengthen, or shorten the expanded gallery so that you can view more or fewer styles (when the gallery is open), as you prefer.

SIDEBAR: The Style Inspector

The Style Inspector

The "**Style Inspector**," first introduced in Word 2007, makes it easy to view – and remove – paragraph and/or character formatting (also referred to as Text-level formatting) within a specific paragraph.

For the example shown below, I typed a few paragraphs and applied the built-in Body Text style, which uses single spacing plus 6 points after. For one of the paragraphs, I applied direct paragraph and font formatting. In particular, I changed the left and right indents to one inch and applied italics to the entire paragraph. Then I applied strikethrough to a portion of the text in that paragraph.

I clicked in the portion of the text with both font changes, then launched the **Style Pane** and clicked the **Style Inspector button** at the bottom of the pane (the one in the middle). The result is shown at right.

The top portion of the Style Inspector Pane shows the paragraph formatting and the bottom portion shows the character (Text-level) formatting. The top box in the section labeled **Paragraph formatting** displays the *style* that has been applied to the paragraph, and the bottom box in that section shows any *direct formatting* (formatting that you've applied manually, usually from the Paragraph dialog). In this case, it displays the 1" left and right indents that I applied.

In the section labeled **Text level formatting**, the top box shows the *font face* that is in use in the paragraph, while the bottom box shows any *character or font attributes* you've applied to the text. In this case, it displays the italics and strikethrough that I added.

To clear paragraph or character formatting, click one or more of the "clear" buttons (the ones with erasers) at the right side of the dialog.[1] The top "clear" button, which shows the label "**Reset to Normal Paragraph Style**" when you hold the mouse over it, resets the paragraph style to the Normal paragraph style for the template on which the document is based. The second "clear" button, labeled "**Clear Paragraph Formatting**," knocks out the direct paragraph formatting, such as the left and right indents that I added. The third "clear" button, labeled "**Clear Character Style**," removes any actual character style that you might have applied (not common with legal document formatting). The fourth "clear" button, labeled "**Clear Character Formatting**," strips any direct character formatting, such as the italics and strikeout that I added.

---

[1] For more about clearing formatting, see the sidebar starting on page 145.

Note that if you wish to clear either type of paragraph formatting, it doesn't matter where your cursor is as long as it's somewhere within the affected paragraph. However, if you wish to clear Text-level formatting, you need to select the text before stripping the formatting, in which case all character formatting will be removed. If you don't select the text, the "Clear Character Formatting" button removes the character formatting of the word that your cursor is in.

The "**Clear All**" button at the bottom right side of the Style Inspector Pane removes both paragraph and font formatting from the entire paragraph – even if you don't select any text first.[2]

Incidentally, just a quick reminder that there is a "Clear All Formatting" icon in the Font group on the Home tab. (As discussed in the section starting on page 145, even though the icon is in the Font group, the button actually clears both font and paragraph formatting.)

Finally, note the other two buttons at the bottom of the Style Inspector Pane. One opens the **Reveal Formatting Pane** (discussed on page 139), and the other, "**New Style**," opens the "Create New Style from Formatting" dialog. (As an aside, if you create a style using the "New Style" button in the Style Inspector Pane, "Add to Style gallery" is checked – enabled – by default.)

---

[2] Interestingly, it doesn't clear highlighting. To remove highlighting, select the highlighted text and click the "Text Highlight Color" icon in the Font group on the Home tab (or press the key combination Ctrl Alt H). If that doesn't work, click the drop-down at the right side of the Highlight icon and choose "No Color."

SIDEBAR: Why the "Automatically Update" Option Is a Bad Idea

If you enable the "Automatically Update" option when you create or modify a style, any direct (manual) formatting changes you make in a single paragraph to which the style has been applied *will redefine the style itself*.[1]

For example, let's say you create a style for indented quotes. You use Exactly 12 point line spacing, a left indent of 1" and a right indent of 1", no "Special" formatting for the first line of a paragraph, and no spacing before or after. You check the "Automatically update" option, as well as the "New documents based on this template" option, before saving the style. Afterwards, you apply the style to several paragraphs in your document. Everything works fine, but then you decide to apply a First-line indent to one of the paragraphs. You click in that paragraph, open the Paragraph dialog, change the "Special" drop-down to "First line" and accept the default of .5", then click "OK."

As you scroll through your document, you notice that the first line of *every paragraph* to which you applied the indented quotes style has been indented half an inch. You remove the indent on one of the paragraphs that you didn't intend to indent, and all of the other paragraphs to which the style has been applied also change. The same type of thing happens if you apply italics or boldface to one paragraph within a lengthy indented quote. Every other paragraph in the indented quote also becomes italicized or bold. Argh!

Without realizing how this innocuous-sounding feature would work, you accidentally modified the style itself. You can see why the "Automatically update" option is a bad idea.

What's confusing is that "automatically update" sounds like something you would want to do. The thing to keep in mind is that when you modify a style, those modifications *are* reflected automatically in every paragraph to which you have applied the style. You don't have to do anything special in order for that to happen.

But what if you truly do want to modify a style "on the fly" to match formatting changes you have made manually in a paragraph to which the style has been applied?

Not to worry. As you know by now, there are other ways of updating a style to match selected text. You can (1) right-click the icon for the style in the Style Gallery, then click "Update [Style Name] to Match Selection"; or (2) right-click the style name in the Styles Pane, then click "Update [Style Name] to Match Selection." (Remember that both of these options will modify the style only in the current document.)

And you always have the option of modifying the style via the "Modify Styles" dialog – available by right-clicking the style name in the Style Gallery or the Styles Pane.

---

[1] For other ways to modify a style, see the section starting on page 391.

SIDEBAR: Creating a Style (and Keyboard Shortcut) for Indented Quotes

If you don't have a pleading template that includes a style for an indented (block) quote, you can set one up yourself.

1. Type some dummy text, then right-click within the text and choose "**Paragraph**."

2. When the Paragraph dialog opens, set both the **Left indent** and the **Right indent** to 1". Leave the **Special** box set to "**(none)**" or, if you prefer, select "**First line**" and either leave the indent set at .5" (the default setting) or choose a different figure. Change the line spacing, too, if necessary, and then click "**OK**."

3. Open the **Styles Pane** by clicking the dialog launcher in the **Styles group** on the **Home tab** *or* by pressing the key combination **Ctrl Alt Shift S**.

4. Click the "**New Style**" button at the bottom left side of the Styles Pane.

5. When the **Create New Style from Formatting** dialog box appears, type a name for your new style (e.g., Indented Quote or Block Quote).

6. In the box labeled **Style for following paragraph**, click the drop-down menu and scroll to "Normal" or "Body Text" or some other text style. (**NOTE**: If you set a different style for the following paragraph, Word "turns on" that style when you press the Enter key after you finish typing your quote so that you can resume typing regular text.)

7. If you forgot to change the line spacing when you set the left and right indents, click the **Format** button at the bottom of the **Create New Style...** dialog box, then click **Paragraph** and change the settings to suit your preferences.

8. To set up a keyboard shortcut for your new style, click the **Format** button again, then click "**Shortcut key**."

9. When the **Customize Keyboard dialog** opens, your cursor will already be positioned in the **Press new shortcut key** box. Press the key combination you wish to assign to your style. If that key combo has been assigned to another feature, Word displays a message to that effect. If not, click the "**Assign**" **button**, and then click **Close**.

10. **IMPORTANT**: Before clicking "**OK**," be sure to click the **New documents based on this template** radio button at the bottom of the dialog box. Otherwise, the style will be available *only in the document in which you have created the style*.

11. Finally, click "**OK**" to save your new style and close the dialog box.

12. To use the style, just press the key combination you assigned and start typing (or start typing, then press the keys).

Creating Your Own Templates

Templates are forms on which various types of documents are based.[1] Common examples include letterhead, a fax cover sheet, a proof of service, a contract, a trust estate document, or a generic pleading that consists mainly of a caption, a footer, and a signature block (with placeholders in lieu of specific information). Many organizations provide several different pleading templates for their employees – e.g., pleadings for state courts and for federal courts, pleadings for motions or complaints, and pleadings for discovery.

The formatting contained in a particular template, along with any boilerplate text, customized styles, Quick Parts, graphics, and the like, is available in documents based on that template.

It's fairly easy to create a template. In this tutorial, I will provide the basic steps for creating and saving simple templates and using documents based thereon.

Creating a Template From an Existing Document

You can create a template from scratch – starting with a blank document and then adding any text, field codes, graphics, and/or formatting you want – or you can turn an existing document into a template. To turn an existing document into a template, locate the document and, in order to avoid overwriting it, open it as a copy. (Just click to select the document, then instead of clicking the "Open" button in the Open dialog, click the arrow at the right side of the button and, when the menu appears, click either "**Open as Copy**" or "**Open Read-Only**." The two commands work more or less the same way.)

When the copy of the file opens, delete any specific information that you don't want to appear in new documents based on the template.[2]

Make any changes you desire. Note that you can add boilerplate text; insert (generic) signature blocks; set up styles for headings, body text, indented quotes, numbered paragraphs, etc.; create and save Quick Parts within the template; and so on.

---

[1] All documents, including blank ones, are based on a template. Under most circumstances, the Normal template (Normal.dotm) – each user has one – is the basis for new documents.

[2] For obvious reasons, templates need to be as generic as possible, although the specific situation will determine which information remains in the template. (As an example, some years ago, a client asked me to help set up a letterhead template that any member of the firm could use, plus individual templates for all of the attorneys. The communal letterhead template used a generic signature block; the other templates contained contact information and signature blocks for the individual lawyers.)

Saving a Template

When you have finished, **press F12** or click the "**Save As**" **icon** on the Quick Access Toolbar (QAT). (Remember that clicking the File tab, Save As takes you to the Backstage view.)

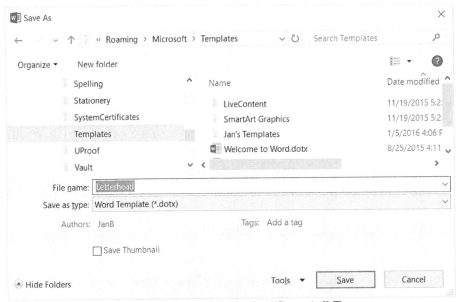

**Save As Dialog – Change the "Save As" Type
to Word Template (*.dotx) or Word Macro-Enabled Template (*.dotm)**

When the "**Save As**" **dialog** opens, give the template a **descriptive name**. For example, you could choose a name such as Letterhead, Inter Vivos Trust, Special Interrogatories, or even simply Pleading. (Do not type the file extension.)

Under "**Save as type**," choose one of Word's template formats: Word Template (*.dotx) or Word Macro-Enabled Template (*.dotm).

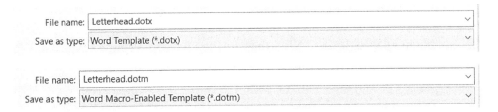

NOTE: As soon as you choose a template file format, *Word automatically changes the "Save As" location* to the default location for saving personal (user) templates – i.e., whatever is set in the **Word Options** under **Save**, "**Save documents**," "**Default personal templates location**."

This behavior – automatically changing the "Save As" location to the default personal templates location when users choose one of the template file formats – is relatively new (it was first introduced with Word 2013). In fact, the ability to set a default personal templates location in the "Save" category of the Word Options is relatively new, and it has important implications, which I will discuss momentarily.

In any case, the fact that Word chooses the "Save As" location means that you don't need to set the location yourself.

Word Template File Formats

As mentioned in the section about file formats starting on page 60, there are two types of Word templates: **.dotx files** and **.dotm files**. The difference is that .dotx files can't contain macros created in Visual Basic for Applications (VBA). By contrast, .dotm files can contain VBA macros. If you are a macro whiz and you want to incorporate VBA macros in your templates, be sure to save them as .dotm files rather than .dotx. Otherwise, you can save your templates in the more common .dotx file format.[3]

Where Personal (Custom) Templates Are Stored

By default, Word 2016 stores each individual's personal (custom) templates in the following location:

C:\Users\<User Name>\Documents\Custom Office Templates

You can change that location if you like. However, be aware that there are *two separate places in the Word Options where this setting is stored*. If you change the default personal templates location in one place in the Word Options, be sure to change it in the other place (the settings in the two places should match).

The reason is that if you inadvertently change the default personal templates location in one place and not the other, *you won't see your personal templates in the Backstage view* when you click **File, New, Custom**. (You still have access to those templates, but only if you add a "New Documents or Templates" icon to your Quick Access Toolbar. For instructions, and more information, see page 414.)

As mentioned on the previous page, the primary place in the Word Options (**File tab, Word Options**) where the default personal templates location is stored is in the **Save** category, under "**Save documents**," "**Default personal templates location**."[4] (See the next screenshot.)

---

[3] Although .dotx templates are not macro-enabled, you can create documents based on those templates that *are* macro-enabled. To do so, you must save those documents in the .docm format (or the old .doc format) rather than the standard .docx format. None of the Open Office XML file formats that end with "x" can store macros. (Think of the "x" as meaning "no.")

[4] This is where Word looks for "Custom" templates to display on the "**New**" screen of the **Backstage view** (i.e., **File, New**). If that box is *empty*, no "**Custom**" heading at all appears on the New screen. (You might see a "**Shared**" heading with access to Workgroup templates.) If the "**Default personal templates location**" in the "**Save**" category of the Word Options doesn't match the "**User templates**" location in the "**Advanced**" category of the Word options, the "Custom" heading appears, along with links to personal templates stored in the "Default personal templates" location, but any personal templates stored in the "User templates" location *do not*.

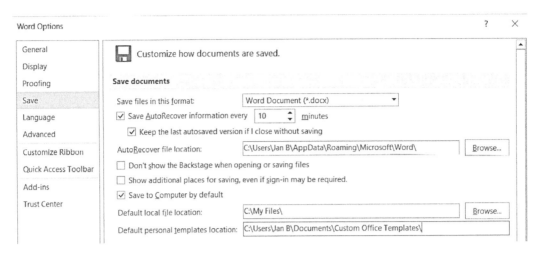

Word Options –Default Personal Templates Location

The other place in the Word Options where the default personal templates location setting is stored, as in previous versions of Word, is in the "**Advanced**" category under "**File Locations.**" (In this location, the templates are referred to as the "User templates.") However, any templates stored in the location set in this part of the Word Options *do not appear* on the "New" screen in the Backstage view (under the "Custom" heading) unless the location matches the Default personal templates location set in the Save category of the Word Options.

To view or change this setting, click the **File tab**, **Options**, and when the Word Options dialog opens, click the "**Advanced**" category at left, then scroll almost all the way down to "**File Locations**" and click the "**File Locations**" **button**. See the screenshot below.

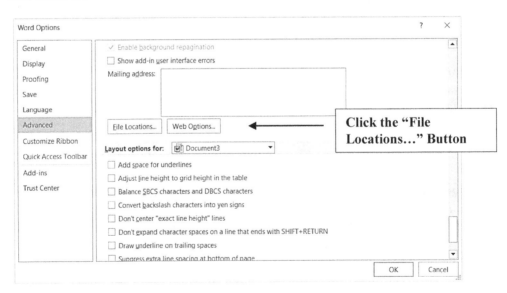

The Word Options – Advanced

A **File Locations dialog** will open, showing the default locations for the various file types, including documents, user (personal) templates, workgroup (shared) templates, and more.

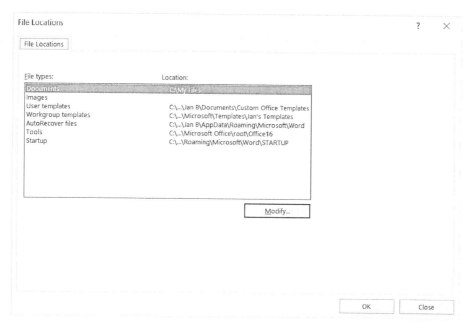

File Locations Dialog

To change the location of the personal templates to match the setting in the "Save" category of the Word Options, click "**User templates**" in the File types list, then click the "**Modify**" button. When the "**Modify Location**" dialog opens, browse to the folder where you want to save your personal templates, then click "**OK**." Click the "**Close**" button at the bottom right side of the File Locations dialog, and finally click "**OK**" at the bottom right side of the Word Options dialog to save your settings.

Where Shared Templates Are Stored

Word stores shared templates in a so-called "**Workgroup templates**" folder, usually on a network drive. If you are creating a template that will be used by other members of your organization, make sure (1) that you save it in the location where other shared templates normally are stored (if you don't know where that is, check with your office administrator and/or your IT department); and (2) that each person's computer points to that location.

To set up individual workstations so that they point to the correct template folders, click the **File tab**, **Options**, and click the "**Advanced**" category. Then scroll almost all the way to the bottom and click the "**File Locations**" **button** to open the **File Locations dialog**.

The screenshot above shows the location for the Workgroup templates. If the Workgroup templates location on your computer is blank, it hasn't been set up yet. If you or someone at your organization adds a Workgroup templates location, that folder will appear on the "New" screen in the Backstage view (File, New) under "Custom" and/or "Shared."

Note that I added a Workgroup templates location – different from my User templates location. As a result, folders for both my shared templates and my personal templates appear on the "New" screen on my computer.

To tell Word where to look for Workgroup templates, **click** "**Workgroup templates**," then click the "**Modify…**" **button**. **Browse** to the folder where your organization stores its shared templates, then click **OK**." Click "**Close**," then click "**OK**" to save your settings.

Creating a Document Based on Your Custom Template

In older versions of Word, creating a new document based on a template was fairly straightforward. You could use either of two methods, both of which opened a "New" dialog box with access to your personal templates:

1. Click the File tab, New, My Templates, and double-click the template you want to use; or

2. Click the "New Documents or Templates" icon on the Quick Access Toolbar (since it isn't one of the default icons, you have to add it to the QAT first), then double-click the template you want to use.

In Word 2016 (as in Word 2013), clicking the File tab, New remains a viable option, but the process has changed – and is somewhat confusing. (Also, it does not produce either a "My Templates" option or the "New" dialog.) As discussed throughout this section, when you click File, New, you might or might not see your personal templates under "Custom." In fact, you might or might not even see a "Custom" heading on the "New" screen.

Moreover, the "New" screen sometimes displays templates that are extraneous (such as the Welcome to Word template), as well as templates that users ordinarily should not edit (such as your Normal template and your Normal e-mail template if you use Outlook).

So I suggest you use the second method. First, you'll need to add a "New Document or Template" icon to your Quick Access Toolbar (QAT). Here are the steps:

1. **Right-click** the **QAT** (or the Ribbon) and choose "**Customize Quick Access Toolbar…**"

2. When the **Word Options dialog** opens, change the "**Choose commands from**" drop-down from "Popular" to "**All Commands**."

3. Click in the commands box and press the letter "**N**" to move the cursor to the first command that starts with that letter, then scroll to "**New Document or Template…**"

4. Click the "**New Document or Template…**" command, then click the "**Add**" **button** in the middle of the screen.

5. If you like, click the "**Up**" or "**Down**" **arrow** at the right side of the screen to move the icon up (to the left on the QAT) or down (to the right on the QAT).

6. Click "**OK**" to save your changes and exit from the Word Options.

414

The "New Document or Template…" icon will appear on your QAT. Note that it looks exactly like the "New" icon that opens a new blank document (so I positioned it farther over to the right on my QAT in order to distinguish the two).

The Left Side of My QAT
"New" at Left, "New Document or Template" Farther to the Right

Close-Up of New Document or Template Icon

When you want to create a new document based on one of your custom templates, just click that icon. Doing so opens the "New" dialog that probably looks familiar from older versions of Word. Your custom templates are located under "General."

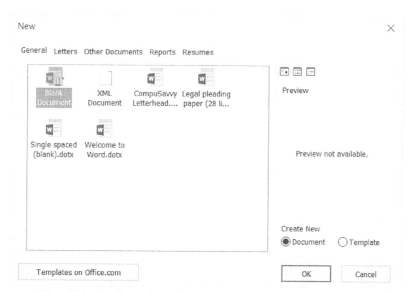

New Dialog Showing My Custom / Personal Templates

Just double-click the template you want to use to open a new document based on that template (or single-click it, then click the "OK" button).

As an aside, note that there is a Blank Document template showing in the General area, which is my Normal template (Normal.dotm).

Creating Another Template Based on Your Custom Template

Take a look at the lower right-hand side of the dialog. Under "**Create New**," the "**Document**" **radio button** is enabled by default. That means that when you either (1) **double-click an icon** for one of the templates *or* (2) **single-click an icon** and click "**OK**," Word will

415

create a brand-new document based on the template. Microsoft made that behavior the default so that the underlying template will remain intact and you can use it again and again to create individual documents.

The other radio button, labeled "**Template**," is used to create *another template* that is based on the existing one. For instance, let's say you already set up a generic letterhead template that can be used by any employee of your organization. You can open the New dialog, click to select that template, click the "Template" radio button, and start working on and customizing a letterhead template for a particular attorney. (The template opens with a name like "Template1," "Template2," etcetera.)

When you finish working on the attorney's letterhead template, press **F12** or click the "**Save As**" icon on the **Quick Access Toolbar**. The **Save As dialog** opens to the same location where you stored the underlying template, so all you need to do is give the new template a different name, such as the attorney's initials followed by the word "Letterhead." Because you opened the file as a template, the "Save as type" drop-down already indicates that the template will be saved as a .dotx (or a .dotm, depending on the file format of the underlying template).

Editing a Template

If at some point you want to revise an existing template, you will have to open the template in the same way you open regular documents for editing. In other words, press **Ctrl F12** and browse to the location of the template, then open it normally. If you open the template from the New Document or Template… icon on your QAT (or from File, New, Custom), you will end up editing either a new document based on the template or a new template based thereon –*not* the template itself. When you have finished editing the template, just save it and close it.

Miscellaneous Tips About Templates

Remember that you can add a code for the file name and path (as explained in the section starting on page 248), create Quick Parts (see the section starting on page 377), and/or add fill-in fields to a template to prompt users to enter specific information (see page 368 and following).

Because this feature is covered in detail elsewhere, I won't repeat the steps here.

416

PART VII: Working With Mailings and Forms

Merges (Mail Merges)

To perform a mail merge[1] in Word 2016, you can do either of the following:

(1) Use the **Mail Merge Wizard**, which walks you through the process step by step; or

(2) Create the necessary form and data files – or use existing ones – and perform the merge **manually** (without the Wizard).

In this section, I provide tutorials for the both methods. The Wizard provides more guidance, but can be a lengthy process. The second method is fairly quick and easy, obviating the need to use the Wizard. In either case, it's important to understand how the merge process works in general.

Overview

Merges involve two different files: (1) a **form file**, such as a form letter you intend to send to multiple people, a fax cover sheet, envelopes, or even a pleading, and (2) a **data file** that contains specific information, such as the names, addresses, and phone or fax numbers of the people to whom you want to send a form letter or a fax. You insert **merge fields** – which act as placeholders or variables for each bit of information – into the form file, and during the merge process, information from the data file is pulled into those fields.

Let's start by taking a closer look at data files.

Data Files

Data files typically are set up as tables.[2] Tables make it easy to store the pertinent information in discrete pieces—such as an individual's first name, last name, street address, city, state, zip, and so on. Those discrete pieces can be pulled into your form file individually, as appropriate.

For example, if you are creating a form letter, you can create a contact list as a table with separate columns for first name and last name. That gives you the option of addressing the individuals by either their first names ("Dear Jan") or their last names ("Dear Ms. Berinstein").

---

[1] The term "mail merge" is somewhat misleading because you can merge information into *any type of document* – not just letters and envelopes. For instance, you can merge names of the parties into a pleading caption, or you can merge case or client information into various types of court or in-house forms. Keep those broader uses in mind and don't be deterred by the fact that Word's Mail Merge Wizard uses terminology that refers to mailings.

[2] That is the case in WordPerfect, as well – and, for that matter, most other programs that make use of merges. You can also use Excel spreadsheets.

Another advantage of using tables with separate columns for each bit of information is that you can *sort* based on different types of information, such as last name or ZIP code.

In tables or spreadsheets, each column represents a **field**, and each row represents a complete **record** (the full information about an individual, such as title, first name, last name, company, street address, city, state, zip, home phone, work phone, e-mail address, and so on; or the full information about a court case, a client, or the like).

If you create a new "recipient list" (Word's terminology for a data file), Word presents you with a blank table (with a header row consisting of labels for the columns / fields). You will have the opportunity to delete, rename, and/or add columns / fields that suit your needs.

TIP: Give some thought beforehand to the exact information to include in the data file. Do you want a prefix field (what Microsoft calls "Title") so that you can address people as "Mr.," "Ms.," "Dr.," etc.? Do you want a job title field? Will you need to sort records by city or zip code? Will you need a fax number to pull into a fax cover sheet? The more thought you give to the project beforehand, the less editing of the data file you'll have to do in the long run.

Using the Mail Merge Wizard

There are six (6) main steps involved in using the Wizard:

1. Select the document type (letter, e-mail messages, labels, envelopes, etc.);
2. Select your starting document (the current / active doc, a template; an existing doc, etc.);
3. Select "recipients," which essentially means choose a data file (existing list, Outlook contacts, type a new list, etc.);
4. Write your letter (create your form file);
5. Preview to make sure everything looks okay; and
6. Complete the merge.

Keep reading for very detailed explanations of each step, or feel free to skip to the section about bypassing the Wizard and performing the merge manually (starting on page 431).

To use the Wizard, navigate to the **Mailings tab**, **Start Mail Merge group**, and click the **Start Mail Merge drop-down menu**. It includes commands for working with letters, e-mail messages, envelopes, labels, and more. Choose the last command, **Step by Step Mail Merge Wizard…**.

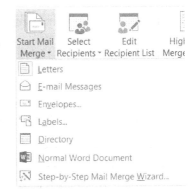

When you click that command, Word opens a **Mail Merge pane** at the right side of the screen that walks you through the six steps involved in setting up a form file and a data file and then merging the data into the form.

NOTE: At every stage, you will be able to go back to a prior step by clicking the "**Previous**" **button** at the bottom of the Mail Merge pane.

TIP: Clicking the "**?**" (Help) button at the top right side of any window during the process produces a Help screen that offers useful guidance.

In **Step 1**, select from a list of **document types**. Because Word doesn't provide a generic "Form" option, choose "**Letters**" to create any type of form that doesn't fit into any of the other categories (e.g., a fax cover sheet, a pleading caption, or a court form). After choosing a document type, click the "**Next**" **button** at the bottom of the pane.

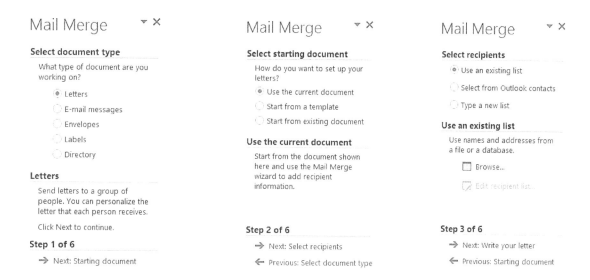

The First Three Steps of the Mail Merge Wizard

In **Step 2**, choose your starting document: the **current document** (typically, but not necessarily, a new, blank document); **an existing template**; or **an existing document**. Click to make your selection (or leave the default set at "current document"), then click "**Next**."

In **Step 3**, choose the recipients (i.e., the data file)[3]. You can use an **existing list**, use your **Outlook contacts**, or start a **new list**. In any case, when you choose a data file, it becomes *associated with* the form file you are using.[4]

<u>Using an Existing List (Data File)</u>

If you previously set up a mailing list or other data file, **click** the "**Browse...**" **button** about one-third of the way down the Mail Merge pane (see the right-most screenshot above). A

---

[3] Think "**data file**" rather than "recipient list." (Instead of *recipients*, you are inserting *data*.)

[4] "Association" means that the merge fields in the data file will be available (from the "Insert Merge Field" drop-down menu in the Write & Insert Fields group) whenever you use the form file. However, you can choose a different data file in the future.

Select Data Source dialog will open, typically to a subfolder within your "Documents" folder (C:\Users\<UserName>\Documents\My Data Sources).[5]

However, your data file – whether an Excel spreadsheet, a Word doc, or something else – could be stored in another location. If necessary, browse to a different folder, select the file you wish to use, then click the **"Open" button**. (See the screenshot below.)

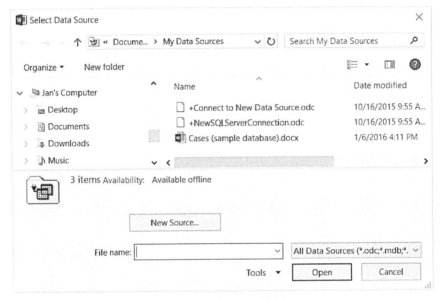

Select Data Source Dialog

Note that clicking "Open" might or might not actually open the data file / recipient list. The most important thing it does is create the association between the data file and the form file. After you do so, the merge pane will indicate which data file you chose ("Currently, your recipients are selected from:").

Editing a List (Data File)

If you need to open the data file for editing, click **"Edit recipient list..."** You should see something like the screenshot on the next page (a fictitious court cases database that I created for testing purposes).

---

[5] When you create a data file from scratch, Word automatically places it in this folder and adds the extension ".mdb," which stands for Microsoft database. You can use other file types, including an Excel spreadsheet, an Outlook contact list, and a regular Word file (but the Word file must be in the form of a table, with a header row consisting of field names).

422

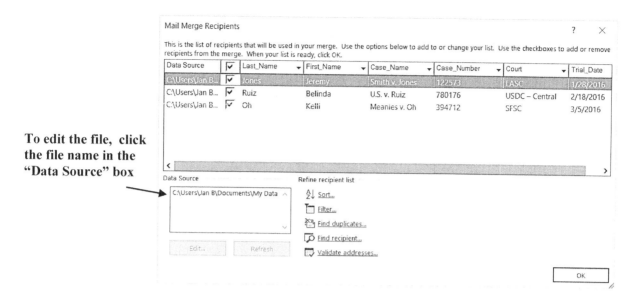

To edit the file, click the file name in the "Data Source" box

Note that the entries are arranged in table form, with each case in a separate row and each type of information about cases (client's first name and last name, case name, case number, court, trial date, etc.) in a separate column.

To add to or edit the list, click the file name in the lower left-hand corner (under "**Data Source**"). Doing so activates the "**Edit**" **button**. Click the button to enter more information and/or modify existing information. (You will be able to change the names of the columns— i.e., the field names—as well as to edit any specific information that you entered previously.)

Creating a New Data File

If you click the "**Type a New List**" **radio button**, the "Browse" command changes to "**Create…**" Clicking the "**Create…**" **button** produces a "**New Address List**" **dialog** – think of it as a "New Data File" dialog – that consists of one blank row (record), plus several columns (fields) with labels assigned by Microsoft.

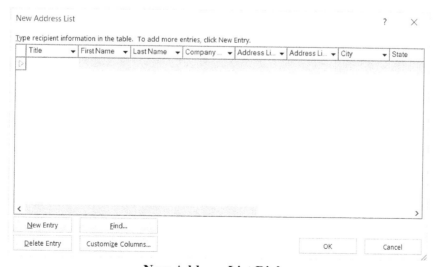

New Address List Dialog

423

To change the column labels, click the **"Customize Columns..." button**. Doing so will open a **"Customize Address List" dialog** where you can delete, rename, and/or add fields.

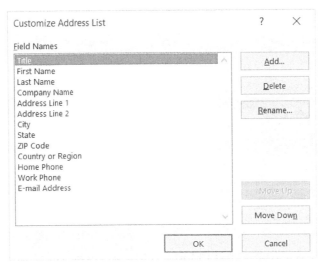

Customize Address List Dialog

As noted on page 420, it's important to figure out in advance which fields to include in your data file. Once you have decided on the fields, editing the fields in the list is fairly straightforward. Just click to select a field, then click **"Delete," "Rename," "Move Down,"** or **"Move Up,"** as appropriate.

To add a field to include in your data file, click the **"Add" button**. (Word will insert the new field below the highlighted field, but you can move it up or down later on.) When you click "Add," a small **"Add Field" dialog** appears where you can type a name for your new field. Afterwards, click **"OK"**, and the new field name will be inserted into the **Field Names list**.

Add Field Dialog

Continue in this manner until you are satisfied with the Field Names list. Then click **"OK"** to save your customized list. Word will prompt you to save the list in the default location for data files. Give the list an easily identifiable descriptive name (and, if you like, change the folder where the list will be stored – but ***be sure to make note of the new location*** if you do so, because you'll have to browse to that location when you want to use the list) and then click **"Save."** See the screenshot on the next page.

424

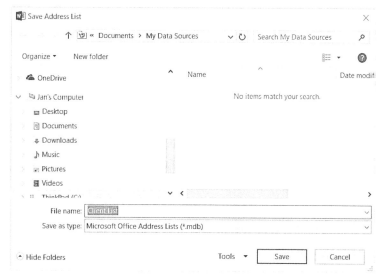

The "Save Address List" Dialog

To start adding information to the list, **click the file name** in the "**Data Source**" area at the lower left-hand side of the Mail Merge Recipients dialog just as you would if you were editing an existing data file. When you click the file name, the "**Edit…**" button will become active. Click the "**Edit…**" **button** in order to open an "**Edit Data Source**" dialog where you can start entering information into the list. (Just click in any field and start typing.)

When you have entered information in the first row and you're ready to create another "record to include in your data file," click the "**New Entry**" **button**. A second blank row will appear.

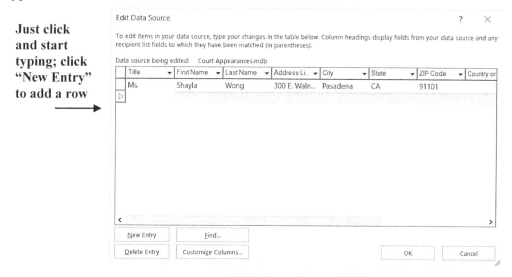

Just click and start typing; click "New Entry" to add a row

Edit Data Source Dialog

Note that if you change or add fields (column headings), Word will warn you that you need to save or discard your changes. To save them, be sure to click "**Yes**." If you click "No," your changes will be lost; if you click "Cancel," you won't be given a chance to edit the field headings (customize the columns).

425

As mentioned previously, you can change the order of the fields by clicking the "**Move Up**" button or the "**Move Down**" button. Be careful about deleting fields; if you delete a field that already contains information, you will lose that information.

Continue until you have finished setting up the data file. (If you don't finish, you can add more information at a later date.) Then click "**OK**" to save your changes. If Word prompts you to update the list and save the changes, click "**Yes**." Otherwise, Word will discard your edits.

After you save the list, click the "**Next**" **button** at the bottom of the Mail Merge pane to move on to **Step 4** (see the screenshot at right) and set up the form file ("Write your letter").

Form Files

This is the step where you set up the form file. Again, the form file might be a letter, but it could be any number of other document types: an envelope, a fax cover sheet, a pleading, a court form, and so forth.

If the file *is* a letter, you can insert codes for the address at the cursor position by clicking the "**Address block...**" **link** in the Mail Merge pane. That will open an **Insert Address Block dialog**, where you can review the way addresses will be inserted into your letters. The "Insert recipient's name in this format" box at left offers various formats; the box at right shows a preview of the selected option.

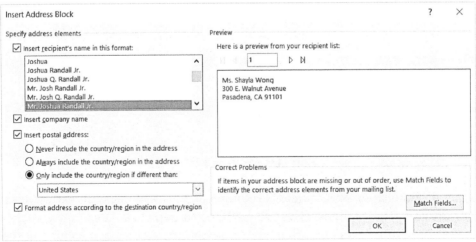

Insert Address Block Dialog

426

NOTE: If you have customized the fields (columns) in your data file, some fields might be missing or out of order in the preview area. In that case, click the "**Match Fields**" button at the lower right side of the dialog and use the drop-downs, if necessary, to ensure that the field names on the right (which are pulled from your data file) side match those on the left, which Word "requires" or "expects" when you use the built-in Address Block field.

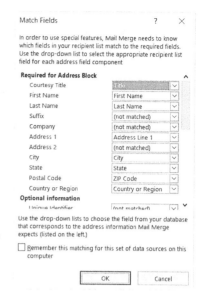

You don't have to match the field names exactly. In the screenshot, the first "required" field name at left is "Courtesy Title," but the field name in my data file is "Title" – which, interestingly, was the default name that Microsoft provided for the field. This match is close enough! (Same for "Postal Code" and "ZIP Code."

When you finish matching the fields, click "**OK**," then click "**OK**" in the **Insert Address Block dialog**. Word will insert an Address Block field, bracketed by double chevrons (arrows), at the cursor position. (The double chevrons indicate that it is a code.) You can move it if you like, but be careful not to delete the chevrons.

«AddressBlock»

You can insert a preformatted greeting line, too. Just click the "**Greeting line…**" **link** in the Mail Merge pane, which will launch an **Insert Greeting Line dialog box**. You can review the way the greeting will appear in your letter and make any changes you want. When you click **OK**, Word will insert a **Greeting Line code** at the cursor position. Again, you can reposition the code if you wish, taking care not to delete the double chevrons.

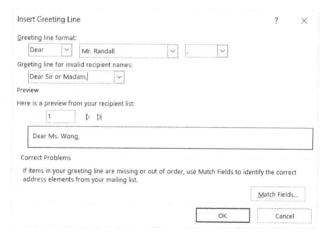

Of course, you don't have to use either the Address Block field or the Greeting Line field. If you prefer, you can insert individual merge codes for portions of the address and the greeting at appropriate places in the form file, as described below.

Inserting Individual Address Fields

If you prefer – and if you want more control over the merge process – you can insert individual address fields (and a code for the greeting) into your form file. To do so, position the cursor where the address will go, and then, instead of clicking the "Address block…" link in the Mail Merge pane, click "**More items…**" An **Insert Merge Field dialog**, displaying fields you can insert into the form file, will open.

427

To insert a field at the cursor position, click the **field name**, then click the "**Insert**" **button**. Unfortunately, you have to click to close the dialog box after inserting each merge field code (the "Cancel" button turns into a "**Close**" **button** that you can click).

Keep in mind that you need to lay out the field codes using spaces, commas, and other punctuation you normally would use in your form document. So, for instance, if you insert a First Name field, you need to press the space bar before inserting a Last Name field. Otherwise, when you perform the merge, the first and last names will run into each other. The same is true with field codes for city, state, and zip code: You need to press the space bar and/or commas between the codes.

Also, if you want to use titles (Mr., Ms., Dr., etc.) for the recipients of the letter, be sure to insert a Title field before the First Name field. With respect to the greeting line, you can type a greeting yourself and just insert a Title Field, a space, and a Last Name field followed by a colon. See the example below.

«Title» «First_Name» «Last_Name»
«Address_Line_1»
«City», «State» «ZIP_Code»

Re: Training

Dear «Title» «Last_Name»:

Typing the Form and Inserting Merge Codes

As you type the text of the letter, stop where you want to insert a placeholder for certain variable information. Click the "**More items…**" **link** in the **Mail Merge pane**. The **Insert Merge Field dialog** will open.

Click the field you wish to insert (you might have to scroll through the field list to find the one you want), then click the "**Insert**" **button**. Again, you can insert individual codes for the first name, last name, address, city, state, and zip rather than using the Address Block code. In any case, Word will insert the merge code at the cursor position. Like the codes you inserted previously, the merge code will be enclosed in double chevrons.

Continue typing and inserting merge codes until the form letter looks the way you want. Then click the "**Next**" button at the bottom of the Mail Merge pane to preview the merge.

428

Previewing the Merge

In **Step 5**, you can preview the merge. This step is critical because it gives you a chance to pinpoint, and correct, any existing problems with the merge setup before you perform the merge.

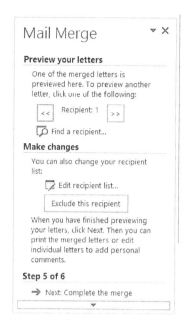

As discussed earlier, when items in the address block are missing or out of order, you need to click the "**Match Fields**" **button** to make sure that your custom fields align with the address codes Word requires in order to perform the merge correctly using the Address Block code.

Note that you don't have to go back two steps to locate the "Match Fields" link. There is a "**Match Fields**" icon, as well as other highly useful icons (including a button that toggles between the preview screen and the form document), on the Mailings tab itself. See the screenshot below.

Match Fields and Preview Results Icons

By default, the preview shows only one of the letters. You can click the "back" or "forward" arrow toward the top of the Mail Merge pane (or in the Preview group on the Mailings tab) to see another letter. Be sure to scroll up and down to make sure the entire letter (or other form file) is formatted to your liking before you move on to Step 6.

Including / Excluding Recipients (or Records)

You can choose to exclude a particular recipient / record from the merge. While you are previewing a specific letter, click the "**Exclude this recipient**" button in the merge pane, and that letter will not be included in the final merge. If you click the "**Edit list**" link, you can see that the record has been unchecked in the **Mail Merge Recipients dialog**, as shown below. (I excluded Dr. Julie Stein.)

If you change your mind and decide to include the record, simply click to check the box again. Also, you can click to exclude other records from this dialog box if you like. Just be sure to click "**OK**" to save your changes.

The unchecked record will not be included in the final merge

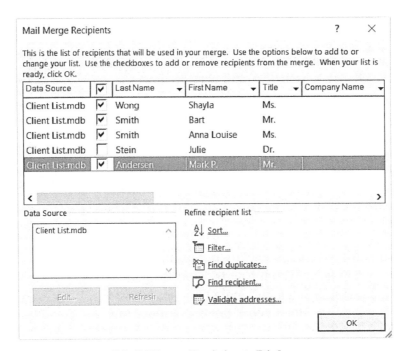

Mail Merge Recipients Dialog

NOTE: If you are merging from an Excel spreadsheet, click "Edit recipient list" to see which records have been checked – and uncheck any records you don't want to include in the merge.

Performing the Merge

When you are ready to perform the merge, click the "**Next**" **button** at the bottom of the **Mail Merge pane** to move to **Step 6**.

The options in the pane are "**Print…**" and "**Edit individual letters…**" Note that if you hold the mouse pointer over the "**Edit individual letters…**" **link**, you'll see a pop-up message with the words, "**Merge to new document**."

Clicking that link opens a "**Merge to New Document**" **dialog** that lets you choose which records to include.

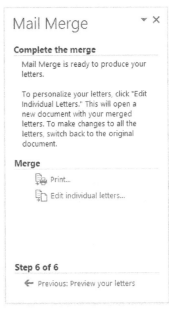

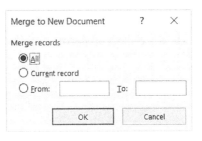

430

The default is "All," but you can click the "Current record" option or specify a range of records (the records must be concurrent, such as 2 to 7 or 14 to 33). If you need to look at the data file / recipient list to determine which records are which, you can either click the "Edit Recipient List" icon in the Mailings tab or click the "Preview Results" icon and then click the forward or back arrow to see individual letters.

The advantage of editing the recipient list (data file) is that you can actually uncheck any records you want to exclude from the merge.

After selecting the records you want to merge (or leaving the default set to "All"), and then click the "**OK**" button to perform the merge.

Once the merge is complete, you can revise individual letters if you so choose.

Printing the Merged Letters / Forms

If you click "**Print…**," a **Merge to Printer dialog** opens. Similar to the "Merge to New Document" dialog, it lets you print all of the records, the current record only, or a range of records.

When you are ready, click "**OK**" to print the records.

Performing a "Manual" Merge (Bypassing the Wizard)

If you prefer, you can perform the merge without using the Mail Merge Wizard. You'll probably find it somewhat faster.

The tricky part of performing a merge without the Wizard is that the commands for inserting merge fields into your form document are grayed out until you click the "**Select Recipients**" **button** and set up a **data file** – or open an existing one. Remember, a data file consists of the information you want to pull into your form document; it can be contact info for a mailing, case info for a pleading, or other info.

Whether you type a data file from scratch, select an existing file, or grab your Outlook contacts, once you click "**Select Recipients**" and choose a data file, you will be able to work with merge fields. (That makes sense if you think about it, because the specific merge fields that you will insert into your form file are based on the fields you set up in your data file.)

Creating the Form File

To get started, navigate to the **Mailings tab** and click the **Start Mail Merge drop-down**. This time, instead of choosing "Start Mail Merge Wizard," click the type of document you want to create. If you want to set up a letter, click "**Letter**." If you want to set up any type of form that doesn't fall neatly into one of the other categories (e-mails, envelopes, labels, directory), click "**Normal Word Document**." You can begin typing the form document at this point or type it later on.

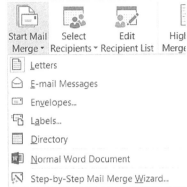

Creating the Data File

Next, click the "**Select Recipients**" **button** and choose from among the three options (Type New List, Use Existing List, or Select from Outlook Contacts). This is a critical step; until you start creating the data file, the commands in the Write & Insert Fields group—including the commands to insert merge fields—are grayed out, indicating that they are unavailable.)

The Commands Are Grayed Out Until You Click "Select Recipients" and Create a Data File

If you decide to type a new list, a "**New Address List**" **dialog** appears so that you can start typing information (records) into the list. When you have finished typing one complete record, either press the **Tab key** or click the "**New Entry**" button toward the bottom left side of the dialog to start a new row (record). Remember that you can customize the field names, add fields, and move fields around by clicking "**Customize Columns**."

When you finish entering data, click "**OK**." Word will open a "**Save Address List**" **dialog** so you can save the form file. The default save location, as mentioned previously, is a "My Data Sources" subfolder of your "Documents" folder. If necessary, browse to a different folder, give the file a name, make note of where you are storing it, and click "**Save**."

After you have saved the data file, the commands in the **Write & Insert Fields group** on the **Mailings tab** become available, and you can insert merge fields into your form file.

**The Write & Insert Fields Become Available
When You Save Your Data File**

Inserting Merge Fields into Your Form File

To insert a merge field, position your cursor at the exact point in your form file where you want the field to go, then click the "**Insert Merge Field**" drop-down and click the field you want to use. Note that the fields that appear on the drop-down derive from the data file / recipient list you have chosen. If necessary, you can browse to and select a different file from the "Select Recipients" drop-down.

If you click the "**Insert Merge Field**" **icon** itself (as opposed to the drop-down), an **Insert Merge Field dialog** will appear.

Insert Merge Field Dialog

433

You can add fields to your form document from this dialog if you like (just click a field and then click the "**Insert**" button). However, you'll have to close the dialog (and reopen it) if you want to tweak the formatting after inserting a field. Otherwise, you'll end up with duplicate fields or other problems.

Continue inserting fields into your form file, then finish typing and formatting the document. When everything looks the way you want, you are ready to preview the merge and then merge the data into the form file.

Previewing the Merge

To preview the merge, click the "**Preview Results**" button in the **Preview Results group** toward the right side of the **Mailings tab**. Doing so will show a preview of one of the merged documents; to see the rest, click the "forward" arrow or the "back" arrow at the top of the Preview Results group. (The single arrows move one record at a time; the arrows with a vertical line next to them move to the beginning of the data file, i.e., the first record, or to the end of the data file, i.e., the last record.)

Preview Results Group

The "Preview Results" button is a toggle, so if you need to review the original form file – and see the fields in it – click the button a second time to turn off the preview.

While in "Preview" mode, you can click the "Find Entry" button to search for a specific entry and display a preview (e.g., for a particular individual in your contact list).

Performing the Merge

If you are satisfied with the way things look in the preview, click the "**Finish & Merge**" drop-down in the **Finish group** on the **Mailings tab**. The drop-down offers three choices: **Edit Individual Documents…**; **Print Documents…**; and **Send E-mail Messages…**.

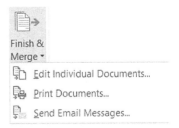

434

The first option, "**Edit Individual Documents**," essentially means that the merge will proceed and you can modify one or more of the merged documents afterwards. If you click that command, a "**Merge to New Document**" dialog will open, giving you the opportunity to include all of the records in the merge (which is the default), to merge only the current record (i.e., the one on the screen), or to specify a range of consecutive records to merge.

Merge to New Document Dialog

After you choose which records to merge, click "**OK**." The merged documents will open in a new document.

TIP / CAUTION: After the merge completes, the form file remains open on another screen.[6] If you haven't saved the final version of that file, be sure to save it at this point for future use. It's easy to forget to take this crucial step.

Also, if you want, you can save the merged documents and print them later on. To do so, be sure to save the file containing the merged documents.

Printing Merged Documents

To send one or more of the merged documents to the printer, click the "Print Documents" command. A "Merge to Printer" dialog will open. Like the "Merge to New Document" dialog, it allows you to include all of the records (the default), only the current record (the one on your screen), or a range of consecutive records.

Merge to Printer Dialog

---

[6] When you switch screens and return to that file, you might see the Mail Merge pane at the right side, even though you didn't specifically invoke it.

435

Make your choice, then click "**OK**" to send the merged document(s) to the printer.
Send Email Messages

This option makes it easy to send the merged documents via e-mail, assuming you have added e-mail addresses to the data file / recipient list. Simply choose the "Email Address" field from the drop-down in the "To:" field. Then type a subject line, select a mail format, choose the current record or consecutive records (or leave the "Send records" default set to "All"), and click "**OK**." (The HTML format inserts the form document into the body of the e-mail message, and retains the document formatting; Plain text inserts the document into the body of the message but strips out formatting; and Attachment adds the form document to the message as a separate attachment.)

If you have left the subject line blank, a prompt will appear asking if you wish to send the messages anyway. If not, you will be returned to the Merge to E-mail dialog so that you can type a subject line.

CAUTION: Clicking "OK" sends the e-mail messages *immediately* – so don't use this option if you wish to compose and review individual e-mails.

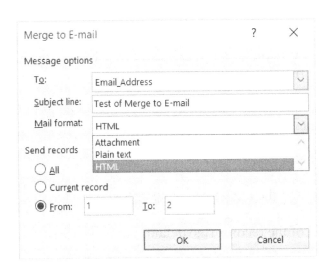

Merge to E-mail Dialog

SIDEBAR: What Is the "SQL Command" Prompt?

If you begin a merge and then open an existing form file that already has a specific data file associated with it, you will see the prompt shown in the screenshot below.

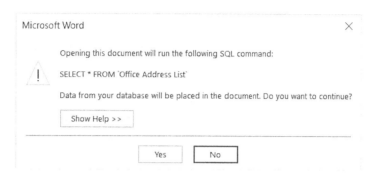

Essentially, it is asking if you want to retain the existing association between the form file and the data file.

Clicking "**Yes**" will open the form file and provide you with access to the merge fields in the associated data file. Clicking "**No**" will open the form file, but you will have to choose another data file / recipient list.

In either case, the form file opens with all of the formatting and merge field codes that you inserted previously.

Creating a Sheet of Different Labels Using Mail Merge

Unlike WordPerfect, Word doesn't provide an easy way to create a sheet of labels and populate the labels with different names and addresses. The only two options are to create and print one label at a time *or* to populate a sheet of labels with ***the same name and address***. To assemble a sheet of labels addressed to different people or entities, you have to perform a mail merge. (Note that the basic instructions for performing a mail merge with labels are almost the same as performing a mail merge with letters and/or envelopes.)

As outlined in the section about merges, you'll use two separate documents: (1) a ***form file*** (in this case, a sheet of labels) into which you will insert merge codes; and (2) a ***data file*** that includes the information that is pulled into the form when you merge the two documents (here, the contact names and addresses).

Setting Up the Form File

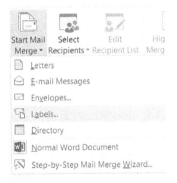

With labels, you'll format the labels first, insert merge codes, and then replicate the merge codes throughout the sheet of labels.[1]

To get started, navigate to the **Mailings tab, Start Mail Merge group,** and click the **Start Mail Merge** button, then click **Labels**. The **Label Options dialog** will open.

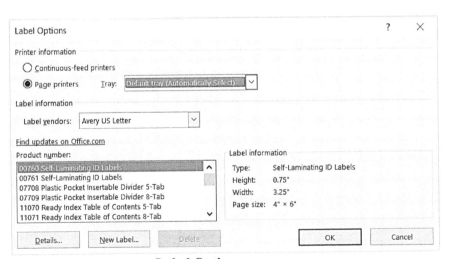
Label Options

---

[1] You might consider creating a separate template for each type of labels you use (such as Avery 5160 or 5162 labels).

438

If this is the first time you have created labels, the **Label Options dialog** will show Microsoft as the **Label Vendor** (about half-way down the dialog). If you use standard Avery labels, click to change the drop-down to "**Avery US Letter**."[2] Then in the **Product number** box, scroll down until you locate the label you wish to use, such as 5160 or 5164.

TIP: Clicking in the Product number box and then pressing the number "5" moves the cursor to the first label that starts with that number.

Click to **select (highlight) it**, then click **OK**. Word might prompt you that it needs to "delete" the content of the document (even if you are using a blank document) in order to set up the label form. Assuming that's what you intended to do—i.e., that it's safe to delete the contents of the document currently on your screen—click **OK**. Word should format the page as a sheet of labels of the type you selected.[3]

In Word, labels are formatted as tables. When you first choose your labels, you might not see the table gridlines – the non-printing borders. To display the gridlines, click the **Layout** portion of the **Table Tools tab** and click the "**View Gridlines**" icon at the left side of the tab.

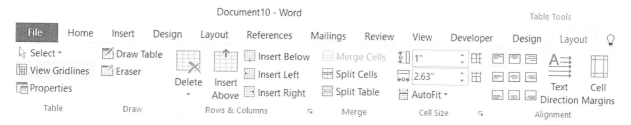

Setting Up the Data File (Recipient List)

Before you can insert merge fields, you have to click the "**Select Recipients**" button in the **Start Mail Merge group** on the **Mailings tab**. (You might have to click the Mailings tab to bring it to the forefront again.) When you do, Word offers you three choices:

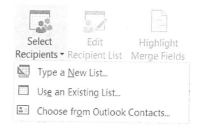

1. **Type a New List**;
2. **Use an Existing List**; or
3. **Choose from Outlook Contacts**.

When you choose the first or second option, Word expects you to insert the contact information in table form, with each discrete piece of information (First Name, Last Name, Company, Address, City, State, Zip, etc.) in a separate cell and each complete contact record in a separate row of the table.

---

[2] There are additional Avery labels available for those who reside outside the United States.

[3] If you know in advance that you will need more than one full sheet (page) of labels, navigate to the last label on the sheet and press the Tab key – several times, if necessary – to create as many additional rows as you need.

Type a New List

If you choose to type a new list, Word opens a **New Address List dialog** in which to enter the information.

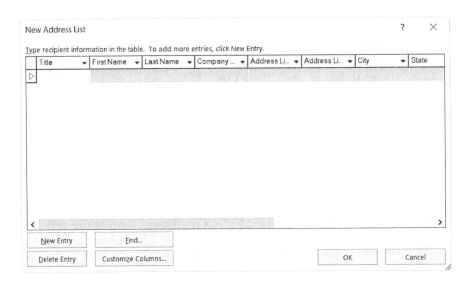

Just click in the first column (field) and start typing. To add another contact, click the "**New Entry**" **button** at the bottom left side of the dialog. Click "**Customize Columns**" to add, delete, change, or move the column headings.

Once you have finished adding contacts, click "**OK**." Word will prompt you to save the list as a database file (automatically adding the .mdb extension) and will place the file by default in your "My Data Sources" folder, located here:

C:\Documents and Settings\<User Name>\My Documents\My Data Sources

It's okay to leave the file there, since Word will look for the file in that location when you perform a merge using that mailing list.

Select From Outlook Contacts

If you maintain all of your contact information in Outlook, the third option is a good choice. When you click that option, Word opens a list of your Outlook contacts—already set up in table format—and you can pick and choose which of those contacts to use in the merge. (If you are prompted to import a file, choose the appropriate one and proceed.)

When the Outlook contact list opens, check to make sure it looks okay. Next, click to *uncheck* any contacts you don't want to include in the merge, then click "**OK**" to dismiss the dialog box.

Use an Existing List

If you choose to use an existing list, Word opens the "**Select Data Source**" dialog so that you can browse for any mailing list you have set up previously.

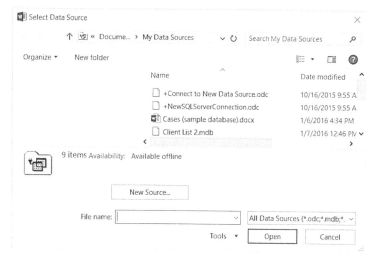

To use an existing list (a data file), click to select it, then click "**Open**."

Word will insert the records from the data file into the sheet of labels. You will see something like the following:

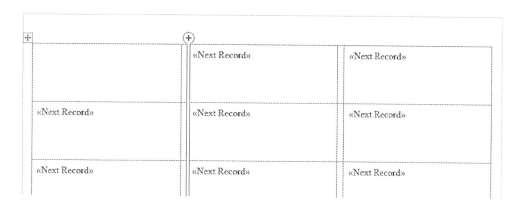

Partial Sheet of Labels With "Next Record" Merge Field

Note that the first label is blank – that is, it doesn't contain any merge fields. You must insert merge fields into the first label in order for the merge to work properly.

Inserting Merge Fields

Begin by clicking within the first label. Then, either (1) click the "**Insert Merge Field**" **button** (located in the **Write and Insert Fields** group) and insert individual fields (laying them out the way you want them to appear in the merged labels) *or* (2) simply click the "**Address Block**" **button**. The second option is particularly easy.

When you first click the "Address Block" button, the **Insert Address Block dialog** appears, allowing you to double-check the information that will be included when you perform the merge and the layout of that information.

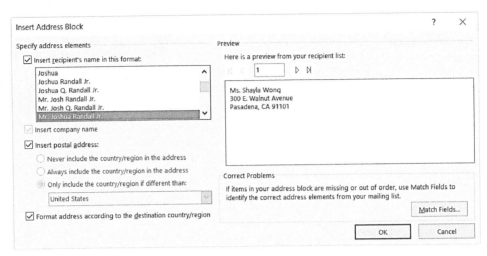

Choose a different format if you wish, then click "**OK**." Word inserts an **<<Address Block>> code** in the label.

NOTE: unless you specifically *unchecked* the first item in the Insert Address Block dialog box ("Insert recipient's name in this format"), the Address Block code *includes the contact's name*. So if you use the Address Block code, don't also insert codes for the contact's first and last names, or you'll end up with the individual's name appearing in the label twice.

After you have set up the first label, click the **"Update Labels" button** at the right side of the Write & Insert Fields group, which will copy the information from Label 1 (i.e., all of the merge fields) into all of the other labels in the sheet.

You're almost ready to start the merge! But first...

Before Proceeding With the Merge

CAUTION: By default, Word inserts extra space between the lines when it merges contact information into a form. Therefore, it is *imperative* that you do the following before you proceed with the merge:

1. Select the entire table that contains your labels, either by clicking the plus sign that appears when you hold the mouse near the upper left side of the table or by clicking the Layout portion of the Table Tools tab, then clicking Select, Select Table; and

2. Launch the **Paragraph dialog** and, if necessary, change **Before spacing** to **0 (zero)**; change **After spacing** to **0 (zero)**; and change **Line spacing** to **Single**.

   NOTE: The menu that appears when you right-click within a table doesn't include a Paragraph command, so you will have to open the Paragraph dialog in some other way – by pressing Alt, O, P, or by clicking the dialog launcher in the Paragraph group on the Home tab, or by clicking the Paragraph Settings icon on the Quick Access Toolbar (if you've added that icon to your QAT).

Performing the Merge

At this point, you're ready to perform the merge. Note that Word will merge the information into a new document, which is ideal because it allows you to keep your label form document and reuse it every time you want to print labels. (You'll simply open the form, select the recipients, and merge.)

Navigate to the **Finish** group at the right side of the **Mailings tab**. Click the **Finish & Merge drop-down**. The available commands are (1) **Edit Individual Documents**; (2) **Print Documents**; and (3) **Send E-mail Messages**.

It's a good idea to perform the merge first and then, if everything looks okay, print the labels. To start the merge, click **Edit Individual Documents**, a somewhat confusingly labeled option that actually doesn't involve "editing" documents (except that it prompts you to select certain records to include in the merge). Doing so will open a **Merge to New Document dialog**, where you can choose to merge all of the records in your recipient list (the default setting), merge only the Current Record (presumably the first one in the list), or select several consecutive records.

When you are ready, click **OK**, and the merged information will appear in a new document.

| Ms. Shayla Wong
300 E. Walnut Avenue
Pasadena, CA 91101 | Mr. Bart Smith
312 N. Spring St.
Los Angeles, CA 90012 | Ms. Anna Louise Smith
9355 Burton Way
Beverly Hills, CA 90210 |

TROUBLESHOOTING TIP #1: If information appears only in the first label after the merge, go back to the form file and be sure to click the "Update Labels" button. Then run the merge again.

TROUBLESHOOTING TIP #2: If the records appear too close to the top of the labels, and you're concerned that information might get cut off when you print, do the following:

1. Select the entire table that contains your labels.

2. Navigate to the Alignment group in the Layout portion of the Table Tools tab.

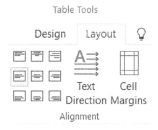

3. Click the middle button at left (the Align Center Left) button – the one that is highlighted in the screenshot above.

4. If you are happy with the results, repeat these steps in the form document (so that the next time you perform a merge with labels, they are aligned correctly).

| Ms. Shayla Wong
300 E. Walnut Avenue
Pasadena, CA 91101 | Mr. Bart Smith
312 N. Spring St.
Los Angeles, CA 90012 | Ms. Anna Louise Smith
9355 Burton Way
Beverly Hills, CA 90210 |

If you are likely to send mail on a regular basis to the recipients whose contact information you've inserted into this sheet of labels, save the sheet as a separate file for future mailings. Be sure to save the form document, too (and make a note – mental or otherwise – of the location where you store it).

<u>Reusing an Existing Form Document</u>

It's fairly simple to reuse an existing form document to perform a merge, as long as you have saved the form (and you remember where you put it). When you are ready to use it for another merge, navigate to and open the form. When you do so, Word will prompt you to run an SQL command (essentially acknowledging that there are merge codes in the file and that the file has been associated with a specific data file / mailing list). Click "**Yes**" to continue and use the same data file (mailing list) or – more likely in this situation – click "**No**" to continue but create or open a different data file.

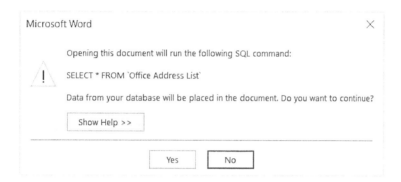

If you click "No," you'll need to click the **Select Recipients drop-down** in the **Start Mail Merge group** in order to choose an existing data file / mailing list or start a new one.

From this point on, just repeat the steps described earlier in this lesson, starting with the "Setting Up the Data File (Recipient List)" section that begins on page 439.

QUICK TIP: Make the Mail Merge Pane Go Away

If the Mail Merge pane keeps popping up when you don't want to see it, try the following:

Navigate to the Mailings tab, Start Mail Merge group, click the Start Mail Merge drop-down, and then click "Normal Word Document."

CAUTION: The Write & Insert fields might become inactive (grayed out) after you click "Normal Word Document." To reactivate the fields, click "**Select Recipients**," choose the "**Use Existing List**" **command**, and locate and **open the data file** that you have associated with the current document. That should do the trick!

Setting Up and Printing Labels

Mail merges work well, but sometimes a less complicated method – creating a sheet of labels and then typing the labels (or copying and pasting some text into each label) is more appropriate. To create a sheet of labels, do the following:

1. Navigate to the left side of the **Mailings tab** and click the **Labels icon**.

2. When the **Envelopes and Labels dialog** opens, click the "**Options**" **button** at the bottom of the Labels tab to open the **Label Options dialog**.

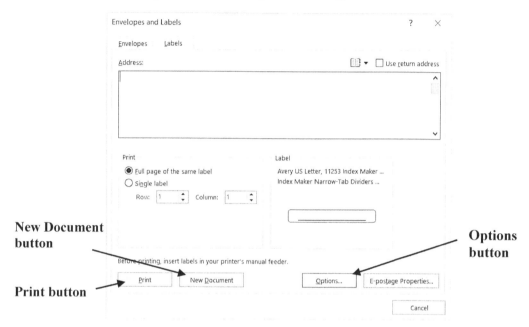

3. If necessary, change the "**Label vendors**" drop-down in the Label Options dialog to **Avery US Letter**.

4. Scroll to the label that you use, such as 5160 or 5164. (**TIP**: You can press the number "5" to move to the first label that starts with that number.) Click to select it.

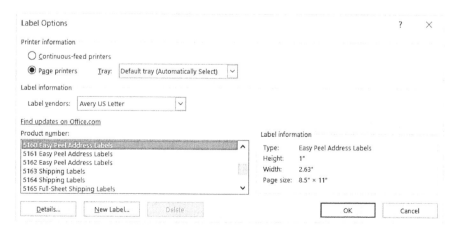

447

5. Click "**OK**."

    Word closes the Label Options dialog and returns you to the Envelope and Labels dialog.

6. Click the "**New Document**" **button** at the bottom of the Envelope and Labels dialog to create a sheet of labels in a separate document window.

    Partial image of a sheet of 5160 Avery mailing labels

    NOTE: Labels are formatted as tables. If you can't see the Gridlines, the non-printing border lines that provide guidance while you type, navigate to the **Layout** portion of the **Table Tools tab**, and click the "**View Gridlines**" icon all the way to the left.[1]

7. By default, the labels are aligned so that the text will start at the top left, as you can tell by the position of the flashing cursor in the first label. You can change this alignment even before typing any text. First, select the entire table by **clicking the plus sign** that appears at the top left side of the table when the mouse is positioned there.

8. Next, navigate to the **Alignment group** and click an alignment icon other than the one that is already highlighted. You'll probably want the one in the center of the left-most column (Align Center Left).[2]

9. While the entire table is selected, you can choose a smaller font size or make other global changes to the label formatting.

10. If you like, save the blank document to use as a form document. Be sure to make note of the location where you are saving the form.

---

[1] After you turn on the Gridlines, they will be visible in any new tables you create.

[2] Selecting the entire table and changing the alignment of the cells is a much better solution than applying "Before" spacing. That is because most people press "Enter" after typing each line of an address, and any "Before" spacing applied to the first line of an address – which Word considers a paragraph – is copied to the next line / paragraph. As a result, there is too much spacing between lines / paragraphs. However, applying "Before" spacing *does* work if you press **Shift Enter** instead of Enter when you finish typing a line of an address. Remember, Shift Enter produces a Line Break / Soft Return, which *extends* the current paragraph rather than creating a new paragraph. So in this situation, the "Before" spacing affects only the first line of the address, since any additional lines created with Shift Enter are not new paragraphs.

11. Then save the document again with a different name and begin typing the specific names and addresses for your contact list.

Printing Labels

Printing labels is fairly straightforward. Make sure that you have loaded one or more sheets of labels (and that they are facing in the correct direction) before you press Ctrl P or click the File tab, Print and send the labels to your printer.

Adjusting Text on the Labels

If the text is getting cut off when you print because it is too close to the top margin or because there is too much text to fit the label, there are a few things to try:

1. **Select** the entire table, then choose a **smaller font size**; or

2. **Select** the entire table, then change the alignment by clicking a different **alignment icon** in the **Alignment group** on the **Layout** portion of the **Table Tools tab**; or

3. Change the top table cell margin by doing the following:

    (a) On the **Layout** portion of the **Table Tools tab**, click **Properties**.

    (b) Click the "**Options**" button at the lower right side of the Table Properties dialog.

    (c) When the **Table Options dialog** opens, change the top margin slightly (e.g., to .15" or .2"), then click "**OK**" twice to save your changes.

NOTE: Although it seems like a logical choice, don't actually change the *left margin* from this dialog box, since that appears to change not the indentation of the text but the actual size of the table (i.e., the sheet of labels). The same appears to be true if you change the left margin from the Page Setup dialog.

The best option for changing the left indentation of text is to select the entire table, then open the **Paragraph dialog** and set the left indent from there. (Note that the left indent might be labeled "Inside," rather than "Left," in the dialog box.)

Labels Tips and Tricks

Creating a Full Sheet of Identical Labels

To create a full sheet of identical labels, start by typing the information that you want to use in the labels. For example, perhaps you need to have a full sheet of labels with a case name, a case number, and the name of the judge, so type that information on separate lines in a blank new document. Then do the following:

1. **Select** (highlight) the block of text.

2. Navigate to the **Mailings tab** and click the **Labels** icon.

    The last label you used should be shown in the box toward the middle of the **Envelopes and Labels dialog**.

3. If you want to use a different label, click the "**Options**" button at the bottom of the dialog.

4. When the **Label Options dialog opens**, scroll to the label you want, click to select it, then click "**OK**."

5. Click "**New Document**."

    Word will create a new document in a different window that consists of a sheet of labels with identical information in each label.

6. If you want to change the alignment, the font formatting, etc., select the entire sheet of labels by **clicking the plus sign** at the top left side, then apply the formatting.

    If for some reason the plus sign isn't visible, select the table by clicking the **Layout** portion of the **Table Tools tab**, then clicking the **Select drop-down** at the left side of the tab and choosing "**Select Table**."

Setting Up and Printing Envelopes

There are a couple of ways to create envelopes from scratch in Word. To start from within an existing letter, do the following:

1. Position your cursor immediately ahead of – or somewhere within – the address block in the letter.

2. Navigate to the **Create group** at the left side of the **Mailings tab** and click the **Envelopes icon**.

3. Word automatically pulls the name and address into the **Delivery address** area of the Envelopes and Labels dialog. (See the screenshot below.)

    If for some reason that doesn't work, close the dialog, select the address block, and click the Envelopes icon again.

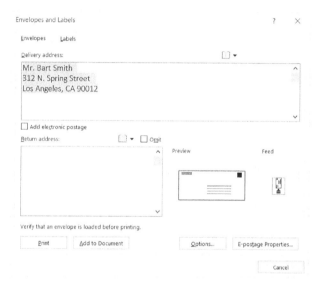

4. Click the "**Add to Document**" button to have Word insert the envelope at the beginning of the letter (with a section break between the envelope and the letter).

5. If you prefer, you can print the envelope directly by clicking the "**Print**" button.

    CAUTION: Make sure you have at least one envelope loaded in your printer before choosing this option.

To create an envelope without starting from within a letter, do the following:

1. Navigate to the **Create group** at the left side of the **Mailings tab** and click the **Envelopes** icon.

2. When the **Envelope and Labels dialog** opens, type the recipient's name and address in the **Delivery address** area (See the screenshot below).

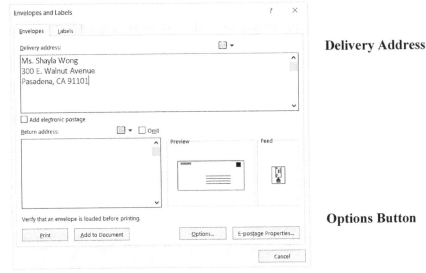

Envelopes and Labels Dialog

3. **OPTIONAL**: If you are not using pre-printed envelopes, you can type a return address in the area labeled "Return Address."

    To print envelopes *without* a return address later on – without deleting the return address in the dialog – just click to check the "**Omit**" **checkbox** above the Return Address" field.

4. Click the **Options button** toward the bottom center of the dialog to select a different envelope size, change the font face and/or size for the return address and/or the delivery address, or change the placement of the Delivery address and/or the Return address.

5. To change the placement of the Delivery address or the Return address, click the "**From left**" and/or "**From top**" spinner arrow(s).

    The **Preview** at the bottom shows where the addresses will appear.

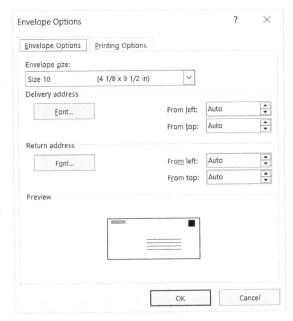

452

6.   To change the font for the Delivery address or the Return address, click the "**Font**" button in the appropriate part of the dialog box and select a specific font (other than the +Headings font).

After you have tweaked the options to your satisfaction, you can do one of two things: (1) click "**Add to Document**," which will append the envelope to a document so that you can print it later or, (2) if you have at least one blank envelope loaded in the printer tray, click the **Print button**, which will send it straight to the printer.

If you append the envelope to your document, be sure to do one of the following when you are ready to print:

- Click somewhere within the envelope before pressing **Ctrl P** or clicking the **File tab, Print** (to open Print Place), then choose "**Print Current Page**" from the **Settings drop-down**; *or*

- Open **Print Place**, choose "**Print Custom Range**," and **specify the page number** where the envelope is situated.

Otherwise, the entire document – both the letter and the envelope – will be sent to the printer.

Changing the Default Address Fonts

Both the Delivery Address and the Return Address are configured to use the **+Headings font**, which is a placeholder. The specific font that is applied is determined by the preexisting **Envelope Address** and **Envelope Return styles**, plus **the active "Theme"** in your document. All other things being equal, the Calibri Light font is used by default (Word 2010 used Cambria), with the font size for the envelope address set at 12 points and the font size for the return address set at 10 points.

To specify a different font face or font size, you can either (1) change the settings in the **Envelope Address dialog**, which will affect only the current envelope, or (2) modify the **Envelope Address style** and/or **Envelope Return style**, which will affect all future envelopes.

To modify one or both of the styles, open the **Styles Pane** (by clicking the **dialog launcher** in the **Styles group** on the **Home tab** or by pressing **Ctrl Alt Shift S**). Click the **Options** link at the bottom right side of the pane and make sure **All Styles** are showing. Then navigate to the **Envelope Address** and/or **Envelope Return style** in the list, **right-click** the style name, and click **Modify…**. Then make any changes you want to the font face and/or size (either from the Font drop-down under "Formatting" or by clicking the "Format" button at the bottom left, then clicking "Font.")

Be sure to click "**New documents based on this template**" (to ensure that the modifications you're making apply to all envelopes you create in the future) before clicking "**OK**."

PART VIII: Working With Pleadings and Contracts

Aligning Text With Pleading Line Numbers

One of the most common problems people in the legal profession encounter with pleadings created in Word is that the text doesn't align with the pleading line numbers.

The discrepancy usually results from an error in the configuration settings described below – and can be fixed by adjusting one or more of those settings. Note, however, that there can be other, less obvious, factors that affect the alignment of text. If the "typical" fixes don't work, try the workarounds suggested toward the end of this section.

The Usual Suspects

1. Mismatched Line Spacing.

In most cases, the problem arises from a mismatch between the line spacing of the document text and the line spacing of the pleading line numbers in the header.[1] The fix involves changing the line spacing of the text to match that of the pleading line numbers.[2]

To determine the line spacing of the numbers, open the header editing screen (either by **double-clicking** in the white space at the top of a page or by **right-clicking**, then clicking "**Edit Header**" in that location). Then right-click anywhere within the line numbers and choose "**Paragraph.**"

When the **Paragraph dialog** opens, note the setting in the **Line spacing** box. (This figure will almost certainly be an **Exactly xx points** figure – it could be 22.75 pt, 23.15 pt, 24 pt, 22.65 pt, or something different, depending on how the underlying template was set up.[3]) That setting is what you will use for all "pleading double-spaced" text in your document.

Close the Paragraph dialog box, close out of the Header editing screen, and check the line spacing of one or more "pleading double-spaced" paragraphs. If in fact there is a disparity,

---

[1] Recall that "Exactly" line spacing based on *points* is more compressed vertically than Double (or single) spacing. If the line spacing of the pleading line numbers is more condensed than the line spacing of the text, the "taller" text won't fit on the numbered lines. That can happen even if both settings use "Exactly" line spacing but the text uses a larger number – for instance, if the pleading line numbers are set to Exactly 22.75 pt and the text is set to Exactly 24 pt.

[2] You might think that it's easier to change the line spacing of the pleading line numbers. However, doing so usually creates a host of other problems. When all is said and done, it's preferable to change the line spacing of the document text.

[3] Because the Pleading Wizard, a feature that was used to create pleading paper in versions of Word prior to Word 2007, set the pleading line numbers at 22.75 pt, some people assume that you should always set the "pleading double spacing" to 22.75 pt. Not so. Many law firms create their own templates or tweak the settings in templates they've acquired, so that there can be a wide variety of settings.

select the relevant portions of the text, open the **Paragraph dialog** again, and configure the **Line spacing** to match the spacing of the pleading line numbers.

After changing the line spacing, click "**OK**" to close the dialog and save your changes.

NOTE: You will have to change the spacing of all "pleading single-spaced" text to *half* the figure you used for the "pleading double-spaced" text. For example, if the line numbers are set at 22.75 pt, that is the figure you'll use for the "pleading double-spaced" text, and the "pleading single-spaced" text must be set at half of 22.75 pt, or 11.375 pt. In this type of situation, Word usually rounds up the spacing (e.g., 11.375 will become 11.4).

ALSO NOTE: It's important that *all* of the text in the pleading be configured to match or be exactly half the setting for the pleading line numbers. Even a few lines in the pleading caption or elsewhere that are set to Single, Double, or some odd "Exactly" spacing can adversely affect the alignment of the rest of the document.

> 2.   **"Before" or "After" Spacing**.

In some pleadings, "Before" or "After" spacing (for example, 12 pt before or after the paragraph) is used to add necessary white space between headings and regular text. If not used appropriately, however, "Before or "After" spacing can throw off the alignment of the text. If you have reformatted the line spacing in the document to match the spacing of the line numbers but things still aren't lining up, try to locate the first place in the document where the spacing looks "off," and check the line spacing of a couple of paragraphs. In particular, look to see if "Before" or "After" spacing has been used and, if so, if the figure makes sense in the context of the line spacing of the pleading line numbers. (There could be a mismatch here, too; for instance, the line numbers might be set at 22.75 pt but the "After" spacing is set at 12 pt.)

If necessary, reset the "Before" and/or "After" spacing and save your changes. You might have to experiment to get the setting just right.

NOTE: In some situations, *adding* space before or after a paragraph can help. But watch out! Remember that pressing the Enter key will copy that additional spacing to the next paragraph.

> 3.   **Different Fonts That Handle "Leading" Differently**.

If the document uses one font for the pleading line numbers and a different font for the text, that can cause problems if the two fonts handle "leading" differently. ("Leading" has to do with the amount of white space inserted between lines of text). Sometimes you can fix things simply by changing either the font used in the pleading line numbers or the font used in the document.

The best way to ensure that the same font is applied to all of the elements of the document – the text, the footnotes, and the headers and footers (including the line numbers) – is to choose a "default font" for the document. To do so, press **Ctrl D** or click the dialog launcher in the **Font group** on the **Home tab**.

458

When the **Font dialog** opens, make sure that the font face, style, and size are to your liking, and click the "**Set As Default**" button at the bottom left side of the dialog.

Set As Default Button

A prompt appears, asking if you want to change the default font for the current document only or for the underlying template. Leave the default setting as is ("This document only?") and click "**OK**."

After you have set the default font for the document, the font in the line numbers should match the font in the text, which might resolve the alignment issue.

4. <u>**Unexpected or Seemingly Random Font Size Changes**</u>.

If you are still experiencing problems with alignment, check the document for unexpected font size changes, especially with respect to blank lines between paragraphs (although it's possible that setting a default font will fix this problem, too). For this task, it can be helpful to turn on **Show / Hide** (by clicking the paragraph icon in the **Paragraph group** of the **Home tab** or pressing **Ctrl Shift *** [asterisk]). Look for any paragraph marks that seem larger than the rest. If you find any, select the paragraph mark itself and change the font size via the font dialog box.

5. __Widows and Orphans__.

Sometimes having **Widow/Orphan control** enabled can cause problems with text alignment. This feature usually isn't enabled in pleadings because typically people want text to fill the page, even if it means one line dangling by itself at the top or bottom of a page. However, *it is enabled by default*, and because many people aren't aware of that fact, they don't think to turn it off. (It's also difficult to turn off in an entire document, even when you select the document, then launch the **Paragraph dialog**, click the **Line and Page Breaks tab**, and *uncheck* **Widow/Orphan control**.)

6. __Different Page Margins in Different Sections__

If your document is divided into sections, it's entirely possible that the page margins are different in different sections. And if so, that can cause alignment problems. It's worth checking (by clicking within a section, then taking a look at the margin settings in the **Page Setup dialog**, which you can open from the dialog launcher in the **Page Setup group** at the left side of the **Layout** tab or by pressing **Alt P, S, P**).

7. __Footers, Footnotes, etc.__

It can be worthwhile to check existing footers and footnotes to see if line spacing, "Before" and/or "After" spacing, or other configuration settings for those specific features could be causing problems with the alignment of the text in the body of the document.

One frequent, but easily overlooked, source of alignment problems is extra hard returns in footers. Turning on Show / Hide sometimes reveals a stray paragraph mark below the footer text; deleting the empty paragraph (or backspacing) often has beneficial results.

__Also Notorious__

Here are a few additional things to investigate:

8. __Layout Options__.

These settings, found under the **File tab**, **Options**, **Advanced** (scroll all the way down to the bottom of the screen to **Layout Options**), can have a significant impact on document formatting. The most important ones to be aware of are "**Suppress extra line spacing at bottom of page**," "**Suppress extra line spacing at top of page**," and "**Don't center 'exact line height' lines**."[4]

9. __"At Least" vs. "Exactly" Line Spacing__.

"At Least" line spacing can be useful in desktop publishing, which often makes use of dropped caps, graphics in line with text, and other special effects. The "At Least" option ensures a minimum height (point size) for text but allows text to expand to accommodate such special

---

[4] When the first line of text starts slightly above the first line number, the "Don't center 'exact line height' lines" option might be the culprit. Typically, you need to *enable* (check) the option.

effects. Pleadings, however, use "Exactly" line spacing. When the "At Least" option is used in pleadings, it can create havoc. For example, years ago I had to troubleshoot a pleading where the text on most pages started at 1" from the top of the page, but started at 0.8" on a couple of pages. Eventually I determined that the line spacing for one or more paragraphs on the problematic pages had been set using the "At Least" option. As soon as I changed the line spacing to "Exactly," the misbehaving pages adjusted and the text moved down to the 1" point. I've also seen pleadings where someone inadvertently set the "pleading single" line spacing to "At Least" 12 pt, and Word changed the spacing to 13 pt – which caused alignment problems. Changing the line spacing to Exactly 12 pt fixed things.

Because Word can – and will – change the line spacing without warning, I strongly advise against using the "At Least" option.

When All Else Fails

10. Page Setup/Margins and Layout for Headers and Footers.

As a very last resort, you can try fiddling with the top margin of the document and/or the header and footer margins. Note that Word uses negative top and bottom margins in pleadings *by design* in order to prevent the header and footer area from expanding (which could cause the body text and the pleading line numbers to become misaligned). You might be able to adjust the margins, but just be aware that doing so could make matters worse. Make a note of the existing margins before changing them, and be prepared to undo if necessary.

Sometimes adjusting the header margin or, more typically, the footer margin, is helpful. It's easiest to do so from within the header or footer editing screen. Keep in mind that the header and footer margins affect the distance of the header or footer from the edge of the page.

Miscellaneous Tips

Always try the least drastic—and most obvious—solutions first. (Sometimes simply bumping text down a "pleading single-spaced" line will solve the problem.)

Remember that more than one setting might need to be adjusted.

Check the options in the Paragraph dialog (both tabs) early in the process. It's possible there's an easy fix (for instance, "Before" and/or "After" spacing might be the culprit).

Never assume that fixing the formatting of one paragraph will fix the formatting of the other paragraphs in the document—or that selecting the entire document and then changing the paragraph formatting options will succeed. Word can be quirky, and sometimes you have to go back in and change the formatting of individual paragraphs. If necessary, check a few paragraphs at random to see if your new settings have, in fact, taken effect.

Using Line Breaks (Soft Returns)
to Fix Formatting in Pleadings

Even in a pleading that is formatted well – where the "pleading double spacing" matches the line spacing of the pleading line numbers and the "pleading single spacing" is half that figure – there can be problems getting the text to align properly in certain situations. One common issue has to do with making the transition from headings and indented "block" quotes, which often use "pleading single spacing," to regular body text, which ordinarily uses "pleading double spacing."

Typically, when a "pleading single spaced" heading or block quote takes up *an even number of lines*[1] (whether 2 lines or 22 lines), pressing the Enter key after typing the text of the heading or block quote puts the cursor between the line numbers, as shown in the screenshot below. (In my sample pleading, the line numbers and the body text style are configured to use Exactly 24 pt line spacing; the heading styles and the block quote style use Exactly 12 pt line spacing with Exactly 12 pt of "After" spacing.)

18	In addition, frivolous lawsuits are prohibited by Code of Civil Procedure §10101(b),
19	which states:
20	"Frivolous lawsuits are a no-no. Don't even think about bringing one, or we'll throw the books at you. Heavy ones, too!"
21	Furthermore, the moving papers reflect that plaintiffs' counsel has only the vaguest notion
22	of how to write a pleading, which suggests that he never took a basic "Law and Motion" class.
23	

Many people attempt to resolve this problem by fiddling with the line spacing of the following paragraph – which usually creates additional problems (and a great deal of frustration). However, if the formatting of the pleading is otherwise correct, there's a fairly simple solution:

Position the cursor at the end of the heading or block quote, and then press **Shift Enter** instead of Enter. Pressing Shift Enter inserts a **Line Break** (sometimes called a Soft Return), which extends the "pleading single spaced" paragraph by one line – rather than creating a new paragraph. That additional line bumps any existing text down so that it is aligned with a line number. (If you haven't typed any text after the heading or block quote, press the Enter key after pressing Shift Enter, and the cursor will move down to a numbered line.)

The next screenshot shows the same text after I inserted a Line Break at the end of the block quote. I turned on "Show / Hide" before taking the screenshot so that you can see the graphic representation of the Line Break; it looks like a broken arrow pointing backwards.

---

[1] You won't experience the problem if your "pleading single spaced" headings and block quotes take up an odd number of lines.

462

18	In addition, frivolous lawsuits are prohibited by Code of Civil Procedure §10101(b),
19	which states:¶
20	"Frivolous lawsuits are a no-no. Don't even think about bringing one, or we'll throw the books at you. Heavy ones, too!"↵
21	¶
22	Furthermore, the moving papers reflect that plaintiffs' counsel has only the vaguest notion
23	of how to write a pleading, which suggests that he never took a basic "Law and Motion" class.¶

As you can see, the Line Break extended the block quote by one line, thereby bumping the next paragraph down to line 22. This solution is much simpler and more elegant than trying to tweak the line spacing of the following text or any of the other kludges that people normally attempt.

Of course, the odds of its success (no pun intended) depend on the pleading being formatted properly in other respects.

Working With Tables

Columnar tables have many uses in the legal field. They are commonly used to set up case captions and signature blocks in pleadings, as well as for exhibit lists and lengthy service lists and for formatting Separate Statements.

Most people use tables rather than columns for formatting legal documents because the only type of columns available in Word is newspaper-style ("snaking") columns – where text typed at the bottom of a page wraps to the next column on the same page, rather than continuing within the same column on the next page – and many legal documents require parallel columns. Fortunately, tables are easy to use in Word (and actually more intuitive than WordPerfect's column feature).

In this section, I'll review the basics and also offer helpful tips for formatting and troubleshooting tables.

Inserting a Table

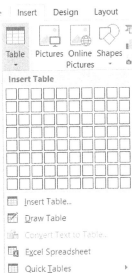

There are a few different ways to insert a table. First, position your cursor where you want the table to go, and then navigate to the **Insert tab** and click the **Table drop-down** (toward the left side). The options are:

- An **"Insert Table" interactive graphic**;
- **Insert Table…**;
- **Draw Table**;
- **Excel Spreadsheet**; and
- **Quick Tables**.

The first option, which is my favorite method, involves moving the mouse pointer over the table graphic to designate how many rows and columns you want to use, then left-clicking to insert the table.

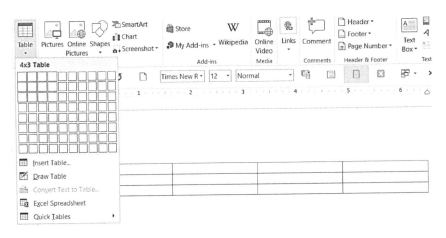

464

The second option, **Insert Table**, opens a small dialog box where you can set the number of rows and columns (by typing the numbers manually or clicking the "spinner" arrows). Clicking "**OK**" inserts the table.

Note that if you use this method, you have the option of configuring a fixed column width (by default, Word automatically determines the column width based on the number of columns you select). "**Autofit to contents**" inserts a small table with columns that expand as you add text (i.e., the columns adjust to fit the contents); "**Autofit to window**" inserts a table that stretches across the entire document (i.e., the table width fits the document window).

The "**Draw Table**" option converts the mouse pointer into a pencil so that you can draw a single-celled table and then drag the mouse pointer (pencil) to add rows and columns where you want them. It works, but is labor-intensive and time-consuming method.

The "**Excel Spreadsheet**" command is a nifty option that inserts an actual Excel spreadsheet into your Word document (as an OLE object[1]). While your cursor is within the spreadsheet, you have access to the entire Excel Ribbon – in other words, you have full Excel functionality within your Word document. Click anywhere outside the spreadsheet to display the Word Ribbon; double-click within the spreadsheet to activate it again. This option is particularly useful for tables that require advanced mathematical functions and/or formulas.

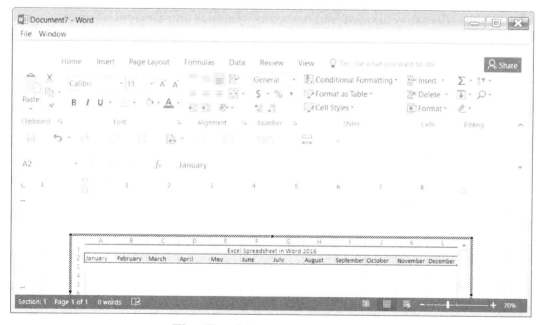

The "Excel Spreadsheet" Option

---

[1] "OLE" stands for Object Linking and Embedding.

The "**Quick Tables**" option offers a gallery of built-in table styles, from calendars to "matrix" tables (rows with alternating shading), tabular lists, and tables with rows set up as "subheads." Scroll down past the calendars to see the other choices. Note that when you insert a Quick Table, it includes the sample text shown in the image, but you can delete it.

If you like the idea of using a pre-formatted table but the Quick Tables don't suit your needs, you can insert a blank table using one of the other methods and then apply one of the available layouts from the **Table Styles gallery** (drop-down) on the **Design** portion of the **Table Tools** tab.

The Table Tools Tab

When you click within a table, a contextual **Table Tools tab** appears. Note that the tab disappears when you click outside the table.

The Table Tools tab is divided into two parts: **Layout** and **Design**. (For convenience, I'll call them the Layout tab and the Design tab.) The Layout tab consists of commands primarily used for changing the table *structure* – adding or deleting rows and/or columns, creating a header row, merging cells, and so forth. It also includes commands for aligning and sorting text. The Design tab consists of commands primarily used to change the *appearance* of the table – e.g., adding borders and/or shading.

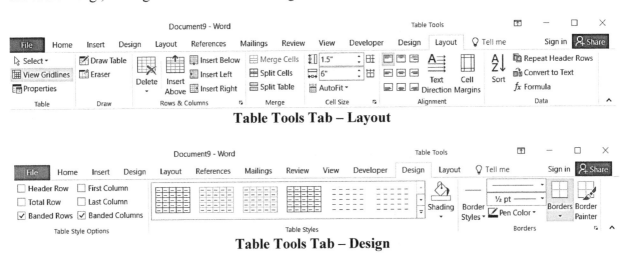

The Layout Tab

The Layout tab contains the most essential commands for working with tables. This section reviews some of those commands and provides various tips for formatting tables. Then I'll take a look at a few of the options on the Design tab.

Adding Rows and Columns

When you click either "**Insert Above**" or "**Insert Below**," Word will add a single row above or below the row your cursor is in. When you click either "**Insert Left**" or "**Insert Right**," Word will add a single column to the left or right of the column your cursor is in.

There are other ways to add a single row or column:

- Right-click within the table and choose the appropriate option; or

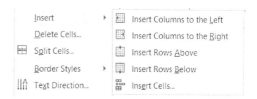

- Click the plus sign on the bar that appears when you position your mouse between rows and columns (see the screenshots below).

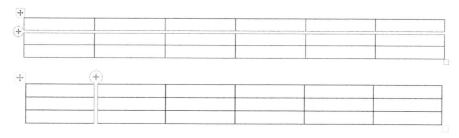

Also, you can add one or more rows by placing the cursor in the bottom right cell of the table and pressing the **Tab key** (keep pressing Tab to add more than one row).[2]

What if you want to insert more than one additional row or column? You can do one of the following:

- Simply press the appropriate "**Insert**" button repeatedly; or

- After inserting one row or column, press **F4** or **Ctrl Y**, the keyboard shortcuts for Repeat Previous Action, or click the "**Redo**" button in the Quick Access Toolbar, as many times as necessary; or

---

[2] This method works in WordPerfect, too.

- **Select multiple rows or columns** within your table (the same number that you want to add, if possible), and then click the appropriate "**Insert**" button in the Ribbon or on the right-click menu.

Deleting Rows and Columns

Position your cursor within the row or column you want to delete or, to delete multiple rows or columns, select the rows or columns.[3] Then do one of the following:

- Click the "**Delete**" drop-down, then click the appropriate option.

- Right-click, then choose "**Delete Cells…**" and choose "**Delete entire row**" or "**Delete entire column**," as appropriate. (All of the selected rows or columns will be deleted.)

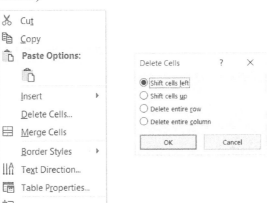

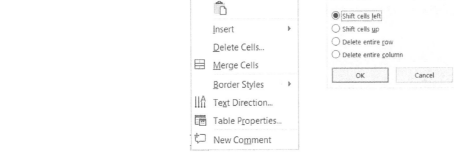

- Right-click within the selected rows or columns, then choose one of the options from the "**Delete**" drop-down in the **Mini Toolbar**.

Deleting the Entire Table

To delete an entire table, do one of the following:

- Click somewhere within the table, then click the "**Delete**" drop-down on the tab and choose "**Delete table**"; or

- Select the table by clicking the **plus sign** at the top left side of the table (or by clicking the Select icon at the left side of the tab and choosing "Select Table"), and then right-click and choose "**Delete table**."

---

[3] When deleting multiple rows, you can just select the rows within a single column (you don't have to extend the selection across the whole table). Likewise, when deleting multiple columns, you can just select the columns within a single row. As long as you choose the "Delete entire row" or "Delete entire column" option, Word will, in fact, delete entire rows or columns.

Selecting Parts of the Table

As mentioned previously, there is a Select drop-down in the Layout portion of the Table Tools tab. From this drop-down, you can select the entire table or the cell, column, or row your cursor is in so that you can apply formatting.

There are other ways to select these table components.

To select a **cell**, do any of the following:

- Position the mouse pointer toward the bottom left side of the cell (move it slightly if necessary) until it turns into a black arrow, then click to select the cell.

- Press and hold the **Shift** key and tap the **right arrow key** (→).

- Triple-click within the cell.

To select a **column**, do any of the following:

- Position the mouse pointer above the column and slowly move it down until it turns into a black arrow, then click to select the column.

- With your cursor in the first cell of the column, press **Alt Shift Page Down** (or, if you are using a laptop, **Pg Dn**).

To select a **row**, do any of the following:

- Position the mouse pointer at the left side of the row (outside the table) and, when it turns into a white arrow, click to select the row.

- With your cursor in the first cell within the row, press **Alt Shift End**.

To select a **table**, do any of the following:

- Click the plus sign at the top left side.

- Press **Alt 5** (i.e., the number 5 on the Numeric Keypad) if Num Lock is *off*; press Alt Shift 5 if Num Lock is *on*.[4]

---

[4] If you are working on a laptop, press **Alt Fn 5** (where "Fn" is "Function" and the "5" is not the one on the row of numbers at the top, but the one in a different color somewhere within the keyboard – if the option is available).

469

Merging or Splitting Cells or Splitting the Table

Other options on the Layout tab involve merging or splitting cells to accommodate text or change the layout of a form. Also, you might want to split a single table into two separate tables.

To merge cells, start by selecting the cells – the Merge Cells command will be grayed out until you do – and then click the "**Merge Cells**" icon or right-click and choose "**Merge Cells**."

To split a cell, click within the cell or select multiple cells (that are adjacent horizontally or vertically) and click the "**Split Cells**" icon or right-click and choose "**Split Cells**." Type a number or click the "spinner" arrows to choose the number of columns or rows you want, then click "**OK**."

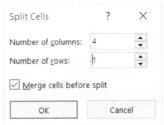

Note that the options available to you (the number of columns or rows into which you can split a cell) might be limited because of the way that surrounding cells are formatted.

To split a table, position the cursor in the row that you want to become the first row of the second table and click the "**Split Table**" icon or press **Ctrl Shift Enter**. (To re-join the table later on, turn on **Show / Hide** and delete the paragraph mark between the two tables.)

Header Rows

If you have added column headings to a table that spans multiple pages and you want those headings to appear on every page, you can designate the first row of the table as a header row. Click anywhere in the first row, and then click the "**Repeat Header Rows**" icon at the right side of the **Layout tab** (in the **Data group**).[5]

---

[5] Alternatively, click the "**Properties**" icon at the left side of the **Layout tab**, and when the **Table Properties dialog** opens, click the **Row tab** and check the "**Repeat as header row at the top of each page**" box.

TROUBLESHOOTING TIP: Sometimes even though you have designated the first row as a header row, no header row appears on subsequent pages. To fix this issue, click the **Properties icon** at the left side of the **Layout tab**, then navigate to the "**Text wrapping**" section of the **Table Properties dialog** (on the Table tab, which should appear at the forefront) and click the box labeled "**None**." (In the screenshot, "Around" is selected, which is the source of the problem.) Click "OK," then take a look at the table. The header row should display on every page, as expected.

CAUTION: There is a **Header Row** option at the left side of the **Table Tools Design tab** (in the **Table Style Options group**). By default, it is checked (enabled).

This feature has nothing to do with creating repetitive content at the top of each page of a table. Rather, it affects the *appearance* of tables that are formatted with alternating shaded rows (it determines whether the first row of the table is shaded). Remember that the commands on the Design tab are primarily used to change the look of a table. (More about the Design tab shortly.)

Adjusting the Column Widths

There are a few different ways to set the width of the columns in your table. One way is by dragging the **column margin markers** on the ruler until the columns are formatted to your liking. (The column margin markers appear when your cursor is within a table cell.)

Column Margin Markers

Or you can move the mouse pointer over a table margin and, when the pointer turns into a double-headed arrow, click and drag the margin to the left or right.   (See the screenshot below.)

Both of those methods work best for people who are highly skilled at using the mouse. Even so, they can be tricky because sometimes the outer margins move when you're adjusting an inner margin. That can cause the table to shrink or expand – and sometimes it expands so far that it's difficult to grab the column margins to resize it. For help with that issue, see the troubleshooting tip below.

TROUBLESHOOTING TIP: Once in a while, when you drag the column markers the table expands so far that you can't grab the column margins to shrink it. The solution is to open the **Table Properties dialog** (click the **Properties icon** at the left side of the **Layout tab**), click the "**Center**" **alignment icon** to center the table horizontally, and set the table width to **6.5"** (or any size you want that is within the page margins). Make sure that the "**Preferred width**" box is checked, then click "**OK**." That should snap the entire table back to the horizontal center of the document.

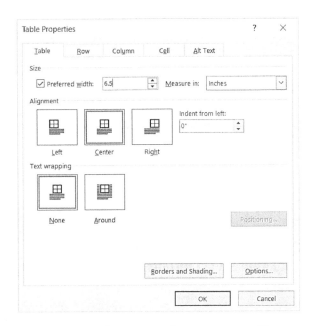

If you still need to change the column margins, use one of the methods described below.

Thankfully for those of us who are not terribly dexterous, there are a few ways to adjust the column margins that don't involve dragging and dropping.

One method is to click within the table, then click in the **Table Column Width** box toward the middle of the **Layout tab** (in the **Cell Size group**) and set the width of each column manually, either by typing a number in the box or by clicking the "spinner" arrows. In the screenshot at right, the Table Column Width box is set to 2".

CAUTION / TIP: If you select part of a column before using this method, only that part of the column will be resized! If that happens, click the **Undo button** on the Quick Access Toolbar (or press **Ctrl Z**) and then click in the first cell of the column and start over.

This same issue can arise if you select multiple columns – but don't select all the way to the bottom – and then click the "**Distribute Columns**" **button** in the **Cell Size dialog** (to the right of the Column Width box) to equalize the width of the columns. Be sure to select the entire columns, from top to bottom, before clicking the button.

If you do select more than one entire column and then **right-click**, a "**Distribute Columns Evenly**" option will be available on the right-click menu.[6] This option is *not* available if you don't select the columns from top to bottom.

Another way to set column widths is to open the **Table Properties dialog box** by clicking the dialog launcher in the **Cell Size group** or by clicking the "**Properties**" icon at the left side of the tab, then clicking the **Column** tab (if it isn't already at the forefront) and setting the column width from there. You can type a number in the "**Preferred width**" box or use the "spinner" arrows.

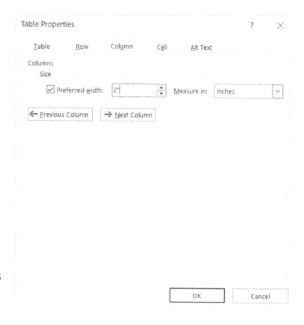

The "**Previous Column**" and "**Next Column**" buttons make it easy to set the widths of all of the other columns at the same time.[7]

Note that you can choose to set the column widths using different units of measurement – either inches or percentage of the table – from the "**Measure in**" drop-down.

TROUBLESHOOTING TIP: If one or more of the columns expands as you type (instead of automatically wrapping the text to the next line within the column margins you set), open the **Table Properties dialog**. Navigate to the lower right-hand corner of the **Table tab** and click the "**Options**" button. When the **Table Options dialog** opens, click to *uncheck* "**Automatically resize to fit contents**." (This hard-to-find option, which means "Automatically resize *the columns* to fit content," actually belongs on the Column tab of the dialog box, in my opinion.)

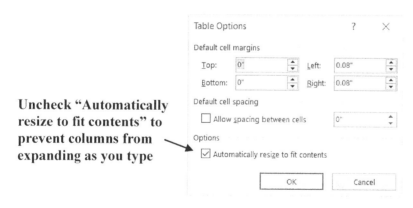

Uncheck "Automatically resize to fit contents" to prevent columns from expanding as you type

---

[6] A "Distribute Rows Evenly" option will be available, as well (but only if you select entire columns from top to bottom). Oddly enough, this option works even if you don't select entire rows.

[7] If you lose track of which column your cursor is in, click "Next Column" or "Previous" column and note which column becomes highlighted.

473

Row Height

The row height is determined by a setting on the Row tab within the Table Properties dialog. See the screenshots below.

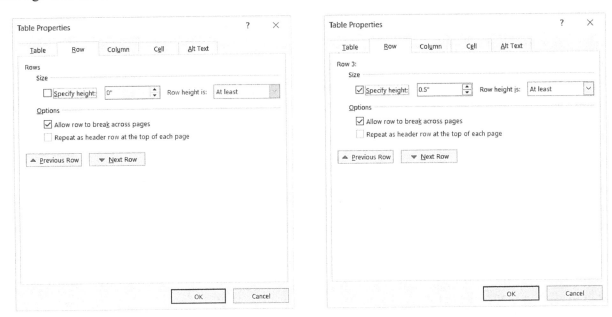

The screenshot at left shows the defaults for the **Row tab** of the **Table Properties dialog** (there is no row height specified – i.e., the "**Specify height**" box is unchecked). The screenshot at right shows the "Specify height" box checked (enabled) and the row height set to "At least" .5".

When you set the row height, the setting affects the row your cursor is in or multiple rows that you have selected. To set a consistent row height for the entire table, select the table beforehand (using any of the methods described on page 469).

CAUTION / TROUBLESHOOTING TIP: Be sure to that the "**Row height is**" **drop-down** is set to "**At least**," *not* "Exactly." Otherwise, your rows will not expand vertically as you add text, and as a result you won't be able to see all of the text that you've typed.

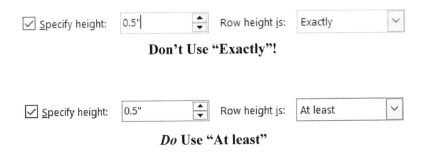

Don't Use "Exactly"!

***Do* Use "At least"**

474

Allowing or Not Allowing Rows to Break Across Pages

By default, Word allows rows to split across pages.[8] However, you can change this setting. Start with your cursor in a specific row or, better yet – because rows expand vertically as text is added, and the current bottom row could get bumped to the next page – select the entire table and then click the **Properties icon** on the Layout tab. When the **Table Properties dialog opens**, click the **Row tab**, and uncheck the "**Allow row to break across pages**" box.

Setting the Table Alignment and Size

As mentioned previously, you can set the table alignment and size from within the Table Properties dialog. (Note that for some reason, the default alignment is Left.) Click the **Properties icon** on the Layout tab (or **right-click** within the table and then click "**Table Properties**"), and change the alignment to **Center** if you prefer. Before closing the dialog, make sure that the table width is set to your liking, click to enable the "**Preferred width**" **box**, then click "**OK**" to save your changes.

The Design Tab

All of the commands on the Design tab affect the table appearance, as opposed to the table structure or the formatting of the table contents. Fully two thirds of the tab is devoted to the built-in gallery of table styles, which most people in the legal profession aren't likely to use. The other third of the tab is devoted to applying and formatting borders and shading (fill).

The Table Styles Gallery

Should you want to apply a pre-set format, just click the Table Styles drop-down. The "plain table" styles appear at the top, and so-called "grid tables" appear in a larger area below. Be sure to scroll to view all of the available table styles. Note that like most galleries in Word, this one affords a "live preview" – in other words, when you hover over one of the table styles, you can see what it would look like in the table in your document. You might have to drag the gallery up and sideways by the "handle" (three dots) in the lower right corner of the drop-down.

You can use the options at the bottom to modify an existing style, clear (remove) a style that you have applied, or create a new table style.

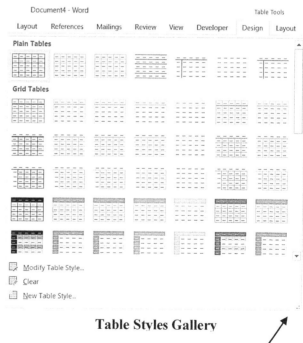

Table Styles Gallery

Handle" for dragging up / sideways

---

[8] WordPerfect's default setting, by contrast, prevents rows from splitting across pages.

475

Table Borders and Gridlines

When you first insert a table in Word, the table ordinarily appears with borders around each cell. These borders print with the document. If you want to remove some or all of the borders – for instance, if you are creating a pleading caption or inserting a signature block in a pleading, you can do so from the Borders drop-down on the Design tab or from within the Borders and Shading dialog, among other methods.

To remove table borders from the Borders drop-down, click within a single table cell, select multiple cells, or select the entire table (depending on which borders you want to remove). Then click to bring the Design tab to the forefront and do one of the following:

1. Click the **Borders drop-down** at the right side of the tab and choose **No Border** (to strip out all of the borders from the single cell, the selected cells, or the entire table).

Or you can use the Borders and Shading dialog:

1. Click the Borders drop-down and click **Borders and Shading…**

2. When the Borders and Shading dialog opens, look at the "**Apply to:**" **drop-down** at the lower right-hand side of the dialog before proceeding. Whichever option is displayed – the choices are "**Table**," "**Cell**," and "**Paragraph**" – is what your settings will affect. To remove borders from the entire table, make sure that "Apply to:" is set to "Table" and then click the "**None**" icon at the top left column in the dialog.

3. When you have finished, click "**OK**" to save your settings and close the dialog.

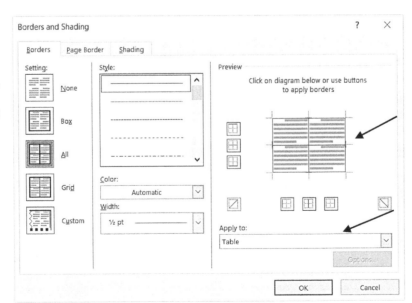

476

Note that there is an identical Borders and Shading drop-down in the **Paragraph group** on the **Home tab**. (See the bottom right button in the screenshot at right.) Although it can be used to apply paragraph borders to plain text, it provides exactly the same options as the drop-down in the Table Tools Design tab.

When you remove the table borders, you may or may not see pale dotted outlines around the cells. These outlines, called "**gridlines**," are non-printing borders that can help you navigate within the table. To toggle the gridlines on or off, navigate to the **Table Tools Layout tab**, then click the "**View Gridlines**" icon at the left side of the tab. (Like other options in the Ribbon, the View Gridlines icon is shaded when it is on / enabled; the shading disappears when it is off / disabled.)

Table (Partial) Showing Gridlines

Gridlines can be turned on or off, as well, from the **Borders drop-down**. The second command from the bottom is **View Gridlines**.

Keep in mind that gridlines do not print. If you want table borders to print, use one of the methods outlined earlier in this section to apply the missing table borders.

CAUTION! There is a "Gridlines" command on the **View tab** that has ***absolutely nothing to do with Table Gridlines***. Rather, it turns on hidden ***drawing gridlines***, a feature that most users never will need. If your documents suddenly appear superimposed on a rather dizzying background consisting of a fine grid, navigate to the **View tab** and uncheck the "**Gridlines**" **box** in the Show group (toward the left side of the tab).

Drawing Gridlines

Practical Applications: Signature Blocks and Pleading Captions

One very common use of tables in legal documents is for signature blocks in pleadings. A two-column table is handy if you need the date at left and the signature block at right, but you can use a single-celled table and position it about halfway across (around the 3" or 3.25") In the example shown below, I inserted a two column table. To indent the name and "Attorneys for" portion below the signature line, I selected the paragraphs, then opened the Paragraph dialog and set the left indent at .25".

DATED: January 11, 2016	VIVALDI, HAYDEN & BACH LLP
	By:_____
	VIVIAN VIVALDI
	Attorneys for Defendant

Note that with the "pleading single" line spacing set at Exactly 12 pt (the pleading line numbers are set at Exactly 24 pt), the dangling portion of the letter "y" and the underline do not display on screen. However, this issue (especially common in pleadings for federal courts, where the required font size is 14 points but the "pleading single" lines typically are set to Exactly 12 pt, affects *the on-screen display only*. In other words, the printed text should look fine.

Another option that can be useful in certain circumstances is to insert a single-celled table and remove all borders except for the one at the top. In the example shown below, I inserted the table first, dragged it over to approximately 3.2", removed all the borders (by clicking "**None**" on the **Borders drop-down** at the right side of the **Table Tools Design tab**), and then added the top border back in (also from the **Borders drop-down**). I could have selectively removed the left, top, and bottom border by clicking those borders in the **Preview** at the right side of the **Borders and Shading dialog**, as well. (Clicking within the Preview removes borders if they have been applied or adds borders if they haven't been applied already.)

You can use this method to create a pleading footer, as well, although I prefer to insert the page number code, then press Enter and create a horizontal line by typing three hyphens and pressing the Enter key (the pressing Enter again to create a blank line for the document title).[9]

---

[9] Or you can insert the page number code, press the Enter key, then click immediately to the right of the page number code and insert a bottom paragraph border from the Borders icon in the Paragraph group on the Home tab.

Incidentally, another way to open the Borders and Shading dialog is by clicking the dialog launcher at the right side of the Borders group in the Design tab.

If you are setting up a pleading caption and you want to add a horizontal line at the bottom and a vertical line at the right side of the parties box, just click in that cell and apply a Bottom and Right border from the Borders drop-down or from the Borders and Shading dialog. (If you use the dialog, make sure that "Apply to:" is set to "Cell" rather than "Table.")

Some Additional Tips About Tables

The following are a few issues that my clients commonly experience. I present them here in no particular order.

Moving Around Within a Table / Adding a "Hard" Tab

As you've probably noticed, pressing the **Tab key** when your cursor is in a table doesn't move the cursor to the next tab stop, as it does when you are working with text outside a table. Instead, it moves the cursor to the next cell (column). (Pressing **Shift Tab** moves the cursor to the previous column.) To tab over within a cell, press **Ctrl Tab** rather than **Tab**.[10] Doing so inserts a "hard" tab. (By default, tab stops are set every .5", but you can add tab stops simply by clicking on the Ruler where you want the additional tab stops to go.)

Watch Out for "Typing Replaces Selected Text"

A configuration option in Word called "**Typing replaces selected text**," which is enabled by default, selects (highlights) text when you press Tab to move to the next column and, when you press any key (except the cursor movement keys), overwrites the existing text.

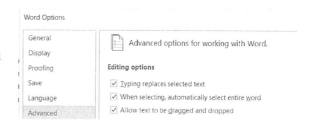

If you accidentally delete text, immediately press **Ctrl Z** or click the **Undo button** on the Quick Access Toolbar. To turn off the "Typing Replaces Selected Text" option, click the **File tab**, **Options**, **Advanced**, **Editing options**, and uncheck the box to the left of that option. Be sure to click "**OK**" at the bottom right side of the Word Options dialog to save your changes.

Bumping a Table Down From the Top of a Page

Sometimes people insert a table at the top of the page, type text within a table, and then decide to put some sort of text above the table – only to find that they can't bump the table down.

A very easy fix for this problem is to position your cursor at the very left side of the very first cell in the table (within the table!), then press the **left arrow key** (←) on your keyboard. It

---

[10] Of course, you can set a left or first-line indent from within the Paragraph dialog instead of using the Tab key.

might not look as though anything happened, but the cursor actually moves outside (and above) the table. Now press the Enter key. Problem solved!

Auto-Numbering Within a Column

Numbering Button

To add automatic numbers to a column, select the column, then click the **Numbering button** in the **Paragraph group** on the **Home tab**.

You can, in fact, add automatic numbers to more than one column and have the numbers start at 1 in each column (as in a Separate Statement of Disputed and Undisputed Material Facts).

To change the indents of the numbers, right-click anywhere within the first number and choose "**Adjust List Indents**." When the **Adjust List Indents dialog** opens, you can change the number position (choosing 0" puts the numbers at the very left side of the column). If you like, you can remove the tab character that, by default, follows the numbers and replace it with "Nothing."

When you have finished formatting the numbers, click "**OK**" to save your changes.

To choose a different number style, click the drop-down arrow to the right of the **Numbering button** and choose an option from the **Numbering Library**.

Sorting Within a Table

In some respects, sorting data within a table is even easier than sorting plain text, because the table columns serve as natural separators for the various "fields" – bits of information such as Prefix, First Name, Last Name, Street Address, City, State, and ZIP Code. If you are creating a table from scratch – whether a service list or a holiday card list – using individual columns for the fields is a good idea. It makes sorting by field extremely easy.

Prefix	First Name	Last Name	Address	City	State	ZIP
Mr.	Bart	Smith	312 N. Spring Street	Los Angeles	CA	90012
Ms.	Shayla	Wong	300 E. Walnut Avenue	Pasadena	CA	91101
Mr.	Mark P.	Andersen	14400 Erwin Street	Van Nuys	CA	91401
Mr.	Efraim	Martinez	111 N. Hill Street	Los Angeles	CA	90012
Dr.	Julie	Stein	1725 Main Street	Santa Monica	CA	90401
Ms.	Anna Louise	Smith	9355 Burton Way	Beverly Hills	CA	90210

Sample Table With Columns for Each "Field"

Start by placing your cursor with the table. The context-sensitive Table Tools tab appears. At the right side of the Layout portion of the tab, there is a Sort icon. Click it to begin the sort.

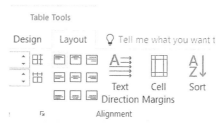

When you perform a table sort, the Sort dialog defaults to sorting by **column**, as opposed to by paragraph. If your table has a header row with names for the columns, the "Sort by" drop down shows a column name rather than a column number. (See the screenshots below; the one on the right shows column names.)

As with paragraph sorts, you can sort text, numbers, or dates.

Sort by Column Number   **Sort by Column Name**

481

Also note that in a table sort, you can exclude the first (header) row from the sort – or indicate that there is no header row, in which case all rows in the table should be included in the sort.[1] (Most of the time, Word senses whether your table does or doesn't have a header row, and makes the choice automatically.)

Start by choosing your primary sort criterion – the column you want to sort first – from the "**Sort by**" drop-down. If your table has a header row with named columns, like my sample, the drop-down displays the column names. If not, it displays the column numbers. In my example, I want to sort by last name and then by first name (because there are two people in my list with the last name "Smith"), so I'll start by choosing "Last Name."

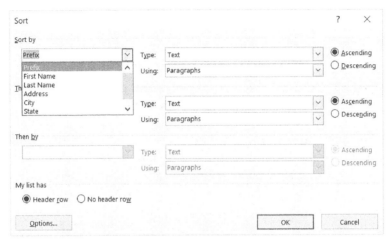

Choose a Primary Column to Sort

Next, navigate to the "Then by" drop-down and choose your secondary sort criterion – your "sort within a sort," so to speak. Again, in my example I'll choose "First Name."

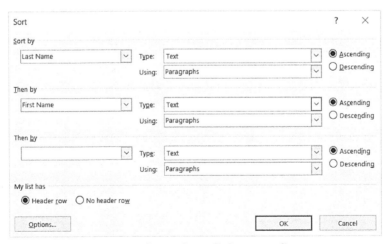

Choose a Secondary Column to Sort

---

[1] In this situation, "header row" means simply a first row with column names. You might or might not have applied the "Header Row" attribute, which causes the first row to repeat at the top of every page if your table is longer than one page.

By default, the sort order is "**Ascending**," which for an alphabetical sort will be in order from A to Z; for a numeric sort will be from lowest / smallest (e.g., 1) to highest / biggest (e.g., 10); and for a date sort will be from oldest to most recent. If you prefer, click the "Descending" radio button at the top right side of the Sort dialog to sort in the reverse order (Z to A; 10 to 1; or most recent to oldest).

Finally, click "**OK**" to perform the sort.

Prefix	First Name	Last Name	Address	City	State	ZIP
Mr.	Mark P.	Andersen	14400 Erwin Street	Van Nuys	CA	91401
Mr.	Efraim	Martinez	111 N. Hill Street	Los Angeles	CA	90012
Ms.	Anna Louise	Smith	9355 Burton Way	Beverly Hills	CA	90210
Mr.	Bart	Smith	312 N. Spring Street	Los Angeles	CA	90012
Dr.	Julie	Stein	1725 Main Street	Santa Monica	CA	90401
Ms.	Shayla	Wong	300 E. Walnut Avenue	Pasadena	CA	91101

Sort Results: Last Name, Then First Name (Ascending Order)

To demonstrate another option, I sorted the same table by ZIP Code (no secondary criterion). I left the sort order at the default setting, "Ascending." Again, keep in mind that "Ascending" puts numbers in order from lowest / smallest number (1) to highest / biggest number (10).

Prefix	First Name	Last Name	Address	City	State	ZIP
Mr.	Efraim	Martinez	111 N. Hill Street	Los Angeles	CA	90012
Mr.	Bart	Smith	312 N. Spring Street	Los Angeles	CA	90012
Ms.	Anna Louise	Smith	9355 Burton Way	Beverly Hills	CA	90210
Dr.	Julie	Stein	1725 Main Street	Santa Monica	CA	90401
Ms.	Shayla	Wong	300 E. Walnut Avenue	Pasadena	CA	91101
Mr.	Mark P.	Andersen	14400 Erwin Street	Van Nuys	CA	91401

Sort Results: ZIP (Ascending Order)

As another example, I've added a column for Court Date and will perform a sort on that column in Descending order (newest to oldest). Screenshots follow. Incidentally, to sort by date, make sure that you use the same date format for all of the dates (e.g., slashes or hyphens).

Prefix	First Name	Last Name	Court Date	Address	City	State	ZIP
Mr.	Efraim	Martinez	12/14/2015	111 N. Hill Street	Los Angeles	CA	90012
Mr.	Bart	Smith	9/22/2015	312 N. Spring Street	Los Angeles	CA	90012
Ms.	Anna Louise	Smith	11/3/2015	9355 Burton Way	Beverly Hills	CA	90210
Dr.	Julie	Stein	1/27/2016	1725 Main Street	Santa Monica	CA	90401
Ms.	Shayla	Wong	2/18/2016	300 E. Walnut Avenue	Pasadena	CA	91101
Mr.	Mark P.	Andersen	10/12/2015	14400 Erwin Street	Van Nuys	CA	91401

Before Sorting

My Sort Criteria

Prefix	First Name	Last Name	Court Date	Address	City	State	ZIP
Ms.	Shayla	Wong	2/18/2016	300 E. Walnut Avenue	Pasadena	CA	91101
Dr.	Julie	Stein	1/27/2016	1725 Main Street	Santa Monica	CA	90401
Mr.	Efraim	Martinez	12/14/2015	111 N. Hill Street	Los Angeles	CA	90012
Ms.	Anna Louise	Smith	11/3/2015	9355 Burton Way	Beverly Hills	CA	90210
Mr.	Mark P.	Andersen	10/12/2015	14400 Erwin Street	Van Nuys	CA	91401
Mr.	Bart	Smith	9/22/2015	312 N. Spring Street	Los Angeles	CA	90012

Sort Results: Court Date (Descending Order)

If there are empty rows anywhere in your table and you perform a sort without selecting only the rows that contain information, the empty rows will rise to the top of your sorted table.

Prefix	First Name	Last Name	Address	City	State	ZIP
Mr.	Bart	Smith	312 N. Spring Street	Los Angeles	CA	90012
Ms.	Shayla	Wong	300 E. Walnut Avenue	Pasadena	CA	91101
Mr.	Mark P.	Andersen	14400 Erwin Street	Van Nuys	CA	91401
Mr.	Efraim	Martinez	111 N. Hill Street	Los Angeles	CA	90012
Dr.	Julie	Stein	1725 Main Street	Santa Monica	CA	90401
Ms.	Anna Louise	Smith	9355 Burton Way	Beverly Hills	CA	90210

Table With Empty Rows – Before Sorting

Prefix	First Name	Last Name	Address	City	State	ZIP
Mr.	Mark P.	Andersen	14400 Erwin Street	Van Nuys	CA	91401
Mr.	Efraim	Martinez	111 N. Hill Street	Los Angeles	CA	90012
Ms.	Anna Louise	Smith	9355 Burton Way	Beverly Hills	CA	90210
Mr.	Bart	Smith	312 N. Spring Street	Los Angeles	CA	90012
Dr.	Julie	Stein	1725 Main Street	Santa Monica	CA	90401
Ms.	Shayla	Wong	300 E. Walnut Avenue	Pasadena	CA	91101

Table With Empty Rows – After Sorting (Last Name, Then First Name)

Of course, you can delete the empty rows, but if you need the additional rows so that you can insert more information later on, just select / highlight only the rows that contain information – but not the header row – before performing your sort.

Prefix	First Name	Last Name	Address	City	State	ZIP
Mr.	Bart	Smith	312 N. Spring Street	Los Angeles	CA	90012
Ms.	Shayla	Wong	300 E. Walnut Avenue	Pasadena	CA	91101
Mr.	Mark P.	Andersen	14400 Erwin Street	Van Nuys	CA	91401
Mr.	Efraim	Martinez	111 N. Hill Street	Los Angeles	CA	90012
Dr.	Julie	Stein	1725 Main Street	Santa Monica	CA	90401
Ms.	Anna Louise	Smith	9355 Burton Way	Beverly Hills	CA	90210

Selected Rows Prior to the Sort

Note that in this situation, the Sort dialog reverts to using column numbers rather than column names (because the header row isn't included in your selection, so Word can't sense that the table has a header row).

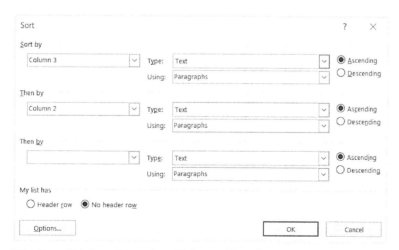

The Sort Dialog (Showing Column Numbers, No Header Row)

485

Because you selected only the rows containing the information prior to carrying out the sort, the empty rows remain at the bottom of the sorted table.

Prefix	First Name	Last Name	Address	City	State	ZIP
Mr.	Mark P.	Andersen	14400 Erwin Street	Van Nuys	CA	91401
Mr.	Efraim	Martinez	111 N. Hill Street	Los Angeles	CA	90012
Ms.	Anna Louise	Smith	9355 Burton Way	Beverly Hills	CA	90210
Mr.	Bart	Smith	312 N. Spring Street	Los Angeles	CA	90012
Dr.	Julie	Stein	1725 Main Street	Santa Monica	CA	90401
Ms.	Shayla	Wong	300 E. Walnut Avenue	Pasadena	CA	91101

Sort Results: Last Name, Then First Name (Empty Rows Remain at the Bottom)

Using the Numbering Button

You can use the **Numbering button** in the **Paragraph group** on the **Home tab** to insert an automatic paragraph number before you have typed any text or, if you like, you can select some existing text and then click the Numbering button. Either way, when you click the button, Word begins a ***single-level list*** using Arabic numerals followed by a period.

By default, the program inserts a number code that is indented .25" from the left margin and formats the paragraph as a hanging indent (indented an additional .25"), like so:

1. This is the default formatting of numbered lists inserted with the Numbering button in Word. Word indents the first line of the paragraph (i.e., starts the number) at .25" and indents the remainder of the paragraph at .5".

Changing the Indents

Because this format isn't suitable for most legal documents – whether pleadings or contracts – you will need to do some tweaking. Fortunately, it is relatively easy to adjust the indentation and other formatting of numbered paragraphs in Word.

After inserting an automatic paragraph number, do the following:

1. **Right-click** within the number.[1]

2. When the pop-up menu appears, click **Adjust List Indents**. The **Adjust List Indents dialog** will open.

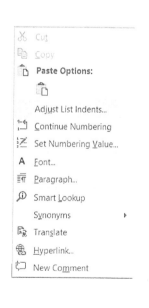

---

[1] The cursor should be within the number when you right-click, if possible. If it isn't, right-clicking might produce a different pop-up menu. Note that the number normally turns gray when you click it, one indication that it is, in fact, a code (i.e., an automatic number). Another indication that it is an automatic number, not plain text, is that the Numbering button appears highlighted when you click anywhere within the paragraph.

487

3. Set the **Number position** and **Text indent** to your liking. (The Number position is like the "First-Line Indent" setting and the Text indent is like the "Left Indent" setting in the Paragraph dialog.) For example, if you want the number to be indented half an inch and the text to wrap to the left margin, set the **Number position** at .5" and the **Text indent** at 0 (zero). (Both settings are relative to the left margin of the document.)

   You don't need to check the "Add tab stop at" box.

4. Click "**OK**" (or press **Enter**) to confirm your settings.

5. When you type some text and press the **Enter key**, Word begins another numbered paragraph with the same indents you set in Step 3.[2]

6. To add white space between paragraphs, **select all of the numbered paragraphs** and then open the Paragraph dialog (by right-clicking, then choosing "Paragraph" or using any other method you prefer) and add some "Spacing After" – keeping in mind that 12 pt is approximately one line.[3]

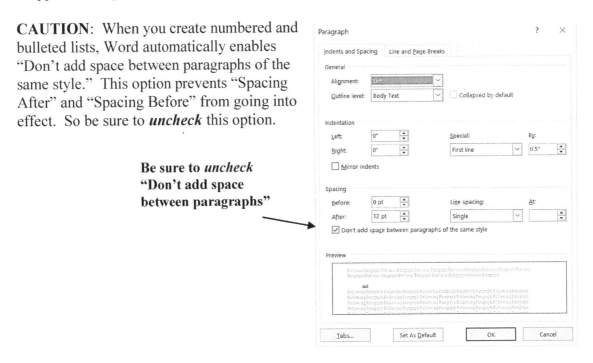

CAUTION: When you create numbered and bulleted lists, Word automatically enables "Don't add space between paragraphs of the same style." This option prevents "Spacing After" and "Spacing Before" from going into effect. So be sure to *uncheck* this option.

Be sure to *uncheck* "Don't add space between paragraphs"

7. Make any other changes you want (such as adjusting the line spacing) and then click "**OK**" to save your settings.

---

[2] The settings in the "Adjust List Indents" dialog affect the entire list – whether you change the indents before or after typing additional numbered paragraphs.

[3] You ***must*** select all of the numbered paragraphs first. Otherwise, Word will add the "Spacing After" only to the paragraph your cursor is in.

To Stop Numbering:

To stop numbering, do one of the following:

- Press the **Enter key** twice;

- Click the **Numbering button** again to toggle it off in the paragraph that your cursor is in; or

- Press **Backspace**.

CAUTION: Clicking the Numbering button a second time removes the number, but typically reformats the paragraph as a hanging indent that starts .25" from the left margin. Pressing Backspace also removes the number, but leaves the cursor in the same position where it was before you pressed Backspace, and keeps the paragraph formatted as a hanging indent.

If you want to add some un-numbered text below one of the numbered paragraphs, press **Shift Enter** (to insert a line break / soft return). Press **Enter** again to insert the next number in sequence.

ANOTHER CAUTION: This method isn't always appropriate. A line break doesn't create a new paragraph; rather, it extends the current paragraph by one line. That is why it has the same formatting as the rest of the paragraph, except for the automatic number. For more about line breaks, see the Sidebar on page 462.

To Resume or Restart Numbering

If you want to turn on numbering again – either to continue the numbering where you left off or to start a new number sequence – click the **Numbering button** again.

NOTE: If your cursor is *below* the first set of numbered paragraphs (the ones with the modified indents), clicking the Numbering button usually starts a new numbered paragraph that uses the same modified formatting. However, if your cursor is *above* the first set of numbered paragraphs, clicking the Numbering button sometimes starts a new numbered paragraph that uses the default formatting – i.e., with the number positioned .25 " from the left margin and the paragraph set as a hanging indent.

The new paragraph usually continues the numbering in sequence, but sometimes it restarts with the number 1 (i.e., Word assumes you are creating a new list). Depending on your preference, you can right-click within the number and choose either "**Restart at 1**" or "**Continue Numbering**." (The "Restart at 1" option is available on the menu only if you haven't already restarted at 1.) If you change your mind, just right-click again and choose the other option.

If necessary, you can right-click and choose "**Set Numbering Value**," which opens the "**Set Numbering Value" dialog**. (See the next screenshot.) Note the handy option labeled "**Advance value (skip numbers)**" under "**Continue from previous list**."

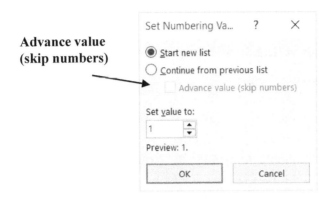

Choosing a Different Number Format

As mentioned at the beginning of this section, the Numbering button by default inserts Arabic numerals followed by a period. To choose a different number format, click the drop-down arrow to the immediate right of the button and click to apply one of the formats in the **Numbering Library**.[4] (See the screenshot at right.) The format will be applied to the entire list.

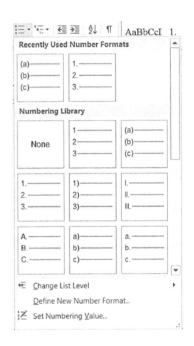

Defining a New Number Format

If you don't see a format that you like, or you want to modify any of the formats, click "**Define New Number Format**."

When the "**Define New Number Format**" **dialog** opens, start by choosing a number style from the "**Number style**" **drop-down** (again, be sure to scroll to see all of the available styles). (See the screenshots on the next page.)

After you choose a number style, you can add or remove punctuation, change the font, and/or change the number alignment (left, centered, or right).

Number alignment can be confusing. As discussed on page 505, the options in the "Alignment" box determine whether numbers align on the first digit, even when the numbers increment above 9 (and above 99, and so on), or whether they align on any punctuation that follows (typically a period/decimal point or an end parenthesis). With Left alignment, the numbers align on the first digit (both "9" and "10" start at the same position); with Right alignment, the numbers align on the decimal point ("10" starts to the left of "9").

---

[4] Be sure to scroll down to see all of the available formats.

490

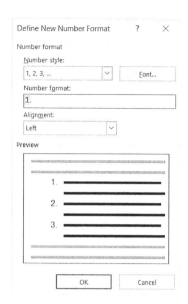 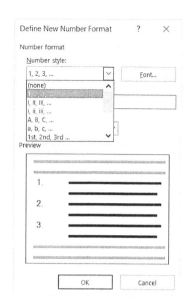

To remove or add punctuation, click within the "Number format" box and make any changes you desire. Just be careful not to delete the gray number code. If you do, close the dialog box and start over. (To avoid deleting the code, either click to the left of the code or use the left arrow key to move the cursor to the left of the code.)

Copying and Pasting Formatting

After you have formatted one or more numbered paragraphs the way you want, you can copy that formatting – automatic numbering and all – to one or more other paragraphs with the Format Painter. In fact, this method is extremely useful for applying numbering to existing text. It's also useful for fixing the indents, line spacing, and Spacing After of "misbehaving" paragraphs.

Start by clicking somewhere within a paragraph that is formatted to your liking. Then double-click the **Format Painter icon** (the paintbrush) at the left side of the **Home tab**, and after the mouse pointer turns into a small paintbrush, either left-click in each paragraph that you want to reformat or, if the paragraphs are adjacent, drag the mouse pointer / paintbrush through the paragraphs. When you have finished, be sure to click the Format Painter icon again to turn the feature off.

If you prefer, you can use keyboard shortcuts to copy and paste formatting, as explained in the section about the Format Painter starting on page 143. Again, start by clicking within the "model" paragraph, and then press **Ctrl Shift C**. To copy the formatting to one or more additional paragraphs, either click in a single paragraph or select multiple paragraphs and then press **Ctrl Shift V**.

Note that copying the paragraph mark at the end of a "model" paragraph and pasting it at the end of other paragraphs works essentially the same way (because each paragraph mark contains the formatting instructions for the preceding paragraph). In order to display the paragraphs marks, turn on **Show / Hide** before you begin, either by clicking the **Paragraph icon** in the **Paragraph group** on the **Home tab** or by using the keyboard shortcut **Ctrl Shift ***.

491

Changing the Paragraph "Level"

Although technically the Numbering button creates single-level lists, you can in fact create a quasi-multilevel list with this feature.[5] You can turn any numbered paragraph except the first one into a subparagraph by doing any of the following:

- Pressing the **Tab** key;[6]

- Clicking the "**Increase Indent**" button in the Paragraph group on the Home tab; or

- Pressing **Alt Shift →** (the right arrow key).

You can "promote" any subparagraph to a higher level by doing any of the following:

- Pressing **Shift Tab**;

- Clicking the "**Decrease Indent" button** in the Paragraph group on the Home tab; or

- Pressing **Alt Shift ←** (the left arrow key).

You must format each paragraph level – though not each paragraph within a particular level – individually. Just right-click within the first subparagraph at a particular level (e.g., the first second-level paragraph), choose "**Adjust List Indents**," and change the indentation of the number and the text from within the "Adjust List Indents" dialog. That will set the indentation for every second-level paragraph you create. You will need to do the same for the first third-level paragraph, as well – and so on.

---

[5] Some trainers discourage using the feature in this way. They recommend using actual multilevel lists (or, preferably, multilevel list styles) instead. However, for certain situations where you need only a few subparagraphs, I think it is acceptable to create one or two additional paragraph levels.

[6] If the Tab key doesn't work to "demote" the paragraph level, it's because of a setting in the Word Options. Click the **File tab**, **Options**, **Proofing**, then click the "**AutoCorrect...**" **button**. When the **AutoCorrect Options dialog** opens, click the **AutoFormat As You Type tab**, then click to put a checkmark in the box labeled "**Set left and first indent with tabs and backspaces**." Click "**OK**" to save your changes and close the Word Options.

Saving Your Modified List Format

Typically, when you modify an automatic numbered list, the modified format is available only in the document in which you made the changes. However, you can turn the formatted list into a style and make it available in future documents based on the underlying template.[7]

In order to save this modified list style so that you can use it in future documents, click within the first paragraph. Then click the "**More**" drop-down at the right side of the **Style Gallery** on the **Home tab** and choose "**Create a Style**."

When the condensed **Create New Style from Formatting** box appears, type a short descriptive **name** for the style (such as Numbered Paragraphs).

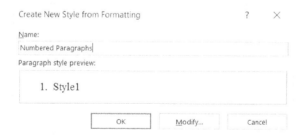

Before OK-ing out of the dialog, click the "**Modify…**" **button**, which will open the full **Create New Style from Formatting dialog**. That will enable you to save the new numbering style to the underlying template so that it is available in future documents.

---

[7] If you don't have rights to modify the underlying template, you can save the list style in a document and then copy and paste the formatting to other documents.

493

When the expanded **Create New Style from Formatting dialog** appears, make any further changes you want.

NOTE: Since numbered paragraphs typically are followed by other numbered paragraphs, you probably don't need to change the setting for the "**Style for following paragraph**" option (by default, Word assigns the same style to follow any given style).

Next, navigate to the bottom of the dialog and click to mark the "**New documents based on this template**" radio button. **NOTE**: This is a critical step!

Click **OK** to save your changes.

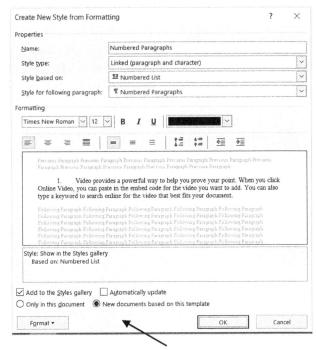

Add to the Styles gallery

New documents based on this template

Because the "Add to the Styles gallery" box is checked by default, the new list style should now appear in the Style Gallery (as well as in the Styles pane).

QUICK TIP: Using the ListNum Field

A lesser-known form of automatic numbering in Word, the ListNum field is extremely useful when you need to insert numbers in sequence *within* a paragraph, using numbering such as (i), (ii), (iii) or (a), (b), (c).

There are three numbering schemes available with the ListNum field, each of which has nine levels: **LegalDefault**, **NumberDefault**, and **OutlineDefault**. (The "**(none)**" option inserts a number code based on the NumberDefault scheme.) The schemes work pretty much the way their names suggest. The Legal scheme uses typical legal-style numbering (1., 1.1., 1.1.1., etc.); the Outline scheme uses a variant of typical outline numbering; and the Number scheme uses a mix of number and letter formats, per the chart below.

	Level 1	Level 2	Level 3	Level 4	Level 5	Level 6	Level 7	Level 8	Level 9
Legal	1.	1.1.	1.1.1.	1.1.1.1.	1.1.1.1.1.	etc.	etc.	etc.	etc.
Outline	I.	A.	1.	a)	(1)	(a)	(i)	(a)	(i)
Number	1)	a)	i)	(1)	(a)	(i)	1.	a.	i

Although ListNum codes are used mainly to insert subparagraph numbers like (a) and (b) within the text of a numbered paragraph, you can use them in other contexts. And, as with SEQ codes, you can have more than one type of ListNum code in the same document – and even within the same paragraph.

To insert a ListNum field code, click the **Insert tab**, **Quick Parts**, **Field** or press **Alt I, F**, then press the letter "L" a few times until the cursor lands on the **ListNum field**. (Alternatively, change the **Category drop-down** at the top left side to **Numbering**, then choose **ListNum**.)

Field Dialog – ListNum Field

Click to select one of the three numbering schemes. If you like, you can check one or both of the checkboxes at the right side of the dialog in order to choose a particular level in the list and/or a default start-at value (the default level and start-at value are both 1).[1]

After you have inserted a ListNum code into your document, you can change the paragraph level or the start value by doing any of the following:

- Select the code and then click the **Increase Indent** or **Decrease Indent** button in the **Paragraph group** on the **Home tab**.

  (Note that this action changes only the *level* of the code; the *indentation* of the code actually remains the same.)

- Select the code and then press the key combination **Alt Shift →** (right arrow key) or **Alt Shift ←** (left arrow key).

- Right-click within a number and choose "**Increase Indent**" or "**Decrease Indent**."

If you like tinkering under the hood, so to speak, you can edit the code directly. Press **Alt F9** to display the code itself (rather than the code results) and then insert the appropriate "switch" (a sort of keyboard shortcut that refines the command). The switch for the list level is \l (a backslash followed by the letter "L"- presumably for "level"), so to change to a level 4 paragraph you would type "\l 4" (without quotation marks) within the French braces after the LISTNUM designation.[2] It does not seem to make a difference whether you press the Spacebar between the "l" and the "4" (as I did).

{ LISTNUM NumberDefault \l 4}

Press **Alt F9** again to toggle back to the code results. A level 4 code using the NumberDefault style produces the number (1).

The switch for the start-at value is \s (a backslash followed by the letter "S" – presumably for "starting value"), so to change to start at 6, you would insert "\s 6" (without quotation marks).

{ LISTNUM NumberDefault \l 4 \s 6

Press Alt F9 again to toggle back to the code results. These particular switches produce the following number: (6).

---

[1] Also, the keyboard shortcut **Alt Ctrl L** inserts a ListNum field (in the NumberDefault style).

[2] Of course, this method assumes that you know which level produces which type of number or letter. But now that you have access to the handy chart on the previous page, you do!

496

Multilevel Lists

When you want to insert an outline into your document, use legal-style numbering in a contract, or create pleading heading styles that incorporate automatic numbers and letters, a multilevel list is the most appropriate tool. You can apply one of the built-in lists or create a new list style and add it to the gallery so that it is available for use in future documents.

Applying a Multilevel List

Microsoft has provided several "built-in" multilevel lists, each with nine different number levels. To apply one of the built-in lists, click the **Multilevel List drop-down** in the **Paragraph group** in the **Home tab**. (It's the button to the right of the Numbering button – the one that is highlighted in the screenshot below.)

Multilevel List Drop-Down

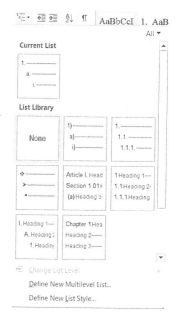

The Multilevel List gallery is divided into several parts: The top shows you the **current list** in effect in your document (if any); the second section shows you a "**library**" of built-in lists; the third sections shows you the **existing list styles** (if any); and, if you have applied one or more lists within in your document, the bottom section shows you those lists. (Click the "All" drop-down at the top right to filter the display and show only one section of the gallery.)

If one of the available lists suits your needs, you can either apply it to existing text or simply start numbering. To apply it to existing text, select the text first. In either case, clicking the icon for the list you want to use applies a first-level number.

To change the number level of any paragraph, you can use any of the methods described in the section about single-level lists.

- Press the **Tab** key to "demote" the level or press **Shift Tab** to "promote" the level (except that you can't "promote" the very first paragraph);[1]

---

[1] If Tab and Shift Tab don't work, it's because of a setting in the Word Options. Click the **File tab, Options, Proofing**, then click the "**AutoCorrect...**" button. When the **AutoCorrect Options dialog** opens, click the **AutoFormat As You Type tab**, then click to put a checkmark in the box labeled "**Set left and first indent with tabs and backspaces.**" Click "**OK**" to save your changes and close the Word Options.

- Click the "**Increase Indent**" button (to "demote") or the "**Decrease Indent**" button (to "promote") in the Paragraph group on the Home tab; or

- Press **Alt Shift** → (right arrow – to "demote") **Alt Shift** ← (left arrow – to "promote").

To change the indentation of any level, **right-click** within the paragraph number, then choose "**Adjust List Indents**" from the pop-up menu. Instead of the small "Adjust List Indents" dialog that appears when you choose this command from within a single-level list, the "**Define new Multilevel list**" **dialog** will open.[2]

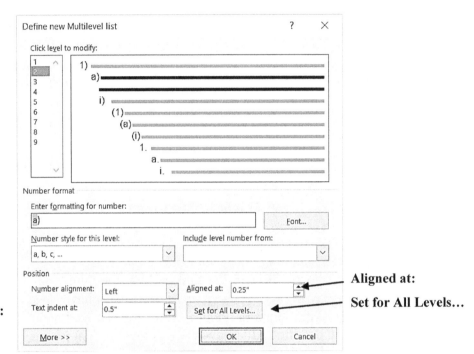

Define New Multilevel List Dialog

Any changes you make from within this dialog will be applied to the level that is highlighted in the narrow box at the top left (below "**Click level to modify**"). To modify settings for a different paragraph level, start by clicking the number for that level. When you do so, the number will be highlighted, as will the sample in the preview area to the right. The settings will be applied to every paragraph at that level in your document.

To change the position of the paragraph number (i.e., the first line of the paragraph), modify the "**Aligned at:**" figure, either by typing a number in the box or by clicking the "spinner" arrows.

---

[2] Although it opens in its "collapsed" form, there is no need to expand it by clicking "More" if all you want to do is change the indentation – or the number / letter format.

To change the indentation of the rest of the paragraph (similar to setting the Left indent for the entire paragraph), modify the "**Text indent at:**" figure, either by typing a number in the box or by clicking the "spinner" arrows.

If you want the indentation of the other paragraph levels to increment by a certain figure – for instance, you'd like every level to be indented .5" more than the previous level – click the "**Set for All Levels…**" button. When the "Set for All Levels" dialog opens, you can modify the "**Additional indent for each level**" setting by typing a number or clicking the "spinner" arrows.

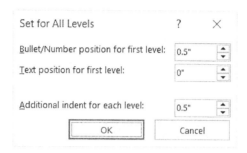

NOTE: This dialog box does not let you change the left indent of the paragraph for every level. That is, if you want the text of every level to wrap to the left margin – a "Text position" of zero (0") – you can't set it from the "Set for All Levels" dialog. You need to change that setting level by level from within the "**Define new Multilevel list**" dialog.

If you like, you can change the number format from within the "**Define new…**" dialog. Start by clicking the paragraph level number at the top left side, and then (1) click the "**Number style for this level**" **drop-down** and choose the basic number format you want; and (2) tweak the formatting by adding punctuation or text within the "**Enter formatting for number**" box.

To change the punctuation, delete any existing punctuation and type your own (e.g., delete an end parenthesis and substitute a period). You can use the left arrow key to move the cursor to the left of the number code. To add text before the number, such as the word "Section," simply type the text plus a space.

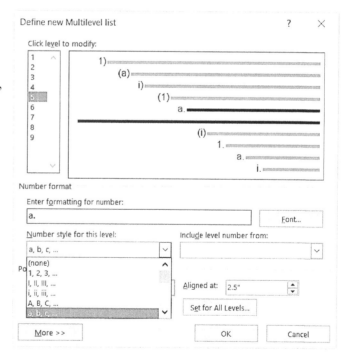

CAUTION: The number or letter in the "Enter formatting for number" box is a code – it turns gray when you click it (not shown in the screenshot). If you accidentally delete the code, you'll lose the paragraph numbering. You can reinsert a number code in the box by choosing a style from the "Number style for this level" drop-down – or just close the dialog and start over.

When you have finished modifying the indents and numbering for the different levels, click "**OK**."

After applying your list within a document, if you need to change the line spacing or the Spacing After, you can do one of two things:

- Click within the first paragraph and change the settings from within the Paragraph dialog (your modified settings will be copied to successive paragraphs when you press the Enter key); or

- Select the entire list, then open the Paragraph dialog and make any changes you desire.

Note that your modified multilevel list is embedded in the current document. It will not be available in future documents *unless* you base a new document on a copy of the document that contains the list. If you do so, you will see your customized list at the top of the gallery under "Current List" and also at the bottom under "Lists in Current Documents." If there are two similar lists shown in the "Lists in Current Documents" section, hold your mouse over each of them to see the number formatting for every level in the list (right-most screenshot below).

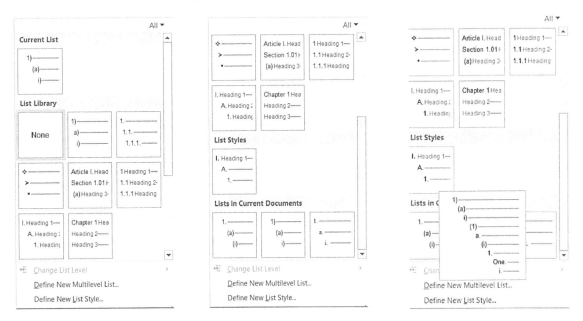

Another way to make the custom list available in future documents is to right-click the list in the gallery, then click "**Save in List Library**."[3]

You also have the option of creating a brand-new list or list style and linking it to heading styles, then saving it within a specific template.

---

[3] Based on my tests, it appears that doing so makes the list available in all new documents, regardless of the underlying template. To be certain, I would need to do more testing.

Creating a New List or List Style

There are a few points to keep in mind before you create a new multilevel list:

1. The "**Define New Multilevel List**" option is somewhat more limited than the "**Define New List Style**" option. You can't name your list and then modify it by right-clicking from within the Multilevel List gallery. For that reason, I prefer to create list *styles* and save them for use in future documents.

2. List styles are especially powerful when you **link each level of the list to a heading style**. You can set up a list without linking to heading styles, but if you want to create custom heading styles that include automatic numbers or letters, this is the method to use.

3. If you are going to create a list style and link it to heading styles, it helps to define the list style first (i.e., the *numbering*), then modify the formatting of the heading styles (indents, line spacing, Spacing After, etc.) as necessary.

4. Unlike in prior versions of Word, you will *not* be able to tinker with the numbering in a heading style by right-clicking the heading style, choosing "Modify," then clicking the "Format" button, then clicking "Numbering." Doing so will lead to a dead end – a dialog that contains only single-level lists (see the screenshot at right). When you need to tweak the number formatting for a heading style, you *must* do it *from within the list style itself* (by right-clicking its image in the gallery)!

5. Be sure to **save your new list style to the underlying template**. Otherwise, it will be available only in the current document.

You can use an existing list as a model for your new style, or you can start from scratch.

Either way, you will need to format **each level** of the list style – or, at least, as many of the nine available levels as you are likely to use. For each level, you will select the *type* (style) of number (Arabic, upper-case roman, lowercase roman, letters, etc.), any surrounding *punctuation* (periods or parentheses), how far the *paragraph number* is *indented* from the left margin, how far the *text* is indented from the left margin and whether the *next line* wraps to the margin or is set up as a *hanging indent*, the *font*, and several other attributes. If you like, you can add text (such as the word "Section") before a number code, as well.

Basing a New List Style on an Existing List

To add your new list to an existing template, first open either the template itself or a new document based on the template. Then position your cursor in a blank paragraph, open the Multilevel List gallery, and click one of the built-in lists that uses a number style similar to what you want to use. If you want to customize heading styles and link those styles to your list, be sure to choose a list that already has heading styles associated with it (i.e., one that displays text such as Heading 1, Heading 2, and Heading 3 next to the level numbers).[4] In practice, the association between the numbers and the heading styles sometimes breaks. However, you can link them manually. Instructions follow later in this section.

When you click a list, Word puts a number code for the first number level into your document or template. (For now, just ignore it; you can delete it after you've created the list.)

Next, reopen the Multilevel List gallery and click **Define New List Style…**. The **Define New List Style dialog** will open. (By default, the name in the "Name" box at the top of the dialog is "Style1"; I replaced the generic name with "Pleadings.")

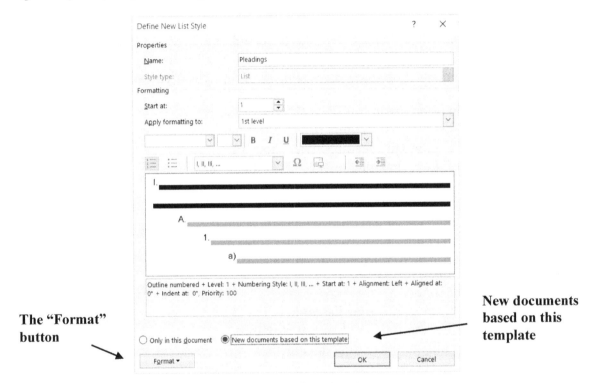

Define New List Style Dialog

At this point, start creating your customized list style. I suggest that you go through this process step by step, formatting all of the levels you plan to use. However, if you do click "**OK**" before you finish customizing the list style, you'll be able to resume later on.

First, type a unique, descriptive name, such as **Outline Numbering** or **Legal Numbering**. This name applies to the entire multilevel list, not to a single level within the list.

Second, click the "**New documents based on the template**" button toward the bottom of the dialog so that the list will be available in future documents based on your template.

---

[4] Thanks to Eva Eilenberg for suggesting this option.

CAUTION: Unless you take this step, your customized list will be saved *only in the document in which you are creating it.* (Technically, you'll be able to save the list as a Style Set after you create it, but it's better to get in the habit of saving new lists to the template as you create them, for a number of reasons.)

Third, don't click "OK" yet. Instead, click "**Format**," then click "**Numbering**." You should see a **Modify Multilevel List dialog** similar to the one in the next screenshot. Don't be concerned if yours differs in some respects from the screenshot.

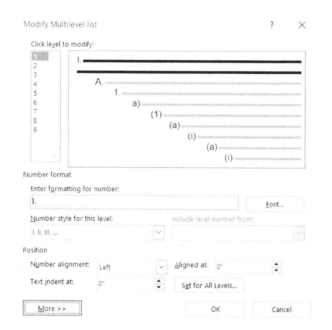

Click "More" to expand the dialog

Modify Multilevel List Dialog

Click the "**More**" **button** in the lower left-hand corner of the dialog. The dialog will expand and provide additional options for setting up the list style.

Take a few minutes to acquaint yourself with the expanded dialog and its options.

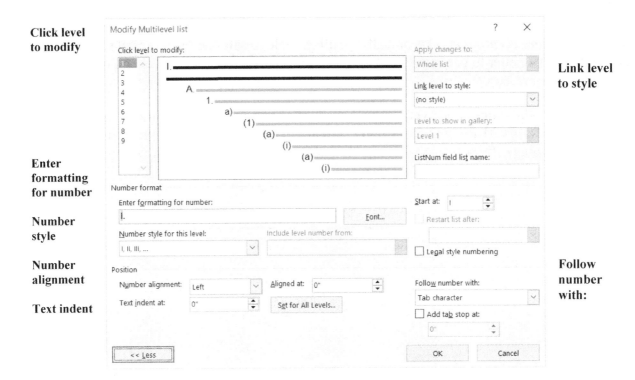

Expanded Modify Multilevel List Dialog

    The "**Click level to modify**" box on the left side of the dialog provides an easy way to modify each level of the list individually. Simply click the level you wish to edit, and the level number becomes highlighted in blue.

TIP: Glance at the blue level indicator from time to time to keep track of which level you're modifying (it's easy to get confused).

    Note the "**Link level to style**" drop-down on the right. When you are creating or modifying heading styles that incorporate automatic numbers or letters, you will use this drop-down to link each list level to a specific heading style. I will walk you through this somewhat complicated process. After setting up a list style and linking each level to a heading style, we'll modify the paragraph and font formatting of the heading styles, as well.

    Underneath the preview windows, you'll see a field labeled "**Enter formatting for number.**" There should be a number in the field, highlighted in gray. The gray portion *is a code* and is based on the "**Number style for this level**" **drop-down** immediately below the field. If you wish to change the type of number or letter for a particular level, use the drop-down. Then, *being careful not to delete the gray number or letter code*, you can edit the characters or text before or after the number or letter.

    For example, there might be an end parenthesis after the gray number code. You could delete the end parenthesis and replace it with a period if you like. Alternatively, you could add an open parenthesis before the number code, or you could delete the end parenthesis and add the word "Chapter" or "Section" plus a space before the number code. It's up to you; just be careful

504

not to delete the code itself. (**TIP**: Click the left arrow key on your keyboard to move the cursor to the left of the code in order to add an open parenthesis, another character, or leading text without deleting the gray code.)

Toward the bottom of the dialog, there are options for setting the number and text positions. The **Number alignment** field is somewhat confusing. Essentially it determines whether numbers align on the first digit, even when the numbers increment above 9, or whether they align on any punctuation that follows (typically a period/decimal point or an end parenthesis). The difference is exemplified by the following series, with the former pair of numbers left aligned and the latter pair right-aligned (aligned on the decimal point):

    9.
    10.

    9.
   10.

Although right alignment seems preferable (especially for lower-case Roman numerals, which can take up a lot of space horizontally), it can result in heading numbers being outside the left margin, so you'll probably want to use left alignment in most situations. Remember that you can modify the list style later on if you decide you prefer to right-align the numbers.

"**Aligned at**" sets the left indent *for the number itself* – i.e., how far over from the left margin the number starts. (This option is the same as the "Number position" option in the "Adjust List Indents" dialog that appears when you right-click a number in a single-level list. It's also the same, essentially, as setting a First-Line Indent within the Paragraph dialog.) For instance, if you are setting up the first level of paragraph numbering in a Complaint, you'll probably use an "Aligned at" setting of .5". However, for a level 1 heading in a pleading, you'll probably use 0" for the "Aligned at" setting (and .5" for a level 2 heading, and so forth). Note that you have the option of setting an indent for all levels at once, which can be very useful if you are creating a list style where each heading level will be indented an additional .5" from the previous level.

By contrast, "***Text indent at***" sets the left indent for every line of text following the number *except* for the first line. (Recall that the first-line indent – the number position – is governed by the "Aligned at" setting.) So, for a for a numbered paragraph in a Complaint, you would set the text indent at 0" – because you want the text of the paragraph to wrap to the left margin. For a level 1 heading, however, you would set the text indent at .5".

Note that Word provides an option to follow the paragraph number with a Tab (the default setting), a space, or nothing (the "nothing" option is useful when you are creating a list that you will link to headings and you want the heading to have a centered number and text centered **below** the number). It also provides an option to add an extra tab stop, which can come in handy in certain situations.

When you start formatting a level other than level 1, you'll see an additional button: "**Restart list after [current level number]**." Ordinarily you will leave this option, which is the default, checked. When it is checked, each *sub-level* starts numbering anew (beginning with "1" or "a" as appropriate), rather than continuing the numbering from the previous level. That is desirable in most circumstances, because otherwise you could end up with a situation where the first sub-level after paragraph 6 should appear as 6.1 but, because the last subparagraph in the previous section was **5.6**, it appears as **6.7** instead.

Once you are familiar with the various options, go ahead and *set up each of the nine levels of the list* (or fewer, if you're absolutely certain you won't use all nine levels). In general, it's a good idea to start with level 1. Just keep track of which level you're modifying by glancing periodically at the highlighted level on the left as you are working.

Checklist for Formatting Each Level of the List Style

For each level, do the following:

✓ Choose a number style from the drop-down.

✓ Format the number (delete and/or add punctuation, such as an open parenthesis, a close parenthesis, and/or a period, and add leading text such as "Section" if you like).

✓ Decide on a number alignment (you can leave it set at Left, which is the default, or experiment with Right or Centered).

✓ Set the "Aligned at" (if you want level 1 to be aligned at the left margin, leave it set to zero; if you want it aligned at the first tab stop, set it to .5"—it's up to you).

✓ Set the "Text indent at" and, if you want all levels indented by the same amount, click the "Set for All Levels…" button (you won't need to do the latter after you create the first level of the list style).

✓ Assuming you want to link the list style with heading styles, click the **Link level to style drop-down** and scroll to **Heading 1**. Click to select it.

This is a critical step. If you are associating the list style with heading styles, make sure that *each list level* is linked to *a corresponding heading style level*, as shown in the screenshot below. Also, note that linking levels and heading styles works best if you start with level 1.[5]

---

[5] Sometimes the links break. If you need to re-set the links, start by positioning your cursor within a level 1 paragraph, even if the level 1 paragraph doesn't need tweaking.

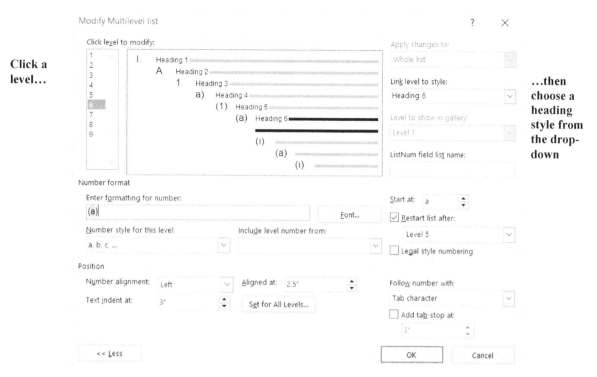

Linking a Heading Style to a Number Level

After you have set up each of the nine levels, click "**OK**," then click "**OK**" again.

If Word inserts a number (or letter) at the cursor position and it appears in a font, font size, and font color you don't want to use (e.g., Calibri Light, 16 points, blue), that is because there is a "Theme" operating in the background that determines the font face and font attributes for all headings – even if you have chosen a default font face, size, and color. (For a review of what Themes are and how they work, see the section starting on page 194.) However, we are going to modify the heading styles in ways that will override the Theme.

Modifying the Heading Styles

The next step, if you are linking the list style to heading styles, is to edit each of the nine heading styles to ensure that the font formatting and the paragraph formatting (indents, line spacing, and so forth) are set up to your liking.[6]

You can edit a heading style from the **Styles Pane** or from the **Style Gallery**. In my example, I'm using the Styles Pane because it's a little easier to display all of the heading styles for editing. To open the Styles Pane, either click the **dialog launcher** in the **Styles group** on the **Home tab** or press **Ctrl Alt Shift S**.

---

[6] If you plan to set up other list styles and associate them with heading styles, you should create additional heading styles for each list and give them unique descriptive names – such as Legal Heading 1 (through Legal Heading 9) or Outline Heading 1 (through Outline Heading 9).

To display all of the heading styles, click the **Options** link at the lower right side of the pane, and when the **Style Pane Options dialog** opens, change the "**Select styles to show**" drop-down to "**All styles**" and change the "**Select how list is sorted**" drop-down to "**Alphabetical.**" Click "**OK**" to save your settings.

Now that all of the heading styles are displayed, **right-click** the Heading 1 style and choose "**Modify.**" When the **Modify Style dialog** opens, immediately click the "**New documents based on this template**" radio button.

Before doing anything else, look at the "**Style for following paragraph**" option toward the top of the dialog. Ordinarily heading styles are set up so they are followed by a body text style (which also usually has been customized). That makes perfect sense, because most people want to add regular text, rather than another heading, after typing a heading. To change the style for the following paragraph, click the drop-down and select the style you want to use.

Next, click the "**Format**" **button** at the bottom left side of the Modify Style dialog and click the **Font button**.

The **Font dialog** opens so that you can choose your preferred font face, font style, font size, and font color.

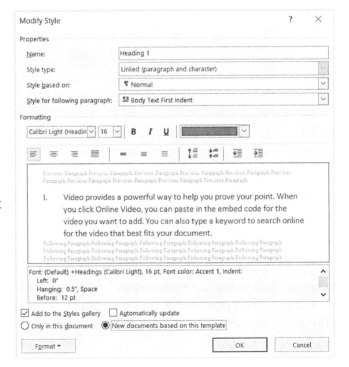

The screenshot at right shows that the current font is **+Headings**, a placeholder for heading styles. Which font actually is applied in lieu of the +Headings placeholder depends upon the theme that is in effect in a given document. The default theme is **Office**, and the Office theme font for headings is Calibri Light. (You can tell which fonts are associated with Microsoft's built-in themes by navigating to the Design tab and clicking the Fonts drop-down. The screenshot immediately below shows a portion of that drop-down, which in turn shows the default heading font and body font for the current theme, "Office.")

Change the settings for the font face, font style, and font size to suit your needs.[7] Before clicking "OK," check to make sure that the font color is set to *black* rather than *Automatic*, since the "Automatic" setting means the color can change unexpectedly according to the theme that is in effect. (To apply black, click one of the black squares, preferably one that displays a pop-up that says "Black, Text 1" when you hold the mouse pointer over it.) Once you've finished, click "**OK**" – but *only once*, because the Heading 1 style needs further customization.

Click the **Format button** again, and this time choose **Paragraph**. When the **Paragraph dialog** opens, check the following settings to make sure they conform to your specifications:

- Indentation
- Special (most heading styles should be formatted as a hanging indent so that if there is more than one line of text, it wraps below the first word in the first line, not all the way to the left margin)
- Before spacing
- After spacing
- Line spacing

---

[7] You also have the option of choosing to apply font formatting such as underlining and all caps to the heading text, although sometimes Word gets confused and continues to apply all caps or other font attributes to the text of the paragraph that follows.

509

The indentation should be fine, assuming you were successful in setting the indents from the **Modify Multilevel List dialog**, but it's a good idea to double-check.

How you set the line spacing depends on whether you are creating styles for a contract or a pleading. If the latter, you will need to use "Exactly" spacing, with your "pleading double spacing" set to match the spacing of the pleading line numbers and your "pleading single spacing" set at half that figure. For more complete discussions of this issue, see pages 128 and 457. For contracts and other types of documents, standard Single and Double spacing should work well.

For my outline-style headings, I have chosen to use Exactly 12 point line spacing with 12 points of "After" spacing (to create white space between the headings and the body text) because I plan to use them in pleadings where the spacing of the line numbers – and hence, the "pleading double spacing" – is set to Exactly 24 points and the "pleading single spacing" is set to Exactly 12 points. (As discussed in the Sidebar about Line Breaks on page 462, you sometimes run into alignment issues when making a transition between "pleading single spacing" and "pleading double spacing," but those issues can be resolved easily by using Line Breaks.)

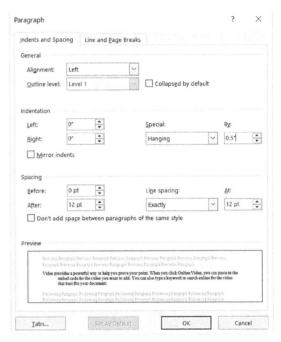

I've also set up my headings to use a hanging indent of half an inch, so that if any heading text wraps to the next line, it will be indented in a way that aligns with the first line of heading text.

Take care to ensure that all of the paragraph formatting options are set the way you want, then click "**OK**." The Paragraph dialog will close, returning you to the Modify Style dialog so that you can finalize the heading style.

Word already has built-in shortcuts for the first three heading level styles (Ctrl Alt 1, Ctrl Alt 2, and Ctrl Alt 3). For the other heading levels, you can create keyboard shortcuts by clicking the **Format button**, and then clicking **Shortcut key…** and, when the **Customize Keyboard dialog** opens, insert your desired keyboard shortcut in the "Press new shortcut key box." (To use Ctrl Alt and a number, press those keys in sequence.) If the key combination isn't already assigned to another feature (as shown in the "Currently assigned to" area at the left side of the dialog), click the "**Assign**" **button**, then click "**Close**."

When you have finished modifying the heading style, click **OK** to save your changes and close the **Modify Style dialog**.

Repeat the above steps for each of the nine paragraph levels.

Double-Checking to Make Sure Everything Works

To double-check to make sure the list style is set up correctly, open the **Multilevel List drop-down** and scroll down to the **List Styles section**. To determine which style is which, hold the mouse pointer over an icon. You should see a pop-up that displays the style name.

Note whether all of the levels are linked to heading styles. (Sometimes even though you have linked all of the list levels to heading styles, the links do not "take," as is the case with my Pleadings list style.) If not, *right*-click the icon for the style, click "**Modify**," and when the **Modify Styles dialog** appears, do the following: (1) click the "**New documents based on this template**" radio button, (2) click **Format**, (3) click **Numbering**, and (4) for each level of the list that isn't associated with a heading style, **link it to the appropriate style**. Be sure to start with the level 1 paragraph (even if it is still linked to a heading style.) When you have finished, click "**OK**" to save your changes and close the dialog.

TIP: Remember that if you need to modify the numbering in a heading style that is associated with a list style, you need to do it by modifying the list style itself, *not* by modifying the heading style. The numbering options available when you modify the heading style are very limited.

Applying Your List Style

After you have created a list style that is linked to heading styles, you can apply it in two different ways: (1) by inserting *the list style* from the Multilevel List gallery; *or* (2) by applying *a heading level style* to text (from either the **Styles Pane** or the **Style Gallery**).

Changing List Levels

As mentioned earlier, there are several ways to change the level of a paragraph:

- Press the **Tab** key to "demote" the level or press **Shift Tab** to "promote" the level (remember that you can't "promote" a first-level number);

- Click the "**Increase Indent**" button (to "demote") or the "**Decrease Indent**" button (to "promote") in the Paragraph group on the Home tab; or

- Press **Alt Shift** → (right arrow – to "demote") **Alt Shift** ← (left arrow – to "promote").

Modifying a Multilevel List: Tips and Caveats

The Right-Click Options

Note that icons in the different sections of the gallery offer different right-click options. Significantly, when you right-click an icon for one of the lists in the **List Styles section,** the resulting context-sensitive menu provides a "**Modify**" option. When you right-click an icon for a list in any other section of the gallery, the menu does *not* provide that option.

Changing the Numeric Formatting

This point is so important—and so confusing to people who are familiar with the way this feature worked in pre-Word 2007 versions of the program—that it bears repeating. In older versions, you could change the numeric formatting of a heading style by modifying the heading style itself. There was a formatting option in the Modify Styles dialog that included so-called outline numbering.

However, the outline numbering option for heading styles was removed, starting with Word 2007. It's somewhat deceptive, because when you right-click a heading style and click "Modify" to open the Modify Style dialog, clicking the "Format" button still produces a "Numbering" command that appears to be active (i.e., it isn't grayed out). But when you click the "Numbering" command, the resulting dialog offers only numbering for a single-level list, which is a non-starter.[8] See the screenshot at right, which shows the "Numbering Library" that appears when you click "Format," then click "Numbering" when modifying a heading style.

The upshot is that if you want to modify the numbering of any of your heading styles, *you must do so via the Multilevel List gallery*. In particular, take the following steps:

1. If you have applied the list in the document on your screen, **navigate to a Level 1 paragraph**—regardless of which level you want to modify—before proceeding. The best way to ensure the integrity of a multilevel list style in Word is to begin the editing process *for any level of the list* from within a Level 1 paragraph. That is true for earlier versions of Word, as well.
If you haven't applied the list in the current document, simply proceed to the next step.

2. **Open the Multilevel List Gallery**, locate the image of the list **in the List Styles section** at the bottom of the gallery, *right*-click it and then click "**Modify**."

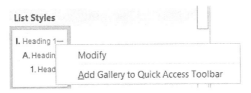

3. Immediately click the "**New documents based on this template**" radio button – something you will need to do every single time you modify the style – so that your modifications will take effect in all new documents based on the underlying template, rather than only in the current document.

---

[8] This option is not appropriate or useful for heading styles because the number level doesn't change when you "promote" or "demote" a heading. Using multilevel list numbering for heading styles is the best – really, the only – way to go.

4. Next, click the **Format** button, click **Numbering**, and when the **Modify Multilevel List dialog** opens, make sure the list level you want to modify is still linked to the heading style. If not, click the level number in the "**Click level to modify**" area at left, then click the "**Link level to style**" drop-down and choose the appropriate heading style for that level. This is a critical step!

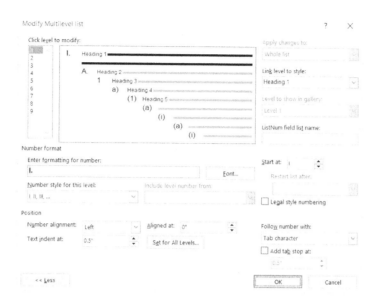

5. After re-linking the heading style, make any adjustments you like to the number style, the number alignment, the aligned-at setting, and/or the text indent setting.

6. To modify other levels, start by clicking the level number in the "**Click level to modify**" area at left, then make any desired changes.

7. When you have finished, click "**OK**" twice to save your changes.

QUICK TIP: Setting Up a "Simple" Multilevel List and Saving It as a Style

This Quick Tip provides somewhat simplified instructions for creating a "simple" multilevel list – that is, one that isn't linked to heading styles – and saving it as a style.

1. Click the **Multilevel List drop-down** in the **Paragraph group** on the **Home tab**.

2. Click the "**Define New List Style…**" command.

3. First, give the list style a **descriptive name**.

4. Before formatting the list style, click the "**New documents based on this template**" **radio button**.

5. Next, click the "**Format**" **button**, and then click "**Numbering.**" Go through level by level, selecting the number and letter types you want to use for each level and inserting any punctuation you like, always being careful not to delete the gray number code.

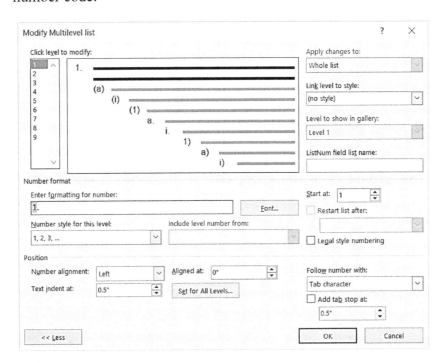

6. Make sure to set the **indents** for each level. You'll probably want each level indented one additional half inch (with a tab half an inch after the letter or number); the easiest method to do so is by clicking the "**Set for All Levels…**" button.

Note that you won't be able to alter the paragraph formatting from this dialog; when you click the "Format" button, you'll notice that the "Paragraph" command is unavailable (grayed out). Rather, you'll have to save the list as a style and then modify the style from either the Style Gallery or the Styles Pane. I will provide instructions momentarily.

7. **OPTIONAL**: Once the list is set up – before you save the list and close the dialog – click the "**Format**" **button**, click "**Shortcut**" **key**, and assign a keyboard shortcut.

8. Finally, be sure to click "**OK**" to save your settings.

<u>Saving the List as a Style</u>

To change the paragraph formatting – for example, to add 12 points of Spacing After to each level of the list – you'll need to save the list as a style. If you haven't done so already, apply the list in a blank document, right-click in or near a paragraph number, and when the **Mini Toolbar** appears, click "**Styles**," and then click "**Create a Style**."

A "**Create New Style from Formatting**" **dialog** will open. Type a **descriptive name** for the style, such as Outline List or Legal List (as appropriate), and then click the "**Modify**" button.

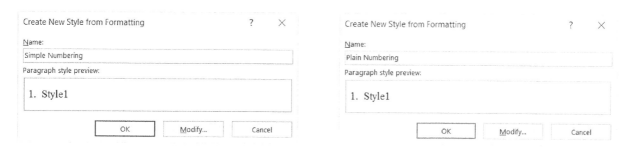

CAUTION: If you click "OK" instead of "Modify," the style will be available only in the current document, not in all future documents.

After you click "**Modify**," an expanded "**Create New Style from Formatting**" **dialog** will open. Immediately click the "**New documents based on this template**" **radio button** at the bottom of the dialog to ensure that the style will be available in all new documents.

515

Then click the "**Format**" **button**, click the "**Paragraph**" **command**, and make any changes you like.

CAUTION: If you add Spacing After, be sure to *uncheck* the "**Don't add space between paragraphs of the same style**" option, which by default is checked (enabled) for numbered and bulleted lists.

When you have finished, click "**OK**" to save the style.

After you save the list as a style, it should appear in the Style Gallery. (It also should be available from the Styles Pane, depending on how the pane is configured – i.e., whether it is set to show all styles.)

If you need to make any further changes to the paragraph formatting, **right-click** the list either in the Style Gallery or in the Styles Pane and click "**Modify**." When the "**Modify Style**" **dialog** appears, click the "**New documents based on this template**" radio button, click the "**Format**" button, click "**Paragraph**," make your changes, and click "**OK**."

QUICK TIP: Sharing Your Custom List Style

To share your custom list style with other members of your organization, apply the list in a blank document and save the document to a shared folder on the network drive. Then ask each user to do the following:

1. Open the document containing the list style. If necessary, click the "**Enable Editing**" button on the Message Bar.

2. With the document on your screen, open the **Styles Pane**. You can either:

    - Click the **dialog launcher** in the lower right-hand corner of the **Styles group** in the **Home tab**; or

    - Press **Ctrl Alt Shift S**.

3. **Locate the style** in the pane. (You'll need to tell everyone the name of the style.)

    - If the style isn't visible in the Styles Pane, click the **Options button** at the lower right-hand side of the pane and, when the dialog opens, (1) make sure "**All styles**" is displayed in the "**Select styles to show**" drop-down and (2) choose "**Alphabetical**" in the "**Select how list is sorted**" drop-down.

    - Optional: Click the "**New documents based on this template**" **button** in order to display all styles in alphabetical order in all new documents.

    - Click "**OK**."

4. Next, click the **Manage Styles button** at the bottom of the Styles Pane. It is the third button from the left (immediately to the left of Options).

Click the **Import/Export button** at the bottom left side of the Manage Styles dialog. The **Organizer** will appear.

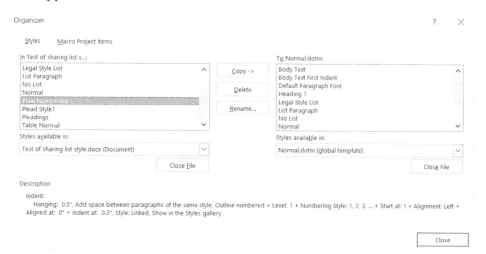

517

- The box at left shows the styles in the current document.

- The box at right shows the styles in your Normal.dotm (your Normal template).

5. **Locate the style** in the box on the left, click to **select it**, then click **Copy** to copy it to your Normal.dotm and click **Close**.

6. Open a new blank document and check to see if the style appears in the **Style Gallery**, which indicates that it is now embedded in your Normal template. If so, click the icon and test to make sure that it works as expected.

7. If you wish to set up a keyboard shortcut to invoke the style, **locate the style in the Styles Pane** and **right-click** it, then click **Modify**.

8. Immediately click the "**New documents based on this template button**" so that the keyboard shortcut will work in all future documents. If you don't click this button, any changes you make to the style will go into effect only in the current document.

9. Click the **Format button** at the lower left-hand side of the Modify Style dialog, then click **Shortcut key**.

10. Position your cursor in the **Press new shortcut key** box, and then press the **key combination** you want to use, such as Alt L (for List). If your key combo has been assigned to another function, you'll see a message to that effect. You can override the assignment or choose a different keyboard shortcut.

11. After you've entered the keystrokes, click the **Assign button**, then click **Close**. Click the "**X**" at the upper right-hand side of the Styles Pane to close it.

12. **NOTE**: When you close Word, the program might prompt you to save changes you have made to the Normal.dotm template. ***Be sure to click OK or Yes to save your changes**, or the modifications you've made – i.e., adding the custom list style to your Normal template – will be lost.*

After they have followed these steps, your co-workers should be able to start using your custom list style. (They can apply the style by pressing the key combination they assigned to the style, if any, *or* by clicking the icon for the style in the Style Gallery on the Home tab, *or* by opening the Styles Pane and clicking the name of the style from there.)

Using the "SEQ" Field for Automatic Numbering in Discovery Headings and Exhibits

The "SEQ" (sequence) field is particularly well-suited for legal documents such as discovery headings and Exhibit letters or numbers because you can insert a number code anywhere within a paragraph – unlike list numbering, which always appears at the beginning of a paragraph. Also, you can create a unique identifier for each type of heading within a document, such as Interrogatories and Interrogatory Responses, and the numbers in each type of heading will increment independently, so that you don't end up with INTERROGATORY NO. 1 followed by RESPONSE TO INTERROGATORY NO. 2.[1]

In this section, you'll learn how to use the SEQ field to set up numbered headings for Interrogatories and Rog Responses. Then I'll explain how to create a Quick Part so that you can insert the headings with just a few keystrokes.

Let's start with the Interrogatories. It's a good idea to create them within an empty paragraph in a pleading that is already formatted with the appropriate line spacing.

1. Begin by typing the heading. For example, for an Interrogatory heading, turn on underlining and bold, as well as CAPS Lock, and type **INTERROGATORY NO.**

2. Press the Spacebar after typing "NO." and then click the **Insert tab**, **Quick Parts**, **Field...** *or* press **Alt I, F** to open the **Field dialog**.

3. When the **Field dialog** opens, scroll down to "Seq" within the **Field Names box** *or* press the "S" key until "Seq" appears. You should also see "SEQ" in the "**Field codes**" box under "**Advanced field properties**" (top right).

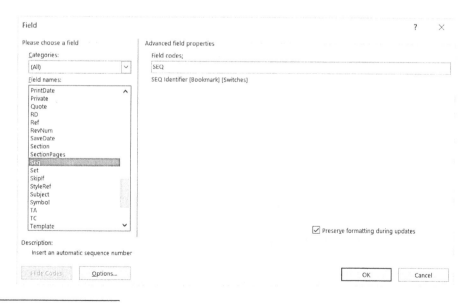

---

[1] In this regard, it's similar to the Counters feature in WordPerfect.

519

4. You're not done yet! The SEQ code requires an "**identifier**." If you click "OK" before typing an identifier, you'll see the following message: "**Error! No sequence specified**."[2]

<u>**INTERROGATORY NO. Error! No sequence specified.**</u>

To avoid that problem, click within the "**Field codes**" box immediately after "SEQ," press the Spacebar once (this is a critical step!), and type a short, unique word such as "Rog" or "Interrogatory" to indicate exactly what this SEQ code does.

<u>**INTERROGATORY NO. { SEQ ROG * MERGEFORMAT }**</u>

The identifier can be up to 40 characters long, but shorter generally is better. Again, you need to create a unique identifier for each type of SEQ code in your document. If your document contains both Interrogatories and Interrogatory Responses, you *must* create one distinctive identifier for the SEQ codes for the Interrogatory headings and another one for the SEQ codes for the Response headings.

5. Click the **Options button** at the bottom left side of the Field dialog to open the **Field Options dialog**.

The "**Formatting**" box on the "**General Switches**" tab of the dialog displays different types of numbering and lettering you can use with SEQ fields. The default is Arabic numerals, which works fine for discovery headings. However, for other number formats, such as for Exhibit letters,[3] **click the appropriate format in the list**, click the **Add to Field button**, then click "**OK**" to add a "switch" for the "ALPHABETIC" letter format to the SEQ code.

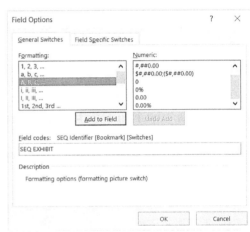

6. After you have typed an identifier, click "**OK**." You should see something like this:

<u>**INTERROGATORY NO. 1**</u>

---

[2] If you accidentally click "OK" before typing an identifier, you can fix the problem without starting over. Press **Alt F9** to display the SEQ code (as shown in Step 7 on the next page), press the Spacebar once, then type an identifier, such as ROG. (**CAUTION**: Be sure to insert a space between the word "SEQ" and your identifier or the code won't work properly.) Press **Alt F9** again to display the results of the code. If you still see an error message, make sure your cursor is somewhere within the error message and press **F9** to update the code.

[3] See the next section, starting on page 525, for more about numbering and cross-references for Exhibits.

7.   If instead you see something like the following, simply press **Alt F9** (the keystroke to toggle between displaying the field codes and displaying the field code results).

<u>**INTERROGATORY NO. { SEQ ROG * MERGEFORMAT }**</u>

8.   Either way, continue to format your heading. As a last step, be sure to turn off bold and underlining so that pressing Enter doesn't carry those font attributes over into the following paragraph.

When you have finished, you can turn the heading-plus-SEQ-code into a "**Quick Part**" (similar to the AutoText feature) so that you can insert it into *any document* with just a couple of keystrokes.[4] Just follow these steps:

1.   Select the heading (*be sure to include the paragraph mark at the end of the heading* so that Word inserts a new blank paragraph underneath the heading when you expand the Quick Part) and then press **Alt F3**. (Alternatively, click the **Insert tab**, **Quick Parts**, **Save Selection to Quick Part Gallery**.)

2.   Next, type an abbreviation for the heading (such as "Rog" or "Interrogatory"), type a description if you like (optional), and click **OK**.

To insert a heading at the cursor position, just type the abbreviation you assigned to it and **press F3** to expand the abbreviation.[5]

NOTE: If you assign a name to your Quick Part that is *at least four characters long* (and if you've used the Alt F3 method, which saves the Quick Part to your Normal template), an AutoComplete prompt will appear after you type the first four characters. To insert / expand the Quick Part after the prompt appears, press **Enter**.

ROGG (Press ENTER to Insert)
ROGG|

IMPORTANT NOTE: SEQ codes are different from most other types of automatic numbering in that *they don't always "update" automatically*. Sometimes they need a little user intervention – an "assist," so to speak. That becomes obvious when you delete or move discovery headings that contain SEQ codes. You'll notice immediately that the numbers don't increment properly. But there's an easy way to update all of the numbers. Simply select the text that includes the numbering, or select the entire document by pressing **Ctrl A**, and then either press **F9** to update the codes or right-click within the selected text and choose "Update Field.") And voilà! All is right with the world again (or at least, with your SEQ codes).

---

[4] By default, user-created Quick Parts are stored in a template called "BuildingBlocks.dotx" unless you use the Alt F3 method to create your entries. See the section that starts on page 377.

[5] You can type the first few letters of the abbreviation and then press F3, as long as the first few letters are unique – that is, none of your other custom Quick Parts starts with those letters.

To create headings for the Rog Responses, repeat the above steps, but be sure to use a different identifier—perhaps something like RogResp.

After you have set up both types of headings using SEQ codes, you'll find that the numbering for the two separate types of headings remains distinct and increments appropriately, even when you alternate Interrogatories and Interrogatory Responses.

Saving the Quick Parts When You Exit Word

As noted in the section about Quick Parts starting on page 377, whenever you create a new Quick Part, a prompt will appear when you exit from Word, asking if you want to save the Building Blocks or other items you created during your work session. ***Be sure to click "Yes," or Word will not save your new Quick Parts.***

Changing the Starting Value

If you need to start numbering with a number value other than 1, you can insert a "restart" switch into the SEQ code.

1. First, press **Alt F9** to display the field codes in your document.

2. Position the cursor in the heading where you want to start renumbering, immediately following the backslash after your identifier (in the screenshot below, "ROG" is the identifier.) Then type the letter "r" (without quotation marks) followed by a space and the number you want to start with. The "r," which is the switch for "restart," can be either lower or upper case.

3. Next, type a space (followed by another backslash, if there isn't one already). So, for example, if you want to start with the number 27, type "r 27 \"

INTERROGATORY NO. { SEQ ROG\R 27 * MERGEFORMAT }:

4. Press **Alt F9** again to display the field code results. If for some reason you get an error message, insert your cursor within the code (or press Ctrl A to select the entire document) and press F9 to update the code(s). The code results should display properly, and the Interrogatory number should be 27.

CAUTION: To ensure that subsequent headings increment properly, ***don't*** copy and paste the heading that contains the "Restart" switch. (If you do, the numbering of all headings will be identical, based on the "restart" number.) Instead, use your new Quick Part to insert the next heading in sequence. If necessary, select the headings and press F9 to update the number codes.

522

Using a SEQ Code for Exhibit Letters or Numbers

To create a SEQ code for Exhibit letters or numbers, type the word "Exhibit" (without quotation marks) and press the Spacebar once. Then do the following:

1. Click the **Insert tab**, **Quick Parts**, **Field…** *or* press **Alt I, F** to open the **Field dialog**.

2. When the **Field dialog** opens, scroll down to "Seq" **within** the **Field Names box** or press the "S" key until "Seq" appears . You should also see "SEQ" in the "**Field codes**" **box** under "**Advanced field properties**" (top right).

3. Click in the "**Field codes**" **box immediately** after "SEQ," press the Spacebar once (this is a critical step!), and type a short, unique identifier such as "EXHIBIT" (again, without quotation marks).

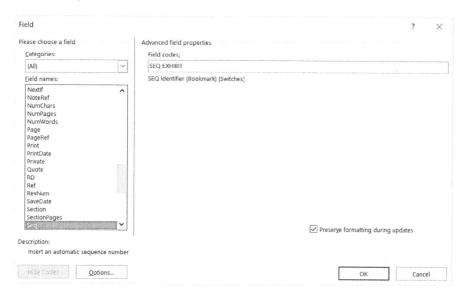

4. Don't click "**OK**" just yet. Instead, click the "**Options**" button at the lower left side of the dialog so that you can choose a letter or number format.

5. After clicking the number format you want to use, click the "**Add to Field**" button (below the "Formatting" box).

6. Click "**OK**" to save the number format, then click "**OK**" again.

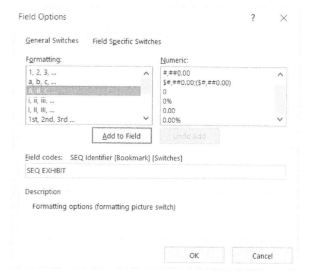

523

7.   The exhibit letter (or number) appears. If you press **Alt F9** to display the actual code, you'll see something like the following:

Exhibit { SEQ EXHIBIT* ALPHABETIC * MERGEFORMAT }

The "ALPHABETIC" switch appears because I clicked on the A,B,C numeric format and then clicked "Add to Field."

8.   Press **Alt F9** again to see the code results. In the screenshot below, you can see that the "A" is a code because codes typically turn gray when you click within them.

Exhibit A

At this point, you can format the text and code to suit your needs (e.g., by adding bold and/or underlining).

9.   To create another Exhibit heading in your document, select the text and code, then copy and paste in the appropriate location.

10.   As with the discovery headings, the exhibit letter (or number) of the pasted code might not "update" (increment) without an additional step. To update an individual SEQ code, click within or select the code and then press **F9** (or **right-click** and choose "**Update Field**." To update all SEQ codes in your document, select the entire document by pressing **Ctrl A**, and then press **F9** (or **right-click** and choose "**Update Field**.").

Cross-Referencing Exhibit Letters and Automatic Paragraph Numbers

Word's Cross-Reference feature can be very useful, particularly when you want to refer to a specific exhibit in a pleading or to a particular numbered paragraph in a contract. In this section, I provide instructions for both types of cross-referencing.

Cross-Referencing Document Exhibits and Similar Items

1. **Select** the item to be cross-referenced, such as an exhibit letter or number.[1]

2. Next, you need to create a unique bookmark for each exhibit. To create a bookmark, click the **Insert tab**, then click **Bookmark** (in the **Links group**).

3. When the Bookmark dialog opens, **type a name** for the bookmark you are creating. The name should be descriptive, so that you remember what it does. A good name might be ExhibitA or Exhibit1 (as appropriate).

    NOTE: Bookmark names cannot contain spaces, cannot begin with a number, and cannot contain non-alphanumeric characters (other than an underscore character at the beginning of the name, which will turn the bookmark into a *hidden* bookmark).

4. Click the "**Add**" **button** at the right side of the Bookmark dialog.

---

[1] This feature works whether you create the exhibit letter manually or with SEQ codes.

5. Next, position the cursor at the point in the document where you want to refer to the bookmarked item (e.g., "see Exhibit X," but without the "X" placeholder), and click **Cross-Reference** (also on the **Insert tab**, in the **Links group**)[2]. The **Cross-Reference dialog** will open.

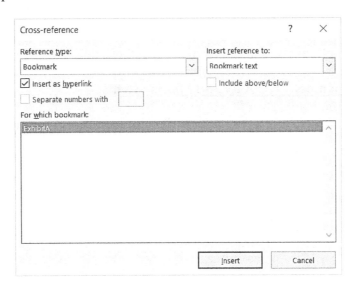

6. From the **Reference type** drop-down list on the left side of the dialog, select **Bookmark**.[3]

7. Click the **Insert reference to:** drop-down and choose **Bookmark text**.

8. Click the bookmark name in the list, click the **Insert** button, then click the **Close** button.

9. Continue setting up Bookmarks and Cross-References for each exhibit (or other item) you wish to refer back to.

10. **NOTE:** If, later on, you add an exhibit to your document in a way that causes the existing exhibit numbers or letters to change, press **Ctrl A** to select the entire document and then press **F9** to update the bookmark and cross-reference codes.

Cross-Referencing Numbered Paragraphs

You can use the Cross-Reference feature to refer to numbered paragraphs in your document. If you use automatic paragraph numbering, you don't need to create bookmarks for the numbered paragraphs; Word recognizes the number codes.

---

[2] There is also a Cross-Reference button in the **Captions** group on the **References tab**.

[3] The other available **reference types** include Numbered item, Heading, Footnote, Endnote, Equation, Figure, and Table.

To insert a cross-reference to an automatic paragraph number, do the following:

1. Position the cursor where you want to insert a cross-reference (for instance, "as mentioned in paragraph XX above," but without the XX placeholder), and click either the **Insert tab** or the **References tab**, and then click **Cross-Reference**.

2. From the **Reference type:** drop-down list on the left-side of the dialog, click to select **Numbered item**.[4]

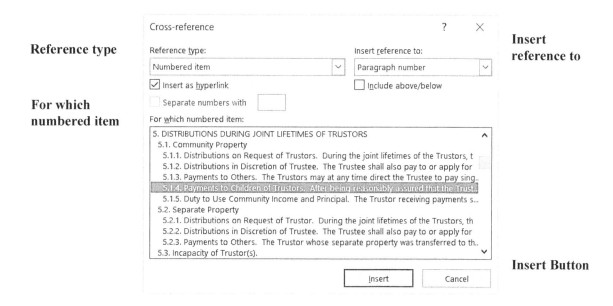

3. Click the **Insert reference to:** drop-down and point to **Paragraph number**, **Paragraph number (full context),** or **Paragraph number (no context)**.[5]

   NOTE: The different options are available only when a subparagraph, such as Paragraph 4(a), is on a separate line from the "parent" paragraph.

   The "**Paragraph**" option inserts a *partial number or letter* – in our example, "(a)" – for a subparagraph if the cross-reference code is located within the parent paragraph (because the full paragraph number is obvious from the context). However, this option inserts a *full number* – "4(a)" – if the cross-reference code is located elsewhere in the document.

   The "**Full Context**" option inserts the complete number (parent and child paragraphs together) – "4(a)" in our example.

---

[4] Alternatively, "Heading" can be a good choice, especially if you use style separators. For an explanation, see the discussion in the sidebar that follows.

[5] The other available "**Insert reference to:**" objects include Page number and Above/below (the latter inserts the word "above" or the word "below" instead of a specific page number reference).

527

The "**No Context**" option inserts only the level of the selected subparagraph – "(a)" in our example.

4.   Navigate to the "**For which numbered item**" section of the dialog and scroll down to locate the paragraph in question. Click to select it, then click the **Insert button**.

5.   Finally, click **Close**. (The label on the Cancel button changes to "Close" when you click the Insert button.)

SIDEBAR: Cross-Reference Tips and Caveats

It is very easy to "break" cross-references because they make use of hidden "target" codes that can be deleted, moved, or otherwise changed accidentally (and without your knowledge). Thus, you need to be extra-careful when *attempting to insert a new paragraph between existing numbered paragraphs* as well as when *adding, deleting, cutting and pasting, or copying and pasting text* to or from a portion of your document that contains bookmarks or cross-references.[1]

In particular, never start a new paragraph by pressing the Enter key from within a paragraph that contains a cross-reference (*especially not* when the cursor is between the paragraph number and the text). This very common practice is almost guaranteed to sever the link between the paragraph and the hidden target code.

If you need to insert a new paragraph, make sure your cursor is *at the end of the previous paragraph* – i.e., *ahead of* where you want the new paragraph to go – before you press the Enter key.

Let's say you want to insert a new numbered paragraph between section 4.2 and section 4.3 (at the same heading / outline level). The new paragraph would become paragraph 4.3 and the existing section 4.3 ("Power of Acting Trustee to Designate Substitute Trustee(s)") would become paragraph 4.4. See the screenshots on the next page.

Don't place the cursor after a paragraph number and press Enter

> **4.2.** **Power of Surviving Spouse to Designate Substitute Trustee(s).** After the death of one Trustor, the Surviving Spouse shall have the power to designate one or more individuals or corporate fiduciaries as Trustee of any trust created hereunder, to serve concurrently with him or her or to serve serially upon Surviving Spouse's death, resignation or incapacity, and any such designation by the Surviving Spouse shall supersede any designation of successor trustees made by Trustors elsewhere in this document.
>
> **4.3.** XX **Power of Acting Trustee to Designate Substitute Trustee(s).** The acting Trustee shall have the power to designate one or more individuals or corporate fiduciaries as Trustee of any trust created hereunder, to serve concurrently with him or her or to serve serially upon acting Trustee's death, resignation or incapacity, and any such designation by the acting Trustee shall supersede any designation of successor trustees made by Trustors elsewhere in this document. The acting Trustee may from time to time revoke or amend any such designation of a successor Trustee. All such designations shall be exercised in writing and shall be effective upon delivery to the beneficiaries of the Trust.

Incorrect Way to Start a New Numbered Paragraph

The screenshot above shows what *not* to do.

Although you might be tempted to position the cursor before the heading text in section 4.3 – that is, between the paragraph number and the heading text (I've inserted two X's to make it easier to see the cursor) – and then press the Enter key, doing so almost certainly would break the existing cross-reference. Any places in the document where you use cross-references to

---

[1] I am indebted to Linda Hopkins and Eva Eilenberg for these tips about methods for avoiding broken cross-references.

point to the paragraph entitled "Power of Acting Trustee to Designate Substitute Trustee(s)" (which becomes section 4.4 after you insert the new paragraph) probably will not update correctly, or at all.

Here's a better way to insert the new paragraph.

Do **place the cursor at the end of the previous paragraph and press Enter**

⟶

4.2. **Power of Surviving Spouse to Designate Substitute Trustee(s).** After the death of one Trustor, the Surviving Spouse shall have the power to designate one or more individuals or corporate fiduciaries as Trustee of any trust created hereunder, to serve concurrently with him or her or to serve serially upon Surviving Spouse's death, resignation or incapacity, and any such designation by the Surviving Spouse shall supersede any designation of successor trustees made by Trustors elsewhere in this document. **XX**|

4.3. **Power of Acting Trustee to Designate Substitute Trustee(s).** The acting Trustee shall have the power to designate one or more individuals or corporate fiduciaries as Trustee of any trust created hereunder, to serve concurrently with him or her or to serve serially upon acting Trustee's death, resignation or incapacity, and any such designation by the acting Trustee shall supersede any designation of successor trustees made by Trustors elsewhere in this document. The acting Trustee may from time to time revoke or amend any such designation of a successor Trustee. All such designations shall be exercised in writing and shall be effective upon delivery to the beneficiaries of the Trust.

Correct Way to Start a New Numbered Paragraph

Instead of putting your cursor at the beginning of the heading text for the existing paragraph 4.3, position it at the end of paragraph 4.2, as in the screenshot above. Now, when you press the Enter key, you get a new paragraph 4.3 *without breaking any existing cross-references*.

In the case of the sample document I used to illustrate this procedure, the situation was a little more complicated than usual because the numbered paragraphs make use of style separators to keep the "run-in" text (text on the same line as the headings) from being pulled into the Table of Contents. The headings are formatted with heading styles, and the run-in text is formatted with a body text style. So positioning the cursor at the end of a numbered paragraph and pressing the Enter key *does* create a new paragraph, but it lacks a paragraph number because pressing Enter copies the body text style contained in the paragraph mark at the end of the paragraph.

As a workaround, after I pressed the Enter key, I inserted the cursor back into the heading for paragraph 4.2, clicked the Format Painter (Home tab, Clipboard group), and then clicked in the new empty paragraph (to copy the heading style to the new paragraph). My second step was to copy and paste the style separator from paragraph 4.2 into the new paragraph. And finally, I clicked within the text of paragraph 4.2, clicked the Format painter, and clicked after the style separator in the new paragraph (to copy the body text style into the new paragraph).

Despite how complicated that might sound, it actually works fairly well. And the advantage is that you can insert new numbered paragraphs without severing the cross-references.

Another possible workaround is to copy and paste an entire paragraph, making sure to position the cursor ahead of the paragraph you wish to copy before selecting that paragraph and then being careful to put the cursor at the end of the paragraph ahead of where you want to paste. The numbering in the new (pasted) paragraph might not increment automatically, but it's a trivial matter to right-click in or near the paragraph number, then click "Continue Numbering." That should fix the numbering of the new paragraph and any paragraphs that follow. You can type over the existing heading and text; just take care not to backspace or otherwise delete anything between the paragraph number and the heading text.

For another workaround, see the Microsoft Knowledge Base article, "Cross-reference links in Word do not update to the correct heading number after you insert a new heading" https://support.microsoft.com/en-us/kb/2630254

Another caution: Be careful not to paste text at the beginning of a paragraph that contains a cross-reference. Doing so could damage or delete the hidden target code. Instead, paste into an "empty" paragraph.

QUICK TIP: Striking Text (Without Using Redlining or Track Changes)

To strike out text in your document without using redlining ("Compare Documents") or Track Changes, **select the text**, then do one of the following:

- Navigate to the **Home tab** and click the **Strikethrough command** toward the bottom center of the **Font group**; or

- Press **Ctrl D** (or click the dialog launcher in the Font group on the Home tab) to open the **Font dialog**, navigate to the **Effects section** and click the **Strikethrough checkbox**, and click "**OK**."

To remove strikethrough marks from text, select the text and use either of the above-described methods.

Note that you can strike out one word at a time by clicking within the word and then applying strikethrough. You can remove the strikethrough marks in the same way.

Generating and Troubleshooting a Table of Contents (TOC)

Generating a Table of Contents (TOC) is easy, but whether you have to mark the headings for inclusion in the TOC depends on how the headings in your document are set up.

Documents That Use Heading Styles

If heading styles – meaning customized versions of the standard Heading 1 through Heading 9 styles that come with Word – have been applied consistently within your document, you don't need to mark the headings manually for inclusion in the TOC. Word automatically pulls such headings into the TOC when you generate.

How to Tell if Heading Styles Have Been Applied

Unless you set up the headings yourself, you might not know whether heading styles have been applied in a particular document. There are a few different ways you can tell.

Check the Style Gallery

One way is to click anywhere within a first-level heading and then look to see if the icon for the Heading 1 style in the **Style Gallery** has a blue or gray border. If so, the Heading 1 style has been applied to the heading. Test some other headings in the document (at least a couple of different levels) to see if they, too, have been "styled."

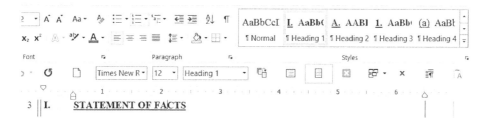

Check The Style Area Pane (Draft View)

Depending upon how the Word Options have been configured, the styles in your document are displayed at left when you switch to **Draft View**. If you don't see any styles when you switch to Draft View, click the **File tab**, **Options**, **Advanced**, scroll to the "**Display**" section, then make sure that the figure in the box labeled "**Style area pane width in Draft and Outline views**" is at least 1". (If it is set to 0 [zero], you won't see the styles when you switch to Draft View.) Click "**OK**" to save your changes.

533

After changing this setting, you should see the styles at the left side of the screen when you switch to Draft View:[1]

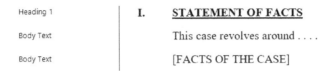

Add a "Style" Icon to the Quick Access Toolbar

A third method involves adding a "**Style**" icon to the Quick Access Toolbar (if your organization hasn't added one already). To do so, either **right-click** within the QAT and choose "**Customize Quick Access Toolbar**…" or click the "**More**" drop-down at the right side of the QAT and choose "**More Commands**." The **Word Options dialog** will open.

For once, the command we're looking for actually is available from the default "Popular" command list. Scroll down to "**Style**" (singular).[2] Click to select the command, then click the "**Add**" button at the center of the Word Options dialog. Click "**OK**" to save your changes.

The Style icon displays the name of the style that has been applied to the paragraph your cursor is in. (In the screenshot below, the drop-down at right is the Style icon.)

---

[1] Note that styles applied to text within a columnar table will not display in the Style Area when you are in Draft View.

[2] When you hold the mouse over that command, a pop-up appears, indicating that the name is "Style (StyleGalleryClassic)."

534

Applying Outline Levels to "Manual" Headings

If you have determined that your document doesn't use heading styles, or if heading styles haven't been applied consistently, you'll need to apply outline levels to each heading.

1. **Right-click** anywhere within a heading (one that has no heading style applied) and choose "**Paragraph**."

2. When the **Paragraph dialog** opens, click the drop-down labeled "**Outline level**" and choose the appropriate level for the heading you are marking for the TOC. (In the screenshot, I've chosen Level 1, which corresponds to a Heading 1.)

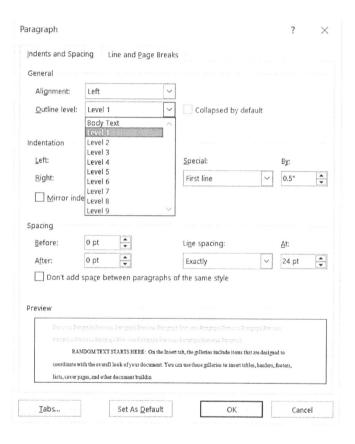

3. Click "**OK**."

4. Use the same method to mark the rest of the "non-styled" headings in your document. (**TIP**: After you have marked one Level 1 heading, you can use the **Format Painter** to mark other Level 1 headings. The Format Painter copies and pastes the paragraph formatting, including the outline level.)

    If you accidentally apply the wrong level to a heading, you can easily change that – either before or after generating the TOC – by right-clicking within the heading, reopening the Paragraph dialog, and choosing the correct level.

Applying TC Codes to "Manual" Headings

You probably won't use this old-fashioned method of marking headings very often – if at all – if one of the other methods works well for you. However, this method, which involves applying "TC" codes to the headings, is extremely useful for pulling headings for "run-in" style paragraphs into the TOC without also pulling in any of the text of the paragraph. (For more information on "run-in" paragraphs, see the discussion on page 537 about the Style Separator.)

To mark "manual" headings (i.e., headings that have not been formatted with heading styles) for inclusion in the TOC, do the following:

1. **Select** (block, highlight) the heading.

2. Press **Alt Shift O** to open the "**Mark Table of Contents Entry**" dialog box.

3. Make sure the "**Table identifier**" displays "**C**" (for Table of Contents) and, if necessary, change the "**Level**" setting to match the level of the selected heading.

4. When everything looks correct, click "**Mark**."

When Word marks the entries, it automatically switches to "**Show**" mode – which displays both the non-printing characters and hidden text – so that you can review the TC code and, if necessary, edit it. (TC codes, like their counterpart TA codes, are normally hidden.)

> B. → PLAINTIFFS·HAVE·NO·STANDING·TO·SUE TC·"PLAINTIFFS·HAVE·
> NO·STANDING·TO·SUE"·\F·C·\L·"2" ¶

You might not need to edit the code immediately after applying it, but you might wish to edit it later on if you revise the text of the heading (the text *within the code*, not the revised heading text itself, will be pulled into the TOC when you generate) or if you realize, after generating the TOC, that you accidentally marked the heading with the wrong level. You can type anywhere within the quotation marks; just be careful not to delete the quotation marks, the backslashes, or the identifiers ("TC" for Table of Contents code; "F" for the type of information that will appear in the TOC; "L" for level).

To toggle between "Show / Hide" modes, click the **Paragraph icon** (¶) in the **Paragraph group** on the **Home tab** or press **Ctrl Shift *** (asterisk).

CAUTION: Because TC codes take up space in the document when "Show" mode is enabled, be sure to switch to "Hide" mode before generating the TOC. Otherwise, the pagination in the generated TOC might be inaccurate (the TC codes can bump text down so much that headings move to the next page in "Show" mode).

The "Add Text" Option

There's another way to mark a paragraph (or other unit of text in the document) for inclusion in the TOC without applying a style to the text. First, select the text (or, to include an entire paragraph, just click within the paragraph). Next, click the **Add Text icon** at the left side of the **References** tab. From the **Add Text** drop-down, choose a level for the text, which automatically *unchecks* "Do not show in Table of Contents."

Conversely, you can prevent text from appearing in the TOC (select the text or click within a paragraph, then make sure that "Do not show in Table of Contents" is *checked*.)

Style Separators

Some documents contain "run-in" paragraphs, where the headings are on the same line as the body text that follows. "Run-in" paragraphs can be problematic because when you apply a heading style, Word applies the style to the entire paragraph (as you would expect). As a result, both the heading and the paragraph are pulled into the TOC when you generate.

To prevent that from happening, you can insert a "Style Separator" between the heading and the body text.[3] Style Separators are special types of paragraph marks, inserted as hidden text, that make it possible to apply two different styles to a single paragraph.

The easiest way to insert a Style Separator is to press **Ctrl Alt Enter**.

CAUTION: By default, a Style Separator will go at the end of the paragraph – regardless of the cursor position when you insert it. That isn't a problem if you insert the Style Separator before typing the body text, but if you've already typed both the heading and the text, you will have to cut and paste the Style Separator. Be sure to turn on Show / Hide first, since Style Separators ordinarily are hidden. After you paste the Style Separator (immediately following the heading), select the text to the right of the Style Separator and apply a body text style to it.

FURTHER CAUTION: In previous versions of Word, the Style Separator caused problems with numbered headings in some situations. Specifically, inserting the Style Separator resulted in paragraph numbers or even entire headings becoming "hidden" (invisible). This problem typically occurred in paragraphs where the numbered heading didn't include any text or caption (for instance, it appeared simply as "Section 1."—as opposed to "Section 1. Parties to the Agreement"). I am not certain if this issue has been resolved. Should you experience this problem, you can use a TC code to mark the heading.

---

[3] There is a feature called "Linked Styles" that some people tout as a solution to the run-in paragraph problem. Linked styles are a sort of hybrid combination of a paragraph style and a character style. In theory, linked styles can be applied either to an entire paragraph or to selected text within a paragraph (you can apply one style to the heading and another style to the text that follows). However, linked styles can be tricky. You might prefer to disable linked styles by launching the Styles Pane and clicking the "Disable Linked Styles" checkbox at the bottom.

Generating the Table of Contents

To generate the Table of Contents (TOC), do the following:

1. Position the cursor at the exact location where you want the TOC to appear. (Word will generate the TOC at the cursor position.)

2. Click the **References tab**, click the **Table of Contents drop-down**, and then choose "**Custom Table of Contents**."[4]

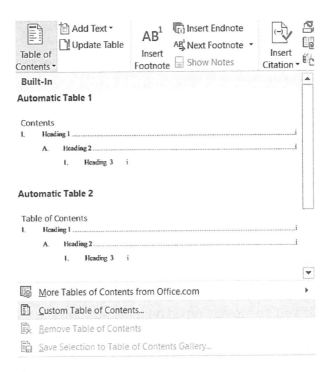

3. When the **Table of Contents dialog** appears, navigate to "**Show levels**" and increase the number from 3 (the default) to 9 (the maximum number of levels available) – or to the actual number of heading levels in the document. If you don't increase the number, only the first three heading levels will display in the generated TOC.[5]

---

[4] In my opinion, this is a much better option than choosing one of the built-in automatic tables. It gives you more control over the process by allowing you to check – and change – various settings before generating the TOC. Also, by default the built-in tables display only the first three heading levels. And the option to insert a "Manual Table" merely sets up *a TOC format* with placeholders for text and page numbering that you type yourself, plus dot leaders. Because nothing updates automatically, this option is of limited utility.

[5] In the event that you forget to change this setting before generating the TOC, simply reopen the Table of Contents dialog, increase the number of levels to show, and regenerate. A prompt will appear, asking if you want to replace the Table of Contents. Click "**Yes**."

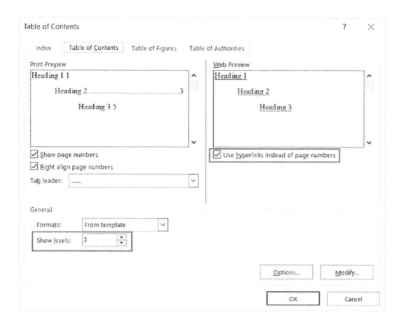

4. Next, *uncheck* "Use hyperlinks instead of page numbers."

5. Double-check to make sure that "**Show page numbers**" and "**Right align page numbers**" are checked and that the "**Tab leader**" drop-down displays the type of leader you want (typically, dots).

6. Click "**OK**" to generate the TOC.

   CAUTION: The generated TOC is a *code* that mirrors the headings in your document (which is why it turns gray when you click within it). To edit the heading text, make your changes in the document rather than in the TOC itself because any revisions you type within the TOC will be wiped out if you regenerate / update the TOC.

7. To regenerate / update the TOC, simply *right-click* within the TOC or press **F9**. The "**Update Table of Contents**" dialog opens, offering two choices: Update page numbers only" and "Update entire table."

"**Update entire table**" is almost always the better choice (because of substantive changes to the headings or because headings have been added, deleted, or moved).

CAUTION: If you have marked headings by applying outline levels to them, right-clicking and choosing "Update Table of Contents" doesn't always work properly. You might find that you have to regenerate the TOC directly from the Table of Contents dialog box instead.

When you open the dialog (by clicking the **Table of Contents drop-down** at the left side of the **References tab** and choosing "**Custom Table of Contents**"), click the "**Options**" button. Make sure that the box labeled "**Outline Levels**" is *checked* so that headings that you manually marked with outline labels are included in the generated TOC. Click "**OK**" and click "**OK**" again to regenerate. If a prompt appears, asking if you want to replace the existing Table of Contents, click "**Yes**.")

Table of Contents Options		? ✕
Build table of contents from:		
☑ Styles		
Available styles:		TOC level:
1.5 Spacing		
Attorney Name		
Balloon Text		
Block Quote		
Body Text		
Body Text First Indent		
☑ Outline levels		
☐ Table entry fields		
Reset	OK	Cancel

Tweaking the Formatting of the Generated TOC

The formatting of the headings in the generated TOC – the indentation, line spacing, text wrapping, and white space between paragraphs – is determined by **TOC styles** that correspond to, but are separate and distinct from, the heading styles. If someone at your organization has created pleading templates and has done a good job of formatting the nine TOC styles (TOC 1 through TOC 9), you probably won't have to do any formatting yourself. But if something doesn't look quite right – there isn't enough white space between the paragraphs, or the text goes over too far toward the right margin – you can improve the appearance of the generated TOC by doing some educated tinkering.

It's easy to reformat the TOC styles because, unlike most styles, they are set to "Automatically Update." That means any direct (manual) formatting actually *modifies the style*. So, for example, if you click within any TOC 2 paragraph and change the left indent from .33" to .5", the TOC 2 style itself changes.[6]

---

[6] For TOC styles, "Automatically Update" is a good option. For other styles, it creates major headaches. See the discussion on page 407.

540

The screenshot below shows some of the formatting issues that you might encounter if the TOC styles in the document you're working on aren't set up well (the default settings for the TOC styles in Word don't work well, at least not for pleadings for the California courts).

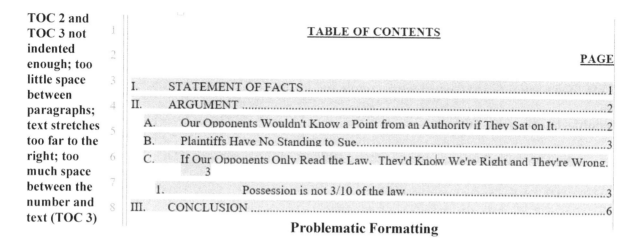

TOC 2 and TOC 3 not indented enough; too little space between paragraphs; text stretches too far to the right; too much space between the number and text (TOC 3)

Problematic Formatting

You can fix each of these issues by applying direct (manual) formatting – for each TOC level – through the Paragraph dialog. (Keep in mind that doing so modifies the TOC styles, although it changes the styles *only in the current document*. The Sidebar starting on page 549 provides instructions for modifying styles in the underlying template. Although the Sidebar deals specifically with TOA styles, the basic steps are the same. See also the section about modifying styles that starts on page 391.)

To fix the formatting of each TOC (heading) level, click within any paragraph at that level, then open the **Paragraph dialog** (by right-clicking within the paragraph and then choosing "Paragraph" or any other method you like).

If necessary, adjust the **Left indentation** of the paragraph – I typically indent each level by an additional .5". To prevent the text from stretching all the way to the right margin, also adjust the **Right indentation**. You might need to experiment with this setting. (Some people find that .5" is sufficient, but others prefer a greater indent, such as .75" or even a full inch.)

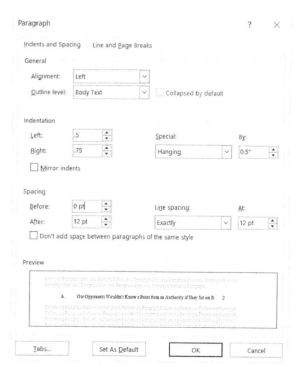

To adjust the white space between paragraphs, you might have to change the **Spacing Before** to 0" (zero) (the default setting is 5 pt) and also add **Spacing After** (to match the "pleading single spacing" that is appropriate for your document, per the discussions on pages 129 and 457 and *passim*).

541

In the "Problematic Formatting" screenshot above, there's also too much space between the number and the beginning of the heading text in the TOC 3 (heading 3) paragraph. That issue might be resolved when you change the left indent, but if it isn't, just click within the paragraph, then click the **Ruler** to place a left tab marker between the number and the beginning of the heading text. I would try to position it about .5" after the number. (Remember that you can reposition the tab markers in the Ruler by dragging them to the left or to the right.)

When you have finished configuring the paragraph formatting for each level, click "**OK**" to save your settings and close the Paragraph dialog.

Troubleshooting the TOC

You might notice a couple of other problems in the generated TOC. One common issue is that some of the generated headings are missing dot leaders. In the screenshot below, the level 2 (TOC 2) headings lack dot leaders.

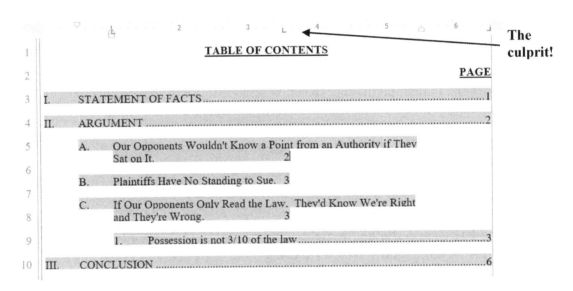

If that happens, click anywhere within one of the problematic paragraphs (I have clicked within paragraph "A," the first TOC 2 paragraph). Turn on the **Ruler** (**View tab**, **Ruler**) if it isn't already displayed, and look to see whether there are any left tab markers – they look like a capital "L" – situated between where the heading text ends and the page number. If so, delete each one by dragging it off the Ruler. (Don't delete the right tab marker – it looks like a backwards "L" – or any tab markers to the left of where the heading text begins.)

Typically, you don't have to delete the tab markers in every other paragraph at that level, but you might have to delete tab markers for the other TOC / heading levels (e.g., a TOC 1 and/or a TOC 3 paragraph). In the screenshot, only the TOC 2 paragraphs are problematic, but I have seen instances where multiple levels lack the dot leaders.

Marking Citations and Generating a Table of Authorities (TOA)

To mark citations (cases, statutes, rules, treatises, and the like) for inclusion in a Table of Authorities, do the following:

1. Select the first instance of a citation, making sure to select the entire cite.

   > As was made plain in the seminal case of *Us v. Them* (1893), 27 Cal.App. 219, 224, 21 Cal.Rptr. 158, a plaintiff must have standing to sue. See also *You and Me v. The World* (1963), 223 Cal.App.2d 506, 508-509, 182 Cal.Rptr. 391. In this case, the plaintiffs clearly lack the

2. Navigate to the right side of the **References tab** and click "**Mark Citation**." (Alternatively, press **Alt Shift I**.)

   The **Mark Citation dialog** will open.

   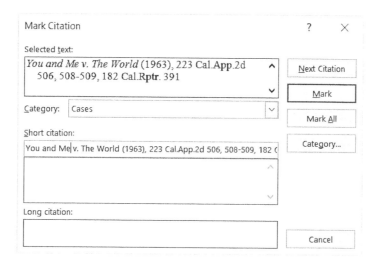

3. Whatever is in the "**Selected Text**" **box** is what will be pulled into the Table of Authorities, so format the citation here.[1] That means:

   a. Position your cursor to the left of any information that you want to appear below the case name (or other type of cite) and bump it down by pressing the Enter key.

   b. Delete any "pin cites" (additional page references). (In the example shown in the screenshot, you would delete "508-509.")

4. Next, make sure the **Category drop-down** reflects the correct category for the citation: Cases, Statutes, Rules, Treatises, or whatever is appropriate. ***This is a critical step***.

---

[1] This step is comparable to editing the Full Form of the citation in WordPerfect.

NOTE: You can add a new category by clicking on one of the numbers in the Category field from 8 to 16, then clicking the **Category button** at the right side of the dialog box, typing a category name in the "**Replace with**" **box**, and clicking "**Replace**."

5.   Next, edit the **Short Citation**.

This is the "nickname" Word uses to identify and mark all instances of the citation in your document. Try to use the most generic Short Citation possible because Word looks for *the exact text string* in this box. For example, when you are marking statutes, if you use C.C.P. in your Short Citation, Word won't find (or mark) any instances of the citation typed as "California Code of Civil Procedure" rather than "C.C.P." Nor will it find or mark the word "section" if the Short Citation uses the section sign. So consider using just the code section number (and letters, if any), such as 127.5(a).

6.   When you have finished, click "**Mark All**" to mark all instances of the citation in the document.

CAUTION: "Mark All" is convenient, but has definite disadvantages. If you use numbers as your Short Citation – say, the full citation is Civil Code §428, and you use "428" (without quotation marks) as your Short Citation – and click "Mark All," you could end up with a page number reference to a phone number or Bar number that includes the digits "428." The same issue can arise if you have a case such as *United States v. Smith*, and you use "Smith" as your Short Citation, but you also make a couple of references in the document to your opposing counsel, Ms. Smith.

7.   Click "**Close**."

When the dialog box closes, Word switches to "**Show**" mode (i.e., it shows the non-printing characters and hidden text) so that you can view the TA code, which normally is hidden. The TA code looks something like the following:

4 | { TA·\l·"*You·and·Me·v.·The·World·*(1963),↵

5 | 223·Cal.App.2d·506,·182·Cal.Rptr.·391"·\s·"You·and·Me"·\c·1·}

- "TA" identifies the code as a Table of Authorities code.

- "\l" (a backslash and a lower case letter "L") identifies the long form of the citation.

- "\s" (a backslash and a lower case letter "S") identifies the short form of the citation as you marked it.

- "\c" (a backslash and a lower case letter "C") identifies the category. In the example, it is followed by the number "1" (it looks identical to the lower case "L" that identifies the long-form citation, but it is in fact a number). The number that follows the "\c" refers to the order of the category in the "Category" drop-down; because "Cases" is the first category in the list, it is identified as "\c 1."

- You can, in fact, edit the TA codes. More about that momentarily.

544

Marking Additional Instances of a Citation – or an "Id."

If you need to mark another instance of a particular citation after you've generated the TOA, position the cursor just to the left of (but touching) the citation. (You don't need to select the citation.) Next, click the "**Mark Citation**" **button** at the right side of the **References tab**. When the "**Mark Citation**" **dialog** appears, navigate to the "**Short Citation**" **box**, scroll to and click the nickname for the citation, click "**Mark**" (*not* "Mark All"), and then click "**Close**."

Short Citation box

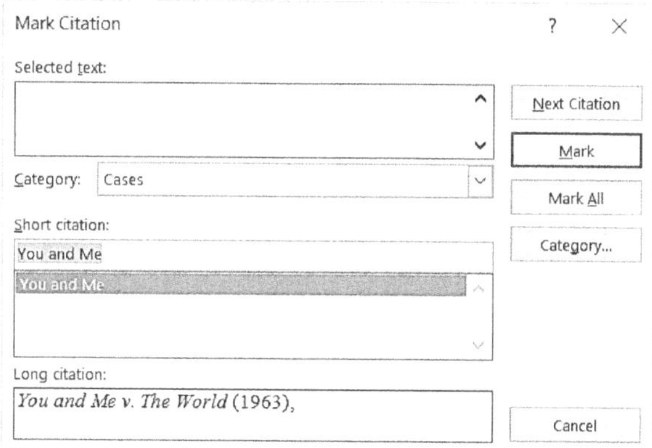

Mark Citation ? ×

Selected text:

Next Citation

Mark — **Click "Mark"**

Category: Cases

Mark All

Short citation:

You and Me

Category...

You and Me

Long citation:

You and Me v. The World (1963),

Cancel

NOTE: This is also how you mark any "Id." designations in your document.

When you mark the first instance of a citation, Word inserts a long TA code, as pictured on the previous page. When you mark additional instances of the citation, Word inserts a shortened version of the TA code that includes only the short form of the citation (screenshot below).

{ TA \s "*Us v. Them*" } *Us v. Them, supra.*¶

TIP: After marking the *second* instance of a particular citation, you can mark the remaining instances of the citation – or any "Id." designations! – by copying and pasting the short TA code, rather than reopening the "Mark Citation" dialog and clicking "Mark" again and again. (I typically paste the code immediately to the left of a citation or an "Id." designation. You can paste it elsewhere, as long as the pasted code is touching the citation or the "Id." designation.)

Continue marking the citations. (If you like, you can click the "**Next Citation**" button to move the cursor to the next citation, but this option is of somewhat limited utility, given that Word doesn't recognize all of the "signals" – such as "vs.," "v.," and "In re" – commonly used in legal documents. Also, it's somewhat tricky to get the next citation into the "Selected Text" box while the "Mark Citation" dialog is open.)

545

Generating the Table of Authorities

CAUTION: Be sure to ***turn off Show / Hide*** (by clicking the Paragraph icon on the Home tab or pressing Ctrl Shift *) before generating the tables.[2] Otherwise, because the Non-Printing Characters take up quite a bit of space in the document – as the screenshot on page 544 shows – citations can get bumped down to the next page. In that event, the generated TOA won't reflect the correct page numbers for citations![3]

1. Position the cursor at the exact spot where you want to generate the TOA, and then click the **Insert Table of Authorities** button at the upper right side of the References tab.

2. When the Table of Authorities dialog opens, *uncheck* the "**Use passim**" option unless you want Word to insert the Latin word "passim" (meaning "throughout") instead of the actual page numbers for citations that appear on more than five different pages.

Uncheck the "Use passim" option, but leave "Keep original formatting" checked

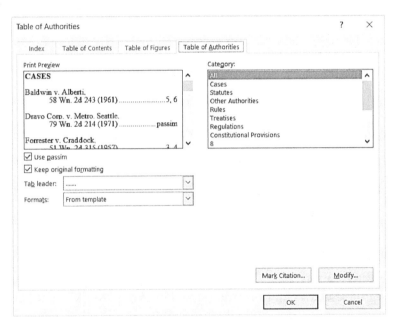

---

[2] If you do so but the TA code remains visible, click the **File tab**, **Options**, **Display**, and look to see if any of the boxes for the formatting marks are checked. If so, ***uncheck*** them and click "**OK**" to save your changes and close the Word Options dialog.

[3] People sometimes tell me they never use Word's TOA feature "because the page numbers in the TOA are always wrong." When I ask them if they turn off "Show / Hide" before generating the TOA, they just look at me blankly. If you are conscientious about turning off "Show / Hide" before generating, the page numbers in the generated TOA should be accurate.

546

3. Leave the "**Keep original formatting**" box checked if you made any changes within the "Selected Text" box, such as deleting pin cites or bumping part of the citation to the next line. (Think of "Keep original formatting" as meaning "Keep *my custom formatting*.")

4. Make sure that the "**Tab leader**" drop-down shows the appropriate type of leader. Dot leaders are the norm for pleadings.

5. Check to make sure that "**All**" is highlighted in the "**Category**" box. If not, only the highlighted TOA category will display when you generate.

6. If everything appears to be in good order, **click** "OK."

The table should generate properly, though you might need to do some "cleanup" similar to that for the Table of Contents. See the discussion about dot leaders on page 542.

Editing the TA Codes

If you made a mistake when you marked a citation – perhaps you forgot to delete the "pin cites"; you selected too much text (or not enough); or you chose the wrong TOA category from the Category drop-down (e.g., you assigned a case to the "Statutes" category or put a federal case into "State Cases") – you don't need delete the code and start over. Rather, you can edit the TA code for that citation.

Because the codes ordinarily are hidden, you have to enable "Show" mode (turn on "Show / Hide") in order to see and edit a code. To do so, either click the Paragraph icon in the Paragraph group on the Home tab or press Ctrl Shift * (asterisk).

```
3   { TA \l "Us v. Them (1893),
4   27 Cal.App. 219, 21 Cal.Rptr. 158" \s "Us v. Them" \c 1 }
```

When the codes are visible, you can edit any text between the quotation marks; be careful not to delete the quotation marks, the backslashes, or any of the identifiers. Also, you can change the category simply by deleting the number after the "\c" and replacing it with the correct category number. But how do you know which number refers to which category?

As mentioned earlier, the numbers are assigned to the categories based on the order in which they appear in the Category drop-down list within the Mark Citation dialog. Simply open the Mark Citation dialog by clicking "**Mark Citation**" at the right side of the **References tab**, click the **Category drop-down**, and then count down from the very top of the list. In my document, "Cases" is Category 1, "Statutes" is Category 2, "Other Authorities" is Category 3, and so forth. (Your document might include different categories.)

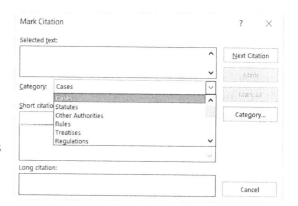

547

After editing the codes, be sure to turn off "Show / Hide" (i.e., switch back to "Hide" mode) before you regenerate the TOA.

Regenerating a TOA is somewhat trickier than regenerating a TOC because of the fact that the TOA is divided into separate categories. If you right-click within a category, such as "Cases," then choose "Update Field" (or if you click within the category and press F9), only that category will update. That can be great if your changes affect only a single category. But what if you just finished editing the category within the TA code for a case that you had accidentally marked as a statute? When you generated the first time, the case appeared in the TOA under "Statutes." Now that you have edited the code, the case should appear in the TOA under "Cases," but if you update only the "Cases" section, the case won't be removed from the "Statutes" section. (See the next screenshot.)

4	**CASES**
5	*You and Me v. The World* (1963).
6	223 Cal.App.2d 506, 182 Cal.Rptr. 391..3
7	**STATUTES**
8	Code of Civil Procedure §10101(b)...2
9	*Us v. Them* (1893).
	27 Cal.App. 219, 21 Cal.Rptr. 158...3, 4

The best practice in these types of situations is to select / highlight the entire generated TOA, then update. If Word prompts you to replace the categories, click "Yes."

Now the citations are in the correct categories (screenshot below).

4	**CASES**
5	*Us v. Them* (1893).
6	27 Cal.App. 219, 21 Cal.Rptr. 158...3, 4
7	*You and Me v. The World* (1963).
	223 Cal.App.2d 506, 182 Cal.Rptr. 391..3
8	**STATUTES**
9	Code of Civil Procedure §10101(b)...2

Modifying Table of Authorities and TOA Heading Styles

The appearance of the citations (and of the category headings) in the generated TOA derives from two different styles: a Table of Authorities style and a TOA Heading style. Unlike TOC styles, neither of these styles is set to "Automatically Update," which means that any direct formatting you apply within the generated TOA will not modify the underlying styles. Therefore, if you regenerate the TOA, the direct formatting will be wiped out.

To modify the styles, see the next section.

548

Modifying the TOA Styles

As discussed in the previous section, there are two styles that determine the appearance of the generated TOA: a TOA Heading style and a Table of Authorities style (the former affects only the category headings; the latter affects the citations). Although you can use direct (manual) formatting to tweak the text within the generated TOA, those changes don't modify the styles themselves, and as a result your changes will be wiped out if you regenerate the TOA.

If you like, you can modify one or both of the TOA styles within the document. If you have the necessary rights / permissions, you can modify the styles within the underlying template so that all future documents based on the template reflect those modifications.

Typically, neither style appears in the Style Gallery, and neither style appears in the Styles Pane unless you change the "Options" to show all styles. However, there's an easy way to modify one or both of the styles. Simply click the "**Insert Table of Authorities**" **button** at the right side of the **References tab** and, when the **Table of Authorities dialog** opens, click the "**Modify…**" **button** at the bottom right side.

When the **Style dialog** opens, click to select the style you want to modify, then click the "**Modify**" button to open the full "**Modify Style**" **dialog**.

549

When the Modify Style dialog appears, click the "**Format**" button at the bottom left side and then click the appropriate button(s) (Font, Paragraph, Tab, etc.), and make all of your desired changes.

Remember to click (check) the **New documents based on this template** radio button if you want your changes saved to the template (for use in other documents), as opposed to saving them just in the current document. (Depending on your situation, you might not have the rights / permissions to modify the underlying template. If not, you can modify the styles in the current document and then copy those styles to other documents with the Organizer, as discussed in the section starting on page 393.)

Finally, click "**OK**."

All instances of the style in your document should change to reflect the modifications you have made. And if you do have the rights / permissions to modify the underlying template, the next time you open a new document based on the template, your changes should be reflected there, as well.

Compare Documents (Redlining)

To compare two different drafts of a document (or two different documents), click the **Compare icon** toward the right side of the **Review tab**, and click **Compare....** A **Compare Documents dialog** will open so that you can choose the documents to compare.

Navigate to the older draft by clicking the "Browse" button in the section labeled ***Original document***, and then navigate to the more recent draft by clicking the "Browse" button in the section labeled ***Revised document***.

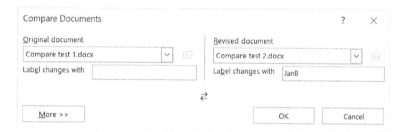

To configure the comparison settings, click the "**More**" button at the lower left side of the **Compare Documents dialog**. You can choose to have the redlined document display – or not display – moves, comments, changes to formatting, case changes, white space, modifications to tables, headers and footers, footnotes and endnotes, text boxes, and/or fields.

In addition, you can fine-tune the comparison to show changes at the character level (word level is the default).

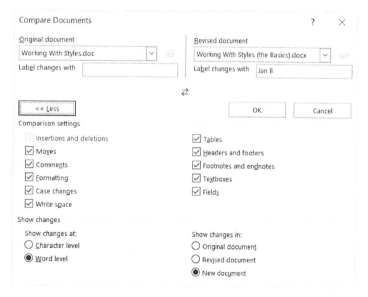

551

And, if you like, you can have Word show the changes directly in either the earlier (original) draft or the revised draft, although the default setting of "New document" has a compelling advantage: It prevents you from overwriting one of the existing drafts by accident.

When you are ready to perform the comparison, click "**OK**." The redlined document will appear on screen, usually in a new window labeled "Compare Result" followed by the document number.

Word displays the results in a split screen similar to that used in some third-party document comparison programs. The **Review Pane** at left summarizes the changes; the **Compare Document pane** in the middle displays the document with redlining, strikeout, and other markup[1]; and the right side is divided into two panes: one containing the older ("**original**") draft and one containing the **revised** document.

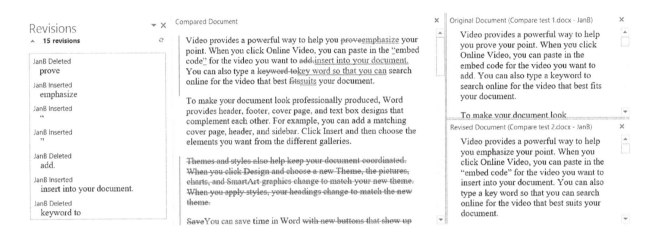

The Compared Document

The appearance and formatting of the markup in the middle pane – including whether or not any of it appears in "balloons" in the margin – are determined by the settings in the **Advanced Track Changes Options dialog**. To open the dialog, click the **dialog launcher** in the **Tracking group**, and when the condensed **Track Changes Options dialog** opens, click "**Advanced Options**" button.

If you aren't seeing any markup other than vertical "Change Lines" in the left margin, navigate to the **Display for Review** options (the drop-down at the top of the **Tracking group**) and choose "**All Markup**."

---

[1] The appearance and formatting of the markup—including whether or not any of it appears in "balloons" in the margin – are determined by the settings in the Advanced Track Changes Options dialog (click the dialog launcher in the **Tracking group**, and then click "Advanced Options.")

552

If you find the profusion of screens overwhelming, just close one or more of the side panes by clicking on the "X" in the upper right-hand corner.[2] Alternatively, you can make them narrower by dragging the vertical margin(s) to one side of the screen. To reopen the Reviewing Pane, click the Reviewing Pane drop-down in the Tracking group and choose "Reviewing Pane Vertical." To reopen one of the other panes, click the Compare drop-down, hover over "Show Source Documents," and choose "Show Original," "Show Revised," or "Show Both."

Saving the Compare Results (Redlined Version)

To save the compare results (redlined version) as a separate document, simply press F12 or click File, Save As (remember that the "File, Save As" method takes you through the Backstage view). Be sure to give the redlined version a descriptive name, such as the matter name and type of document followed by "Redline – 3rd draft to 2nd draft" or something similar.

Accepting and Rejecting Changes

After performing a comparison, you can go through the redlined document and selectively accept or reject changes that you or other reviewers have made to the document (or accept or reject all of those changes at once). This process is similar to accepting or rejecting tracked changes (see the section starting on page 555).

To accept or reject changes, you can do any of the following:

1. Click the appropriate choice under the "**Accept**" and "**Reject**" **drop-down menus** in the **Changes group** on the **Review tab**; *or*

2. Right-click within the redlined text, then click **Accept Insertion** (or **Deletion**) or **Reject Insertion** (or **Deletion**)[3]; *or*

3. Right-click an item in the **Reviewing Pane**, then click **Accept Insertion** (or **Deletion**) or **Reject Insertion** (or **Deletion**).

---

[2] To re-display the left-hand pane, click **Reviewing Pane** in the **Tracking group**, and click **Reviewing Pane Vertical**. To re-display the right-hand panes, click "**Show Source Documents**" in the **Compare group**, then choose Show Original, Show Revised, or Show Both.

[3] If balloons are enabled in the Track Changes Options, right-click within a balloon to accept or reject the deletions.

After you finish reviewing the changes, you can save the document as a "cleaned" version of the redline if you like.

Comparing and Combining Documents

Word provides two "comparison" options: (1) **Compare Documents** and (2) **Compare and Combine Documents**. The essential difference between the two is that option (1) typically is used for redlining sequential drafts of a document (ordinarily authored by a single individual) and option (2) typically is used for merging versions of a document worked on separately by different authors or reviewers in a collaborative environment.

The **Compare and Combine** process is very similar to that of comparing drafts of a document. One notable difference has to do with the way Word treats revision marks inserted into the documents before the comparison (i.e., as a result of a document author using **Track Changes**). When you use the simple **Compare Documents** feature, any markup existing in either the earlier draft or the revised draft *is blended into the redlined document as if you had clicked "Accept Change."* Also, Word labels insertions and deletions (etc.) as if all changes were made by one author.

By contrast, when you use **Compare and Combine**, the redlined document shows *all* markup, including markup that existed in one (or both) of the documents prior to the comparison. It also attributes changes (insertions, deletions, formatting, moves, comments, etc.) to the specific people who made those changes.

NOTE: As discussed in the section about Track Changes, settings in the **Display for Review** and **Show Markup** drop-downs in the **Tracking group** of the **Review tab** affect which revision marks are visible in the combined (redlined) document. If for some reason you are seeing fewer changes than you anticipated, check the settings on both of those drop-downs to make sure that they allow for the display of all markup.

Track Changes

The Track Changes feature, as its name implies, applies revision marks as you type (i.e., in real time) to text that you insert, delete, and/or move within your document.[1] In this respect, the feature is different from Compare Documents – covered in the previous section of the book – which typically is used for comparing / redlining different drafts of a document.

The feature also is a useful collaboration tool that displays revision marks made by multiple document authors in different colors.[2]

To start tracking changes, you can do any of the following:

- Press **Ctrl Shift E** (press the same keys a second time to turn Track Changes off);

- Click the top portion of the **Track Changes button** toward the middle of the **Review tab** in the **Tracking group** (click it again to turn Track Changes off);

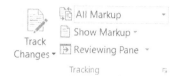

- Click the bottom portion of the **Track Changes button** and then click the "**Track Changes**" command (click it again to turn Track Changes off); or

- Click the "**Track Changes**" **indicator** on the Status Bar once. When you're ready to turn Track Changes off, click it again (it's a toggle).

    NOTE: The Track Changes indicator is not displayed on the Status Bar unless you specifically add it. To do so, right-click the Status Bar and then click "Track Changes." Click somewhere outside the menu to close it. (The indicator is one way to tell if Track Changes is on or off. Another way to tell at a glance is by looking at the top portion of the Track Changes button on the Review tab. If Track Changes is on, the button is highlighted / shaded. If Track Changes is off, there's no highlighting / shading.)

- Right-click within any revision mark, then choose "**Track Changes**." (Repeat the steps to turn Track Changes off.)

Track Changes will remain in effect, adding revision marks to your text, until you actively turn it off.

---

[1] In early versions of Word, this feature was called "Revisions."

[2] When you hover over a particular revision, a pop-up window displays the initials of the author, the date and time of the modification, the nature of the change (insertion, deletion, formatting, or comment), and the content.

Track Changes Options

Word is pre-configured to use certain colors and formatting attributes to highlight your edits. However, you can change the appearance of inserted and deleted text. To do so, start by clicking the **dialog launcher** in the **Tracking group** on the **Review tab**, then click the "**Advanced Options…**" **button** in the **Track Changes Options dialog**. That will open the **Advanced Track Changes Options dialog** (shown below at right).

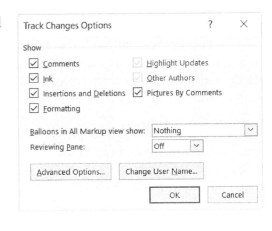

There are several different options you can set.[3] You can change the formatting and color for any or all of the following:

- **Insertions** (by default, formatted with underlining)

- **Deletions** (by default, formatted with strikeout marks, referred to as "strikethrough" in Word)

- The appearance of vertical lines in the margins that flag changes ("**Changed lines**")

- **Comments**

- **Moves** (different marks indicate where text was moved *from* and where text was moved *to*)

- Changes to **table cells**

- **Formatting** changes (e.g., bolding, underlining, italics)

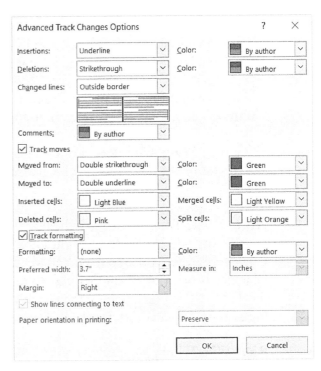

The default color setting for Insertions, Deletions, and Comments is "**By author.**" The "By author" setting is useful because if several different individuals end up working on the document, Word will assign different (unique) colors to the different authors to indicate each person's changes.[4]

---

[3] These settings are specific to each individual user (i.e., the person whose name and initials are shown on the "**General**" page of **Word Options**).

[4] According to Microsoft, the colors can change if a document is opened on a different computer, or even if the document is closed and reopened on the same computer.

Click the drop-downs to change the settings to suit your preferences. (On my own computers, I like inserted text to appear in blue with double underlining and deleted text to appear in red with strikethrough.) To save your customized settings, click "**OK**."[5]

Comments

To insert a comment, position your cursor where you want the comment to appear, then click the "**New Comment**" icon in the **Comments group** on the **Review tab**.

A **Reviewing Pane** (labeled "Revisions") opens at the left side of the screen, displaying your comment as you type it (and also showing any existing revisions).

To close the Reviewing Pane, either click the "X" at the top right side or click the **Reviewing Pane** icon in the **Tracking group**.

Depending on how the **Display for Review options** are set (see the section starting on page 559), you will see either a pink rectangle within the text or a small comment balloon in the right margin. To see the text of the comment, hover over the pink rectangle or click the comment balloon. (See the screenshots below.) Or, if you closed the Reviewing Pane, click the Reviewing Pane icon again to reopen it.

Balloons

Word provides an option to display insertions, deletions, formatting changes, and/or comments in "**balloons**" in the document margins, rather than within the body of the document.

CAUTION: If this option is enabled, balloons appear on screen and also print with the document, which can be confusing, especially if you've never used this feature.

To enable balloons, navigate to the **Tracking group** in the **Review tab** and either:

---

[5] You can change these settings again at any time.

- click the **dialog launcher** to open the **Track Changes Options** dialog, click the drop-down labeled "**Balloons in All Markup view show**," and choose "**Revisions**"; or

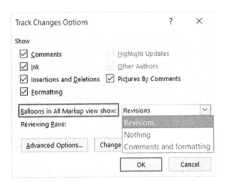

- click the "**Show Markup drop-down**," hover over **Balloons**, and choose "**Show Revisions in Balloons**."

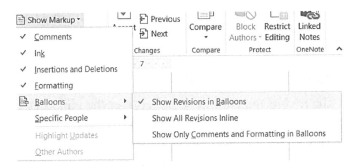

To disable balloons, choose the "**Nothing**" option within the Track Changes Options dialog or the "**Show All Revisions Inline**" option on the "Show Markup" drop-down. There is also an option to use balloons only for comments and formatting changes.

With balloons enabled, insertions appear in-line (within the document text), while deletions, moves, formatting changes, and comments appear in balloons. If change lines are enabled – as they are by default – they will appear in the opposite margin. See the screenshot below for an example of how a document looks when balloons are enabled.

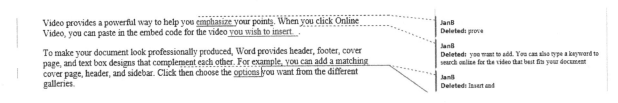

To change the width of the balloons (the default appears to be 3.7"), balloons must be enabled. Otherwise, that option – under "**Track Formatting**" in the **Advanced Track Changes Options dialog** – is grayed out. (To adjust this setting, click the dialog launcher in the **Tracking group**, then click "**Advanced Options**.")

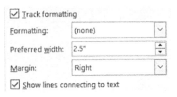

558

Viewing Only Certain Types of Markup

If you don't wish to see revision marks for every type of edit, you can click the **Show Markup drop-down** in the **Tracking group** on the **Review tab** and turn off the display for one or more categories of "markup." These include: **Comments**, **Ink** (for hand-written comments if you use a touch-enabled device), **Insertions and Deletions**, **Formatting**, **Balloons**, and **Specific People** (formerly labeled "Reviewers"; if several people have worked on the document, you can show or hide the markup by specific reviewers).

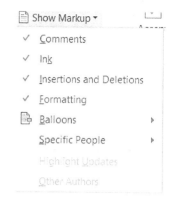

Display for Review[6]

While you are revising a document, you can preview how the document would look if you *accepted* all the changes – insertions, deletions, moves, etc. – made thereto.

To do so, navigate to the **Review tab** in the **Tracking group**, click the **Display for Review drop-down** (the one at the top right), and choose the **No Markup** option. (In versions of Word prior to Word 2013, the Display for Review option that displays the document as if all revisions had been accepted / incorporated is called **Final**.)

CAUTION: No Markup is merely a display option – a hypothetical, if you will. Switching to the No Markup display option *does not actually remove the revision marks from the document*. The only way to strip the revision marks from the document is to accept or reject every change.

To see how the document looked before any insertions, deletions, moves, and/or formatting changes, choose the **Original** display option.

There are two other Display for Review Options that you need to be aware of. They are:

Simple Markup

Simple Markup also shows the document as if all of the changes have been accepted – that is, as if insertions and deletions have been made – but displays thin vertical lines ("Change Lines") in the margins next to portions of the document to indicate where text has been inserted, deleted, reformatted, and/or moved.

- Red vertical lines indicate that markup exists, but is hidden. To display the markup, left-click any of the red lines.

- Gray vertical lines appear when the markup is displayed (i.e., the display switches to the All Markup option). To hide the markup again, left-click any of the gray vertical lines.

---

[6] **CAUTION**: The Display for Review options have changed dramatically since Word 2010.

Video provides a powerful way to help you prove your point. When you click Online Video, you can paste in an "embed code" for the video you want to insert. You can also type a key word to search online for the video that best suits your document.

Simple Markup

In simple markup, comments appear as small balloons in the right margin. To see the text, click the balloon.

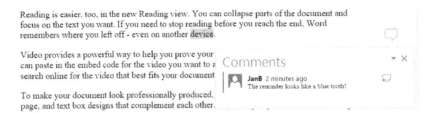

As should be obvious, Simple Markup is a somewhat dangerous option because, depending on how much markup exists in the document, it can be easy to overlook the vertical Change Lines and assume – wrongly – that all changes have been accepted and the revision marks have been purged.[7] It is a good idea to change the Display for Review drop-down, if necessary, to show **All Markup** instead.

All Markup

The **All Markup** option shows revision marks for all insertions, deletions, moves, formatting changes, etc. that have been made in the document.

If you have enabled balloons, insertions appear inline, whereas deletions (along with moves, formatting changes, and comments) appear in balloons in the margin.

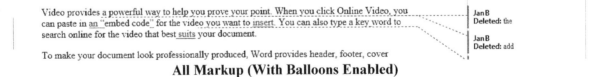

All Markup (With Balloons Enabled)

---

[7] Because of possible malpractice exposure, many law firms have asked their IT people to make sure that "All Markup" is the default setting in order to reduce the likelihood of accidentally sending documents containing markup outside the organization.

Accepting or Rejecting the Changes / Removing Revision Marks

TIP: You can't undo finalization of a document, so if there's any chance you'll want to re-create your edits at some later date, *save a copy of the document* before proceeding to this next step. Give it a distinctive name, and be sure to choose a name that will help you remember not to send the version that contains markup outside your organization!

When you are ready to finalize the document, navigate to the **Review tab, Changes group**. You can accept or reject all revisions (by clicking the "**Accept All Revisions**" option in the "**Accept**" drop-down or the "**Reject All Revisions**" option in the "**Reject**" drop-down), or click "**Next**" or "**Previous**" and accept or reject one revision at a time.[8]

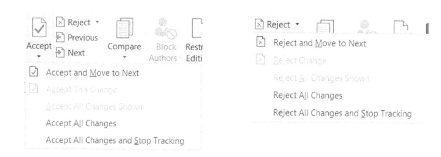

CAUTION: In order to remove the markup from the document permanently – so that no one else is able to display it – you *must* accept or reject every single revision. If you fail to do so, you will leave metadata in your document.

In most situations, you should turn off Track Changes after accepting or rejecting all of the revisions, which people sometimes forget to do. A relatively new option on the "Accept" drop-down menu, "**Accept All Changes and Stop Tracking**," makes it easier to remember. (There is a comparable option on the "Reject" drop-down menu.)

Note that there is a new option on the **Track Changes drop-down**, "**Lock Tracking**," that prevents other people from turning off tracking. If you choose this option, you will assign a password to the document so that only someone who knows the password can turn off tracking. Be careful, because according to Microsoft, while the lock is in effect, you won't be able to turn off tracking either – and no one (including you) will be able to accept or reject revisions.

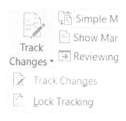

---

[8] **TIP**: You can use this same process if you accidentally turn on Track Changes and can't figure out how to get rid of tracking marks you've inserted unintentionally.

When you are ready to finalize the document, also be sure to delete all of the comments, unless you have a specific reason for leaving them in the document. Deleting comments can be tricky because the "**Delete**" **icon** in the "**Comments**" **group** is grayed out unless your cursor is within a comment. To activate the button, click within any comment, *or* click the "**Next**" (or "Previous") **button** to move to a comment. You can then click the top portion of the "**Delete**" **icon** to delete the comment your cursor is in *or* click the **drop-down menu** and choose "**Delete**."

Note, as well, that even when it is grayed out, you can click the "**Delete**" icon to open the **drop-down menu** and choose "**Delete All Comments in Document**."

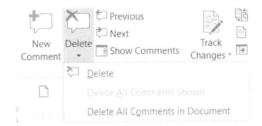

After accepting or rejecting all of the changes and deleting the comments, *be sure to save the finalized document*. Otherwise, the markup will remain in the doc.

To be absolutely certain that you have removed the revision marks and comments (as well as other metadata in the document), you can run the Document Inspector. For instructions, see the next section.

Removing Metadata With the Document Inspector

Word 2016 comes with a metadata removal tool called the Document Inspector. This tool combs through your document, looking for comments, revision marks, annotations, document properties, personal and company information, data in headers and footers (as well as watermarks), and hidden text. You can have the Inspector remove any or all of the items it finds.

Before running the Document Inspector, ***make a copy of your document***. It's a good idea to create a backup copy (and possibly even inspect the copy) because after certain items are eliminated from the document, it can be difficult – or impossible – to restore them without going through the laborious process of re-creating them manually. In other words, some metadata removal can't be "undone." That can be problematic, especially because:

(1) you can't see exactly which information the Document Inspector has identified before you decide to remove it;

(2) you don't have an opportunity to pick and choose which items in any given category to remove (it's an all-or-nothing proposition); and

(3) in an attempt to be meticulous, Word sometimes gets rid of innocuous information, such as entire headers and footers.

With your document open, click the **File tab** and take a look at the **Info screen**. To the right of the "Check for Issues" button, you should see a warning that your document contains certain items that you might wish to remove. In the case of my test document, Word found comments and revisions, as well as certain document properties and the author's name. Word might identify different items that merit a closer look in your various documents.

To run the Document Inspector, click the **Check for Issues drop-down**, then click **Inspect Document**. You will see a dialog similar to the one depicted in the screenshot on the next page. It consists of checkboxes for various types of document content the Document Inspector can examine for metadata: Comments, Revisions, Versions, and Annotations; Document Properties and Personal Information; Task Pane add-ins; Embedded Documents; Macros, Forms, and Active X Controls; Collapsed Headings; Custom XML Data; Headers, Footers and Watermarks; Invisible Content; and Hidden Text.[1]

---

[1] "Hidden Text" means text to which the "Hidden" property has been applied through the Font dialog. The Document Inspector will ***not*** identify and remove text to which the color white has been applied (to make it invisible on a white background) or text that has been sized so small that it is not visible at normal screen magnifications.

Microsoft has added several content types since Word 2010; you will need to scroll through the Document Inspector dialog box to see all of them.

All of the boxes are checked by default, but you can uncheck any types of content that you don't want the Inspector to review.

CAUTION: I *strongly* recommend that you *uncheck* Headers, Footers, and Watermarks before you begin so that the program doesn't even search for those screen elements. If you include them in the search, Word will flag them – and if you get distracted, you could inadvertently remove them.

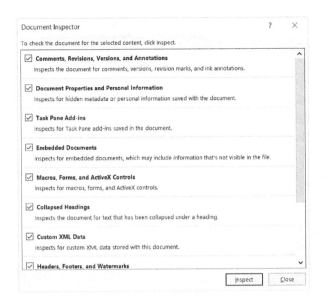

There's no way to undo that action and restore the deleted headers and/or footers, and re-creating them could involve a great deal of effort. So I think makes sense not to have the Document Inspector search for them in the first place.

To begin, click the **"Inspect" button** at the bottom right side of the dialog. The Inspector will go through the document, searching for various types of metadata. If it finds any, it will alert you with an exclamation point next to the type of content it located, as in the screenshot below.

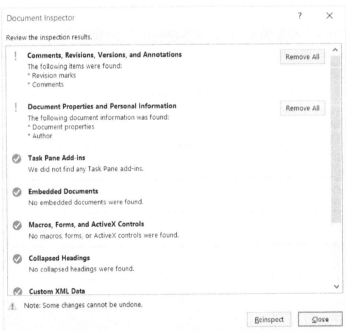

Again, the mere fact that the Document Inspector has found some "metadata" doesn't necessarily clue you in to what, exactly, that information includes. (In the screenshot, we see

564

that Word found Revision marks and Document Properties including the Author name, but we don't know the specifics.)

If you click the "**Remove All**" **button** next to a category of data, the Inspector will remove everything in that category. You can take an incremental approach and "Remove All" items in one category and then check the document, or you can click each of the "Remove All" buttons to scrub the suspect items in all of the categories tagged by the inspection utility.

After you click "Remove All," the Inspector does its thing and then shows you the results, which might look something like the following (depending on whether you clicked "Remove All" for each category of metadata). The exclamation point next to that category will be gone, replaced by a checkbox in a blue circle.

Even though everything looks fine, I usually click the "**Reinspect**" **button**, then click "**Inspect**," to have the Inspector make another pass through the document again.

When you're finished, click the "**Close**" button.

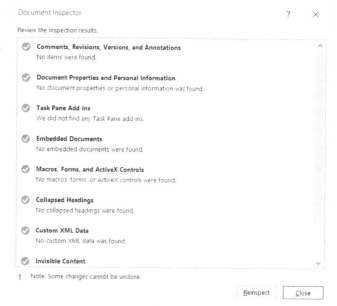

CAUTION: After running the Document Inspector, immediately save the cleaned document. This is a critical step because if you close it without saving, the metadata you thought had been removed will remain in the document!

To see how effective the Document Inspector was, click the **File tab** and take a look at the right-hand side of the **Info screen**. Most of the information under "**Properties**" has been cleared. (You'll probably still see the author's name, but you can backspace over it and then save and close the doc. In my test, the author name did not repopulate when I reopened the document.)

However, if you click the "**Properties**" drop-down and choose "**Advanced Properties**," you'll notice that you can see the document type and location (i.e., its path in your computer) on the **General tab** of the **Properties dialog**.

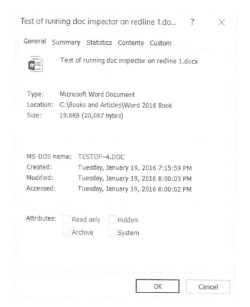

More About Metadata

Metadata: Definition and Origins

Metadata, sometimes called "data about data," refers partly to information that is embedded automatically in a document by software,[1] as well as document properties and other information that can be inserted deliberately by a human author.

This information, much or all of which is "hidden" under normal circumstances – such that the person writing, editing, or typing the document might not realize it exists – can include the identity of the author(s) and any reviewer(s), the company where the document author works, the software used to create the document, the computer and the exact path where the document is stored, the date and time the document was created and/or modified, the title of the document and any keywords or summary used to identify it, the amount of time spent on editing the document, the template on which it was based, and so on. If a document was routed by e-mail to other people in your firm, detailed routing information could be hidden in the document.

In addition, revisions intended to be confidential – insertions, deletions, and comments – can be stored in a document. Even if you don't see any "markup" on your screen, such material could remain in your document unless you took active steps to remove it. And if so, others will be able to view the markup simply by changing a setting or two.[2] As Microsoft warns:

> "...hidden text, revised text, comments, or field codes can remain in a document even though you don't see such information or expect it to be in the final version. If you entered personal information, such as your name or e-mail address, when you registered your software, some Microsoft Office documents store that information as part of the document. Information contained in custom fields that you add to the document, such as an 'author' or 'owner' field, is not automatically removed. You must edit or remove the custom field to remove that information."

From "Remove personal or hidden information,"
http://office.microsoft.com/en-us/word/HP051901021033.aspx

Limitations of the Document Inspector

Again, keep in mind that the Document Inspector, although useful, is a blunt instrument (you can't fine-tune it; it removes all or none of the items in the various categories of metadata that Microsoft included). Also, there are certain types of information that might remain in your document even after you use the Document Inspector. For example, the document location (i.e.,

---

[1] Some of this information is added/tracked by the operating system, as well as by the application used to create the document (in this case, Word).

[2] In particular, if you did not accept or reject all of the changes, delete the comments, and then save the scrubbed document, the revision marks will be visible when someone chooses the "**All Markup**" option in the **Display for Review drop-down** on the **Review tab**.

its path in the computer), as well as the document type, still appears when you click Advanced Document Properties and open the traditional Properties dialog.

Some Items That the Document Inspector Might Not Remove

Besides the above-mentioned items, there are other types of information or objects that can be embedded in your documents and potentially can be viewed by others. These additional items, which the Document Inspector might not flag or remove, include:

- Bookmarks
- Creation date
- Document variables
- Field codes
- Hyperlinks
- Linked objects
- Modified date
- OLE graphics
- Print date
- Smart Tags
- Text that is hidden by applying a very small font size (so that it is invisible, or nearly so, at a normal screen magnification)
- Text that is hidden by coloring it white (so that it is invisible on a white background)
- Unlink document property fields
- Unused styles
- Visual Basic for Applications (VBA)

Some of these items might not be problematic, but it's worth further investigation, given the risk of malpractice exposure.

Third-Party Metadata Removal Programs

Because the Document Inspector doesn't eliminate all types of metadata from Word documents, consider purchasing a third-party metadata removal program and using it in conjunction with (or instead of) Word's built-in utility. There are several such programs available. I don't have enough personal experience with any of them to enable me to make a recommendation, but you can request evaluation copies (usually good for 30 days). That might be a good way to compare the various utilities.

Before downloading a trial version, be sure to inquire about any possible incompatibilities with other software you have and make sure you can uninstall the trial version easily. Also, you might want to install trial versions of different metadata scrubbers on different computers, just in case they are incompatible with one another (and also to make it easier to differentiate among them).

SIDEBAR: What Does "Mark as Final" Do?

Word 2016 comes with a feature, introduced in Word 2007, called "**Mark as Final.**" When Mark as Final is applied, the document is saved in read-only mode and formatting commands are disabled / grayed out so that other people with whom you are collaborating are discouraged from making changes. However, it is of limited utility, for the following reasons:

- Although it makes the document read-only, anyone who receives the document can change the document status easily and make it editable again.

- Despite the feature's name, it doesn't work like Track Changes, and shouldn't be thought of as a substitute therefor.

- And finally, if someone opens a "Marked as Final" document in an older version of Word that lacks this feature, the read-only status is removed.

Still, you might find the feature useful as a reminder to others (or to yourself) that a document is a final draft and shouldn't be modified. To use it, click the **File tab**, **Info screen**, **Protect Document**, **Mark as Final**. You'll see the message box depicted at right.

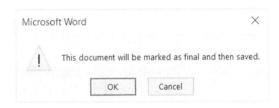

After you click "**OK**," another message box will appear:

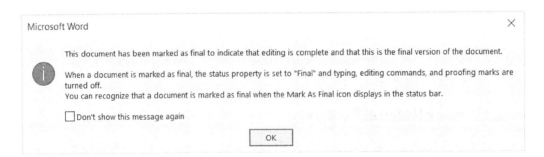

After you click OK again, a "**Marked as Final**" icon will appear in the Status Bar (though it's tiny and you might not notice it).

Most icons in most tabs on the Ribbon will be grayed out (and the Ribbon will be collapsed) so that – in theory – no one can apply any formatting to the finalized document. But there's an easy workaround: Anyone who opens the document can just click the "**Edit Anyway**" **button** displayed in the Message Bar above the document *or* click **File**, **Info**, "**Protect Document**," and click "**Mark as Final**" again in order to *unmark* the document.

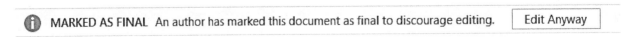

Restrict Editing (Apply a Password for Editing)

As mentioned on page 569, a better option than Mark as Final might be **Restrict Editing**, a feature that lets you limit the types of editing that certain people can do. Restrict Editing is on the **Review tab**, all the way to the right under **Protect**. You can also get to this feature by from the **File tab**, **Info**, under the "**Protect Document**" drop-down.

Click to open the **Restrict Formatting and Editing Pane** (screenshot below).

The first option on the pane, **Formatting restrictions**, lets you limit the *styles* other people working on the document can use (click **Settings…**, then choose the allowable styles from the resulting list).

There is also an option called **Editing restrictions** that permits only certain types of editing: Tracked changes, Comments, Filling in Forms, or No changes (Read only). You can specify exceptions – that is, individuals who are allowed to edit all or a portion of the document.

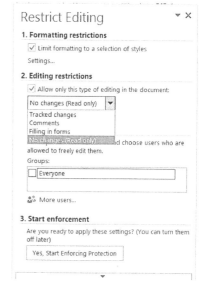

Either before or after you have checked one or both options, navigate to **Groups** and choose the individuals you wish to restrict. If their names are not listed, click "**More users…**" and, in the "**Add Users**" box, type the e-mail addresses of specific people. Then click "**OK**."

Add Users

569

When you are ready to apply the restrictions, click the "**Yes, Start Enforcing Protection**" **button**. When the **Start Enforcing Protection dialog** opens, type and confirm a password – to restrict editing, not to prevent opening the document – and click "**OK**." **CAUTION**: Be sure to make note of the password and keep it in a safe, easy-to-remember location.

To disable protection, open the document, go to the **Protect group** on the **Review tab**, click **Protect Document**, then click "**Stop Protection**." (If you prefer, you can do the same thing from the **File tab**, **Info**, **Protect Document**.) You'll have to enter the correct password and then click **OK** in order to remove the password.

PART IX: Troubleshooting Tips

Troubleshooting Tips and Best Practices

Troubleshooting can be tricky. Sometimes it's hard to figure out whether the problem you're experiencing is document-specific, is a bug in Word, is a Windows glitch, is the result of a hardware or software conflict, or derives from something else altogether. And even if you determine that the problem is confined to one ornery document, how do you know whether it's a simple formatting error or something more serious, like document corruption?

That is the crux of the matter: You have to isolate the problem, which essentially means focusing on the most likely causes and then testing each one in turn. To some extent troubleshooting is an art, and it involves a certain amount of educated guesswork, but you're more likely to get results if you proceed in a careful, methodical manner. These tips are intended to give you some guidance as you try to diagnose your issues with Word.

Consider the Context

The context matters. If a problem occurs only with one document, or only on one computer, that is an important clue. If it occurs only when you print, only when you print envelopes, or only when you exit from Word, that is an important clue. If it occurs only when you are working with styles, that is an important clue.

Under what circumstances do you experience the problem? Does it seem to be associated with one particular task? Does it trigger any error message? (If so, take a screenshot of the message and pass it along to your IT department – or, if you don't have an IT department, look up the error message on Google or some other Internet search engine.)

Do other members of your organization report the same type of trouble? If not, is there anything in their setup – their computer, their attached printer(s), specialized software that not everyone else uses, other hardware (such as a scanner), the way they've configured Word, etc. – that might explain what's going on?

Does the problem occur only in documents that have been converted from WordPerfect? In documents that have been "round-tripped" between Word and WordPerfect?

Does the problem occur only in .doc files or files labeled as being in "Compatibility Mode"?

Did the unruly document originate in house or at another company? Was it scanned in and converted from scanning software?

Is it a document that you have been reusing repeatedly – saving as a new document – since the beginning of time (rather than copying and pasting without formatting into a new blank document and then applying styles or direct formatting)?

Is it laden with a large number of styles or complex formatting, such as nested tables?

These sorts of questions can help you pinpoint the problem.

Test One Potential Cause at a Time

It is important to test, and rule out, *one potential cause at a time*. Keep track of what you have tested so that you don't duplicate your efforts.

In addition, you need to narrow your focus to those items that are *the most likely reasons* for the specific problem you're dealing with. For example, if the way that a document appears on the screen has changed—if it suddenly seems larger or smaller than usual—it's probably just a display issue, and you should check the View tab (and possibly the Zoom dialog) to see if anything there is out of the ordinary. Has the Draft document view been enabled? If so, that might explain why you can't see the pleading lines and line numbers.

If underlining doesn't appear on the screen but does appear in the printed document, that probably is a display issue, too. Try changing the magnification of the document (zoom to about 115%) and see if that makes a difference.

Start With the Simple and Obvious Solutions

When you're troubleshooting, it's always best to start with the simplest and most obvious solution and work your way toward more complex fixes. More often than not, whatever is causing the problem is something fairly straightforward. (It's almost never something that can be solved by uninstalling and reinstalling the software; such a drastic move should always be a last resort.) In fact, formatting issues often can be traced to a setting in either the Paragraph dialog or the Page Setup dialog.

In the next few pages, I've listed some other common sources of formatting issues that you might want to check, depending on the symptoms.

The Paragraph Dialog

As I've recommended throughout the book, many problems result from erroneous settings in the **Paragraph dialog box**. Depending on the symptoms, that can be a good starting point for your troubleshooting efforts. Review both the **Indents and Spacing tab** and the **Line and Page Breaks tab**. Look for any setting that doesn't seem "normal." Is there a hanging indent – or no indent at all – where you intended a first-line indent? Does the Spacing After box show 3 points instead of 12? Is "Page Break Before" checked even though the paragraph ought to be on the same page as the previous paragraph?

If nothing in those settings appears unusual or unexpected, display the **Non-Printing Characters (Ctrl Shift * [asterisk])** and/or invoke **Reveal Formatting (Shift F1)**. Again, look for anything out of the ordinary.

Line spacing and "Before" and "After" spacing can cause all kinds of havoc in your documents. As an example, a few years ago one of my clients had an issue in a Word document that had been converted from WordPerfect. The document contained a table with text that was squished up toward the top of the cells. It seemed logical to deduce that the problem might have resulted from the vertical text alignment in the cell (Table Tools, Layout, Alignment). So I changed the text alignment so that it was centered vertically, as opposed to being at the top of the cell. No difference. I checked the row height (Table Tools, Layout, Cell Size dialog or Table Tools, Layout, Properties, Row tab) to make sure there wasn't a setting that was limiting the height of the cell such that it was too narrow for the text. There wasn't.

Finally, with my cursor in one of the problematic cells, I launched the Paragraph dialog. And voilà! As it turned out, the line spacing was set to 6 points – approximately half the height of a standard line. As soon as I changed the setting to single spacing, the text appeared normal. (Changing to Exactly 12 pt would have resolved the issue, too.)

Another client had a problem with a footnote that was too close to the pleading footer; the bottom line of the footnote was cut off. One of the staff members suggested changing the bottom page margin (increasing the margin to accommodate all of the footnote text). That worked, but it affected every page of the document, leaving big gaps at the bottom of most of them.

I thought it might be preferable to add some extra white space after the footnote by using the "Spacing After" option. So we opened the Paragraph dialog and added 6 points of space after the footnote text. It was a great solution because it bumped the footnote text up enough to be completely visible without having an effect on any other pages.

Sometimes it takes a little imaginative thinking to figure out what's going on and devise an elegant solution – one that doesn't create new problems. (And the more you work with Word, the better you'll become at this sort of troubleshooting.)

The Page Setup Dialog

If nothing is amiss with the paragraph formatting, perhaps the problem lies with the page formatting. To rule out that possibility, open the **Page Setup dialog** (by clicking the **dialog launcher** in the **Page Setup group** on the **Layout tab**) and look for any odd settings. Review both the **Margins** and **Layout tabs**.

In particular, check the **page margins**. In addition, note whether the **header** and/or **footer margin** (on the Layout tab) is larger (or smaller) than you meant it to be. And be sure to check the **Preview area (Applied to:)** toward the bottom of each tab to see if settings that should have been applied to the whole document were applied, incorrectly, to "This Section Only" or "This Point Forward" instead of "Whole Document" – or vice versa.

It might not occur to you to review the "**Multiple pages**" **option** in the "**Pages**" **section** of the **Margins tab**, but if your pleading looks funky, with a wide left margin on the odd pages and a wide right margin on the even pages, it's possible that this setting has gotten changed from "Normal" to "Mirror Margins." If so, change it back, then click "**OK**" to save your changes.

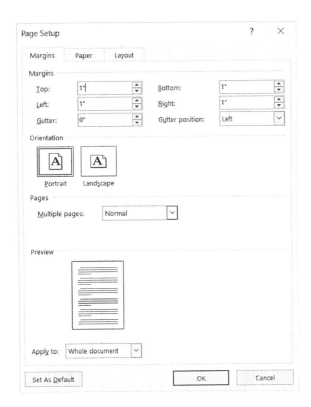 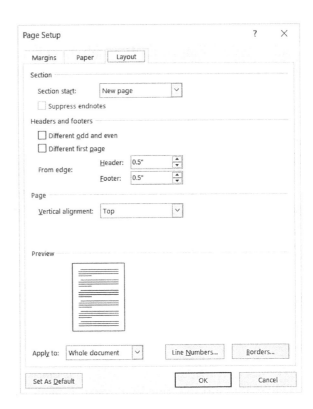

The Word Options

If you have reviewed both the Paragraph dialog and the Page Setup dialog, enabled "Show / Hide" (i.e., displayed the Non-Printing Characters), and checked Reveal Formatting and you're still stumped, take a look at the Word Options (**File tab**, **Options**). Unfortunately, these settings can be somewhat daunting, not only because it is hard to figure out where the settings are located, but also because the labels are pretty obscure.

Still, it's possible that some setting buried in the Options is the reason your document is misbehaving. Be sure to check the following (if they strike you as possible culprits):

The AutoCorrect Options

AutoCorrect Options (under **Proofing**)—especially the **AutoFormat As You Type** tab. The settings for bulleted lists, numbered lists, border lines, and "**Set left- and first-indent with tabs and backspaces**" can cause unexpected behavior. In particular, if the latter option is enabled, pressing the Tab key will produce not a left tab, but a first-line indent (formatting that will carry over to the next paragraph automatically when you press Enter).

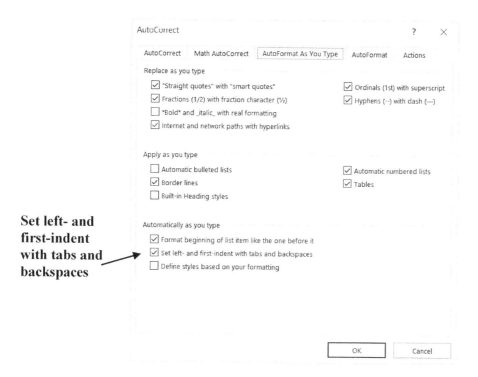

The Display Options

There are a couple of Display options that could throw you off your stride.

Many people don't realize that if any of the boxes under "**Always show these formatting marks on the screen**" is checked, those mark(s) will display in your document no matter whether you've manually toggled "**Show / Hide**" on or off via the **Paragraph icon** in the **Paragraph group** on the **Home tab** (or by pressing **Ctrl Shift * [asterisk]**). In other words, the settings in Word Options take precedence over your manual settings.

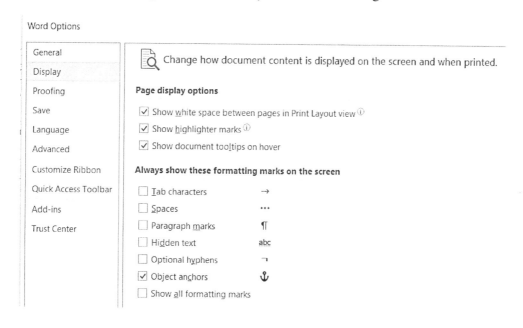

Also, if "**Update fields before printing**" is turned off (which it is by default), certain items in your document might not look correct when you print your document because the underlying field codes (SEQ codes, page number codes, cross-references, indexes, etc.) are not updating. To change this behavior, click to check (enable) the option.

Word Options, Display, Printing Options
"Update fields before printing"

Advanced Editing Options

There are a few **Editing options** in the **Advanced** category that are worth reviewing.

One Editing option to watch out for is "**Typing replaces selected text**." If that option is checked, you can delete text accidentally. For example, when you tab to the next column in a table, Word by default selects the text in the table cell to which you tab. If you then press a key (other than one of the arrow keys), Word will delete the selected text and replace it with whichever character is on the key you pressed.

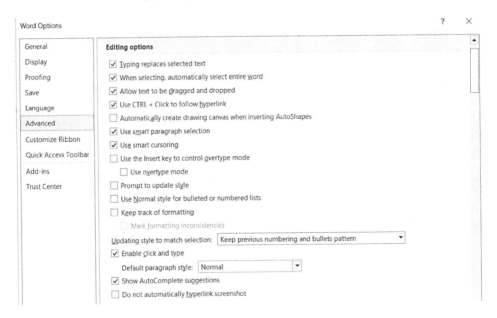

An Editing option you might want to enable (it is disabled by default in Word 2016) is "**Prompt to Update Style**." If the option is enabled, a message box pops up and warns you when you reapply a style to text after changing the formatting of the text. It lets you choose

578

between updating the style to reflect the modifications you've made – which may or may not be a good idea – and reapplying the formatting of the style to the selected text. Note that the message box also gives you the option of automatically updating the style when you make manual formatting changes, something you ***should not*** do because of the havoc that option can wreak with your documents. See the Sidebar about automatic updating that starts on page 407.

To enable the Prompt to Update Style option, click the **File tab**, **Options**, **Advanced**. Under "**Editing options**" (which appears at the top of the Advanced category), navigate to and **click** to check the option labeled "**Prompt to update style**." Be sure to click "**OK**" to save your changes when you exit from the Word Options.

For information about some additional Word Options you might want to tweak, see the section starting on page 97.

These tips, while not exhaustive, should give you some useful ideas about how to begin the troubleshooting process, as well as some common sources of formatting problems. A solid understanding of Word's logic, as well as a methodical approach, will go a long way toward helping you to diagnose the occasional, but inevitable, difficulties that are endemic to working with computers.

SIDEBAR: Conflicts Between Word and Other Programs (Add-Ins)

Some problems can be traced to conflicts between Word and other software on your computer. In particular, there can be conflicts with the so-called add-ins, third-party programs that integrate with Word but that also – on occasion – can cause problems. (Microsoft also creates some of its own add-ins for the Office programs.)

One potential source of trouble, ironically, is the Data Execution Prevention (DEP) function built into Office. This important security measure, which helps to block so-called "overflow exploits" that allow viruses and worms to run on your machine, also can cause add-ins to fail – which can cause Word to crash. As explained in a "Help" article:

"Introduced in Microsoft Office 2010, Data Execution Prevention (DEP) helps prevent badly-written code from running and harming your computer. When an add-in that isn't designed to function in a DEP-enabled environment tries to run, the Office program you're using stops working (crashes) to help protect your computer."

The excerpt is from the article entitled "Why is my add-in crashing?"; see also "View, manage, and install add-ins in the Office programs." To locate these articles, type "DEP" or "add-ins" in the "Tell me what you want to do" box. (Alternatively, you can open Word Help by pressing F1 and search directly from there, or go to the Microsoft Support site, located at http://support.microsoft.com, and enter your search term in the box toward the top of the page.)

Sometimes, Word will prompt you to disable an add-in that caused the program to crash. You might or might not want to do so, but if Word continues to crash, click "Yes" (or "OK") when the prompt appears and see if that makes a difference. (If the problem recurs and you need to use both the add-in and Word, contact the add-in manufacturer; the company might have a patch that will resolve the issue. Also, sometimes a different version of the add-in program will run without problems.)

You can disable certain troublesome add-ins yourself. To do so, click the **File tab**, **Options**, click the "**Add-ins**" category, then navigate to the "**Manage**" drop-down at the bottom of the dialog. Choose an add-in type and click "**Go**" to review the add-ins and disable any that appear to be causing issues. **USE CAUTION** (and take notes) when changing these settings, especially if you are not an advanced user!

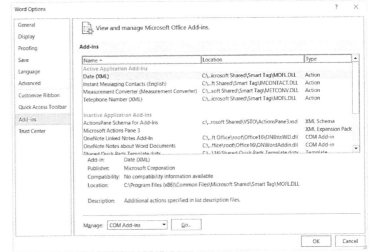

Preventing, Diagnosing, and Repairing Document Corruption

Because document corruption is a fact of life, the best strategy for dealing with it is a defensive one: namely, (1) practice good computer "hygiene"; and (2) back up critical files frequently (and back them up to many different storage media, including online sites such as OneDrive, Google Drive, or Dropbox; external drives; USB drives; CDs and/or DVDs; and so forth). If you are diligent about both types of prevention, you are less likely to experience corruption, and you'll probably suffer less damage – and be in a better position to recover your work – if it does strike.

Common Causes of Corruption

Document corruption can occur for a wide range of reasons, including (but not limited to) the following: a sudden power surge or outage; saving a document while your computer resources are low; saving a file directly to or opening a file directly from a USB drive, a CD or DVD, or another removable storage medium (you should copy the file to your computer and always open it from there); "round-tripping" a document between Word and WordPerfect formats (i.e., saving the same document first in one format and then in another format); macro viruses; a corrupted printer driver; a bad sector on your hard drive; problems with / incompatibilities related to third-party "add-in" programs that work with Word; using the Master Document feature, Fast Saves, Versioning, Nested Tables, or certain other complex features (some of which are no longer available in Word).

You can't prevent all of those events, but you can reduce the likelihood of at least a few of them. For ideas, see the section about good computer "hygiene" starting on page 584.

Symptoms of Corruption

First, it's worth pointing out that many phenomena besides corruption can produce unusual formatting or unexpected behavior. Before deciding that a file is corrupt, be sure to investigate other, less serious possibilities—and always try less drastic remedies first.

Suspect corruption if you experience one or more of the following problems:

- Difficulty saving a file;

- Inability to open a file;

- Opening a file causes Word to crash or freezes the computer;

- Uncontrollable cursor movement (and/or the cursor skips past certain sections or pages);

- Improper display of certain characters or the presence of "garbage" characters in the document;

- Constant repagination;
- Sudden changes in formatting;
- Error messages about document corruption;
- Error messages about "insufficient memory."

This is not an all-inclusive list, but it includes many of the most common symptoms of document corruption.

Some Possible Remedies and Workarounds

Depending on the problem(s) you are experiencing, try one or more of the following remedies or workarounds. They might help in some circumstances, although it is possible that they won't work for you.

CAUTION: To avoid making matters worse, always make at least one a backup copy of the problem document before attempting any repairs. That way, if the remedy doesn't work—or creates new problems—you can try something else.

If you are having trouble opening a Word document, use the "**Open and Repair**" **command** on the "Open" button at the lower right side of the Open dialog.

Type an "X" at the top of a blank document, then click the **Insert tab**, click the "**Object**" **drop-down**, and click "**Text from File...**" (to insert the text from the file into the blank document). Then **delete the "X"** and **save the document with a new name**. This procedure (occasionally referred to as the "X-retrieve" method) sometimes removes corruption because it inserts the content of the file without the so-called "file header," which can become corrupted.

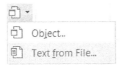

If you can work with a document but you are experiencing problems such as the cursor skipping certain sections of the document, turn on the Show / Hide (click the **Paragraph icon** in the **Paragraph group** on the **Home tab** or press **Ctrl Shift *** [asterisk]), and then select the entire document *up to, but not including, the very last paragraph mark*. (The last paragraph mark in a document can contain corruption.) Copy the selected portion and paste it into a new blank document screen, then save the copy with a new name.

Alternatively, try selecting the portion of the document up to the point where the cursor is skipping, copy that portion, and **paste it into a new blank document**. Then copy and paste the next "good" portion. Test to make sure the new document doesn't experience the same problem. If all seems well, save it with a new name. You might have to re-create the corrupted section of the original document from scratch, but at least you will have salvaged the bulk of the document.

Another possible solution is to copy the text of the document and paste into a blank document *as **unformatted text*** (the "Keep Text Only" paste option). Sometimes that strips out the corruption. Of course, it also strips out styles and most other formatting, so you will have to reapply the formatting from scratch.

You can try saving the file **in a different format** – if the original file was saved as a .docx, try saving it as a .doc, or vice versa. Or try saving the file to RTF, which will preserve most of your formatting, or to Plain Text, which will discard your formatting (you'll have to reapply the formatting from scratch, a less-than-desirable option, but one that might be necessary under the circumstances). Then reopen the document in Word and check to see if the problem persists.

Deleting or Renaming the Normal Template

One common cause of document corruption in Word is a corrupted Normal template (Normal.dotm). If you have reason to believe your Normal template has become corrupted, try the following:

1. Exit from Word;

2. Locate the Normal.dotm template;

3. Delete the template altogether *or*, if you haven't made a backup copy, rename it (perhaps giving it a name such as "Normal-Old.dotm")[1]; and

4. Reopen Word.

When you reopen the program, Word will re-create a ***generic*** Normal template (Normal.dotm) - one that uses Microsoft's default settings – from scratch. If having a new Normal template resolves the problems, you should be able to copy at least some of your customizations (styles and macros) from a backup copy, if any (or possibly from the original [renamed] Normal template), to the new template via the Organizer. For instructions on using the Organizer to copy customizations between documents (or templates), see the section starting on page 393.

---

[1] People sometimes delete the Normal.dotm rather than renaming it. However, the Normal template stores customized macros, styles, and AutoText entries; if you delete the template, those customizations will be lost – unless you had the foresight to create a backup copy of the template before problems arose. It's a good idea to ***make a backup copy while the program is functioning normally*** (and to create updated backups periodically). That way, if the original template becomes corrupted, you can delete it and copy any customizations from the backup copy to the new, generic Normal.dotm template that Word will create the next time you launch the program.

If having a new Normal template ***doesn't*** resolve the problems, you can restore the original template (assuming you renamed it rather than deleting it) or the backup copy (if you deleted the original template).

To replace the generic new Normal template with the template containing your customizations, do the following:

- Exit from Word;

- Rename (or delete) the new Normal.dotm template;

- Give the backup copy (or the original template) the name "Normal.dotm" (without quotation marks); and

- Restart Word.

Good Computer "Hygiene"

There are several steps you can take to reduce the likelihood of computer problems and minimize the damage in the event of a serious issue such as a power outage. Some of these preventative steps are fairly obvious, but I will point them out anyway because the consequences can be serious. As the saying goes, an ounce of prevention is worth a pound of cure. And on occasion, I have learned that lesson the hard way; my hope is that these gentle reminders will help you avoid similar ***tsouris*** (heartbreak, calamity, trouble).

- Don't place beverages within spill distance of your computer keyboard. We've all done it, but it's better to learn from someone else's sad experience than from your own why it's not a good idea. The more important your document, the farther away the beverage should be. (Preferably, on a different table...)

- Invest in (or ask your firm to invest in) a heavy-duty surge suppressor so that normal power spikes don't damage your computer.

- If you work on a laptop, make sure your machine is plugged into an outlet (or, better yet, a heavy-duty surge suppressor that is plugged into an outlet) at all times and that the electrical connection is good.

- Save your documents frequently (every few minutes). Automatic backups are not an adequate substitute for frequent manual saves.

- Make copies of critical files, including the Normal template and any other template(s) that you've customized.

- Make frequent backups onto external media, such as "cloud" (online) storage, an external hard drive, a USB drive, and/or a CD or DVD. However, be sure to do so with the next tip in mind.

- Never save a file directly to or open a file directly from a floppy disk, a USB drive, a CD, a DVD, etc. Instead, ***copy the file to your hard drive***, then open it into Word ***from the storage location on hard drive*** by using the keyboard shortcut Ctrl F12 or Ctrl O or by clicking the File tab, Open.

- Don't round-trip documents between Word and WordPerfect—or, for that matter, between Word and RTF, or even between different Word file formats (.doc and .docx).

- Watch for signs of macro viruses, including the inability to save a regular file (a .docx or a .doc) as anything other than a .dot, a .dotx, or a .dotm

Resources

There are lots of good articles available online about recovering / repairing corrupted documents. Here are a few to get you started:

"How to troubleshoot damaged documents in Word":
http://support.microsoft.com/kb/918429

This extensive article from the Microsoft Knowledge Base suggests numerous ways to diagnose and repair documents that appear to be damaged (corrupted). If you experience any of the problems identified in the article, or any other unusual behavior that you suspect is a result of corruption, read each of the proposed solutions to try to determine which one(s) apply in your specific situation. Make a backup copy of the document, if possible, before attempting any repairs – just to be on the safe side.

http://word.mvps.org/FAQs/ApplicationErrors.htm

The Microsoft MVPs (volunteer experts in the various Microsoft Office programs) have an entire page with links to articles about troubleshooting Word problems. Although many of the articles deal with older versions of Word, you'll probably find the advice helpful.

http://word.mvps.org/FAQs/AppErrors/CorruptDoc.htm

This article from the MVPs site discusses some causes of document corruption and a few remedies / workarounds. Note in particular the points they make about the features that increase the likelihood of corruption, as well as the fact that corruption often is stored in a section break or a paragraph mark, especially the very last paragraph mark in a document.

SIDEBAR: Backing Up Your Normal Template

Be sure to back up your Normal template (Normal.dotm) after you have customized styles, AutoText entries, Quick Parts that you have stored in the Normal.dotm template, and formatted AutoCorrect entries. Start by exiting from Word. Then do the following:

1. Locate your Normal template (the file name is Normal.dotm). Ordinarily, the file is stored here:

    C:\Users\<UserName>\AppData\Roaming\Microsoft\Templates

    If you don't see a recent file named Normal.dotm in that location, look in this location instead:

    C:\Users\<UserName>\Documents\Custom Office Templates

2. Copy the Normal.dotm template and paste the copy in the same folder where you found the original.

3. Give the backup copy a name such as "NormalOld.dotm," "NormalBackup.dotm," or "Normal 1-25-2016.dotm" (i.e., use the current date in the name of the file to differentiate it from earlier or later backup copies).

    CAUTION: Don't change the file extension!

4. Consider saving a copy of the backup copy to the cloud or to an external drive or similar medium.

If Word crashes and then creates a new Normal.dotm – and you find that your customizations are missing – do the following:

1. Exit from Word.

2. Browse to the folder where your backup copy of Normal.dotm is stored.

3. Before renaming your custom Normal.dotm, rename the generic Normal.dotm. Consider calling it something like "NormalGeneric.dotm."

4. Next, make another copy of your backup copy so that you will be prepared if Word crashes again at some point.

5. Rename one of the backup copies "Normal.dotm."

6. Reopen Word.

Your customizations should be available again.

PART X: File Conversion Issues

Opening .docx Files With Older Versions of MS Word

As you know, by default, Word 2016 saves documents in a new file format, ".docx," which is a form of Extensible Markup Language or XML. Microsoft chose that format in part to allow Word users to share documents with users of Open Office (another word processing program). Other reputed advantages of the .docx format are that it produces smaller files and supposedly is less prone to corruption than the standard file format used by earlier versions of MS Word (.doc).[1]

Because the .docx format is not "backwards compatible" with any version of Word prior to Word 2007, people who still use Word 2003 (or any older version of Word) could have difficulty opening documents created in Word 2016 unless they use a special converter. That converter, also referred to as a "Compatibility Pack" is available online from Microsoft free of charge.

If you regularly exchange Word documents with clients or others who use a very old version of Word, you can save those documents in the .doc file format (i.e., change the Save as type to "Word 97-2003 Documents (*.doc)"). That is probably a better choice than changing your default file format to .doc – a rather drastic step – because certain newer features won't work, or will have more limited functionality, within .doc files.[2]

Another option is to let your clients know about, and perhaps even send them a link to, the Compatibility Pack, and send them a link to, the "Compatibility Pack." For more information, see the following:

"Microsoft Office Compatibility Pack for Word, Excel, and PowerPoint"
https://products.office.com/en-us/microsoft-office-compatibility-pack-for-word-excel-and-powerpoint

"How to use earlier versions of Excel, PowerPoint, and Word to open and save files from 2007 Office programs"
http://support.microsoft.com/kb/924074

---

[1] Or, at least, it reportedly does better at recovering and fixing corrupted files.

[2] If you do save files in .doc format, don't convert them back to .docx files. As with WordPerfect to Word conversions, going back and forth between file formats can trigger document corruption – even though .doc and .docx are both Word files.

WordPerfect to Word Conversions

Word 2016 can "read" native WordPerfect files.[1] However, some features of WordPerfect won't translate well if you open a WP file directly into Word. In general, the more complex the formatting of the original document, the less successfully it will convert. Word just doesn't "get" all of WordPerfect's codes. And, of course, macros, QuickWords, and similar automated features won't convert at all.

Don't even think about opening pleadings directly into Word. Doing so creates too many intractable problems and will result in much frustration and lost time. I speak from experience (I had many opportunities to test this option during my 18-month stint as a consultant at the Department of Justice in Southern California during their conversion from WordPerfect to Word).

The best practice for dealing with pleadings is to copy the body of the document, then open a Word pleading, position the cursor in an empty (blank) paragraph, and paste the text without any formatting – i.e., using the "Keep Text Only" paste option. The text from the WordPerfect document will take on the formatting at the cursor position.

Most of the body text will not need much reformatting (although for some reason, pasting from WordPerfect into Word using "Keep Text Only" does not remove first-line tabs, so you will have to delete them[2]). However, you'll have to apply heading styles and do some other cleanup. It's somewhat time-consuming, but ultimately results in a reasonably clean and trouble-free document.

Here are a few other methods you can try with WordPerfect docs that are not as heavily formatted:

- Open the WordPerfect document directly into Word using **File**, **Open** or any other method you like. This method works pretty well with documents containing plain text and also with documents containing elements such as columnar tables. (Watch out for text in one or more rows of the converted table possibly being truncated as a result of the line spacing changing to Exactly 6 pt, which is about half of a standard line. If that happens, select the entire row, open the Paragraph dialog, and change the line spacing to Exactly 12 pt or Single.)

- Pull the text of the WordPerfect document into Word by clicking the **Object drop-down** toward the right side of the **Insert tab** and choosing **Text From File**.

---

[1] Whether you use the File, Open method or the Insert Text From File method, you might find that only Word files are visible in the **Open dialog** or the **Insert File dialog**. In that case, navigate to the File Type drop-down at the bottom right side of the dialog (it isn't labeled, but you'll recognize it as a File Type field) and choose "**All Files**."

[2] For a quick way to delete these tabs, see the instructions starting on page 295 about using Find and Replace to replace tab characters with nothing.

Again, this method works pretty well with documents that don't contain much complex formatting.

- Save the WordPerfect file as a Word document, and then open the converted document into Word. The most recent versions of WordPerfect (X7 and X6) allow you to save files in .docx format (choose "**MS Word 2007/2010/2013**" or "**MS Word 2007/2010**" from the "File type" drop-down) or in .doc format (choose "**MS Word 97/2000/2002/2003**" from the "File type" drop-down).

- Save the WordPerfect file as **RTF** (Rich Text Format), an "intermediate" format invented by Microsoft that both Word and WordPerfect can read, and then open the file into Word. (It might be a good idea to make a copy of the document before experimenting, even though you're not likely to overwrite the original file when you save it as an RTF. [3])

There's no way to tell whether any of these methods will work until you try. Keep in mind, though, that if all else fails, you can copy and paste text without formatting and then apply styles and other formatting to the pasted text. Also keep in mind that after you have applied a style and/or direct (manual) formatting to one paragraph, you can copy and paste that formatting to other paragraphs with the Format Painter. That can be a significant time-saver.

---

[3] When you save a file in RTF format, it takes on the file extension .rtf, leaving the original file intact.

Word to WordPerfect Conversions

You can no longer save Word documents in WordPerfect format, but recent versions of WordPerfect (starting with WP X4) can convert .docx or .doc files without difficulty with either File, Open or Insert, File. If you have a version of WordPerfect earlier than version X4, you will have to do one of the following:

- Save your Word file **as a .doc (a Word 97-2003 file)** and then open it into WordPerfect via File, Open or Insert, File; *or*

- Save your Word document **in RTF format** (which preserves much of the formatting) or **as plain text (.txt)** (which will strip out all the formatting), and then open the converted file into WordPerfect; *or*

- **Copy and paste** text from the Word document into WordPerfect, which will wipe out most or all of the formatting.

    CAUTION: You might get an error message if you try to paste text from Word 2016 into a legacy version of WordPerfect. If so, use the **Paste Special** command (found on the **Edit menu** in WordPerfect) and then paste the text either as **Unformatted Text** or, if it possible, as **Rich Text Format**. I say "if possible" because that option, despite being available in the Paste Special dialog, doesn't work in some older versions of WordPerfect, and you'll get an error message if you attempt to use it.

    Typically, Word files that are opened directly into WordPerfect bring a lot of extraneous codes with them, including First Ln Ind (First Line Indent) codes and Lft Mar Adj (Left Margin Adjustment) codes. If the profusion of codes is problematic, you can clean up the document with WordPerfect's **Find and Replace** feature, using either **Match Codes…** or **Type, Specific Codes…**, and replace each instance of a particular code with **<Nothing>** (the "**Replace All**" option makes relatively short work of this process). Note that you might have to run through the document more than once.

    As with WordPerfect-to-Word conversions, the translation often leaves something to be desired. Still, in some situations it might be preferable to the tedious alternative of copying and pasting unformatted text and then reapplying formatting to the document line by line.

Avoid Round-Tripping Your Documents

One of the most important bits of advice consultants offer to people who work in both Word and WordPerfect is not to "round-trip" documents between the two formats. In other words, avoid bringing a WordPerfect file into Word, saving it as a Word doc, and then pulling it back into WordPerfect. Doing so is a well-known – and a leading – cause of file corruption. A one-way conversion isn't particularly risky, but going back and forth is just asking for trouble. *Don't do it!*

APPENDIX A:
Quick Start Guides and Other Resources

This section lists a few resources that you might find helpful. They include Microsoft's Quick Start Guides and some other informative sites. Note that I have not personally reviewed all of these resources, and by listing them here, I am not necessarily endorsing them (with the possible exception of my own blog).

Quick Start Guides

Office 2016 (for Windows) Quick Start Guides

https://support.office.com/en-us/article/Office-2016-Quick-Start-Guides-25f909da-3e76-443d-94f4-6cdf7dedc51e

> Microsoft has made available for download (for free) PDF versions of Quick Start Guides for Office 2016 and for the individual Office 2016 programs: Word, Excel, PowerPoint, Access, Outlook, and OneNote.

Office Mobile Quick Start Guide

https://support.office.com/en-us/article/Office-Mobile-Quick-Start-Guides-c957c048-00fa-4793-8b40-4f564f9d58c6?ui=en-US&rs=en-US&ad=US

Office 2016 for the Mac Quick Start Guides

https://support.office.com/en-us/article/Office-2016-for-Mac-Quick-Start-Guides-5bccb480-0e5b-4b51-b072-66d3793ccad8?ui=en-US&rs=en-US&ad=US

Explore Word 2016 – Microsoft web site
https://support.office.com/en-IN/article/Explore-Word-2016-eb385404-cb97-4b41-b2aa-1c18d05cd383

Microsoft's Knowledge Base (MS Word, Excel, Access, Windows XP, etc.):
https://support.microsoft.com/en-us

> On-line technical support for all Microsoft products. You can run searches (queries) using natural language or key words. (Note, for example, that searching for the word "pleading" returns several articles dealing with pleading paper.) Some of the results are from Microsoft's "community" (user forums).

Microsoft's Word Support Page
https://support.office.com/en-us/word

> Tutorials, known issues, "trending topics" (in the forums), and more.

Keyboard Shortcuts for Microsoft Office Word

https://support.office.com/en-US/article/Keyboard-shortcuts-for-Microsoft-Word-2016-for-Windows-95ef89dd-7142-4b50-afb2-f762f663ceb2

Lengthy list of keyboard shortcuts for Word 2016, categorized by function.

Microsoft Word MVP Site

http://word.mvps.org/

The Word "MVPs" are experts who – although none of them actually works for Microsoft – write definitive articles (and respond to user questions in various forums) about Word and other Office programs. The site hasn't been updated since early 2014, but it remains a treasure trove of useful information.

Microsoft Word MVP FAQ Site

http://word.mvps.org/FAQs/index.htm

Very helpful site, albeit even less current than the Word section. Lots of tips and workarounds, as well as explanations of how Word works. (Note that if you type "html" instead of "htm," you'll get a "404 Not Found" error.)

Links to Web Sites of Various Word "MVPs":

http://www.mvps.org/links.html

Scroll down almost to the bottom for links to web sites run by Word gurus.

Word FAQs site (by Suzanne Barnhill, Word MVP):

http://sbarnhill.mvps.org/WordFAQs/

Barnhill is one of the best MVPs (and that's saying a lot). Her explanations tend to be unusually clear and readable.

Making the Most of Word (by Shauna Kelly, Word MVP):

http://www.shaunakelly.com/word/index.html

Lots of terrific tips here from the incomparable Shauna Kelly. Kelly's instructions for using automatic numbering are especially useful, even though she wrote them for older versions.

Windows Secrets Forums

http://windowssecrets.com/forums

Very helpful user support site started by Microsoft guru/gadfly Woody Leonhard. The Word Processing section of the Lounge is a great place for posting questions about MS Word because there are many highly knowledgeable moderators and others who will work with you to try to resolve your issues. You must create a user login in order to post.

Office Watch:
http://new.office-watch.com/

Another site started by Woody Leonhard (although I'm not sure whether he's still involved). Free information, although you must join to get full access. Helpful articles, but a rather dizzying interface.

CompuSavvy's Word & WordPerfect Tips (blog)
http://compusavvy.wordpress.com

My blog offers article-length tips, mostly about Word and WordPerfect but also about other software and technical topics. I add posts periodically, as my schedule permits.

APPENDIX B:
Where Important Word 2016 Files Are Stored

It can be helpful to know where key files such as the Normal template and the template where Building Blocks / QuickParts are stored in the computer. Because some of these files contain your customizations, it's a good idea to create backup copies from time to time (and save them to the "cloud" and/or to an external device). That way, if something happens to your computer and one of the files is damaged or is inaccessible, you don't have to re-create all of your customizations from scratch.

What follows is a list of some of the most important files and their typical locations.

Normal Template (Normal.dotm)

The Normal template (Normal.dotm) is the basis for all new (blank) documents in Word. Each user has one. Many customizations are stored in your Normal template, including your default Normal Paragraph style, certain other styles that you have created or modified, AutoCorrect entries, and macros (but *not* your personalized Quick Access Toolbar or Quick Parts / Building Blocks, which are located in separate files).

Ordinarily the Normal template is stored in the following location:

In Windows 7, 8, and 10:
C:\Users\<UserName>\AppData\Roaming\Microsoft\Templates

CAUTION: Although the "AppData\Roaming" location is where Word stores your Normal.dotm by default, you might actually have more than one Normal.dotm on your system if you have tinkered with the settings in the Word Options. For more information, keep reading.

In Windows 10, your Normal.dotm template might be located here:
C:\Users\<UserName>\Documents\Custom Office Templates

Starting with Word 2013, Microsoft created *two different places in the Word Options* that point to a user's personal / custom templates. One is located in the "**Save**" category of the Word Options and is labeled the "**Default personal templates location.**" The other is located in the "**Advanced**" category of the Word Options under "**File Locations**" and is labeled the "**User templates.**" If neither you nor anyone else at your location has changed these settings, the "Default personal templates location" points to C:\Users\<UserName>\Documents\Custom Office Templates, whereas the "User templates" location points to C:\Users\<UserName>\ AppData\Roaming\Microsoft\Templates. Under those circumstances, your Normal.dotm will be stored only in the latter location.

However, if *both* locations point to C:\Users\<UserName>\Documents\Custom Office Templates, Word apparently creates a copy of the Normal.dotm template, puts it in *that* location, and relies on that copy for everyday document formatting. At least, that appears to be the case based on fairly extensive testing that I have done in late January of 2016.

Custom Templates

By default, each user's customized (personal) templates are stored in this location on a Windows 10 computer:

C:\Users\<User Name>\Documents\Custom Office Templates

This is the location that is set, by default, in the **Word Options** (File tab, Options) in the **Save** category under "**Default personal templates location.**" Note that this is *not* where custom (personal) templates were stored in versions prior to Word 2013 (they were stored in C:\Users\<UserName>\AppData\Roaming\ Microsoft\Templates).

As mentioned above, in both Word 2016 and Word 2013, there is another location in the Word Options that points to custom (personal) templates. That location is in the **Advanced** category under "**File Locations**" and is labeled "**User templates.**"

What is exceptionally confusing is that the second location by default points to C:\Users\<UserName>\AppData\Roaming\ Microsoft\Templates.

To make things worse, the **File tab's** "**New**" **screen** displays only the custom templates that are stored in the folder listed under "Default personal templates location," but the traditional "**New**" **dialog** – which you can add to the Quick Access Toolbar by browsing to a command labeled "**New Documents or Templates**" – displays only the custom templates that are stored in the folder listed under "User templates."

Thus, you will find different templates depending on where you look for your custom templates – either File, New or the "New" dialog / "New Documents or Templates" – unless you take pro-active steps to change one of the settings in the Word Options so that they point to the same location in the computer!

Obviously, then, the best practice is to make sure that both settings in the Word Options point to the same location – and store all of your custom templates there!

Microsoft's Built-In Templates

In Windows 8 and10, you will find a bunch of built-in templates here:
C:\Program Files (x86)\Microsoft Office\root\Templates\1033
or
C:\ \Program Files\Microsoft Office\root\Templates\1033
or some variation thereof that might include the number "16" (without quotation marks) after the words "Microsoft Office."

In Windows 7, 8, and 10, at least some built-in templates are located here:
C:\Users\<UserName>\AppData\Roaming\Microsoft\Templates

Building Blocks

Word 2016 comes with two different Building Blocks templates. One contains items pre-formatted by Microsoft – various cover pages, footers, headers, page numbers, tables, text boxes, watermarks, and the like – and should not be edited directly; the other is a working copy that contains your custom Quick Parts / Building Blocks.

The template containing the pre-formatted content, called **Built-In Building Blocks.dotx**, is stored in this location in Windows 7:
C:\Program Files\Microsoft Office\Office16\Document Parts\1033\16

In Windows 8 and 10, there is a new "root" folder:
C:\Program Files (x86)\Microsoft Office\root\Office16\Document Parts\1033\16
or
C:\Program Files\Microsoft Office\root\Office16\Document Parts\1033\16

The customizable user copy is located here in Windows 7, 8, and 10 (confirmed):
C:\Users\<UserName>\AppData\Roaming\Microsoft\Document Building Blocks\1033\16

If something happens and the user-customized file becomes corrupted, Word creates a new customizable file based on the original template. (You likely will lose your Quick Parts if that happens, which is why it makes sense to *make a copy of the customized file* every so often.)

List styles gallery

The **ListGal.dat** file contains the user's customized gallery of numbered lists (i.e., it includes the lists that came with the program as well as any list styles you've created).

In Windows 7, 8, and 10:
C:\Users\<User Name>\AppData\Roaming\Microsoft\Word

Heading styles

Heading styles ordinarily are stored either in the Normal template (**Normal.dotm**) or in the document or template in which they were created. In fact, most built-in styles are saved in Normal.dotm.

Note that whenever you create a new style or modify a built-in style, the default setting in the Modify Style dialog is to store the style *in the current document*. You can choose to save the new style to the underlying template (if you have rights to modify that template), and you can use the Organizer to copy styles to other templates. (Also, you can copy styles between documents; see page 392 for instructions.)

Style Sets

Built-in Style Sets are stored here:

In Windows 7, 8, and 10:
C:\Program Files (x86)\Microsoft Office\root\Office16\1033\QuickStyles

In Windows 7, 8, and 10, custom Style Sets (if any) are stored here:
C:\ Users\<User Name>\AppData\Roaming\Microsoft\QuickStyles

Themes

Theme files have the extension **.thmx**.

Built-in themes are located here in Windows 7, 8, AND 10:
C:\Program Files\Microsoft Office\root\Document Themes 16
or
C:\Program Files (x86)\Microsoft Office\root\Document Themes 16
or some variation thereof that might include the number "16" (without quotation marks) after the words "Microsoft Office."

User-created custom themes (if any) are located here in Windows 7, 8, and 10:
C:\Users\<User Name>\AppData\Roaming\Microsoft\Templates\Document Themes

AutoRecover Files

Temporary files that Word automatically recovers in the event of a "crash" or other serious problem have the extension .asd. Normally you don't have to look for them because Word opens them in a separate pane at the left side of the screen after a power outage or similar event. They can be found here:

In Windows 7, 8, and 10:
C:\Users\<User Name>\AppData\Roaming\Microsoft\Word
(This location is automatically entered into the "Save" category of the Word Options under "AutoRecover file location.")

"Unsaved Documents" Temporary Backup Files ("Never-Saved Documents")

Note that actually there are two types of "Unsaved Documents," and the two types are saved in different locations.

In Windows 7, 8, and 10 you can find files you closed without ever saving in this folder (they are saved for approximately four days):
C:\Users\<UserName>\AppData\Local\Microsoft\Office\UnsavedFiles

"Unsaved Documents" Temporary Backup Files ("Previously-Saved Documents")

In Windows 7, 8, and 10 you can find files that you saved at least once, and named, but then closed without saving your changes (or that were on your screen when the program crashed):
C:\Users\<User Name>\AppData\Roaming\Microsoft\Word

These files, sometimes stored within temporary folder within this location, are saved for approximately four days.

QAT (Quick Access Toolbar)

The file that contains settings for your customized Quick Access Toolbar, called Word.officeUI, is stored in the following location:

In Windows 7, 8, and 10:
C:\Users\<UserName>\AppData\Local\Microsoft\Office

CAUTION: There is also a file called "Word16.customUI." This file stores Ribbon customizations. It is not a good idea to share this file with other users because it will wipe out all of their existing customizations.

AutoCorrect Files

Unformatted AutoCorrect entries (i.e., those that consist of plain text – as opposed to, say, bolded text or text to which a different font color has been applied – and that use the default character set) are stored in files that use the extension .acl (for AutoCorrect List). They are located here (the one called MSO1033.acl is the American English-language version):

In Windows 7, 8, and 10:
C:\Users\<User Name>\AppData\Roaming\Microsoft\Office

Formatted AutoCorrect entries are stored in your Normal template (Normal.dotm).

Custom Dictionaries

Custom dictionaries have the file extension .dic.

In Windows 7, 8, and 10:
C:\Users\<User Name>\AppData\Roaming\Microsoft\UProof

INDEX

A

Account Screen 96
Aligning Text 209, 457, 505, 539
Alignment .... *See* Justification
Alignment Tabs 209, 228
All Caps
    Keyboard Shortcut for 348
Authorities, Table of ...... *See* Table of Authorities
AutoComplete 378, 380, 381
AutoCorrect 30, 195, 219, 271, 596, 600
AutoCorrect Options..... 150, 218, 219, 229, 231, 576
AutoCorrect Options Icon......................218, 223
AutoFormat As You Type......150, 218, 219, 229, 231, 576
Automatic Borders..218
Automatic Bulleted Lists................................229
Automatically Update 386, 391, 407, 579
AutoRecover Files................. 50, 53, 54, 55, 599
AutoText...521

B

Backstage View.... 35, 36, 37, 39, 41, 52, 57, 70, 73, 105, 358
    Bypassing Backstage 105
Badges 357, 358, 359
Balloons...552, 557
Bookmarks 94, 299, 349, 525, 526
    Names...525
Bottom of Page *See* Page Numbering, Bottom of Page
Browse by Object 284, 301, 302, 303
Building Blocks..... 353, 377, 378, 383, 521, 596, 598
Building Blocks Organizer 379
BuildingBlocks.dotx 377, 378, 380, 381
Bulleted Lists 232
    Changing the Bullet Character 231
    Changing the Bullet Size 230
    Changing the Spacing Between Bulleted
      Paragraphs 230

C

Center Justification.................... *See* Justification
Change Case 270, 353, 355
Character Styles...385
Clear All..406
Clear Formatting 146
Click and Type 209
Co-Authoring 63

Codes

Codes.......................................*See* Field Codes
Codes, Locking .... *See* Locking Codes
Codes, Unlinking................... *See* Unlinking Codes
Codes, Unlocking...................*See* Unlocking Codes
Collapsible Headings 10, 289, 291
Compare and Combine Documents 554
Compare Documents.........................551, 554
Compatibility Mode 60, 193
Compatibility Pack 60, 589
Contents, Table of........... *See* Table of Contents
Contextual Tabs................................. 19, 26, 28
Copyright Symbol
    Keyboard Shortcut for 348
Corruption ....*See* Document Corruption
Cross-References 525, 526
Custom Dictionary.............................325, 327
Custom Templates.................................72

D

Date Code..............245, 361, 363, 364, 367, 370
Default Font 185, 187, 188, 191, 352, 389
Default Template............195, 210, 240, 368, 391
Default.dotx 186
Design Tab13, 18, 19, 23, 26, 30, 111, 202, 213, 261, 471
Developer Tab 372
Dialog Launcher......16, 112, 237, 258, 267, 388, 390, 401, 408, 507, 517, 532
Dictionary 86
Different First Page 134, 245, 247, 250
Digital Signature.......................................64, 66
Direct Formatting 125, 309, 310
Display for Review . *See* Track Changes, Display for Review
doc File Format...60
docm File Format...95
Document Corruption.........44, 45, 394, 589, 592
Document Defaults 186
Document Inspector 67, 290, 291, 562, 563, 564, 565, 566, 567
Document Map................... *See* Navigation Pane
Document Views.....................................21, 107
docx File Format 60, 589
Don't add space between paragraphs of the
    same style 130, 149, 230
Don't Center "Exact Line Height" Lines ..98, 103, 460
dot File Format...60
dotm Files (Templates) 411
dotx Files (Templates) 95, 370, 411
Draft View 22, 259

601

E

Encrypt with Password....................*See* Password
Envelopes............................ 426, 452, 453, 454
Excel............................ 316, 317, 422, 589, 593
Exit (From Word)......................................358
Export Screen 91

F

Field Codes 83, 142, 300, 343, 344, 353, 355,
    361, 368, 369, 409, 428, 519, 521, 522, 523,
    566, 578
    Allow fields containing tracked changes to update
      before printing...84
    Fill-In Fields..368
    Locking...353, 367
    Page X of Y 364
    Print field codes instead of their values 83
    Shading...361
    Switches..361
    Toggle Between Codes and Results .252, 353, 361
    Unlinking.......................................353, 367
    Unlocking.......................................354, 367
    Updating..353, 362
File Conversions 592
    Word to PDF...94
    Word to WordPerfect................................592
    WordPerfect to Word...............................590
File Formats 60, 95, 411, 585
File Tab 17, 36, 39, 41, 53, 56, 57, 82, 94, 95,
    150, 152, 157, 169, 209, 229, 231, 303, 313,
    314, 315, 318, 325, 345, 357, 368, 369, 370,
    373, 374, 396, 413, 460, 479, 568, 579
Fill-In Fields...368, 370
Find 301, 303, 349
    "Find in" Option 298
    "Reading Highlight" Option.........................298
Find and Replace 301, 303, 352, 592
Find Options..285, 288
First Line Indent 133, 221, 222
Font Color...188, 268
Font Dialog... 187, 269, 348, 349, 352, 359, 532,
    563
Font, +Body..188, 193
Font, +Headings.....................................188, 193
Footers ... 26, 133, 135, 138, 150, 209, 210, 239,
    240, 241, 385, 460, 551
Footnote Separator 260
Footnotes 133, 256, 257, 460
Format Painter 15, 109, 139, 143, 229, 230,
    351, 530
Formatting Marks .. *See* Non-Printing Characters
Full Justification....................... *See* Justification

G

Galleries 111, 112, 382
Grammar Checker...............................324, 329

Advanced Grammar Settings 330

H

Hanging Indent...............................221, 222, 350
Hard (Non-Breaking) Hyphen 351, 354, 356
Hard (Non-Breaking) Space 351, 354, 356
Header 240
    Different First Page 244
Header & Footer Tools Tab 239
Headers ..26, 133, 135, 138, 150, 209, 210, 239,
    240, 241, 242, 551
Heading Styles.....................................188, 385
Highlighting
    Keyboard Shortcut for 348
Home Tab 15, 18
Hyphenation...131

I

Incremental Find 277
Indent Markers......................................221
Indentation 126, 132, 133, 220
Indented Quotes
    Setting Up a Keyboard Shortcut for.................408
    Setting Up a Style for 408
Indents
    First Line Indent..................................221
    Special 221
Info Screen.......................52, 57, 65, 81, 358
Insert Tab 44, 111, 239, 270, 348, 357, 358,
    377, 380, 495, 519, 521, 523, 525, 526, 582

J

Justification 208, 352, 360
    Center Justification................................349
    Full Justification..................................349
    Left Justification...................................349
    Right Justification 349

K

Keep Lines Together 130
Keep With Next....................................130, 131, 133
Keyboard Shortcuts
    for "File" commands 343
    for Tabs and Dialog Boxes 357
    Listed by Feature...................................355
    Listed by Keystrokes.............................353
    Miscellaneous (and "Cool") 348
    Setting Up Your Own.............................345, 347
    that Use the Ctrl Key 349, 352

L

Labels 438, 439, 441, 443, 447
Layout Options......................................460
Layout Tab 18, 125, 131, 136, 138, 237, 241,
    358

Left Justification .... *See* Justification
Line Break 448, 462, 463
Line Height 217
Line Spacing 124, 128, 133, 189, 211, 214, 408, 460
Line Spacing, "At Least"..............................460
Line Spacing, "Exactly" 128, 217, 457, 461
Linked Styles...537
ListNum...495, 496
Lists, Bulleted...........................*See* Bulleted Lists
Live Preview.......................................110, 399
Locking Codes 353, 367
Logic, WordPerfect's 135
Logic, Word's...135

M

Macros.................. 345, 371, 372, 373, 374, 375
Mail Merge.......................................419, 438
  Data File... 419, 420, 421, 422, 424, 425, 426, 427, 431, 432, 433, 434, 438, 441, 446
  Form File..419, 420, 421, 426, 427, 429, 432, 433, 434, 435
    Match Fields 427, 429
    Merge Fields..........................419, 420, 424
    Record..420, 425
    Wizard.......................................419, 420
Manage Document.............................52, 53, 70
Manage Styles 393
Margins.. 124, 133, 134, 135, 209, 237, 240, 461
Mark as Final.................................64, 568, 569
Merges .... *See* Mail Merge
Metadata 563, 564, 565, 566
Mini Toolbar 109, 110
Mnemonics............................. 36, 357, 358, 359
Multilevel Lists..... 497, 501, 502, 503, 510, 511, 512

N

Navigation Pane...... 20, 275, 276, 277, 280, 283
Nested Lists 232
Never-Saved Documents 599
New Screen...71
Non-Printing Characters..............................114
Non-Printing Characters, Display..136, 139, 142, 350, 354, 356, 377
Normal Paragraph Style.......................187, 189
Normal Template.... 81, 185, 187, 188, 347, 373, 415
Normal.dotm.......... 188, 268, 347, 377, 415, 596
  Backing Up 583
Numbered Lists 221, 487, 598
Numbering Button 480, 487, 489, 490, 492

O

Office 365 ....3, 47, 96

Office Button 150, 218, 345, 368, 576
Office Theme 13, 14, 15, 20, 193
OneDrive....................................2, 3, 48, 84, 87, 89
OneNote...593
Open and Repair..............................44, 45, 582
Open as Copy..43, 44
Open Office XML 29, 209, 228
Open Read-Only 43, 44
Organizer 393, 394, 395, 598
Outline View...22
Outlook.......89, 90, 421, 422, 432, 439, 440, 593

P

Page Break Before...................................574
Page Formatting 233, 235
Page Layout...133, 237
Page Numbering 251
  Bottom of Page..251
  Current Position.......................................252
  Suppress 252
Page Setup dialog.....79, 80, 108, 112, 136, 138, 225, 237, 238, 263, 264, 359, 574, 575, 576
Page X of Y...246
Paragraph Dialog..124, 125, 129, 130, 131, 132, 133, 136, 137, 149, 212, 217, 220, 221, 225, 343, 349, 352, 359, 360, 387, 405, 407, 443, 457, 458, 460, 461, 509, 510, 574, 575, 576
Paragraph Formatting...123, 124, 125, 131, 135, 139, 141, 377, 396, 461
Paragraph Indentation 220
Paragraph Mark 123, 135, 139, 142, 218, 230, 250, 377, 392, 459, 521
Password 64, 65
  Remove..65
Paste Options 304, 308
  Default Settings.................99, 102, 305, 307, 315
  Keep Source Formatting 308
  Keep Text Only....................................310
  Merge Formatting 309
  Use Destination Styles 310
  Use Destination Theme.............................311
Paste Options Button....150, 304, 305, 306, 307, 313, 317
Paste Special...350
PDF 94
  Create 92, 93
  Open Directly into Word 10, 319
Permissions 173
Pilcrow 123, 135, 142, 218, 230, 271, 392
PowerPoint............................. 192, 317, 589, 593
Previously-Saved Documents.......................600
Print Layout View......21, 22, 107, 150, 249, 259, 348
Print Markup...82
Print Place............37, 73, 74, 105, 177, 353, 358
Print Preview.......................73, 74, 75, 177, 353

603

Print Preview Edit Mode 73, 74, 75
Printing
    Print What option...............................80, 81, 82
Protect Document 63, 568, 569, 570
Protected View 45, 118

Q

QAT .... *See* Quick Access Toolbar
Quick Access Toolbar 22, 31, 103, 106, 175,
    176, 249, 357, 479, 600
    Adding a "Close" Command 180
    Adding Commands...176
    Backing Up (Exporting) 179
    Changing the Order of Icons 179
    Customize 74
    Removing Icons...179
    Show Below the Ribbon 74
Quick Parts... 353, 377, 378, 379, 382, 383, 519,
    521, 523, 596
    Saving 522
Quick Style 113
Quick Tables 466

R

Read Mode....................................21, 22, 107
Real-Time Co-Authoring 85, 87
Recent Screen 38, 39, 358
Recover Unsaved Documents 42, 52
Redlining 552, 554
References Tab.... 256, 259, 260, 358, 526, 527,
    537, 545
Registered Symbol
    Keyboard Shortcut for 348
Remove a Password ..... *See* Password, Remove
Restoring the Pleading Paper 250
Restrict Editing 64, 66, 569
Reveal Codes...................................135, 136, 137
Reveal Formatting...... 136, 139, 140, 353, 355,
    406, 574
Review Tab 86, 322, 331, 359, 551, 553, 554,
    555, 559, 561, 569
Ribbon...... 15, 27, 31, 106, 175, 239, 256, 343,
    344, 345, 357, 358
    Built-in tabs...151, 157
    Context-sensitive tabs 26, 28
    Custom tabs 151, 157, 168, 226
    Customizing...151
    Main tabs..15
    Optional tabs 27
    Permanent tabs 15
Rich Text Format...............................591, 592
Right Justification .... *See* Justification
Round-Tripping 592
RTF 591, 592
Ruler..................... 108, 210, 221, 222, 224, 225
    Vertical Ruler...108

S

Screen Color .... *See* Office Theme
Scrollbars 108
Section Breaks......133, 134, 235, 241, 242, 243,
    249, 259
    Continuous 241
    Next Page...241
    Troubleshooting..263
SEQ Codes 362, 368, 519, 520, 521, 523
    Change the Starting Value 522
    Updating...521, 524
Share Menu 37
Share Screen 84, 358
SharePoint 47, 48, 84, 87, 89
Show / Hide...114, 136, 139, 142, 207, 250, 339,
    350, 354, 377, 392, 459, 460, 470, 491, 536,
    537, 546, 547, 548
Show Markup 559
Shrink One Page...155
Single-Level Lists...487
Small Caps
    Keyboard Shortcut for 348
Smart Tags 567
Soft Return.............................. *See* Line Break
Sorting...335, 481
    Within a Table 481
Spacing After 129, 130, 133
Spacing Before 129, 130, 133
Special .... *See* Indents, Special
Spell-Checker .30, 107, 322, 325, 326, 327, 329,
    348
    Keyboard Shortcut for 348
Start screen..1
Status Bar 13, 106, 107, 182, 183, 241, 248,
    372, 397, 555, 568
    Add a Section Indicator 248
    Add a Track Changes Indicator 555
    Add an "Overtype" Indicator 99
    Customizing...182
    Proofing Errors 107
    View Shortcuts 22
    Word Count 107
    Zoom Slider..107
Strikethrough...532
Style Area 397
Style Area Pane 533
Style for Following Paragraph 391, 408, 494, 508
Style Gallery....18, 110, 113, 132, 387, 391, 398,
    399, 400, 401, 402, 404, 494
Style Inspector 136, 405
Style Separator 350, 356, 536, 537
Style Sets......131, 185, 186, 190, 193, 213, 389,
    599
Styles 385, 386, 390, 397
    Apply Styles Dialog 387, 389
    Automatically Update 386, 391, 407, 579
    Copying Between Documents 392, 598

604

Creating Your Own 389
Manage Styles Dialog 402, 517
Modify Style Dialog....258, 508, 510, 512, 518, 598
Modifying..188, 210, 258, 385, 391, 402, 407, 454, 501, 507, 510, 515, 598
Options 388
Style for Following Paragraph 391
Styles Pane .. 258, 259, 359, 388, 390, 392, 393, 395, 397, 401, 402, 407, 408, 494, 507, 511, 515, 516, 517, 518, 537
Subscript 351, 354, 356
Superscript 351, 354, 356
Suppress Page Number... *See* Page Numbering, Suppress
Symbol dialog...270
Symbols...270, 345
Most Recently Used 270

T

Table of Authorities 142, 543, 546
Adding a New Category 544
Editing the TA Codes 547
Generating..546
Keep Original Formatting 547
Legal "Signals" 545
Mark All...544
Mark Citation...543
Modifying the TOA Styles....................................549
Short Citation...544, 545
TA Codes 536, 544, 547
Updating (Regenerating) 548
Table of Contents 142, 533
Add Text..537
Applying Outline Levels......................................535
Applying TC Codes 536
Generating..538
Mark TOC Entry Dialog 536
Marking "Manual" Headings 536
Reformatting..540
Run-in Paragraphs 536, 537
TC Codes 536
TOC Styles...540
Troubleshooting...542
Updating (Regenerating) 539
Table Tools Tab
Design 466
Layout 466
Tables...464
Adding Rows and Columns 467
Adjusting the Column Width 471
Alignment 475
Allow row to break across pages.....................475
Borders...476
Deleting Rows and Columns 468
Draw Table...465
Excel Spreadsheet 465
Gridlines 439, 448, 477
Header Row 470
Insert Table..465
Merging Cells 470

Pasting Into 318
Quick Tables 466
Row Height 474
Selecting Components 469
Sorting...481
Splitting 470
Turning Off Borders..210
Tabs 133, 224, 225, 227
Alignment 209, 228
Bar..227
Center 224, 227
Decimal 224, 227
Leaders 227
Page Layout 133
Right..227
Setting 224, 226
Templates 72, 81, 368, 369, 393, 411
Creating Your Own...................................409, 416
Custom...72, 370
Default personal templates location 46, 70, 410, 411, 412, 596
Featured..1
Macro-Enabled...95, 411
Modifying...416
New Documents or Templates Icon 411, 414
Personal (Custom) 411
User templates 103, 411, 412, 596
Workgroup templates ...70, 72, 100, 103, 369, 411, 412, 413, 414
Text Effects...............................63, 111, 203, 532
Text-Stream Formatting 135, 209
Themes 185, 192, 387, 599
Thesaurus 348, 353, 355
Keyboard Shortcut for 348
Thunderbolt.........*See* AutoCorrect Options Icon
TOA.................................... *See* Table of Authorities
TOC styles ....*See* Table of Contents
Track Changes......................182, 555, 556, 561
Display for Review.............10, 552, 554, 557, 559
All Markup 560
No Markup 559
Original 559
Simple Markup 559
Show Markup 554
Trademark Symbol
Keyboard Shortcut for 348
Troubleshooting 136, 141, 573
Typing Replaces Selected Text 479

U

Underlining Words
Keyboard Shortcut for 348
Unlinking Codes 353, 367
Unlocking Codes....................................354, 367
Unsaved Documents ..50, 51, 52, 53, 54, 55, 70, 599, 600
Update Fields Before Printing........362, 370, 578
Updates Available 183

605

V

Vertical Ruler..*See* Ruler
View Tab 224, 249, 259, 275, 357, 359, 371, 372, 397, 477, 574

W

Watermark Gallery 111
Watermarks.............. 18, 30, 167, 202, 235, 261
    Picture 262
    Remove 262
    Text 261
Web Layout View 22, 107
Widow/Orphan Control.................130, 133, 460
Wildcards...286, 287
Word 2003....................................191, 389, 589
Word 2007...... 35, 56, 63, 67, 92, 109, 110, 113, 131, 132, 149, 151, 165, 198, 228, 239, 398, 399, 405, 512, 568, 574, 589, 594
Word 2010.... 30, 32, 36, 38, 41, 47, 60, 61, 62, 63, 91, 116, 154, 167, 173, 211, 251, 275, 278, 284, 310, 330, 364, 454, 559
Word 2013............................. 8, 13, 19, 32, 107

Word Count.............................20, 106, 107, 183
Word MVPs...594
Word Options 150, 177, 229, 231, 303, 318, 345, 347, 358, 372, 374, 396, 460, 479, 556
WordPerfect....13, 123, 135, 137, 182, 209, 217, 220, 239, 343, 352, 353, 368, 386, 590, 592
    Conversion to Word...590
    Indent 352
    Keyboard Merges 368
    Line Height 217
    Logic...135
    Paste Special 592
    Switch Screen 353

X

XML....... 45, 60, 62, 67, 95, 131, 151, 186, 411, 563, 589
XPS
    Create 94

Z

Zoom Slider..107

Made in the USA
Middletown, DE
22 May 2019